EXAMPLES & EXPLANATIONS

Criminal Law

EDITORIAL ADVISORS

EXAMPLES & EXPLANATIONS

Criminal Law

Seventh Edition

Richard G. Singer
Distinguished Professor of Law, Emeritus
Rutgers, The State University of New Jersey School of Law

John Q. La Fond
Edward A. Smith/Missouri Chair Emeritus in Law,
the Constitution, and Society
University of Missouri–Kansas City School of Law

Shima Baradaran Baughman
Professor of Law and Presidential Scholar
S.J. Quinney College of Law
University of Utah

Published by Wolters Kluwer in New York.

Wolters Kluwer Legal & Regulatory U.S. serves customers worldwide with CCH, Aspen Publishers, and Kluwer Law International products. (www.WKLegaledu.com)

To contact Customer Service, e-mail customer.service@wolterskluwer.com, call 1-800-234-1660, fax 1-800-901-9075, or mail correspondence to:

Wolters Kluwer
Attn: Order Department
PO Box 990
Frederick, MD 21705

Printed in the United States of America.

1 2 3 4 5 6 7 8 9 0

ISBN 978-1-4548-6842-2

Library of Congress Cataloging-in-Publication Data

Names: Singer, Richard G., author. | La Fond, John Q., author. | Baughman, Shima Baradaran, author.
Title: Criminal law / Richard G. Singer, Distinguished Professor of Law, Emeritus Rutgers, the State University of New Jersey School of Law; John Q. La Fond, Edward A. Smith/Missouri Chair, Emeritus in Law, the Constitution, and Society University of Missouri–Kansas City School of Law; Shima Baradaran Baughman, Professor of Law and Presidential Scholar, S.J. Quinney College of Law, University of Utah.
Description: Seventh edition. | New York : Wolters Kluwer, [2018] | Series: Examples & explanations
Identifiers: LCCN 2018009875 | ISBN 9781454868422 (hardcover)
Subjects: LCSH: Criminal law—United States—Outlines, syllabi, etc.
Classification: LCC KF9219.85 .S58 2018 | DDC 345.73—dc23
LC record available at https://lccn.loc.gov/2018009875

About Wolters Kluwer Legal & Regulatory U.S.

Wolters Kluwer Legal & Regulatory U.S. delivers expert content and solutions in the areas of law, corporate compliance, health compliance, reimbursement, and legal education. Its practical solutions help customers successfully navigate the demands of a changing environment to drive their daily activities, enhance decision quality and inspire confident outcomes.

Serving customers worldwide, its legal and regulatory portfolio includes products under the Aspen Publishers, CCH Incorporated, Kluwer Law International, ftwilliam .com, and MediRegs names. They are regarded as exceptional and trusted resources for general legal and practice-specific knowledge, compliance and risk management, dynamic workflow solutions, and expert commentary.

To Karen: For twenty-three years of laughter, and love
—R.G.S.

To my wife, Evelyn
—J.Q.L.

To all my boys, Ryan, Kian, Darian, & Milo
—S.B.B.

Summary of Contents

Contents

Preface

Criminal law forces us to confront the most important moral dilemmas of our times. More than most law school courses, criminal law engages our emotions as well as our intellects. This book will encourage that engagement. Many of our examples are taken from current topics of intense public debate such as euthanasia, abortion, rape, and even fantasy Internet crime. But the underlying normative challenge of the criminal law—justifying the coercive use of state power against individuals—transcends particular controversies. Indeed, this debate has challenged great thinkers of the past like Plato, Socrates, Aquinas, and Kant. And it will certainly challenge us and future generations. This text keeps that tension in sharp and continuous focus.

This book helps students master a broad range of criminal law doctrines. But it does not merely present a collection of "rules." It also explains and analyzes those doctrines and the problems they generate in a cohesive and comprehensive way. Where there are ambiguities—either theoretical or practical—we discuss them. Not to do so would mislead students and trivialize the criminal law. By recognizing how complex the tapestry is and how interwoven are its various threads, students can appreciate the rich nuances of its doctrine and policy. This book examines that complexity, while remaining easy to read and to understand. Its sole purpose is to help students learn.

We were attracted to the format of the *Examples and Explanations* series long before we began work on this book. The format fits the typical law school classroom experience by posing challenging problems first (without answers, of course!) and then offering solutions. We also enjoyed the humor evident in other volumes in this series. Learning is serious business—but no business is so serious that it cannot be approached with an occasional smile. We have tried to sprinkle humor generously throughout the book.

From all reports, students have found the earlier editions of this book very helpful, not only for mastering criminal law, but also for learning what is expected of them on law school exams. We are pleased that the earlier editions were so successful. We have maintained the same basic approach, but we have thoroughly updated the seventh edition. New material has been added on important and current topics, like which facts the prosecution must prove beyond a reasonable doubt, homicidal liability for deaths resulting from the transmission of AIDS, torture (and the liability of those who relied upon administration policy while administering the "enhanced interrogation" techniques), necessity and terrorism, and the implications of new discoveries in neuroscience on criminal law. Examples have been drawn from newspaper headlines, such as terrorism prosecutions, testosterone overload, sexual abuse by clergy, male rape, the San Francisco "dog mauling" case, and the New York "cannibal cop." We think that you will enjoy this book and that it will help you, as it has helped many other students to succeed in criminal law.

Finally, a plea for your help. This book can be successful in helping students only if the authors know what works—and what doesn't. We are anxious for your comments—negative and positive—either on specific topics or hypotheticals, or generally. Please contact us at our e-mail addresses and give us your criticisms and comments. We can't promise we'll respond directly, but we can promise that we'll consider every point as we move toward an eighth edition. A number of the hypotheticals, or at least their topic areas, have been added as the direct result of student comments to earlier editions. We have also benefited from observations about the accuracy of citations, format, etc. Keep those cards and letters coming in.

To all who read this book, we hope that you learn from it and enjoy it.

Richard G. Singer
John Q. La Fond
Shima Baradaran Baughman

rsinger@camlaw.rutgers.edu
lafondj@comcast.net
Shima@law.utah.edu

April 2018

Acknowledgments

This book bears the name of its "authors." But it required the hard work, assistance, and sacrifice of many people. Our students contributed helpful comments on many of the examples in this book, thereby protecting future students from the foibles found in earlier versions. Research assistants, particularly Madeline Aller, Emily Swenson, Lauren Martinez, Marina Pena, Helena Jordan, and Amylia Brown at the University of Utah and Laura Anglin, Jenifer Hanlon, Tara Manley, and Anne-Marie Sargent at Seattle University School of Law, and Rebecca Abeln, Deawn Hersini, Christin Keele, Chris Moberg, Tina Parsley, and Katherine Schoofs at the University of Missouri-Kansas City School of Law. Moral support was provided by our respective deans—Rayman Solomon, Jim Bond, and Burnele Powell. The tedious and frustrating job of reading our scribbles and editing for errors fell to wonderful and indefatigable administrative staff: Noreen Slease at Seattle University, Norma Karn at the University of Missouri–Kansas City School of Law, Debi Leak at Rutgers University, and Patti Beekhuizen, Baiba Hicks, and Angela Turnbow at University of Utah, whose good humor and positive approach kept us all on an even keel. We wish especially to thank our respective spouses, Karen Garfing, Evelyn La Fond, and Ryan Baughman, for their continuing tolerance and patient support.

We wish to thank the following copyright holder, who kindly granted permission to reprint excerpts from the following material:

EXAMPLES & EXPLANATIONS

Criminal Law

CHAPTER 1

The Sources and Limitations of the Criminal Law

OVERVIEW

Ever since Cain slew Abel, societies have had to deal with those whose acts seem "wrong." A conclusion that an act is wrong may be simply innate.[1] Some wrongs, however, seem worse than others. Thus, breaking a promise or tripping someone seems wrong, but homicide, rape, and maiming seem "really" wrong. If a general consensus arises that specific acts are really wrong, there will be laws against such acts. Some acts will be criminally punished, while others will be handled by civil parts of the legal system. This book focuses on how that behavior is defined and punished as "criminal."

American criminal law has three main sources: (1) the common law, (2) statutory law, and (3) constitutional law. Of these, the most important is statutory law, since it is now accepted that it is unconstitutional to punish someone unless her conduct was previously proscribed by the legislature. Nevertheless, criminal statutes are interpreted in light of an 800-year history of common law principles and against more modern constraints imposed by constitutional doctrines. The criminal law is yet further limited: Since most of criminal law consists of statutes, courts have established maxims of statutory interpretation, some rooted in the Constitution, others

1. G. Fletcher, Rethinking Criminal Law 115-118 (1978).

not. Of these, the most important are examined on pages 9-12, including the void-for-vagueness doctrine and the rule of lenity.

Finally, this chapter explores, if only briefly, the procedural limitation that requires the prosecution to persuade a jury beyond a reasonable doubt that the defendant is guilty. Just as important as the standard and its articulation are the reasons why the Supreme Court has held this standard to be required by the Constitution.

SOURCES OF CRIMINAL LAW

The Common Law as a Source of Criminal Law

Early English custom condemned as felonies seven offenses: mayhem, homicide, rape, larceny, burglary, arson, and robbery. All other offenses were misdemeanors, and they ranged from serious crimes (kidnapping) to less serious crimes (assault). These classifications became known as the "common law" because they were commonly shared.[2]

The term "common law" is usually employed to refer solely to judge-made law, typically in the areas of torts and contracts. However, legislatures early on became interested in defining crimes; therefore, in the context of criminal law, the term "common law" incorporates both statutes and judge-made law as well as judicial interpretations of statutes. The power of courts to "create" crimes existed until well into the nineteenth century and in some rare instances, continues even today.

Initially, English law treated all injuries, except homicide, as inflicting private harms that could be compensated. If the injured party accepted compensation, the defendant could not also be criminally sanctioned. After the Norman Conquest, however, the new kings, unhappy with leaving such decisions in private hands, sought to establish their power over crimes by punishing these actors. Although this divergence between torts (compensable acts) and crimes (punishable acts) began more than 800 years ago, and took centuries to complete, even today, many acts that constitute crimes also often constitute torts. Therefore, it is still helpful to compare the common law rules of tort, in which compensation to the plaintiff is the major concern, with the common law rules of crimes, in which punishment of the defendant is the sole concern.

2. Because it was an evolutionary process, however, there is no "starting point" to the common law, although Hale has urged 1192, the date of the ascension of Richard I to the throne of England, as the "best" starting date. Matthew Hale, The History of the Common Law in England (3d ed. 1739).

Legislative Sources

The legislature increased in importance when the procedures for torts and crimes divided. The English Parliament codified the common law of crimes and—slowly at first, then rapidly—enlarged the list of felonies beyond the initial seven. In the United States, legislative dominance in defining crimes through statutes has continued on the ground that the protection of citizens was too important to leave to the gradual development by judges of the common law. In addition, courts decided that applying newly defined crimes retroactively would violate the requirement of fair notice, a basic doctrine of English-American law.

In political theory, legislatures should be at least predominantly, if not exclusively, the source of criminal law in a democracy. To the extent that criminal law reflects moral sentiments of the community, the legislature, as the most democratically elected institution, should prevail. Courts, which are often appointed, should be subordinate to the representative body; even where judges are elected, they are not as frequently reviewed by the populace.

Statutes are usually written not one provision at a time but address many issues that are considered in a relatively short time. It would be unrealistic to expect legislatures to focus on the precise questions that litigation may pinpoint. Moreover, no matter how carefully written, statutes are in English, a notoriously ambiguous and opaque language. Thus, judicial interpretation of statutes is inevitable.

The interplay between the common law (developed by courts) and statutes (developed by legislatures) is dynamic. American courts can no longer "create" crimes, as their English forebears did in earlier times (see Chapter 10 (theft) and Chapter 13 (conspiracy)). There is also agreement that there can be no crime unless there is a statute prohibiting the conduct.[3] Still, courts can construe statutes either broadly or narrowly, thus effectively broadening or narrowing the reach of the statutory criminal law.

The Model Penal Code as a Source of Criminal Law

In our federal system, each state is free within constitutional limits to develop its own common and statutory law. Consequently, state and federal legislatures have enacted differing statutes, and the courts have interpreted English common law principles differently. As a result, American criminal law, while sharing a common basis, is quite diverse. Prior to 1960, it was difficult to speak of "the criminal law of the United States."

---

3. S. Pomorski, American Common Law and the Principle *Nulla Crimen Sine Lege* (1975).

In 1962, the American Law Institute (ALI), a private organization comprised of leading lawyers, judges, and scholars, adopted the Model Penal Code (MPC), intended as legislation for states to adopt or reject. Since its promulgation in 1962, the MPC has been adopted in whole or in part by legislatures in over 35 states. Because of that general acceptance, no survey of current criminal law could omit the MPC. This book compares the doctrines of the MPC with the previous doctrines of law. Those earlier doctrines, whether statutory or judicial, are referred to together here as the "common law." Be warned, however—our comparison is with the MPC *as adopted by the ALI*. No state has adopted the MPC precisely as proposed by the ALI, and many jurisdictions (most importantly, the federal Code and that of California) still have not adopted the MPC in any way. Thus, while it may be generally true that the MPC is "American law," any specific provision may not be "the law" in a particular jurisdiction. Still, even in jurisdictions that have not enacted the MPC, courts sometimes look to it for guidance because it is thought to embody neutral and carefully constructed approaches to criminal law doctrine.

Constitutional Sources and Limits

Many decisions you will read in your constitutional law class are criminal law cases. In this sense, many constitutional guarantees in the Bill of Rights *directly* limit legislative policy. Thus, under the First Amendment, Congress and state legislatures may not pass *any* law (including a criminal law) that restricts freedom of speech, religion, or the press. In addition to these well-recognized constitutional rights, decisions of the last 30 years have recognized a "right of privacy" that legislatures may not infringe. It was under this theory that the Supreme Court decided the famous case of *Roe v. Wade*, 410 U.S. 113 (1973). Although procedurally that case was a civil matter, it held that states could not criminally punish persons performing or undergoing abortions. Similarly, *Bowers v. Hardwick*, 478 U.S. 186 (1986), was a civil suit to enjoin enforcement of a criminal statute. There, however, the court held that the right to privacy did not forbid states to punish criminally homosexual sodomy. (In 2003, the Court, in a case involving a *criminal* conviction, overruled *Bowers*; but the point still remains that crucial criminal matters may arise by the civil process. *Lawrence v. Texas*, 539 U.S. 558 (2003).)

The precise contours of these rights, including the right to privacy, are not clear. Nonetheless, each of these constitutional rights reminds us that the criminal law is not merely a means of punishment—the doctrines of the criminal law also protect those whose conduct does not fall directly within its clear meaning.

Beware—for those who have not yet studied constitutional and federal law (and perhaps for those who have), in this book (and in your casebooks) you are likely to find several cases decided by the United States Supreme Court. With one or two exceptions, those decisions are NOT based on the federal Constitution, but construe federal statutes. Neither the decisions, nor their rationale, "bind" state courts. The decisions may, or may not, be good policy. But the United States Supreme Court has been extremely wary of "constitutionalizing" criminal law, and thus "requires" states to follow specific rules with regard to crimes. There are exceptions to this statement, but they are unusual. Don't "overread" decisions by the United States Supreme Court.

While it is true that only legislatures can define crimes, courts give less deference to the legislative power in the criminal arena than in other areas. Whether that is due to the unique sanctions that criminal law carries (see Chapter 2 on punishment) is not clear. However, recognizing the interplay of these three sources—common law, statutes, and constitutional precepts—is essential to understanding American criminal law.

LIMITATIONS ON THE CRIMINAL LAW

Law-abiding people should not have to guess whether there is a criminal law forbidding their conduct or, if there is, what that law means. Likewise, the police, who enforce the law, should not have the power to decide what behavior the law covers. Finally, both trial and appellate courts need to know what the law is in order to apply it fairly and consistently in numerous cases.

Several doctrines, including the principle of legality, the constitutional doctrine of "void for vagueness," and the rule of lenity, address these concerns. The principle of *legality* provides that before individuals can be convicted and punished for engaging in such conduct, it must be legislatively prohibited. The constitutional doctrine of *void for vagueness* requires the criminal law to be sufficiently clear so that individuals of ordinary ability can understand what their legal obligations are. The rule of *lenity* requires a court to construe criminal statutes strictly, resolving doubt in favor of the defendant.

The Principle of Legality

The Common Law in England

The common law method of formulating new crimes virtually stopped in the mid-nineteenth century. Nonetheless, English judges still occasionally apply common law crimes to novel situations that are not expressly covered by a criminal statute. Thus, in *Shaw v. Director of Prosecutions*,[4] the defendant published a "Ladies Directory" of prostitutes, which contained their names, pictures, addresses, and telephone numbers. Prostitution itself was not a crime, but soliciting in public was. The House of Lords upheld the defendant's conviction for "conspiracy to corrupt public morals" even though there was no criminal statute forbidding the publication of such a directory. Viscount Simonds concluded that courts retained:

> residual power to enforce the supreme and fundamental purpose of the law, to conserve not only the safety and order but also the moral welfare of the State. . . . [I]t is their duty to guard against attacks which may be the more insidious because they are novel and unprepared for. . . . Such occasions will be rare, for Parliament has not been slow to legislate when attention has been sufficiently aroused. But gaps remain and will always remain since no one can foresee every way in which the wickedness of man may disrupt the order of society.[5]

The Common Law in the United States

The early colonists brought with them the common law of England and its statutes, both civil and criminal.[6] Thus, most states had common law crimes. A number of states enacted comprehensive statutory criminal codes in the nineteenth century. In most states, common law crimes were displaced by specific statutory declaration; in others, the common law was preserved, but today, only legislators can create new crimes.

The Strengths and Weaknesses of Common Law Crimes

Common law crimes have some strengths. As Viscount Simonds observed, they ensure that the criminal law is always available to punish harmful conduct even if the legislature failed to anticipate its occurrence by enacting an applicable criminal statute. They also discourage the imaginative exploitation of loopholes in the criminal laws. Common law crimes provide flexibility, which permits adjustment to new and unanticipated situations. In the arena of drug crimes, for example, "designer drugs" are created so quickly that Congress (or state legislatures) cannot keep up with statutes that incorporate their names (or chemical compositions) and prohibit their manufacture. Consequently, federal statutes now allow the Attorney General, working with the Department of Health, to add a newly created drug to the list, for a limited period of time; the listing is valid only for a

---

4. House of Lords, [1962] A.C. 220.

5. Id.

6. See Jerome Hall, The Common Law: An Account of Its Reception in the United States, 4 Vand. L. Rev. 791 (1951).

period sufficient to allow Congress to decide whether to amend the statutorily designated list of drugs.

Common law crimes, however, also have serious weaknesses. First, unless there is a clear precedential case available, an individual could not know beforehand if her contemplated conduct is lawful or criminal. Only when a court decides after the fact, using analogies or cases from other jurisdictions, would a defendant learn whether she had committed a crime. Even someone trying to obey the law must act at her own peril as the defendant in *Shaw* unhappily learned. Faced with such uncertainty, many individuals may play it safe and avoid engaging in conduct that would not be declared criminal.

Second, under a common law system, the limits on governmental authority are not clear. The criminal law is a restriction on individual liberty, but it is also a restriction on governmental authority. Unless the law draws a clear boundary between permissible and impermissible behavior, the government can more easily use the awesome power of the criminal law to convict and incarcerate individuals it considers its enemies for behavior that may have actually been innocent.[7]

The absence of a clear set of rules embodied in criminal statutes thus creates uncertainty in predicting the future. It also weakens the moral justifications for conviction and punishment and diminishes the restraints on government.

Principle of Legality

Today, most jurisdictions have enacted comprehensive modern criminal statutes and have abolished courts' authority to create new crimes. This clear preference for a statutory criminal law reflects a collective sense of justice that individuals are entitled to the protection afforded by clearly announced rules that both protect individual autonomy and limit governmental authority. Fair warning is an essential part of due process which is the foundation of the American criminal justice system. Relying on statutes rather than cases to create crimes also supports separation of powers: The legislature *makes* the law; courts *interpret* and *apply* the law.

The *principle of legality* is an important part of American criminal law today, a principle expressed in the often-cited Latin maxim: "*Nullum crimen, nulla poena, sine lege*" ("There is no crime without law, no punishment without law"). Today, a defendant cannot be convicted of a crime unless the legislature has enacted in advance a statutory definition of the offense.[8]

---

7. Pomorski, supra n. 3; Jeffries, Legality, Vagueness, and the Construction of Penal Statutes, 71 Va. L. Rev. 189 n. 15 (1985).

8. H. Packer, The Limits of the Criminal Sanction (1968).

Providing prior notice of illegality by statute also supports the reasons for convicting and punishing lawbreakers. Utilitarians would concede that, before deterrence can be effective, an individual must be able to know what conduct is forbidden and the consequences of breaking the law. Most retributivists conclude that the fundamental purpose of punishment is to blame those who choose to do wrong. Unless adequate notice of criminal behavior is provided, it is difficult to argue that the defendant has "chosen" to commit a wrongful act. Moral condemnation and punishment without such notice are indefensible.

Ex Post Facto

The Constitution expressly forbids both Congress and state legislatures from passing ex post facto criminal laws.[9] Legislatures cannot enact statutes that criminalize acts that were innocent when done or that increase the severity of the crime or the punishment after the fact. Such laws are a form of retroactive criminalization. This constitutional restraint ensures that the legislature give fair warning of criminal conduct and its consequences.[10]

The ex post facto prohibition is expressly limited to legislatures. Nonetheless, American courts today are sensitive to the basic unfairness created by *unforeseen* judicial interpretations of criminal statutes that expand their reach and, in effect, retroactively criminalize behavior or aggravate the severity of the crime or its punishment. Concern that due process prohibits such judicial construction of criminal statutes and respect for the separation of powers have influenced courts to avoid such interpretations.[11]

A good example of this cautious judicial approach is *Keeler v. Superior Court*.[12] The defendant was charged with murder (killing a "human being") under California law after he intentionally shoved his knee into the abdomen of his former wife, who was in an advanced state of pregnancy, and said: "I am going to stomp it [the unborn fetus] out of you." The fetus was delivered stillborn with a fractured head.

The majority, rejecting the prosecution's argument that the statute should be interpreted in light of changing medical technology, interpreted the phrase "human being" as used in the California murder statute as having the common law meaning of "born alive," which was the generally understood meaning of "human being" when the statute was enacted first in 1850 and reenacted in 1872. The majority decided that a court should

---

9. U.S. Const. art. I, §9 (federal) and §10 (state).

10. *Calder v. Bull*, 3 U.S. (3 Dall.) 386 (1798); *Bouie v. City of Columbia*, 378 U.S. 347 (1964).

11. *Bouie*, 378 U.S. 347.

12. 2 Cal. 3d 619 (1970).

not expand the reach of a criminal statute to include conduct beyond that intended by the legislature. In its view, to do so might violate the separation of powers by judicially rewriting a law enacted by the legislature, thus usurping the legislature's law-making authority.

Interpreting the phrase "human being" to include a viable fetus might also violate federal and state due process, according to the majority. Providing a new judicial definition of this material element of murder was constitutionally impermissible. Under the applicable law in effect when the defendant struck his wife, he had only committed an assault on his former wife (and possibly an abortion). Deciding after the fact that his conduct actually constituted murder would be an exercise in retroactively increasing the severity of the defendant's crime and its penalty.[13]

However, the Supreme Court has since given courts greater authority to expand retroactively the scope of the criminal law. In *Rogers v. Tennessee*, 532 U.S. 451 (2001), the defendant stabbed the victim, who died more than one year and a day after the stabbing. Even though Tennessee at the time followed the common law rule that the victim must die within one year and a day of the defendant's act to establish murder, the state supreme court retroactively abolished this rule and upheld the defendant's murder conviction. Without this authority, courts could not engage in "incremental and reasoned development"[14] of precedent. So long as a court's decision is not "unexpected and indefensible,"[15] it has the power to broaden the reach of the criminal law.

The Rule of Lenity

This fear of improper judicial expansion of a statutory definition of crime is also reflected in the *rule of lenity*, also referred to as the *rule of strict construction*.[16] English courts originally developed this principle to restrict capital punishment in response to the increasing number of felonies punishable by death.[17] This rule of strict judicial construction requires courts to "construe a penal statute as favorably to the defendant as its language and the circumstances of its application may reasonably permit."[18] Simply put, ambiguity in the statutory language should be resolved in the defendant's favor. This

13. Subsequent to this decision, the California legislature amended the state murder statute to include the unlawful killing of a "fetus." 1970 Cal. Laws ch. 1311, §1. This amended statute would punish as murder what Keeler did.

14. 532 U.S. at 461.

15. 532 U.S. at 462.

16. Paul H. Robinson et al., *Criminal Law Case Studies and Controversies* 39 (5th ed. 2017).

17. Jeffries, supra n. 7, at 198.

18. *Keeler*, 2 Cal. 3d at 631.

rule works to advance the legality principle by deeming an individual's conduct legal if a law is ambiguous and can be read as to not criminalize the individual's behavior.[19] Some courts, however, will apply the rule of lenity only if other strategies for interpreting a criminal statute fail to make its meaning clear.[20] Because this rule is not a constitutional requirement, courts do not have to follow it and legislatures may supersede it by statute.[21]

The Model Penal Code did not expressly adopt the rule of lenity. Instead, it requires that criminal statutes be "construed according to the fair import of their terms." In cases involving ambiguous language, however, it directs courts to construe statutory language to further both the general purposes of the criminal law and the specific purposes of the statute under consideration.[22] A number of jurisdictions subsequently followed suit and adopted a defense for "*de minimis* infractions."[23] This defense rests on the notion that a defendant should not be culpable for an act that can be deemed criminal under the law, but that was not an act the legislature sought to prohibit when enacting the law.[24]

Void for Vagueness

The United States Supreme Court has consistently struck down criminal laws that are so vague that ordinary people could not reasonably determine their meaning and application from the language of the statute.[25] The Court has also consistently struck down statutes which confer excessive discretion on law enforcement authorities to arrest or prosecute,[26] or on judges and juries to determine what conduct is prohibited.[27] The "void for vagueness" doctrine is based on the due process clauses of the Fifth Amendment (when a federal statute is involved) and on the Fourteenth Amendment (when a state statute is involved). It helps ensure that the American criminal law implements the principle of legality.[28] There is an important distinction in regarding a statute as vague as opposed to ambiguous. An offense is vague when an individual is unsure what the illegal conduct is. By contrast,

---

19. Robinson, supra at 50.
20. Id. at 42.
21. Id.
22. Model Penal Code §1.02(3). Providing "fair warning" of criminal conduct is one of the general purposes of the MPC. §1.02(d).
23. Robinson, supra at 51.
24. Id.
25. *Connally v. General Constr. Co.*, 269 U.S. 385 (1926).
26. *Papachristou v. City of Jacksonville*, 405 U.S. 156 (1972).
27. *Giaccio v. Pennsylvania*, 382 U.S. 399 (1966).
28. Packer, supra n. 8, at 93. But see Jeffries, supra n. 7, at 200-201.

an ambiguous law allows for multiple readings of the same law, none of which are inherently incorrect.[29]

The doctrine ensures that criminal statutes provide fair notice of what behavior is forbidden. It requires the legislature to define the elements of the crime clearly in advance rather than require the judiciary to do so retroactively and additionally requires the legislature to provide notice of potential sanctions.[30] The vagueness doctrine also prevents police from arbitrarily choosing which persons they will arrest. Finally, it helps ensure a consistent and equal application of the criminal law. Void for vagueness does not preclude the legislature from passing a criminal law to accomplish a legitimate law enforcement goal. It simply requires the legislature to use clear and focused language. Of course, it is not always clear when a law is too indefinite so as to be unconstitutional. Courts are more likely to strike down laws as unconstitutionally vague when they are very general in scope, are overly broad or too readily reach innocent behavior (especially if the First Amendment is involved), and confer very broad discretion on police officers to arrest whom they choose (especially if racial discrimination appears to be involved).[31] Thus, in *Papachristou v. City of Jacksonville*, the Supreme Court struck down a broadly worded vagrancy ordinance because it gave the police "unfettered discretion" to decide whom to arrest. Justice Douglas noted: "The rule of law, evenly applied to minorities as well as majorities, to the poor as well as the rich, is the great mucilage that holds society together."[32] More recently, in *City of Chicago v. Morales*,[33] the Court agreed with the Illinois state supreme court that a Chicago ordinance that prohibited criminal street gang members from "loitering" with other gang members or non-members was unconstitutionally vague because it failed to give ordinary citizens adequate notice of what conduct is criminal and conferred too much enforcement discretion on police officers.

There is an emerging issue in the void for vagueness context—an increasing number of statutes are being written to prohibit a great amount of behavior. Additionally, these statutes are broadly written which allows for the executive to find whichever undesirable behavior they choose to be criminal.[34] Most recently, in *United States v. Jonson*, the Supreme Court used the void for vagueness doctrine to hold a law defining a violent felony as

29. Robinson, supra at 41.

30. Carissa Byrne Hessick, Vagueness Principles, 50 Ariz. St. L.J. 1137 (2017) ("Courts should instead revisit current doctrines which regularly permit insufficient notice, arbitrary and discriminatory enforcement, and unwarranted delegations in the enforcement of non-vague criminal laws.")

31. *Papachristou*, 405 U.S. 156; *Kolender v. Lawson*, 461 U.S. 352 (1983).

32. *Papachristou*, 405 U.S. at 171.

33. 527 U.S. 41 (1999).

34. Hessick, supra.

a crime that "otherwise involves conduct that presents a serious potential risk of physical injury to another" unconstitutional.[35] The Court took issue with the presence of the disparity of risk associated with the listed crimes in the statute in combination with the use of the word "otherwise" as an overly broad catch-all phrase. The combination of these factors left the public uncertain as to what could constitute a "potential risk" and therefore what was prohibited.[36]

However, courts have a pattern of upholding statutes against a vagueness challenge if the statute alerts an ordinary person that there is a reasonable risk that his conduct would violate the law. As Justice Holmes said in *Nash v. United States*, "the law is full of instances where a man's fate depends on his estimating rightly, that is, as the jury subsequently estimates it, some matter of degree."[37] Finally, a court can construe the statute more narrowly so that, as interpreted by the court, it is not unconstitutionally vague.[38]

The Burden of Proof

A final "limit" on the criminal law's reach is the procedural protection afforded to a criminal defendant. In this book, we discuss only one[39]—the high standard of proof required in criminal cases.

In virtually all legal proceedings, the person who wishes to change the status quo must demonstrate that there is good reason for doing so. Thus, she must carry the burden of proof that some legal harm has been inflicted, and that some legal remedy should be provided. In most civil lawsuits, the standard by which this proof must be established is articulated as a "preponderance" of the evidence. In a few suits, the standard is "clear and convincing," which is assumed to be "more than" a mere preponderance. In 1972, the United States Supreme Court confirmed in *In re Winship*[40] what had been the rule in the United States for over two centuries: In a criminal case, the United States Constitution requires that the prosecution has the burden of proof, and the standard of proof is beyond a reasonable doubt (BRD). The Court gave two reasons for this requirement: (1) defendants *might* face loss of liberty if convicted; (2) defendants would *certainly* be stigmatized as having committed immoral acts. In later cases, the Court made clear that

35. Id.
36. Id. at n.15.
37. 229 U.S. 373, 377 (1912).
38. *Winters v. New York*, 333 U.S. 507 (1948).
39. See R. Bloom & M. Brodin, Criminal Procedure: Examples and Explanations (4th ed. 2005), for a discussion of many others. R. Singer, Criminal Procedure II: From Bail to Jail: Examples and Explanations (3d ed. 2012).
40. 397 U.S. 358 (1972).

both of these factors must be present to require this level of proof. In civil commitment cases, where there is a potential loss of liberty but no stigmatization as a criminal, for example, the standard is "clear and convincing," not BRD.[41]

It is fairly easy to quantify the preponderance standard: 50.01 percent of the probabilities. And "clear and convincing" is "somewhat more" (70 percent?). But how much is "beyond a reasonable doubt"? In *United States v. Fatico*, 458 F. Supp. 388 (S.D.N.Y. 1978), a United States district court judge polled his colleagues and found that they "quantified" BRD as low as 76 percent and as high as 95 percent. As it turns out, there is no uniform national standard for beyond a reasonable doubt.

Nor can words better capture the heart of the standard. Since *Winship*, the Court has continuously questioned attempts to explicate more fully the purport of the words. In *Sandoval v. California* and *Victor v. Nebraska*, 511 U.S. 1 (1994), the Court upheld instructions that defined reasonable doubt as "not a mere possible doubt, because everything relating to human affairs and depending on moral evidence is open to some possible or imaginary doubt" or as requiring proof beyond a "moral certainty" and an "actual and substantial doubt." The Court's opinions, however, clearly demonstrated that the Justices were troubled by *any* attempt to define the term. Indeed, it has been suggested that trial judges should *never* try to do so.[42]

Debate has recently arisen about "what" the prosecution must prove beyond a reasonable doubt. One question involves the degree of factual particularity about which the jury must be unanimous. If the charge is carrying a concealed weapon, for example, and eight jurors find that the gun was in the defendant's right pocket, and four believe that it was in his left pocket, this lack of unanimity does not invalidate the conviction. But if eight jurors believe that the defendant, charged with grand larceny, stole a lamp on Thursday, and four believe that he stole a car worth the same amount of money on Friday, this is a sufficient difference to preclude a conviction.

A second issue has been addressed by the Supreme Court in a series of opinions. Suppose that a statute declares that possession of cocaine is illegal but imposes different sentences depending on the amount of cocaine involved. May a judge decide the question of *amount* (by a preponderance standard), or must this issue be left to the jury, in which case the standard of proof is beyond a reasonable doubt? In *Apprendi v. New Jersey*, 530 U.S. 466 (2000), the Court held that the Sixth Amendment required that any fact

---

41. *Addington v. Texas*, 449 U.S. 418 (1979).

42. Note, 108 Harv. L. Rev. 1955 (1995).

that *increased the potential maximum sentence* had to be proved to the jury BRD.[43] Thus, in this example, if the statutory maximum for 5 grams was a year, but the statutory maximum for 50 grams was 10 years, the amount must be submitted to a jury. On the other hand, suppose that one statute allows a sentence of 1 to 20 years for possession of cocaine but that sentencing guidelines establish the "usual" sentence to be 1 and 10 years, respectively, depending on the amount. In *Blakely v. Washington*, 542 U.S. 296 (2004), the Court held that even within the statutory framework, if the *sentencing guideline maximum* were to be increased, *Apprendi* required the court to submit the issue to the jury. Thus, if kidnapping carried a 10-year statutory maximum, but sentencing guidelines provided for a 2-year cap unless the kidnapping was done "for ransom"—in which case the guideline maximum was 5 years, still below the statutory maximum of 10 years—the jury would have to decide, BRD, whether ransom was involved. Six months later, the Court ruled the federal mandatory sentencing guidelines constitutionally invalid under *Apprendi-Blakely*. The Court reinterpreted the federal statutes establishing the guidelines as making them advisory, and not mandatory upon judges. If the guidelines are merely mandatory, an issue such as ransom need not be submitted to the jury, because even if the judge found ransom to be a factor, she would be under no compulsion to increase the sentence she would otherwise have imposed. *United States v. Booker*, 543 U.S. 220 (2005). *Booker*, which involved the interpretation of a federal statute, does not apply to the states; however, *Blakely* continues to require proof BRD of any fact that would increase the maximum sentence possible.

The *Apprendi-Blakely* cases' emphasis on the effect on maximum sentences is somewhat puzzling. Suppose that a statute establishes two different maximums (1 year vs. 3 years) between two different levels of larceny, depending on the value of the items stolen. Under a literal reading of *Apprendi*, the value of the goods must be submitted to the jury, although the increase in potential sentence (2 years) is only a small fraction of the increase in potential sentence under the drug guidelines. On the other hand, if *Apprendi* reaches the drug statute, many people argue that recent salutary reforms in sentencing processes will be threatened. Some people, however, have suggested that *Apprendi* would allow the jury to find the facts that potentially affect a sentence while allowing the judge to decide the precise quantity of that effect, much as a jury's finding that the defendant assaulted the victim "with intent to kill" allows the judge to increase the sentence based upon that finding.[44]

---

43. The Court recognized one exception—past criminal record—but its reasons for so doing are sui generis and need not detain us here.

44. See Richard G. Singer, Criminal Procedure II: From Bail to Jail: Examples and Explanations (3d ed. 2012).

EXAMPLES

Examples

1. Bobby was pulled over for speeding. When the officer stepped up to her window he noticed an open gas can on the floor of her car. The officer issued Bobby two tickets, one for speeding, and another for the unsafe handling of explosives. Bobby did not know that the gas can in the back of the car did not have the cap on. The relevant statute states "it is a criminal action to knowingly transport highly flammable or toxic materials in an unsafe manner." Bobby wants to rely on the lenity doctrine; as her attorney, how would you make this argument?

2. Tarrance promotes "rave" concerts in San Francisco. These concerts are one-time events featuring rock bands and are put on in secret locations on short notice. The promoters often sell drugs at these events.

   Tarrance receives anonymous calls from the producers detailing their plans to put on an all-night "Techno-Funk" rave concert and also to sell esctasy, an illegal designer drug. They tell Tarrance the date and location of the concert and hire him to print up catchy flyers advertising the event and the directions to the secret location. He is also hired to find friends who will pass out flyers to individuals who might be interested in attending the concert.

   Tarrance knows that ecstasy is often sold at rave concerts, but he has never been to a rave concert, does not sell drugs, and has never taken ectasy. He is hired only to promote the concert.

   A teenager passing out flyers is stopped and questioned by the police. She tells the police that Tarrance hired her to pass out the flyers. The police obtain a warrant and search Tarrance's home. They find no drugs or drug paraphernalia; they find only a printer and the printed flyers.

   A creative prosecutor charges Tarrance with "advertising an event at which drugs will be sold," even though there is no statute defining this offense. Can Tarrance be convicted on this charge?

3. Benton, a convicted felon, is arrested after he is caught buying a gun that has been transported across state lines. The prosecutor initially charges him with violating Title IV of the Omnibus Crime Control Act, which prohibits a convicted felon from buying a gun that has been transported in interstate commerce and provides a maximum penalty of two years in prison.

   Unfortunately for Benton, the prosecutor does some additional research and discovers that the Safe Streets Act of 1968, using the same language as Title IV, proscribes the very same conduct but provides a maximum sentence of 7 years. The prosecutor amends the charge, dropping the Title IV charge and adding the Safe Streets charge, hoping to obtain a longer prison term.

The defense counsel moves to dismiss the prosecution, claiming the statutes are void for vagueness because the law does not clearly set forth the penalty for this offense. What result?

4. Gabriela is an attorney for Scussy Scum, who has been charged in Las Vegas with solicitation to commit murder in a high-profile case. After the grand jury indicts Scussy, Gabriela holds a press conference where she states that the police fabricated stories and tampered with evidence in this case, and that these practices have become "all too common in Nevada."

   Two weeks later Gabriela is charged with violating a criminal statute that forbids a lawyer to speak about a pending case in ways that "a reasonable lawyer should know would have a substantial likelihood of materially prejudicing an adjudicative proceeding." Section (b) of the law provides that a lawyer "may state without elaboration . . . the general nature of the . . . defense." Statements by an attorney are permitted under this section even though they may "materially prejudice" the case.

   Gabriela claims she reasonably believed she could speak generally about her client's defense because of the language in section (b). She claims that the statute is constitutionally void for vagueness because attorneys, the group targeted by the law, must guess at its meaning.

   What result?

5. Russ, a convicted sex offender, was driving to his job at 7:00 a.m. The most direct route took him past the entrance to a five-acre city park. He ran out of gas just outside the park entrance. A police officer, who stopped to assist Russ, ran a license check and found that Russ was a convicted sex offender. The officer had just passed a mother with a baby in a stroller on the other side of the park. Russ was charged and convicted for violating a city ordinance that prohibited "a convicted sex offender from being within 2,000 feet of a park, playground, school, day care center, bus stop, or pool when children are present."

Explanations

EXPLANATIONS

1. The government will argue that Bobby knew that the gas can was in the vehicle and was transporting it in an unsafe manner and therefore she acted criminally. To make the best argument for Bobby using the lenity doctrine, a defense attorney will argue that although Bobby knew the gas can was in the car, she did not know that the cap was off and that she was therefore transporting the gas can in an unsafe manner. The statute is not clear as to whether or not it requires knowledge of only the transportation of the highly flammable material, or the knowledge of both the transportation and the unsafe manner of said transportation.

Because this statute can be read two different ways, it is ambiguous. Resolving this ambiguity in accordance with the rule of lenity, Bobby did not act criminally. If the court is persuaded by the rule of lenity, it will resolve the ambiguity in favor of Bobby (the defendant). However, the rule of lenity works more like a suggestion than an absolute rule, so courts may ignore it and rule against Bobby.

2. At one time, many American jurisdictions recognized "common law crimes," thereby allowing prosecutors to charge new crimes even though there was no statute specifically forbidding the defendant's conduct. If the evidence established that the defendant had injured social interests generally protected by the law, judges and juries were allowed to determine the criminality of the defendant's behavior based on the evidence presented.

   In such a common law jurisdiction, the court might well conclude that Tarrance had committed a crime because his behavior helped other individuals violate a specific statute that forbids selling drugs. This approach provides the criminal law with sufficient flexibility to meet new and unanticipated dangers. It also discourages creative criminals from taking advantage of the legislature's failure to pass a criminal law that prohibits such harmful behavior.

   Today, however, virtually every American jurisdiction has abolished common law crimes and, instead, requires the legislature to pass laws that specifically state what conduct is criminal and what punishment can be imposed. This provides individuals with adequate notice of what they can and cannot do and avoids retroactive punishment. It also ensures that prosecutors and juries are not making law, thereby preserving the important role of the legislature in our constitutional system of separated powers.

   Tarrance will not be convicted of the charged offense because there is no law that criminalizes his conduct—promoting concerts. He did not attend the concert nor did he supply or sell drugs there. If the legislature wishes to prohibit the act of promoting events at which drugs will be sold, it must enact a law specifically making such conduct criminal. This principle of legality will help ensure that the legislature has thought about the problem and also will limit police and prosecutorial discretion. More importantly, it will provide sufficient guidance to individuals about what conduct can expose them to criminal responsibility.

3. The void for vagueness doctrine also applies to punishment. At first glance, Benton's case seems to be one of unacceptable ambiguity. Two different laws provide different punishments for the very same offense. Can Benton successfully argue that these laws are void for vagueness because the statutes do not clearly set forth what penalty can be imposed for this offense?

In *United States v. Batchelder*, 442 U.S. 114 (1979), the Supreme Court held that two similar criminal statutes were *not* unconstitutionally vague. Each statute clearly set forth the conduct proscribed and the punishment authorized. The Court then concluded that two different statutes prohibiting the same conduct but providing two different penalties create no more uncertainty than does a single statute authorizing alternative penalties. These laws provide Benton with adequate notice of the range of punishment that can be imposed for his conduct and impose a reasonable limit on sentencing discretion.

4. The court might well find this statute void for vagueness. The "safe harbor" provision of section (b), which allows attorneys to describe the "*general* nature" of the defense "without *elaboration*," may mislead them into believing that they cannot be prosecuted for publicly discussing possible defenses even if they should reasonably know that the discussion might "materially prejudic[e] an adjudicative proceeding."

   Gentile v. State Bar of Nevada, 501 U.S. 1030 (1991), involved a Nevada supreme court rule (uncannily similar to the criminal statute in our example) that governed what lawyers may say about a case outside a judicial proceeding.

   The United States Supreme Court concluded that the Nevada rule failed to provide "fair notice to those to whom [it] is directed," and that a lawyer would have to guess at whether section (b) protected his discussion of his client's defenses. Section (b) was not sufficiently clear because the terms "general" and "elaboration" are classic terms of degree, which in this context have no settled usage or traditional legal interpretation. As a result, section (b) does not provide sufficient guidance for lawyers trying to fit within its "safe harbor." The Court held that the court rule as applied in Mr. Gentile's case was void for vagueness.[45]

   A statute can be constitutionally void on its face or as applied in a specific case. The standards are the same in each instance. The statute must (1) give adequate notice of what conduct is forbidden and (2) provide adequate enforcement standards. There is a difference between the two instances. A statute that is unconstitutionally vague *on its face* does not satisfy this two-part test for *any* conduct. A statute that is vague *as applied* does not satisfy the two-part test when applied to *specific* conduct. However, there is some conduct to which the statute can readily be applied without violating the test. In our example the statute would be considered impermissibly vague when applied to what Gabriela actually did.

45. Though agreeing that courts may adopt ethical rules that regulate what lawyers can say publicly about pending cases, the Court was also concerned that the rule as applied in this case could impermissibly infringe on Mr. Gentile's First Amendment right to criticize public officials.

5. Russ would argue that this criminal law is unconstitutionally vague. While driving his car, he had no way of knowing whether the road came within 2,000 feet of one of these prohibited locations, and he certainly could not be expected to know that a child was physically present, especially this early in the morning. Thus, a reasonable person in these circumstances could not know when he is engaging in the forbidden conduct. Moreover, the statute interferes with his First Amendment right to travel and, because it is virtually impossible *not* to inadvertently violate this city ordinance with great frequency, it confers excessive discretion on police officers to decide when they will arrest sex offenders for doing what ordinary citizens do every day.

   The prosecutor would respond that a reasonable person would have no difficulty understanding what the law prohibits. Convicted sex offenders surely would comprehend that they cannot come near these specified sites when children are there and that it is their responsibility to take all necessary precautions to comply with the law. To be safe, Russ should simply avoid coming near these places. This is a reasonable measure to prevent sex offenders from committing more sex crimes against children.

   How would you rule?

The Purposes of Punishment

OVERVIEW

Why do we punish? Why isn't requiring a defendant to pay damages to his victim "enough"? These are hardly new questions; philosophers have debated them for millennia. This chapter explores some of the answers philosophers have given, upon which modern criminal law is founded. We explore two of the usual answers—utilitarianism and retributivism—and assess them within the context of current legislative efforts to broaden the reach of the criminal law.

DEFINING PUNISHMENT

In general discussions we often use the term "punishment" as the equivalent of any hardship or loss that a person endures. Thus, if *A* has recklessly killed his beloved child in a hunting accident, we may be loath to prosecute him criminally because "he has been punished enough." That usage of the term "punishment," however, is both inadequate and inaccurate in the law (and in philosophy, as well). Punishment is hardship (1) *purposely* inflicted (2) *by the state* (3) because one of its laws was violated.

Thus, if Carl negligently injures Alice, compelling him to compensate Alice for the injury he caused, while causing loss to Carl, it is not punishment.[1] Punishment, instead, connotes a *blaming*, a *stigmatizing*, of the perpetrator as a choosing agent.

In the criminal system, it is often said that the individual victim is not relevant, and that the actual victim is the state.[2] Compensating Alice, therefore, does not compensate the victim of the criminal act, the state. Instead, the state *punishes* the offender—purposely inflicts discomfort upon him—*because* he has broken the law. In fact, no individual "victim" is required. Consider the fact that there are statutes punishing "victimless" crimes such as bribery, failure to pay taxes, or drug use.

THE PURPOSES OF PUNISHMENT

As we saw in Chapter 1, criminal law and tort law were once joined in the same proceeding. Even today, most acts that constitute crimes also constitute torts. Thus, if Charlie purposely hits Doug with a baseball bat, Charlie will have to pay Doug for the injuries for the tort of battery. Why, then, also punish Charlie criminally? What does criminal punishment add to the goals of the civil legal system?

Traditionally, two different responses are given to this question. One suggests that punishment serves *utilitarian* ends, such as (a) deterring persons who might be thinking about committing crimes, (b) incapacitating those who, if released, are likely to commit additional serious and violent crimes, or (c) rehabilitating those who have already committed offenses. The other explanation of criminal punishment (*retribution*), argues that persons who have committed crimes have acted immorally and must be punished to atone for the immoral action.

These two basic philosophies of punishment theory have clashed for centuries. Each has strong proponents, but each has significant weaknesses; supporters select one over the other based more on faith than proof.

Utilitarianism

The basic premise of utilitarian explanations of punishment is that punishment is itself an evil because it deliberately inflicts harm on a human being.

1. Zedner, Reparation and Retribution: Are They Reconcilable?, 57 Mod. L. Rev. 228 (1994); Barnett, Getting Even: Restitution, Preventive Detention, and the Tort/Crime Distinction, 76 B.U. L. Rev. 157 (1996).

2. There is a growing view that the individual victim should not be barred from some parts of the criminal process—e.g., at sentencing. Indeed, there have been attempts to enact a constitutional amendment explicating "victims' rights." See Richard G. Singer, Criminal Procedure II: From Bail to Jail: Examples and Explanations (3d ed. 2012).

Therefore, we should punish criminals only if some "good" is achieved by this act. That "good reason" is found in various social benefits to the law-abiding—primarily reduction of future crimes, producing unity, or promoting social welfare[3]—that are said to result from punishing criminals.

Deterrence

Deterrence theory posits that punishment of a criminal should be set to most efficiently prevent, avoid, or deter future offenses. This theory can be divided into two categories: specific deterrence and general deterrence. Aiming to deter the offender at hand from committing additional offenses in the future is specific deterrence; aiming to deter other potential offenders is called general deterrence.[4] If Joan never speeds because she fears a ticket, this is general deterrence. If, just as Bob decides to speed, he sees a police car and does not speed, he demonstrates specific deterrence.

General deterrence and specific deterrence may rely on different factors in determining punishment. For example, general deterrence would impose greater punishment in cases receiving greater media coverage. The broad reach of the message sent by punishment in these cases would give a greater general-deterrent payoff for the punishment-cost investment. Specific deterrence has little reason to care or consider the degree of media coverage, as the target audience is only the offender at hand.[5]

Deterrence depends on an offender's consideration of the "costs" of punishment, and those costs depend on both the amount of punishment and the likelihood of punishment.[6] Both general and specific deterrence are based on the ability of the law to threaten potential Ds with a penalty serious enough to dissuade them from acting. The pain threatened must be greater than the pleasure that D thinks he will attain by committing the crime. The premise is that criminals balance these pleasures and pains; indeed, Jeremy Bentham, the founder of utilitarianism, called this the "felicific calculus."[7]

There are simply too many variables to accurately measure the actual deterrent effect of a threatened punishment. For example, if the legislature increases the penalty for burglary, and the rate of burglaries thereafter decreases (assuming that we are relatively sure of that), it is very difficult to prove that the threat of increased punishment *caused* the decline. After all, all the burglars may have already been put in jail, or (if unemployment is

---

3. Paul H. Robinson, Shima Baradaran Baughman, & Michael T. Cahill, Criminal Law: Case Studies and Controversies 80 (4th ed. 2017).

4. Id.

5. Id. at 81.

6. Id. at 80.

7. Principles of Penal Law, in J. Bentham's Works 396, 402 (J. Bowring ed., 1843).

related to crime) the unemployment rate might have dramatically decreased, making fewer people "turn to" crime. After examining all the studies on this subject, the National Research Council of the National Academy of Sciences concluded that we "cannot yet assert that the evidence warrants an affirmative conclusion regarding deterrence."[8]

To be effective, deterrence requires that *D* receive *notice* of the threat of punishments. However, how members of society learn of the possible punishments threatened if they violate the criminal law is uncertain. Obviously, few citizens read the statute books to determine the possible punishments. Most of us probably learn simply by experience that crimes are "bad," and that some crimes are "worse" than others. We also sense that "worse" crimes are punished more severely than others.

The theory of deterrence requires not only that *D* hears the threat of the criminal law, but that he hears it *accurately*. Thus, if the law threatens a punishment of five years, but *D* believes the punishment is only three years, he will be less deterred than he should be. (On the other hand, if he believes that the punishment will be ten years, he will be overdeterred.)

A more sophisticated version of providing notice assumes that there are "target" groups who are more likely to commit certain kinds of crimes. Consequently, it is more important to ensure that they hear the threat than that the general public hear it. Thus, for example, to deter embezzlement, we might ensure that bank tellers or others entrusted with large amounts of funds are expressly and continuously reminded of the penalties associated with that crime.

In addition to being heard, the threat must be *credible*. This requires two further suppositions: (1) *D* thinks he will be captured; (2) *D* believes that, if captured, he will be punished as threatened.

Most criminologists believe that the *certainty of capture* deters much more than severity of punishment.[9] Unfortunately, both theory and practice undermine both hopes: The FBI Uniform Crime Report of 2015 indicates that police "clear" (believe they have found the guilty party) in only a small percentage of most crimes. For example, police "cleared" 61.5 percent of murders and 37.8[10] percent of rapes, but only 21.9 percent of larceny-thefts,

---

8. Deterrence and Incapacitation: Estimating the Effects of Criminal Sanctions on Crime Rates (1978). See also Law Reform Commission of Canada, Fear of Punishment (1976).

9. See Fear of Punishment, supra n.4, at vi.

10. In 2013, the FBI's UCR Program revised the definition rape and removed the term "forcible" from the definition. (UCR Handbook, 2004, p. 19) The revised definition defines rape as: "Penetration, no matter how slight, of the vagina or anus with any body part or object, or oral penetration by a sex organ of another person, without the consent of the victim." *Summary Reporting System User Manual*, Version 1.0 dated June 20, 2013. According to the FBI Uniform Crime Report, the clear rate is 37.8 percent for rape offenses (revised definition) and 36.2 percent for rape offenses (legacy definition).

29.3 percent of robberies, and 12.9 percent of burglaries.[11] These figures remain distressingly consistent year after year. Changes in the crime rate do not appear to alter the clearance rate in any significant way.

Furthermore, every criminal, even if he knows that the capture rate is high "in general," believes that *he* is smart enough to avoid capture. If that were not the case, he would not commit the crime. Bentham's "felicific calculus" requires that the defendant accept the possibility of capture, but most actual criminals do not do so.[12] Indeed, critics of the deterrence theory point out that when pickpockets were publicly hanged, many pockets were picked at the public executions, thus suggesting that the pickpockets did not expect to be caught (since the penalty, if caught, was obvious).

Even when defendants are captured, these same FBI data show that most persons are prosecuted for and convicted of less serious offenses than those for which they were "cleared." Assuming for the moment that the police clearance rate is accurate, this means that many persons who actually commit crime A are punished for a less serious crime B; unless the threatened punishment for B is (almost) as severe as that for A, the threatened punishment for A has become irrelevant.[13] Thus, such practices as pretrial diversion, plea bargaining, early release on parole, and so on, all undercut the deterrent impact of the threatened punishment. These realities are exacerbated by the fact that the persons most likely to avoid punishment for crime A are those who know how to manipulate "the system." Paradoxically, a professional criminal (especially one with financial means) may well be more able to obtain a lesser sentence than the first-time offender.

Critics of the deterrence theory argue that many crimes are *not* crimes of calculation. Indeed, current analysis argues that deterrence theory is most applicable in white collar crimes, which often take long periods of planning, followed by long periods of implementation, and that "street crimes," such as muggings and burglaries, are far less amenable to the deterrence calculus. Yet most current concerns about crime focus on street crime rather than white collar crime.

---

11. Federal Bureau of Investigation, Uniform Crime Report (2016). These figures, of course, relate to "reported" crimes. There is wide consensus among experts that the reported crime figures are substantially below actual crime figures, except possibly for homicide. Estimates based on victimization studies suggest that only one-third to one-half of all rapes are reported, and that anywhere between one-third to four-fifths of all property crimes are unreported.

12. A 1996 study of nearly 500 armed robbers showed that 83 percent of them believed affirmatively that they would not be caught. R. Erickson, Armed Robbers and Their Crimes 38, 39, 89 (1996). This was true even though 48 percent had been previously imprisoned. An unspecified additional percentage had been caught and put on probation.

13. This, of course, is true only if D *knows* of these facts. To the extent that he overestimates either the possibility of capture or the possibility that the threatened punishment will actually be imposed, he is "overdeterred."

Finally, though the evidence is slim, several studies have concluded that peer pressure and the threat of losing status among friends and friendships have much more influence on a potential criminal than does the threatened criminal penalty.[14]

None of these criticisms necessarily demonstrates the invalidity of the deterrence model. Most likely, criminal punishment achieves some "general prevention" and "educates" us to both the threat and the morality of the criminal law as we grow up.[15]

Note that it is the *threat*, and not the actual punishment, that brings about deterrence. Under utilitarian theory, if it were possible to threaten punishment but never impose it and yet achieve the same amount of deterrence, punishment itself would be unnecessary. Thus, if Professor Wing convinces her students that she lowers grades on the basis of poor class performance—even if she never does—she may obtain better participation in class. And if Ezekial performs poorly, Professor Wing may merely have to *appear* to note his poor behavior in her class notes in order to increase preparation.

Incapacitation

A second utilitarian explanation[16] of why we punish is that those who commit criminal acts have rejected important social norms and have thereby demonstrated their willingness to continue to do so in the future. Thus, for the good of those who abide by the law, these offenders must be prevented (incapacitated) from reoffending via imprisonment, execution, or any other restraint or impairment that disables a potential offender.[17]

Incapacitationists must either (1) punish equally, for lengthy periods of time every person committing the same crime or (2) assume that they can accurately identify those who are most likely to reoffend and impose on them lengthy periods of incarceration. This latter premise partially explains the establishment of parole boards, which are theoretically composed of experts who can determine when an offender has "learned his lesson," and no longer needs incapacitation.

Opponents of incapacitation pose several objections. First, they assert it is not possible to predict accurately who will recidivate. Thus, if incapacitation is to reduce the crime rate, many offenders must be incarcerated at

---

14. F. Zimring & G. Hawkins, Deterrence (1973).

15. Even here, however, there are cavils. What of the person who grows up in a "criminal" milieu? Can he be deterred? Suppose that, in his subculture, capture and punishment are *not* seen as stigmatizing but are approved? These issues are now being raised in the area of "rotten social background" or "cultural defense."

16. For a thorough study of this view, see F. Zimring & G. Hawkins, Incapacitation (1995).

17. Robinson, Baughman, & Cahill, 82.

very high cost for long periods of time. Assume, for example, that statistics indicate that 10 percent of all burglars actually commit 80 percent of all burglaries. Out of a group of 100, unless we can identify the 10 high repeaters, we must incapacitate for long terms 90 who will not "seriously" recidivate. Some argue that this is too high a price to pay both economically and morally.

Supporters of incapacitation respond by saying that it *is* possible to predict some kinds of recidivism within "acceptable" limits. We have come a long way as far as prediction in crime before arrest, after arrest, and after conviction.[18] Furthermore, they suggest, if there *is* overprediction, and some offenders are kept unnecessarily long, the pain imposed on them is outweighed by the pain not imposed on those putative innocent victims of the 10 who would be "improperly" released.

A major critique of incapacitationist theory is that it ignores the so-called replacement phenomenon in crime. Many criminal activities are "market" driven. If there is a demand for contraband goods (drugs, prostitutes, stolen TVs), someone will supply them. Thus, when one supplier of goods is convicted and incapacitated, another supplier will replace him. While it may be true that when Aloysius is incarcerated, *he* will not push drugs on the corner, it is still likely, given no reduced demand, that someone else will.[19] Whether crimes of violence, rape, homicide, or robbery follow this same pattern is less clear. Some criminologists argue that even these crimes have "markets," in the sense that the arrest of one robber simply widens the possibilities for those who have not been arrested. If so, incapacitating one robber will result in no reduction of the overall crime rate for that offense.

Rehabilitation

Between 1800 and 1975, American jurisdictions seemed dominated by a third utilitarian theory, rehabilitation. This theory holds that offenders can be "changed" into nonoffenders by taking away the offender's desire or impulse to engage in criminal conduct if given proper "treatment."[20] Common forms of rehabilitation include medical treatments, rehabilitation programs, psychological counseling, and education and training programs.[21] The idea of rehabilitation emanated from the Quakers who, in the first decade after the American Revolution (and as a reaction to the widespread use of capital punishment for virtually all felonies), invented

18. See e.g., Shima Baradaran & Frank McIntyre, Predicting Violence, 90 Tex. L.R. 497 (2012).
19. This is also true, of course, if *A* is part of a gang, which will continue without him. If *A* is replaced by B, we may paradoxically have created a new criminal, B.
20. Robinson, Baughman, & Cahill, 82.
21. Id.

the penitentiary, where a criminal would become "penitent" by reading the Bible and renounce further criminality.

During its ascendancy, rehabilitation took several different modes. Between (roughly) 1800 and 1870, crime was often seen as a "social" disease generated by conditions in industrial cities. Hence, many prisons were built in places remote from those cities. From 1870 to 1900, crime was analogized to a medical disease, and the proper "care" would cure the offender. Parole boards, consisting of experts who could best detect whether a defendant was cured, would release the offender when he was no longer in need of treatment. In a subsequent wave from 1900 to 1940, criminality was seen as inherited. Many states provided for the sterilization of criminals to avoid crime by their progeny.[22] Finally, between 1940 and 1975, crime was seen primarily as a symptom of psychological disturbance; psychiatrists were added to parole boards, and "behavior modification" programs blossomed in prisons.

Each of these models resulted in other changes in the criminal justice system. The rehabilitationist theory (like an incapacitationist one) required an indeterminate sentence for each criminal because the "symptoms" and cure would differ with each individual. Similarly, judges would require "presentence reports," which would inform them of the social background of the defendant, the likelihood that he needed rehabilitation, and for how long. Indeterminate sentencing was adopted in virtually every state.[23]

Critics of rehabilitationist theory generally argued that there was no evidence that "treatment" during punishment worked. No data showed that persons put in treatment programs while in prison were less likely to recidivate.[24] This skepticism was strongly supported by a landmark paper in the mid-1970s that, after reviewing studies of scores of such programs, was interpreted as concluding that "nothing works."[25] In fact, that was not

---

22. In *Skinner v. Oklahoma*, 316 U.S. 535 (1942), the Supreme Court invalidated an Oklahoma statute that provided for the sterilization of some thieves, but not all, on the grounds of *equal protection*, since the Court found no basis for distinguishing among thieves. There was no suggestion that the penalty itself would be unconstitutional (although that view might hold sway in today's Court).

23. Prior to 1976, California adopted the most indeterminate adult system in which many crimes were punished by "0-life." The most indeterminate system, of course, was the juvenile justice system, which was also seen as the most "rehabilitative" in nature. Juveniles would be sentenced to totally indeterminate terms (capped only by reaching their majority) without regard to the crime at all. Thus, assuming a majority age of 21, a 17-year-old would receive essentially a 4-year term for an offense for which a 12-year-old would receive a 9-year term.

24. Whether this is due to the inadequacy of resources devoted to rehabilitative programs or to some notion that criminality is "inborn" is unimportant to these critics.

25. Robert Martinson, What Works? Questions and Answers About Prison Reform, 35 Pub. Interest 22 (1975).

the conclusion of the piece, as its author thereafter recognized,[26] but by that time, it was too late. The "nothing works" message had been generally accepted by legislatures around the country.

Empirical Critiques

Each of the utilitarian theories claims to reduce the crime rate. When, as in the rehabilitation study cited above, the efficacy of the practice is questioned by empirical studies, the validity of the theory is similarly questioned. This may be unfair, since there are so many other variable factors that affect the crime rate (including, for example, the reporting rate) that have nothing to do with any of the theories. Moreover, much of the data may be soft. Assertions about the incapacitative effect, for example, often rely on self-reports by prison inmates concerning how many crimes they "really" committed before being captured. Therefore, the very claims about reducing crime rates that make the utilitarian theories attractive also tend to make them susceptible to empirical attacks. (The retributive theory, discussed below, is not subject to the same critique, since it explicitly rejects any claims of real-world effect.)

Normative Critiques

In addition to the practical questions that confront utilitarian theory, there is a separate issue: Is it fair? Retributivists argue that utilitarians are willing to use the defendant as a "pawn" for purposes other than fair punishment. It is sometimes suggested that utilitarians would even be willing to punish a person they know is innocent if they could hide that fact from the "target population."

The great philosopher H.L.A. Hart attempted to reconcile these problems by suggesting that the "General Justifying Aim" of the criminal law could be utilitarian, but that the "General Distributive Aim" could be retributivist.[27] That is, we would punish only those who, by committing crimes, deserve punishment, but we would punish them with utilitarian, rather than retributivist, goals in mind. Even if one accepts Hart's accommodation, it does not fully meet the critique made by Immanuel Kant of any utilitarian theory. Kant argued that the "categorical imperative" of morality forbade treating a human being for any social purpose whatever. Utilitarians, he argued, did exactly that, thereby ignoring the difference between civil law (which is utilitarian) and criminal law (which, he asserted, should be based on moral judgments).

---

26. Robert Martinson, New Findings, New Views: A Note of Caution Regarding Sentencing Reform, 7 Hofstra L. Rev. 243 (1979).
27. Punishment and Responsibility (1968).

Retribution

The alternative major explanation for punishment is *retribution*. Retribution argues that persons who choose to do wrongful (i.e., criminal) acts *deserve* punishment, and punishment should be imposed on them even if it serves no utilitarian purpose. Indeed, an argument accepted by many retributivists is that punishment *must* be imposed because the offender deserves to be treated as a moral agent who has earned punishment by his crime. Failure to impose such punishment refuses to recognize this moral capacity. Thus, there is a "right to punishment." An individual is punished if and only if they are blameworthy of the offense and the degree of punishment is determined by the degree of blameworthiness.[28] Furthermore, the degree of blameworthiness depends on the seriousness of the violation as well as the extent of the actor's accountability.[29]

Unlike utilitarianism, which looks to effects in the future to justify the imposition of punishment, retributivism looks at the *past* act that the criminal chose to commit. Retributive theory restricts punishment only to those who have made moral, willing choices; it would not allow the state to punish those who, such as the mentally ill or the duressed, had no (or little) choice. Nor would retribution allow *criminal* confinement based on prediction of *future* acts.

Most retributivists focus on the ability of the defendant to "choose" at the time of the crime. In the past few decades, however, a variation of retributivism has emerged that suggests that we can and should punish persons because of their *character*—as exemplified by their choices. This school of thought argues that if a "criminal" act is not "in character" for the defendant, then she should not be punished at all, or as gravely, as would be a "real" criminal.[30]

When the theory of retribution is pressed, however, many of its supporters seem to explain it by referring to the need to reaffirm society's mores, which seems like a utilitarian objective. Another weakness in the retributive theory is the difficulty with which it explains how punishing the criminal "makes up for" the injury that *D* inflicted on society. Some argue that *D* has obtained an unfair advantage through his crime, and that only by punishing him can that advantage be balanced. But that claim surely is not clear: If *D* has stolen $100 from *Z*, and *D* has been captured and the $100

---

28. Robinson, Baughman, & Cahill, 83.

29. Id.

30. Samuel Pillsbury, The Meaning of Deserved Punishment: An Essay on Choice, Character, and Responsibility, 67 Ind. L.J. 719 (1992); Dan Kahan & Martha Nussbaum, Two Concepts of Emotion in the Criminal Law, 96 Colum. L. Rev. 269 (1996).

returned, it would seem that *Z* is already back in the status quo ante. One response to this is to suggest that *Z*'s psychological state has been affected in a way that requires that *D* be punished, but to some this seems like vengeance. Another response is that the rest of society, possible future victims of *D*, are put in psychological fear and need reassurance that *D* will not commit more crimes. However, this sounds like incapacitation, which retributive theory expressly rejects as a basis for punishment.

Yet another criticism of retributivism is its ambiguity. Retributive schemes of punishment require proportionality. While the *lex talionis* (an earlier version of retribution) established the notion of "an eye for an eye," retributivists point out that their theory is also one of limits. The principle of an eye for an eye is no longer allowed, even if total blindness would deter (or incapacitate) more offenders. Perhaps such a proportionality was possible when most crimes (and punishments) were corporal in nature, but when a society refuses to use certain methods of punishment—death, torture, maiming—even if the defendant used them, the concept is difficult to apply. Determining the "proportionate" length of imprisonment for theft or for bribery or, for that matter, the purposeful infliction of the loss of an eye—known as the problem of *cardinality*—is surely difficult if not impossible. Furthermore, proportionality requires *ordinality*, ranking crimes according to their seriousness. Again, while robbery is clearly more serious than jaywalking, there seems to be no objective basis for at least some ordinal rankings.

Notions of proportionality are extremely fluid. When retributivists argue that one should be punished "for the crime," the seriousness of the crime is in the eyes of the beholder. If *A* wishes to impose more punishment than would *B*, there is no obvious way to resolve that dispute except to say that one of these punishments "feels" wrong. Thus, capital punishment for jaywalking may "feel" disproportionate, but articulating why that is true is more difficult. In recent years, the United States Supreme Court has confronted several challenges, based on an alleged constitutional doctrine of proportionality, to punishments of life imprisonment for (1) three-time bad check passers, *Solem v. Helm*, 463 U.S. 277 (1984), and (2) one-time possessors of significant amounts of drugs, *Harmelin v. Michigan*, 501 U.S. 957 (1991). The Court appears to have decided that there was a requirement of proportionality.

The Court has reaffirmed the existence of a proportionality principle in the Eighth Amendment but held that a state statute that imposed a minimum term of 25 years' imprisonment before eligibility for parole for a third felony (the latest of which was the theft of three golf clubs worth $400 each) did not violate that principle. *Ewing v. California*, 538 U.S. 11 (2003). During the same term, however, the Court also held that punitive damages awards in civil cases could be so disproportionate as to violate the due process clause. *State Farm Mutual Automobile Ins. Co. v. Campbell*, 538 U.S. 408 (2003).

In addition to these concerns, critics argue that the theory validates hatred. Indeed, one major advocate of retributivism once said it was morally right for the public to hate criminals.[31] That view is often taken to justify vengeance. Phrases such as "an eye for an eye" seem to suggest not only that the anger raised by a crime is acceptable (which it may be), but that any actions taken as a result of that anger are also acceptable (which a retributivist would reject).

In the past three decades, retributivism has experienced a resurgence, in part because of the perceived empirical uncertainties of utilitarian claims, and in part because of the inherent attractiveness of a normative approach to punishment.

The Relationship of the Theories

Proper analysis of criminal law doctrines requires that we keep these various theories of punishment separate and assess doctrines according to each of these theories. In practice, however, the theories frequently reach the same result. A deterrence theorist would support a claim of self-defense because persons who are, or who believe themselves to be, under imminent attack cannot be deterred from defending themselves, and because allowing such a response might deter future aggressors (see Chapter 16). A retributivist would agree that the claim should be recognized, but on the grounds that an actor is not morally blameworthy for taking action to prevent injury to himself. A rehabilitationist would probably conclude that the defendant is in no need of treatment, since he acted (ex hypothesis) as most persons would act. And an incapacitationist would not need to incarcerate a self-defender since he will use deadly force only in such situations. Thus, all four theories support a claim of "self-defense," but for different reasons.

It is when this harmony does not occur that the criminal law must choose among those conflicting purposes. A deterrence theory might support a claim of insanity because the insane cannot be deterred, and a retributivist would argue that the insane person is not blameworthy because he is not a freely choosing agent. However, the incapacitationist and the rehabilitationist might well want to confine the insane actor to prevent future harm to others or to have the opportunity to treat him. Therefore, whether we recognize a claim may depend on what we see as the purpose of the criminal law.

---

31. James Fitzjames Stephen, A History of the Criminal Law 81 (1883).

The Importance of Sentencing

The theories of punishment outlined above impact not only on doctrines of the substantive criminal law but on sentencing, as well. Far too often, courses in criminal law ignore the sentencing process and focus solely on assigning criminal liability. While we cannot here discuss that process in any detail, it is critical for students to recognize the way in which sentencing schemes can undo the doctrines of substantive criminal law.[32]

Much of the course in criminal law is spent in differentiating one crime, or one level of crime, from another. Thus, for example, criminal law usually treats persons who "purposely" commit some act as different from (and hence, deserving of more punishment than) persons who commit the same act "recklessly" or "negligently." Each offense will have a general classification or grade (for example, third-degree felony or first-degree misdemeanor) that will establish a range of possible punishments.[33] However, if the sentencing scheme in a particular jurisdiction allows both to be punished equally, the distinctions drawn by the criminal law are undermined. For example, substantive doctrine distinguishes between a premeditated killing (Melinda wants to kill Bill, lies in wait for Bill, puts the gun to Bill's head, and pulls the trigger six times) and a reckless killing (Constance, while twirling a loaded gun, drops it; it discharges and kills Dudley). The first of these is called "first-degree murder," the second "manslaughter." However, suppose the sentencing system provides that either killer can be sentenced to zero to life. If a judge sentences Melinda to 5 years and Constance to 20 years, the doctrinal differences that are debated in criminal law courses become less important (one might say meaningless) to Constance. Conversely, to the extent that sentencing systems provide for no overlap between similar crimes (in the example above, 0-15 years for manslaughter and 20 years-life for first-degree murder), they reinforce the distinctions drawn by the substantive criminal law.

The criminal law is drafted to make the assignment of liability a matter of rules rather than discretion.[34] This articulation of liability rules is called the principle of legality.[35] Many jurisdictions have established sentencing guidelines that purport to limit judicial discretion in sentencing. It is not

32. We have here chosen to focus on sentencing discretion because it most obviously undercuts criminal law doctrine. However, at every stage of the criminal justice system, discretionary decisions can have this effect. Thus, if police do not arrest, prosecutors do not prosecute, or fact finders do not convict obviously guilty persons, the substantive law is frustrated. After conviction and sentencing, if parole boards release offenders "too early," they arguably undermine the intended legislative effect of the statute.

33. Robinson, Baughman, & Cahill, 20.

34. Robinson, Baughman, & Cahill, 21.

35. Id.

clear, however, that these guidelines were intended to, or will, lessen the tension between goals of the criminal law and those of sentencing policy. Uniformity in enforcing sentences imposed primarily for the purpose of incapacitation, for example, will not reduce the conflict if the goal of the substantive criminal law is seen as deterrence, or retribution, or rehabilitation.

The sentencing system should reflect the theories of punishment as much as the substantive criminal law. Thus, suppose that the reason substantive criminal law distinguishes between murderers and manslaughterers is that it endorses retributivism. It may turn out that Melinda really regrets her act, whereas Constance is not at all sorry that the gun discharged and would commit the same reckless act again if given the chance. Under an incapacitationist sentencing scheme, Melinda *should* receive a lighter sentence than Constance, but under the retributivist criminal law, Constance should receive less punishment than Melinda. This would seem to require that the substantive criminal law and the sentencing schemes be based on the same theories. If those two processes are based on different theories, a significant conflict can arise that undermines each part of the system.

The relative disappearance of rehabilitation as a goal of punishment has resulted in the reduction of indeterminacy in sentencing. In the last three decades, at least half the states have adopted some form of restrictions on such discretion. Mandatory minimum sentences are one example. Sentencing guidelines, usually established by sentencing commissions, are another. These approaches do not necessarily avoid the clash between theories we have outlined above. Commissions can still use a different basis for setting sentences than did the legislature in establishing definitions of crimes. Many states are beginning to regret moves towards determinate sentencing that provide less flexibility when it comes to reducing sentences for offenders in jurisdictions facing overcrowded jails.

"CIVIL" VS. "PUNITIVE"

The Difference Between "Criminal" and "Civil" Confinement

Our constitutional system provides vigorous protection for individual liberty. Thus, under the criminal law, a person can lose his liberty only *after* the government proves beyond a reasonable doubt that he has committed a crime. But our system also allows the government, in limited situations, to take away an individual's freedom to *prevent* him from committing additional harmful acts. The government may civilly commit someone to a mental health facility to prevent such harm and to treat him if it can prove that he suffers from a *mental condition* that *causes* him to be *dangerous*. These laws are "civil" because they do not further either retribution or deterrence. Instead, they are intended to incapacitate and treat mentally disturbed and dangerous individuals who do not respond to the threat of criminal punishment. Every state has an involuntary civil commitment law.

A Contemporary Example: Sexual Predator Laws

Since 1990, at least 19 states and the federal government have also enacted "sexual predator laws." They allow the government to civilly commit sex offenders about to be released from prison if it can prove they suffer from a "personality disorder" or "mental abnormality" that makes them likely to commit another serious sexual crime. Commitment is to a secure mental health facility for an indefinite period. The government must provide treatment and periodically review their condition to see if they are no longer a danger to society and can be released. The Supreme Court upheld the constitutionality of these laws in *Kansas v. Hendricks*, 521 U.S. 346 (1997), provided the government can prove the person suffers from a condition that makes it "difficult, if not, impossible for the person to control their dangerous behavior." The mental condition that causes loss of volitional control need not be recognized by mental health professionals. In *Kansas v. Crane*,[36] the Court clarified its earlier decision in *Hendricks* by requiring the government to prove that the defendant's mental condition significantly impaired his ability to control his sexual conduct.

The *Hendricks* Court set forth criteria for determining when laws that deprive a person of their liberty to prevent crime should be considered "civil" rather than "punitive" and, thus, not violate either the constitutional prohibitions against ex post facto or double jeopardy:

> Where the State has "disavowed any punitive intent"; limited confinement to a small segment of particularly dangerous individuals; provided strict procedural safeguards; directed that confined persons be segregated from the general prison population and afforded the same status as others who have been civilly committed; recommended treatment if such is possible; and permitted immediate release upon a showing that the individual is no longer dangerous or mentally impaired. . . . [*Hendricks* at 368-369.]

Supporters claim these laws are necessary to prevent dangerous sex offenders from committing another serious sex crime after they are released

36. 534 U.S. 407 (2002).

from prison. Critics argue they allow unconstitutional preventive detention under the guise of "civil commitment," and cannot in theory be limited in their reach.[37]

Examples

1. After a spree of burglaries in a suburban neighborhood, the police work with city officials to put up neighborhood watch signs to try to avoid home break-ins. This approach most closely aligns with which theory of punishment?

2. A number of towns in the United States have adopted ordinances holding parents criminally liable for the acts of their children. What are the theoretical arguments for and against such provisions?

3. Congress and many state legislatures have adopted "three strikes and you're out" statutes, which provide that a person convicted three times of a felony (sometimes limited to violent felonies, sometimes not) must be sentenced to mandatory terms of life imprisonment. What are the theoretical bases for such provisions, and what are the critiques?

4. Recent developments in genetics have suggested that some violent conduct may be greatly influenced by genes. On the basis of such preliminary suggestions, some social critics have proposed testing all six-year-old children to determine if their genetic makeup or behavior suggests that they are likely to commit violent criminal acts. If the finding is affirmative, they would confine and (if possible) treat such persons. What theories support such a proposal?

5. State X provides a term of 0-20 years for burglary. Sentencing guidelines, which are very strict in the state, require a sentence of no more than 5 years for the "usual" burglar. If, however, the offender is proven to be a "patterned sex offender," the judge must impose the maximum term of 20 years. What are the theoretical bases for this statute?

6. Kim has been convicted of aggravated assault of his wife with a weapon for a second time and is about to be released from jail. The prosecutor has filed a petition to send him to a mental health facility as a "dangerous, violent person" under a recently enacted law that authorizes involuntary civil commitment for any person "convicted of a crime of violence against the person who suffers from a personality disorder or mental abnormality that makes him likely to commit another serious assault." A

37. See Bruce J. Winick & John Q. La Fond (eds.), Protecting Society from Sexually Dangerous Offenders: Law, Justice, and Therapy (2003); John Q. La Fond, Preventing Sexual Violence: How Society Should Cope with Sex Offenders (2005).

mental health professional will testify that Kim suffers from an "antisocial personality disorder," a recognized mental disorder, which is based in part on a history of "irritability and aggressiveness, as indicated by repeated physical fights or assaults." Otherwise, the law is identical to the one upheld in *Kansas v. Hendricks*. Is this law constitutional?

7. Most states have adopted "Megan's Laws," statutes requiring that communities be warned of convicted sex offenders about to be released from prison to that community. Are these laws "punitive"?

Explanations

1. The signs are aimed to deter all potential offenders, not necessarily the offender(s) at hand, from committing additional offenses. This approach most aligns with general deterrence, a subcategory of utilitarianism. The objective of general deterrence is to deter all potential offenders as opposed to specific deterrence, which aims to deter the specific offender at hand. In this case, there have been a number of burglaries in a suburban neighborhood. It may be possible that there is only one offender or that there are many offenders, however, the purpose of the signs is to discourage or intimidate *any* potential offender(s) from committing a burglary in that neighborhood.

   This approach does not align with specific deterrence because the main objective of the signs is not to punish or discourage the actual offender(s) from reoffending. Specific deterrence would be the correct answer had the police discovered who was offending and punished them directly.

   For example, police discover that Katey and Gabriela are responsible for the burglaries. Katey and Gabriela are convicted of burglary, a second-degree felony, and sentenced to 1-15 years in prison. Under the theory of deterrence, the purpose of the sentence is to prevent Katey and Gabriela from reoffending. Imprisonment will prevent them from reoffending while they are serving their sentence. Additionally, the conviction will discourage them from reoffending in fear of being convicted again.

2. Most retributivists would find such a statute repugnant because the parent has not, by their definition, committed any morally blameworthy act. Utilitarians, however, might support some versions of these ordinances: The threat of imprisonment might coerce parents to supervise more closely their children. This would result in fewer juvenile crimes and thus less pain to the entire populace. (Some utilitarians might argue, however, that parents might *oversupervise*, thereby becoming disutilitarian.) A rehabilitationist might similarly argue that the parent needs

"training" in how to supervise a child. An incapacitationist, however, would find it hard to support this approach, since the incarceration of the parent might mean less supervision of the child.

Some retributivists, and most utilitarians, might conclude that, although the parent has not affirmatively committed a criminal act, the failure to properly supervise may be morally blameworthy. This would be particularly cogent if the provision were restricted (as is tort liability) to parents who were on notice that their child had committed, or was likely to commit, criminal acts. If negligence can be a proper basis for criminal liability (see Chapter 4, infra), such negligence may be blameworthy.

3. Retributivists would oppose such statutes, since the punishment proposed is, by definition, in excess of that required *for this* crime. Deterrence theorists might argue that such statutes are desirable because the mandatory nature of the penalty might deter felons from engaging in even "minor" crimes. (Of course, since "major" crimes would already carry long penalties, the issue for the deterrent theorist is whether the life sentence carries sufficient "marginal deterrence.") The primary explanation for such statutes is, of course, incapacitationist: The confinement of all such offenders ensures they would not offend again in society. This, however, raises several empirical issues: (1) are we "over-incapacitating," in the sense that not all three-time felons will continue to commit future crimes? (2) can we accurately predict those who will recidivate a fourth time? Experts disagree on the accuracy with which such predictions can be made, although there is general agreement that accuracy increases with an increase in the number of prior felonies. In addition, there is the question of whether the economic cost of lifelong incarceration is outweighed by the hoped-for reduction in crime in the community. This is a normative, not an empirical, question.

4. No theory of *criminal* liability supports incarceration in this manner. There is no deterrence to be gained since, by hypothesis, the defendant's conduct is caused by noncognitive facts (his genes). Similarly, unless therapy can be an effective treatment, there is no rehabilitative support for confinement. And the retributivist would strongly reject the argument that the child is responsible for his genetic makeup. Only an incapacitationist approach supports such a proposal. However, this kind of confinement, if allowed at all, would surely not have to be "criminal" in nature. The child *may* be dangerous, but since she has done nothing yet to demonstrate that, civil incapacitation would serve society just as well. Indeed, since "criminal" confinement requires more procedural safeguards and hence more chance of not confining the child, it would be burdensome and hence, counter-utilitarian. There are other, perhaps

determinative, arguments against such a project because the prediction of future behavior, even if highly accurate, would not be entirely certain. In a society that favors freedom, we have to take risks rather than incarcerate the child before she has injured anyone. However, these arguments go generally to the moral desirability (and possible constitutionality) of such a proposal, not its link to criminal law generally.

5. How can burglary be sexually motivated? Burglary is defined as the "breaking and entering of [a place] with the intent to commit a felony therein." In one case, decided under such a statute, the court found that the presence of a condom in the defendant's pocket was sufficient to warrant finding that his motivation for the break-in was sexual in nature. *State v. Christie*, 506 N.W.2d 293 (Minn. 1993). The question here is why sexual motivation justifies the quadrupling of the normal sentence. Again, incapacitationists would argue that sexually-motivated offenders might be less deterrable than others, and therefore more in need of long-term incarceration. Rehabilitationists might agree. Retributivists would argue that the sentence is disproportionate to the harm actually inflicted, since the legislature has determined that 5 years, not 20, is the appropriate penalty for non-sexually motivated burglary, and the defendant's motive is irrelevant.

6. The answer to this question depends on whether the court concludes the "dangerous violent person" law is "civil" or "punitive." Under *Hendricks*, a court would probably uphold the law, provided it meets the requirements set forth in that case. The state must prove that Kim suffers from a mental condition that so impairs his ability to control himself that he is likely to commit another assault. It must also provide treatment, periodically review his condition, and release him when he no longer suffers from this condition *or* is not dangerous.

   Why do you think states would enact a civil commitment law that can only be used *after* the person serves his full prison term? To provide needed treatment? To extend incapacitation after the state's authority to confine someone under the criminal law has ended? Other good reasons?

   Should an individual be considered both *criminally* responsible and punished for his conduct and then *civilly* committed to a mental health institution for care and treatment because of a mental condition that it defined in large part by the same criminal acts? (You might want to reconsider this example after you have read "The Insanity Defense" in Chapter 17.)

7. In *Smith v. Doe*, 538 U.S. 84 (2003), the Court held the Alaska statute (and presumably all other such registration and notification laws) to be non-punitive and hence not governed by the ex post facto clause. In reaching this conclusion, the Court looked to the *intent* of the legislature, which

it said was to protect the public from sex offenders, and not to punish sex offenders. The Court then considered whether the law's *effect* was so punitive as to negate its civil purpose. Even though it required offenders to register periodically with local law enforcement authorities and to provide extensive personal information including where they lived (much of which is made available to the public), the Court concluded that the statute did not have a punitive effect. Instead the law simply imposed restrictive measures on sex offenders considered dangerous. Protecting the public is a legitimate government objective.

What if convicted sex offenders could prove that, as a result of registration and notification laws, they were unable to get jobs, find housing, live safely with their families, and return to a normal life in the community? Should courts consider those consequences in deciding whether they are punitive or regulatory? Are there any limits on what measures can be used to protect the public? What if a law prohibited convicted sex offenders from living near schools, parks, bus stops, and day care centers, effectively preventing them from living in most neighborhoods of a major city (like San Francisco), civil or punitive?

CHAPTER 3

Actus Reus

OVERVIEW

The criminal law needs a practical and consistent method to describe the behavior for which its special power of arrest, conviction, and punishment may be used. Simply put, it needs a basic architecture to define crime. Although they may differ on their reasons, most utilitarians and retributivists agree on the basic elements of a crime.

Voluntary Act. Subject to some exceptions we will discuss shortly, the criminal law only punishes voluntary action; it does not punish inaction or mere thinking. The "voluntary act" element of a crime is usually called the *actus reus*.

Many utilitarians would argue that involuntary behavior should not be criminalized because it cannot be deterred. Retributivists would claim that an individual who did not choose to do a wrongful act does not deserve punishment. Moreover, other systems of care and control, such as involuntary hospitalization, are used for individuals perceived as posing an ongoing threat of harm by involuntary acts.

There are good reasons for why the criminal law does not punish thoughts without action. First, it is extremely difficult to tell what a person is thinking, let alone whether he will act on those thoughts by committing a crime. Second, without this limitation, perhaps most of us would be subject to the reach of the criminal law because we fantasize about committing a crime at one time or another! Note, however, that speaking words is usually considered an act rather than "mere thoughts" in the criminal law.

Intangible Acts. In some cases, "the law assumes that an act has occurred although the actor has performed no muscular movement."[1] These circumstances will typically arise in the context of a conspiracy, where the party who physically commits the crime is indirectly instructed by another party. For policy reasons, the criminal law has created an avenue for holding the instructor culpable for the crime that he did not necessarily commit.

Omission and Legal Duty. The criminal law generally punishes an individual only for the affirmative harm she herself inflicts; it does not punish for failing to prevent harm caused by others or by natural forces.

In limited cases, however, the failure to act—usually called an *omission*—may be a crime if the defendant had a *legal duty* to act. Of course, the defendant must have been capable of doing the legally required act because "the law cannot hope . . . to stimulate action that cannot physically be performed."[2]

Legal duties may arise from a number of different sources. For example, sometimes a criminal statute explicitly requires an individual to act. A common example is the federal statute requiring most people to file an income tax return. Failure to file the return is considered a voluntary act rather than an omission because the statute specifically defines the failure to file as the prohibited "voluntary act."[3]

Mental State. Some type of mental state or attitude—i.e., *mens rea*—is usually (though not always) necessary for the commission of a crime. One exception is strict liability crimes, which do not require a mental state (see Chapter 6). The mental state requirement reflects a community consensus that the attitude with which the actor performed a voluntary act is important in determining whether to punish and, if so, how severely. Generally, the mental state component of a crime requires some degree of intentionality or carelessness. At common law, the mental state was called "mens rea"; the Model Penal Code calls it "culpability." We will discuss mental states more fully in Chapter 4.

Prosecutors often use the defendant's conduct or actus reus as their primary evidence in proving the defendant's mental state. This makes sense because human conduct is generally the product of mental processes. Moreover, an individual's behavior is usually easier to establish than her internal thought processes.

---

1. Paul H. Robinson, Shima Baradaran Baughman, and Michael T. Cahill, Criminal Law: Case Studies and Controversies, 505 (New York: Wolters Kluwer, 2017).

2. Model Penal Code and Commentaries 214-215 (1985).

3. In the real world, we think of a failure to file as an omission because the taxpayer has not done what he was supposed to do.

Summary. The definitional components of crime are straightforward. Most crimes consist of an actus reus and a mens rea. Both must occur together. In limited cases, an omission or failure to act, together with a legal duty, may also be a crime.

THE COMMON LAW

Crime requires either a voluntary physical act or an omission when there is a legal duty to act.

Voluntary Act

A *voluntary act* is a movement of the human body that is, in some minimal sense, willed or directed by the actor. A straightforward example is when a professional killer deliberately points a loaded pistol at his victim's head and pulls the trigger.

A voluntary act can also be the result of habit or even inadvertence as long as the individual *could* have behaved differently. Driving to the child care center to pick up your child even though your spouse told you the child did not need a ride qualifies as a voluntary act. This is the case even though you made the trip purely out of habit or while you were daydreaming.

Involuntary acts are those over which the individual had no conscious control. These may include acts done while unconscious or sleepwalking or acts resulting from health conditions, such as an epileptic seizure. They also may include bodily movements caused by being struck by another person or object. If *A* pushes B off the dock, B's plunge into the water is not a voluntary act. There is controversy over whether some behavior, such as that occurring while one is hypnotized, is voluntary or involuntary.

Usually, a voluntary act is essential for criminal responsibility—even for strict liability crimes that do not require any mental state (see Chapter 6). However, not all of the behavior must be voluntary before criminal responsibility attaches. As long as there is at least *one voluntary act* in the defendant's course of conduct, he may be criminally responsible. For example, in *People v. Decina*, 2 N.Y.2d 133, 138 N.E.2d 799 (1956), the defendant, knowing he was subject to epileptic seizures, nonetheless voluntarily drove a car and subsequently killed four people when he lost control of the car during an epileptic seizure. He was convicted of negligent vehicular homicide even though the actual "act" that killed was itself "involuntary" because it occurred during a seizure. The *earlier* voluntary act of getting into the car and driving it satisfies the voluntary act element of the crime.

Sometimes people do harmful acts because they are threatened with death or serious injury or to avoid a greater harm or because of serious mental impairment. Though these acts are often done under a great deal of pressure, the criminal law usually considers them "voluntary." Whether someone will be punished in such cases usually depends on whether a defense based on justification or excuse is available (see Chapters 15-17).

Intangible Acts

Under certain circumstances, the criminal law has allowed a voluntary act to be assumed where no physical movement has occurred. "'Let me know if I shouldn't kill him like the rest, Boss,' may allow the Mafia chief to direct a killing by doing nothing."[4] Under this scenario, the Mafia chief may be held liable for the murder despite the fact that he made no literal physical movement to perpetrate the crime. This can also be observed in the context of conspiracies, where courts have held the "agreement" requirement of one party to be satisfied by an intangible act.[5] The policy for allowing culpability in these cases "focuses on the special circumstances that express the actor's intention and willingness to carry out the act"; these circumstances are "adequate to serve the primary rationales of the act requirement as effectively as an affirmative act does."[6]

Omission and Legal Duty

Though usually concerned with preventing individuals from doing affirmative harm to others, the criminal law is occasionally used to motivate individuals to perform obligations imposed on them by other laws. The threat of criminal punishment may provide this extra motivation. Thus, the failure of a person to act when he is under a legal obligation arising from civil law also satisfies the actus reus requirement for crime.

The legal duty may be based on (1) *relationship* (e.g., a parent must provide food, shelter, and clothing to a child); (2) *statute* (e.g., many states have a law that requires medical providers and others to report suspected child abuse); (3) *contract to provide care* (e.g., nursing homes often enter into a contract to provide medical services to residents); (4) *voluntary assumption of care that isolates the individual* (e.g., taking a sick person into one's home may result in a duty to provide care); (5) *creation of peril* (e.g., someone who pushes

---

4. Paul H. Robinson, Shima Baradaran Baughman, and Michael T. Cahill, Criminal Law: Case Studies and Controversies, 505 (New York: Wolters Kluwer, 2017).
5. Id.
6. Id.

another who cannot swim into a deep lake must take reasonable steps to rescue him); (6) *duty to control the conduct of another* (e.g., a business executive may have a duty to prevent the company chauffeur from speeding); and (7) *duty of a landowner* (e.g., a theater owner has a duty to provide reasonable emergency exits for his patrons). Limiting *criminal* liability to cases where the *civil* law imposes a legal duty at least provides "notice" to individuals that they are legally required to act and fail to perform that duty at their peril.

Generally, a defendant must know the facts from which the duty to act has arisen. However, he may not avoid criminal responsibility by claiming he was unaware that a legal duty to act arose from those facts. Thus, a nursing home operator who entered into a contract to care for elderly patients cannot claim he did not know he had a legal duty to provide them with care. Nor can he claim he did not know that he could be held criminally liable for breaching that duty by failing to provide such care. Such a claim is, in reality, a defense based on ignorance of the law and is not a valid defense (see Chapter 5).

What About Almost Family? Courts have reached different conclusions on whether to impose a duty to prevent harm on someone who is a member of the victim's "extended family." The Connecticut Supreme Court initially upheld a first-degree assault conviction of a live-in boyfriend who did not stop his girlfriend (and mother of the victim) from beating her child because he had a family-like relationship with the victim.[7] Subsequently, however, it reversed course, holding that only individuals with a legally established family relationship with the victim have a duty to act.[8] Other courts would impose a duty of care on those who act as the functional equivalent of a parent in the household setting.[9]

Expanding the duty to act on a case-by-case basis may well protect more children from harm in the future. However, such fact-specific analysis makes it more difficult for individuals to know when they must act or face criminal prosecution. It might also discourage individuals from becoming part of an extended family.

What About When a Parent Is Also a Victim? Several recent cases have confronted the question of whether a parent can be criminally punished for failing to prevent someone else from abusing a child in situations where the parent also feared violence at the hands of the abuser. Some courts have found mothers who knew of ongoing sexual abuse of their young daughters by a father, stepfather, or boyfriend, guilty of child abuse for failing to take steps reasonably calculated to prevent the abuse. See, e.g., *Commonwealth*

---

7. 715 A.2d 680 (Conn. 1998).

8. *State v. Miranda*, 274 Conn. 727, 878 A.2d 1118 (2005).

9. See, e.g., *People v. Carroll*, 93 N.Y.S.2d 564, 715 N.E.2d 500 (1999).

v. Cardwell, 515 A.2d 311 (Pa. Super. 1986). Other courts, however, have reached a contrary conclusion. See, e.g., *Knox v. Commonwealth*, 735 S.W.2d 711 (Ky. 1987). These tragic cases place victims of past violence in a difficult position: Should they protect their child and run the risk of violent injury, or face prosecution if they fail to intervene? Most courts conclude that a parent does have a legal duty to act, and that failure to prevent the abuse can result in criminal responsibility.

Moral Duty

In general, our society expects people to do the right thing, which includes fulfilling their moral duties. Moral duties are those obligations that, according to our basic sense of right and wrong, people should live up to. However, the criminal law does not impose responsibility for failure to live up to a moral duty to act unless it is embodied in a civil law duty. Though we may hope or even expect our fellow citizens to be good Samaritans and prevent serious harm to others when they can do so at little or no risk to themselves, the criminal law generally does not impose this affirmative obligation.

Several arguments can be made in favor of this approach. They include a preference for personal autonomy and laissez-faire government. Law should only prevent individuals from affirmatively harming others; it should not compel citizens to help one another, especially when resources are limited. Moreover, requiring assistance may cause overreaction that could overwhelm or even harm the victim. Finally, the "slippery slope" argument asks where we should draw the line.

Some states, however, have enacted "good Samaritan" statutes that make it a criminal offense to refuse to help those known to be in serious peril when aid could be provided without danger.[10] Other states impose the duty only in more limited circumstances. These laws typically provide modest penalties, including fines only, or fines and very short sentences. This approach may strengthen a sense of community, make society safer, and prevent serious harm with little or no cost to the rescuer. It may also bring the law into closer conformity with our sense of moral decency and send a message encouraging cooperation rather than isolation.

Possession

Many criminal statutes forbid possession of specified items, such as laws punishing the possession of burglar tools or illegal drugs. In a sense, this

---

10. See, e.g., Vt. Stat. Ann. tit. 12, §519 (West 2006).

type of law does not require the defendant to "do" anything. Rather, mere possession—or the failure to terminate possession once the defendant learns of the item's presence—is sufficient. Nonetheless, these statutes comply with the requirement of a voluntary act because they are generally construed as requiring active or constructive knowledge on the defendant's part of the nature of the item he has under his control or custody. Thus, knowingly taking or keeping a forbidden item is a voluntary act.

What if someone does not know he possesses a legally forbidden item? Suppose a drug smuggler sneaks heroin into an innocent person's luggage, hoping to steal the suitcase after the innocent traveler successfully passes through customs. If the heroin is discovered in a border search, can the traveler be convicted of possessing drugs? Most courts require the defendant to be aware that he actually has whatever item the statute forbids possessing, even if he need not have the knowledge that the possession is illegal. But some courts do not require this awareness.[11]

Frequently, courts conclude that an individual or several individuals had "constructive possession" of forbidden items even though they did not individually exercise physical dominion and control over the items. Instead, courts often base their conclusion on the proximity of these individuals to the items or their ability to reduce an object to control and dominion.

THE MODEL PENAL CODE

Voluntary Act

The MPC defines an act or action as "a bodily movement whether *voluntary* or *involuntary*." MPC §1.13(2). It also provides that a person is not guilty of a crime under the MPC unless "his liability is based on conduct that includes a voluntary act or the omission to perform an act of which he is physically capable." MPC §2.01(1). However, the MPC does not define a "voluntary act." The Commentary suggests that it is essentially behavior that is "within the control of the actor."[12]

In addition, MPC §2.01(a) describes certain types of action that are *not* voluntary acts. These include "(a) a reflex or convulsion; (b) a bodily movement during unconsciousness or sleep; (c) conduct during hypnosis or resulting from hypnotic suggestions; and (d) a bodily movement that

11. *State v. Bradshaw*, 989 P.3d 1190 (Wash. 2004).

12. Model Penal Code and Commentaries 215 (1985).

otherwise is not the product of the effort or determination of the actor, either conscious or habitual."

Section 1.02(1) makes it clear that only the individual's *own* conduct will support criminal responsibility. Section 1.05 speaks of "conduct" that can "constitute an offense."

Omission and Legal Duty

Like the common law, the MPC permits an omission or failure to act to satisfy the conduct element of a crime in two different types of cases: (1) when the statute defining the offense expressly states that failure to act is a crime, or (2) the defendant has a duty to act imposed by civil law. MPC §2.01(3)(a) and (b). Failure to file an income tax return is an example of the first type; the law expressly states that such failure to act is a crime. A parent's failure to provide necessary food, shelter, and clothing to her child is an example of the second type because most states have laws that require parents to do this.

Though not entirely clear from the text, the MPC effectively requires a voluntary act—or an omission and legal duty—for criminal responsibility.

A More Precise Definition for Actus Reus

The MPC also provides a more thorough analytic framework for the actus reus component of a crime. It breaks it down into three separate components—conduct, circumstance, and result—called "material elements." MPC §1.13(9)(i), (ii), and (iii). These components or material elements describe more precisely what the defendant did. Since they are the basic building blocks for defining each crime and for assessing blame and imposing appropriate punishment, a prosecutor must show evidence for each material element to prove actus reus.

Conduct is the physical behavior of the defendant. Driving a car or shooting a gun, for example, would be considered conduct under the MPC.

A *circumstance* is an objective fact or condition that exists in the real world when the defendant engages in conduct. Many criminal statutes include circumstances in the definition of the crime. For example, if a defendant enters a residence at night to steal something inside, the fact that his conduct occurred "at night" is a circumstance that describes what he did with more precision. If the burglary statute so requires, the prosecution will have to prove that the defendant entered a residence "at night."

A *result* is the consequence or outcome caused by the defendant's conduct. If a defendant points a loaded pistol at another human being, pulls the trigger, and causes a bullet to strike and kill him, the death of that human being is the result of defendant's conduct.

Distinguishing Voluntariness Requirement from Act Requirement. As previously mentioned, MPC §2.01(1) requires a *voluntary* act. It is important to note when analyzing the above "material elements," that even if an action fulfills the actus reus requirements, it may nonetheless be involuntary.[13] For example, imagine that a woman sleepwalks into a neighbor's home. Her walking meets the conduct element; depending on the trespassing law in her jurisdiction, she likely meets the circumstance element; and the result of her conduct is a trespass. However, the woman may not be culpable if her actions are deemed to be involuntary. If her actions are involuntary, she would not establish actus reus.

Possession

The MPC explains when possession is an act or conduct. This provision applies when someone takes possession of an item—illegal drugs, for example. If the defendant knows that he is accepting custody of illegal drugs, then his "possession" is clearly a voluntary act under the MPC and he can be convicted of illegally possessing drugs.

What about someone who initially does not realize that he has drugs in his control but subsequently realizes that he does? The MPC states that the person's possession is sufficient for criminal responsibility if, after becoming aware of the fact that he has drugs in his control, he does not terminate his possession within a sufficient period. His failure to act (i.e., terminate possession) is an omission in the face of the legal duty to do so.

EXAMPLES

Examples

1. Brooke is a loving single mother of three boys. One day while she is working from home, she allows the children to play at their neighborhood park. A half hour later, two of her children run through the door frantically, informing Brooke that a man had kidnapped the third child. She then receives a phone call from an unknown number. The voice on the other end instructs: "I have your child. If you ever want to see him again, you will get me $300,000 dollars within the hour" and promptly hangs up. Brooke knows she does not have nearly that amount of money. In her desperate state, she decides her only option is to rob a local bank. She retrieves her gun, drives to the nearest bank,

13. Paul H. Robinson, Shima Baradaran Baughman, and Michael T. Cahill, Criminal Law: Case Studies and Controversies, 507 (New York: Wolters Kluwer, 2017).

and successfully acquires the money—only to be apprehended by police when she runs out. When her child is safely recovered, she cries, "I thought I had no other choice."

2. Sarah is the owner of the Sunshine Daycare Center, which is celebrating its twentieth year of being in business. As an anniversary promotion, Sarah is offering new families one day of care free of charge to try their services. One day, a mother brings in her five-year-old daughter to take advantage of the promotion. When the mother leaves, Sarah immediately notices the girl exhibiting some troubling behavior. The girl is withdrawn, seemingly depressed, and has several bruises on various areas of her body. When the girl's mother returns at the end of the day, the girl kicks and screams, "I don't want to go home!" Sarah recognizes these all as likely signs of physical abuse, but says nothing. The girl and her mother never return, and Sarah chalks the incident up to overthinking. Several months later, the girl's mother is arrested for severe physical abuse of her daughter. Authorities interview Sarah, informing her that state law makes clear that daycare centers are requires to report signs of abuse and asking whether she observed any such signs when the girl was there. Sarah admitted that she did, but insisted she had no idea about the reporting obligations. Can Sarah be convicted of a crime?

3. Elizabeth, jealous that her boyfriend, Bob, was also dating Connie:

3a. drove her car directly at Connie while Connie was crossing the street, hoping to kill her while making it look like an accident. Her car struck and killed Connie.

3b. took a gun she knew was loaded over to Connie's apartment and waved it at Connie, yelling that Connie had better not see Bob again or else. The gun discharged and killed Connie.

3c. while driving her car, failed to see Connie crossing the street in a pedestrian crosswalk because Elizabeth was totally distracted by her own jealous rage.

3d. while driving her car, suffered a heart attack for the first time in her life and lost consciousness. Unfortunately, her car struck and killed Connie while Elizabeth was unconscious.

3e. while driving her car, started to feel drowsy. Rather than pull over, Elizabeth continued driving. Soon thereafter, Elizabeth fell asleep at the wheel and her car struck and killed Connie.

3f. while driving her car, started to feel drowsy. Pulling her car over to the curb, Elizabeth took a nap so she would not fall asleep while driving. She left the motor running to provide heat because it was so cold outside. Awaking suddenly from a deep sleep, Elizabeth's hand struck the automatic gear shift, putting the car into drive. Unfortunately, the car struck and killed Connie.

In which of these instances could Elizabeth have committed a voluntary act?

4. Jasmine is subject to a court order forbidding her from being physically present between the hours of 2:00 p.m. and 2:00 a.m. in an area designated as a known prostitution district. Failure to comply with this order is a criminal offense. At 10:00 p.m., Jasmine was released from the county jail after serving a 30-day sentence for prostitution. Unfortunately for Jasmine, the county jail is located within the district from which she is banned. While walking to a bus stop a few blocks away to catch a bus home, she is arrested and charged with violating the court order.

5. Gunter, a salesman, was driving along a road using his talking GPS to direct him to a company he had never been to before. Suddenly, the friendly voice of the GPS said, "Turn right now." Gunter did, running over a curb and getting stuck on a light-rail track. A few minutes later a light-rail train struck his stuck car and several people were injured.

6. Jack is a highly respected golf pro. While on an airplane flight to California to play in the U.S. Open, Jack started to act very strangely, taking off his clothes and speaking incoherently. He then broke into the plane's cockpit and wrestled with the co-pilot, trying to grab the controls and yelling, "I'm going to kill you." Several passengers helped the co-pilot subdue and restrain Jack. After his arrest, doctors discovered that Jack was suffering from encephalitis, a viral infection of the brain that can cause confusion, altered consciousness, fever, and other symptoms. The disease is transmitted by mosquitoes and can be controlled by medication if the person knows he has it.

7. Scott is seated in a large auditorium with thousands of people watching his niece's college graduation. Halfway through the ceremony he thinks he smells smoke, so he shouts: "Fire! We all have to get out of here! There's a fire!" There is no fire. Unfortunately, everyone panics and, as a result, many people are injured and three people die. The smoke Scott smelled was actually the result of an uncinate fit—an episodic seizure of the uncinate lobe of the brain that can cause abnormal sensations of smell. This smell of smoke led him to believe that there really was a fire danger.

8a. Because Aaron had suffered through too many sleepless nights, his doctor prescribed Ambien, a top-selling prescription sleeping pill. He took the drug just before going to bed, as prescribed. At 3:00 a.m. that morning, Aaron was arrested for driving an automobile in the wrong lane while impaired. He had no recollection of awaking from a deep sleep, let alone driving a car. Recent studies show that Ambien increasingly is involved in similar impaired-driving cases. Drivers have no recollection of getting into their cars and driving them. Does Aaron have a viable defense?

8b. Sally was sleepless in Seattle. Her doctor also prescribed Ambien. Because the drug took a while to work, Sally disregarded the directions on the label and took a pill as she drove home late one evening so she would be ready to fall asleep at bedtime. Surprise! The pill kicked in before she reached her home. Sally was arrested for hitting a telephone pole. She remembers nothing after taking the drug.

9. Seth was civilly committed as a sexual predator because he suffers from a mental abnormality or personality disorder that makes it difficult, if not impossible, to control his dangerous sexual behavior. He was on conditional release from a secure facility, living in a halfway house and working in a grocery store. Suddenly overcome by a sexual compulsion, he groped a women's breast for sexual pleasure. Can he be criminally convicted and punished for an act that is very difficult—perhaps even impossible—for him to control?

10. Ten years ago, Rusty, a graduate assistant at a major college football powerhouse, saw a senior assistant coach raping a 10-year-old boy in the locker room showers. Appalled, he immediately intervened and stopped the abuse. The next day Rusty told the head coach, a legendary figure at the university and Rusty's boss, what he saw the assistant coach doing and what Rusty did to stop it. To his dismay, the assistant coach continued to serve on staff for several more years. Even after retiring as a coach, he continued to have access to the university's athletic facilities where he continued to bring young boys. Recently, the senior coach was charged with sexually abusing many young boys. Some of these crimes occurred in the school's athletic facilities after Rusty had reported what he saw to his boss. State law only required Rusty to report suspected sexual abuse to a university superior; he was not required to inform the police. Can he be convicted of a crime?

11. Senator Duck Chainsaw was bird hunting with his rich buddies. Thinking he heard a flushed quail, Duck turned quickly and shot at a moving target. Unfortunately, he shot Daddy Warbucks in the chest. Duck told Daddy he would get help immediately, but first he called his chief political adviser, King Kove. Kove told Duck to treat the wound himself rather than summon medical aid, because the publicity could be very damaging to his upcoming reelection campaign. Duck and

his buddies bandaged the wound, but the bleeding did not stop. Two hours later Duck called for an ambulance, which arrived in 15 minutes. Unfortunately, Daddy died on the way to the hospital. Daddy would have survived if the ambulance had been called right after the accident.

12. Bishop Olson assigned Pastor Lothar to his fourth new congregation in six years. Yet another series of numerous, verified complaints about Pastor Lothar touching young children in an inappropriate manner in his current parish necessitated this new assignment. Bishop Olson did not inform the police of these allegations, nor did he inform any member of the new congregation about them. Shortly after taking up his new position, in which he had daily contact with young children, Pastor Lothar was arrested and convicted of sexual battery of two young children. Can the prosecutor bring any charges against Bishop Olson?

13. Stuart works for Harvey Made-Off, soon to be convicted of running a giant Wall Street Ponzi scheme. Harvey took money from investors telling them he would buy stocks and bonds for them; instead, he simply pocketed their money. He paid off early investors using money from later investors. Stuart's job is to prepare monthly reports, based on information provided by other members of the company, for individual investors, showing how much money they "made" and the current "value" of their investments. Stuart was completely unaware of the fraud being committed until one day he mistakenly received a memo from Harvey to his second-in-command, completely outlining the scheme and asking how it could be covered up should the SEC ever audit the company. Stuart quits immediately but does not report the scheme to any public authority.

14. Patricia wore her black leather jacket to school. During recess she accidentally put on a similar looking jacket that, unknown to her, had a gun in its pocket.

    a. Just as Patricia finished putting on the jacket, a school security officer noticed the gun protruding from the jacket Patricia was wearing. He took Patricia immediately to the principal's office where the gun was removed. Patricia was charged with possession of a gun on school premises, a strict liability offense that has no mens rea element.
    b. Feeling a hard object in her pocket, Patricia put her hand into the pocket and found a pistol. For the next ten minutes she walked around the school looking for someone who might have put her coat on by mistake so they could exchange jackets. A school security officer noticed the gun protruding from the jacket Patricia was wearing. He took Patricia immediately to the principal's office where the gun was removed. Patricia was charged with criminal possession of

a gun on school premises, a strict liability offense that has no mens rea element.

15. At work during his lunch break, William frequently browsed the Internet for child pornography sites. William looked at child pornography on these sites very briefly so that he wouldn't be observed and then closed them. At one site, a small dialog box appeared on the screen. He entered it and then quickly closed it and left the site. Though William did not realize it, this command caused the computer to immediately download child pornography onto his computer's hard drive. An internal company audit uncovered child pornography on William's computer, and he was charged with the federal crime of knowingly possessing materials involving the sexual exploitation of minors.[14]

16. Roro, a member of an ethnic group trying to secede from a foreign country, inadvertently overheard several of his friends finalizing their plan to board a plane belonging to the national airline of their country later that evening with bomb material hidden in their clothing. At a predetermined time, they would assemble the bomb in the plane's toilet and trigger an explosion, causing the airplane to crash and killing many people. He knew in his heart they were deadly serious and would carry out their plan. Although he had not been involved in any way and learned of the plan accidentally, Roro did not report what he had heard to the police. His friends successfully carried out their plan. When interviewed by the police afterward, Roro told them everything he had heard about their plan.

Explanations

EXPLANATIONS

1. Unfortunately for Brooke, her actions in robbing the bank constitute a voluntary action in the criminal law. Recall that the law finds a voluntary action even when threatened with death or serious injury or to avoid greater harm. While one may certainly be sympathetic with Brooke because of the predicament she faced, these particular circumstances do not influence whether or not her actions were voluntary.

   Note, however, that finding an action to be voluntary is not equivalent to finding the perpetrator culpable. Brooke's attorney will certainly explore various options of defenses, such as those based on justification

14. 18 U.S.C. §2252(a)(4)(B) (2003). This statute prohibits: "(B) knowingly possess[ing] . . . any visual depiction that has . . . been transported in interstate or foreign commerce . . . by any means including by computer, if—(i) the producing of such visual depiction involves the use of a minor engaging in sexually explicit conduct; and (ii) such visual depiction is of such conduct."

or excuse (see Chapters 15-17), which may ultimately relieve her of culpability. A possibility, here, might be an argument for duress.

2. Sarah's failure to report blatant signs of child abuse is an omission. And since the law in her state creates a legal duty for daycare employees to report any signs of abuse they observe, the omission will be considered a voluntary action. Given Sarah's decades-long experience in the child care industry, she should have been well aware of her obligation to report signs of abuse. However, even assuming Sarah truly was ignorant of her reporting obligation, ignorance of the law is not a valid defense (see Chapter 5) and does not negate the voluntariness of her action. There may be an argument Sarah can make that she didn't have a duty given the fact that the child was only under her care for one day. However, given what she observed, her experience in the industry, and her voluntarily undertaking the care of the child, this argument would not likely be successful.

3a. Elizabeth's driving the car directly at Connie is a voluntary act. She moved her hands on the wheel and pressed her foot on the gas pedal so that the car would collide with Connie. She consciously directed her body to engage in behavior that constitutes a "voluntary act."

3b. Elizabeth's waving a loaded gun at Connie is a voluntary act that satisfies the criminal law's requirement of an actus reus. The fact that the gun discharged "accidentally" (i.e., arguably without any mental determination on Elizabeth's part) does not preclude criminal responsibility for a homicide charge. A voluntary act is not rendered involuntary simply because it may include an involuntary act or because it had unintended consequences.

3c. Elizabeth's driving her car is still a voluntary act for the same reasons described in 3a. The fact that the car struck Connie because Elizabeth inadvertently did not see her does not alter the essential nature of Elizabeth's driving as a voluntary act.

3d. Because Elizabeth lost consciousness as a result of an unforeseeable heart attack, her behavior during this time period is not considered a voluntary act. She did not, in any sense, control the vehicle and her physical incapacity to change or alter her conduct make this an "involuntary act" as far as the criminal law is concerned.

3e. Though Elizabeth was sleeping when her car struck and killed Connie and was not itself a voluntary act, Elizabeth has still engaged in a voluntary act by driving even though she was tired. Thus, this aspect of her behavior satisfies the criminal law's general requirement of at least one voluntary act in the course of conduct before criminal responsibility can attach.

3f. This is a tough call. Elizabeth may have been in an unconscious state when her hand engaged the gear shift of the car. The prosecutor would argue that this case is like the case in 3e above; that is, Elizabeth engaged in a voluntary act when she went to sleep leaving the car engine running. The defense would argue that the relevant course of conduct is Elizabeth's "act" of engaging the gear shift while sleeping; consequently, there is no act that can satisfy the criminal law's insistence on a voluntary act. It is not clear how this case would come out.

4. The prosecutor would argue that this is a strict liability offense (see Chapter 6). No mens rea or state of mind about being present in an area from which she has been judicially excluded is required. There can be no doubt that Jasmine was, in fact, physically present here in violation of a valid court order.

   However, recall that even strict liability offenses require a voluntary act to be punishable. The defense would argue that Jasmine did not commit a voluntary act. Officials released her from the jail at 10:00 p.m. and had no choice but to violate the court order. Surely she cannot be required to stay in jail overnight, assuming this was even an option for her. Implicit in the court order under these circumstances must be a condition that she leave the district in a reasonable period of time. She was trying to do just that. Otherwise, the police could manufacture crime by simply releasing individuals subject to similar exclusion orders at a time that would automatically generate new offenses.

5. Gunter would argue that he did not commit a voluntary act. He simply obeyed the command of the GPS, assuming it knew a safe route. The prosecution would argue that Gunter still had a choice to turn or not to turn. Moreover, Gunter had to deliberately move the wheel so his car would make the necessary course adjustment. Gunter had no right to delegate important decision-making over a moving car to a machine. The prosecutor should prevail. But what if this were a self-driving car? Now that would be a different story.

6. Jack did not commit a crime if he did not perform a "voluntary act." The viral infection may have physically affected his brain and seriously impaired Jack's ability to engage in volitional and conscious behavior. Because he may have acted in a fugue state without any memory of the incident, Jack's conduct may not satisfy the actus reus requirement for committing a crime—even though his behavior seemed conscious and rational to other passengers. Note that the prosecution must prove a voluntary act beyond a reasonable doubt and that, without such proof, a defendant cannot be convicted of *any* crime, even a strict liability offense (see Chapter 6). If Jack was aware of his illness and could have prevented the symptoms by taking medication, he may be responsible

based on his earlier "omission" (failure to take medication) and his duty to do so. This example is based on a real case.[15]

7. This is a real brainteaser. An uncinate fit, which consists of smelling or tasting hallucinations, has been connected by medical experts to a type of brain tumor. Scott will argue that he did not commit a voluntary act because he was subjectively experiencing the "smell" of smoke. In fact, his defense attorney will argue Scott should be praised for his behavior because he acted as a "good Samaritan" and warned people of what he honestly sensed to be imminent danger to life. Thus, Scott cannot be punished for his reasonable response to an unwilled, but actual sensory sensation. (Of course, if Scott had experienced these false smells before and did not take steps to determine what caused them or to stop acting on them, he may have committed a prior "voluntary act" by not taking appropriate precautions; this would be similar to someone who drives a car knowing he suffers from epilepsy. See the *Decina* case in this chapter.)

   The prosecution will argue that Scott voluntarily did yell "Fire!" in a crowded room when there was, in fact, no fire. She will insist that Scott's imagined smell of smoke should be analyzed as a "circumstance" element of actus reus rather than as a part of the "conduct" element. Consequently, Scott's criminal responsibility under the MPC will depend on what, if any, culpability or mental state is required with respect to this element (see Chapter 4). If it is a strict liability element, then Scott may be convicted if the prosecutor's analysis prevails. If, however, knowledge or recklessness about real danger is required, Scott will probably not be convicted. What if negligence is required? Should the objective standard of negligence include Scott's physical illness?

   Under the common law, Scott might have a "mistake of fact" defense. But he must prove by a preponderance of the evidence that he honestly and reasonably believed that there was smoke in the room. As with negligence, should Scott's physical ailment be considered in the jury's determination of "reasonable"? How would you instruct the jury if you were the judge? Should the law emphasize the harm done or the actor's behavior and attitude?

   Note how careful analysis is often required in determining what is included in the criminal law's definition of a *voluntary act*.

8a. Aaron would argue that he was "sleepwalking" while driving, through no fault of his own. The drug's label warns that it can, on very rare occasion, cause sleepwalking as a side effect, and experts have seen such cases. Nonetheless, Aaron had no reason to believe that the drug would

15. See "Illness Cited in Cockpit Attack," Kansas City Star, June 19, 2000, p. B-1.

affect him that way. Thus, he would claim that he did not engage in the voluntary conduct of driving a car because he did not consciously decide to get into his automobile, start it, and operate it on a public road.

The prosecutor would claim that Aaron was faking, falsely using the drug as an "alibi" for his criminal act, or that, even if Aaron was sleepwalking, he was responsible for inducing this condition.

If you were the prosecutor, would you dismiss the charge, insist on a guilty plea with a light penalty, or prosecute to the full extent of the law?

8b. Sally did not follow the directions for taking this powerful drug. She consciously and voluntarily took the pill before she should have, and it caused the very condition she could reasonably expect. Thus, taking the pill while driving is a voluntary act sufficient for imposing criminal responsibility, even if she was, in fact, "sleepwalking" behind the wheel when she crashed.

9. The prosecutor would claim that Seth committed a voluntary act and is, therefore, criminally responsible for his conduct. He purposely put his hands on his victim's breast for his own sexual pleasure. His consciousness was not impaired in any way. He knew exactly what he was doing and why. His conduct was the result of a clear intention, determination, and desire and, thus, willful. Even hard choices are the result of "free will" and, consequently, constitute voluntary acts.

   Defense counsel would argue that Seth's behavioral controls were so severely impaired by an underlying mental condition (which he did not cause) that the government had already established in a trial that he could not refrain from engaging in precisely this type of criminal conduct. Nor can the prosecution point to an earlier voluntary act, such as taking an intoxicating drug or substance that induced this mental condition. How can the government both civilly commit an individual because the criminal law is unable to deter this type of behavior, while at the same time insisting that he acted voluntarily? How would you rule?

10. Though conceding that Rusty complied with the law by reporting the sexual abuse to a superior and that there is no statutory legal duty to report it to the police, the prosecutor would claim that Rusty's failure to inform the police after knowing the assistant coach was still on staff, had access to the school's athletic facilities, and continued to bring young boys there is an omission that allowed a known sex offender to commit numerous crimes that have caused enormous harm to many young and vulnerable victims. Surely, the moral duty to prevent this ongoing victimization is so compelling in this situation that Rusty can

be criminally punished for his inaction. Even though Rusty did bring the coach's criminal conduct to the attention of a superior with authority to take appropriate preventive action, he knew that the coach was still in a position to commit more crimes like the one he saw. The criminal law cannot be powerless to prevent such tragic and predictable harm. There must be a duty to act here when the burden on the individual is so minimal—just call the police—and the harm prevented is so damaging.

The defense counsel would argue that the criminal law is clear: Without a legal duty to act, the failure to do so does not satisfy the necessary elements of criminal responsibility. Rusty did not affirmatively harm any of the victims. He actually acted to prevent future harm. He did exactly what the law required; he informed a person in the organization with authority over the coach of what he saw. Rusty must be able to rely on the law in determining his legal responsibility. Expanding criminal responsibility in this case would be a trap for the innocent and violate the principle of legality. Where would the "slippery slope" of extending criminal responsibility stop? Who would know the scope of her criminal responsibility? This is why there is no common law of crime in this state.

If you think Rusty is criminally responsible for not doing more, what should his punishment be? A modest fine? Conviction of the same crime as the perpetrator? Is this a just result?[16]

11. Duck is not criminally responsible for the accidental shooting of Daddy. Because he caused the injury to Daddy, however, Duck had a legal duty to summon medical aid immediately. Duck's failure to provide medical assistance to his victim was an omission that caused Daddy's death. Duck can be convicted based on his inaction.

12. If there is a statute requiring clergy to report to the police known or suspected cases of child sexual abuse, Bishop Olson's failure to comply would satisfy the actus reus of a crime. Note that it would not be an "omission" because the bishop did not do what the statute expressly requires. His failure to report would be similar to not filing an income tax return when required by law. If there is no criminal statute imposing this duty on clergy, then the bishop's failure to report is a true "omission," which does not generate criminal responsibility unless there is a legal duty to report imposed elsewhere in law. Although he has a strong moral duty to report these past cases, the criminal law does not enforce every moral obligation.

16. This is factually similar to the Jerry Sandusky sexual abuse allegations at Penn State University.

The prosecutor might argue that because of his status, Bishop Olson is under a legal duty to prevent Pastor Lothar from committing future sex crimes against children. Again, this would depend on whether there is a duty in civil law to take such action. If there is no such duty, Bishop Olson's failure to act is not a crime.

13. Stuart would argue that he is an "innocent agent" (see Chapter 11). Admittedly, he helped cause terrible financial harm to thousands of victims; however, he had no awareness of this fact. Thus, so long as he quit at once and did no further harm, he has no duty to prevent future harm. The government would counter that, although he was an innocent agent and therefore not responsible for his past acts, Stuart has induced reliance by the victims of this Ponzi scheme on the integrity and accuracy of the financial reports, and investors would rely on them even after Stuart quit. Thus, Stuart has a duty to undo this misplaced trust and inform authorities. Otherwise, he is responsible for these subsequent acts of fraud. Who has the better argument?

14a. In the first example, Patricia does not know or have reason to know that the jacket she has mistakenly put on has a weapon in it. Thus, in most states her physical possession is not a voluntary act, and she cannot be convicted of the charged offense, even if it is a strict liability offense.

14b. The second example is more difficult. Though Patricia does not know there is a gun in the jacket when she first puts it on, she soon realizes that a weapon is located in the jacket pocket. At this point Patricia is under a legal duty to terminate her possession within a reasonable time; failure to do so may lead to a possession charge. Patricia would argue that she was trying to terminate her possession by attempting to locate the original owner. The prosecution may argue that Patricia should have immediately removed the jacket or gone to school authorities to turn in the weapon. A conviction on these facts is possible.[17]

15. To be guilty of possession of child pornography, an offender must knowingly have the prohibited material. William intentionally searched for these websites and viewed child pornography. He also intentionally entered and closed the dialog box. However, he was unaware that this act automatically downloaded the prohibited pornography onto his computer's hard drive, and did not know that it was on his computer's hard drive until he was arrested. Thus, he will argue that he was never cognizant of this crucial fact and, therefore, did not "knowingly possess" the child pornography.

17. See *In the Matter of Ronnie L.*, 121 Misc. 2d 271, 463 N.Y.S.2d 732 (1983).

The prosecution may argue that simply viewing this material is possessing it; possession does not require downloading or printing it. This argument will probably fail. The prosecutor will then argue that William committed a "voluntary act" by opening the site, viewing child pornography, and entering and closing the dialog box. This satisfies both the actus reus requirement of the common law and the conduct element of the MPC. He may not have known the result of his conduct, but that should be construed as a strict liability element.

This is a tough case and could go either way. Because William did not voluntarily engage in conduct that would normally result in downloading material from a website onto a computer hard drive, he has a strong case that he did not engage in the voluntary act necessary for possession.

16. Roro's failure to tell the police what he had learned is clearly an omission, one that allowed his friends to cause the loss of many innocent lives. But does his failure to warn law enforcement authorities trigger criminal responsibility?

    The prosecutor would argue that Roro was under a legal duty to prevent this tragedy because of the incredible magnitude of the harm planned and because Roro could prevent it with no risk to himself (he could have called the police anonymously).

    The defense would argue that Roro is not a co-conspirator (see Chapter 13) nor an accomplice (see Chapter 14) and there is no civil duty to report crimes planned by others. There can be no criminal responsibility for an omission unless there is a legal duty to act to prevent the harm. An individual is personally responsible only for the harm he causes; generally, he is under no obligation to prevent others from committing crimes. Only a duty to act imposed by civil law could provide adequate notice to Roro and others that failure to act in such situations carries the threat of criminal sanction.

    Without a duty in civil law, an individual cannot be held criminally responsible for doing nothing. Roro's failure to interrupt human causal forces already at work is morally reprehensible and indefensible. But it is unlikely that he could be convicted of any crime. In states with Good Samaritan laws, which require individuals to prevent harm if they can do so with no risk, Roro could be convicted of a crime. But his punishment would be extremely light (a modest fine and perhaps a six-month sentence) given the number of people who die as a result of his inaction. Should the law criminal be used as an instrument to induce people to do the right thing when the stakes are so high?

CHAPTER 4

The Doctrines of Mens Rea

OVERVIEW

As we saw in Chapter 2, criminal law is distinguished from all other fields of law because of the sanctions it can impose: loss of liberty and moral stigmatization. We regularly incarcerate, or otherwise deprive of freedom, persons who are not morally blameworthy — the mentally ill, the addicted, the fatally contagious, and so on. However, only criminal punishment declares that defendants are to blame for their acts; the essence of the judgment is not that they should be incarcerated for our sakes, but that they deserve punishment because they have chosen freely to violate the criminal law. Such a free choice appears to require that they *knew* what they were doing, and were aware, or at least should have been aware, that it was morally blameworthy. For centuries, the law has captured this notion of free will and knowledge by looking for *mens rea* — Latin for "guilty mind." This chapter is concerned with the basic definitions of mens rea.

Until 1900 or so, many different terms were used to describe states of mind that seemed to reflect aspects of moral blame. However, behind each of these statutory terms stood the larger backdrop of mens rea itself: the broader notion of looking for a truly "immoral" person. We will refer to that notion as *traditional* mens rea. In the past century however the term "mens rea" has lost much of that moral connotation and has come to mean merely the mental state required by statute. We will call this *statutory* mens rea.

Unfortunately, neither courts nor commentators differentiate consistently in their use of these concepts.

This chapter examines various aspects of mens rea: (1) defining the relevant mental states; (2) investigating the relation of mens rea to motive; and (3) interpreting statutes that use mens rea words. Succeeding Chapters 5 and 6 continue this exploration in the specific contexts of mistake and strict liability.

The Model Penal Code effected many changes in both the substantive criminal law and in the way criminal statutes are interpreted. Beginning with this chapter, the text will constantly compare and contrast the positions taken by the common law with those of the Code. This kind of comparison should help you understand both approaches. Although the MPC is not "the" law in the majority of jurisdictions today, it cannot properly be understood without an awareness of how it differs from the common law and why its drafters took the approach they did.

THE CONCEPTS OF MENS REA

Criminal law is not tort law. While that may seem obvious, the point is critical to understanding the central importance of mens rea to criminal law. Because tort law also deals with conduct that often results in physical injury, and because, historically, criminal and tort causes of action were joined in the same proceeding, it is helpful to contrast the two systems of law. In tort, where the prime aim is to compensate the innocent plaintiff, an objective standard ("the reasonable person") is used to assess the actions of the defendant. Criminal law, however, has other concerns. Under most of the four theories of punishment discussed in Chapter 2, the defendant's mental state is critical in determining whether to punish him. The entire theory of general deterrence—especially as articulated by its preeminent founder, Jeremy Bentham—requires that the potential criminal "calculate" the gains and benefits of committing a crime and then *choose* to commit it. If the defendant does not know the punishment, or that the act is even criminal, the defendant is unlikely to be deterred. A utilitarian who seeks to rehabilitate the defendant needs to know whether the defendant *needs* "treatment," which means that he knew—or was capable of knowing—the harm risked by his conduct. If so, then the defendant needs to be trained to avoid such injuries; if not, he needs to be trained to be aware of possible injuries.

It might appear that an incapacitationist might think mental state is not relevant. If the defendant is dangerous, she should be locked up without regard to her mental state. However, the criminal process and criminal incarceration are a costly business. If we are only interested in confinement, we can use the less costly and less burdensome civil process. If the criminal process is to be relevant to an incapacitationist, it must be because the defendant will continue to be dangerous because she is dangerous.

The notion of blame, however, fits most easily in the retributivist's theory. To a retributivist, a person is morally culpable, and therefore properly subject to punishment, only if she had a "real choice" in her conduct and knowingly exercised her free will to execute that choice. As Justice Jackson put it in a frequently repeated observation:

> The contention that an injury can amount to a crime only when inflicted by intention is no provincial or transient notion. It is as universal and persistent in mature systems of law as belief in freedom of the human will and a consequent ability and duty of the normal individual to choose between good and evil. A relation between some mental element and punishment for a harmful act is almost as instinctive as a child's "But I didn't mean to. . . ." Unqualified acceptance of this doctrine by English common law . . . was indicated by Blackstone's sweeping statement that to constitute any crime there must first be a "vicious will."[1]

No state has fully adopted any one of these goals of punishment as "the" purpose. Indeed, most observers argue that the criminal law should adopt all these purposes, at one time stressing one purpose, at another time another. Where the legislature is silent on the purpose of a particular statute, and where the different philosophies would result in different interpretations, however, a real dilemma arises.

Suppose a statute prohibits "selling drugs," and Rob sold a white powder that he thought was salt, but was actually heroin. He would contend that the statute should be interpreted as requiring knowledge of the nature of the item sold. A deterrence theorist might argue that the statute should not be interpreted to require mens rea, because by punishing Rob, others might be deterred from selling white powder unless they assured themselves it was salt. An incapacitationist might similarly argue that the statute should not be interpreted to require knowledge because Rob's failure to perceive or check the nature of the powder makes him dangerous enough to be imprisoned. A rehabilitationist, on the other hand, would most likely contend that persons who make these mistakes should be trained to be more careful, but not punished as though they knew the powder was heroin; the statute should be required to show knowledge. Finally, a retributivist would adamantly demand that the statute be interpreted to require that a defendant knew it was heroin; a person who sells what he believes to be salt is simply not morally culpable if it turns out that he was wrong.

1. *Morrissette v. United States*, 342 U.S. 246 (1952).

"Traditional" and "Statutory" Mens Rea

Clearly heavily influenced by religious notions of sin, the criminal law as early as the thirteenth century encapsulated the need for a "vicious will" in the Latin term "mens rea." This view that a defendant could be punished only if he were a "sinner" influenced the common law, and created the *traditional mens rea* concept described earlier. Between that time and the middle of the twentieth century, both common law courts and legislatures used a dizzying variety of adverbs in an attempt to capture the notion of general malevolence and blameworthiness at the heart of the original, Latin term. These adverbs included "feloniously," "unlawfully," "maliciously," "corruptly," "fraudulently," "spitefully," and "willfully." The Model Penal Code found that there were 76 terms in federal statutes alone that were used to describe mens rea.[2] This abundance of terms might have been amusing except that, under the principles of legality (see Chapter 1), courts, faced with this wide variety of legislative terms, felt compelled to conclude that there must be differences among *each* of them.[3] Explaining the nuances between 76 different terms challenged the creative limits of the courts' ingenuity. As courts focused on the statutory words, however, the moral content of mens rea became diluted. If Mary, for example, is given a box to deliver to Jessica, and is told that it contains books, when she is charged with "intentionally transporting heroin" (the real content of the box), under traditional mens rea, she will claim lack of moral blameworthiness. As we will see, she will likely be exonerated. Under a *statutory mens rea* approach, however, the court might ask only whether she "intentionally" "transported" the box. If so, she will be found guilty. Again, as we will see, recent court decisions seem to be moving toward providing rules of statutory construction that would "readopt" the common law approach and exculpate Mary.[4]

---

2. Model Penal Code §2.02, commentary at 230 n. 3 (1980).

3. Thus, in *Rex v. Davis*, 168 Eng. Rep. 378 (1788), a statute prohibited "wilfully and maliciously" shooting, but the indictment charged that the defendant "unlawfully, maliciously, and feloniously" shot. The indictment was ruled invalid because "wilfully" must mean something different than "unlawfully and feloniously." There was certainly no doubt that the indictment charged the defendant with having *traditional* (i.e. blameworthy) mens rea, but that was insufficient: There was a requirement that the prosecution charge and prove *statutory* mens rea as well.

4. "Once upon a time, mens rea meant culpability. . . . During the Enlightenment, its essential normativity remained, wrapped in the language of evil and wickedness, malice and passion. . . . For much of the past fifty years, the conventional view has tried to bury this judgmental feature. It has attempted to isolate the individual as the object of mens rea and to make mens rea look less like 'guilty mind' than simply 'mind.'" V.F. Nourse, Hearts and Minds: Understanding the New Culpability, 6 Buff. Crim. L. Rev. 361, 365-6 (2002).

The distinction between *traditional* and *statutory* mens rea can work either to the benefit or detriment of a person charged with crime. Assume, for example, that recklessness is morally blameworthy. Under this premise, a defendant who is charged with "intentionally" doing *x* would be convicted under traditional notions of mens rea. But under statutory notions of mens rea, the defendant could be acquitted because he did not "intend" to do *x*. On the other hand, if "intentionally" doing *x* means that the defendant must intend only the conduct, then a non-blameworthy actor who intentionally does an act might be found guilty under the statute, even if they are not aware of the facts giving rise to culpability, and did not intend the result.

As discussed later in this chapter and in Chapters 15-17, it is now fairly clear that there is no federal constitutional requirement that states observe "traditional" mens rea notions of blameworthiness before imposing criminal liability. Nevertheless, the division between the two types is still useful, both theoretically and practically. An example may help. In *Regina v. Cunningham*, 41 Crim. App. 155 (Ct. Crim. App. 1957), the defendant tore a gas meter off the wall of a house. The gas escaped, and *V* (an occupant of the house) was nearly poisoned. Defendant was charged with "unlawfully and maliciously" causing *V* to inhale the gas, to which he responded that he had absolutely no intent that she inhale the gas. The trial judge instructed the jury that it would be sufficient for conviction if they were persuaded that the defendant had acted "wickedly." The defendant's conviction was reversed on appeal because, although he intended to remove the gas meter (and thus commit theft), he did not intend (even obliquely or by transfer) to hurt *V* in any way. In the terminology we are using here, the trial court instructed the jury that if the defendant had traditional mens rea (just plain wickedness), that was enough. But the appellate court held that that was not enough; the defendant had to have statutory mens rea, as well.[5] The moral: keep in mind "traditional" as well as "statutory" mens rea when analyzing criminal charges.

Motive and Mens Rea

A person's motive for committing a crime may tell us a great deal about her and particularly whether we should view her as a "criminal." But the law says that motive is not intent—and not even mens rea.[6]

---

5. *Cunningham* is often interpreted as saying that whether the defendant has traditional mens rea is irrelevant, but that is not the holding. The holding is that traditional mens rea is not sufficient; whether it is necessary is not raised by the case.

6. Elaine M. Chiu, The Challenge of Motive in the Criminal Law, 8 Buff. Crim. L. 653 (2005); Martin Gardner, The Mens Rea Enigma: Observations on the Role of Motive in the Criminal Law Past and Present, 1993 Utah L. Rev. 635; Michael Rosenberg, The Continued Relevance of the Irrelevance-of-Motive Maxim, 57 Duke L.J. 1143 (2008).

Considering the defendant's motive complicates matters. If Robin Hood intentionally robs the Sheriff (statutory mens rea), the fact that his motive for doing so is to give the proceeds to the poor (arguably a morally good reason, and thus denying "traditional" moral blameworthiness) is irrelevant to his guilt.

Euthanasia raises most directly the difference between the two kinds of mens rea in dealing with motive. A person who (often with the victim's consent) intentionally disconnects life-prolonging devices or kills with a shotgun at point-blank range for the sole purpose of relieving that person's suffering certainly has statutory mens rea. However, is he blameworthy? Does he have traditional mens rea? Motive suggests he does not have traditional mens rea. Yet most courts today would exclude evidence of such a motive.

Motive is admissible, however, to bolster the prosecutor's case, since the jury may well infer mens rea from the motive. For example, Gertrude, who has just run over Jillian with her car, claims she did not see Jillian. So far as we initially know, they are total strangers. Charged with purposely killing Jillian, Gertrude is likely to be acquitted. We simply can't see why Gertrude would purposely kill the victim, even if the external evidence suggests that (1) it was a bright and sunny day; (2) Gertrude traveled over 500 feet before she hit Jillian, who was on the sidewalk; (3) Gertrude never hit the brakes. However, if we discover that Jillian is having an affair with Gertrude's husband, or that Gertrude stood to inherit from Jillian, or that Jillian was blocking Gertrude's advancement in her field, we might *now* be willing to infer that Gertrude purposely killed Jillian, *because she had a motive for doing so*. It is the lack of apparent motive that spurs Hitchcock's great film, *Strangers on a Train*, where strangers agree to "swap murders" in the belief that the police will not suspect them of "motiveless" crimes.

If motive is not relevant to the determination of guilt, the judge may—or may not—consider it at the time of sentencing. Even if Robin Hood and Smokey the Rat are both robbers, we may tend to think Robin deserves less punishment. Similarly, a bad motive may seem to warrant increased punishment. Assault alone may be a crime. If it is motivated by racial animosity, we may consider it worthy of more punishment.

Motive and Defenses

If motive means the reason why the defendant acted with the requisite statutory mens rea, the criminal law sometimes does consider motive, but it has cloaked this consideration by calling some motives "defenses." Thus, if Hillary claims that she purposely killed Andrew because Andrew had fired four shots at her, or that she purposely stole the painting because Andrew had a gun trained on her (or on her son), these *reasons* (motives) are relevant under standard criminal law doctrine because they constitute defenses (self-defense and duress, respectively). We will explore the rules as to those defenses in Chapter 16, but it is useful, even now, to at least recognize that there are motives that the criminal law does consider.

Specific Kinds of Mens Rea

In an attempt to define mens rea, courts divided the concept into three major sub-concepts: (1) intent; (2) knowledge; (3) recklessness.

Intent (Purpose)

In General

A person who *intends* harm is clearly a proper subject for punishment under any theory of punishment. He is dangerous, in need of rehabilitation, and a morally culpable actor. To the extent that general deterrence works at all, it is also likely that his punishment can deter others like him. It is the defendant's subjective malevolence, not the likelihood of result, that determines his liability. Suppose, for example, that Hector wants to kill Achilles and, with this purpose in mind, aims at him a feather that is unlikely to harm him in any way. The feather, however, hits Achilles in a vital spot and, wonder of wonders, Achilles dies. If Hector had not wanted to kill Achilles, this would be a tragic accident, and probably Hector would not be punished at all. Should Hector be able to claim that he did not intentionally kill Achilles because the physical facts made it unlikely, almost fantastic? The common law answer to this was no; if Hector really wanted to kill Achilles, the fact that he did so by what would ordinarily be ineffective means was irrelevant. If Hector intended the death, and the death occurred, Hector was liable for intentional homicide.[7]

However, it is not that easy. We must distinguish between *intending the conduct* and *intending the result*. Suppose that Peter Pumpkin has intentionally pulled the trigger of a gun, and a bullet from the gun has killed Lucretia. If Peter is charged with "intentionally killing a person," he may admit he pulled the trigger intentionally (intended the conduct) but still respond that he is not guilty of the offense for several reasons:

7. Of course, this hypothetical rests mostly in the minds of law professors: Imagine that someone sees Hector aim a feather at Achilles, and Achilles dies. Unless Hector admits his intent, no one, including the witness, is likely to deduce Hector's actual mens rea.

1. He did not intend to shoot the gun (e.g., he thought it was empty).
2. He did intend to shoot the gun, but he did not intend the bullet to hit anyone (e.g., he was aiming at a tree and did not know Lucretia was in the tree).
3. He did intend to shoot the gun but meant to hit not Lucretia but the Joker, who was assaulting him.
4. He did intend to shoot the gun and to hit Lucretia, but earnestly hoped that this would not kill her (e.g., he was trying to *wound* her in the heart).

Can one characterize Peter's mens rea as intentional? We will leave Cases 1 and 2 for Chapter 5, which treats the subject of mistake. However, in Cases 3 and 4, there is at least *some* intention on Peter's part to inflict harm. How should the law resolve these cases?

Transferred Intent: Case 3

The third case incorporates a fiction borrowed from tort law, transferred intent. Here, the conclusion is that the intent follows the bullet. Transferred intent, however, is limited to results that create *the same type of harm* as was actually intended. Thus, if Mary throws a stone at Jim and hits John, the intent is said to transfer, and Mary will be convicted of intentionally hitting John. If, however, the stone misses Jim and breaks a plate glass window behind him, the intent is not transferred. *Regina v. Pembliton*, 12 Cox C.C. 607 (1874).

Some commentators argue that the doctrine is not necessary: Mary intended to assault a human being and she did just that. However, suppose that the actually injured party is not just "a" human being but a "specially protected" human being—the King, the Pope, a federal judge—for whose intentional assault the penalty is enhanced. Should Mary pay the extra penalty? At least arguably, no. Mary threw the stone intentionally, but did not hit the Pope intentionally; Mary should be punished for *attempting* to hit Jim and for negligently or recklessly assaulting the Pope. The transferred intent analysis ignores Jim as a victim, and concentrates all its attention on punishing Mary for hitting the Pope.[8] When the defendant aims at *A* but kills B, the intent is transferred; when he kills both *A* (his target) and B with the same bullet, some courts hold that the intent does *not* transfer because it is "used up."

---

8. One might find an echo in the theory of transferred intent of the "greater crimes" theory. See Chapter 6. Under that approach, since Mary was willing to engage in some criminality, she should be required to take the risk that her actual crime is greater than she expected it to be.

Oblique Intent: Case 4

Most courts deal with Case 4 by treating the defendant *as though* he had intended the actual result. Some courts explain this by using the term "oblique" intent. The defendant didn't really "intend" the result but knew that if he acted, the result (death) was practically certain to happen if he achieved his actual goal (wound in the heart). In other cases, courts simply have said that if the defendant knew that the result was almost certain to occur, even if he did not in fact want it to happen, he would be deemed to have intended it.

The typical classroom hypothetical to illustrate "oblique intent" concerns John, who purposes to kill his wife by putting a bomb on a plane she is taking. The bomb explodes, and his wife is killed. But so are 30 other passengers. As to them, John will probably say that he did not "purpose" or "intend" their deaths—he would have been ecstatic had they somehow survived. Nevertheless, the law will treat him as though he intended their deaths, because those deaths were virtually certain to occur.

The policy behind the doctrine of oblique intent is fairly clear: The defendant is almost as morally blameworthy, or as much in need of rehabilitation or incapacitation, as the defendant who *actually* intended to kill the person he shot. This explanation can also explain the transferred intent doctrine, which held Mary guilty of intending to hit John, but it will not explain her acquittal when she breaks the window. If anything, she is *more* morally culpable (and in need of rehabilitation or incapacitation) than a person who actually intends to break a window. Only adherence to the *statutory* meaning of mens rea and the view that this outcome is mandated by the principle of legality can explain that result.

"Specific" and "General" Intent: An Island of Confusion in an Ocean of Chaos

Every student must try to learn the difference between *specific* intent and *general* intent, although all criminal law scholars (and many courts) believe the distinction to be totally meaningless and unrelievedly befuddling. As one authority puts it, "In confusing circularity, a general intent offense can be said to be any crime that requires *mens rea* and that has no special or specific intent required."

Often, the legislature will help out by using the phrase "with intent to" when designating a specific intent offense. Thus:

1. Assault is a general intent crime, *People v. Hood*, 1 Cal. 3d 444 (1969); assault *with intent to rape* is a specific intent crime.
2. Breaking and entering is a general intent crime; breaking and entering *with intent to commit a felony* therein is a specific intent fix crime.

3. Burning down your house is a general intent crime; burning down your house *with the intent to obtain insurance* thereon is a specific intent crime.

Often, but not always. And therein lies the rub. While the presence of "with intent to" almost always indicates that a crime is a specific intent crime, the absence of that phrase does not necessarily indicate that it is a general intent crime. Moreover, the same conduct can often be described (and charged) as *either* a general or specific intent offense. For example:

1. Aggravated assault (a general intent offense) may also be described as assault with intent to kill or maim (specific intent).
2. Burglary is defined by common law as a breaking and entering (usually a dwelling house) with intent to commit a felony therein (and therefore a specific intent offense). However, aggravated (or second-degree) trespassing *can* be defined to reach the same conduct without using the magic words "with intent to."

Virtually no one—courts, commentators, defendants—thinks the specific-general intent distinction is very helpful. Only prosecutors, whose charging discretion is enhanced by these differences, seem to support the idea. However, courts sometimes candidly acknowledge that they will (re)define an offense as general or specific intent because of the effect of other doctrines on the charge. See *People v. Hood*, supra.

In mens rea terms employed by the common law, a specific intent crime is one done "purposely" or "intentionally." If the defendant can be convicted for "knowingly, recklessly or negligently" committing the offense, it is often referred to as a general intent crime.

What, then, is "general intent"? Often, courts define it as requiring that the defendant "intended to perform the physical act proscribed by the statute." But that is not very helpful, as we shall see. Suppose the crime is "possessing cocaine." Is the "physical act" "possessing"? Or is it "possessing cocaine"? We'll come back to that.

Knowledge

"Willfully" and "Knowingly"

In many modern codes, "oblique intention" is now called "knowingly." Knowingly, while close to intentionality, does not have the same exact meaning of intentionally. The defendant need not intend a result; she need only know that the result is virtually certain. In inchoate crimes (see Chapters 12-14) and in accessorial liability (Chapter 14), which are said to be "specific intent" crimes, a person who knows that a crime *might* occur, but does not intend that the crime occur, is not guilty. On the other hand, "knowingly" sometimes means *less* than meets the eye. Thus, if Tom is handed a glassine envelope of white powder, and told to sell it to Helen for $100 a gram, and says he will do it, "just don't tell me what it is," he is treated as though he knew that the substance was cocaine. He is said to have made himself "willfully blind" to the facts.

Many statutes and common law crimes used the term "willfully." "Willfully" was often interpreted to mean "by one's will," which, as discussed in Chapter 3, would reduce that term to mean only that the defendant acted in a voluntary way. This was too narrow a reading. Other courts required that the prosecution prove the defendant "knew" what the consequences of his action were likely to be.

Recklessness

The *Cunningham* decision discussed on page 67 is known for its holding that "recklessness" is the "lowest" mental state required for criminal mens rea. Recklessness is not a concept familiar to tort law, and therefore perhaps not even to law students who have struggled through torts. Some courts have used terms like "gross negligence" as a synonym for "recklessness," but recklessness stands between intent on one side and criminal negligence on the other. It is usually defined as a *conscious decision to ignore a risk, of which the defendant is aware,* that a "bad" result will occur or that a fact is present. The essence of recklessness, therefore, is that the defendant *knows* injury is being risked but proceeds anyway.[9]

Not every risk, of course, is to be condemned. In everything we do—driving a car, walking down steps, hitting a golf ball—we knowingly take risks that serious bodily injury or death might ensue. However, these risks are acceptable because they are outweighed by the social good that occurs: commerce, autonomy, pleasure. Only if the social good does not outweigh the possible harm (e.g., speeding, walking down steps while carrying a loaded gun, hitting a ball with persons standing only ten feet in front of the ball) do we say that the risk is unacceptable.

Caveat. The term "recklessness" is often misused in general language and occasionally in court decisions, as well. As used in the criminal law, and particularly in the Model Penal Code, recklessness requires that the defendant recognize that there is a particular risk and *subjectively choose to disregard that risk.* Thus, as with negligence (remember *Palsgraf* from your torts class?), there is no such thing as recklessness in the air. If LeeAnn drives

9. If the defendant does not know that there is such a risk, then the defendant is not reckless but at worst, criminally negligent. See the next subsection.

90 miles an hour on a crowded city street, she may be acting *dangerously* but cannot be accurately described as driving *recklessly* with regard to the risk of death or serious injury unless she *actually, subjectively recognized* and shrugged off that risk.[10] If LeeAnn did not consider the possibility of death, and she kills someone in such a situation, it would be incorrect to say that she killed recklessly. Again, it is important to distinguish between being reckless as to the conduct and as to the result. Do not be misled on exams (or in other contexts either).

Of course, when LeeAnn tells the jury that it never occurred to her that she might injure or kill someone, a jury could simply disbelieve her—based on its realistic sense that any person driving the way she did "must have" recognized the risk. But before they can convict her, they will still have to find that LeeAnn had the capacity, at the time, to recognize the risk and did so.

Take a classic example. In *Regina v. Faulkner*, 13 Cox C.C. 550 (1877), the defendant, a sailor, went to the hold of the ship to steal some rum. When he was finished imbibing, he attempted to replace the cork in the rum keg. To help him see where to put the cork, he lit a match, which then ignited the rum and the rum fumes, burning down the ship. If he were charged with "recklessly" destroying the ship, the prosecutor would seek to prove that Faulkner knew that rum was combustible. If Faulkner denied that charge, the prosecutor would have to rely on inferences from other evidence: (1) Faulkner had cherries jubilee every night for desert; (2) other persons had heard Faulkner talk about the flammability of rum; (3) all sailors know that rum is flammable, and Faulkner has been a sailor for 30 years.

Although there must be "a" risk of the result occurring, there is no minimum level of probability that must be met before a risk will render a defendant potentially liable. For example, assume that Peter Pumpkin is put in a room with 10,000 guns and told that one (and only one) is loaded. He selects one at random, aims it directly at Lucretia's head, and pulls the trigger. If death results, Peter is reckless with regard to that result, even if, statistically, the chances of the gun firing were very, very small (.0001).

Some courts and commentators have suggested that a balancing test should be used to define recklessness. Thus, if the resulting harm is severe, a minimum degree of recklessness may be required; if, however, the resulting harm is less serious, the same defendant may not be found reckless. Thus, Peter may be a reckless murderer, but it is possible to argue that he is not guilty of "recklessly" discharging the gun in public.

---

10. Many statutes, of course, use the term "recklessness" to describe such driving, but that usage is incorrect, at least under most definitions of recklessness, because there is no requirement that the government prove that the defendant had a mens rea with regard to any injury.

Negligence as a Predicate for Criminal Liability

"Negligence," at least as the term is used in tort law, does not ask anything about the individual defendant's mind. It focuses only on whether the defendant *acted* as a reasonably prudent person would. If he did, then he's not liable, even if his *mind* was "evil." Similarly, a person who is merely negligent has not *subjectively* foreseen even the remotest possibility that harm may occur. This is the distinguishing factor between negligence and recklessness. Should persons who are merely negligent be punished as criminals?

Surprisingly, the different theories of punishment are divided on this question. Some retributivists argue that a person who has not paid attention to a risk has not chosen to create that risk, and therefore is not morally culpable. Other retributivists argue that a person who has the *capacity* to be non-negligent but fails to use that capacity *is* morally blameworthy, either because he has not used his capacity at the time of the event, or because he has not honed his skills and character better in the past to allow him to have perceived and avoided the risk when it arose.

Utilitarians are no more united on this issue. Some argue that punishing negligent defendants may encourage others to become more careful, thereby deterring future harms. Others, however, argue that persons rarely act without believing that they *are* acting rationally and reasonably, and that they will not teach themselves to be more careful than what they believe is reasonable. Therefore, there will be no educative (deterrent) effect, and the punishment of the negligent actor will have no beneficial effect in the real world.

Some utilitarians argue that if the law does not punish those who are negligent, nefarious evildoers will escape criminal liability by duping juries into believing that they were not reckless, but "merely" negligent. This argument, however, proves too much. At its most extreme, it would require strict liability for all harm since any requirement of proof of mens rea, or even actus reus, could be abused by a duplicitous defendant and falsely believed by a sympathetic (or misled) jury.

Defining Criminal Negligence

The common law in very limited circumstances allowed *criminal* negligence as the basis of some liability. But what does the term mean? The basic definition can be easily stated: Mere tort negligence is insufficient to ground criminal liability; the negligence must be "criminal." This is obviously not helpful, so try these definitions:

1. "That degree of negligence or carelessness which is denominated as gross, and which constitutes such a departure from what would be

the conduct of an ordinarily careful and prudent man . . . as to furnish evidence of that indifference to consequences which in some offenses takes the place of criminal intent." *Fitzgerald v. State*, 112 Ala. 34, 20 So. 966 (1896).

2. "Negligence, to be criminal, must be reckless and wanton." *State v. Weiner*, 41 N.J. 21, 194 A.2d 467 (1964).

As these (not very helpful) "definitions" illustrate, many courts invoke words that are so close to recklessness as to make criminal negligence indistinguishable from that concept. Some decisions even talk about advertent negligence, a notion that is even harder to explain than jumbo shrimp.

Analytically, one might try to explain the concept of degrees of negligence in various ways. "Criminal" negligence might differ from "tortious" negligence by requiring (1) a subjective recognition of the harm, and/or (2) a risk of only some, very serious, harm (see below) and/or (3) a statistically greater risk of harm. While we might find the defendant tortiously liable if the risk were 40 percent, we would find her criminally liable only if the risk were 70 percent because *virtually every person*, not merely the average person, would see the risk. The cases seem to endorse something like this latter view: Only if the defendant's failure to recognize the risk was "really outrageous" or "really stupid" should he be convicted. We could refer to this as the "really stupid reasonable person" test.

There is also some question about whether criminal negligence applies to most offenses. Most cases defining criminal negligence (including the two quoted above) involved charges of homicide. More modern cases involving charges of nonhomicidal acts, have allowed conviction on the basis of "tort" negligence.

For example, in *United States v. Garrett*, 984 F.2d 1402 (5th Cir. 1993), the defendant was charged with attempting to board an airplane with a concealed weapon. She claimed that she had forgotten that the gun was in her purse. Moreover, she had been late in getting dressed that morning and had hastily picked up a purse that she used only infrequently. The court held that a jury could nevertheless convict her if they found her mistake to be tortiously (civilly) negligent.

States have also allowed tort negligence to be sufficient for criminal liability in such areas as child abuse and neglect. Some state legislatures have enacted statutes dealing with very specific and discrete behavior and results—for example, negligent operation of a vehicle resulting in death, which is punished less seriously than other types of homicide.

As a general matter, courts will not permit mere tort negligence as a basis for criminal liability. If, of course, the legislature has unequivocally allowed conviction on the basis of such a low mens rea, the courts will enforce that. In *State v. Williams*, 4 Wash. App. 908, 484 P.2d 167 (1971), the defendants, poorly educated American Indian parents whose infant child had developed a severe abscess in his teeth, but who did not realize the severity of the illness, and who were afraid that the child would be removed from their home if they took him to a doctor for treatment,[11] were convicted of the death of their infant child based on a statute that appeared to allow such a conviction on mere negligence. That statute was later amended by the Washington state legislature to require at least "criminal" negligence.

Subjectivity vs. Objectivity

As every torts student knows, adoption of an objective standard is hardly the end of the question. Even in torts, where the prime objective is compensation to innocent plaintiffs injured by unreasonable defendants, the question constantly arises as to what characteristics of the defendant are relevant in the test of the reasonably prudent person (RPP). Characteristics that increase the defendant's duty of care—higher degrees of expertise, training, or learning—are routinely added to the RPP (e.g., the reasonable brain surgeon). There are also relevant characteristics that lower the possible level of care. In torts, age (the children's rule) and long-term or permanent physical characteristics (e.g., blindness, deafness) are frequently added to the RPP standard.[12] It should not be surprising, therefore, that wherever the RPP test is used in criminal law, these kinds of characteristics are easily incorporated. Because the criminal law focuses much more on the actual subjective blameworthiness of the defendant, however, the impetus to further "subjectivize" the objective reasonable person test is strong, indeed virtually irresistible, particularly for the retributive—just deserts—theorist. As an example, American courts have held that in self-defense cases, the RPP defendant is the type of person who (1) reads police gazettes and has been the victim of a mugging, as has his doorman[13]; (2) has been socially acculturated to use only deadly force to reply to non-deadly force[14]; (3) has been battered by the victim's spouse over so long a period of time that (s)he suffers from "battered spouse syndrome."[15] We

---

11. These fears were not necessarily unreasonable. Even Congress later recognized that many American Indian families had been "unnecessarily" broken up by overly aggressive employees of the Bureau of Indian Affairs.

12. On the other hand, in tort law, the defendant's mental illness or insanity is irrelevant, whereas in criminal law, insanity is a full excuse (see Chapter 17).

13. *People v. Goetz*, 68 N.Y.2d 96 (1986).

14. *State v. Wanrow*, 88 Wash. 2d 221 (1977).

15. Schopp, Sturgis & Sullivan, Battered Woman Syndrome, Expert Testimony and the Distinction Between Justification and Excuse, 1994 U. Ill. L. Rev. 45.

will examine these issues in more depth later on, especially when we deal with specific defensive claims.

Given this trend toward increasingly subjectivizing the RPP, there is now substantial debate whether the concept of objective criminal negligence using a tort standard is sensible.

Proving Mens Rea

The first three kinds of mens rea (intent, knowledge, and recklessness) require that the state prove the defendant's actual mental state with regard to facts and result. But how can the state prove that? Other fields of law have concluded that it is simply too hard and too costly to prove what was actually in the defendant's mind.[16] However, criminal law does focus on individual blameworthiness as a basis for punishing.

Can we ever know what someone else is thinking? Some philosophers and psychiatrists argue that we never even know what *we* are thinking.[17] How, then, can we determine whether the defendant in a criminal case had the requisite mens rea for conviction?

The answer is *inference*. We can only infer, primarily from the defendant's conduct and words and secondarily from other facts that help us assess those inferences, what the defendant was thinking. Perhaps because we recognize the fallibility of such inferences we require that the jury be persuaded beyond a reasonable doubt that the inference of mens rea is a reasonable one to draw in this case.[18]

Again, an example may be helpful. Peter Pumpkin, who shot Lucretia, claims that he did not know the gun was loaded. If Peter is proven to be an expert gun handler, we may begin to doubt his denial. If the evidence also shows that Peter spent 10 minutes looking at the weapon before he fired it, we may find further reason to reject his claim. And if more evidence shows that Peter actually loaded the gun, we may think the case clinched. *But be careful*. Peter may claim that he thought the items he placed in the gun were blanks, and he may show us the box, marked "blanks," that he used.

---

16. In *Vaughan v. Menlove*, 132 Eng. Rep. 490 (1837), for example, the court explicitly rejected a subjective standard of negligence because it would require "measuring the feet" of every defendant. Thus, tort law uses an objective, fictitious person to assess the defendant's liability and does not actually care what was actually going on in *this* defendant's mind.

17. See I. Buford, Essays on Other Minds (1970); Comment, Motive, Crimes and Other Minds, 142 U. Pa. L. Rev. 2071 (1995).

18. Prior to the twentieth century, defendants were generally prohibited from testifying in their own behalf. The common law, seeking some way in which to allow the prosecutor to establish mens rea, and particularly intent, established a "presumption" that a person "intends the natural and probable consequences of his act."

Much of our decision will depend on Peter's credibility, should he choose to testify. If we believe Peter about other items, we are more likely to infer that he is telling the truth about this item, as well. However, inference is our best, perhaps our only, guide.

CONTEMPORANEITY, PRIOR FAULT, AND TIME FRAMES

It is frequently said that a defendant is liable only if the actus reus and the mens rea coincide. Like many other truisms of the law, this is true only if it is understood properly. If not, it can prove to be a trap for the unwary.

A defendant is not liable if, at one point in time (T), she has formed the requisite mens rea upon which she does not act but, at a later time (T2) when that mens rea is not present, the harm that she had envisioned occurs. For example, Carmen, in a blue funk, decided to kill her toreador lover, Chuck, by shooting him the next time he brought her a rose. However, as (his) luck would have it, Chuck stops bringing Carmen roses, and the thought disappears. Two weeks later, choking in daffodils, but fully reconciled with Chuck, Carmen is taking pot shots at a tree in the backyard. You guessed it: Chuck walks out from behind the tree (carrying a rose yet), and the next bullet terminates his breathing. Quite obviously, Carmen is not guilty of purposely killing Chuck, even though she has killed him (actus reus) and has previously intended to kill him (mens rea). To explain this result, the common law courts said that the mens rea and actus reus must coincide.

But take a different case. Sarah decides to kill her lover, Clancy, for exactly the same reasons that energized Carmen. She gets a vial of arsenic and pours the contents into Clancy's sugar bowl. She knows that, sometime within the next three weeks, Clancy will use the sugar. Immediately after this event, Sarah leaves the house and is trampled by a rogue elephant. She goes into a coma and is kept alive only by a respirator; no part of her body is acting voluntarily (see Chapter 3). Sure enough, two weeks later, with Sarah in the coma, Clancy takes the poison and dies. Miraculously, Sarah awakes from her coma 10 seconds after his death and shouts out: "Someone warn Clancy. I don't want him to die." If Sarah is prosecuted for murder, she will raise the doctrine of contemporaneity. At the moment Clancy died, she was not acting at all; the actus reus (Clancy's death) and the mens rea (purpose to kill) did not coincide. Nice try, Sarah. The *relevant* actus reus here is not Clancy's death, but Sarah's *act* of putting the poison in the sugar bowl although the *result* occurred much later. When *that* actus reus occurred, Sarah did have the requisite mens rea.

One way of conceptualizing this analysis is to say that we can move the time frame back to see if, at some relevant time, the defendant, with the requisite mens rea, acted in a way that ultimately caused the harm. Consider *People v. Decina*, discussed in Chapter 3. At the time his car hit the four school children (the time of the harm), Decina was suffering an epileptic seizure, and neither acting voluntarily nor entertaining a mens of any kind. However, by moving the time frame back to before the seizure (indeed, perhaps to the time he entered the car and turned on the ignition), the court found both an act (beginning to drive) and a mens rea (criminal negligence or recklessness as to the possibility that he would have a seizure, lose control of the car, and cause death or serious injury).

STATUTORY INTERPRETATION AND MENS REA

Principles of Statutory Construction

Because modern criminal law consists of interpreting statutes, it is important to have some grasp of general rules of statutory construction and how they apply to criminal cases. Writers and courts debate whether the "maxims" of statutory interpretation are meaningful, not only in criminal law, but in law generally.[19] We will not enter that debate here. Instead, we assume the general usefulness of such maxims, particularly in interpreting criminal statutes, where the policies of lenity and legality attain constitutional, or quasi-constitutional, status (see Chapter 1). Similarly, many of the rules of interpreting criminal statutes are generated by the substantive policy positions of the criminal law. For example, under the common law, courts require the prosecution to prove mens rea, even if the legislature has not explicitly required a mental state.[20] This specific result could be seen as an application of the maxim that *penal statutes are to be construed narrowly and against the state*.

Other maxims dealing with legislative silence are also important in construing criminal statutes. If, for example, a statute does not require an element of proof that the common law did require, courts would probably apply the general maxim that *statutes in derogation of the common law are to be construed narrowly* and require a mens rea.[21]

19. K. Llewellyn, The Common Law Tradition (1960) (maxims of statutory interpretation can conceivably be manipulated to include or exclude anything).
20. Exceptions to this practice are considered in Chapter 6.
21. *Morrissette v. United States*, 342 U.S. 246 (1952).

Furthermore, the general rule of *in pari materia*—statutes dealing with similar subjects should be construed similarly—often has particular impact. Consider the following statutes:

A. Whoever sells cocaine shall be fined $1,000.
B. Whoever knowingly sells heroin shall be fined $1,000.

Can a person violate statute A without "knowing" that he is selling cocaine? The two statutes *seem* to deal with the same basic evil, the sale of drugs. Assume (for the moment) that statute B requires that the defendant know that he is selling heroin (and not merely that he is selling something that turns out to be heroin). Since statute B tells us that the legislature has articulated a requirement of "knowingly" on occasion, should we infer that its failure to do so in statute A means that the omission was purposeful?

The argument that the two are to be read *in pari materia* because they deal with drugs is strengthened by the fact that the punishments are identical. However, suppose that statute B prohibited knowingly selling poisoned food (or stolen pencils) and specified the same fine of $1,000. It would then be harder to use the *in pari materia* approach because drugs and pencils (or even poisoned food) might not be seen as the same "matter." On the other hand, if the punishment is the same, that might be the same "matter." Or suppose that the punishment for selling heroin, in statute B, is raised to 5 years. Now it might be argued that statute A does not require proof of knowledge, because knowledge must be proved only if the punishment is "very" severe.

Another maxim of statutory construction tells us to read *any* statute in its "plain meaning." As noted in Chapter 1, the rule of lenity holds that if the legislature has not clearly spoken, the statute's ambiguities should be construed against the legislature and in favor of the defendant (and the defendant's freedom).

The above remarks should be regarded as an introduction to the problems of interpreting statutes generally, and not solely those in the criminal law. General rules of interpretations may or may not be applicable to the exotic field you are about to enter. However, it won't hurt to keep those rules in mind.

Element Analysis

Little Red Riding Hood has been instructed by her mother to deliver a package to her grandmother. Red, who had been planning a round of golf, is not pleased. As she is walking through the woods, she comes across a great bonfire. Herman is standing there and shouting "No more books" as he throws volume after volume of Charles Dickens on the fire. Angry that she cannot play golf, Red throws the package into the fire and watches it burn. It turns out that the package contains a first edition of *Dickens*! Red is charged under a statute that punishes anyone who "purposely hides, destroys, or mars a book." Is Little Red guilty under this statute?

If the prosecutor has only to prove that Red purposely destroyed the *package*, that hurdle is easily cleared: Red obviously purposely destroyed whatever were the contents of the package. But does the prosecutor have to prove that Red knew the package contained a "book"? This problem raises the issue of how far down the statute the mens rea word ("purposely") goes. Prescient lawyers call this the "traveling" question.

The first approach to this problem is grammatical. "Purposely" is an adverb; "book" is a noun. Since adverbs modify only verbs, "purposely" cannot apply directly to the word "book" in the statute. A number of common law decisions therefore concluded that Red would be guilty of the crime, even though she did not know that it was a book she was destroying, since she "purposely" destroyed it.[22]

However, this result seems wrong. The legislature was not concerned with persons who purposely destroyed *packages*, only with persons who purposely destroyed *books*. No one would condone what Red did and she might be sent to bed without supper, but the issue here is not *only* whether she has acted in an immoral way (traditional mens rea) but whether she has also acted in a way proscribed by the statute (statutory mens rea). Whether *traditional* mens rea is always necessary, *statutory* mens rea is necessary to meet the principle of legality. To use our earlier terms, Red may have been *reckless* or *negligent* (even criminally negligent) as to what was in the package. If the legislature had prohibited recklessly or negligently destroying books, Red might (given further facts, such as the shape of the package or her ability to feel the contents) be guilty of one of those offenses. However, she was not acting "purposely" with regard to the result of a destroyed book, and is therefore not guilty under the statute. Moreover, to punish Red for purposely destroying the book would mean that she would be treated as being equally bad as Herman, who was well aware that the items he was throwing on the bonfire were books.

The common law's response to this dilemma was to create a separate set of doctrines dealing with mistake. We shall investigate those doctrines in the next chapter. Here, however, we focus solely on statutory interpretation, apart from the independent question of the law of mistake. One method of resolving this question would be to define in general terms what a particular mens rea word such as "purposely" *means* with regard to each of the words in the statute. For example, we could say that a person acts

22. *Cotterill v. Penn*, 1 K.B. 53 (1936).

"purposely" with regard to the "book" in the statute only if she knows that the book exists. This approach of applying a statutory mens rea word to every significant part of the statute is now called *element analysis*.

The United States Supreme Court appears to have adopted element analysis in interpreting federal statutes. In *X-Citement Video v. United States*, 513 U.S. 64 (1994), the defendant distributed a sexually explicit film whose cast included minors. A federal statute punished anyone who "knowingly ships" such a film involving the "use of a minor." The Court held that the word "knowingly" modified not only the verb "ships" but the phrase "use of a minor." Thus, a defendant who knows that he is shipping a film, and even knows that what he is shipping is a sexually explicit film, is not guilty of this offense unless he *also* knows that the film includes a minor. Note that unless this approach to statutory interpretation is adopted (or an additional set of rules created), the statute essentially establishes strict liability (see Chapter 6) for the element of "minor" (or "book" in Little Red Riding Hood's case). Under that interpretation, any person who handled the film (the FedEx deliverer, the developer of the film, etc.) would be potentially liable, a result that the Court said would cast the net far too wide.

In 2009, the Court once again embraced element analysis, even calling it a "presumption" that a mens rea word modified everything in a statute. *United States v. Flores-Figueroa*, 129 S. Ct. 1886 (2009). The statute involved there made it a felony to "knowingly" use an identity card "of another person." The Court concluded that the trial court had erred by not requiring that the government prove that the defendant knew the identification number was that "of another." The decision is important because, unlike *X-Citement Video*, it did not involve a potential First Amendment issue. *Caveat:* *X-Citement Video* and *Flores-Figueroa* apply only to federal statutes—this does not mean that a state court must adopt the same approach.

Even if the common law requires a mens rea with regard to the "really important" parts of the statute, there may be "less important" parts to which such a requirement does not apply. Consider, for example, a New York statute that makes "stealing a car in New York City" punishable by 5 years in prison, while another statute makes "stealing a car" punishable by 2 years. Even assuming the defendant has to know that what he is stealing is a car (as opposed to a minivan, which is legally a truck), does he have to know that he is in New York City? Many, if not all, courts have answered that question in the negative by differentiating between "real" and "jurisdictional" elements. Although the prosecution must prove that the crime occurred in New York, it need not prove that the defendant *knew* he was in that city.

This result is not as obvious as it may first appear. After all, the New York legislature doesn't seem to care as much about cars stolen in places other than New York City. One might think that the fact that it happened in

New York City really *is* important, and that a mens rea should apply to this fact, as well. That, however, has not been the general result in the courts.

Another example may be helpful. State statutes often distinguish between assaults upon persons generally, and assaults upon "especially protected persons," such as law enforcement, firefighting personnel, and judges. In these statutes, the status of the person is *not* a jurisdictional element; the same court would have jurisdiction over both types of assault. Some statutes specifically require that the defendant know the protected status of the victim; where the statutes are silent, courts are divided on whether such knowledge is required.[23]

The "Default Position"

Suppose that Red Riding Hood had been prosecuted under a statute punishing "anyone who destroys a book." This statute, unlike the first one, contains no mens rea word at all.

Courts confronting such a statute are faced with a dilemma. The plain words of the statute do not require a mens rea. Does the omission of a mens rea word reflect a firm legislative decision to impose strict liability? Should we assume that the legislature *intended* to omit mens rea? Or should we assume that the omission was a mere oversight? (Or, only somewhat more impishly, that the statute was drafted on a Friday, when everyone was tired and wanted to get home for the weekend?)

The problem is that to argue about what the legislature *could* have done is sterile: Just as it *could* have written in the word "knowingly," it *could* just as easily have said, "Anyone who destroys a box, whether or not they know, suspect, or could have known it was a book, is guilty of an offense."[24] In the end, the legislative intent argument leads us nowhere unless we have a starting point. Some courts have provided that starting point by asserting that the legislative intent to do away with mens rea must be "patently" clear.[25]

When mens rea was used in its "traditional" sense, the problem was perhaps less evident. The basic question then was whether Red had acted in a blameworthy way. This revived the debate as to whether negligence could amount to blameworthiness (see supra), but beyond that, the courts

23. A federal statute that prohibits assault against "a federal officer" may well be different; a federal court would not have jurisdiction over an assault against a nonfederal person. See *United States v. Feola*, 420 U.S. 671 (1975). In that event, the status of the victim is in fact jurisdictional and might not require a mens rea.

24. For example, the New Jersey "drug-free school zone" statute expressly provides: "It shall be no defense . . . that the actor was unaware that the prohibited conduct took place while or within 1000 feet of any school property." N.J. Stat. Ann. 2C: 35-7.

25. *People v. Hager*, 476 N.Y.S.2d 442 (Nassau Cty. Ct. 1989).

did not need to go. Any level of blameworthiness would suffice. As the principle of legality took hold, however, and statutory mens rea became ascendant, courts could no longer ask merely whether the defendant was blameworthy. They had to decide as well which of the statutory mens rea words would apply. Traditional mens rea, even if necessary, was no longer a sufficient condition for liability. Since there were scores of statutory mens rea words from which to choose, this was a daunting task.

Most courts adopted the view that criminal punishment should not be imposed unless the defendant was at least reckless (actually foresaw a possibility of criminal harm) and went ahead anyway. The United States Supreme Court has gone beyond that. It now appears to have adopted the view that in interpreting federal statutes that are silent on the mens rea issue, it will begin with the presumption that the defendant must act *knowingly* as to each element of the statute. The case, *United States v. Staples*, 511 U.S. 600 (1994), involved a defendant who was charged with failing to inform the federal government that he owned an automatically firing weapon—an AR-14. Federal law did not require that all gun owners register all guns with the government; only owners of "firearms which shoot, or can be readily restored to shoot, automatically" had to register them. The statute contained no mens rea word at all. The defendant acknowledged that he had purchased an AR-14 but maintained that when he purchased it, it was not capable of firing "automatically," and that he did not know when or by whom the gun had been altered after the purchase. The Court concluded not only that some mens rea would be required, but that the level of mens rea required was "knowingly." *Staples* is an important decision regarding strict liability, and we will discuss it in that context, as well. But it is important here because it appears to adopt "knowingly" as the default position—if Congress does not specify recklessness (or some lower standard of mens rea), federal courts should construe such a criminal statute to require actual knowledge of the facts.[26] This is not merely a statutory interpretation point; the decision carries significant moral weight, as well, because it appears to adopt the subjectivist view.

MENS REA AND THE CONSTITUTION

For decades, law professors (at least) have debated whether the Constitution requires that the government prove some form of mens rea for any criminal statute. Declarations, such as those in *Staples* and *X-Citement Video*, strongly

26. Again, the same caveat as with *X-Citement Video* and *Flores-Figueroa*: *Staples* applies (at best) only to interpreting federal statutes; it has no applicability (except as persuasive authority) in interpreting state statutes.

suggested that mens rea would be read into every federal statute. But the most recent statements from the Court appear to put this question to rest, at least for the foreseeable future. In *Dixon v. United States*, 548 U.S. 1 (2006), the Court repeated that the decision as to whether to require mens rea at all was a legislative, and not a judicial, one. In *Clark v. Arizona*, 548 U.S. 735, the Court held that state legislatures have the authority to define (and limit) mens rea, and the defenses to crime, virtually without limit. See also *Montana v. Egelhoff*, 518 U.S. 37 (1996).

THE MODEL PENAL CODE

Perhaps the greatest contribution that the Model Penal Code has made is in the area of providing rules for statutory interpretation. The Code:

1. distinguishes between "elements" and "material elements" of a statute
2. reduces statutory mens rea culpability to four mental states
3. adopts element analysis by applying the four mental states to each of the material elements of a statute (indeed, the Code really invented the idea of element analysis)
4. adopts subjective liability (recklessness) as the default position.

"Elements" vs. "Material" Elements

In order to apply the four mental states (see infra) and "element analysis" (see infra), the Code first establishes the distinction between (nonmaterial) "elements" of a statute and "material elements." Under section 1.13 of the Code, "nonmaterial" elements are those terms "unconnected with the harm or evil, incident to conduct, sought to be prevented by the law defining the offense."

Consider the Red Riding Hood statute, which made it a crime to "destroy a book." What is the "harm or evil" sought to be prevented by this statute? Clearly, the legislature here is concerned with books. It does not care, at least in this provision, about the destruction of movies, porcupines, or buildings. And it is concerned not with the mutilation, or the hoarding, of books—only with their destruction. Thus, the "harms or evils" about which this statute are concerned is "destroying" "books." These, then, are the "material elements." Most words in a statute are likely to be "material" elements—after all, why is the legislature acting at all and using these words if it is not concerned with all of those words? On the other hand, had the statute added "in New York City," it is arguable that this is not a "material element," but only an "element." Indeed, the Code expressly says that words relating to "venue, jurisdiction, or the statute of limitations" are not "material" elements (although, as we saw earlier, an argument could be made that the statute shows that the legislature is only concerned with New York City books, rather than Albany books).

Defining the "material" elements in some statutes may be more difficult. A statute that punishes any person "who discharges a gun in public" may be concerned with (1) loud noises in public places or (2) possible endangerment of persons in public. The statute is unclear. Usual approaches to statutory interpretation may assist, but the courts will have to try to interpret the statute as the legislature wanted them construed. Here the "statutory maxims" mentioned, above, may be useful. For example, a court might rely on the legislative history, or the placement of the statute (is it in a section on noises or on harm to the person) in deciding whether an "element" is a "material element."

Kinds of Material Elements

Having defined what the "material elements" are, the Code then subdivides these into (a) conduct, (b) attendant circumstance, and (c) result, and applies each of the four mental states to these material elements. Before discussing the mental states, however, we should differentiate the kinds of material elements.

Conduct and Result

Clearly verbs are "conduct," so "destroys" is conduct. But, like many other verbs in the English language (kill, touch, hide), it can also describe a result. This can sometimes create a problem. Suppose a statute declares that "Whoever employs fire and destroys . . . " has committed a crime. Even if "destroys" is both conduct and result, what is "employs"?

Attendant Circumstances

An attendant circumstance is any material element that is not a result or conduct. If most "conduct" words are verbs, most attendant circumstances are nouns or adjectives. In the statute in question, "book" is a material element, and since "book" is rarely a result or verb except to a theater entrepreneur ("book that act"), it is an attendant circumstance. Similarly, had the legislation prohibited destroying (only) "purple" books, "purple" would also be a "material element" since the legislature didn't care about whether orange or green books were destroyed.

Be careful here. The state must prove, beyond a reasonable doubt, ALL the "elements"—material or nonmaterial—in the statute. Thus, it must prove that the item was a "book," that it was "destroyed," and that it was destroyed "in New York City." With regard to "material" elements, however, the state must also prove one of the requisite mental states, to which we now turn.

Levels of Mental States

Section 2.02 of the Code replaces the confusing and innumerable mental states used by state and federal legislatures in a plethora of criminal statutes with four, in "descending order" of culpability[27]:

1. purposely
2. knowingly
3. recklessly
4. negligently.

Purposely

This is roughly the equivalent of the common law term "intentionally." To prove that a defendant had "purpose" with regard to an attendant circumstance, the Code requires that the defendant "be aware or hope or believe" that fact is true. If the material element is a "result" element, he must entertain the "conscious object" to achieve the proscribed result. Note that, unlike the remaining three levels of mental state, likelihood of a consequence is never part of the "purposely" analysis. If Steve—who has never shot a gun before—shoots at his wife 400 yards away, the likelihood that he will hit and kill her is slim. However, the low probability of success would not be a defense if his ultimate purpose was to kill her. As a practical effect, "reckless conduct, as manifested in risk taking, can be elevated to purposeful conduct if the actor hopes that the risk will come to fruition."[28] In the above example, a prosecutor would not have a difficult time making an inference to the jury that Steve's shooting in his wife's direction was evidence of his intent to kill her, despite a low probability of doing so.

---

27. The greater culpability includes the lesser. Thus if a prosecutor proves that the defendant "purposely" destroyed the book, the defendant is guilty of "recklessly" destroying it.
28. Paul H. Robinson, Shima Baradaran Baughman, and Michael T. Cahill, Criminal Law: Case Studies and Controversies, 131 (New York: Wolters Kluwer, 2017).

Knowingly

This Code term is essentially the equivalent of "oblique intention" under the common law. The critical distinction between "purpose" and "knowledge" is that the purposeful actor *desires* a specific result, whereas the "knowing" actor foresees the result as highly likely but doesn't really care whether it occurs or not. The Code also expressly provides that "willfully" is equivalent to "knowingly" (§2.02(8)) and adopts the general notion of "willful blindness." Section 2.02(7).

Recklessly

As with the common law, the Code provides that the defendant is reckless only if he *actually foresees* that a harm may occur or that an attendant circumstance is present. Thus, subjective liability is continued. There is, however, one major possible problem with the Code's approach to recklessness. The Code requires that the risk that the defendant foresees (and thereafter consciously disregards) be "substantial and unjustifiable." The latter term is understandable, and it clearly puts on the prosecution the burden of proof as to lack of justification (see Chapter 15). The difficulty, however, is in the apparent requirement that the risk be *substantial*. Taken literally, this requirement might lead to a different result in the hypothetical, discussed above (page 74), where Peter Pumpkin takes the one loaded gun out of 10,000 and kills Lucretia. There, we concluded that Peter was reckless. However, a chance of .0001 is not really "substantial." To avoid the absurd result that Peter is not reckless as to death under the Code's definition therefore, requires that the word "substantial" be read as qualitative ("of real importance") rather than merely quantitative ("highly probable").

Negligently

Section 2.02(2)(d) of the Code proposes criminal negligence as a possible predicate for criminal liability—that is, not tort but criminal (or wanton or culpable) negligence, as understood under the common law. However, the Code, in fact, only allows criminal negligence in one crime, homicide, in which case the penalty is less than that for manslaughter (which is usually the level of punishment for negligent homicide in common law jurisdictions). Thus, while appearing to embrace negligence as a basis of liability generally, the Code really uses this approach as a way of mitigating punishment for those who might otherwise be convicted of manslaughter (see Chapter 8).

The Code also retains two of the subsidiary doctrines of the common law of mental states. Transferred intent is now viewed as a matter of causation (§2.03(2) and (3)) (see Chapter 3). Similarly, while the Code generally rejects the "specific-general" intent notions, it does occasionally talk in terms of a crime being committed "with the purpose of" achieving a result, a rough analog to specific intent. But the common law rules relating to general versus specific intent, and mistake (see Chapter 5), are essentially eliminated.

Also note that the key distinction between "negligence and recklessness is the actor's *awareness of the risk*."[29] If a substantial risk is present, but the actor was not aware of the risk, she was not capable of ignoring the risk so as to meet the recklessness mental state. In such a case, the actor would only be liable for a negligence offense.

Faultless (Strict) Liability

On some occasions, no level of mental state is required to impose liability for a crime. These are called strict liability crimes. These types of crimes generally arise from conduct that the legislature has deemed such an interest to the public that it warrants the potentially harsh outcomes that arise from eliminating the mental state requirement. For example, in most statutory rape statutes, an offender may be punished without regard to otherwise mitigating circumstances or mistake of fact. As the Supreme Court noted, there is an important interest there to protect that can only, or best, be accomplished through strict liability.[30]

Element Analysis

Now comes the Code's monumental achievement—"element analysis."[31] The Code merges its definitions of culpability with its establishment of material elements, and provides that *every material element in every statute must be modified by one of the mental culpability states* (§2.02). This simple but elegant move solves many of the dilemmas we have confronted in the earlier sections of this chapter. The result is best shown graphically in Table 4.1.

Let's take the case of Little Red Riding Hood, who is charged with "purposely destroying a book." Since the statutorily stated mens rea is

29. Paul H. Robinson, Shima Baradaran Baughman, and Michael T. Cahill, Criminal Law: Case Studies and Controversies, 131 (New York: Wolters Kluwer, 2017).

30. See Paul H. Robinson, Shima Baradaran Baughman, and Michael T. Cahill, Criminal Law: Case Studies and Controversies, 130 (New York: Wolters Kluwer, 2017).

31. See Paul H. Robinson & Jane Grall, Element Analysis in Defining Criminal Liability: The Model Penal Code and Beyond, 35 Stan. L. Rev. 681 (1983); Kimberly Ferzan, Don't Abandon the Model Penal Code Yet! Thinking Through Simon's Rethinking, 6 Buff. Crim. L. Rev. 185 (2002).

4.1 Mens Rea and Section 2.02 of the Model Penal Code

Culpability Level	Conduct	Attendant Circumstances	Result
Purposely	Defendant's conscious object is to engage in such conduct.	Defendant is aware or hopes or believes the circumstance exists.	Defendant's conscious object is to cause this result.
Knowingly	Defendant is aware his conduct is of this nature.	Defendant is aware the circumstances exist.	Defendant is aware that the result is practically certain.
Recklessly	Defendant consciously disregards a substantial and unjustifiable risk that he is engaging in this proscribed conduct.	Defendant consciously disregards a substantial and unjustifiable risk that the proscribed circumstances exist.	Defendant consciously disregards a substantial and unjustifiable risk that the result will occur.
	This disregard involves a gross deviation from the standard of conduct that a law-abiding person would observe, considering defendant's purpose and the circumstances known to him.		
Negligently	Defendant fails to recognize a substantial and unjustifiable risk he is engaging in this conduct.	Defendant fails to recognize an unjustifiable risk that the proscribed circumstances exist.	Defendant fails to recognize a substantial and unjustifiable risk that the result will occur.
	The failure to recognize the risk, given defendant's purpose and the circumstances known to him, involves a gross deviation from the standard of care a reasonable person would observe.		

"purposely," and since "book" is an attendant circumstance material element, the state must show that Red either was "aware of the existence of such circumstance or believe[d] or hope[d]" that it exists—i.e., that the package contained a book. We have already posited that Red did *not* know, or even suspect, that the package contained a book. Thus, she does not meet the Code's requirement and is not guilty of the crime charged. Herman, on the other hand, *did* know that he was burning a book and it was his conscious object to cause the destruction of the book. He is guilty under the statute.

Suppose, instead, that Little Red was charged under a different statute, punishing anyone who "recklessly" destroyed a book. Here, the analysis is the same: "Book" is an attendant circumstance material element. Under the recklessness provision, Red is guilty if she "consciously disregards a substantial and unjustifiable risk" that the item she is destroying is a book. That disregard must involve "a gross deviation from the standard of conduct that a law-abiding person would observe" in Red's situation. So if Red manipulated the package and it felt like a book, or she saw that an attached sales receipt was from a bookstore, she might be found guilty of violating this statute. Note that the difference between her possible liability under "knowingly" and "recklessly" depends on the degree of probability that Red recognizes that the item might be a book. If she is aware that it is a book or that there is a high probability that the package contains a book, she is "willfully blind" under §2.02(7) of the Code and hence acts "knowingly." If, on the other hand, she is aware of a substantial (but not highly probable) risk that the package contains a book, she is reckless, and not knowing, with regard to that material element.

In the Red Riding Hood statute, "purposely" is the only mens rea word articulated in the statute, and thus modifies all the material elements in the statute. But the legislature may require different mental states with regard to different material elements in a statute. Thus: "Whoever, while purposely destroying a package, recklessly destroys a book, is guilty of a crime." Here, purposely requires that the defendant *know* (or hope) that it is a package, but merely be reckless as to whether it contains a book. If the statute read "Whoever, while destroying a package, recklessly destroys a book," the defendant obviously must be reckless as to (1) whether a book is involved or (2) whether the item was "destroyed." But what is the mens rea as to whether a package is involved? This involves the default position.

The Code's analysis makes statutory interpretation easy. In *X-Citement Video*, for example (see page 83), it is clear that "minor" is a material element—the "harm or evil" here is using minors; Congress couldn't care less if adults were involved in pornography. And "minor" is an "attendant circumstance." The adverb "knowingly" modifies every material element of the statute wherever found; the defendant is guilty only if he "is aware" that the person in the film is a minor.[32] Rather than the very long opinion it filed, the Supreme Court could have solved this issue in two paragraphs—if Congress had adopted the MPC (which it has not).

The Default Position Under the Code

The Code establishes recklessness as the default provision of mens rea. Section 2.02(3) provides that if there is no mens rea stated in the statute, the element is proved if a person acts purposely, knowingly, or recklessly with respect thereto. In our cocaine statute, for example, there is no mens rea stated. Thus, the prosecution will be successful only if it proves the defendant was reckless (or worse) with regard to the item being cocaine. In the case suggested above, the government would have to prove that Red was reckless as to a package being involved (and as to whether she was destroying it), *not* because "reckless" is used somewhere in the statute, but because the default provision applies.

The Code's position on default does two things (at least). First, it rejects the view, apparently adopted by the United States Supreme Court in *Staples*, supra, as a matter of interpreting federal criminal statutes, that "knowingly" is the presumed mens rea requirement. Thus, the Code seems to accept a lower default standard of culpability than did *Staples*. Second, the Code rejects, at least as a presumptive matter, imposing criminal liability on the basis of criminal negligence; all criminal liability is *presumed* to be based on subjective moral culpability. Unless the legislature expressly allows criminal negligence as a predicate for criminal liability, the statute will be interpreted as requiring subjective culpability.[33]

In *United States v. Flores-Figueroa*, 129 S. Ct. 1886 (2009), the Court seemed to adopt "element analysis" for interpreting federal statutes. In 2000, to secure employment, Flores gave his employer a false name, birth date, and Social Security number, along with a counterfeit alien registration card. The Social Security number and the number on the alien registration card were not those of a real person. In 2006, Flores presented his employer with new counterfeit Social Security and alien registration cards; these cards (unlike Flores' old alien registration card) used his real name. But this time the

---

32. Note that if the statute had used the adverb "purposely," the defendant could be guilty not only if he was "aware" of the actor's age, but also if he "hoped or believed" that the actor was a minor.

33. At least 11 states have adopted the Code's use of recklessness as the default provision, six use negligence, and one uses knowledge. Holley, The Influence of the Model Penal Code's Culpability Provisions on State Legislatures: A Study of Lost Opportunities, Including Abolishing the Mistake of Fact Doctrine, 27 Sw. U. L. Rev. 229 (1997).

numbers on both cards were in fact numbers assigned to other people. The federal statute that he violated provided, additionally, that:

> Whoever, during and in relation to any felony violation enumerated in subsection (c), knowingly transfers, possesses, or uses, without lawful authority, a means of identification of another person shall, in addition to the punishment provided for such felony, be sentenced to a term of imprisonment of 2 years. 18 U.S.C. §1028A.

The Court, in an opinion by Justice Breyer, held that the "natural reading" of the statute was that the government had to prove that the defendant knew that the false papers and numbers he used belonged to "another person." Thus, the mens rea term (knowingly) "traveled" throughout the statute to the "material attendant circumstance" of "minor."

Summary

It would be too much to say that the Code solves the issues of interpretation raised earlier in this chapter. However, it gives more guidance and more serious consideration to these problems than any other tool we know. Moreover, since the Code has been adopted in a majority of states, and has influenced common law courts even when the legislature has not adopted the Code, it may now be suggested that element analysis is part of the American law of crimes.

EXAMPLES

Examples

1. Lisa's parents were incredibly wealthy entrepreneurs who earned hundreds of millions of dollars through the course of their careers. After her mother passed away recently, her father's health began declining rapidly. It was no secret that he likely would not make it much longer. Lisa secretly anticipated his death. Her relationship with her parents was always turbulent, and she assumed she had half of a large fortune coming her way. Lisa visited her father one day and found his will, which left most of his and his wife's estate to Tom—the golden child—and a modest sum to Lisa. The will stipulated that if either child was not alive upon the will's execution, the living child would inherit everything. Furious, Lisa ran home and began plotting to kill Tom. She knew his wife would be out of town that weekend, so she bought a gun and made plans to stage a robbery gone wrong. That weekend, she broke into his house, snuck into his room, and unloaded her entire gun in the direction of his bed. Unfortunately for Lisa, she is a horrible shot and missed Tom entirely. Also unfortunate was that she struck and

killed Tom's wife, who had cancelled her weekend plans. What result if Lisa is charged with intentionally killing Tom's wife?

2. Gilberto—a disturbed police officer—has recently begun having fantasies of killing and cooking various women. The idea thrilled him so much that he spent hours in online chatrooms discussing how to kill (and then eat) over 100 women with other similarly interested people. He even goes so far to discuss cooking and eating his wife (slowly) but never engaged in any of these actions. His wife happens to find these chats and reports her husband to the FBI right away. Has his behavior risen to the level of a crime?

3a. One fine October day, Napoleon, an avid hunter, goes hunting for deer. An animal scurries across the path, and Nappy, in a flash, shoots. He discovers that he has killed a rabbit, which is prohibited in this jurisdiction. Just at that moment, Odie, the friendly game warden, appears and arrests him. Nappy is prosecuted for knowingly killing the rabbit.

3b. Same facts, except that the charge is "recklessly" killing the rabbit.

3c. Same facts as in 3a, but this time the statute prohibits "negligently" killing a rabbit.

3d. Same facts as in 3a, except that it is a child who is killed. Is Nappy guilty of any form of homicide ("purposely," "knowingly," "recklessly," or "negligently" killing a human being)?

4. Later in October, Napoleon again goes hunting, this time in the woods in Smith County. Unbeknownst to him, his trek takes him across the county line into Jones County. As (good) luck would have it, he spots a rabbit and kills it with a single shot. As (bad) luck would have it, however, as he goes to pick it up, Odie, the friendly game warden, shows up again, and again arrests him. This time the charge is "knowingly killing a rabbit in Jones County"; killing a rabbit is not illegal in Smith County. What result?

5. In Stephen King's book *Misery*, an obsessive fan of a mystery writer nurses him back to health when he is injured in an automobile accident. When he informs her that he intends to leave her house, she smashes his legs with a sledge hammer. If she is prosecuted in a common law jurisdiction for (1) assault with intent to kill or (2) aggravated assault, defined as "assault with a deadly weapon, inflicting great harm," is she guilty of either offense?

6. Barney goes into FAO Schwarz to buy toy dinosaurs for his children. He pays for the toys with a VISA credit card. Unknown to Barney, the card has expired. He is prosecuted under a statute that punishes anyone who "purposely uses an expired credit card to obtain goods or services."

7a. Jacob is a devout Snaker. His religion teaches him that no bite of a snake will be harmful, much less deadly, if the handler of the snake has true belief in God. Jacob does. He therefore takes his six-month-old son to church one day and, handling the snakes himself, allows them to bite the boy three times. The boy dies. Assume that a statute penalizes, in varying degrees, anyone who "intentionally, purposely, knowingly, maliciously, or recklessly" causes the death of another. Of which of these crimes, if any, is Jacob guilty?

7b. Same facts. The statute penalizes anyone who "causes the death" of another person.

8. Diana, an actress, picks up a gun and, just as the script requires, carefully and deliberately loads it with bullets from a box plainly marked "bullets." She then walks over to Charles, who is studying pictures of his newest polo ponies, and, holding the gun to Charles' temple, pulls the trigger, shouting, "And that's for Camilla, you bastard!" Charles drops to the floor, blood spurting from the wound. Diana immediately screams, "Someone get a doctor!" When she is charged with "purposely" killing Charles, she claims she did not know the gun was loaded. What result?

9. Cary is driving his new Rolls Royce one night at ten miles per hour *under* the speed limit. He is keeping a careful watch on the road. Suddenly, a child runs out in front of the car. Cary presses his foot to the brakes, but there is no response. Desperately, he screams at the child and veers his car hard to the left, applying the emergency brake at the same time. Nothing works. The child is killed. Cary is prosecuted for "reckless homicide." What result?

10. Helen, a burglar, has decided to burglarize a warehouse. She has "cased" the place for three weeks and is sure that everyone leaves by 10 p.m. On the night in question, she double-checks the parking lot and waits until 2 a.m., just in case anyone has stayed late. She then breaks in to the building by smashing a window and jumping through. As she lands, her foot hits the windpipe of Harry, a homeless person who has sneaked in through the back door and is sleeping there. Harry dies. Has Helen killed Harry "purposely, knowingly, recklessly, or negligently"?

11. Louis carefully "cases" a bank for two weeks, noting the times that every employee enters and exits. He knows that by 2 a.m., the only person in the bank is a guard. He arranges for someone to call the guard at 1:45 a.m. and tell him that his wife has just been taken to the hospital. Sure enough, the guard leaves by 1:50 a.m., giving Louis at least two hours to commit his theft. He breaks though the back door, opens the vault, and begins removing money, when he discovers a bank teller

who was unwittingly locked inside the vault. Louis calls the hospital and waits until the paramedics arrive. The teller is saved. Louis is then prosecuted for "knowingly breaking and entering a building which is occupied by one or more persons." Is he guilty (a) under the common law? (b) under federal law? (c) under the Model Penal Code?

12. Abbie enlists in the United States Army in November 2002. Six months later, while stationed at Ft. Riley, Kansas, he is ordered to a post in Iraq. Convinced that the invasion of Iraq constitutes a war crime, he leaves Ft. Riley and appears on numerous television shows condemning the war and denying its legitimacy. Three months later, he returns to Ft. Riley. He is charged with "desertion with intent to avoid hazardous duty and shirk important service." He seeks to introduce evidence that he wished to protest the Iraq war, not to avoid hazardous duty. May he do so?

13a. Riffi is charged with intentionally (purposely) running down and killing Constantine. Riffi argues that Constantine was a complete stranger, and that the death was an accident. The prosecutor seeks to introduce evidence that Riffi is of Armenian background, and that Constantine is Turkish American. The prosecutor's theory is that Riffi is seeking revenge on the Turks for the genocide committed against the Armenians in the early twentieth century. Riffi argues that motive is not relevant to the criminal law, and that the evidence should be precluded. What result?

13b. Riffi is charged with intentionally murdering Constantine. Riffi wishes to introduce evidence that Constantine is the lead hit man of the "Turkish mafia," and has personally killed 25 people. He argues that his motive should suggest that the killing was not socially undesirable.

14a. Al has a license to carry a concealed .45 Colt revolver. On Mother's Day, he takes his entire family, including his wife, two children, and both his and his wife's mothers, to Boliva's, his favorite family restaurant, which he has frequented at least monthly for the past two years. As he sits down to dinner, he is tapped on the shoulder by Pablo, the local sheriff, who charges him with violating the following statute: "It is illegal to carry a firearm in an establishment licensed to dispense alcoholic beverages." It's a fourth degree felony, punishable by a maximum sentence of 18 months. It turns out that Al forgot that his Colt was in his jacket pocket. What result?

14b. Al knows that he has the gun on his person. What he doesn't know is that that on May 1, Boliva's obtained a liquor license, which it had never had before. This is Al's first visit since May 1. What result?

15. Miniver has been sitting in a plane on the tarmac for over two hours, waiting for his "one-hour" flight to Boston to take off. As he rises to stretch his legs, Louis, the flight attendant, says to him, sternly, "Sir, you must remain in your seat so that we can taxi as soon as possible." "As soon as possible," rages Louis. "I'm already supposed to be in Boston," and he swings at Louis, missing him. He is charged with violating 49 USC §46505, which provides that "[a]n individual on an aircraft . . . who, by . . . intimidating a flight crew member . . . interferes with the performance of the duties of the members, or lessens the ability of the member of attendant to perform those duties, shall be fined . . . imprisoned for not more than 20 years, or both." Miniver argues that the government must prove he had the specific intent to interfere with Louis's duties. He urges two grounds: (1) one cannot "intimidate" without having the specific intent to do so, and (2) the predecessor statute prohibited assaulting "so as to" interfere with the attendant's performance. That statute, he contends, required specific intent to interfere, and the successor statute should be so construed, as well. How should the judge rule?

EXPLANATIONS

Explanations

1. It is clear from the facts that Lisa did not intend to kill Tom's wife. In fact, she took active precautions to ensure that his wife would not even be home when she committed the murder. For this reason, it is unlikely that she even recklessly killed Tom's wife Lisa. However, Lisa will still be on the hook for the crime. Under the common law, the prosecutor will rely on the doctrine of transferred intent. Here, Lisa intended to kill Tom but, in an effort to do so, ended up killing Tom's wife. Recall that this doctrine requires that the actor's actual harm matches the intended harm. Lisa's intent was to cause death, which matches the ultimate result—death.

   The result is the same under the MPC, although it is not explicitly referred to as transferred intent. Instead, the MPC specifies that an element is established even if the actual result differs from the intent, if the only difference is the person injured or affected. (Section 2.03(2)).

2. Sadly, this example is based on a real case. Gilberto Valle, known as the Cannibal Cop from Queens, New York was arrested and served jail time for conspiracy to commit kidnapping. He claimed that he was simply fantasizing and never committed a crime. Many experts agreed that his activities did not amount to anything criminal, but were simply "mens rea" without adequate actus reas. Gilberto's state of mind showed that he would be culpable for a purposeful murder if he went through with

his plans to kill any of these women. However, the problem here is that after planning and plotting to eat and kill over 100 women, he never went through with any of his plans. Thus, a murder charge is out of the question, and so is conspiracy if he never commited any "overt acts" in support of his fantasies. It will make you feel really safe that Gilberto is now home still fantasizing and discussing killing and eating women in the safety of his home. See https://nypost.com/2017/02/08/cannibal-cop-still-fantasizes-about-being-an-actual-cannibal.

3a. Under the common law, Napolean would likely be found to have had the requisite mes rea, but he'll clearly be exculpated under the Model Penal Code. Many common law courts concluded that the mens rea word modified only the verb. Napoleon has clearly "knowingly" killed something—indeed, he wanted to kill what he shot at. Thus, under this common law approach, he has "knowingly" killed the rabbit. Don't despair, however—under that same common law, most courts developed a separate doctrine of mistake, which we will examine in Chapter 5. Suffice it here to say that if Nappy's mistake was "reasonable," he may ultimately be exculpated.

Under the MPC, the answer is easy—Napoleon has a good chance of being acquitted. "Rabbit" is clearly an attendant circumstance material element. Thus, under a statute requiring "knowingly," the Code allows conviction *only* if the defendant was aware that the attendant circumstance existed. Since Nappy was not aware that the animal was a rabbit, he is not guilty. Reasonableness is not—at this point—a relevant consideration.

3b. Again, we have to know what was going on in Nappy's mind, and what was reasonable for him to believe, depending on the language of the statute in this jurisdiction. One consideration here is whether the factual circumstances might have alerted a "reasonable person" that she was shooting a rabbit. Another way to think about it is whether the defendant himself, with all his foibles, weaknesses, and incapacities, was consciously aware of a substantial and unjustifiable risk that what he was shooting was a *rabbit*. If not, he was not reckless, under either the common law or the MPC.

Caveat. The problems of proof go both ways here. If the prosecutor shows that the area was infested with rabbits, that there was only one deer, that deer are much larger than rabbits, that Nappy had plenty of time to see the animal, and so forth, the jury might not credit Nappy's statements as to his ignorance. But they cannot convict him on the basis of what an RPP would have figured out; they must be convinced that he really knew the risk.

3c. Here, the problem is the same under the common law and the Code: Does "negligently" require tortious, or criminal, negligence? Most courts required "culpable" negligence, but in most instances, those decisions involved homicides (of people, not rabbits). Moreover, since only "reasonable" mistakes of fact exculpated when there was no mens rea word (see below), some courts in nonhomicide cases concluded that "tortious negligence" could suffice here. Under the MPC, the resolution of this question is clear: Nappy's acts must constitute a "gross" departure from the conduct of an RPP. Mere tortious negligence is insufficient. Of course, trying to distinguish between "tort" and "gross" negligence is not easy, but the prosecutor could try. In addition to the facts suggested in 3b, the prosecutor would try to prove, for example, that the papers were full of stories about the influx of rabbits and that rabbits are easy to spot because of their white tails.

3d. Almost certainly not. Under the common law, Nappy's mistake will exonerate him; under the MPC, while Nappy clearly intended the death of what he shot, he did not hope or believe that it was a child, nor was he aware that it was. On the question of recklessness or negligence, we would have to explore the possibility that a child would be in the middle of a forest without a parent. This risk seems so unlikely that its disregard is neither reckless nor negligent.

4. Napoleon may have met his Waterloo. He obviously knew he was killing a rabbit. He did not know that he had wandered into nearby Jones County, however. Many common law courts concluded that a mens rea word modified only the verb, thereby imposing strict liability (so far as mens rea is concerned) as to the remaining parts of the statute. This was especially true in the later words related to "jurisdiction," which seems to be the case here.

   Caveat. No one doubts that "Jones County" is an element of the offense, and the prosecution must prove that the killing occurred there. The issue here is whether the prosecutor must also prove, beyond a reasonable doubt, a relevant mens rea (here, knowingly) with regard to that element.

   The Model Penal Code will provide the same result, but for a different reason. It requires culpability with regard to any "material" element, but not with regard to an "element." The Code's distinction, however, is stated in the negative: a material element is an element that "does not relate exclusively to the statute of limitations, jurisdiction, venue, or any other matter similarly unconnected with (i) the harm or evil incident to conduct, sought to be prevented by the law defining the offense." This would seem to mean that only if the prosecution can show that Jones County is exclusively related to jurisdiction, it is not a "material element"; if the prosecutor cannot carry that burden, then the item is a material element, and mens rea must apply.

But how does one determine that? One position is that nothing can relate "exclusively" to jurisdiction: that by prohibiting rabbit killing only in Jones County, the legislature was after an evil unique to Jones County, and therefore, that the location is incident to the conduct sought to be prevented by the law defining the offense. This argument, though appealing, is certainly wrong, for it would make the Code's attempted distinction between an "element" and a "material element" meaningless. Thus, one must conclude that "Jones County" (which certainly sounds as if it is solely related to jurisdiction) is not a material element, but only an element, and mens rea does not apply to that element. So long as Napoleon knew he was killing, and that what he was killing was a rabbit, he's a gone goose.

5. Because the common law required a "specific intent" when a statute used the words "with intent to," the defendant will not be guilty, assuming she can convince the jury that her intent was only to make sure that the writer remained in her house. On the other hand, aggravated assault, which may carry an even greater penalty, does not use the term "with intent to," and is likely to be construed as a general intent crime, requiring only that the defendant intended to assault, and knowing that she was using a sledge hammer (assuming that the sledge hammer is a "deadly weapon" within the meaning of the statute, which it almost surely is).

6. Barney seems like a nice enough chap, but he may well have violated this statute under the common law. Different common law courts might have defined "purposely" differently; for this example, we will equate it with "intentionally," a much more frequently used adverb, whose meaning is more or less self-evident. The first question, of course, is whether Barney "purposely used" the credit card. This seems fairly straightforward: Barney used what he knew to be a credit card and therefore "purposely" used it. But is that sufficient for liability? Or must Barney's "intent" be to use an "expired" credit card? How far down the statute does the word "purposely" run? Many common law courts would conclude that "purposely" does not modify "expired" or even "credit card"; as long as Barney "intentionally used" something that was in fact a credit card, and that was in fact expired, that would have been enough. His mens rea as to what it was, or whether it was expired, would have been irrelevant. Moreover, if "purposely" modifies "expired," what does "purposely" mean? Would it require that Barney intended to cause the card to be expired? Or would it require that he know that it was expired? Or that he know that it "might be"

expired? Common law courts wrestled with these statutory interpretation problems and came to different conclusions.

Under the Model Penal Code, the answer is easy. The mens rea word modifies every material element of the statute. Obviously, it is material that the card be "expired." If it were *not* expired, there would be no harm (assuming, for example, it was not stolen). Under §2.02(1), "purposely" modifies every material element. Since "expired" is not a result (at least not of Barney's conduct), it must be an "attendant circumstance" material element. And, by §2.02(a)(ii), Barney must "be aware of the existence of such circumstances or . . . believe or hope that they exist." Unless Barney knows or hopes the card is "expired," he is home free.

7a. Surprise. Under the Model Penal Code, Jacob is not guilty of any of these crimes. Each of these mens rea words requires, with regard to the result element of death, that the defendant either "consciously desire death," "know that it is practically certain," or "consciously disregard a substantial . . . risk" that death will occur. None of these describes Jacob's mental state with regard to death. Jacob honestly believed that there was no risk to his son. Therefore, he did not "consciously disregard" any such risk.

Under the common law, the question is closer because Jacob did "intend" that the snakes bite the boy. However, at least in homicide cases, the courts looked beyond the "statutory mens rea" and often inquired about the "traditional mens rea" issue of moral culpability. From his own viewpoint, certainly, Jacob is not "morally culpable." That may mean that he did not have the requisite mens rea. See the discussion of homicide in Chapter 8. See also *People v. Strong*, 37 N.Y.2d 568, 338 N.E.2d 602 (1975).

7b. More difficult at first blush. Clearly, Jacob "caused" his son's death. However, common law courts, certainly when faced with a severe punishment (possibly execution), would usually read into a statute like this some level of mens rea. Almost certainly they would have required at least recklessness. *Staples*, discussed in the text, adopted "knowingly" as the position in a nonhomicidal (federal) case. Even if recklessness were the requisite mens rea, Jacob is not guilty, since that mens rea requires subjective awareness of the risk. The result under the Code is the same. Section 2.02(3) establishes recklessness as the "default" position in such statutes. Since, as discussed above, Jacob did not consciously disregard the risk of death for his son, he was not reckless.

This is an unsettling result. Obviously, Jacob is a dangerous person, at least to his own children. Is there nothing the law can do? There is, in fact, much that the "law" can do. Jacob might be civilly committed for mental illness (assuming the jurisdiction has the properly drawn statutes and Jacob fits within them). The state could also take away Jacob's other children. Very frequently the undoubted need of society often persuades courts or legislatures to "find" some crime of which Jacob could be convicted, rather than rely on processes of civil commitment, confinement, quarantine, reeducation, and so on. See, e.g., *State v. Williams*, 4 Wash. App. 908, 484 P.2d 167 (1971).

There is one crime of which Jacob is almost surely guilty (aside from child abuse). If "negligent" homicide were punished in the state, and negligence were measured by an objective, rather than a subjective, standard, Jacob would almost certainly fall within that statute.

8. Whether or not Diana will be convicted will come down to how successful the prosecution is in proving the requisite mens rea. If the prosecutor cannot show, beyond a reasonable doubt, that Diana knew the gun and bullets were real, she will likely be acquitted. Our first inclination, of course, is to believe Diana—after all, as she claims, she was just following the script. Her claim that she did not know the bullets were real seems perfectly acceptable. The prosecution's best strategy will be to find additional facts from which a jury may make an inference that Diana did in fact act intentionally.

   Suppose, for example, that we were to discover that, in addition to being thespians, Diana and Charles were longstanding competitors in art collecting, and that only moments before the play began, Diana had discovered that Charles had destroyed all of her Picassos. Or that Diana and Charles were brother and sister, and that Diana had just learned that their ailing mother had left everything to Charles, but if Charles died first, then the entire $100 million estate would go to Diana. From these facts about motive we might begin to reevaluate our first inference (and our willingness to believe Diana) and draw others.

9. It depends. At the time of the injury, Cary is anything but reckless. However, if his brakes fail because he has consistently refused to have them adjusted, and they have been slowly deteriorating, then his prior fault (indeed, his getting into and driving the car that night, if he took cognizance of that risk) could render him liable. Remember that the principle of contemporaneity does not require that the mens rea coincide with the *harm*, but with the *act* that causes the harm. (Of course, if the evidence shows that even if the brakes had been in superb condition, the child would have been killed, then Cary's negligent act is not a cause in fact of the death.)

10. Helen is surely not guilty of any kind of homicide that requires a mens rea. Her care that there be no one present demonstrates that she did not even consider that there was a risk, much less consciously disregard

such a risk, that injury, much less death, could result from the burglary. She took every precaution that injury would not happen. Moreover, given all the circumstances, it is hard to say that she was "negligent" or criminally negligent *with regard to the risk of death*. *Caveat*: In Chapter 8, we will discuss Helen's possible liability under the felony murder doctrine, which does not require mens rea of any kind as to a death occurring during a felony.

11. The question, of course, is whether Louis must "know" that there was a person in the building. (Contrast the Model Penal Code definition of "occupied structure," which includes any building that MAY be occupied, whether or not it is at the time of the crime. MPC Section 221.0(a).) Louis did not "know" that—indeed, he was convinced that no one was in the bank. Under the common law, the answer is unclear: While most courts would say that "knowingly" modifies that phrase, some courts have held that the adverb stops at the verb, and that it is enough if the defendant knows the "general nature" of his conduct, rather than the specifics.

    If the statute is federal, the answer will revolve around whether the decision in *Flores-Figueroa* (discussed in the text, at page 83) applies to this statute. Although the court relied upon legislative history and intent, it also announced the general proposition that the "natural reading" of any criminal statute is that the adverb (mens rea word) applies to all the critical parts of the statute. Therefore, it is *likely*, but *not assured* that Louis will not be guilty of the crime.

    Under the Model Penal Code, the answer is really easy. Surely "occupied by one or more persons" is a material element of the offense, and Louis is off the hook.

    Caveat. At least so far as the common law response, there is one possible hook—the "greater crime" theory, discussed in more detail in Chapter 6. That theory is that if the defendant knows he is engaged in a crime (and breaking into the bank would itself be criminal trespass at least), then he is guilty of any "greater" crime that he happens to commit. We'll get to that question when we get to it.

12. Held, in *United States v. Huet-Vaughn*, 39 M.J. 545 (1994): yes. While motive is not relevant to whether Abbie "deserted," it may be relevant to the actual charge, which requires the government to prove that his "specific intent" (reason) was to avoid hazardous duty. It is possible that this holding may be limited to military law, and may not apply to civilian law, but the military court in this case cited many non-military decisions. Indeed, the court found that there was enough evidence to support the lesser (general intent) charge of being absent without authority.

13a. Motive is not an element of an offense—any offense—and so one would think that Riffi's motive would be inadmissible. But Riffi's motive here supports an inference that he acted "intentionally," and not accidently. The evidence is likely admissible.

13b. If evidence of motive is relevant in (a), surely it's also admissible here—right? No. Riffi's claim does not dispute that he killed Constantine intentionally—only "why" he did so. And while his motive may well be considered in assessing Riffi's sentence (although taking the law into one's own hands is rarely considered mitigation even in sentencing), it's not relevant to his guilt (consider, as well, that once again Riffi's motive supports the prosecution claim of intentionality).

14a. At least in New Mexico, Al will be back on the ranch in no time. Even though the statute doesn't use the term "knowingly," the court in *State v. Powell*, 115 N.M. 188, 191 (Ct. App. 1993), noted that the intent to possess a firearm requires "the knowledge that the object possessed is a firearm." The same result will be reached under the MPC—under §2.02(3), the default provision is recklessness, and there are no facts here to suggest that Al "consciously disregarded" the risk that he was taking the gun into the restaurant.

14b. Al will be spending Mother's Day in prison next year. The statute does not require that Al "know" that the restaurant has a liquor license. *State v. Torres*, 134 N.M. 194, (N.M. App., 2003). The *Torres* court held that the knowledge requirement did not apply to the liquor store; as to that, the statue was a "strict liability" offense (see Chapter 6).

If New Mexico were a Model Penal Code state, however, the result would be different. Under the MPC, the mens rea requirement applies to each material element. Given the specificity of the language in the statute, which singles out "establishments licensed to dispense alcoholic beverages," it is clear that the location is material to the statute's overall purpose—i.e., the evil sought to be prevented. Therefore, Al must have known that the establishment was licensed to dispense alcoholic beverages to be culpable under the MPC.

15. There's absolutely no doubt that waiting on the tarmac is exasperating—and waiting for two hours may have other consequences. Nevertheless, courts have been clear that this is a crime of general, not specific, intent. In *United States v. Grossman*, 131 F.3d 1449, (11th Cir. 1997), the court concluded that even if the prior statute *might* have been interpreted to require a person to actually interfere with the attendant, the amendment made clear that no such specific intent was required under the statute as rewritten. It may not be irrelevant that

intoxication can exonerate a defendant charged with a specific intent crime, and many "airplane rage" instances occur after the passenger's gotten a lift out of spirits (see Chapter 17). Miniver, drunk or sober, will be grounded for a significant period of time.

CHAPTER 5

Mistake

OVERVIEW

We all make mistakes—even criminals. However, suppose someone who thinks that what he is doing is legal turns out to be mistaken, and the act is a crime. Is he guilty? The common law answered this question as it often does: "It depends." Consider a *factual* mistake. As a general rule, if Angelica reasonably thinks the white powder in her vial is salt, though it is really cocaine, she is not guilty of transporting cocaine. The law treats *legal* mistakes, however, strikingly differently. Arthur has been told by a state EPA director that he may, without a permit, dump what he knows to be toluene. The advice turns out to be a misinterpretation of the environmental statutes. Such a mistake would never exculpate. This tension between legal and factual mistakes and the exceptions to these general rules create ulcers in law students—not to mention in clients.[1]

The Model Penal Code takes a somewhat different, more subjective view. Angelica's *factual* mistake will exculpate her unless the statute punishes "criminally negligent transportation," and then only if her mistake was a "gross deviation" from the Reasonably Prudent Person (RPP) standard of care. Arthur's *legal* mistake, if constituting a reasonable reliance upon the agency's advice, would likely be a defense under the Code.

1. For a careful and nuanced discussion of the various kinds of mistake, see Kenneth W. Simons, Ignorance and Mistake of Criminal Law, Noncriminal Law and Fact, 9 Ohio St. J. Crim. L. 487 (2012).

MISTAKE AND IGNORANCE OF LAW

Perhaps no rule of criminal law is better known than the doctrine *ignorantia lexis non exusat*—"ignorance of the law is no excuse." Thus, in the example in the Overview, even if Arthur has gone to five lawyers, four priests, three government officials in charge of pollution control, and read the statute books himself, he is still liable if the advice he has received has been erroneous. He will be convicted and punished as though he were just as culpable as Dave, a midnight dumper who dumped toluene in the river, knowing it was illegal and dangerous.

Supporters of the ignorantia rule argue that people *should* know the law and not act until they do. They argue, further, that anyone could claim reliance on the advice of others, and that this would either be too hard to (dis)prove or generate collusion between defendants and others, who would claim to have given such advice. (As one writer said nearly three centuries ago, "Ignorance of the law excuses no man; not that all men know the law, but because it is an excuse every man will plead, and no man can tell how to confute him." J. Selden, Table Talk—Law 61 (3d ed. 1716).) A more recent argument sustaining part of the doctrine is that persons who are, or should be, aware that their conduct might be regulated have a "duty to inquire" about the law and are morally blameworthy for failing to ascertain its reach.

Opponents of the doctrine contend that failure to know every statute and administrative regulation, and the interpretation of every statute and administrative regulation, does not reflect moral blameworthiness. (Indeed, if it did, every lawyer, indeed every judge on every court, should beware.) A person who is truly ignorant or mistaken about whether his conduct is unlawful, particularly one who has actively and fairly sought to determine the law, is neither morally culpable (in the "traditional" sense of mens rea) nor purposeful or reckless about breaking the law (in the "statutory" sense of that term).

The rule is sometimes rephrased as saying that everyone is conclusively presumed to know the law. When Blackstone wrote, such a view was at least plausible. A claim that one did not know that rape, murder, robbery, or mayhem was illegal (or immoral) would hardly be taken seriously. Yet the rule continues to be followed today, when criminal law applies to many new areas of activities, and encompasses literally hundreds of thousands of administrative regulations, as well.[2] If this explanation of the rule were

2. E.g., *United States v. Freeman*, 535 F.2d 1251 (4th Cir. 1976) (ignorance of any rule in the Federal Register is irrelevant). See also *United States v. Freed*, 401 U.S. 601 (1971); *United States v. International Minerals and Chemical Corp.*, 402 U.S. 558 (1971). In *Freed* and *IMCC*, the holding was that the prosecutor need not allege in the indictment knowledge of the law, which leaves

tested against modern methods of assessing presumptions,[3] it would be clearly unconstitutional.

The argument that the claim of ignorance is too easily made and too difficult to refute was rejected by Justice Holmes, who pointed out that that concern was present for virtually all defensive claims. To the extent that it was easier to make than some of those other claims, the law could place on the defendant the burden of persuasion. O.W. Holmes, The Common Law (1881).

Holmes proffered another support for the rule, however—that we wish to encourage people to learn what the criminal law is. Moreover, as an ardent utilitarian, he argued that it is occasionally necessary to sacrifice the morally innocent person to achieve the better good of establishing an incentive for learning the law. However, the doctrine has been applied even where the defendant has actively sought legal advice from various sources, including court opinions, judges, prosecuting attorneys, and lawyers. Still, there is the problem that Selden raised: Even if Arthur at trial produces those lawyers, priests, and government officials, and they affirm *their* advice, how will the prosecutor ever find the 30 lawyers, priests, and officials who gave Arthur different advice? Should he put Arthur's picture in the newspaper with the caption "If you gave this man legal advice on dumping toluene, call my office"?

Similarly unsuccessful has been the argument that, even if ignorance of the *criminal* law should not excuse (in order to encourage persons to learn what the criminal law is), ignorance (or mistake) as to other laws, which are then incorporated into the criminal law, should excuse.[4] Suppose the criminal law prohibits blocking public roads, and Yehudi knows that he is blocking a road but he believes the road to be private. Unknown to him, the road has become "public" under condemnation just a few hours before. Yehudi should not be punished, the argument goes, because he has learned what the criminal law prohibits. His mistake is about condemnation law, not criminal law.

Until very recently, the rule has reigned virtually unchallenged. However, the Model Penal Code and several recent United States Supreme Court cases discussed below suggest that future decisions may be more open to changing the rule, at least in some contexts.

---

open the possibility that the defendant could raise ignorance; who then would carry the burden of persuasion was not discussed. The language of each opinion, however, certainly leaves the impression that ignorance of the law is still irrelevant. *Cheek* and *Ratzlaf*, more recent cases discussed in the text below, may narrow the implications of these two decisions.

3. See Chapter 15.

4. Professor Jerome Hall argued that to allow a defendant to exculpate himself by simply claiming his interpretation of a law would negate the law and elevate that defendant to the status of lawmaker. J. Hall, General Principles of the Criminal Law (2d ed. 1961).

Ignorance of the Law

We can distinguish between a defendant who does not know that a particular act is even arguably criminal and a defendant who knows that there is a law generally applying to his area of activity, but believes that the law does not cover his particular act. The first is *ignorance* of the law; the second, *mistake*.

The few reported decisions of ignorance of the law usually involve aliens to a particular culture[5] and epitomize the injunction, "When in Rome (or at least a common law country) do as the Romans do." Thus, in *In the Matter of Etienne Barronet and Edmund Allain*, 118 Eng. Rep. 337 (1852), the defendants, Frenchmen who had taken political asylum in England, acted as seconds in a duel fought on English soil. Dueling was not merely legal in France; participation was a "matter of honor." The defendants were unaware that dueling was illegal in England. The court declared their ignorance of the law to be irrelevant.

This rigor is still in force. In *United States v. Moncini*, 882 F.2d 401 (9th Cir. 1989), the defendant, who lived in Italy and who was interested in pornographic pictures, was contacted by an undercover FBI agent in the United States and induced (but not entrapped) to send such pictures to the agent. When the defendant arrived in the United States for unrelated business, he was arrested and charged with "using the mails to send child pornography." He contended that since dissemination of such materials was not a crime in Italy, he should be excused in the United States, as well. The court rejected his claim of ignorance of the law.[6]

A more recent opinion of the United States Supreme Court *may* suggest a slight movement away from this doctrine, at least in interpretation of federal statutes. In *Ratzlaf v. United States*, 510 U.S. 135 (1994), the defendant owed over $100,000 to a gambling casino in Reno, Nevada. When he tried to pay off most of this debt in cash, he was informed that if he paid $10,000 or more in one lump sum, the casino would have to report this to the United States government under anti-money-laundering statutes. For

---

5. *Star Trek* fans will recall that in both the original series and in *The Next Generation* the issue of ignorance is raised. In *Star Trek*, a crew member, while visiting a planet for recreation, picks a flower; this turns out to be a capital offense in that culture, and he is accordingly tried for that crime. In *The Next Generation*, Wesley Crusher inadvertently enters an area that, under the law of the planet, is forbidden. He, too, is tried capitally. In both episodes, the Captain (Kirk or Picard) persuades the rulers that the doctrine is too harsh. Fortunately for the crewmen, they never landed in a jurisdiction governed by the common law.

6. The court did note that, even in Italy, the kinds of photographs involved, while not illegal, were regulated, thereby putting the defendant on notice to inquire about the laws of other jurisdictions to which he might send such pictures. Although not critical to its holding, the court's position could be read as portraying the defendant as reckless and hence morally blameworthy in this regard.

reasons known only to Ratzlaf, he did not wish the government to know of his transactions. The casino thereupon drove him (in a limousine) to a number of banks in the town, at each of which he could obtain a cashier's check for an amount under $10,000, in which case neither the casino nor the bank would have a duty to report the transaction. Ratzlaf agreed that he had willfully structured his transactions so as to avoid reporting, but argued that he did not know that this was illegal. The trial judge instructed the jury that this ignorance was irrelevant, as long as Ratzlaf in fact "willfully structured" the transaction. The Supreme Court reversed, holding that his ignorance of the legal duty not to structure the transaction made his act "nonwillful" under the statute.[7]

Mistake of Law

In many cases, defendants "rely" on their own "understanding" of the law, informed by either "general custom" or a "hunch," although in some rare instances defendants will attempt to find and read the applicable criminal statute. Far more common are cases where a defendant suspects that his activity may be subject to government, even criminal, regulation, but concludes, as the result of advice that he has sought, that his actions are not criminal. In all of these cases, the defendant has sought to discover what the law is, as Holmes hoped. Yet in virtually none is he exculpated. For example, a minister charged with erecting in his front lawn a sign declaring that he performed marriages was precluded from presenting evidence that he relied on advice from a county attorney that the sign was acceptable. *State v. Hopkins*, 193 Md. 489 (1959). Similarly, a restauranteur who relied on the judgment of a municipal court (given in another proceeding) that the device he was installing was not a "gambling device" within the meaning of the criminal law was held liable for his mistake of law. *State v. Striggles*, 202 Iowa 1318 (1926). And a fisherman was precluded from introducing evidence that he had obtained advice from both an attorney and a

---

7. One other ignorance case should be mentioned here. In *Lambert v. California*, 355 U.S. 255 (1957), the Court held that constitutional due process was denied a defendant who was precluded from introducing evidence that she was unaware of a city ordinance requiring her, as an ex-felon, to register her presence with the city. Some commentators thought that the decision would lead to a series of constitutional challenges to the entire "ignorantia lex" rule, but it has been restricted to cases involving (a) ignorance of (b) a local ordinance (c) imposing a duty to act (in contrast to imposing a prohibition against acting). It has become, as Mr. Justice Frankfurter predicted in his dissent in the case, a "derelict upon the waters of the law." For a broad attempt to resurrect *Lambert*, see the dissenting opinion of Judge Bennett in *United States v. Hutzell*, 217 F.3d 966 (8th Cir. 2000).

commissioner of fishing licenses that his method of fishing for smelts was not illegal. *State v. Huff*, 89 Me. 521 (1897).

Reliance on a lawyer's advice was never an acceptable defense under the common law. In *Staley v. State*, 89 Neb. 701 (1911), the defendant and his cousin, both of whom lived in Nebraska, wanted to marry but knew that their marriage would be illegal under Nebraska law. They then were married in Iowa, which did not prohibit marriages between cousins. When they returned to Nebraska, the county prosecutor told the defendant that he would be prosecuted for fornication if he continued living with his cousin. The defendant then went to three attorneys, each of whom informed him that the Iowa marriage was indeed not valid in Nebraska. Consequently, the defendant left his cousin. A year later, he married another woman in Nebraska and was then prosecuted for bigamy. It turned out that the Iowa marriage *was* valid in Nebraska, and that he was therefore still married to his cousin when he "remarried." On the basis of "ignorantia lex," the defendant was precluded from presenting any evidence of the legal advice given him by the three lawyers or by the county prosecutor concerning the (in)validity of his marriage to his cousin.

Thus, under common law, the defendant's mistake of law was usually held to be irrelevant to his guilt. A recent decision from the United States Supreme Court, however, casts doubt on this rule, at least in federal cases involving the statutory word "willfully." In *United States v. Cheek*, 498 U.S. 112 (1991), the Court held that even an *unreasonable* mistake of law could negate liability. Cheek, an airline pilot, was repeatedly told that his wages constituted "income" for purposes of the federal income tax laws. However, he was also told by anti-income tax zealots, and by lawyers who agreed with them, that this was *not* the proper interpretation of the tax laws. He was also told (notwithstanding numerous court decisions to the contrary) that the income tax law, as well as the amendment that allowed it, was itself unconstitutional. He claimed he honestly relied on this advice, but the trial court instructed the jurors that unless his reliance was reasonable, they could not consider it. In reversing Cheek's conviction for "willfully" failing to file tax returns and pay taxes, the Supreme Court concluded that the jury should have been instructed that *any* reliance, however unreasonable, on *any* advice would exculpate.[8]

Some have argued that if mistake of law is to exculpate, it is because it is an excuse, rather than a justification (see Chapter 15 for a discussion of the difference). However it is characterized, mistake—particularly

8. The *Cheek* decision was muddled by the Court's conclusion that, while Congress intended ignorance of tax law to negate liability, it did not intend ignorance or mistake of *constitutional* law to do so. One could easily argue, of course, that constitutional law is even murkier than tax law.

one generated by reliance on what appears to be a reasonable source, such as a court opinion, government official, or even a lawyer—should be granted, since the defendant has not acted in a morally blameworthy way.[9]

Exceptions to the Rule

"Specific Intent" Crimes

Common law courts carved out minor exceptions to the harsh rule of "ignorantia lex." One was the rule that any mistake of law, no matter how unreasonable, would be a valid "defense" to a specific intent crime (but not to a "general intent" offense). Larceny is a "specific intent" crime (see Chapter 10). If Abraham believes, however unreasonably, that by law he is the owner of Esau's car and proceeds to take it "back," Abraham is not guilty of larceny because larceny requires that one intends to take the property of "another." Since Abraham thinks that he is the owner of the car, he has not intentionally taken property he knows to be "another's."

It may well be that Abraham is not morally culpable, given his belief, and therefore should not be punished. *Ratzlaf* and *Cheek* both involved the mens rea word "willfully," and might be seen as examples of the "specific intent" exception. Yet it is uncertain whether legislatures actually think about the specific-general intent division when writing statutes—surely the best result would be for legislatures to adopt a general statutory interpretation rule regarding the impact of mistake or ignorance of law, whether the crime is considered one of "general" or "specific" intent. And, once again, our caveat: It is easy to think that a decision of the United States Supreme Court is "the law of the land." But not if, as in *Ratzlaf* and *Cheek* (or even other cases discussed in this book), the Court is merely interpreting federal statutes. Be careful to distinguish *constitutional* decisions from *statutory interpretation* decisions.

Most crimes are NOT specific intent crimes—although many "economic" and "white collar" crimes, such as most tax offenses or frauds, are. Defendants in those crimes cannot only claim their own lack of specific intent, but, as well, rely upon advice of lawyers and others because any advice could negate their "specific" intent.

---

9. See Gur-Arye, Reliance on a Lawyer's Mistaken Advice—Should It Be an Excuse from Criminal Liability?, 29 Am. J. Crim. L. 455 (2002) (recognizing that "reasonably unavoidable mistakes of law" negate culpability in Germany, France, and Israel, among other countries, but arguing that a mistake made in reliance on a lawyer is not "reasonably unavoidable").

Noncriminal Law Mistake

Commentators have suggested another possible "exception" to the ignorantia lex doctrine. If the defendant is mistaken (or ignorant) not as to the criminal law, but as to a part of the civil law that is incorporated in the criminal law, they contend that the doctrine should not apply. Here, the reason for the rule (enhancing knowledge of the criminal law) does not apply. Suppose that Abraham, in the car problem above, has adversely possessed the car for 11 months, believes the law requires 10 months to possess adversely a chattel, but the time period is really one year. His mistake then is not one of criminal law. He knows there is a law against *larceny*, but he believes that, as a result of *property law doctrine*, the car is his.

Staley is an even more attractive case for this exception. Staley knew that there was a criminal law against bigamy. He also knew that, under Nebraska domestic relations law, cousins could not marry. His mistake, and that of the three attorneys he consulted and the county prosecutor who threatened him, was one of *federal constitutional law*. They all failed to understand that, under the full faith and credit clause of the United States Constitution, Nebraska had to honor a marriage that is valid where it was performed.[10] While it may be desirable that citizens know the criminal law, and perhaps even the domestic relations law, of their home state, it seems unduly optimistic to think that we can encourage every citizen to become a constitutional law scholar.

Estoppel

When a defendant relies explicitly on the advice of a government official in charge of a particular activity, the government may sometimes be "estopped" from prosecuting an individual. This is a relatively new idea, and is a sea change from the ancient notion that "the king can do no wrong." Although the Court itself has never used the term "entrapment by estoppel," one of the leading United States Supreme Court cases involved a witness who was told by the commission of a legislative committee that he could invoke the privilege against self-incrimination, at which point he was held in contempt of the committee. *Raley v. Ohio*, 360 U.S. 423 (1959). And in *United States v. Pennsylvania Industrial Chem. Corp.*, 411 U.S. 655 (1973), the Court held that a defendant charged with discharging refuse into navigable waters without a permit (often seen as a strict liability offense—see

10. See, e.g., *Williams v. North Carolina*, 317 U.S. 287 (1942); *Loughran v. Loughran*, 292 U.S. 216 (1934).

Chapter 6) should have been allowed to show that it was affirmatively misled by the Corps of Engineers—the responsible administrative agency.[11]

The Model Penal Code

Retention of the "Ignorantia Lex" Doctrine

The Code retains the basic doctrine. Section 2.02(9) expressly provides that "neither knowledge nor recklessness or negligence as to whether conduct constitutes an offense or as to the existence, meaning or application of the law determining the elements of an offense is an element of such offense unless the definitions of the offense or the Code so provides." There is one exception to the "no ignorance" position of the Code. If the statute or regulation in question "has not been published or otherwise reasonably made available" to the defendant, the claim is allowed. See §2.04(3)(a).

The "Reasonable Reliance" Approach to Mistake

In General

On the other hand, the Code takes a significant, though cautious, step to protect defendants who "reasonably" rely on advice as to the legality of their proposed conduct. Section 2.04(3) provides that a defendant has a defense[12] to a charge if he can show that he has acted "in reasonable reliance" on:

> (b) an official statement of the law, afterwards determined to be invalid or erroneous, contained in (i) a statute or other enactment; (ii) a judicial decision, opinion or judgment; (iii) an administrative order or grant of permission; or (iv) an official interpretation of the public officer or body charged by the law with responsibility for the interpretation, administration or enforcement of the law defining the offense.

Notice that this provision helps persons in Striggles' position because it allows reliance on *any* judicial opinion. And it probably helps Hopkins, if the county attorney falls within the words of subsection (iv). But Staley's

11. See generally John T. Parry, Culpability, Mistake, and Official Interpretations of Law, 25 Am. J. Crim. L. 1 (1997).

12. Reasonable reliance is indeed a "defense," which the defendant has to prove by a preponderance of the evidence. See §2.04(4). This stands in stark contrast to most of the rest of the Code, which puts on the prosecution the burden of disproving defensive claims, including all justifications and excuses, once properly raised. See §§1.12 and 1.13. This topic is discussed in Chapter 15. Eighteen states have adopted the MPC provision in whole or in part.

reliance on his lawyers is not relevant even under the Code, for reasons we will explore in a moment.

First, however, let us assess the general purpose of this provision. Surely, in a maze of government bureaucracy, citizens have come to rely on all levels of government bureaucrats to help them stay within the law. The Code provides some amelioration of the common law rule in light of this reality, but *only* if the defendant relies on persons whose *official tasks* involve statutory interpretation or enforcement. This seems unduly narrow.

Consider Butch, who goes to his local zoning ordinance office to get advice about building an addition to his house. Jocelyn, an employee there, tells him, incorrectly, that he needs no permit for it. She's wrong, and he is prosecuted. If Butch *knew* that Jocelyn was not so authorized, his reliance on her advice might be unreasonable. However, few citizens would be likely even to raise the question of whether the person behind the desk who gives them the answer to their question fits the statutory definition: To consumers, persons working in a government office are probably fungible.[13] And even if they asked, could they be sure that they have gotten "the right person"? Furthermore, is *any* prosecutor sufficient under subsection (iv), or must the interpretation come from "the" county prosecutor? Laymen are unlikely to make such a distinction. Also, the reliance must be on "an *official* interpretation" by that office. What makes the interpretation "official"? The Code and Commentary are silent. Surely, however, any reliance by a citizen on the word of a governmental official who works in the relevant office or *appears* authorized should be sufficient to exonerate.

Some courts have interpreted the MPC provision so narrowly that it is almost irrelevant. In *Hawaii v. DeCastro*, 913 P.2d 558 (Haw. App. 1996), for example, DeCastro, driving a van, stopped to write down the license plate of a patrol officer who, in DeCastro's view, had been recklessly chasing a speeding motorist. The officer then threatened DeCastro with arrest. DeCastro called a 911 operator, who "gave him permission" to leave the scene. When DeCastro did so, the patrol car followed and arrested him. The court, interpreting its version of the MPC, concluded that, even if the operator's authorization to leave the scene was a "statement of the law . . . contained in . . . an administrative grant of permission," the statement was

---

13. See Cremer, The Ironies of Law Reform: A History of Reliance on Officials as a Defense in American Criminal Law, 14 Cal. W. L. Rev. 48 (1978). For example, in *Miller v. Comm.*, 492 S.E.2d 482 (Va. App. 1997), agents of the Federal Bureau of Alcohol, Tobacco and Firearms and Virginia Department of Game and Inland Fisheries both told defendant that he was not prohibited by state law to possess a firearm based on his conviction of possession of a hunting rifle. Since these persons were not charged by law to define the relevant statute, defendant's reliance was held irrelevant. Fortunately for him, his probation officer, who was charged with defining defendant's permissible conduct (but not directly the firearms statute), also gave him the same advice, and the court held that this advice was legally relevant.

not "official," and DeCastro's reliance therefore was unreasonable as a matter of law.

Reasonable Reliance and Lawyers

The Code confirms the common law rule, exemplified by *Staley*, that reliance on a lawyer's advice is not a defense. Supporters of this position argue collusion may occur between a lawyer and his client. However, this is a dubious explanation: Some government employees, like some lawyers, may collude with clients, but the Code does not blanketly prohibit reliance on their advice.

A better explanation, perhaps, is not that lawyers are too ready to break the law, but that they are trained to assist the client to obtain what she wants. Lawyers, some argue, will be too tempted (subconsciously) to give the "desired" advice. And certainly law students know that there are at least two possible interpretations and arguments to every legal question. Thus, to be not snide but realistic, it may be that *no* reliance on the word of an attorney is "reasonable."

New Jersey, however, allows *any* reasonable reliance, including on the advice of an attorney, as a defense. N.J. Stat. §2C:2-4d (1994). (Perhaps, because New Jersey has more lawyers per capita than any other state in the country, it is impossible *there* to avoid advice from a lawyer.)

Does the Code really change everything? Does it change anything? The fear that the Code's reasonable reliance doctrine would exculpate too many defendants seems overdrawn. Mr. Ratzlaf would be worse off under the Code than under the United States Supreme Court decision. He relied on no "official interpretation," and his claim of ignorance of the law is not explicitly recognized in the statute (unless one interprets willfulness as a "specific intent" word). Moreover, it is quite possible that many of the defendants in the other cases summarized above would still be found liable under a "reasonable reliance" doctrine.

MISTAKE OF FACT

Reasonableness and Specific Intent

In stark contrast to the doctrine of mistake of law, the common law acquits persons who, because of mistakes of *fact*, commit what turn out to be crimes. Thus, Little Red Riding Hood (see Chapter 4) would have been held not guilty of "knowingly" destroying a book, because she had made a "mistake of fact" (i.e., she didn't know she was burning a *book*). Although most statutes were silent as to the importance of mistake, the common law courts created a whole doctrine of mistake, which held that some mistakes of fact "negated" mens rea.[14]

The reasons for not finding Red guilty seem obvious: A retributivist would not convict her because she is not morally blameworthy; and because people will not be deterred from doing what they believe to be innocent acts, there is no utilitarian need to punish either. The one possible exception to this last statement has created much uncertainty in the law of mistake of fact, and involves the question, already discussed, whether negligence is a proper basis for criminal liability. Prior to the nineteenth century, if Red honestly believed that she was not burning a book, Red was exculpated whether her belief was reasonable or not.[15] Within the last 200 years, however, this view has changed dramatically.

In the nineteenth century, the courts embraced the emerging notion of the "reasonable person" as a standard in both tort and crimes. People who made unreasonable mistakes would not be acquitted; only reasonable mistakes would now acquit. However, if the defendant were charged with a "specific intent" crime, the legislature had effectively indicated that only the "really" bad (not merely the unreasonable) should be convicted. Thus, in these crimes, an unreasonable mistake of fact, if honestly held, became a relevant claim.

As in other areas of the law, the invocation of a term such as "reasonable" only begins the inquiry: What does it mean? As discussed in Chapter 4, when the crime is defined as "negligently" doing *x*, the criminal law requires more than a showing that the defendant was "merely" (tortiously) negligent; he has to be "criminally" negligent. By analogy, if the criminal law wanted to punish only the "really negligent" defendant, then even

---

14. The metaphor that mistake of fact (or other relevant claim by the defendant) "negates" mens rea is misleading and can have significant practical importance. The mere wording of the concept suggests that the defendant "had" mens rea (i.e., that her mens *was* "rea") but that somehow the "mistake of fact" (or other claim) "threw the reus part out of her mens." Obviously, this is not true. If the jury believes that the defendant was mistaken, it will conclude that she never harbored a mens rea of any kind. More accurate, though still somewhat tricky, is the explanation that we assume *not* that the defendant *had* mens rea, but that the prosecutor's evidence raises an *inference of mens rea that is negated by the defendant's claim*. The inference of blameworthiness effectively "disappears" when the jury believes the defendant's claim that she was harboring a mistaken view of the world. But even then, the metaphor could lead, and has led, to the conclusion that a defendant can be required to carry the burden of proof on defensive claims because (after all) the mens rea has been shown to be present. See *State v. Smith*, 576 P.2d 1110 (Mont. 1978). We will discuss this issue in Chapters 15-17, but keep it in mind as you read through this and the next chapter.

15. See Richard Singer, The Resurgence of Mens Rea II: Honest But Unreasonable Mistake of Fact in Self-Defense, 28 B.C. L. Rev. 459 (1987).

an "unreasonable" mistake, unless truly outrageous and one that "everyone" (certainly not just the reasonable person) would have avoided, should exculpate.

As in some other areas of the common law, the view here is "all or nothing." If the defendant makes a reasonable mistake, she is exculpated. However, if she makes an honest, but unreasonable, mistake, she is punished for the crime as though she had made no mistake at all. Thus, if Paul sells what he knows to be cocaine, he will be punished for doing so. If Hermione honestly though unreasonably believes the white powder she is possessing is salt, but it turns out to be cocaine, then (if her mistake must be reasonable) she is convicted of possessing cocaine, and assumedly punished as much as Paul. Those who oppose the requirement that the mistake be reasonable argue that the unreasonably mistaken person is significantly less culpable than the knowing actor and, if convicted at all, should be punished less.

One final reminder—a mistake will not necessarily exonerate if the fact is a "jurisdictional" element (see Chapter 4 supra, page 86), and goes only to where the crime will be prosecuted, rather than if there is a crime. Thus, if Melissa, who knows she possesses cocaine, believes she's in Albany, but she's really in Poughkeepsie, and the penalty in Poughkeepsie is twice as high as that in Albany, she'll be prosecuted in Poughkeepsie. There aren't too many real cases where this issue arises—but sometimes it turns up on law school exams.

Knowledge and Willful Blindness

In the Red Riding Hood hypothetical, we assumed that Herman *knew* that he was burning a book. And in Red's case, we have concluded that if she did not "know" it was a book, she should be exculpated. However, suppose the defendant strongly suspects a fact but purposely avoids actually "knowing"? For example, suppose that Red knew that her grandmother loved books, that her mother had just bought a book for the grandmother the day before, and that the package was "big enough" for a book. Red doesn't actually "know" that it's a book inside the package; it could be a box that "feels like" a book. Can Red claim a mistake of fact or lack of knowledge?

The common law's commonsense answer was no. Red has made herself "willfully blind" to the facts and should be treated as though she knew the facts. This fiction allows us to punish Red on the ground that anyone confronted with facts that should alert them to the "relevant" facts is as morally blameworthy as someone who actually knew. In essence, it establishes a duty to inquire when the facts are highly suspicious. Because this is a fiction, however, the idea of willful blindness, while generally accepted in every jurisdiction, has been severely criticized by many commentators as vague and unfair. The danger here is that the willful blindness principle, sometimes called the "ostrich" doctrine,[16] may lead the jury to convict if they find that the defendant "should have" known it was a book—a negligence standard.[17] Some courts, in fact, appear to use an objective "reasonable person" standard, but most take care to instruct the jury that guilt clearly requires something very close to knowledge. Compare *United States v. Alston-Graves*, 435 F.3d 331 (D.C. Cir. 2006), with *United States v. Carrillo*, 435 F.3d 767 (7th Cir. 2006) ("A reasonable person standard is not the proper measuring stick for deciding whether to give an ostrich instruction . . . the instruction 'calls for a subjective inquiry, rather than an objective one'"). The doctrine has been criticized by many commentators.[18]

	Statute Requires Specific Intent	**Statute Requires General Intent**
Reasonable Mistake of Law	Exonerates	Guilty
Unreasonable Mistake of Law	Exonerates	Guilty
Reasonable Mistake of Fact	Exonerates	Exonerates
Unreasonable Mistake of Fact	Exonerates	Guilty

MISTAKE OF LEGAL FACT

A defendant's liability for a mistake (reasonable or unreasonable) thus depends on whether that mistake is characterized as one of fact or law. The doctrinal difficulties become even more complex when the defendant's mistake is one of "legal fact"—a word or phrase that is defined by law in

16. Professor David Luban has distinguished ostriches, who merely do not want to know, and foxes, who contrive deniability. See Luban, Contrived Ignorance, 87 Geo. L.J. 957 (1999).
17. For example, 21 U.S.C. §841(c)(2) makes it a crime to know, or to have reasonable cause to believe, that a substance will be used to manufacture a controlled substance, methamphetamine. Such statutes criminalize negligence and usually impose a lesser sentence; in contrast, a defendant who is found to be willfully blind is treated as "knowingly" acting. Since the legislature has indicated it wants to punish only those who knowingly burn books, the willful blindness doctrine may result in more convictions than the legislature intended.
18. *United States v. Jewell*, 532 F.2d 697 (9th Cir. 1976); J.L. Edwards, Mens Rea in Statutory Offenses (1955); Perkins, "Knowledge" as a Mens Rea Requirement, 29 Hastings L.Q. 953 (1978); Williams, The Theory of Excuses, 1982 Crim. L. Rev. 157-159.

a strange way. But be careful. The law can, for various purposes, define a word to mean something other than its usual meaning. And there are many "facts" in our lexicon that depend, in whole or in part, on the implicit incorporation of a legal norm.[19]

For example, "we all know" whether a person is a "female" or a "male." But do we? The definition of that term may depend on the context. Years ago, a male professional tennis player underwent a sex change operation. There was then a dispute as to whether she could play in women's tournaments. Was she a female? The Lawn Tennis Association said yes. However, that same person may not be a "female" for purposes of inheriting money ("I leave all my money to be divided among my female descendants"). Similarly, "we all know" whether a person is "married" or "single." However, that status is not a "natural" one. It depends solely on a legal norm—whether the ceremony (or the divorce) followed specific legal requirements. Consider as well:

1. Whether a person is "Caucasian" or "Negro" was explicitly a matter of legal definition in this country during the Jim Crow days of the nineteenth century.
2. Whether the gun that Staples (see Chapter 4) owned was a "firearm" was purely a matter of legal definition; as the dissenters argued, no one would have even questioned whether the AR-14 was a "firearm" in the usual meaning of that term.
3. Whether property is "stolen" or not usually depends on a legal definition.
4. Whether a liquid is "intoxicating" or a "hazardous waste" may depend not on our common experience with the particular liquid but on a legal (almost chemical) definition.

These examples could be multiplied endlessly, but the point here is how these issues affect the mistake doctrine. Suppose that I snub the tennis player and am prosecuted for snubbing a "red head"? My liability may well depend on how the question is characterized rather than on my culpability as such. If it is viewed as a *legal* mistake, no amount of reasonableness on my part will exculpate. If it is viewed as a *factual* mistake, however, reasonableness may exculpate.

---

19. One commentator has called the category of legal fact "an unfruitful" approach to discussion of mistake. Kenneth W. Simons, Ignorance and Mistake of Criminal law, Noncriminal Law, and Fact, 9 Ohio St. J. Crim. L. 487 (2012).

THE MODEL PENAL CODE

The Code's approach to mistake of fact is straightforward. Section 2.04(1) provides that "ignorance or mistake as to a matter of fact . . . is a defense if: (a) [it] negatives the purpose, knowledge, belief, recklessness or negligence required to establish a material element of the offense." This approach rejects the idea that mistake of fact is a separate doctrine and treats it as being among the basic notions of mens rea. A reference back to Chapter 4, and especially to the table on page 91, will show that as to crimes committed purposely, knowingly, or recklessly, the defendant must *know* either that a fact (attendant circumstance) exists, or that there is a substantial probability that it exists. Definitionally, a defendant who honestly, no matter how unreasonably, believes that the fact does not exist (the white powder is not cocaine, but salt) does not know the contrary. Thus, at least for these three states of mind, any mistake "negatives" the requisite mental state. In cases of "negligence," however, a mistake as to fact that is a "gross deviation" from what a reasonable person would understand will suffice for liability.

The Code also retains willful blindness, treating those who see a "high probability" of a fact as "knowing" that fact. See §2.02(7).

A NOTE ON THE FUTURE OF MISTAKE

The doctrines regarding mistake of both fact and law, however, seem to be changing. The Model Penal Code is one harbinger, but common law courts on their own have increasingly reverted to the nineteenth century view of the impact of mistake.

The Supreme Court also appears to be adopting the subjectivist approach, at least for federal statutes. Throughout this chapter and Chapter 4, we have referred to four United States Supreme Court cases[20] that portend changes, at least in the way in which the Court approaches issues of mistake in federal statutes. It is possible to state narrowly the holding of each of these four cases. *Ratzlaf* and *Cheek*, each dealing with legal mistake, involved a statute that proscribed a mens rea of "willfulness." This is a form of "specific intent" mental state, and the cases might be limited to such statutes. Similarly, *X-Citement Video* trod near First Amendment issues; had the shipment been of contraband cigarettes rather than free speech materials, it is possible that the Court would not have required the mens rea word to travel all the way down the statute, thus holding the defendant liable for

20. *Ratzlaf v. United States*; *Staples v. United States*; *Cheek v. United States*; and *X-Citement Video v. United States*.

his mistake. And although *Staples* could be read as endorsing a requirement of knowledge in all federal statutes, thus establishing mistake as a defensive claim in all such instances, it could also be read as a case where the government conceded that if mens rea were required at all, the proper level would be knowledge.

But a fair reading of these cases, individually and collectively, suggests that this is too narrow a view.[21] In each of these four cases, the Court exhibited a concern with "innocently" mistaken behavior. In each case, the Court interpreted the statute to require mens rea because a contrary holding might criminalize thousands of innocent persons. The Court rejected the argument that the defendant was "nefarious" in his acts or his motivations.

Just as important for the purposes of this chapter, the Court seemed to see no difference between *legal* and *factual* mistake; the "innocence" rationale was enunciated in each case. It is, of course, too early to be sure whether these cases are indications of future decisions or merely isolated instances. But if you like to gamble, bet that they will be followed again. A recent United States Supreme Court case seems to affirm the view that the Court is moving even further toward subjectivity. In a unanimous opinion, the Court, in *Arthur Andersen LLP v. United States*, 544 U.S. 696 (2005), reversed the conviction of the accounting firm of Arthur Andersen for destroying hundreds (perhaps thousands) of papers that were relevant to an SEC investigation of its client, Enron. The Court spoke of the "level of culpability . . . we usually require in order to impose criminal liability." It appears that this language is not limited to the statute's wording, but embraces a broad notion of moral wrongdoing as a predicate for criminal sanctions.

Examples

EXAMPLES

1. Officer Steiner observed Cottrell give Nath three or four chunks of what he believed to be rock cocaine in exchange for money. Nath was then observed a few yards away smoking the chunks in a pipe. After Officer Steiner observed what appeared to be another sale of rock cocaine by Cottrell, Cottrell was arrested. While Cottrell believed that Nath was about 19-20 years old, Nath was in fact a minor. As such Cottrell was charged with selling cocaine to a minor. Does Cottrell's mistake about Nath's age provide a defense to selling cocaine to a minor?

21. Douglas Husak and Richard Singer, Of Innocence and Innocents: the Supreme Court and Mens Rea Since Herbert Packer, 2 Buff. Crim. L. Rev. 859 (1999); Alan Michaels, Constitutional Innocence, 112 Harv. L. Rev. 819 (1999); Susan Pilcher, Ignorance, Discretion and the Fairness of Notice: Confronting "Apparent Innocence" in the Criminal Law, 33 Am. Crim. L. Rev. 1 (1995).

2a. Sylvester manufactures widgets. As a side effect of the manufacturing process, he creates "crud," a messy looking but otherwise apparently innocuous substance. For years, Sylvester has simply put the "crud" in a barrel with other trash and had it carted off to the local dump. Unknown to Sylvester, the Environmental Protection Agency, after years of internal debate, has just issued a regulation that lists "crud" as a substance that must be disposed of according to specific procedures. Weeks after publication of this new rule, Sylvester puts some of the "crud" into his garbage can and is prosecuted for "willfully disposing in an improper manner of a substance designated by the EPA. . . ." Does Sylvester have a defense?

2b. Would there be a different result if the statute omits the word "willfully"?

2c. Same facts as in 2a, except that Sylvester has kept apprised of the regulations, which require only that crud A, which has a specific percentage (20 percent) of toluene, be disposed of as required; crud B is not covered. Sylvester is not sure, however, whether the substance he has is crud A or crud B. He calls in his chemist, who tells him that the material is not crud A. The chemist's conclusion, alternatively (1) is wrong because the material contains 24 percent toluene, but he believes that only material containing more than 30 percent toluene is crud A; (2) is wrong because his analysis erroneously shows that the material Sylvester has contains less than 20 percent toluene, and therefore is not crud A. What is the result?

3. Julio, a guard at a federal prison, is charged in state court for carrying, while off duty, a weapon in a grocery store in violation of a state law. He argues that the state statute allows "peace officers" to carry a weapon, and that he carried the weapon in reliance upon the wording of the statute. If Julio is not, as a matter of statutory interpretation, a "peace officer" within the meaning of the statute, is he guilty of the crime?

4. Five years ago, Boris was convicted of larceny, a felony punishable by 2 years in state prison. He was put on and successfully completed probation. Today, Boris and his friend Fyodor went hunting with shotguns, where they were accosted by a federal agent, who arrested Boris and charged him with a violation of 18 U.S.C. §922(G)(1), which prohibits anyone who has been convicted of a felony from possessing a firearm. Boris was unaware of the statute, and also believed that his successful completion of probation meant that any collateral consequences were abolished. What is the likelihood that he will be successful?

5a. Harold Homeowner wishes to avoid another sultry summer by installing an air conditioner in his study. He installs one and is then prosecuted for not having obtained a building permit. He claims he did not know, and could not reasonably have known, of the requirement for a permit. Will he succeed in this defense?

5b. Now assume that Harold is told by a friend that if he installs a unit that has a rating of more than 500 BTUs, he must obtain a building permit. Careful not to break the law, he calls the local housing authority and speaks to a Mr. George Pepper. Mr. Pepper tells him that the limit is not 500, but 1,000 BTUs. Harold puts in a unit of 450 BTUs, only to learn, to his horror, that the limit is actually 400 BTUs. The violation is a felony. May Harold successfully defend his actions if prosecuted?

6a. Joan is prosecuted for "knowingly killing a homing pigeon." She seeks to introduce evidence that she believed the bird was a golden eagle. She concedes that her mistake was unreasonable. Should the evidence be admitted?

6b. Same facts, but the charge is "killing a homing pigeon."

These examples demonstrate the link between common law doctrines of mistake and current definitions of mens rea. In addition, a statute such as the one in 2b would raise questions of strict liability, discussed in Chapter 6. You must keep the interrelationship of Chapters 4-6 in mind whenever confronting a mens rea problem, be it of statutory interpretation or common law liability.

7. Michelle is indicted under a federal statute that makes it a felony for "any person to . . . knowingly deliver or cause to be delivered . . . any false or misleading or knowingly inaccurate reports concerning" certain kinds of information. She concedes that she knowingly delivered reports that, as it turned out, were false, but she claims that she did not *know* the reports were false, and that this is a valid defense. Is she right?

8. Johnboy is vacationing with his family near the Painted Desert, which is, as he knows, a national park. He sees a particularly attractive shard, about the size of a dime, which he puts in his pocket. The shard turns out to be more than 100 years old and is therefore an "artifact." He is prosecuted for "removing an artifact from a national park." What results under the following three circumstances? (a) Johnboy honestly and reasonably believes that he is not in the park. (b) Johnboy honestly and reasonably believes that the shard is a piece of plastic. (c) He honestly but unreasonably believes that the shard is a piece of plastic.

9. Dorothy asks Megan to deliver a transparent package, obviously containing some white powder, to George, and she says (a) "Remind George he owes me $10,000"; (b) "Tell him it's $10,000." Is Megan guilty of "knowingly" transporting (or selling) cocaine if she transports the powder without asking more?

10a. In 2009, the Obama Administration announced that it would not criminally charge CIA and military officers who had arguably tortured detainees in Guantánamo Bay and Iraq. The relevant statute, 18 U.S.C. §2340, defines torture as an "act . . . specifically intended to inflict severe physical or mental pain or suffering." The Administration gave several different reasons—either the actions were not torture under international or domestic law or the actual interrogators had relied on opinions from the Department of Justice's Office of Legal Counsel (OLC) assuring them that the methods they were using were not illegal. That memorandum, signed in 2002, declared: "Because specific intent is an element of the offense, the absence of specific intent negates the charge of torture. . . . We have further found that if a defendant acts with the good faith belief that his actions will not cause such suffering, he has not acted with specific intent." Was OLC correct?

10b. If so, was the Obama Administration correct in not charging those who relied on the OLC memo?

Explanations

EXPLANATIONS

1. No. In *People v. Williams* (1991) 223 Cal. App. 3d 407, 284 Cal. Rptr. 454, the Court of Appeal held that Cottrell Williams' mistake about Nath's age was not a defense to the charge of selling cocaine to a minor. The court noted that a prior decision, *People v. Lopez* (1969) 271 Cal. App. 2d 754, 77 Cal. Rptr. 59, held that a "mistake of fact relating only to the gravity of an offense will not shield a deliberate offender from the full consequences of the wrong actually committed." The *Williams* court further explained that the specific intent required for selling cocaine to a minor is the intent to sell cocaine, not the intent to sell it to a minor. Since the requisite intent is not negated by the mistake of the buyer's age, Cottrell Williams' mistake about Nath's age was not a defense.

2a. Under the traditional common law, Sylvester would be convicted. His ignorance of the regulation would be no defense. Under the common law, some courts interpreted the term "willfully" to require "specific intent" (which means that Sylvester would have a claim), while other courts would simply require that he act "voluntarily" (as a matter of will) (in which case he would not have a claim). After *Cheek* and *Ratzlaf*, however, the result is even more clear. Given that this statute establishes "willfulness" as the mens rea, the court would interpret that word as essentially requiring a "specific intent." This would require that the government prove that Sylvester *knew* that he had a duty to dispose of crud in a particular way. Since those decisions are not based on the Constitution, however, they do not necessarily affect the interpretation of state statutes. Thus, the usual ignorantia lex rule might apply, and Sylvester would be convicted. The Model Penal Code would reach the same result as the states. Under §2.02(9), ignorance of the law is irrelevant, where the statute establishes knowledge, recklessness, or negligence as the mens rea. The implication, not expressed in the Code, is that ignorance might be relevant if the statutory mens rea were purpose. Because that is not the case here, Sylvester's ignorance, however reasonable, is irrelevant.

2b. If *Cheek* and *Ratzlaf* are limited to statutes involving the word "willfully" (and a requirement of specific intent), Sylvester is in trouble. However, if the cases apply to "complex" regulatory schemes, Sylvester still might be exculpated. Under the Model Penal Code, the requisite mens rea under §2.02(3) is recklessly, knowingly, or purposely (see Chapter 4). Since, by operation of §2.02(9), ignorance of the law is irrelevant unless purposely is the requisite mens rea, Sylvester will have no defense of ignorance of law.

Note that the entire difference depends on the legislature's use of the word "willfully," and the assumption that the presence or absence of this mens rea word was intended to change dramatically the defendant's liability, even though his behavior is exactly the same.

2c. These variations raise the question of the relation of mistake of law and mistake of fact. In (1), Sylvester's "mistake" is one of law, derivative of the chemist's mistake of law. Since the mistake really involves a definitional error (what is the legal meaning of "crud"?), it can be characterized as a mistake of legal fact. Under earlier common law views, this would not have been relevant; Sylvester's error would be seen as one of law, and it would be irrelevant. Under *Staples*, however, the mistake might be exculpatory. *Staples* requires that the government show that the defendant knew every "fact" that gave rise to his legal obligation. Since the definition of crud A is a "legal fact," one could argue that *Staples* gives Sylvester a plausible claim of mistake. If the statute requires "willfulness," then *Cheek* and *Ratzlaf* arguably affect the case as well and allow Sylvester's claim that he did not know of the duty to dispose. On the other hand, Sylvester's reliance on his own employee might be unreasonable per se, since employees are likely to tell the boss what he wants to hear. At least in one New York case, *People v. Marrero*, 69 N.Y.2d 382 (1987), a state court required an official interpretation of law (rather than an employee's) in order to justify a mistake of law. This would require an official interpretation by the state attorney general of a statute, and an employee's view of the statute would not suffice.

In (2), Sylvester's claim comes closer to a mistake of fact. He knows that he must dispose properly of anything that contains more than 20 percent toluene, and is told that this substance does not contain that percentage of toluene. He may have a mistake of fact (or a mistake of "legal fact") here; his action looks reasonable, and most people would (or could) rely on a chemist for this information.

3. Held, in *People v. Marrero*, 69 N.Y.2d 382 (1987): Julio is guilty, both under the common law and under the state's version of the Model Penal Code. The opinion, which is scathingly criticized in Comment, 54 Brook. L. Rev. 229 (1988), rejected any weakening of the ignorantia lex rule because "Any broader view fosters lawlessness." Under the MPC, which is somewhat different from New York's version, Marrero will still be guilty, since §2.04(3) does not allow mistakes of law that are simply the defendant's personal misinterpretation of law; only official (mis)interpretations, reasonably relied upon, are relevant. Prof. Kahan has argued that Marrero was properly convicted because he was looking for a "loophole" rather than legitimately believing he could carry the gun into the bar. See Dan Kahan, Ignorance of Law Is an Excuse—but Only for the Virtuous, 96 Mich. L. Rev. 127 (1997).

4. Zero. The Circuit courts are unanimous that Boris need not know of the federal statute, nor of the effects of his felony conviction. Boris's failure to know of the statute constitutes ignorance of law, which, as we know, is never (well, almost never) a relevant claim. His failure to understand the impact of his conviction is, at best, a mistake of law, which is also never a claim. See, e.g., *United States v. Leahy*, 473 F.3d 401, 408 (1st Cir. 2007). Jeffrey A. Meyer, Authentically Innocent: Juries and Federal Regulatory Crimes, 59 Hastings L.J. 137, 170 (2007) (collecting cases); Brian E. Sobczyk, 18 U.S.C. §922(G)(9) and the *Lambert* Due Process Exception Requiring Actual Knowledge of the Law: *United States v. Hutzell*, 217 F.3d 966 (8th Cir. 2000), 80 Neb. L. Rev. 103 (2001).

5a. No. Harold's ignorance of the law is no excuse. Even in a day and age when there are literally thousands of city regulations and ordinances that govern our lives and with which we cannot possibly be familiar, the ignorantia lex doctrine lives on. These are also examples of strict liability crimes that are discussed later in the book. The same result holds under the Model Penal Code, so long as there is no potential jail time (see Chapter 6).

5b. Harold still loses at common law, unless Pepper's misstatement could be found to be intentional, in which case, under a very few scenarios, the government might be "estopped" by Pepper's words from prosecuting Harold. Under the Model Penal Code, Harold will still have virtually no chance of exculpation. Although he relied, perhaps reasonably, on Pepper's words, those words have never been reduced to a *written* interpretation, which the Code requires before a defendant can claim reasonable reliance on a misstatement of the law. Harold will just have to sweat this summer out—hopefully not in the cooler.

6a. Under common law, unless "knowingly" is interpreted as a specific intent requirement, Joan's evidence is irrelevant, since only reasonable mistakes "negate" "general intent" crimes. If she's free (as a bird?), "knowingly" is interpreted as a specific intent requirement. This is particularly true after *Staples* and *X-Citement Video*. Thus, her mistake, even though unreasonable, will exonerate. This result, of course, should be reached even without deeming the statute one requiring "specific intent." It seems clear that Joan, whatever her faults, is not the evil malefactor—purposeful killer of homing pigeons—that the legislature is after. Perhaps she should be required to wear glasses or take bird recognition courses, but sending her to prison is unlikely to achieve any goal, including deterrence.

Under the Model Penal Code, Joan must be "aware" that the bird was a pigeon (as required by the word "knowingly"). Since her actual belief contradicts that requirement, the evidence is admissible.

6b. Under the Code, "recklessness" is the default position when the statute contains no mens rea word (see Chapter 4). Since recklessness requires that Joan be aware of a substantial risk that the bird could be a pigeon, the evidence should be admitted. Under the common law, the evidence appears inadmissible, since there is no statutory mens rea. But under the separate doctrine of mistake of fact, Joan's mistake would be relevant if reasonable. Since she concedes it is not reasonable, Joan is heading for the big house.

7. This example, based on *United States v. Valencia*, 394 F.3d 352 (5th Cir. 2004), demonstrates the problems of statutory interpretation created by an ambiguous statute. Clearly, the legislation requires that the defendant "knowingly" deliver information and that the information be "knowingly" inaccurate. But the word "knowingly" does *not* appear before "false." Since the legislature *could have* written the statute to prohibit delivery of "knowingly false and knowingly inaccurate" information, it can be argued that it did not intend to require the government to prove that Michelle knew the information to be false. In *Valencia* itself, the court concluded that *X-Citement Video* (see page 83) required construing the statute as mandating that the government prove that Michelle *knew* the information was false.

Under the Model Penal Code's "element analysis," this is an easy case. "Falsehood" of the information is clearly a "material element," and the mens rea word "knowingly" clearly modifies "false."

8. This scenario demonstrates the (indefensibly) different results the common law gave between unreasonable and reasonable mistakes as to fact and law. In (a), Johnboy will not be allowed to present evidence as to his *reasonable* belief as to his location, because he was ignorant of the law that applied where he actually was. Under the MPC, because "national park" is likely to be determined to be an element "exclusively related to jurisdiction," which does not require a mens rea, he's guilty. Johnboy will be held guilty under the common law under (c) but not (b) because the mistake in (b) is reasonable, whereas the mistake in (c) is unreasonable. If the statute had proscribed "willfully" removing the artifact, however, the question is then (1) whether *Cheek* and *Ratzlaf* apply, in which case even an unreasonable mistake would seem to exculpate, or (2) whether "willfully" otherwise connotes a "specific intent" crime, in which case an unreasonable mistake of fact exculpates. Under the MPC, since there is no stated mens rea, the "default" position of "recklessness" applies, and Johnboy's mistake now negates the mens rea, since recklessness requires a conscious disregard of a substantial risk that the shard might be an artifact (which, by hypothesis, he could not entertain if he honestly believes it is plastic).

   Claims by the Johnboys of the world—that they failed to recognize an object as an "artifact"—have been treated as a mistake of fact, which, if reasonable, will be exculpatory. See *United States v. Quarrell*, 310 F.3d 664, 184 A.L.R. Fed. 625 (10th Cir. 2002). Closer analysis, however, suggests that even the mistake as to whether the shard was an "artifact" is, at best (or worst), a "legal fact": Johnboy may know that the shard is old, but unless he's a law student, he is unlikely to know that the statute defines how old a shard must be to be an "artifact." Nevertheless, surely the *Quarrell* court (and others) are right: Congress did not intend to make felons out of casual visitors who pick up items that are not obviously protected. The example shows, moreover, the thin line between mistake of law (which does not exculpate, no matter how reasonable), and mistake of fact (which does exculpate, often even if unreasonable).

9. The concept of willful blindness (or "ostrich culpability") allows conviction for a crime of "knowledge" even if the defendant did not actually know the facts. Courts have differed as to the wording of the test, concerned that the use of wording, such as "should have known," would risk punishing a merely negligent (or reckless) actor as seriously as one who actually knew. The cases require that the government not merely show facts from which a reasonable person could have deduced the relevant fact, but also show that the defendant strongly suspected the facts. In neither (a) nor (b) is there any evidence that Megan actually suspected that the powder was cocaine. But the statement in (a) could easily be interpreted as relating to a preexisting debt, while the statement

in (b) is more likely to be construed by the jury as putting Megan on notice that the $10,000 was in payment for the white powder actually being delivered. Contrast the situation where, in response to either statement, Megan had said, "That's a lot of money for a canister of sugar." Or suppose she had merely said, "That's a lot of money," not explicitly connecting the $10,000 with the powder.

10a. It is true that if the interrogators did not intend to inflict severe harm, the statute was not violated. But if they did intend to inflict pain, but thought their doing so was legal, then their mistake of law would be a defense only if the statute required specific intent to violate the law, that is, if the statute was either interpreted as were the statutes in *Cheek* and *Ratzlaf* (which required "willfulness," a word which is not present in this statute), or the statute was otherwise interpreted to require specific intent to violate a "known legal duty."

10b. Whether the interrogators could rely on the view of OLC that the actions were not torture is a different question. Reliance on anyone is not a relevant claim, unless the crime is one of specific intent, which is what OLC appears to be arguing. The specific intent exception, however, operates where a crime requires a specific intent and the mistake or ignorance of law negates that intent. Moreover, as we have seen in the text, the law is especially averse to allowing reliance on counsel; the MPC excluded even reasonable reliance on counsel as a relevant claim.

CHAPTER 6

Strict Liability

OVERVIEW

Notwithstanding the law's general insistence that the state prove the defendant had a mens rea, in a very few instances, courts interpret statutes that have no mens rea words as allowing criminal liability to be imposed even though the defendant had *no* mens rea *with regard to one or more material elements of the offense* (see Chapter 4 for a discussion of "elements analysis"). A common example is a statute that makes it a crime to sell alcohol to a minor. Most courts would require that the government prove that the defendant knew he was selling liquor; a mistake of fact that the item sold was water would usually exonerate.[1] If there is strict liability in such a statute, it is with respect to the material element of the customer's age.

Suppose that Gregori, a bartender, makes it a practice to "card" every new customer. In walks Herbert. Gregori asks for identification as to age, and Herbert produces a driver's license and a union card, each of which shows him to be 24. Since such documents can be easily forged, reliance on them might not be deemed reasonable by a court or a jury. But *assume* that Herbert, though 17, looks 24, and that Gregori has acted reasonably. Under a strict liability approach Gregori's reasonableness is irrelevant; Gregori is guilty of serving a minor. Now suppose that Gregori, having

1. See Richard Singer, The Resurgence of Mens Rea III: The Rise and Fall of Strict Liability, 30 B.C. L. Rev. 337 (1989). Also, some courts, particularly with regard to liquor or drugs, have held that no mistake, however reasonable, as to these two items will exculpate.

been stung (not to mention convicted) once, takes "super care" the next time. When Isaiah comes in, Gregori asks for his driver's license, his university or union ID, his birth certificate, and a notarized letter from his parents, whose signature Gregori has obtained in advance, all attesting to Isaiah being over the legal drinking age. If Gregori serves him, and Isaiah is underage, too bad! Gregori is still liable. Wait—it gets worse. Suppose that in the Isaiah example, the documents were not forged, and that *everyone* (including Isaiah's parents) was wrong about his birth date. Even then, Gregori is liable. When the courts say *no* mens rea—not even tort negligence—is required, they mean it.

One further distinction must be drawn. There are many other areas of the criminal law, felony murder (discussed in Chapter 8) and mistake of law (discussed in Chapter 5) among them, where the common law has, for decades if not centuries, imposed liability without regard to mens rea as to one or more elements of the crime. Yet they are not generally referred to as strict liability "crimes." Perhaps they are better thought of as strict liability "doctrines," because they apply to virtually all underlying crimes, rather than to a specific statutory offense. For example, the "ignorance of law" doctrine applies to virtually *any* crime and imposes liability without regard to the defendant's moral culpability. Similarly, the felony murder doctrine, as discussed in detail in Chapter 8, imposes added liability for a death that occurs during virtually "any" felony.[2]

THE REACH OF STRICT CRIMINAL LIABILITY

Strict criminal liability was only established during the second half of the nineteenth century. Early cases in which some courts upheld strict criminal liability usually involved either sexual acts (e.g., adultery, bigamy, and statutory rape) or the protection of minors (serving or selling alcohol; allowing minors to be present during gambling, billiards, or other such act; or both). Thus, a defendant who remarried, believing that he was divorced or that his first wife was dead, was guilty of bigamy if his belief, no matter how reasonable, turned out to be erroneous. Similarly, if a defendant had intercourse with a female whom he reasonably believed to be over a stated statutory age, he was guilty of rape if his partner turned out to be younger

2. For a lucid and challenging exploration of these issues, see Douglas Husak, Varieties of Strict Liability, 8 Canadian J.L. & Jurisprudence 189 (1995).

than the statute allowed.[3] Similar results occurred in cases involving the possession of or the serving of liquor.

The courts here relied on two main premises: (1) legislatures were unrestrained in their ability to proscribe conduct and did not have to require mens rea (a jurisprudential philosophy known as legal positivism); (2) there was a compelling need to protect society, particularly minors, against such evils (sex, liquor, etc.), and it was too hard to prove mens rea.

During the first half of the twentieth century, some courts applied these decisions to newly enacted "regulatory" statutes, such as those prohibiting (1) the sale of oleomargarine; (2) the possession or sale of alcohol generally (during Prohibition); and (3) environmental damage. For example, since requiring a license in order to engage in a home improvement business is for public protection, a defendant's lack of knowledge of this requirement is irrelevant. See, e.g., *People v. Stephens*, 937 N.Y.S.2d 822 (2011). In the last half of the twentieth century, prosecutors argued (not surprisingly, since their burden is eased) that statutes not specifying a mens rea should be construed as establishing strict criminal liability in numerous new settings, such as environmental, endangered species, or traffic cases.

Decisions in the United States Supreme Court have been equivocal. In *United States v. Dotterweich*, 320 U.S. 277 (1943) defendant, and the pharmaceutical company of which he was CEO, were charged with shipping "adulterated" drugs, which in this case involved an innocent misrepresentation on the label of the contents of the item; there was no actual threat to the safety or health of anyone who consumed the drug. Defendant argued that the word "person" under the statute reached only corporations; the narrow holding of the case was simply to reject that interpretation. But Justice Frankfurter's opinion had broad language endorsing, and even encouraging, strict criminal liability:

> Congress has preferred to place [any hardship] upon those who have at least the opportunity of informing themselves of the existence of conditions imposed for the protection of consumers before sharing in illicit commerce, rather than throw the hazard on the innocent public, who are totally helpless [320 U.S. at 285 (emphasis added)].

Much more recent, and even more ambiguous, is *United States v. Park*, 421 U.S. 658 (1975). Park was the president of a national food chain, one

---

3. This is so-called statutory rape. Note that the defendant must still have mens rea as to the conduct element (intercourse) and the result. His liability is strict only with regard to the age element. See *People v. Hernandez*, 61 Cal. 2d 529 (1964). At least seventeen states now allow a reasonable mistake as to age to avoid liability. See *Garnett v. State*, 632 A.2d 792 (Md. 1993); Catherine L. Carpenter, On Statutory Rape, Strict Liability, and the Public Welfare Offense Model, 53 Am. U. L. Rev. 313 (2003).

of whose warehouses in Baltimore inadequately protected against rodent infestation, causing some of the food in the warehouse to become "adulterated." Park did not know of the actual contamination before he was notified of it by the Food and Drug Administration; he then ordered his subordinates to clean up the warehouse. When this was not done, the FDA prosecuted him for possessing adulterated food for sale. The trial judge instructed the jurors that they could convict Park if they found that he was in a position of power to avoid the adulteration even if he was unaware of its existence.

The Court upheld the conviction, finding that the jury instruction was not critically misleading. Both the holding and much of the language in the opinion seem to support strict criminal liability. However, the facts demonstrated that the persons to whom Park delegated the cleanup of the Baltimore warehouse had previously allowed a warehouse in Philadelphia to become similarly contaminated. As the Supreme Court put it, "[Defendant] was on notice that he could not rely on his system of delegation to subordinates to prevent or correct insanitary conditions of [the] warehouses, and . . . he must have been aware of the deficiencies of this system before the Baltimore violations were discovered." 421 U.S. at 678. This language suggests that Park was willfully blind, reckless, or at least negligent. It emphasizes that Park's moral culpability lay not in his ignorance of the facts in the Baltimore warehouse, but in his *knowing* reliance on people who he knew had previously been unable to keep his warehouses clean.

DEFINITIONS AND INDICIA OF STRICT LIABILITY

How does a court (or, more to the point, a student) tell whether a statute should be construed as one involving strict liability? The courts have established several guideposts, but they are hard to read and often point in different directions. Good luck!

Public Welfare Offenses

In his classic article discussing strict liability decisions, Professor Francis Bowes Sayre used the term "public welfare offenses" to describe these kinds of crimes. Sayre, Public Welfare Offenses, 33 Colum. L. Rev. 55 (1933). At first blush, the phrase seems fairly understandable: It appears to refer to instances where the "public" rather than a single individual is endangered.

Dotterweich, which involved the sale of mislabeled drugs, would seem to involve danger to many. It is certainly true that individuals are usually unable to protect themselves against the dangers lurking in a can of soup. But a rock band using pyrotechnics in a crowded nightclub may endanger at least as many lives as a company executive who fails to protect against salmonella in his packaged food. Yet the rock band is seen as perpetrating a "real" crime that requires proof of mens rea, whereas the manufacturer of the food product is not. The number of victims, actual or potential, seems not to be a useful criterion here.

The kinds of cases in which the courts have employed the "public welfare offense" language do not always fit even the "public endangerment" thesis expounded by Justice Frankfurter. Thus, some courts have upheld strict liability for persons who kill migratory birds or endangered species, or remove artifacts from national parks. While these are important interests to protect, it is hard to see how the public is "endangered" or even "affected" by these crimes in a way distinct from the way in which it is affected by other, non-strict liability, crimes (e.g., bribery of an official). The argument that the public is more endangered in "public welfare offenses" than in non-strict liability offenses is, at best, tenuous.

In *Staples v. United States*, 511 U.S. 600 (1994), the United States Supreme Court appeared to limit the reach of strict liability federal crimes to those involving items that were *both* (1) dangerous (such as drugs, grenades, or explosives) *and* (2) highly regulated and, by their nature, would alert the defendant to the possibility of regulation, thus putting her under a duty to inquire about those regulations and ensure her compliance. Whether lower federal courts will follow that lead, however, is uncertain. Moreover, state courts are obviously not required to follow the *Staples* lead, since it was a statutory interpretation case.

Mala in Se ("Real") vs. *Mala Prohibita* ("Unreal"?) Crimes

When lawyers don't understand what they're doing, they often try to make it seem more defensible by clothing it in Latin. (Does "res ipsa loquitur" ring a bell?) In seeking to determine which crimes can be interpreted as allowing strict liability and those that cannot, courts have invented the terms (respectively) of *malum prohibitum* and *malum in se*. The reference is to crimes that are "merely" prohibited by statute and those that are both prohibited by statute and that are "in their nature" bad. Initially, this distinction seems confusing. As we discussed in Chapter 1, the principle of legality requires that *all* crimes now be statutory: In the twenty-first century, actions are criminal only because the legislature has prohibited them by statute. How can we formally distinguish between two statutes, one that punishes burglary and one that punishes a parking violation? On the other hand, the distinction seems to reflect common sense. Parking in violation of a statute or ordinance (malum prohibitum) doesn't "really" seem bad; burglary (malum in se) does.

An everyday example of a malum prohibitum crime that will illustrate this distinction is a statute that requires everyone to drive on the right side of the road. There is nothing inherently wrong with driving on the left side of the road: People in many countries do it all the time, and properly so. Yet this regulation (or an opposite one) is clearly necessary to maintain order and safety, both of which would collapse if people refused to play by a common set of rules. Without such regulations, there would be little reason to pay taxes, get a license before driving, or park in appropriate areas if the law could not penalize failure to do so.[4]

Some courts have expanded on these Latin phrases by explaining that if the offense was punishable under common law, it is a "real crime" (malum in se), while if the offense is a "new" crime, it is not a "real" crime (malum prohibitum).[5] If the latter, the defendant can be convicted without proof of a mens rea with regard to some element of the offense.

Again, there is a surface plausibility to this distinction. Those acts that all societies regard as heinous—rape, homicide, theft—must require a mens rea, or they are not "really" crimes at all. The grain of truth here, however, undermines the central point. If something isn't "really" a crime, then why use criminal sanctions to indicate displeasure? Moreover, such an approach does little to help us determine whether some "new" crimes, which seem as serious or as evil as the "old" ones, should be strict liability offenses. For example, burying toxic wastes or discharging particulates into the air was not a common law offense. However, today these acts seem both highly obnoxious and at least as life-threatening as burglary. Most federal environmental offenses were misdemeanors when originally enacted, but most are now felonies.[6] Morals and perceptions of dangers change over time. There is a possibility that the "malum in se" notion freezes the criminal law, or at least that part of it requiring mens rea, in the amber of the nineteenth

---

4. For these examples and more, see Paul H. Robinson, Shima Baradaran Baughman, and Michael T. Cahill, Criminal Law: Case Studies and Controversies, 8 (New York: Wolters Kluwer, 2017)

5. The United States Supreme Court distinguished between "common law" and "statutory" crimes in determining whether duress could be a relevant claim to the non-common law crimes of "receiving a firearm while under indictment" and "making a false statement to purchase a firearm" and, if so, whether Congress could put upon the defendant the burden of proof. *United States v. Dixon*, 548 U.S. 1 (2006).

6. See Avi Samuel Barbow, The Federal Environmental Crimes Program: The Lorax and Economics 101, 20 Va. Envtl. L.J. 47, 54 (2001); Michael Parker, Categorizing Environmental Crimes: Malum in Se or Malum Prohibitum?, 40 Tex. Envtl. L.J. 93 (2010); David Uhlmann, Environmental Crime Comes of Age: The Evolution of Criminal Enforcement in the Environmental Regulatory Scheme, 2009 Utah L. Rev. 123 (2009).

century (or earlier). "[B]oundary cases were so plentiful that even as early as 1822 the malum in se/malum prohibitum distinction was said to have 'long since exploded.'"[7]

Finally, many would argue that to say that malum prohibitum acts are wrong solely because they are prohibited is not entirely accurate. Most statutory rules[8] seek to prevent some real harm from occurring. Parking by a fire hydrant would normally not be "wrong," except that it endangers lives by blocking firefighters' access to water. Carrying or selling cocaine is not "wrong," except that the legislature has made a judgment that cocaine involves a public danger. Thus, *all* statutory rules appear to prevent some "real" harm and are not merely the whim of a legislature.

In addition to the confusion sometimes generated by "mala in se" and "mala prohibita," courts sometimes refer to those offenses that may be strict liability as "regulatory" or "police" offenses. Again, the terms are confusing. Perhaps when the only sanctions were fines, this distinction was meaningful. In a governmental system suffused with many regulatory agencies, the phrase seems less limiting.

Innocent Actors

In the *Staples* case, the Court reinvigorated another criterion to the strict criminal liability analysis by declaring that strict criminal liability would be inappropriate if it criminalized ostensibly innocuous conduct.[9] The Court pointed to two cases to demonstrate the difference. In *United States v. Liparota*, 471 U.S. 429 (1985), the Court had decided against strict liability in a case involving a restaurant owner who had accepted food stamps in a way that, unknown to him, violated federal law. He was, suggested the Court, morally "innocent." On the other hand, the Court had upheld an indictment against a possessor of hand grenades, even though the indictment did not allege that

---

7. Daniel Yeager, Kahan on Mistakes, 96 Mich. L. Rev. 2113 (1998) (Citing *Bensley v. Bignold*, 106 Eng. Rep. 1214, 1216 (1822)).

8. Some statutory rules do not have any moral basis. Thus, for example, it is imperative that we all drive on the same side of the road. Whether that is the right- or left-hand side is morally neutral, as long as we all follow the same rule once established.

9. "The government protests that guns, unlike food stamps, but like grenades and narcotics, are potentially harmful devices." Under this view, it seems that *Liparota*'s concern for criminalizing ostensibly innocuous conduct is inapplicable whenever an item is sufficiently dangerous, that is, dangerousness alone should alert an individual to probable regulation and justify treating a statute that regulates the dangerous device as dispensing with *mens rea*. But that an item is "dangerous," in some general sense, does not necessarily suggest, as the Government seems to assume, that it is not also entirely innocent. Even dangerous items can, in some cases, be so commonplace and generally available that we would not consider them to alert individuals to the likelihood of strict regulation. *Staples*, 511 U.S. at 619-620.

he knew the grenades were unregistered, because "innocent" persons do not possess hand grenades. *United States v. Freed*, 401 U.S. 601 (1971).

This criterion initially seems relatively easy to apply. Most people do not possess what they know to be hand grenades unless they have nefarious schemes, while many people possess food stamps without intending to commit a crime. To impose strict liability with regard to food stamps might expose tens of thousands of morally innocent persons to criminal liability and punishment.

The distinction, however, seems less obvious when applied to other strict liability items. Thousands of persons transport, deliver, trade, or sell canned food every day, yet *Dotterweich* seems to allow legislatures to impose strict liability on all of them if the food in the can is adulterated. But *Staples* suggests that gun owners are not strictly liable, even though (surely) guns are more dangerous than cans of food. And the Court in *X-Citement Video* (see page 83) expressly declared it did not want to hold strictly liable the FedEx carrier who delivered the video containing pornographic child sex. What, then, are "dangerous" items after *Staples*, and who, then, is "innocent" is still unclear, although the trend seems manifest.[10]

The Litmus Test of Available Punishments

Professor Sayre, after reviewing the various attempts to distinguish strict liability offenses from others, concluded that there was only one rational distinction:

> The real distinction depends on the nature of the penalty involved and the character of the offense. If the penalty is a serious one, particularly if it involves imprisonment . . . [strict liability is improper]. But if the maximum penalty consists in no more than a light fine, and if the character of the offense is such that infraction involves wide-spread public injury [strict liability may be proper].[11]

Sayre's suggestion seems straightforward. However, other courts have upheld strict criminal liability where the penalty is very significant, sometimes up to 10 years' imprisonment. See, e.g., *United States v. Freed*, 401 U.S. 601 (1971) (dictum). In *Staples v. United States*, 511 U.S. 600 (1994),

---

10. The "apparent innocence" language has been challenged as too harsh on the ground that it allows trial courts to exclude a great deal of evidence that would persuade a jury that the defendant was morally innocent. Jeffrey A. Meyer, Authentically Innocent: Juries and Federal Regulatory Crimes, 59 Hastings L.J. 137 (2007). See also Susan L. Pilcher, Ignorance, Discretion and the Fairness of Notice: Confronting "Apparent Innocence" in the Criminal Law, 33 Am. Crim. L. Rev. 1 (1995).

11. The Present Significance of *Mens Rea* in Criminal Law, Harvard Legal Essays 399, 408 (1934).

however, where the maximum penalty possible was 10 years' imprisonment, the United States Supreme Court explicitly rejected the intensity or duration of punishment as "the" litmus test of strict criminal liability, choosing instead to consider it as but one (albeit a very important one) of a list of factors in making such a determination.[12] The Canadian Supreme Court has actually taken such a step, holding that what we would call "strict liability" would violate the Charter of Human Rights if imprisonment were even possible, *Martineau* [1990] 2 S.C.R. 633.

STRICT VS. VICARIOUS LIABILITY

Strict liability must be distinguished from vicarious liability. In a case involving only vicarious liability, *someone* (usually the person who actually met the conduct element of the offense) has entertained the requisite mens rea; the issue is whether the defendant should be held responsible for that person's acts and mental states. Differently stated, the issue is whether the actus reus element of the crime should be *imputed* from the actual actor to the *putative* actor, our defendant. The answer is easy if the defendant has *told*, or encouraged, the actor to act as he did; we call this accomplice liability, and it is discussed in Chapter 14. Thus, if *A* tells B to shoot *C*, *A* is responsible for B's shooting of C, even if *A* never held the gun and even if *A* was not present at the shooting. Suppose, however, that the defendant's connection is less direct than that. The classic case involves a bartender who *knowingly* serves a minor: Should the owner be held liable, even though the owner was not present and perhaps even admonished the bartender against such sales? However one resolves that question, there is mens rea present; the bartender knew that the customer was a minor. Though it is true that the employer is morally innocent, and that as to him, the liability is in some sense strict, at least there is someone present who has acted in a morally blameworthy fashion.[13]

---

12. "[W]here, as here, dispensing with *mens rea* would require the defendant to have knowledge only of traditionally lawful conduct, a severe penalty is a further factor tending to suggest that Congress did not intend to eliminate a *mens rea* requirement. In such a case, the usual presumption that a defendant must know the facts that make his conduct illegal should apply." 511 U.S. at 624.

13. Most courts would hold the employer strictly (and vicariously) liable in either case, but at least two state courts have held that vicarious liability violates the due process clause of their *state* constitutions. *Davis v. City of Peachtree City*, 251 Ga. 219, (1983); *State v. Guminga*, 395 N.W.2d 344 (Minn. 1986). In each case it was unclear whether the bartender knew the age of the minor, but each court's opinion seems to preclude conviction of the owner unless the owner personally knew the purchaser's age.

One must distinguish the more difficult case, the one that raises all the policy issues in this area. It involves the bartender who does everything humanly possible to ensure that the customer is over the drinking age (recall the Gregori/Isaiah hypothetical at the outset of this chapter). If his customer now turns out to be one day under that age, should the bartender be held liable? If he is, *strict* liability holds. If the *owner* is held on the basis of the bartender's acts, *strict vicarious* liability operates. Before concluding that a case imposes strict liability, be sure that it is not "only" one of vicarious liability.

ARGUMENTS FOR AND AGAINST STRICT LIABILITY

Proponents of strict liability contend that strict liability is acceptable where (1) the need for deterrence is great and the ability to prove mens rea is difficult (e.g., food adulteration); (2) the penalty is small and the number of cases large (e.g., parking violations); (3) there is no stigma attached to the conviction; and (4) the use of strict liability will lead people to be more careful in carrying out certain types of conduct.[14]

Each of these arguments, taken separately, seems unable to carry the day. Strict liability obviously clashes dramatically with the view that mens rea is a bedrock of criminal liability. If one believes that persons who are not at least criminally negligent are "morally innocent," then strict liability means punishing the morally innocent. Moreover, mens rea is always difficult to prove. Although it is difficult for the prosecution to prove that the defendant knew that the milk was less than 2 percent cream, it is equally difficult to prove that the defendant "purposed" death in a homicide case.

Nor is court backlog a persuasive reason. Having too many cases is always a problem, and there are far too many "real" crimes today on the courts' dockets. Moreover, as we have seen, the Supreme Court has recently opined that the larger the number of potential defendants, the *weaker* the argument for strict liability becomes because of the danger of ensnaring truly innocent parties.

As for the third justification, stigma may well be in the eye of the beholder. As summarized by one panel of dissenting judges:

---

14. See generally, Appraising Strict Liability (A.P. Simester ed., 2005); see also Paul H. Robinson, Shima Baradaran Baughman, and Michael T. Cahill, Criminal Law: Case Studies and Controversies, 147 (New York: Wolters Kluwer, 2017).

> We undermine the foundation of criminal law when we . . . vitiate the requirement of a criminal state of knowledge and intention as to make felons of the morally innocent.[15]

Some supporters of strict liability argue that strict liability is necessary to prevent real criminals from fooling juries or escaping conviction because of proof problems, but this concern would exclude all claims that would exonerate a defendant, since juries sometimes do make mistakes.

Finally, although there is some merit to the argument that strict liability will encourage people to be more careful, there may be better means to justify that end. A negligence standard already requires an actor to do everything reasonably within their power to act with care. Demanding any more care than reasonableness may be asking too much from society. Moreover, proponents' argument that strict liability is necessary for the most serious of crimes is undermined by the fact that strict liability is used most commonly for minor offenses.[16]

Proponents of strict liability may also argue that many such crimes involve regulated businesses into which defendants voluntarily enter (e.g., banking, food manufacturing, waste management), and therefore it is not unfair to require them to take the risk of strict liability since the defendants knew of this risk when they undertook the activity. Furthermore, the argument goes, the government regulates this activity because it is potentially harmful to society, and the risks to the public at large that the risks to the public at large outweigh the risk that a truly innocent defendant will be criminalized.[17]

Empirical studies show rather conclusively that regulatory agencies do not enforce these regulations on a strict liability basis, but give the defendants frequent and constant notice of known or suspected violations before bringing criminal charges. Richardson, Strict Liability for Regulatory Crime: The Empirical Record, 1987 Crim. L. Rev. 295.

In addition to this empirical evidence, juries themselves may well nullify strict liability when confronted with actual defendants. Some may argue that the debate over strict criminal liability is a tempest in a very small teapot indeed, but this may not be so. First, juries *do* listen to instructions and follow them (see *Park*, supra). Second, there is surely something unsettling about a system that must rely on jury nullification or executive discretion

15. *United States v. Weitzenhoff*, 35 F.3d 1275, 1299 (9th Cir. 1993).

16. Paul H. Robinson, Shima Baradaran Baughman, and Michael T. Cahill, Criminal Law: Case Studies and Controversies, 149 (New York: Wolters Kluwer, 2017).

17. The argument somewhat begs the question of whether there should be strict liability by assuming that the acquiescence of the defendant answers the question. Suppose the government were to notify every car owner that, by virtue of using the public roads, he "consented" to a search at random of his car or his house. Would that consent be valid?

in order to achieve justice. Finally, to the extent that strict liability (or any other legal doctrine) fails to comport with the community's moral norms, it may bring the entire system into disrepute.

ALTERNATIVES TO STRICT LIABILITY

The strongest argument against strict liability is that it authorizes the criminalization of the morally innocent. Opponents also point out that no other country embraces strict liability, either rejecting it entirely or adopting one of several options. If compromise were necessary, they posit, the following alternatives could be explored. For example, one could

1. restrict such liability only to fines and preclude loss of freedom as a sanction. If deterrence seems necessary, the legislature could add a crime of "recklessness" and severely increase the penalty;
2. require the state to prove negligence;
3. permit the state to prove its prima facie case on the basis of strict liability, but then allow the defendant to avoid conviction by proving that he was not negligent (usually in a tortious sense). Canada and many other Commonwealth countries have taken this path. *Regina v. City of Sault Ste. Marie*, 85 D.C.R.3d 161 (1978).

"GREATER CRIME" THEORY

If *A* does not know he possesses cocaine at all, throwing him in prison seems unfair. Suppose, however, that B knows that he possesses cocaine but is unaware of the quantity involved. If the statute provides for stiffer penalties depending on the amount of cocaine possessed, it does not intuitively seem unfair to impose on B the larger penalty. B, after all, is not an innocent party to begin with; he knows he is engaging in a crime. Similarly, if C purposely punches D in the nose, C knows he is committing a criminal assault. If it turns out that D is a police officer, and a statute penalizes assaults on police officers more severely, it is arguably acceptable to impose on C the higher penalty.[18]

18. The suggestion was first made in dictum in *Regina v. Prince*, 80 All Eng. Rep. 881 (1875). For current applications, see annotations at 114 A.L.R. Fed. 355; 32 A.L.R. Fed. 2d 371; and 27 A.L.R. Fed. 2d 297. In *United States v. Feola*, 420 U.S. 671 (1975), the Court appeared to hold that a defendant did not need to know his assault victim was a federal officer. However, that

The general approach has been termed the "greater crime" theory. The "greater crime" theory can lead to other, even more expansive, notions. Thus, in the classic case of *Regina v. Prince*, 80 All Eng. L. Rep. 881 (1875), the defendant and his girlfriend, Annie Phillips, ran off to Leeds. When prosecuted for taking a girl under the age of 16 from her parents without their consent, Prince argued that he believed Ms. Phillips was over 16. The jury found this belief to be reasonable. Under normal common law rules, a reasonable mistake of fact would have been a total defense (see Chapter 5). Nevertheless, a majority of the judges subscribed to two theories that went beyond the "greater crime" to uphold Prince's conviction. They would hold the defendant guilty if he knew either (1) that he was committing a possible tort, and therefore should take the risk that he was committing a crime ("greater legal wrong" theory) or (2) that he was committing an immoral (though not necessarily illegal) act, and therefore should take the risk that he was committing a crime ("greater moral wrong" theory).[19] Some would argue that each of these approaches expands the net of criminality far beyond what theories of deterrence or retribution would allow.

In 2009, within one week, the Supreme Court issued two opinions that reflect the tension in the criminal law generated by the greater crime doctrine. In *Dean v. United States*, 556 U.S. 568 (2009), the Court confronted this statute:

> (A) any person who, during and in relation to any crime of violence or drug trafficking crime. . . . uses or carries a firearm, or who, in furtherance of any such crime, possesses a firearm, shall, in addition to the punishment provided for such crime of violence or drug trafficking crime—
>
> (i) be sentenced to a term of imprisonment of not less than 5 years;
>
> (ii) if the firearm is brandished, be sentenced to a term of imprisonment of not less than 7 years; and
>
> (iii) if the firearm is discharged, be sentenced to a term of imprisonment of not less than 10 years.

Dean robbed a bank, using a gun. As he was collecting the money, the gun discharged, leaving a bullet hole in the partition between two teller stations. He cursed and dashed out of the bank. Witnesses later testified that

---

issue was not briefed or argued in the Supreme Court, and the decision is therefore on shaky grounds. See Laura Bishop, Whether and at What Cost Section 111 Protects Federal Officers from Assault, 40 Sw. L. Rev. 355 (2010). Many states require such knowledge where there is an additional penalty. See Richard Singer, supra, n. 1.

19. *Prince* and all its progeny now seem to be dead in English law; any belief as to the victim's age, no matter how unreasonable, will be a defense to virtually any sexual crime. See *B (a Minor) v. DPP* (2000) 2 W.L.R. 452 (House of Lords); *R v. K* (2001) 3 W.L.R. 471 (House of Lords); Myerscough, Commentary: The Retreat from *Prince* and *Pointers* to Reform of Age-Based Sexual Offences, 2000 Child & Fam. L.Q. 12.4 (401).

he seemed surprised that the gun had gone off. For purposes of the appeal, the government conceded that the discharge was accidental, and, at best (or worst), negligent. Although no one was injured, Dean was sentenced to 10 years for the discharge (in addition to the sentence for his bank robbery). He argued that since subsections (i) and (ii) required some mens rea, subsection (iii), which had a longer additional penalty than either of those two, should be similarly interpreted. Instead, the Court, in an opinion written by Chief Justice Roberts, concluded that defendants who commit "violent offenses" "take the risk" that they will end up with longer sentences than they knew they were risking.

The *Dean* opinion was entirely consistent with the greater crime theory, although Chief Justice Roberts never mentioned that concept by name. Nor did he argue that clause (iii) constituted "merely" a sentencing factor, for which no mens rea was required (see below). One could, therefore, read *Dean* as embracing the greater crime theory.

One week later, however, in *United States v. Flores-Figueroa*, 556 U.S. 646 (2009), the Court totally ignored that same theory. As discussed in Chapter 4, the government in *Flores-Figueroa* argued that while it was required to prove that the defendant knew he was engaged in identify theft, it did not have to prove that he "knew" that the card he used actually belonged to another person in order to obtain a sentence enhancement of two more additional years. This, of course, was the greater crime theory—the *Dean* rationale would have upheld the government's argument. But the Court, in an opinion by Justice Breyer, rejected the government's argument, relying primarily on a reading of the statute that closely resembled "element analysis" (see page 83 for a more detailed examination of this part of the opinion). Nowhere in the opinion did Justice Breyer cite, much less discuss or distinguish, the *Dean* decision, nor was there any reference to the possibility that someone who knew he was involved in identity theft should take the risk that the false identity belonged to a real person.

Dean and *Flores-Figueroa* are reconcilable, of course, on a narrow reading: *Flores-Figueroa* involved a statute that explicitly used the term "knowingly," while the statute in *Dean* did not. Moreover, the *Dean* statute looked more like a "sentencing statute" than did the one involved in *Flores-Figueroa*. And Dean was involved in a violent offense, whereas Flores-Figueroa was not. Still, that *Flores-Figueroa* did not discuss these differences makes the two opinions together clash at least in approach, if not in actual outcome.[20]

---

20. The lower federal courts have been slow to apply *Flores-Figueroa*. See *Loenid* (Lenny) Traps, "Knowingly" Ignorant: Mens Rea Distribution in Federal Criminal Law After Flores-Figueroa, 112 Colum. L. Rev. 628 (2012). More generally, see Darryl K. Brown, Federal Mens Rea Interpretation and the Limits of Culpability's Relevance, 75 Law & Contemp. Probs. 109 (2012).

ONE MORE WAY OF IMPOSING STRICT LIABILITY: ELEMENTS, MATERIAL ELEMENTS, AND SENTENCING FACTORS

The courts have sometimes taken another approach to allowing legislatures to impose strict liability. Remember that mens rea only applies if there is a "material element" involved. If the element relates "exclusively" to jurisdiction, not even the Model Penal Code requires the government to prove any mens rea with regard to that fact. (*Caveat*: The government must still prove beyond a reasonable doubt that the element exists, e.g., that the crime occurred within the relevant statute of limitations period or in the relevant city, county, state, etc.)

And if the factor is not even an element, it is even clearer that the government need not prove mens rea. In the past 20 years, the Supreme Court has grappled, in a slightly different context, with statutory facts that appear to relate primarily, if not exclusively, to sentencing. For example, in *Apprendi v. New Jersey*, 430 U.S. 466 (2000), the defendant was convicted of possessing a gun for an illegal purpose, for which the maximum sentence was 10 years in prison. A separate statute provided that if the judge found that the defendant intended to use the gun for a racially motivated crime, the maximum sentence could be doubled. The Court held that the motive had to be proved to the jury beyond a reasonable doubt. But it did not say that the motive was an element, instead it said that since the motive increased the *maximum* sentence, it *acted like* a material element. In the intervening decade, many opinions, and literally hundreds of law review articles, have tried to determine the impact of *Apprendi* and its progeny.[21] For our purposes, however, the question is whether a fact that potentially increases the sentence carries with it a mens rea (which the government would clearly have to prove beyond a reasonable doubt).

CONSTITUTIONALITY

Although the United States Supreme Court has frequently talked about strict liability crimes, a careful reading of the decisions demonstrates that the Court has never actually rendered a holding on whether such offenses are

21. See Richard Singer, Examples and Explanations, Criminal Procedure II: From Bail to Jail, Ch. 12 (3d ed. 2012). See also Richard Singer, The Model Penal Code and Three, Two (Possibly Only One) Ways Courts Avoid Mens Rea, 4 Buff. Crim. L. Rev. 139 (2000).

constitutionally permissible. This is due, in large part, to the fact that virtually all of the cases concern federal statutes, and therefore are technically decisions involving statutory construction rather than constitutional limitations. The Court also has frequently indicated its refusal to become enmeshed in deciding the constitutional implications of the mens rea doctrine. Finally, the procedural posture of some of the cases has frequently been such that no "holding" on the issue is necessary. Thus, for example, in each of three of the leading cases, *United States v. Balint*, 258 U.S. 250 (1922); *United States v. International Minerals and Chemical Corp.*, 402 U.S. 558 (1971); and *United States v. Freed*, 401 U.S. 601 (1971), the lower court dismissed an indictment that had not alleged knowledge on the part of the defendant. Each case held that such an allegation is not necessary, but no decision states what should be done when the defendant raises the issue at trial.[22]

Similarly, the *Morrissette* opinion (see page 65), whose language strongly supports a "presumption" that all statutes require mens rea, ultimately avoids the constitutional issue by construing the statute to require mens rea. Even in *Staples*, the Court explicitly acknowledged in dictum in a footnote[23] the possibility of strict criminal liability.

The only United States Supreme Court case *holding* that a conviction dispensing with mens rea is unconstitutional is *Lambert v. California*, 355 U.S. 255 (1957). The Court held that the conviction of an ex-felon for not registering with the police in Los Angeles, as required by a city ordinance, violated the Fifth and Fourteenth Amendments because there was no showing that the defendant knew, or should have known, of a duty to register. That decision, however, has been a "derelict on the waters of the law," precisely as Justice Frankfurter, in dissent, predicted. There may be several reasons for the failure of *Lambert* to start a flood of anti-strict-liability decisions. First, it involved a city ordinance rather than a state statute. It is one thing to require defendants to be familiar with state statutes; it is a burden of a different order to require them to be familiar with every ordinance of every city in which they happen to find themselves (see Chapter 5). Second, the ordinance imposed a duty to register rather than imposing a duty *not* to do something. The common law has always been wary of imposing duties to act (see Chapter 3).

In short, the United States Supreme Court has given mixed signals on the constitutional significance of mens rea and its counterpart, "strict liability."

---

22. There are many other issues that the prosecution need not allege, but upon which the state may have to carry the burden of proof beyond a reasonable doubt once defendants raise them. See Chapter 15.

23. "[I]f Congress thinks it necessary to reduce the Government's burden at trial to ensure proper enforcement of the Act, it remains free to amend §5861(d) by explicitly eliminating a *mens rea* requirement." *Staples*, 511 U.S. at 1802. See also *Bouie v. City of Columbia*, 378 U.S. 347 (1964).

There has been much eloquent language repeated in several recent decisions about the crucial role that mens rea plays in all criminal charges. However, there is also some language, usually in the earlier decisions, that both supports the concept of strict liability, and in some instances endorses the application of strict liability in particular areas.

THE MODEL PENAL CODE

The Model Penal Code takes what it calls a "frontal attack" on strict criminal liability. Section 2.05 provides expressly that culpability is not required *only* with regard to "[o]ffenses which constitute violations." "Violation" is, under the Code, a term of art meaning an act for which imprisonment, even for a day, is not an available sentence (§1.04(5)). This, of course, follows precisely the line that Professor Sayre proposed in his article some 80 years ago. Even where the defendant is charged with a violation, a court may still interpret a statute to require mens rea if the court determines that requiring the state to prove mens rea is "consistent with effective enforcement of the law defining the offense" (§2.05(1)(a)).

The Code also rejects the "greater crime" theory. Section 2.04(2) provides that mistake is not a defense "if the defendant would be guilty of another offense had the situation been as he supposed." *However*, the next sentence provides that "In such case . . . the . . . mistake . . . shall reduce the grade and degree of the offense of which he may be convicted to those of the offense of which he would be guilty had the situation been as he supposed."

A RECAP AND A METHODOLOGY

How, after all this, can one begin to assess a statute to decide if it even arguably imposes strict liability? Under the Model Penal Code, the answer is fairly straightforward: If imprisonment is possible, the statute cannot impose strict liability. Under common law:

1. First determine that the statutory word is a "material element" and not a sentencing factor nor a "mere" element of the crime. If it's either of the latter two, STOP.

2. If the statute contains a mens rea word, then it is likely that the mens rea word modifies all material elements of the offense (see *X-Citement Video*, Chapter 4, supra).
3. If the statute does *not* contain any mens rea word, then:
   a. If it prohibits something like a common law crime, it is probably not strict liability (*Morissette*, supra).
   b. If it carries a severe penalty (usually more than one year of imprisonment, but this is very shaky), it is probably not strict liability.
   c. If it involves a complex regulatory scheme, it may be strict liability as long as (a) and (b) are not true, and possibly even if they are. (Boy, was that some help!)
   d. If the defendant would have been guilty of a crime even under the facts as he supposed, many states will impose strict liability on the "greater crime" theory.

Remember that these are only guidelines. If state legislatures declared expressly when an offense is strict liability, most of *these* questions would be answered,[24] and we would be left only with the (easy?) issues of fairness and constitutionality. Good luck in the woods.

Examples

1. Mike, a 25-year-old man, is out at a 21-and-over bar with some friends. He meets and begins talking to a girl named Jenna. At one point in the night, Jenna has her driver's license out and Mike notices they were born in the same year. When he mentions this, Jenna confirms that she is 25. At the end of the night, Jenna invites Mike back to her apartment, where they engage in consensual sexual acts. Eventually, Mike learns that Jenna is actually a 17-year-old high school student who regularly

24. In most instances, the absence of a mens rea word, or the failure to specify strict liability, is merely legislative oversight or sloppiness. In Utah, however, the legislature declared that, prior to 1983, a crime was considered strict liability "only when a statute defining the offense clearly indicate[d] a legislative purpose to impose strict liability for the conduct by use of the phrase 'strict liability' or other terms of similar import." Utah Code Ann. §76-2-102 (1982). However, this statute was amended in 1983 to require only that "the statute defining the offense clearly indicates a legislative purpose to impose criminal responsibility for commission of the conduct prohibited by the statute without requiring proof of any culpable mental state." Utah Code Ann. §76-2-102 (1999). Arizona has adopted the contrary statutory interpretation rule: "[i]f a statute defining an offense does not expressly prescribe a culpable mental state that is sufficient for commission of the offense, no culpable mental state is required for the commission of such offense, and the offense is one of strict liability unless the proscribed conduct necessarily involves a culpable mental state." Ariz. Rev. Stat. §13-202(B) (2001).

goes to bars using her fake ID. "Her" apartment is actually her older sister's apartment, which she uses when her sister is out of town. Mike is arrested for statutory rape, which criminalizes an adult engaging in any sexual acts with a minor under the age of 18. Mike argues that he sincerely believed—based on the facts that Jenna was in a bar, had an ID that showed she was 25, and seemed to have her own apartment—that Jenna was an adult. What result?

2. Chris parks his car, puts sufficient money in the meter for one hour, and walks into a meeting. Later, noting that his watch indicates that he has eight minutes left, he leaves the meeting and returns to put more money in the meter, only to find Rita, a meter reader, writing him a parking ticket for overtime parking. The meter reflects a violation. Unknown to him, Chris' watch stopped three times for a period of four minutes each during the hour, although on each occasion the watch began running again. The offense is punishable by a fine of $50. Is Chris guilty of a parking violation?

3. Bjorn is driving his van through a 60 m.p.h. zone. He sets his cruise control at 58 and takes his foot off the pedal. The control malfunctions, and the car's speed slowly rises to 72. It sticks there, and Bjorn carefully darts in and out of traffic, honking his horn as he goes. He finally pulls over and pulls out the ignition key, stripping the gears and causing $6,000 damage to his van. At that point a friendly state trooper points out to Bjorn that haste makes tickets as well as waste. The maximum penalty for speeding is $500. The maximum penalty for reckless driving is 30 days' imprisonment. Is Bjorn guilty of both these offenses? Or of either?

4a. Jack is a cook at Burger Prince; Jill is the cashier. A customer purchases from Jill a burger that was cooked by Jack and becomes ill. It is determined that the meat that Jack used contained bacteria that were not destroyed by the cooking process, although a properly working stove would have killed them. Neither Jack nor Jill is responsible, as a matter of employee functions, for cleaning the stove. Jack and Jill are prosecuted under a statute that prohibits the "manufacture or selling of dangerous food." The penalty is up to 2 years in jail. What result?

4b. Jack and Jill's supervisor, John Schmidlap, who was not present at the time, is also charged with selling adulterated food. Is John Schmidlap guilty?

5. On a dark and rainy night, Harvey, driving a pickup truck, is unable to stop and runs through a stop sign. His truck hits Matilda, killing her. He is charged with "motor vehicle homicide," which carries a maximum sentence of one year and a substantial fine. At trial, the prosecutor

argues that he need not even prove that John was negligent—the crime is one of strict liability. What result?

6. Emily purchases a white powder in a small glassine envelope from a friend. She is told and believes (reasonably) that it is sugar. Guess what? It's not. Is Emily liable for possession of a controlled substance?

7. Striker, a star pitcher for the local baseball team, is also a leading cocaine pusher. He has arranged to meet his latest purchaser near a movie theater in a section of town with which he is not familiar. As the sale goes down, he is arrested and charged with "knowingly selling cocaine within 1,000 feet of a school property." Some 900 feet away, hidden by trees, a railroad trestle, and an interstate highway, is a warehouse owned by the Board of Education and used to store books. The penalty for knowingly selling cocaine (a different statute) is 5 years. The penalty for this statute is 20 years. Striker argues that he did not know, and could not reasonably have known, that he was near school property.

8. Marty wants to surprise his wife, Mary Lou, with a diamond necklace. He steals from a jewelry store a box that contains such a necklace, without knowing that the owner, Diamond Lil, has rigged a bomb inside the box. When Marty gives the "necklace" to Mary Lou, she opens the box, the bomb detonates, and it's so long, Mary Lou. Has Marty committed homicide?

9. Mary, seeking to rent an apartment in a very tight market, falsely tells the Realtor that she works for the Defense Department. Unknown to her, the Realtor is an FBI agent. Mary is prosecuted for knowingly providing false information to a federal employee. What result?

10. Remember Johnboy from Chapter 5 (on pages 125 and 130)? Is it possible that a court could interpret this statute to impose strict liability as to either his mistake of law or his mistake of fact, however reasonable?

11. Quincy was convicted in state court of child molestation in 1992, and became subject to the state's Sexual Offender Registration Act (SORA). In 2008, as a result of the economic downturn, he lost his job and then his house. For four months he was homeless. He then found another job, and moved into an apartment. Two months later he was arrested and charged with violating SORA, which requires "[w]ithin 48 hours after any change in the offender's permanent or temporary residence . . . the offender shall report in person to a driver's license office." Failure to register is a felony. Quincy requested a jury instruction that the state must show that he knowingly or recklessly did not register, but Bryan, the prosecutor, objected on the ground that this was a public welfare, strict liability statute. The trial judge rejected Quincy's request and Quincy was sentenced to 6.5 years in prison. What result on appeal?

12. Osama purchased, at $4.00 a pack, several packages of Marlboro Lights. He then resold them to Gregory for $6.00 per package. Osama is charged with violating subsection (2) of the following statute: "Whoever

    1. makes a first sale of unstamped cigarettes;
    2. sells, offers for sale, or presents as a prize unstamped cigarettes; or
    3. knowingly consumes, uses, or smokes cigarettes taxed under this chapter without a stamp affixed to each individual package is guilty of a misdemeanor."

    The offense carries a maximum $4000 fine and a jail term of up to 1 year. The indictment does not charge any mens rea. Osama moved to quash the indictment. What result?

13. Remember Napoleon, who in Chapter 4 shot a rabbit, not knowing that he was even shooting a rabbit? Now assume that the rabbit was a snowshoe rabbit, which is listed as an endangered species under a state endangered species statute, which provides that "[i]t is unlawful to shoot a snowshoe rabbit." (a) He didn't know it was a rabbit he was shooting; (b) he knew it was a rabbit, but not a snowshoe rabbit; (c) he knew it was a snowshoe rabbit, but he had no idea that it was endangered; (d) the rabbit, which is rather large, actually attacked him, and he killed it, fearful for his life.

14. In a series of cases, the federal courts have interpreted the Migratory Bird Treaty Act, 16 U.S.C. §703 as imposing "strict criminal liability" for the death of any migratory bird. On January 15, 2009, U.S. Airways flight 1549 crash-landed in the Hudson River when several birds, including several migratory birds, flew into the jet engines. While all passengers were saved, the birds died. Is Captain Sully Sullenberger, the pilot of Flight 1549, criminally liable for the birds' deaths?

15. Liam buys a Coke at the nearby convenience store. He sees a donation box marked "For the orphans of Sudan." He sees several coins and a $5.00 bill in the box, so he grabs the box and runs. When he shakes the box open, he counts the loot. "Seven dollars! All that effort for seven bucks!" Unhappily for Liam, Chris Columb, the local police officer, hears him and arrests him for larceny, which would normally carry a six-month sentence. Even more unhappily for Liam, it turns out that one of the coins was not merely a nickel, but a "buffalo nickel" worth $50,000. He is charged with grand larceny (anything over $500) and is sentenced to the maximum 10 years. Has Liam been nickled and dimed?

16. Ansel Jefferson, CEO of Green Energy, Inc., is an ardent environmentalist and conservationist. While building his new company headquarters,

Ansel became aware that it was on the flight path of robins, which migrated past this spot every year. He sought the advice of the best engineers and environmental groups to assure that the birds would not fly into the building. At a cost of over $5,000,000, the building was oriented away from the flight path and made as apparent to birds as possible. One dark and stormy night, however, Hurricane Adams blows three robins and a Canadian goose into the windows, and they are all killed. The goose is significantly off-course; the ferocity of the winds had essentially blinded him to his route. Ansel is prosecuted for the violation of the Migratory Bird Treaty Act, 16 U.S.C. §703, which makes it a misdemeanor to "pursue, hunt, take, capture, kill, attempt to take, capture" a protected bird (which a Canadian goose is, but a robin is not). Ansel argues that (1) he has been "super cautious" and that (2) it was totally unforeseeable that a Canadian goose would be injured by his building. Assume that actus reus is established. What result?

Explanations

EXPLANATIONS

1. The first thing you would examine in this case is the statutory language of the offense. Statutory rape is "commonly defined as requiring no culpability as to the offender's sexual partner being underage."[25] In other words, it is often designated a strict liability crime by statute. It is unclear what the statute in Mike's jurisdiction says, however, so we must look to other indicia that the crime should or should not be construed as having strict liability.

   The most common and convincing argument would be that statutory rape is a public welfare offense. Undoubtedly, there is strong public policy in favor of protecting youth in society from sexual predators. Making statutory rape a strict liability crime would prevent predators from claiming they were mistaken of their victims' ages. However, such a strong position by nature will make arguably innocent actors culpable of a serious crime. Mike, for example, seemed to have acted in the most prudent way possible; all signs seemed to point to Jenna being of age.

   The Model Penal Code seems to take the middle road on this issue. While most crimes in the MPC are not strict liability crimes, §213.6(1) instructs that, in the context of rape, "[w]henever . . . the criminality of conduct depends on a child's age . . . to be older than 10, it is not defense that the actor did not know the child's age, or reasonably believed the child to be older than 10." This effectively makes statutory

25. See Paul H. Robinson, Shima Baradaran Baughman, and Michael T. Cahill, Criminal Law: Case Studies and Controversies, 147 (New York: Wolters Kluwer, 2017).

rape of a child under 10 a strict liability crime. Since Jenna was 17, it seems, the crime would not be strict liability in an MPC jurisdiction.

2. This is the prototypical strict liability offense. Whether Chris knew that he was overparked or not, he will be found liable. The penalty is low, and it is at least plausible that there are too many such offenses to allow or require a prosecutor to prove and a court to inquire about the defendant's actual state of mind. It is also unlikely that there is any moral stigma to such an offense. (But in a world where people kill for parking spaces, who knows?) The Model Penal Code would agree, since there is no imprisonment possible.

3. Even assuming that the malfunction of the cruise control occurred for the first time and was a complete surprise, Bjorn is likely to be found strictly liable of speeding, primarily on the flood-of-cases rationale, but also due to the potential harm involved. This will be true even if Bjorn just had had his car, including the cruise control, checked and serviced 10 minutes before the event. Tough luck, Bjorn. Next time, don't be so decadent. Bjorn's best argument is that he was not *driving*, not that he was not speeding (no actus reus). He is not reckless—the chances that the control would stick are not "substantial."

   The Model Penal Code would allow strict liability if the charge is *speeding*. However, Bjorn would not be guilty of the *reckless* driving charge because imprisonment is possible. The state would have to prove recklessness, which under the Code requires a subjective awareness of the risk of committing the crime (in this case speeding).

   Note: This is a real case. *State v. Baker*, 571 P.2d 65 (Kan. App. 1977). However, the court's analysis in *Baker* is not technically based on strict liability. It distinguished two earlier decisions in which drivers involved in accidents because of failing brakes and failing throttles were not held strictly liable on the grounds that those items were "essential" to the operation of a car, whereas a cruise control was not. Perhaps using cruise control is simply too decadent.

4a. Unless the court reads a mens rea requirement into the statute (see Chapter 4) or they are in an MPC state, Jack and Jill should pack for Statesville now. Food and other health offenses are frequently deemed "public welfare offenses," allowing strict liability even if imprisonment is possible because the public generally is endangered and cannot protect itself. However, the owner of the restaurant, not the employees, may be responsible for this strict liability crime. If the two were charged with "reckless" sale of dangerous food, they might have a good claim because they did not know there was a risk of contamination. They will stay home in an MPC state, which precludes imprisonment without mens rea.

4b. Jack and Jill could have a cellmate, John. Even if John wasn't present in the building, he may be held on a vicarious strict liability basis, even if the punishment is incarceration (except in an MPC state or those states that have held vicarious liability involving imprisonment to be unconstitutional).

5. In *State v. Perina*, 282 Neb. 463 (2011), the Court held that motor vehicle homicide was a public welfare offense not requiring mens rea. The court relied heavily on *Morrissette*'s observation that crimes "derived from" the common law often required mens rea but concluded that because this statute had no common law roots, *Morrissette*'s presumption of mens rea did not apply. Remember, too, that this is the opinion where Justice Jackson spoke so eloquently about the usual need for mens rea (see page 65). The Nebraska court also noted, however, that the crime was a misdemeanor, rather than a felony—which is a significant distinction. Other courts have reached similar conclusions. See, e.g., *State v. Wojahn*, 204 Or. 84 (1955); *Haxforth v. State*, 117 Idaho 189 (1990). Under the Code, it's easy—any jail time requires the state to prove at least (criminal negligence) and recklessness unless negligence is stated.

6. Emily clearly did not have any mens rea as to possession of a controlled substance, so she will only be liable if this is a strict liability crime. There is no clear legislative intent to impose strict liability, so we must first determine if there is an argument to urge a court to impose strict liability anyway. Emily undoubtedly violated a "material element" when she was in possession of a controlled substance. Moreover, there is no mens rea word (purposefully, knowingly, etc.) that would give us any indication that mens rea is required. Therefore, the prosecutor's best argument will be that strict liability should be imposed because possession of a controlled substance is not a common law crime and the maximum sentence is relatively light. If the court agrees with this argument, then Emily's subjective thoughts do not matter and she is responsible for the crime.

   The answer in an MPC jurisdiction would be simple: Since there is a possibility that Emily can be sent to prison, there is no strict liability and Emily is off the hook.

   As an aside, the real-world answer to this would depend, incredibly enough, on *when* the event occurred. Prior to 1970 or so, virtually every state—following the Uniform Narcotic Drug Act suggested in 1932 by the Conference of National Commissioners on Uniform State Laws—held that drug crimes, including possession or sale, could be prosecuted on a strict liability basis. The defendant's belief, no matter how reasonable, about the nature of the item was irrelevant. In 1970, the Commissioners revised their view and required mens rea. Within 15 years, every state had followed this lead, either legislatively or judicially. Whether this had to do with possible increased punishments, or a sense that drug deals were now "mala in se" rather than "mala prohibitum," or for some other reason is unclear. So, in reality, Emily stays home, even under the common law.

7. This is an example of the "greater crime" theory. Drug sale, after all, is a crime by itself. Many states, following the example of the federal government, have passed "drug-free school zone" statutes such as the one involved in this example. These statutes vary in form. Some, such as the one here, are "free-standing" crimes. Others, including the federal statute, build on a preexisting statute that bans drug sales, and declare that any sale that occurs near a school yard doubles the maximum penalty. With the latter, the argument that "school property" is not a material element of the crime, but merely a "sentencing enhancer," is plausible. Under the statute, as presented in this example, however, it is much more likely that a court should find it to be a "material element" of the crime, thus requiring the state to prove mens rea with regard to the proximity of school property. Some courts, however, have simply ignored this distinction and held that there is no mens rea requirement as to that element. Several states have expressly declared in a statute that lack of knowledge that the event occurred near school property is irrelevant as to guilt. Under the Code, Striker's term will be much shorter. He can be convicted of selling near a school yard, but his sentence can't be more than that for "merely" selling. The Code totally rejects the idea of punishment for a "greater crime." See generally Annot., School-Zone Statutes, 27 A.L.R.5th 593 (1995). It looks like Striker will be pitching for the state prison team for the next few years.

8. This example tests the outer limits of the greater crime theory. To the extent that the issue arises at all, it usually involves a fact that makes the first crime a "higher-level" offense of the same kind. The courts usually are not confronted with, and therefore do not discuss, whether the theory would apply to a different kind of crime (property vs. personal injury; possession of diamonds vs. possession of drugs, etc.). Even more than a century ago, one court expressed great concern over exposing a defendant who knew he was committing larceny to the far more serious crime of arson, when the method by which he committed the larceny resulted in the burning down of a ship. *R v. Faulkner*, 13 Cox C.C. 550 (1877). The court rejected what it called a "very broad" claim by the prosecutor that anyone involved in any crime should be held liable for any greater crime that happened (however accidentally) to ensue. Under the MPC, Marty can be punished only for the larceny,

not the death. *But be careful*: When we get to felony murder (Chapter 8), the same question may be answered in a different way.

9. Believe it or not, under both the common law and the MPC, it is likely that Mary will be on her way to prison. This is a variation of *United States v. Bakhtiari*, 913 F.2d 1053 (2d Cir. 1990), which actually has much more bizarre facts than the example. Some courts would explain that "federal employee" here is not a "material" element, but only a "jurisdictional" element of the offense, and no mens rea is required. If this is a valid argument, the Model Penal Code would agree. Other courts might consider this an example of the "greater moral wrong" theory; while still others might consider a mistake (or ignorance) as to the legal status of the Realtor a legal mistake, and hence governed by ignorantia lex.

10. You guessed it. It's not only possible—it's happened. Courts applying statutes similar to these have held that the statutes are strict liability offenses, immune to both mistake of law and mistake of fact claims. Note that it is virtually impossible to see this statute as a "public welfare offense" in the sense that the public is "endangered" in a way against which it cannot protect itself (the original explanation of that phrase). Here, the only viable explanation is that public policy requires us to sacrifice Johnboy so as to deter real looters from even raising mistake.

11. This sounds like *Lambert* (Chapter 5), right? But Bryan argued that (a) sex offenders were much more likely to repeat than "felons generally," and thus the public welfare (and particularly children's welfare) was more clearly involved; and (b) this was a regulatory provision and thus plausibly strict liability. This sounds like a close question. Even if the state's suggestion that Quincy is "in the business" of offending, he had registered with SORA before and certainly "should" or "might" have been informed of his duty to inform the state of his movements. Moreover, the argument that the state is merely "regulating" this "business" is clever. But the Florida Supreme Court rejected these contentions, pointing out that the penalty for non-registration was severe (particularly in contrast to that in *Lambert*). *State v. Giorgetti*, 868 So. 2d 512 (Fla. 2004). Nice try, Bryan.

12. This is a real case. *State v. Abdallah*, 64 S.W.3d 175 (Tex. App.-Fort Worth 2001). The first issue is a matter of statutory construction—does the presence of a specific mens rea in §(3) imply that there is no mens rea required to violate §(2)? Given the presumption that there is always a mens rea, the court in *Abdallah* proceeded to discuss whether this offense could (or should) otherwise be a strict liability offense, in which case the absence of a mens rea word in §(2) might be persuasive. But the

court, in a careful opinion, then examined each aspect of the crime: (a) whether there was a risk of serious harm to the public; (b) the legislative history and the severity of the punishment; (c) defendant's ability to ascertain the facts; and (d) the number of expected prosecutions, and concluded that this statute should not be interpreted as establishing a strict liability offense. There might be some argument here because subsection (1) appears to punish even the first offender, whereas subsection (2) seems to deal with a "second offender," but the court rejected that suggestion. A later decision, *State v. Walker*, 195 S.W.3d 293 (Tex.-Tyler App. 2006) applied *Abdallah* to a charge of filing for record an unapproved plan for real estate development to reject strict liability there, as well.

13. In Chapter 4, we asked how to interpret the statue under "normal" mens rea analysis. By now, however, we have several new questions, and we will discuss them together. The first question is whether this is a strict liability statute. There are now many such statutes, both state and federal, premised on the need to preserve species. The more noted federal laws include the (1) Endangered Species Act, (2) Lacey Act, (3) Marine Mammal Protection Act, (4) Bald Eagle Protection Act, (5) Migratory Bird Treaty Act, and (6) African Elephant Conservation Act.

    In addition, there are a number of federal laws that address the protection of both heritage and habitat, such as the Wild Free-Roaming Horses and Burros Act. If the species is listed by either the EPA or a state agency as "endangered," the liability is usually strict—no matter how careful he was, Nappy would be liable. David P. Gold, Wildlife Protection and Public Welfare Doctrine, 27 Colum. J. Envtl. L. 633 (2002). If there were some mens rea requirement, but he knew it was a horseshoe rabbit, his failure to know that it was "endangered" would not be helpful—it's a mistake of law, or of legal fact (see Chapter 5), and he's liable. For a claim of self-defense (necessity), Nappy's belief might have to be reasonable. If he had shot a charging (protected) Florida panther, for example, it is more likely that he'd be able to claim necessity than for a charging rabbit, even a snowshoe one. There is, however, still a question of whether one can claim necessity if a crime is one of strict liability. See Chapter 16 for more details.

14. Yes. Although the Justice Department had the good judgment not to attempt a prosecution of Captain Sully, the precedents are clear—so long as the penalty is merely that of a misdemeanor (a maximum sentence of one year in prison), the provision may be applied without requiring a mens rea. See Larry Martin Corcoran, Migratory Bird Treaty Act: Strict Criminal Liability for Non-Hunting, Human-Caused Bird Deaths, 77 Denv. U. L. Rev. 315 (1999). Under the MPC, of course,

the answer is simple—if there is even one day of confinement possible, the statute must be construed as requiring at least negligence, and it is hard to argue that if birds fly into your plane, *you* are the negligent party. Captain Sullenberger might argue that he did not "act" in this regard—that birds flew into his plane, rather than his plane killing them. But the possibility of criminal liability is striking. See Marc R. Greenberg, Captain "Sully" Sullenberger, Charles Dickens, and the Migratory Bird Treaty Act, 25 SPG Crim. Just. 12 (2010).

15. Under the common law, you bet your dollar. This would be the epitome of the "greater crime." A thief never (or rarely) knows the value of what he steals—it could be paste, or it could actually be the Hope Diamond. Liam's going to be flipping coins for a very long time. The issue here is the MPC. It would convict Liam of the crime of which he would be guilty "had the situation been as he supposed." Now Liam can probably make a fairly good case here that he "supposed" the facts to constitute petit, rather than grand, larceny. But if a thief never really knows how much is in the box, wallet, or whatever he takes, what crime does he "suppose" he's committing?

16. First, note that the MBTA provision appears to be *mala prohibitum*—i.e., a regulatory crime—rather than a *mala in se*, or inherently bad, crime. This fact would weigh in favor of an argument for imposing strict liability. Also in favor of strict liability are the facts that Jefferson's crime violated a material element of the law and that the law is a misdemeanor, likely carrying a light sentence or fine. Moreover, the prosecution will argue that environmental law and the protection of endangered animals involves a highly complex regulatory scheme, which favors imposition of strict liability.

    Jefferson's only argument against imposing strict liability is that he was an innocent actor, similar to the *Liparota* case discussed above. Jefferson spent millions of dollars to take every precaution to protect the endangered birds from his building. Arguably, he succeeded, since the only reason the birds flew into his building were because they were thrown off course by unusually high winds. Surely, this makes Jefferson "morally innocent." If Jefferson can successfully make this argument, he will likely be off the hook.

    What result in real life? The MBTA has been the subject of much litigation, and even more law review analysis. The misdemeanor provision has been consistently interpreted as imposing strict liability, on the premise that it is an environmental statute which could be easily evaded if the government were required to prove any level of mens rea. See Kalyani Robbins, Paved with Good Intentions: The Fate of Strict Liability Under the Migratory Bird Treaty Act, 42 Envtl. L. 579 (2012). In strict liability, foreseeability and great care are both irrelevant. The harms are the only issue. But there are two glimmers of hope for Ansel: First, over 30 years ago, the court in *United States v. FMC Corp.*, 572 F.2d 902 (2d Cir. 1978) actually foresaw (in dictum) the possibility that birds might fly into buildings and suggested that the owners should not be liable for such unforeseeable deaths. But that's only dictum. Second, the court in *United States v. Apollo Energies*, 611 F.3d 679 (10th Cir. 2010), embraced a notion of proximate cause that supplements (or replaces) strict criminal liability. See Alex Arensberg, Are Migratory Birds Extending Environmental Criminal Liability?, 38 Ecology L.Q. 427 (2011). (Wind turbines now kill between 5,000 and 275,000 birds each year.) (at fn. 115). But as the law stands now in most circuits, Ansel's going to pay a fine and possibly go to jail for a year. On the other hand, the MBTA was amended to include a felony offense as well; that provision has been interpreted to require mens rea.

CHAPTER 7

Causation

OVERVIEW

Some crimes require the prosecution to prove that the defendant caused a particular result. Proving this fact is usually not difficult. However, challenging issues of causation sometimes occur in the criminal law, most frequently in homicide cases. Homicide requires the prosecutor to prove the defendant caused the death of another human being. (See Chapter 8.)

Causation often can be established by showing that the defendant's action directly brought about the resulting harm. In most cases, causation is simply a question of physical occurrence. Did the defendant initiate physical forces that, according to the laws of nature, led to a particular result?

Establishing that the defendant's conduct caused the proscribed result ordinarily is not difficult. If a professional killer shoots the victim in the head and the victim dies, a pathologist can conduct an autopsy and then testify at trial that the bullet fired by the defendant brought about the victim's death by producing massive injury to the victim's brain. Because the defendant produced the victim's death in exactly the manner he intended, there is no controversy about his criminal responsibility for causing death. Likewise, when a defendant engages in risky conduct that brings about death in exactly the way his conduct made probable, proving that the defendant's conduct caused the prohibited result is not hard. The actor is rightly blamed for the predictable consequences of natural events that he intentionally set in motion.

However, as in all human experience, the unusual or unexpected sometimes happens. What if the defendant did not intend or anticipate the harm, or the harm occurs in an improbable manner? Is she criminally responsible for that harm? Judges, juries, and especially law students have difficulty determining when the criminal law will conclude the defendant has "caused" the harm and when she did not. In such cases, what started out as a simple inquiry into what caused a physical occurrence often requires a moral judgment, as well.

The analytic tools developed by the criminal law to resolve difficult causation issues are not always clear or easy to apply. This doctrinal difficulty is prompted, in part, by the ongoing debate concerning the relevance of harm in determining and grading criminal responsibility.[1]

Utilitarians are less concerned with the occurrence of harm than some retributivists. Some utilitarians argue that the defendant's *attitude* toward harm—not the *causation* of harm—is critical in determining whether he needs to be punished. They point out that whether harm occurs is often a matter of luck or skill and that the dangerousness of the individual is the same regardless of what harm his conduct actually causes.[2]

Some retributivists, on the other hand, argue that humans intuitively feel that the harm done is an important element in determining criminal responsibility and setting an appropriate punishment.[3] This particular retributive theory requires that individuals be punished only for harm they caused.[4] Otherwise, punishment is disconnected from a moral concept of just deserts.

THE RATIONALE OF CAUSATION

A primary goal of the criminal law is to prevent harm. Individuals may be punished for the harm they cause, provided other necessary elements like mens rea are satisfied. However, there must be a connection between someone's conduct and the resulting harm sufficient to justify the infliction of punishment.

---

1. The moral debate over the relevance of harm to criminal responsibility also occurs in attempt. See Chapter 12.
2. Schulhofer, Harm and Punishment: A Critique of Emphasis on the Results of Conduct in the Criminal Law, 122 U. Pa. L. Rev. 1497, 1514-1516 (1974); Alexander, Crime and Culpability, 5 J. Contemp. Legal Issues 1 (1994).
3. M. Dan-Cohen, Causation, 1 Encyclopedia of Crime and Justice 165-166 (S. Kadish ed., 1983); Crocker, A Retributive Theory of Criminal Causation, 5 J. Contemp. Legal Issues 65 (1994). But see H.L.A. Hart & A.M. Honore, Causation in the Law 395 (2d ed. 1985).
4. Michael S. Moore, Causation and Responsibility, 16 Soc. Philos. & Policy 1 (1999).

The causation requirement limits criminal responsibility to those individuals whose conduct has been essential in bringing about harm. To ensure freedom from government interference, it must be shown that a prohibited result occurred because the actor's conduct caused that result. This required relationship between an actor's conduct and the result derives from the notion of causal accountability. A result should only affect an actor's liability if the actor is responsible for it, and responsibility demands some causal connection. In other words, liability should only be established against an actor if the actor is responsible for it.[5]

One approach to determining causation in the criminal law is analogous to how a scientist might examine cause and effect in the physical world. The scientist might examine the natural forces that brought about the harm and determine whether the defendant's act played an essential part in physically causing the harm. Another approach focuses on the defendant's moral culpability; that is, did she act with the intention or contemplation that she might cause harm? If not, *should* she have contemplated the harm?

The former approach stresses the mechanisms by which harm occurs in the real world. The latter approach focuses more on the defendant's attitude and intent toward the occurrence of harm.

Causation is also an important element of tort liability. An individual who commits a tort may be required to pay compensation only for the damage he has caused. However, the goals of tort law are different from criminal law goals. Tort law seeks in part to distribute the risk of harm to those most able to bear the cost as well as to those who benefit from the activity that produced the harm. Moreover, negligent conduct is usually sufficient for the imposition of liability in tort. Thus, the concept of causation in tort is quite broad so that these goals can be more easily accomplished.

Criminal law punishment, on the other hand, is aimed both at deterring and at "paying back" intentional or risky harmful conduct. Thus, the concept of causation in criminal law may be more narrow.

There is an ongoing debate in criminal law on whether tort law concepts of causation should become part and parcel of what criminal law requires or whether criminal law should have a more narrow concept of causation. Needless to say, this debate has not been resolved.

---

5. P. H. Robinson, S. Baradaran Baughman, & M. T. Cahill, Criminal Law: Case Studies and Controversies 302 (4th ed. 2017).

THE ELEMENTS OF CAUSATION

The Common Law

Responsibility for Causing Harm

As in tort, to be held criminally responsible for causing a proscribed harm under the common law, the defendant's conduct must have been both the "cause in fact" and the "proximate cause" of the harm.

Cause in Fact

Cause in fact is "but for" causation. If the harm would *not* have occurred *unless* the defendant had engaged in the conduct, there is "cause in fact." This inquiry is essentially one of fact. Was the defendant's conduct necessary or a substantial factor for the harm to occur? Frequently, the analysis will conclude that the defendant's conduct started a chain of events that eventually resulted in the proscribed harm. Put simply, "but for" defendant's conduct, this chain of events would never have begun and the harm would not have occurred.

Cause in fact ("but for" causation) is required before an individual can be convicted of a crime that requires him to *cause* a result. Without it, the harm that has occurred cannot be linked to the defendant's behavior. After all, the harm may have happened even if the defendant had done nothing. To punish someone in these circumstances is arbitrary and unfair because it is not based on what the defendant did. Thus, "but for" causation must be established whenever causation is necessary for criminal responsibility. However, as we shall soon see, cause in fact is not enough for criminal responsibility under either the common law or the Model Penal Code.

Omission as a Cause

An act requires affirmative conduct while an omission is the failure to act.[6] Though the rule raises interesting philosophical questions, an omission can also satisfy the legal requirement of causation.[7] This is so even though it is difficult to think of "doing nothing" as bringing about a result. In reality, an omission fails to interrupt other forces already at work and, as a consequence of the defendant's not intervening, a harm that was avoidable occurs.

6. David A. Fischer, Causation in Fact in Omission Cases, 1992 Utah L. Rev. 1335, 1339.

7. See Leavens, A Causation Approach to Criminal Omissions, 76 Cal. L. Rev. 547 (1988).

Concurrent Causation

Concurrent causation is the one situation when the cause in fact requirement does *not* have to be met. It occurs when *two* independent causes in fact occur at the same time, and *either* of them would have caused the result by itself.

If two gang members intentionally shoot a victim (*V*) at the same time with the intent to kill him and each of their bullets inflicts a mortal wound, *each* has been the cause of *V*'s death. This is true even though the victim would have died had either of the defendants not intentionally shot the victim. This is a case of concurrent causation: Each defendant's conduct is considered the "cause in fact" because both acted with the intention of killing the victim and the conduct of either would have been effective in bringing about the proscribed result. The criminal law does not excuse the intentionally harmful conduct of one actor just because another actor also caused the same harm.

People v. Arzon, 92 Misc. 2d 739, 401 N.Y.S.2d 156 (1978), is a close case of concurrent causation. Defendant (*D*) started a fire on the fifth floor of an abandoned building to keep warm. Firefighters responded to fight the fire. Meanwhile, another fire started independently by *B* on the second floor trapped the firefighters. Overcome by smoke from the first and second fires, *V*, a firefighter, sustained injuries from which he died. Has *D* caused the death of *V*? In all likelihood, *V* would not have died had someone else not set the second-story fire. Nonetheless, *D*'s fire satisfied the "but for" requirement. If *D* had not set the chain of events in motion, *V* would not have died. Moreover, the court could point to *D*'s conduct—starting the fire—as one component of the forces that caused the firefighter's death.

In *Quintanilla v. State*, 292 S.W.3d 230 (2009), Defendant (*D*) was driving while intoxicated. The car crashed into a ditch and ejected *D* and his passenger from the vehicle. The passenger was left in a vegetative state and eventually died. The death certificate stated that the immediate cause of death was a "right lung empyema due to a chronic vegetative state that was the result of a closed head injury."[8] *D* was charged and convicted of intoxication manslaughter. *D* appealed his conviction contending that the evidence was insufficient to sustain a guilty verdict because the prosecution had failed to prove that he had caused the deceased's death. *D* argued that there were concurrent causes of death: a lung infection and the family's decision to discontinue efforts to prolong the decedent's life. The court disagreed, stating that the fatal lung empyema was a sole result of *D*'s conduct. The right lung empyema was the immediate cause of death, however that condition was caused by a chronic vegetative state, which was due to a

8. *Quintanilla v. State*, 292 S.W.3d 230, 233 (Tex. App. 2009).

head injury obtained in the car crash. The court held that the lung empyema and the discontinuance of life support were not concurrent causes of death. But for D's conduct, the lung empyema would not have occurred and the decedent would never have been on life support.

Direct Cause

Direct causation occurs when the defendant's act is the only causal agent in bringing about the harm. Simply stated, there is no other causally connected act that could have caused the harm.

In most criminal law cases, the defendant's conduct *is* the only cause of harm and, therefore, is also the *direct cause* of the harm. No one else even partially helps produce the harm. In the case of our professional killer discussed earlier, the defendant's intentional act of shooting the victim in the head is the only act necessary to bring about death.

Direct causation always satisfies the requirement of proximate cause. The defendant is the sole causal agent, and she brought about the harm in precisely the manner intended or made likely, therefore she is criminally culpable.

Proximate Cause

Is the defendant criminally responsible when another actor or event (called an "intervening cause" since it generally occurs *after* the defendant has engaged in his conduct, but *before* the harm results) plays a causal role in bringing about the harm?

Proximate cause is the doctrine the criminal law generally uses to decide when the defendant *should* be held criminally responsible for causing harm even though an intervening cause helped bring about the harm. The actor's conduct must be related to the result in a sufficiently strong way in order to be held responsible. Proximate cause is satisfied if the intervening cause was (1) intended or reasonably foreseeable and (2) not too remote or accidental as to fairly hold the defendant responsible. "Foreseeability" does not require that the defendant subjectively knew the intervening cause could bring about the harm. It only requires that she *should* have known. There can be more than one proximate cause of a particular harm. (Note, however, that some jurisdictions require direct causation for criminal responsibility because proximate causation is considered too broad.)

Proximate cause questions cannot be answered solely by the physical sciences; thus, they are not "facts" that can be uncovered by scientifically examining cause and effect in the real world. Instead, their answers will depend to a large extent on public policy and the value judgments made by judges and juries about a defendant's moral culpability and their intuitive sense of justice in a particular case. To hold that an act proximately caused a harm is to say that it seems fair, or just, to hold the actor responsible for that harm. This sense of fairness in imposing accountability cannot be measured scientifically.[9]

Dependent Intervening Cause

A dependent intervening cause is one that was intended or reasonably foreseeable by the defendant, or sufficiently related to his conduct, to impose criminal responsibility for causing the harm. Characterizing the intervening cause as *dependent* results in a finding that the defendant *proximately caused* the harm. In more simple terms, the fact that another causal agent contributed to the result will not relieve the defendant of responsibility.

If a defendant forces a man into a car and states that she is going to kidnap him, and he subsequently leaps out of the moving car and seriously injures himself, his conduct will be considered a dependent intervening cause because human experience shows that victims will take serious risks in trying to escape from their captors. Thus, even though the man chose to leap out of the car, the defendant has proximately caused his injuries.

Independent Intervening Cause

Occasionally, however, another actor or event causes the harm in such an unexpected or unusual manner that the defendant will not be held criminally responsible for causing it. This is true even though the defendant's conduct set in motion the chain of events that produced the harm, thereby satisfying "but for" causation. An additional actor may remove the first actor from the result, weakening the chain of causation.

To find that the intervening cause is *independent*, the fact finder must conclude that (1) the harm was not intended by the defendant or was not reasonably foreseeable, or (2) that it is simply unfair and unjust to hold him responsible for the harm that has occurred. Put more simply, the direct cause of the harm was sufficiently fortuitous or coincidental in its occurrence and unconnected to the defendant's conduct so as to make it unjust to punish him for causing that harm.

A finding of *independent* intervening causation breaks the chain of events that the defendant started and results in a finding of no proximate cause. It thus prevents his being convicted of any crime that requires the prosecution

9. P. H. Robinson, S. Baradaran Baughman, & M. T. Cahill, Criminal Law: Case Studies and Controversies 304 (4th ed. 2017).

to prove the defendant *caused* the harm. (Note: Some courts and commentators as well as the Restatement of Torts call this *superseding causation.*)

Consider a case in which the defendant inflicts a minor wound on a victim, and afterwards the victim is driven by a friend to a doctor's office for some stitches. While sitting in a waiting room, a disgruntled patient enters the doctor's office and opens fire with a gun, killing the victim. The defendant's initial assault satisfies the "cause in fact" requirement. But for his conduct, the victim would not have been at the doctor's office at that particular moment. However, the killing by the former patient is really a coincidence; it is just bad luck that the assault victim became a murder victim. Even though the defendant initiated the sequence of events that eventually resulted in the homicide, the death was not foreseeable nor made more likely by the defendant's act. Thus, the disgruntled patient who fired the fatal shots would be considered an *independent intervening cause*, and the defendant would not be considered the "proximate cause" of death.

For a visual summary of proximate causation, see Table 7.1.

Judicial Rules of Thumb for Finding Dependent Intervening Causation

As noted at the outset, the definitions of proximate cause and intervening cause do not provide much help in analysis because they require both a factual inquiry and a moral judgment. As a result, courts often use rules of thumb to justify their conclusion that the defendant *should* be held liable in a particular case. There are some generalizations from the case law that may be useful.

Harm Intended or Risked Versus the Manner in Which It Occurs. If a defendant intended a particular harm or created a risk that a particular harm would occur but it occurs in a manner different than intended or expected, courts generally will find the intervening cause to be dependent, provided the specific causal mechanism was not entirely unexpected or coincidental. In such cases, when the court finds the interning cause to be dependent, the defendant will be held liable.

This principle is illustrated in *People v. Kibbe*, 35 N.Y.2d 407, 321 N.E.2d 773 (1974). Late in the evening, two defendants robbed a nearsighted and very intoxicated victim on a cold winter night in upstate New York where heavy snow had fallen. They left him without his glasses near the side of a road surrounded by steep snowbanks. The victim, unable to see clearly and somewhat immobile, sat down in the middle of the roadway. Soon a truck driver, who was speeding, struck and killed the victim. The defendants argued that they did not cause the victim's death. They claimed that either the victim—by putting himself in such obvious peril of being hit by

7.1 Proximate Causation

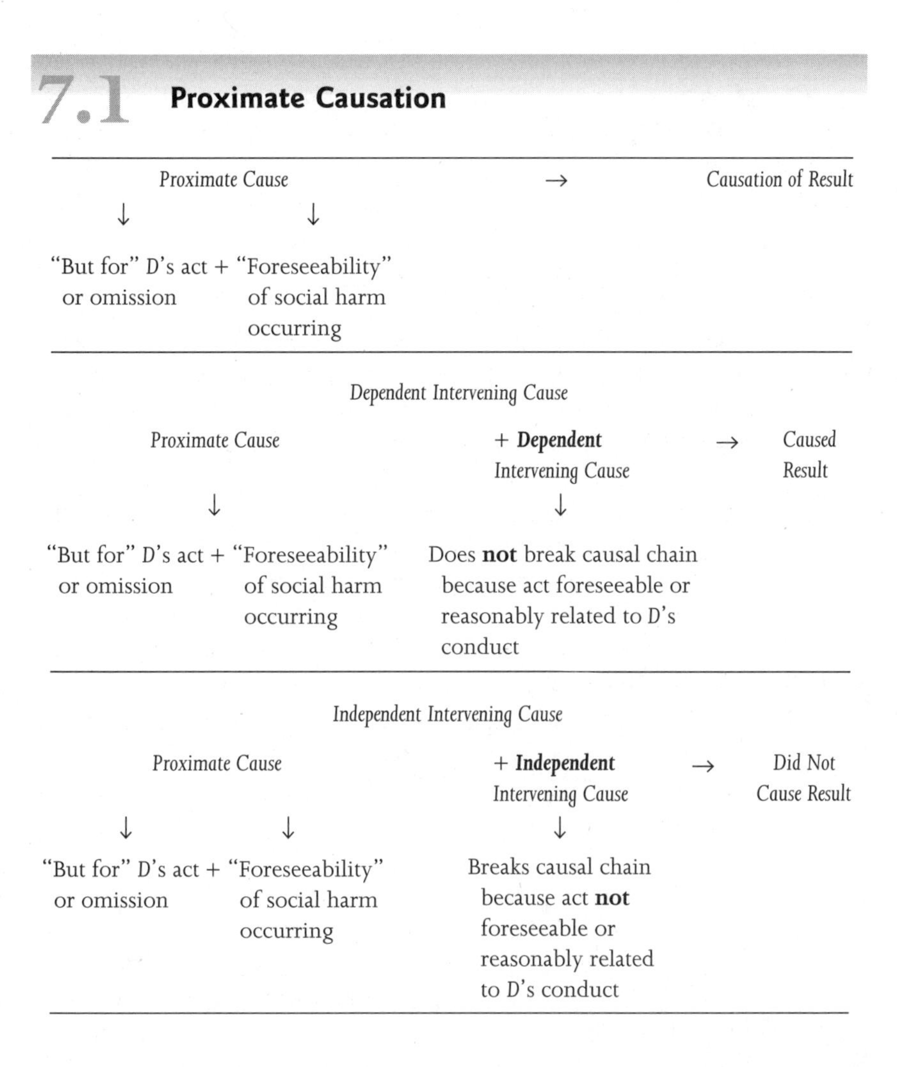

a vehicle—or the truck driver—who could not brake in time because he was speeding—was an *independent* supervening cause.

The New York Court of Appeals disagreed with the defendants. It concluded that the defendants, in committing armed robbery and leaving their intoxicated victim in these harsh and perilous conditions, could anticipate that he would seek help by moving onto the road, especially because he had trouble seeing and walking. Nor was it unusual for drivers to be driving over the speed limit at that hour.

In this case, defendants surely knew they created a strong possibility that the victim might die from exposure to the cold. They might even have anticipated his being struck by a vehicle while walking alongside the road. However, it is unlikely they anticipated, or should have anticipated, the particular manner in which the defendant was killed because most people, even if drunk and unable to see or walk well, do not sit in the middle of a highway. Though conceding that it was somewhat unusual for someone to sit down in the middle of the road, the court concluded that the victim's *death* was foreseeable, even though the *particular manner* in which it occurred may not have been. Only if the victim had died in a manner that was not related to what the defendants did—perhaps by having a meteor fall on him because *that* would be a matter of pure chance—would the court probably find an independent intervening cause.

Preexisting Conditions and Negligent Medical Treatment. Most jurisdictions will consider the victim's preexisting medical condition as a *dependent* intervening cause. Thus, in *People v. Stamp*, 2 Cal. App. 3d 203, 82 Cal. Rptr. 598 (1969), the court found the defendant had proximately caused the victim's death during the commission of an armed robbery when the 60-year-old victim, who was extremely overweight and had a history of heart disease, died during the robbery.[10]

Likewise, subsequent negligent medical treatment is usually considered a dependent intervening cause even though it contributes to the victim's death.[11] We expect medical care to be furnished to individuals who have been assaulted. Because medical aid is so likely and because the possibility of negligent medical aid is a fact of life, the criminal law considers this intervening cause *dependent*. It is foreseeable and sufficiently related to what the defendant did. Consequently, negligent medical care usually does not break the causal chain of events set in motion by the defendant, and proximate causation will be found.[12]

In *United States v. Rodriguez*, 754 F.3d 1122 (9th Cir. 2014), three defendants were charged with "knowingly and willfully conspir[ing] and agree[ing] with each other to murder" a fellow inmate.[13] The defendants stabbed an inmate, and the inmate was hospitalized. At the hospital, the medical staff allegedly removed the victim's breathing tube, but this evidence was omitted from trial. The defendants claimed that the improper removal of decedent's breathing tube during his hospitalization may have been the proximate cause of his death, not the stabbing. Therefore, it was inappropriate to omit the evidence. The court determined that medical treatment was a foreseeable response to defendants' conduct of stabbing the decedent; any error by the district court in excluding the evidence was harmless. Furthermore, the court explained that the defendants failed to show that there was medical

---

10. See also *State v. McKeiver*, 89 N.J. Super. 52, 213 A.2d 320 (1965); *Komlodi v. Picciano*, 217 N.J. 387, 89 A.3d 1234 (2014).
11. See, e.g., *Hall v. State*, 199 Ind. 592, 159 N.E. 420 (1928).
12. *United States v. Rodriguez*, 754 F.3d 1122 (9th Cir. 2014).
13. Id.

negligence and that the removal of the breathing tube was "so extraordinary that it would be unfair to hold [defendants] responsible."[14]

Foreseeable Human Action. Action taken in response to the danger created by the defendant is also considered foreseeable. Thus, persons in danger will try to escape and others will try to rescue them. The police will also try to apprehend criminals.

Defendants who create peril to human life should realize that their conduct elicits precisely this kind of human response. They should not be surprised if harm occurs as a result of what they did. Consequently, an actor will be held responsible even if another person, including the victim, a would-be rescuer, or a police officer, actually brings about the harm. Increasingly, courts are holding fleeing criminals responsible for the death of police officers giving chase even when the conduct of the pursuing police officer is itself extremely reckless and, therefore, arguably unexpected.[15]

Contributing Cause. Occasionally, a defendant will hasten the death of a victim who is already suffering from a mortal wound inflicted by another. Or the victim himself, suffering from a mortal wound, will hasten his own death by inflicting another mortal wound.[16] Most courts do not allow the individual who inflicted the initial mortal injury to avoid responsibility by claiming that the subsequent voluntary act of another human being was an intervening independent cause. They conclude instead that *both* acts (i.e., those of the initial actor and of the subsequent actor) caused the harm. This situation is often called a case of contributing causation because both acts are effective in bringing about the harm. It can also be considered a case of "concurrent causation." (See pages 167-168.)

Judicial Rules of Thumb for Finding Independent Intervening Causation

Not surprisingly, courts also use judicial rules of thumb to support their conclusion that the defendant *should not* be held responsible in a particular case.

Grossly Negligent or Reckless Medical Treatment. If a physician provides grossly negligent or reckless medical treatment, a finding of *independent* intervening causation is likely (but not inevitable),[17] cutting off the

14. *United States v. Rodriguez*, 754 F.3d 1122, 1133 (9th Cir. 2014) (citing *United States v. Pineda-Doval*, 614 F.3d 1019, 1034 (9th Cir. 2010).

15. See, e.g., *People v. Acosta*, 284 Cal. Rptr. 117 (1991).

16. See, e.g., *People v. Lewis*, 124 Cal. 551, 57 P. 470 (1889).

17. See, e.g., *State v. Shabazz*, 719 A.2d 40 (1998) (holding subsequent gross negligence of hospital treatment precludes criminal liability for actor who inflicted wounds that would have

defendant's responsibility for causing death.[18] The logic in such cases is that the defendant's conduct set in motion a chain of events that would normally not result in the victim's death. Death was actually caused by extremely poor medical treatment, which is a very unusual event. Consequently, the grossly negligent treatment, rather than the defendant's initial conduct, will be considered the cause of death.

Irresponsible Human Agent. As we will see in the discussion of accomplice liability in Chapter 14, the criminal law generally does not look beyond the last human actor for a causal explanation of events. Because every human being is presumed to have free will, the last actor is considered capable of deciding whether to engage in conduct intended to cause harm. Thus, in *People v. Kevorkian*[19], the Michigan Supreme Court concluded that Dr. Kevorkian, who gave the deceased his (in)famous "suicide machine" (a device that, when hooked up to a person, and activated by that person, released a lethal dose of chemicals into the individual's bloodstream), did not cause his death. Kevorkian simply furnished the means for causing death, but the deceased, as a responsible agent, then had to choose to commit the final, overt act that directly killed him. (Dr. Kevorkian was later convicted of other crimes.)

Suppose, however, that a defendant engages in conduct, such as continuous rape and other assaultive behavior, that renders another human being so distraught that she cannot make rational decisions; if she were to intentionally take poison that contributes to her death, the defendant may be held responsible for causing her death.[20] (This approach is very similar to how the law attributes the act of an innocent agent to the principal. See Chapter 14.)

In *Stephenson v. State*, 205 Ind. 141, 179 N.E. 633 (1932), the defendant held the victim prisoner against her will for several days and committed various sexual assaults on her. The victim consumed a poisonous substance in an attempt to commit suicide. Subsequently, she died from several causes, including the self-administered poison. The court held the defendant responsible for the victim's death, rejecting his argument that, in taking poison, the victim was an intervening independent cause. It concluded that the victim's becoming irresponsible was a "natural and probable result" of defendant's conduct.

---

caused death in the absence of medical treatment only when it was the *sole* cause of death; otherwise, the hospital's gross negligence is a contributing factor).

18. See, e.g., *Regina v. Cheshire*, 3 All E.R. 670 (1991).

19. *People v. Kevorkian*, 447 Mich. 436, 527 N.W.2d 714 (1994).

20. See, e.g., *People v. Roberts*, 2 Cal. 4th 271, 826 P.2d 274 (1992).

Unforeseeable Human Action. Courts will generally find intervening causation to be *independent* when a person subsequently acts in a very unusual or unlikely manner. A defendant who swindles retired people out of their life savings will probably not be found guilty of homicide if one of the victims, distraught by his financial losses, commits suicide. Based on human experience, the law will generally assume that most fraud victims, even though suffering severe financial and psychological harm, would not take their lives as a consequence of being so victimized.

Identifying the Specific Causal Mechanism. Some cases hold that the defendant cannot be held responsible for causing a harm if the specific causal mechanism cannot be identified. Thus, in *People v. Warner-Lambert*, 51 N.Y.2d 295, 414 N.E.2d 660 (1980), the defendant knowingly used two explosive ingredients in its manufacturing process and had been warned that high concentrations of these chemicals were creating dangerous conditions in its factory. Several employees were killed after an explosion occurred in the factory. The corporation and several of its officers and employees were convicted of second-degree manslaughter. The prosecution could prove that defendant had knowingly created the dangerous conditions. It could not establish the specific mechanism that triggered the explosion.

The court of appeals concluded that cause in fact ("but for" causation) was insufficient to hold the defendants responsible. Though this case seems wrongly decided, one can argue that, without knowledge of what exactly triggered the explosion, it is impossible to know if the manner in which the harm came about should have been within the defendant's contemplation. Thus, it is possible (though highly unlikely) that a burglar entered the factory late at night and deliberately sparked the explosion. Of course, it is more likely that the explosion occurred in precisely the way the defendants knew it might. The probability that one set of circumstances is more likely or probable is not enough to hold the defendants responsible.

The cases go both ways on this question. However, the prosecution's case is stronger if it can show the precise manner in which the harm occurred. This will then enable the fact finders to conclude that the defendant should have foreseen that this particular causal mechanism could occur.

Contributory Negligence and Proximate Causation

Conduct by a victim that would be considered contributory negligence in a tort case does not prevent a finding that the defendant was the proximate cause of the victim's death. Thus, if *A* engages in a high-speed drag race with B, who dies in a car crash during the race, *A* can be prosecuted for proximately causing B's death even though B's survivors could not successfully sue *A* in tort because B's own act of driving was contributory negligence.

The Model Penal Code

Responsibility for Causing Harm

The Model Penal Code dramatically revises the role of causation in assessing criminal responsibility. In effect, the MPC transforms much of the analysis of causation into an inquiry about the defendant's culpability.

"But For" Causation

To be held criminally responsible for causing a proscribed harm, the MPC requires the prosecution to establish "but for" causation (cause in fact under the common law approach) and any other specific causal requirement "imposed by the Code or the law defining the offense."[21]

Causation is established under the MPC if "but for" the actor's conduct, the result in question would not have occurred. Additional analysis, is required only when the result that occurs is different from the result intended or contemplated. Consequently, in most cases it is very easy for the prosecution to establish the causation necessary for criminal responsibility under the MPC.

The "but for" inquiry is essentially a hypothetical question asking what the result would have been had the actor not done the act. If the result would not have occurred, then the actor's conduct was necessary to the result and "but for" causation would apply. If the result would have occurred regardless of the actor's conduct, then the result would not be a "but for" cause.[22]

Other Causation, Concurrent Causation, and Transferred Intent

The MPC allows legislatures to impose traditional causal elements in a statute if they wish,[23] but it does not directly address "concurrent causation." Common law cases of "transferred intent" are treated by the MPC as cases of causation, requiring causation analysis; that is, did the defendant *cause*

---

21. MPC §2.03(1)(a) and (b). Section 1(a) and (b) provides:

> (1) Conduct is the cause of a result when: (a) it is an antecedent but for which the result in question would not have occurred; and (b) the relationship between the conduct and result satisfies any additional causal requirements imposed by the Code or by the law defining the defense.

22. P. H. Robinson, S. Baradaran Baughman, & M. T. Cahill, Criminal Law: Case Studies and Controversies 304 (4th ed. 2017).
23. MPC §2.03(1)(b). In most jurisdictions the "law defining the offense" will require "proximate causation."

the result? This question arises only if the result that occurs is *not* within the purpose or contemplation of the actor.

Culpability as to Result

The MPC focuses on the defendant's culpability toward the result.[24] It compares what *actually* happened with what the defendant *thought* or *should have thought* would happen. When results different from what the defendant intended, contemplated, or should have contemplated occur, subsections (2)(a) and (2)(b) (purposefully or knowingly) or (3)(a) or (3)(b) (recklessly or negligently) are applied, depending on the culpability required for conviction.

Section 2(a), Purposefully and Knowingly

If the actual result differs from what the actor purposed or knew would occur, then he is *not* responsible for the actual result unless (i) a *different person* or *property* was harmed, or (ii) the defendant actually caused a *lesser* harm than contemplated.[25] In either of these two situations, the defendant is responsible for the actual harm he causes.

The MPC approach in holding the defendant responsible for injuring a different person or property than he intended or contemplated is just like the common law's use of "transferred intent." If *D* shoots at *A* and hits *B*, then the MPC treats *D* as having caused *B*'s injury. Likewise, if *D* sets out to burn down *A*'s house by use of an incendiary device and instead only produces some charring of *B*'s house, then *D* has caused the harm to *B*'s house. (Note that the defendant must cause a harm equal to, or less than, the harm he intended or contemplated.)

Section 2(b)

Under this section, even though the same kind of injury occurred as the actor intended or contemplated, he will not be held responsible if unusual

24. To refresh your memory on culpability, see Chapter 4.

25. Section 2.03(2)(a) of the MPC is difficult to read. It provides in part that the actual harm or injury is not within the purpose or contemplation of the actor unless the "injury or harm designed or contemplated would have been *more serious* or *more extensive* than that caused." The effect of this language is to make the actor responsible for an injury or harm that he causes, provided it is *not* as serious or extensive as that he designed or contemplated. Put another way, the actor is not held responsible for causing a more serious injury than the one he intended or contemplated. To punish in such a situation would impose disproportionately more punishment than his culpability deserved.

and unexpected causal mechanisms actually caused the harm. Thus, the jury must decide whether the actual causal agent is "not too remote or accidental in its occurrence to have a just bearing" on the actor's liability or the severity of the offense.

The approach in subsection (b) lets the fact finder conclude that the mechanism that caused the harm is simply too coincidental or unexpected to impose liability. It is a very open-ended approach, inviting subjective judgments about moral culpability, chance, desert, and whatever else the fact finder considers relevant. Thus, if the victim in the *Kibbe* case discussed above was killed in a random drive-by shooting, a jury might conclude that the defendants should not be held responsible for causing the harm.

Recklessly or Negligently

Section 2.03(3) of the MPC uses the same approach here for these culpability requirements as described above for purposefully and knowingly in §2.03(2).

Again, the MPC compares the harm that actually occurred with the harm risked by the actor and asks the same questions. A person is responsible for the harm that actually occurs if the harm simply involves injury to a different person or property or was less serious than the harm risked. Likewise, if the harm that occurs is the same kind as the harm risked, the actor is responsible unless it is "too remote or accidental in its occurrence" to fairly blame the actor.

Strict Liability

Section 2.03(4) sets forth how causation is analyzed in a strict liability offense that contains a result element. The actual result must be a "probable consequence of the actor's conduct."

Examples

1. Sam, a drug dealer, uses a pharmaceutical drug to produce Drug X. Two teenagers purchase and consume Drug X. Both teenagers overdose on the drug and suffer from permanent brain damage. The parents of both teens sue the Manufacturing Company of the pharmaceutical drug claiming negligence. The plaintiffs argue that the Manufacturing Company should have foreseen that the pharmaceutical drug would be used by drug dealers to produce Drug X. The Manufacturing Company filed a Motion to Dismiss asserting that the plaintiffs cannot show that the Manufacturing Company's actions were the proximate cause of the injuries sustained by the teens. How would the court rule?

2a. Adrian, a mechanic, accidently spills gasoline on the shop floor and forgets to clean it up. Jaden, a customer, is walking by and throws his cigarette butt and it lands on the spilled gasoline. The gasoline catches fire causing burns to Jaden. Is the cigarette butt a dependent intervening cause or an independent intervening cause?

2b. Jaden is so frightened by the fire that he suffers a heart attack. Is the cigarette butt a dependent intervening cause or an independent intervening cause?

3. Roberta, angry at Raoul and wanting to kill him, pointed a loaded pistol at his head while Raoul was asleep and pulled the trigger. The gun discharged, killing Raoul. Did Roberta cause Raoul's death?

4. Charlie enters a hotel room to steal valuables left behind by the guests. Unfortunately, Edna is still in the room and sees Charlie. Charlie hits her over the head with a heavy object, intending to kill her because she could potentially identify him to police. Charlie leaves Edna lying in a pool of blood. A maid discovers Edna, who is then rushed to the hospital. Edna, still unconscious, is diagnosed as having suffered serious brain damage. Did Charlie cause Edna's death in the following examples?

4a. Dr. Able skillfully performs complicated and risky brain surgery, reasonably concluding that otherwise Edna will surely die within a few days. Despite the surgery, Edna dies from excessive bleeding resulting from the surgery.

4b. Edna would have survived if Dr. Inept had not provided negligent medical treatment.

4c. Edna would have survived if Dr. Hopeless had not provided grossly negligent medical treatment.

5. While driving along the highway with Tara in the passenger seat, Jennifer spotted Bob, her fiancé, several car lengths ahead of her. She sped up to wave at him. Bob, recognizing Jennifer in the car behind him, waited until she almost caught up to him and then sped away. Jennifer then increased her speed so she could catch up to Bob once more. Again, Bob, laughing, waited until Jennifer almost caught up and then increased his speed even more. This game of "cat and mouse" continued until suddenly Jennifer, traveling well above the speed limit, lost control and hit a tree. Tara died instantly. Jennifer and Bob are both charged with homicide. Did Bob cause Tara's death?

6. Jason and Keefer agree to race their cars on a winding public street. Jason drives a BMW, which is extremely fast. Keefer drives a Honda,

which has more agility but is slower. Without Jason's knowledge, Keefer adds a nitrous oxide system ("NOS," in professional racing circles) to his engine to boost its power and speed if necessary. (NOS allows the driver to inject gases into his engine that alter combustion and dramatically increase power and speed.) During the race, Keefer, aware that he is losing, decides to use his NOS and presses the activating button. Unfortunately, the NOS explodes, killing Keefer. Moreover, shrapnel from his car flies through the air and kills Ashley, who is walking on a nearby sidewalk. Did Jason cause the death of either Keefer or Ashley?

7. The U.S. Army charged eight soldiers, including a platoon leader, with manslaughter and involuntary manslaughter after Daniel, a 19-year-old soldier of Chinese descent, killed himself while on solitary guard duty in Afghanistan.[26] The soldiers had bullied Daniel mercilessly, including—among other abusive acts—dragging him across a floor while pelting him with rocks, forcing him to hang upside down with water in his mouth, and taunting him with ethnic slurs. Can the soldiers be convicted of homicide?

8. Luke, drunk as a skunk, crossed over into the oncoming traffic lane, slamming his macho SUV into a car driven by Rebecca, who suffered devastating injuries, including a spinal column fracture that caused paralysis from the chest down, broken ribs and hip, brain damage, and recurring infections. Unable to breathe on her own, Rebecca was placed on life-support systems in a hospital for several weeks. Before the accident, Rebecca had made it clear that she did not want to live on life support, and during lucid moments after the accident, she made it apparent that she did not want to live in this condition. Rebecca requested that she be removed from life support. Her request was honored and she died shortly thereafter. Did Luke cause Rebecca's death?

9. Finally ending a series of random sniper killings, the police arrested Allen and Boyd and charged them both with capital murder for the "willful, deliberate, and premeditated killing of a person by the use of a firearm." The police seized a .22 caliber Bushmaster rifle and scope from their car. Ballistics matched the gun to the bullets recovered from the first victim, Calvin. Fingerprints from both Allen and Boyd were found on the trigger. The prosecutor is unable to prove which of the two suspects actually pulled the trigger and killed Calvin. Only the *shooter* can be sentenced to death under the statute. Can the prosecutor obtain a death sentence for Allen and Boyd?

---

26. N.Y. Times, Dec. 22, 2011 at A-6.

10. Martin was desperate for money. One night he deliberately set fire to a large, abandoned warehouse he owned in order to collect the fire insurance. The fire department responded and started to fight the fire.

    Sven, a firefighter, wearing a breathing apparatus with a 30-minute tank of oxygen, entered the burning building without a buddy. When the alarm signaled that Sven had only five minutes of oxygen left in his tank, Sven disregarded it and stayed to fight the fire. Almost five minutes later, Sven died from suffocation. Fighting a fire "solo" (without a buddy) and failing to immediately leave a fire when the warning signal sounds on the oxygen tank are both serious violations of department regulations. Should the judge instruct the jury that Martin could not have caused Sven's death?

11. Nyguen walked into the bank, pulled a gun, and told the teller to put money in a bank bag. Betty did this while triggering a silent alarm. Seeing a police car pull up in front of the bank, Nyguen grabbed Betty by the arm, pointed his gun at her head, and used her as a shield while leaving the bank from a rear exit. A police sharpshooter, stationed in the alley, saw Nyguen leaving the bank with Betty in front of him and his gun pointed at her head. Taking very careful aim at Nyguen, the sharpshooter waited for a clear shot and fired. Unfortunately, Nyguen turned at the same moment. The bullet struck and killed Betty instantly. Is there a viable theory that the prosecutor can use to hold Nyguen responsible for Betty's death?

12a. Hal, tired of living, jumped off the top of a 15-story office building. Just as Hal was passing by the twelfth floor, Julia, angry that her boyfriend, Chet, was leaving her, fired a pistol at him intending to kill Chet. Fortunately, Chet moved and the bullet missed him. Unfortunately, it went through the window of the twelfth-floor apartment, killing Hal instantly in mid-flight. The prosecutor has filed a murder charge against Julia. Is she guilty?

12b. What if Cindy had pushed Hal off the building, intending to kill him, after he told her their relationship was over? Who killed Hal? Cindy? Julia?

13. Kyra, a high-ranking police detective, arrests Wayne, a gang member, in his neighborhood where a fatal armed robbery recently occurred in a grocery store and brings him to the police station. She grants him immunity from the use of any confession. Wayne then admits to needlessly killing two beloved members of the neighborhood who owned the store during the robbery. He also identified two other gang members who participated in the robbery. Kyra cannot use his statement as evidence against Wayne. But, knowing that word of his confession implicating other gang members has spread in his neighborhood, she drives Wayne in her marked police car to the corner where the killing took place, and,

over his strenuous objection that his life is in danger, tells him to get out. Thirty minutes later, Wayne is killed by his fellow gang members.

Can Kyra be charged with homicide?

14. Ian was jealous of his coworker Craig, who had been promoted over Ian by Otto, their boss. Otto was obsessively possessive and jealous of his wife, Mona. Ian knew that Otto had a reputation for violent outbreaks when he suspected his wife of cheating. He also knew that Otto had been convicted several times for beating Mona for alleged flirting and for assaulting the men he erroneously believed were involved with Mona. Hoping that Otto would kill Craig, Ian sent an anonymous e-mail message to Otto telling him that Mona was having an affair with Craig. Ian made up scandalous details to make Otto furious. Otto flew into a rage and wanted revenge.[27]
    a. Otto went straight to Craig's office and shot him dead.
    b. When Otto got home, he shot and killed Mona in a rage of jealousy before she could deny the accusations.
    c. When Otto found out that Mona in fact had not had an affair with Craig, Otto was devastated and killed himself.

15. Vic was diagnosed with lung cancer at age 50. He underwent chemotherapy treatment, and his cancer went into remission. Two years later, his oncologist discovered that the cancer was back. Vic began the same chemotherapy, taking daily intravenous doses of the drug, Taxol. Vic died four months later from this cancer, which never remitted. Vic's oncologist was stunned because he was very confident that Taxol would cause Vic's cancer to remit again. He filed a report with the FDA expressing suspicion about the drug's potency. The FDA investigated Vic's pharmacist, Richard Courtney, and discovered that he had drastically diluted Vic's Taxol. An expert oncologist concluded that (a) Taxol was prescribed to Vic at a high potency and should have checked his cancer; (b) Vic's chance of remission was moderate without chemotherapy and increased significantly with the use of Taxol at the prescribed dosage; and (c) had Vic been injecting the prescribed dosage of Taxol, he probably would have lived at least several more years.

    Courtney admitted that he understood the dosage of Taxol prescribed and intentionally had significantly diluted every dosage of Vic's Taxol. Can Courtney be charged with murder?

16. Joe Camel, president of Federated Tobacco, recently testified before a congressional committee that cigarette smoking is not addictive and that there is no evidence scientifically establishing that smoking causes cancer.

27. The Riverside Shakespeare, *The Tragedy of Othello, the Moor of Venice* 1198-1248 (G. Blakemore Evans ed., 1974).

Rusty Lunchpail, a lifelong smoker of cigarettes made by Federated, died recently of lung cancer. On his deathbed Rusty swore in a videotaped deposition that he knew cigarette smoking was harmful to his health, but that he could not break the habit.

Billy Jackson, a crusading prosecutor from Mississippi, has indicted Federated and Joe Camel, as its president, for murder in connection with the death of Rusty Lunchpail. Billy can prove that the United States Surgeon General has publicly warned that smoking cigarettes is harmful to human health and that nicotine, a primary ingredient in cigarette tobacco, does create a physiological craving for its continued consumption. He also has a witness who will testify that Federated carefully monitored the amount of nicotine in its cigarettes and always blended in sufficient amounts of nicotine-rich tobacco to ensure that its cigarettes contained at least a specified amount of nicotine. Finally, he can prove that Joe Camel knew nicotine was addictive.

17a. Justin unlawfully sold Erica a new prescription drug patch containing fentanyl, a pain-killing drug more powerful than morphine. The patch releases the drug over a three-day period and was intended for use only by cancer patients and others with serious chronic pain. Justin showed Erica how she could bite down on the patch and release the entire drug dosage instantly. Erica took the patch home, bit down on it, and died. Did Justin cause Erica's death?

17b. Justin unlawfully sold Aaron, who he knew was addicted to pain-killing drugs, the same patch and also showed him how to release the entire dosage with one bite. Aaron took the patch home, bit down on it, and died. Did Justin cause Aaron's death?

18. Roberta, angry at Raoul and wanting to kill him, pointed a loaded pistol at his head while Raoul was asleep and pulled the trigger. The gun jams and does not fire. Raoul wakes up and grabs the gun from Roberta before she can pull the trigger again. What would be the result?

Explanations

1. The court would likely grant the Motion to Dismiss. The parents are not able to show that the Manufacturing Company's actions were the proximate cause of the plaintiffs' injuries. The sole or supervening cause of the injuries to the teens was a criminal act committed by the drug dealer. The Manufacturing Company had no duty to anticipate or prevent the criminal actions.

2a. Adrian may argue that the lit cigarette was the intervening cause that broke the chain of events between Adrian spilling the gasoline and Jaden's burns. However, Jaden may argue that it would be foreseeable that such a flammable liquid would catch on fire in a mechanic shop, and he received no warning, and therefore the cigarette butt is not an independent intervening cause.

2b. Adrian may be held liable for Jaden suffering a heart attack. Most jurisdictions consider the victim's preexisting medical conditions as a dependent intervening cause therefore holding the defendant liable for any resulting injuries. However, the lit cigarette could be seen as an independent intervening cause because Adrian could not have foreseen that the spilled gasoline would result in someone having a heart attack.

3. In firing a loaded pistol at the head of another human being, Roberta intended to cause a particular result, Raoul's death. In a homicide prosecution the prosecutor should easily establish causation as required by the law. Roberta's conduct was the cause in fact and direct cause of Raoul's death. The very same harm she intended to bring about occurred in exactly the manner Roberta intended.

4a. Under the common law, Charlie's conduct satisfies both cause in fact and proximate cause. Hitting Edna with a heavy object satisfies cause in fact; but for this conduct, Edna would be alive. It was also foreseeable that Edna's death was a natural and probable result of Charlie's conduct.

    True, Edna died as a direct result of Dr. Able's skillful and high-risk surgery. However, only such surgery might interrupt the fatal causal forces that Charlie had previously set in motion. Thus, such invasive medical treatment was a likely and natural result of the chain of events put in motion by Charlie. The surgery will therefore be considered a dependent intervening cause, and Charlie will be held responsible for proximately causing Edna's death.

    The MPC would also find Charlie responsible. The actual result, Edna's death, is the same as that intended or contemplated. Although the operation was the immediate and direct cause of Edna's death, it is highly likely that medical professionals will undertake high-risk surgery to avoid the harm Charlie's actions will otherwise cause. Thus, the surgery is not too remote or accidental to have a just bearing on Charlie's guilt.

4b. Charlie's conduct satisfies "but for" causation. Edna's injury and subsequent medical treatment would not have occurred unless Charlie had struck her. However, there is an intervening cause—the negligent treatment provided by Dr. Inept.

    In most jurisdictions negligent medical treatment is considered foreseeable and the natural and probable result of the actor's harmful conduct. Thus, it is a *dependent* intervening cause that does *not* defeat a finding of proximate cause. Charlie would be found to have caused

Edna's death in most jurisdictions and could be convicted of a homicide charge.

The outcome under the MPC is not clear. Charlie's conduct satisfies its "but for" causation requirement. The jury would then have to decide whether the actual mechanism of death, Dr. Inept's negligent medical care, was "too remote or accidental" to convict Charlie.

4c. The initial analysis here is the same as in Example 4b. *Grossly negligent* medical treatment is generally not considered foreseeable or the natural and probable result of the defendant's conduct. Such a deviation from the standard of medical competency is unusual as a matter of human experience. Thus, it is an *independent* intervening cause that precludes a finding of proximate causation for Charlie.

Under the MPC, there is a strong case for concluding that the grossly negligent medical treatment provided by Dr. Hopeless is too remote or accidental to fairly hold Charlie responsible. This will be a value judgment that the fact finder will have to make.

5. At common law, Jennifer is both the cause in fact and the proximate cause of Tara's death. Jennifer can easily be convicted of vehicular homicide.

The MPC would reach the same conclusion. Jennifer's driving is the "but for" cause of Tara's death. The analysis then turns to the culpability required under the relevant statute. Most vehicular homicide statutes require recklessness. The prosecutor should be able to prove that, while driving the car, Jennifer acted with conscious disregard toward a substantial and unjustifiable risk of a fatal car accident. Moreover, the victim was the very same person whom she put at risk and the actual result, Tara's death, was the very same risk that she contemplated.

Bob, by initiating and continuing to play car tag, satisfies the common law's cause in fact requirement. He might argue that Jennifer's driving is the only cause in fact; had she not driven recklessly, the accident would not have happened. Nonetheless, his conduct will probably be found also to have been a proximate cause of Tara's death. (Remember that there can be more than one proximate cause.) Thus, *both* Jennifer and Bob have legally caused Tara's death.

Jennifer's response to Bob's game of car tag is foreseeable because Bob knew she would continue to speed to catch him. Thus, it was foreseeable that either he or Jennifer might lose control of their respective vehicles and cause someone's death. Note that the foreseeability analysis here does not depend on what Bob subjectively expected or contemplated. Rather, it depends on what human experience indicates can happen. At common law, proximate causation is not dependent on the actor's subjective awareness of risk or probable consequences.

Under the MPC, Bob's driving satisfies the "but for" requirement of §2.03(1)(a). The analysis then focuses on the culpability required in the relevant statute. The prosecutor could establish that Bob acted with conscious disregard toward a substantial and unjustifiable risk that either he or Jennifer might lose control of their respective cars, resulting in a fatal accident. The actual outcome is the same as the contemplated outcome, and the result is not "too remote or accidental" as to justly blame Bob.

6. If the jurisdiction requires *direct* causation, then Jason clearly did not cause Keefer to install the NOS nor to use it; thus he was not the direct cause of either Keefer's or Ashley's death. Keefer's installation and use of the NOS was a but for cause (or "cause in fact") of both deaths, and the resulting explosion was the "direct" cause. Only Keefer's conduct brought about these results.

   If the jurisdiction requires only *proximate* causation, the prosecutor must prove that the defendant's conduct was a "but for" cause and that the harm was "foreseeable." Had Jason refused to compete, Keefer and Ashley would still be alive. His conduct probably satisfies "but for" causation. Were their deaths foreseeable?

   The prosecutor would argue that death during a drag race is known to happen, including deaths caused by unusual mechanisms. Moreover, installation of a volatile NOS is not uncommon in racing circles. Thus, he would maintain that its installation and explosion were foreseeable.

   The defense might agree that drag racing contestants are generally held responsible for actions of their competitors that *typically* occur during such heated and risky competitions, such as speeding, and passing in prohibited zones. However, it would claim that there was no reason to expect that a competitor's secretly installing a volatile NOS system is typical or even remotely expected in these already dangerous activities. Consequently, both Keefer's and Ashley's deaths occurred in a very unusual manner and through a bizarre causal mechanism and were not foreseeable.

   Ultimately, this is a jury question. Again, note that "foreseeability" does not require Jason to be aware of the NOS; rather, the question is whether there is some reasonable possibility that competitors might use this type of system.

   Under the MPC, Jason is a "but for" cause of these deaths. His conduct was necessary for these deaths to have occurred. Although the same kind of injury occurred as the actor contemplated (death of a competitor and a bystander), the causal mechanism may be "too remote or accidental" to "have a just bearing" on Jason's liability. If so, then Jason has not caused these deaths. The jury must decide this question. Would you convict Jason?

7. A significant issue is whether the defendants *caused* Daniel's death. The prosecutor may have at least two theories available to prove causation. She would concede that Daniel, by discharging a loaded weapon into his head, was the direct cause (cause in fact) of his own death. However, she would argue that, if direct causation is required, the defendants' conduct had done so much physical and psychological harm to Daniel that he had become an "irresponsible" human agent, no longer rational and able to see a way out of his unbearable situation. Thus, defendants are the last responsible actors in this sad case and become the direct cause of Daniel's death by rendering him incapable of free will, including rational decisionmaking.

   If she must prove proximate causation, the prosecutor would probably have a somewhat easier road to conviction. She would argue that suicide was a reasonably foreseeable outcome of such intensive bullying over an extended period of time, especially when it occurs in a war zone and breaks the bond of brotherhood crucial to soldiers' survival on the battlefield. Even his platoon leader did nothing to prevent this hazing. No wonder Daniel concluded that going through the chain of command would not end his ordeal. Thus, Daniel's self-destructive act cannot be considered an independent intervening cause because his death in this manner was foreseeable. Note that the prosecutor does not have to prove that the defendants *actually* foresaw this outcome; she must only persuade the jury they *should* have. This issue is a mixed judgment of fact and values for the military jury based on their assessment of the defendants' moral culpability and their intuitive sense of justice in this case.

   Under the MPC, the prosecutor would only have to establish "but for" causation; this terrible death would not have occurred if the defendants had not engaged in such brazen and terrible acts of human degradation. Can she prove this? Soldiers in combat have been known to commit suicide. Can the prosecutor persuasively claim that Daniel would not have killed himself if the defendants had not bullied him? On the other hand, this type of violence against fellow soldiers is very unusual. If she can establish "but for" causation, the issue for the jury then becomes one of culpability. In this case, were the defendants either reckless or negligent as to the result of death? The prosecution would argue that though the defendants did not intend Daniel to kill himself, they surely were aware he might, or at the very least, should have been aware he might. Thus, Daniel's taking his own life was not too remote or accidental to have a just bearing on the defendants' liability. Again, this would be a judgment call for the jury. (See pages 209 and 214 in Chapter 8.)

   The defense will argue that Daniel took his own life and all responsibility for homicide stops with the last responsible human agent. Though defendants' conduct is reprehensible and worthy of punishment for less serious crimes like assault, Daniel had free will and could have—and should have—taken less extreme measures to stop the bullying. He could have reported the hazing to officers higher up the chain of command than platoon leader, spoken with the chaplain, or taken other steps that virtually every other soldier would take. Thus, the prosecutor cannot prove direct causation in this case, and homicide of any degree cannot be established. Neither can the prosecution establish proximate causation here. The defense would argue that neither the defendants nor other soldiers would expect a combat soldier would kill himself simply because he was subjected to harsh hazing or racial slurs. Hazing occurs with some frequency on the battlefield and victims do not take their own lives. This proves that the result here—the unfortunate death of a soldier—was too remote or accidental to be reasonably related to their behavior. Thus, under either common law or the MPC, the defendants cannot be convicted of homicide.

If you were the prosecutor, would you charge the defendants with homicide? Would you vote to convict as a juror?

8. Luke is clearly the "but for" cause of Rebecca's death. Had he not driven while intoxicated and recklessly crossed into her lane, she would not have been severely injured and required life support. Thus, his conduct started a chain of causality that resulted in Rebecca's death. But should her removal from life support be characterized as a *dependent* or *independent* intervening cause of her death?

   Under the common law, the defense will argue that removing life support caused Rebecca's death and that removal was so unexpected and out of the ordinary in relation to Luke's conduct that it was an independent intervening cause. Moreover, the defense will point out that Rebecca was a competent and responsible decision maker who, in effect, ended her own life. In a MPC jurisdiction, the defense will claim that Rebecca's death was too dependent on another's volitional act, that is, Rebecca's own decision to discontinue life support, to have a "just bearing" on Luke's liability.

   The prosecutor will respond that this jurisdiction recognizes an individual's right to refuse medical treatment and, consequently, Rebecca's decision cannot be considered unexpected or extraordinary. Physicians had no duty or right to continue life support in this case. Thus, stopping life support was clearly foreseeable. Moreover, Luke's conduct generated the need for life support in the first place, so its removal is not the cause of Rebecca's death. It simply allowed fatal forces already at work to continue. The prosecutor will argue that removing Rebecca from life support was a dependent intervening cause that does not break the causal chain or responsibility.

These are difficult value judgments for juries to make. How would you vote?

9. To obtain a death sentence under this statute, the prosecutor must prove that the defendant *personally* and *directly* caused Calvin's death. It should be easy to prove that the shooter caused Calvin's death and that either Allen or Boyd was the shooter. Calvin died from gunshot wounds. The bullets taken from his wounds were fired from the rifle found in the possession of Allen and Boyd. Fingerprints from both Allen and Boyd were on the rifle and its trigger. Either Allen or Boyd shot Calvin, and therefore one of them is guilty of capital murder.

   But can the prosecution prove beyond a reasonable doubt that either Allen or Boyd was the shooter? Though theoretically both could have pulled the trigger at the same time, this is highly unlikely given the need to aim and fire carefully. Since Allen's fingerprints are on the trigger, there is reasonable doubt that Boyd shot Calvin. Likewise, since Boyd's fingerprints are also on the trigger, there is reasonable doubt that Allen shot him. Without other evidence, like a confession or an eyewitness, establishing who actually fired the shot that killed Calvin, it is unlikely that the prosecutor can prove who killed him. Both Allen and Boyd can be convicted of murder as accomplices or as co-conspirators, but neither will be sentenced to death.

10. In charging Martin with felony murder (see Chapter 8), the prosecutor will argue that an arsonist creates a risk that a firefighter may die fighting the fire. Thus, this particular harm is, or should be, within Martin's contemplation and occurred during the course of the victim doing his job. Martin's setting the fire was the proximate cause of Sven's death.

    Martin will respond that he did not proximately cause Sven's death. Sven should be considered an independent intervening cause of his own death because Sven would not have died if he had complied with the department's regulations. By disregarding two separate regulations, Sven acted negligently, or even with gross negligence, and such negligence by a professional firefighter is simply not foreseeable.

    The court will probably conclude that an arsonist has no right to expect that a fire will be fought carefully, and that any negligence by a firefighter that contributes to his death does not preclude a finding of proximate causation.

    Under the MPC, Martin's conduct satisfies cause in fact. Though the MPC does not provide for felony murder, in analyzing causation the Code asks whether the causal agency for this harm is "too remote or accidental" in its occurrence to have a "just bearing" on Martin's responsibility. A jury could go either way in this case. It might find no causation here if it concluded that Sven acted in a very unprofessional and reckless manner. Or, angered by the death of a public servant in the course of his duties, the jury might want to blame Martin and, in order to achieve this goal, find that Martin did cause Sven's death and thus convict him of some form of homicide. Ultimately, causation in this case is a value judgment to be determined by the fact finder.

11. Nyguen would not be liable under a felony murder theory in most jurisdictions because neither he nor another co-felon killed an innocent person during the commission of a felony. (See Chapter 8.) Causation theory, however, would allow a conviction of Nyguen for proximately causing the death of Betty even though she was killed by a police officer trying to rescue her.

    By using Betty as a human shield, Nyguen satisfies cause in fact; but for his act, she would not have been killed. Moreover, by using her as a shield, Nyguen placed Betty in harm's way. It was foreseeable that a police officer would try to rescue her from this dangerous situation by using deadly force against Nyguen. By keeping Betty so close to him while threatening her with imminent death, Nyguen started a chain of events, the natural and probable consequence of which was her accidental death.

    This example demonstrates how conduct that manifests extreme indifference to the value of human life that proximately causes the death of either a felon or an innocent person can generate responsibility for homicide. For a good example of this approach, see *Taylor v. Superior Court*, 3 Cal. 3d 578, 477 P.2d 131 (1970).

    Under MPC §210.2(1)(b), the prosecutor could argue that, in using Betty as a shield, Nyguen committed murder "recklessly under circumstances manifesting extreme indifference to the value of human life." To satisfy causation, she would prove that Nyguen's act was the "but for" cause of Betty's death and that, because the police often use deadly force to rescue hostages, the result was contemplated by Nyguen. Note that the MPC requires the prosecutor to prove culpability with respect to result in this example.

12a. Hal would have died in a few seconds, and he certainly would have been the direct cause of his own death in that event. Nonetheless, Julia has *directly* caused Hal's death because it was her shot that actually ended his life. Thus, under the common law, her intent to kill Chet is "transferred" to Hal (see Chapter 4) and she can be convicted of intentional homicide. Even though the chance of Julia's shot hitting anyone else (let alone *killing* anyone else) other than Chet was a million in one, her actions satisfy the common law's causation requirement.

    Under the MPC, a jury could conclude that Julia has caused Hal's death because her errant shot caused the death of a "different" person than she intended. Because Julia has brought about a harm *equal to* the one she intended (the death of a human being), conviction and punishment would not be disproportionate to the harm she intended to cause. However, the MPC would also allow the jury to conclude that she did not cause Hal's death. The jury might decide that the causal mechanism of his death (Julia's shooting at Chet and killing Hal) was "too remote or accidental" to have a "just bearing" on her liability. What are the odds of anyone dying in this manner? And yet, Julia surely intended to kill someone. Should attitude or harm be more important? How would you vote as a juror?

12b. Cindy would argue that Julia is the "direct" cause of Hal's death. Furthermore, she would argue that the manner in which Hal died was absolutely unforeseeable and accidental. Thus, Julia was the *independent* intervening cause and Cindy can only be convicted of attempted murder.

The prosecutor would argue that this is a case of *concurrent* causation and that both Cindy and Julia caused Hal's death. He will argue that either Cindy's or Julia's conduct would have caused Hal's death and that Julia's conduct merely hastened an inevitable result set in motion by Cindy. Thus, this must be a case of two *independent* causal agents who must bear joint responsibility for causing Hal's death. The prosecutor probably has the better argument. Cindy intended to cause Hal's death. She should not escape responsibility simply because the particular harm she intended came about in such a bizarre and unexpected manner. But, it is a close call!

Under the MPC, Cindy is a "but-for" cause of Hal's death; Hal would not have been in Julia's line of fire had Cindy not pushed him off the building. But was Julia's errant shot "too remote or accidental in its occurrence to have a just bearing" on Cindy's responsibility? One suspects that a jury would not let Cindy, the primary actor who set out to kill Hal, off the hook just because Julia was trying to kill someone else and did the job for her.

13. Clearly, Kyra did not directly kill Wayne—gang members did. Thus, she cannot be convicted of homicide unless proximately causing his death is sufficient in this jurisdiction and the prosecutor can establish it. The prosecutor has at least two theories of responsibility. She would first argue that Kyra proximately caused Wayne's death by deliberately putting him "in harm's way," thereby satisfying the requirement of "but for" causation. Kyra knew that word of his confession had already spread in this neighborhood and that gang members would try to silence Wayne. In addition, Wayne had pleaded with her not to release him publicly in his neighborhood precisely because he knew his life was in danger. Thus, Kyra was subjectively aware that this particular harm, Wayne's death, was very likely to occur and she knew how it would most likely occur—gang members would shoot him. Moreover, as a

police officer, Kyra had a duty to prevent Wayne's death and failed to take reasonable steps to prevent this terrible harm. At the very least, she should have released him in a safer location and, even better, given him police protection. Her omission or failure to act together with her duty to prevent this harm is an independent ground for finding proximate causation here.

Defense counsel would claim that Kyra acted professionally in obtaining useful information implicating other gang members from Wayne. Kyra only knew that information about her grant of immunity to Wayne and his subsequent confession implicating other gang members had reached some members of Wayne's community. She could not know or expect, nor should she have known or realized, that other gang members would actually kill Wayne. And even if she did, counsel would argue that Kyra was not a "but for" cause of Wayne's death. Wayne's killers might well have shot and killed him regardless of what Kyra did or didn't do. Thus, his death cannot be linked to Kyra's conduct, which is neither a necessary nor sufficient condition for the occurrence of this particular harm. Moreover, Kyra was only obligated to return Wayne back to where she initially arrested him. The police department would be available to protect Wayne on the same basis as it protects everyone living in this neighborhood. Wayne is not entitled to special protection. Thus, the prosecutor's alternative theory—omission and duty—though clever, does not apply because Kyra satisfied any duty applicable to police officers. And even if she did not, her omission was not a "but for" cause of Wayne's death.

Under the MPC, the prosecutor would have to prove "but for" causation and then proceed to establish the culpability required by the homicide statute. As noted above, it may be difficult for the prosecution to establish that Kyra's conduct was required before Wayne could be killed. If she is successful in establishing "but for" causation, however, it might be easier to establish criminal culpability (rather than foreseeability) with respect to result here. After all, Kyra knew or should have known that she was risking Wayne's life by returning him to his neighborhood under these circumstances.

On balance, it will be very difficult for the prosecution to prove "but for" causation, which is required in establishing criminal causation. Thus, Kyra would probably be acquitted even though she may well have expected this result. The prosecutor might use an alternative theory—accomplice liability—if she could prove that Kyra acted with the *purpose* of aiding and abetting Wayne's unknown killers. (See Chapter 14 and *State ex rel Attorney General v. Tally*, at page 435.)

This is a real brain teaser. In all likelihood, Kyra knew that she was creating a greater risk and probability that Wayne would die, but her conduct was not essential for the harm to occur. Should this relieve her of criminal responsibility?

14a. *The Death of Craig.* Ian acted with premeditated intent to cause Craig's death. This satisfies the mens rea requirement for first-degree homicide. But did Ian *cause* Craig's death? Otto—not Ian—shot and killed Craig. Under the common law, Otto is the "cause in fact" (direct cause) of Craig's death. Should the law look beyond the last human actor and moral agent to establish causation?

The prosecution will argue in the affirmative, claiming that Ian proximately caused Craig's death. Ian's conduct satisfies both requirements of proximate cause: but for causation and foreseeability. Otto would not have killed Craig unless Ian had sent the e-mail that incited Otto's predictable rage and violence. The prosecutor will insist that Otto's killing of Craig was the "natural and probable consequence" of Ian's conduct. Because Otto's jealous rage and violence were foreseeable, his shooting Craig does not break the chain of causal connection between Ian's e-mail and the subsequent harm. Thus, Otto's conduct was a dependent intervening factor because it was expected and integral to bringing about Craig's death. Ian preyed on Otto's insecurity, jealousy, and fury with the actual purpose of causing Otto to kill Craig; logically, he should not now claim that Otto's actions were unforeseeable.

The defense will claim that jealousy and anger do not preclude moral choice and intentional conduct. Thus, the law cannot look beyond Otto as the legally relevant cause of Craig's death. Thus, Otto is an independent intervening cause of Craig's death.

Under MPC analysis, Ian may also have caused Craig's death. Under §2.03, Ian satisfies the "but for" requirement of §2.03(1)(a). Under §2.03(2)(a), the result that occurred is precisely the same result as that purposed by Ian. Thus, Ian has caused the result—Craig's death.

If Ian is found to have proximately caused Craig's death, the defense might argue that Otto acted in the heat of passion and can be convicted only of manslaughter. Ian would then claim that accomplice liability limits his responsibility to the same crime committed by Otto, his principal. Depending on the law of complicity in this jurisdiction, this argument might succeed.[28] As a matter of causation, however, the question is simply whether Otto's intervening act was foreseeable; if it was, then it is a dependent intervening cause that does not preclude Ian's being held responsible.

14b. *The Death of Mona.* Ian's responsibility for the killing of Mona is harder to establish. Ian did not intend to cause Mona's death. But if Ian had not sent the e-mail, Otto would not have been incited to kill Mona. Because

28. For complicity, see Chapter 14.

Ian knew that Otto was extremely jealous and violent when Mona's fidelity was questioned, a strong argument can be made that Ian acted *recklessly* (with gross and callous disregard of the risk that Otto might also kill Mona) or *negligently* (he should have known of the substantial and unjustifiable risk that Otto might kill Mona). These mental states satisfy the respective mens rea requirements of manslaughter.

But has Ian *caused* Mona's death? The pivotal question now is whether it was *foreseeable* that Otto would kill Mona. The prosecutor would argue that, because Ian knew that Otto's prior violent outbreaks were sometimes directed at Mona, it was even more foreseeable that Otto might harm Mona rather than Craig, her alleged lover. Thus, the jury could find that Otto's homicidal act was a *dependent* intervening cause, which will not defeat a finding of proximate causation. Note that foreseeability is an objective test; it does not depend on what Ian actually did anticipate would happen. Instead, it depends on what a jury determines about Ian's moral culpability and its sense of justice in this case. Clearly, Ian did not expect that Mona would die as a result of his actions, but a jury could find that, nonetheless, her death was foreseeable. It could also find that Ian acted with recklessness or negligence with respect to that result. That determination would reduce the severity of the crime to manslaughter rather than murder.

Under the MPC, this is a more difficult problem. Ian did not intend or contemplate Mona's death. But did a *different* harm occur than that intended? Not really; Mona was killed rather than Craig. Thus, Mona's death is not a case of "transferred intent," and §2.03(2)(a) probably does not apply. More likely, §2.03(2)(b) applies. Mona's death is the same kind of harm as that intended by Ian, and because Ian knew of Otto's past jealous violence against Mona, Otto's killing her (instead of Craig) is not "too remote or accidental in its occurrence to have a just bearing" on Ian's liability.

14c. *The Death of Otto.* Although moral theory might hold Ian responsible for Otto's suicide, legally he is not culpable. The suicide will probably be considered as an *independent* intervening causation that breaks the causal chain of events from Ian's e-mail to Otto's death. Ian never intended Otto's death, nor did anything in Otto's history suggest that he might turn his jealous rage into violence against himself. Thus, Ian will argue this risk was not foreseeable.

Under the MPC, the analysis is the same as for Mona's death in (14b) above. However, because Ian had no reason to anticipate that Otto might take his own life, a jury would probably conclude that this harm is "too remote or accidental in its occurrence" to hold Ian responsible. This is essentially a value judgment for the jury to make.

15. The prosecution has the burden of providing beyond a reasonable doubt that the defendant proximately caused Vic's death. Here causation is complicated because the direct cause of Vic's death was his cancer. Courtney's attorney would claim that the cancer would have killed Vic anyway.

    However, the prosecution can readily prove that Taxol had been effective in treating Vic's cancer before; Courtney knew that this type of cancer is usually fatal without treatment; and highly diluted Taxol would be ineffective in arresting Vic's cancer. Thus, Courtney could readily predict that, at the very least, Vic's death from the cancer would be accelerated because he was not receiving a treatment proven to be effective. In all probability, Courtney's conduct hastened Vic's death. A jury could find that Vic would not have died when he did if Courtney had not diluted the Taxol. It could also determine that his conduct was readily foreseeable as a contributing cause of Vic's (early) death because the untreated cancer did not go into remission as before, but spread. Thus, the jury could conclude that Courtney's conduct was a *concurrent* cause (together with the cancer) of Vic's death. Remember that shortening the life of a human being for even a few moments is legally sufficient to "cause" death.

16. Billy Jackson will argue that selling cigarettes to Rusty was the cause in fact and the proximate cause of his death. Billy will claim that Joe Camel knew cigarettes are dangerous to human health and that many smokers cannot break their "habit."

    Joe will respond that the available evidence does not establish that lung cancer is a foreseeable result of smoking cigarettes. Moreover, Joe will maintain that Rusty was forewarned about any possible health risk and that, consequently, Rusty's decision to smoke and to continue smoking broke any causal chain that Federated may have put in motion by selling cigarettes.

    This is a hard case. If the jury finds that lung cancer is a natural and probable result of smoking cigarettes and that nicotine is physically addictive, making it difficult for individuals to discontinue smoking, it might find that Federated and its president caused Rusty's death and return a homicide verdict.

    In *Commonwealth v. Feinberg*, 433 Pa. 558, 253 A.2d 636 (1969), the defendant, who stocked and sold regular-strength Sterno (which contains methanol) to alcoholics on skid row, was convicted of 32 counts of manslaughter after selling industrial-strength Sterno, which contains a much higher percentage of methanol, to customers who then drank the product. The Pennsylvania Supreme Court held that the voluntary acts of the victims, though considered contributory negligence in a tort action, were not independent supervening causes in the criminal case.

17a. The prosecutor would argue that Justin was the proximate cause of Erica's death. A reasonable person would anticipate that Erica would release the entire dosage by chomping down on the patch just as Justin had showed her. He or she would also understand that consuming such a large amount of this powerful drug could well be fatal. In illegally selling her such a powerful drug *and* showing her how to consume three days' dosage at once, Justin surely foresaw (perhaps even intended) that Erica would engage in very risky behavior that could well result in her death. Though Erica was the direct cause of her own death, Justin was the proximate cause by setting into motion the very chain of events that he expected or should have expected.

Justin would argue that Erica was the direct and only cause of her own death. She was a responsible human agent who chose to consume the entire drug at once; thus, she, not Justin, caused her death. He is not criminally responsible for her independent decision.

The prosecutor has the better argument here. Justin provided Erica with the illegal drug and showed her how to short-circuit the time-release mechanism so she could get high. Thus, Erica's risk-taking behavior, which directly caused her death, was reasonably foreseeable (and probably intended) by Justin. Thus, it was not accidental or remote in the least, and the jury would likely decide that she was a *dependent* intervening cause and hold Justin responsible.

Justin would probably be found guilty under the MPC, as well. By making the powerful drug available and showing her how to misuse it, he is the "but for" cause of Erica's death. And since the result here is the same result as Justin expected (or should have expected), he has caused her death. The only serious issue is what level of culpability the jury would find.

17b. The prosecutor has a stronger argument here. Justin knew that Aaron was addicted to pain-killing drugs. He illegally sold Aaron the "loaded" patch and showed him how to ingest the entire drug in one swallow. It is much harder for Justin to argue that he did not intend or foresee that Aaron would do exactly what Justin enabled him and showed him how to do. Justin also knew that Aaron was not a fully responsible human agent since his control over his risk-taking use of drugs was substantially impaired.

The MPC analysis is the same here as for Erica's death, with the same outcome: Justin caused Aaron's death.

18. Roberta has acted with the same mens rea as in Example 3, yet she has not caused Raoul's death. Roberta could be convicted of attempted murder, probably in the first degree. However, why should she be punished less severely than in Example 3? She acted with the same state of mind and took the last step she could to bring about the result.

The fact that she did not actually kill Raoul was fortuitous. Only luck saved her from causing his death.

Some would argue that causing harm should not be an important consideration in determining the severity of punishment. Rather, the defendant's attitude toward causing harm and her conduct designed to bring it about should be the primary considerations. Others argue that the public is rightly angered by the fact that harm has occurred and that more severe punishment should be imposed in such cases.

CHAPTER 8

Homicide

OVERVIEW

Homicide is defined by the common law as the unjustified and unexcused killing of a human being. Most American jurisdictions in the nineteenth century divided homicide into two major categories, *murder* or *manslaughter*, and then subdivided these categories to reflect differences in available punishments. Murder was divided into *first degree* (for which a defendant could be executed) and *second degree* (which did not carry the death penalty). Manslaughter was viewed as a less serious killing and was not initially divided into degrees. However, over the years many states divided manslaughter into *voluntary* (or first degree) and *involuntary* (or second degree) manslaughter.

The Model Penal Code abolishes the "degrees" of murder, and makes all murders subject to the death penalty. The availability of the death penalty is a major, though unseen, factor in the development of homicide law. It is, indeed, the gorilla in the closet.

HUMAN BEING

The definition of homicide includes the killing of a "human being." This term was once self-evident, but current medical technology now raises questions about both the beginning and end points of life's temporal spectrum.

When Does Life Begin?

Death comes to fetuses just as it does to full-born persons. Most courts have held that a viable fetus, even if the obvious target of a purposefully homicidal act, is not a "human being" within the meaning of the homicide statute. In *Keeler v. Superior Court*, 2 Cal. 3d 619 (1970), the defendant purposely kicked his former wife, whom he knew was pregnant, in the abdomen, threatening to "stomp it out of you." The fetus died. Reluctantly, but on the theory of narrow interpretation of criminal statutes (see Chapter 1), the court held that the fetus was not a "human being." But see *Commonwealth v. Cass*, 392 Mass. 700 (1984). A rarer question is whether a fetus, even at the moment of birth, qualifies as a "human being." Thus, in *People v. Chavez*, 77 Cal. App. 2d 621, 176 P.2d 92 (1947), Defendant (*D*) delivered her baby into a toilet bowl where it drowned. *D* testified that the baby did not cry, and that she did not tie its umbilical cord. The court held that the fetus became a "human being" after the child passed through the birth canal and took a breath; it was irrelevant that the baby may have been dead by the time the process was finished.[1]

These cases, though rare, raise serious questions about the degree to which the criminal law should broaden its net to capture persons who seem as evil and malevolent as persons already captured by the "normal rules." Against this goal is the general belief that criminal statutes should be construed narrowly, in order to avoid judicial expansion of legislative determinations of the proper scope of the criminal law. Legislatures, reacting to these decisions, have either broadened the definition of "person" to include fetuses or created a separate offense, called feticide, as did California after *Keeler*. Cal. Penal Code §187.

When Does Life End?

At the other end of life's path is the question of whether the victim of an unlawful act was "dead" (and hence no longer a "human being") before the defendant acted. In past centuries, death was assessed practically. The

1. The question sometimes arises in nondeath cases. Thus, in *Johnson v. State*, 602 So. 2d 1288 (Fla. 1992), the mother, who was addicted to cocaine, was charged with delivering the drug through the umbilical cord to a "human being," her newly born child, in the 90 seconds between the time the child was "born" and the time the cord was severed.

majority rule was that a "human being" ceases to exist once the heart stops functioning. The majority of states today, however, now define death as "brain death," although there are various definitions of this event.

Cause and Death

A related question arises as to whether a defendant's act "causes" death, particularly if the actual cessation of breathing (or brain death) is due to the intervention of a third party. Most of these causation issues were discussed in Chapter 7, but one aspect must be addressed here. In earlier days, when victims tended to die soon after an assault, the common law established a rule that any death that did not occur within a "year and a day" of the assault was not "caused" by the assault. If the victim could survive for more than a year, it was at least arguable that something else (extraneous disease, incompetent medical assistance) had in fact caused the death. In such ambiguous circumstances, the better rule is to favor the defendant and find that the defendant's act did not cause the death. Modern medical technology, however, has again created problems. We can now extend, sometimes by years or decades, the "life" of a person who, in other times, clearly would have "died" at an earlier date. Courts and legislatures confronted with cases of this kind have abolished the year-and-a-day rule as inconsistent with modern technology.

MURDER

"Original" Murder: Killing with "Malice Aforethought"

The common law and statutes of fourteenth-century England originally defined "murder" as a killing with "malice prepense (aforethought)." There were no "degrees" of murder under the common law. The words meant precisely what they suggested in ordinary English: an intentional, preplanned, deliberate killing, motivated by ill will (malice) toward the victim.[2] Over a period of several centuries, however, judges redefined the

2. This is what we earlier referred to in Chapter 4 as "traditional" mens rea. In a recent case, not involving a homicide, the court embraced that concept of malicious. In *State v. Burgess*, 205 W. Va. 87 (1999), defendant admitted that he had killed Henry's cow in order to steal the meat, and that he shot it—once—through the head. Charged with "maliciously" killing the cow, defendant argued successfully that the most humane way to kill an animal was with one shot. Said the court, reversing his conviction: "(This) is the same method used throughout West Virginia by farmers and slaughterhouses every day . . . when one unlawfully dispatches

term "malice aforethought" to encompass not only these calculated killings (often labeled "express" malice), but also those that resulted from extremely reckless or wanton conduct (often labeled "implied," "universal," or "constructive" malice). In this way, the courts substantially broadened the legislature's net for "murderers." By the mid-nineteenth century, the term "malice aforethought" had come to mean in England any killing with

> (a) intention to cause the death of, or grievous bodily harm to, any person. . . .
> (b) knowledge that the act which causes death will probably cause the death of, or grievous bodily harm to, some person . . . although such knowledge is accompanied by indifference or by a wish that it may not be caused. . . .[3]

As Stephen shows, "malice" no longer required an intent to kill; the term "malice aforethought" acquired a much broader meaning. It was no longer limited to ill will toward the victim or preplanned killings, as Parliament originally intended; it had been broadly "reinterpreted" by the courts to have little, if anything, to do with either malice or aforethought.

Part (a) of the definition above seems obvious as to why such persons might be labeled as serious offenders. People who *intend* to kill are arguably the "worst" killers. Part (b) of the definition is less evident; not everyone who sets out to hurt someone severely by, for example, stabbing them in the arm, intends death. Perhaps, in past centuries, when serious bodily harm often led to death because of inadequate medical treatment, an intent to kill could be inferred from any intent to inflict serious harm. That inference is less sound today.

The common law developed a set of romantic terms to describe the second kind of killings done with "malice aforethought," sometimes called *implied malice*. Persons who, though not intending to kill, nevertheless acted in a way that they knew created a very high risk of death, and not caring whether death occurred or not, were said to act with a "depraved heart" or one "disregarding social duty" or having an "abandoned heart." Such, for example, was the case of a defendant who, for no apparent reason, fired a rifle into a train, killing (by mere fortuity) a trainman. Under this approach someone who knowingly creates a great risk of death generally, and actually kills someone, can be found to have acted with "malice aforethought" toward the victim.

In sum, both those who *wanted* to kill and those who engaged in very dangerous conduct that they actually foresaw almost surely would (and did) result in death could be convicted of murder with "malice aforethought."

---

a domestic animal belonging to another person by using a commonly accepted, humane method, and there is no evidence of any other form of malice, the killing is not malicious."

3. James Fitzjames Stephen, A Digest of the Criminal Law 161-162 (1887).

If this all sounds confusing, don't be too alarmed. The definition of "malice aforethought" continues to perplex courts. In 2007, more than six centuries after it was first used, the California courts stumbled as they tried to define the term. In *People v. Knoller*, 41 Cal. 4th 139, the trial court concluded that the term, as used in California, meant conduct "that involved a high *probability* of resulting in the *death* of another." The California appellate court disagreed, concluding that the term meant "a defendant's conscious disregard of the *risk of serious bodily injury* to another." The California Supreme Court determined that BOTH courts were wrong—the term meant "an act, which is *dangerous to life*, deliberately performed by a person who knows that his conduct endangers the life of another and who acts with conscious disregard for life." Thankfully, at least the seven California Supreme Court justices were unanimous. But if the trial court, and the three judges on the appellate division, can err on such a fundamental point, you have every right to be uncertain of the precise meaning of the term.

Is the "substantiality" of the risk, or the recklessness of an act quantifiable? Consider *Comm. v. Malone*, 354 Pa. 180 (1946). Defendant, a juvenile, put one bullet in a five-chamber gun. According to his testimony, he did not expect the bullet to discharge until the fifth pull of the trigger. He then "pretended" to play Russian roulette with Billie, his 13-year-old friend. There was no evidence that he spun the chamber. On the third pull of the trigger the gun fired, killing Billie. The court, ignoring the defendant's testimony that he did not anticipate any risk at all, sustained a conviction of "depraved heart" murder, concluding that the risk of death was 60 percent (three pulls of a five-chamber gun). As every law professor in the country points out in class, however, that is incorrect—the actual chance of the gun firing on the third pull was 33 percent, since there were only three chambers left (assuming no spinning of the chamber after each pull of the trigger), the chances were one in three that this chamber held the bullet. Despite the court's bad math, however, if the defendant's testimony is ignored, the fact that the chances of firing were less than 50 percent is irrelevant—indeed, as the hypothetical with Peter Pumpkin in the room of guns (page 74) shows, even a .0001 percent chance of death may indicate a "depraved heart" when there is "no reason" for generating the risk at all.[4] (On the other hand, if the defendant's testimony is credited, he did not "consciously disregard" any risk that the gun would fire, unless one takes the position that anyone who "plays" with a gun, even what he believes to be an "empty" gun, is consciously disregarding a risk that he is wrong.)

---

4. The other prototypical malice aforethought murder is *Banks v. State*, 85 Tex. Crim. 165 (1919) (where the defendant fired a shotgun into a passing train, killing someone inside the train). Surely the risk of actual death from such an event is small—perhaps less than .0001. But the court had no trouble finding the defendant guilty not only of murder, but of capital murder.

These common law labels reflect a deeper, ethical assessment of the defendant's conduct. No one's heart (or mind) can be "depraved." The latter word connotes a judgment that the defendant's *conduct* (not his heart, or liver, or brain) is unacceptable on a moral level. While a doctor might be able to tell us whether a heart (or mind) is "malignant," whether it is "depraved" is not a medical question. And how a heart could be "abandoned," and still beat within the defendant's body is unclear. The words are merely metaphors to convey what, in the twenty-first century, we might call (in an obviously legal phrase) a "scumbag."

Presumed Malice

Prior to the end of the nineteenth century, criminal defendants were not allowed to testify in court (even if they wanted to), and current constitutional prohibitions preclude the prosecutor from compelling the defendant to testify. The common law therefore established several "presumptions" with regard to malice. Of these, two are of interest here. The first was that a person is "presumed" to intend the "natural and probable consequences of his act." The other was that a killing committed with a deadly weapon (defined as a weapon calculated to or likely to produce death or great bodily injury) was presumed to have been committed with malice. Although some courts today continue to rely on these doctrines, the better view is that these are not "presumptions" at all but merely permissive inferences, which the jury may use or disregard at its discretion. See *Bantum v. State*, 85 A.2d 741 (Del. 1952). See also Chapter 15.

Gradations of Murder

"First-Degree" Murder

After the American Revolution, many state legislatures—aware that English courts had expanded the meaning of "malice aforethought" to include those who, while not intending death, created a great risk of death—responded by dividing "murder" into two "degrees." These statutes provided the death penalty only for "first-degree" murders—that is, only those "murders"[5] that were "premeditated, willful and deliberate."[6] In

5. Some state statutes used the word "killing" rather than "murder." Although it was probably inadvertent, the distinction was relatively unimportant in most instances. However, in *People v. Aaron*, 409 Mich. 672 (1980), the court seized on this semantic difference to abolish judicially the doctrine of felony murder. See pages 218-225.

6. The first such statute was enacted in Pennsylvania in 1794 and was quickly followed by other states. The statutes also defined as first-degree murder killings by "lying in wait, torture,

so doing, state legislatures clearly intended to recapture the original meaning of "malice aforethought," that is, killings committed by individuals who (1) thought about killing their victim (premeditated), (2) brooded over it for some significant period of time (deliberated), and (3) then killed willfully. The openness of the phrase has split courts on whether it is overly vague (*State v. Thompson*, 34 P.3d 382 (Ariz. App. Div. 2001)), or, on the other hand, whether it needs to be defined at all (*State v. Patton*, 102 P.3d 1195 (Kan. App. 2004)). Neither a "depraved heart," nor even intent, were sufficient to constitute "premeditation, deliberation and willfulness." The legislature had redefined those eligible for the death penalty by focusing on the "coldbloodedness" of their killings.

As in England, however, many American courts quickly thwarted this ameliorative legislation by construing the term "premeditation" to encompass even split-second decisionmaking. Thus, in *State v. Arata*, 56 Wash. 185, 105 P. 227 (1909), the court declared that

> the law knows no specific time; if a man reflects upon the act a moment antecedent to the act, it is sufficient; the time for deliberation and premeditation need not be long. . . . [Emphasis added.][7]

Although it is possible to argue—and some courts have tried—that the three words do indeed connote different levels of mental state, by the early twentieth century, the term was a "term of art," without reflecting much difference among the words (much less "malice aforethought," really). As a consequence, the death-eligible group of killers was once again judicially broadened. In recent years, an increasing number of courts, rejecting this expansion, have required a "reasonable period of time" to find premeditation or deliberation. In the well-known case of *People v. Anderson*, 447 P.2d 942 (Cal. 1968), the court listed three elements tending to show the requisite premeditation and deliberation—(1) planning activity, (2) motive, and (3) manner of killing—which would combine to establish that the defendant acted with a preconceived design. This is very close to the fourteenth-century view of what "malice prepense" meant.

This struggle between the judiciary and the legislature over which killers should be death-eligible is neither surprising nor difficult to explain.

---

and poison." The first of these is virtually taken verbatim from the fourteenth-century statute first establishing malice prepense as the critical distinction for murder. All three types of killing require premeditation. It is difficult (though not impossible) to conceive of an intended *poisoning* that was not premeditated. And it is only slightly less possible to think of an *intentional* death by torture that does not require preplanning. One might conclude, therefore, that these phrases are superfluous, if not redundant.

7. This view continues. See *State v. Harms*, 643 N.W.2d 359 (Neb. 2002): "The purpose to kill may be formed at any moment before the homicide is committed."

While the legislature must define general categories of offenders eligible for the death penalty, courts encounter specific instances where the defendant, though perhaps not fitting within the precise words of the legislation, falls within its spirit. As the court said about the defendant described above who, for no apparent reason, and with no apparent intent to injure, much less kill, shot into a passing train:

> That man who can coolly shoot into a moving train . . . in which are persons guiltless of any wrongdoing toward him . . . is, if possible, worse than the man who . . . waylays and kills his personal enemy.[8]

Confronted with persons they considered "as morally bad" (or as dangerous) as the killers clearly falling within the legislatively defined group, courts frequently construed the statute's words to meet their views. Because they could not expressly *say* they were "adding" to the category of death-eligible killers a new category, they merely "redefined" the terms to encompass killers they saw as equally blameworthy (and dangerous).

"Second-Degree" Murder

The statutory division of murder into two "degrees" meant that second-degree murder became the "default" ("catch-all") position. If a killing was murder (committed within the broadened notion of "malice aforethought") and was not premeditated, it was second degree. These killings were not capitally punishable, although they might result in a sentence of life imprisonment.

To determine under a statute dividing murder into two degrees whether a murder was first or second degree requires three steps:

1. Was the killing a "murder" (was it done with malice aforethought)?
2. If so, was it "premeditated, deliberate and willful"?
3. If yes, it was first-degree murder; if not, second-degree.

The Model Penal Code Approach

The Model Penal Code essentially agrees with the policy views of the nineteenth-century courts that no single set of general words describing an actor's state of mind can adequately encompass all the factors that should

8. *Banks v. State,* 85 Tex. Crim. 165 (1917).

go into deciding whether to execute a particular killer.[9] Section 210 of the Code abolishes both the term "malice" and the distinction between first- and second-degree murder. Instead, it characterizes as "death eligible" all killers who cause the death of another human being

1. purposely;
2. knowingly; or
3. recklessly under circumstances manifesting extreme indifference to the value of human life.

These words closely parallel the notions enunciated in pre-Code law. Any "premeditated and deliberate" homicide would fit within the Code's definition of "purpose" or "knowing." The Code's third category can encompass those killers said to have a "depraved heart." Thus, a person who acts "recklessly" neither "purposes" death, nor does he know that death is "practically certain." Instead, he simply "consciously disregards" a "substantial and unjustifiable risk" that his actions (like shooting into a passing train) might result in death. On the other hand, the Code does not explicitly include the "intent to inflict serious bodily injury" category of murder (unless such intent can be said to imply recklessness under "extreme circumstances"). It is critical to remember that the Code's definition of "reckless" would require that the defendant *subjectively recognize* the risk of death. Even if the defendant is reckless, the death must *also* occur under "circumstances manifesting extreme indifference." If the defendant is "merely" reckless or negligent, the death is manslaughter, not murder. (See below.)

Some Further Thoughts

The common law's preoccupation with mens rea as "the" dividing line in grading homicides is not the only approach that could have been chosen. One might, for example, distinguish, even among premeditators,

---

9. Although the Code provides that all "murderers" may be eligible for the death penalty, that penalty is not imposed on all murderers. Instead, the Code establishes a procedural scheme that requires specific findings on a list of "aggravating" *and* "mitigating" circumstances that must be considered in determining whether the killer should be sentenced to death. The aggravating factors, taken together, are intended to cover most of the killings that motivated earlier courts to interpret broadly the words ("premeditation and deliberation") of the earlier statutes. The list of mitigating factors is intended to cover most of those cases where a jury would usually decide that the defendant is not so blameworthy as to be sentenced to death. Because of several decisions by the United States Supreme Court on the constitutionality of the death penalty, a significant number of states that have the death penalty have adopted a procedure similar to that recommended by the Code. See MPC §210.6.

depending on (a) the victim,[10] (b) the method of killing, (c) whether it was done for hire, and (d) whether there were multiple possible victims. Thus, a torturer of a two-year-old child or a premeditated killer of a police officer might well be seen as "worse" than a poisoner of a 50-year-old man even though all three killings are premeditated murder. Similarly, one could conclude that a reckless killer of an infant is more culpable or dangerous than one who poisons an adult who happens to be his worst enemy. The Code allows some of these factors to be considered in sentencing.

Although historically the availability of the death penalty was thought to require gradations among offenders, even some countries that have abolished the penalty have consciously decided to retain the label "murderer" because of its association with the "worst" kind of killer.[11] The argument is that criminal law does and should make moral distinctions among offenders, and that simply calling all criminal killings "homicide" would weaken the law's moral status.

Examples

1. Karen learns that her worst enemy, Rick, is coming to town in two days. She buys a gun and decides to kill Rick as he steps off the train. Two days later, she takes the gun with her to the station, loads it there, and walks up to Rick and shoots him at point-blank range in the head five times, killing him instantly. What level of homicide?

2. Karen has watched her brother, Rick, die slowly and painfully from cancer over the last six months. Totally distraught, she buys a gun and decides to kill Rick. Two days later, she walks into the hospital room, deceives a nurse into leaving the room, and then shoots Rick at point-blank range in the head five times, killing him instantly. What level of homicide?

3. Geraldo is waiting for a bus one day when he sees a four-year-old boy nearby, walking on the sidewalk. He instantly pushes the boy off the sidewalk into the path of an oncoming car (which Geraldo saw), killing him. Is this murder? What level?

4a. Tom is in love with Mary, but Mary doesn't return his affection. She is, however, in love with Romero. Tom, hoping to scare or injure his rival, puts a nonpoisonous snake in Romero's mailbox. Unknown to

10. The word "murder" actually stems from a fine (the "murdrum") imposed by the first Norman kings of England upon a town if the town refused to disclose the murderer of a Norman. If the victim was proven to be a Saxon, however, no fine was imposed. Thus, "the worst kind of killing" was initially designated by victim rather than by mens rea.

11. N. Cameron & S. France, The Bill in Context, in Essays on Criminal Law in New Zealand 1, 4-5 (1990).

Tom, Romero has always been afraid of snakes. He looks into the mailbox and has a coronary. Is Tom guilty of murder?

4b. Suppose, instead, that the snake is a cobra, but that even before it can bite Romero, he has that same coronary. Murder this time?

5. Laurie and Michael are the last two contestants for a major job opportunity. Laurie, wearing a ski mask, kidnaps Michael and puts him in a locked room. She has provided two weeks' worth of food in a refrigerator and freezer. The room is escape proof. She tells Michael that he will be released in seven days. She has also pre-timed a set of videotapes, so that Michael will see one each day, assuring him he would be released. On the fourth day, Laurie gets the job in part because Michael is not able to make the final interview.

   a. After landing the job, Laurie writes an anonymous and nontraceable e-mail to the police, telling them where to find Michael. Unfortunately, just as she is about to press "Send," she is struck by a car and goes into a coma; her computer is totally destroyed. She awakens two weeks later, and immediately shouts, "Find Michael!" and gives the location. Michael is dead when the police arrive.

   b. The videotape for the seventh day told Michael that the key to the room was in ice cubes in the freezer, so that he could escape on that day. Unfortunately, Michael became so despondent over the situation, believing it to be hopeless, that he killed himself on the fifth day. Is Laurie a murderer in either, both, or neither of these scenarios?

6. John and Evelyn have a heated dispute over John's excessive golfing, an issue that has divided their marriage for years. After five hours, John, more in frustration than anything, reaches into his golf bag and pulls out a five iron. After 10 seconds, he swings it once at Evelyn and hits her in the head, killing her instantly. Is this murder?

7. Widgets Inc. manufactures widgets. A by-product of the process is "gooey," which is extremely toxic and has been declared by the state Environmental Protection Agency to be a hazardous waste. Daniel, vice president of Widgets, knows of gooey's characteristics but, needing money, decides to dispose of the gooey by dumping it into a nearby river and pocket the money that is otherwise earmarked for disposal processes. Six months later, Billy, age 5, dies from swimming in the river. An expert will testify that gooey, still present in the river, caused Billy's death. Dan is charged with Billy's death. What result?

8. Reba, aware that she is "drunk," nevertheless attempts to drive home. She weaves across a median and collides with another car head on, killing two occupants. Of what level of murder, if any, is she guilty?

9. Jack is a telephone operator for 911 Emergency Services. He agrees with Fast and Speedy Ambulance Service that he will divert at least 20 calls a day to them, for $50 a call. This arrangement continues for two months, with no ill effects. One day, Jack receives a call from Joseph Johnson, who screams over the phone: "My wife is having trouble breathing. Please get down here soon!" Jack obtains basic information, and concludes that the situation is not as bad as Johnson believes. Rather than calling the nearest ambulance, Jack diverts the call to Fast and Speedy, who this time isn't. Johnson's wife dies. Assuming that the prosecutor can establish causation, of what level of homicide is Jack guilty, if any?

10. Bob and Marjorie own two, 120-pound dogs. Sometimes Bob walks them, sometimes Marjorie; on rare occasions, both do. On several walks, the dogs have lunged at passersby, but no person has ever been injured. On at least one occasion, the dogs pulled Marjorie for several hundred feet. One day, while Marjorie is walking both dogs alone, the dogs attack and kill a neighbor. The dogs were not muzzled. Marjorie tried, but was unable to stop them. At trial, Marjorie and Bob present evidence that although other dogs have killed strangers, (a) none of this breed has ever been involved in a lethal attack, and (b) no lethal attack, involving any breed, has occurred while the dogs were being walked. Is either Marjorie or Bob guilty of murder, and if so, what degree?

11. Michael is told by his doctor that he has AIDS. He continues to have sex with various partners without telling them of his condition. Two of his partners die. Is he guilty of murder? If so, what degree?

12. Lamont, a trial judge who had desperately and unsuccessfully sought to be promoted to the appellate bench, becomes so despondent that he decides to take his own life. He turns on all the burners in his gas oven, seals the windows and doors, takes six sleeping pills, and lies down to die. A spark from his refrigerator ignites the gas. An explosion kills four neighbors, but Lamont survives. Is he guilty of any level of homicide?

13. Albert, a 36-year-old software developer, bicycles to work every day in San Francisco. On several occasions, he has just missed hitting pedestrians. On the fateful day, he was not so lucky. While biking downhill, and being clocked by various monitors at a speed of over 35 miles per hour, Albert sees a yellow light ahead of him but claims, "I was too committed to stop." The light turns red, and he collides with two pedestrians, one of whom is killed. (a) Of what level of homicide, if any, is Albert guilty? (b) May the prosecutor introduce evidence that four pedestrians have been killed in the city in the past year?

14. Janet and her husband, Bob, often get into heated arguments; sometimes Janet even turns violent. Janet has been known to strike or

kick Bob in the middle of arguments, or even throw objects at him. However, Janet has never seriously injured Bob. One day, Janet and Bob are in the middle of one of their biggest arguments to date and Janet, in the heat of the moment, grabs a nearby pocket knife and stabs Bob in the leg. Shocked at what she had done, she called 911, but it was too late by the time they arrived. Janet had hit an artery in Bob's leg and he bled out in minutes. When the police arrived, Janet insisted that she did not intend to kill Bob, only hurt him a little; she never imagined a thin, 2-inch knife to the leg could actually kill someone. Assume Janet is of sound mind. For what level of homicide, if any, is Janet culpable?

Explanations

EXPLANATIONS

1. Karen intended to kill, and thus, under the common law, has "malice aforethought" and a "depraved mind" (not to mention heart). She is thus guilty of at least second-degree murder. The jury may readily find that she premeditated the event, deliberated and mulled it over, and then willfully killed. She is thus guilty not merely of murder but of first-degree murder. Under the Model Penal Code, Karen has acted "purposely" and is therefore guilty of murder.

2. This case is intended to be almost precisely the same as that in Example 1 to illustrate a point: The "premeditation" formula sometimes is *over*-inclusive as well as *under*-inclusive in assessing moral blame. *This* Karen thought for a long period of time, about taking life before acting, and thus, like the first Karen, "premeditated." Under the common law, she, too, would be found guilty of first-degree murder and of murder under the Model Penal Code. But Karen's premeditation does not indicate that she is a "wicked" or "depraved" person. On the contrary, she has tried to do the right thing (as she saw it) and has, arguably, acted from the best of motives. (See Chapter 4.) There is something jarring about treating her as equally "culpable" or equally "bad" as Karen in Example 1, no matter how one feels about euthanasia as a general matter. We will explore and explain this tension at various points in the book, especially in the materials on "new excuses" (Chapter 17). However, as the law now stands, Karen is a first-degree murderer—or, under the MPC, simply a murderer—and may be executed. Of course, it is not certain the prosecutor will charge Karen with any homicide, nor that the grand jury will indict, nor that the petit jury will convict. Often, at some level of discretion, the decision is made not to move forward. But that is discretion, not law.

3. There is little argument that Geraldo's actions would not satisfy at least second-degree murder under the common law. He purposely pushed

the boy into the path of the car that he clearly saw coming, demonstrating malice aforethought. Also recall that the common law presumes that Geraldo intended the "natural and probable consequences of his act." So, the bulk of our concern will be whether there was the requisite premeditation to elevate Geraldo's charges to first-degree murder.

It is unlikely that the legislature intended such a killing to fall within the term "premeditated." But it is precisely because this term fails to capture such killers that nineteenth-century American courts often declared that juries could conclude that a person premeditated "in an instant." See, e.g., *People v. Waters*, 118 Mich. App. 176 (1982), in which the defendant, a youth armed with a gun, became annoyed with the victim's husband. He fired his gun into the victim's car once and then, within five seconds, but with both hands on the pistol, fired the gun a second time, killing the victim. The trial court found premeditation, which was upheld on appeal.

Caveat. Merely because the jury *could* find premeditation does not mean it must. And mere time alone, in the absence of other factors, may not be sufficient even to allow a jury finding of premeditation. Thus, in *State v. Bingham*, 105 Wash. 2d 820 (1986), the defendant spent five minutes strangling his victim. The (very divided) court, however, said that there was no other evidence of premeditation, and that "time alone," without more, would not support such a finding.

As already noted, the Model Penal Code eliminates the concept of "premeditation" precisely because of these ambiguities. The Code's formulation is significantly more helpful here. A jury could easily find "purpose" or "recklessness under circumstances manifesting extreme indifference to the value of human life." Whether the death penalty would then be imposed would depend on a series of factors rather than merely one.

4a. Tom is clearly a rapscallion. But it is hard to argue that his conduct, however scandalous and outrageous, evinced a "depraved heart" under the common law, or a "conscious disregard of a substantial and unjustifiable risk" that Romero would have a heart attack upon seeing the snake. Without evidence of these mental states, it would be difficult, if not impossible to prove malice aforethought, which is necessary to find Tom guilty of murder under the common law.

Moreover, it would be equally difficult to prove negligence or recklessness, let alone the lowest necessary mental state for a murder charge under the MPC: recklessness *under circumstances manifesting extreme indifference to the value of human life*. Even assuming the prosecutor could find evidence that Tom was aware of Romero's fear of snakes, that would be clear evidence of Tom's intent to scare Romero, not to kill him. Tom's behavior demonstrates a disregard for common decency at most.

4b. Much more likely this time. Tom clearly had a "person-endangering state of mind," and a "malignant heart," which would support at least a second degree murder charge under the common law. And Romero's death was clearly caused by Tom's action, even if the result didn't come about quite the way Tom had envisioned (see Chapter 7 on causation).

Under the MPC, Tom's behavior would likely constitute murder for the same reason. His actions show at least an extreme indifference to the value of human life, given the immense risk of mortal injury from a cobra bite.

5a. Even though she didn't intend Michael's death, Laurie is clearly a "but for" cause of Michael's death. But was her heart "malignant and abandoned"? Kidnapping someone is no laughing matter. But her steps suggest that she did not disregard a substantial risk that Michael would die. On the other hand, there are a million ways in which Laurie could become unable to inform the police of Michael's location. A jury might well infer a bad heart (or mind) or a "conscious disregard" of the risk that Michael would die, sufficient to satisfy either a charge of first-degree murder under the common law or murder under the MPC. This is a jury question, but it is very likely that a jury would convict Laurie.

5b. This is a version of the *Stephenson* case, discussed in Chapter 7 on causation. In that case, and similar ones, the defendant was found liable when the victim committed suicide. But in those cases, the defendant did "more" than kidnap—rape or other personal injury was involved. Here, again, even if Laurie is found to be the "proximate cause" of Michael's death, the question of the level of her liability (manslaughter or murder) will depend on whether the jury finds that she had the relevant mens rea. In the rape-suicide cases above, it is easy to envision that a victim might seek any form of escape. But here, Laurie has given Michael food for two weeks, and promised release in a week (which she intended to observe). Probably not murder. Whether she was "reckless" (voluntary manslaughter) or "criminally negligent" (involuntary manslaughter) or guilty of felony murder is another matter—see the discussion infra pages 236-241; 244-246.

6. This is a difficult case. Under the common law, a jury could find that John intended to kill or seriously injure Evelyn, or that he "thought about the risks involved and went ahead anyway," thereby demonstrating a "depraved heart." He therefore has "malice aforethought" and is guilty of common law murder. But did he premeditate so as to be guilty of "first-degree murder" under American statutes? As in Example 3, John's 10 seconds is probably sufficient time to allow a jury to find not merely intent, but premeditation. In a similar case, a court found

the defendant guilty of first-degree murder and sentenced him to life in prison. *Commonwealth v. Carroll*, 412 Pa. 525 (1963).

Under the Model Penal Code, "premeditation" is not the key. The jury could easily find "purpose" and thus render the defendant eligible for the death penalty. And they could even more readily find that John was "reckless under circumstances manifesting extreme indifference to the value of human life." Who said golf was not a dangerous sport?

7. Clearly, Daniel is not guilty of first-degree murder under the common law. He did not intend, much less premeditate, the death of anyone. Whether he had a "depraved heart" is less clear. He knew of "some" risk, perhaps even a substantial risk, that someone might be injured. However, that might not qualify as actually foreseeing that death might "probably" result.

   Under the MPC, the result is likely to be the same. Even assuming that there was a "substantial risk" of death, it is not obvious that Daniel foresaw the risk as substantial and therefore "consciously disregarded" it. However, if this part of the Code's test were met, since Daniel was aware that the substance was potentially dangerous to human life, he could be found to have acted under circumstances "manifesting extreme indifference to human life" as required by §210 of the Code.

   Alternatively, under the common law "felony murder" doctrine, Daniel might be found guilty of murder if his failure to follow EPA disposal methods qualified as a felony. See the next section.

8. There is no evidence that Reba had the intent to kill anyone when she began driving, let alone that she premeditated the victim's death, so she would not be guilty of first-degree murder under the common law. This would almost certainly not have qualified as "depraved heart" murder under earlier views. However, an increasing number of courts, outraged by the number of highway fatalities caused by drunk drivers, have allowed second-degree murder charges to go to the jury, at least where it can be shown that the defendant was "excessively" drunk and had been warned and cautioned about his driving. *Jeffries v. State*, 169 P.3d 913 (Alaska 2007); *People v. Murray*, 225 Cal. App. 3d 734 (1990). Given the increasingly widespread knowledge of the risks associated with driving drunk, this comports with the second definition of "malice aforethought," requiring knowledge that the act will probably cause the death of, or grievous bodily harm to, some person.

   Reba's culpability under the MPC would likely be dependent on her criminal history. If Reba has an extensive history of DUIs, there may be an argument that her behavior was reckless *and* manifesting extreme indifference to human life, amounting to murder. However, the strongest argument would be that her behavior was reckless, or at least negligent, calling for a manslaughter charge.

9. Is this common law murder? Does Jack have "malice aforethought"—a mind "disregardful of social duty"? Under the Model Penal Code terms, is the risk "substantial" enough to warrant imposition of liability for murder? Remember—even under the common law, and clearly under the Model Penal Code, the prosecutor must show not merely that the RPP "would have" recognized this risk as substantial—he must show that *Jack saw* the risk as substantial. This is surely a jury question, and a jury could conclude that Jack must have considered the fact that he is involved in a business that literally involves life and death decisions, and must have considered the risk that something like this would happen.

10. This, is the infamous "dog maul" case, discussed supra, page 210. This example contains some of the key facts. In the actual prosecution, the jury convicted Marjorie of second-degree murder, apparently finding that her refusal to muzzle the dogs, combined with her knowledge of the breed's general reputation for violence and prior incidents with passersby, constituted a "depraved heart." The jury also convicted Robert of involuntary manslaughter. The trial judge overturned Marjorie's murder conviction, however, holding that under California law (1) there had to be a high probability of death on any given occasion, and (2) the defendant had to *know* that there was a high probability of death. After declaring that Ms. Knoller had lied continually on the stand, the trial judge concluded that she had told the truth when she said that she did not know that death was a highly probable result. The California Appellate Division reversed the trial judge. The appellate opinion held that the jury could have found that the prosecution proved that there was a "base, antisocial motive and wanton disregard for human life or [knowledge] that one's conduct endangers the life of another and consciously disregards that risk." The murder verdict was reinstated. *People v. Noel*, 28 Cal. Rptr. 3d 369 (Cal. App. 1 Dist. 2005).

    As noted in the text, the California Supreme Court reversed, finding that both the trial judge and appellate courts had used erroneous definitions of "malice aforethought." Instead, said the court, the prosecutor need prove only that the act was "dangerous to life" and that the defendant was "consciously aware" of that risk. On remand, a new judge found Ms. Knoller guilty of second-degree murder and reinstated the original jury verdict.

    A number of state legislatures have considered, or enacted, legislation imposing criminal liability on dog owners when the owner knew or should have known that a dog was potentially dangerous. See ABA Journal 26 (Jan. 2003).

11. A number of cases reported in newspapers have involved persons charged with "attempted" murder in similar situations; that issue is

discussed in Chapter 12 infra. Many states have made, the knowing or reckless transmission of AIDS a crime by itself. See State Criminal Statutes on HIV Transmission, https://www.aclu.org/other/state-criminal-statutes-hiv-transmission (last visited Jan. 25, 2018). If death were to occur, as in the example here, a jury could easily find the defendant had a "depraved mind" with regard to *all* of the possible victims. But if (as in the *Malone* case) we consider the victims one by one, it is a more difficult question. The chances of infecting "someone" may be significant, but the odds of infecting any one victim are relatively insignificant. Still, on the "traditional" notion of "morally bad behavior" as the premise of mens rea, Michael seems to qualify. It is also possible, if the state has made sexual contact without disclosure a felony, that Michael could qualify for second degree felony murder (see the next section). Failing that, Michael is surely "grossly negligent" for not having informed his partners of his condition and is therefore guilty of involuntary manslaughter (see pages 244-246 infra). Under the MPC, the analysis is really the same—does the "unjustifiable" risk for recklessness have to be "quantifiably" substantial or only "qualitatively" substantial (i.e., disproportionate to the gain). Another consideration is that an AIDS transmission is no longer the death sentence it used to be, as many are able to live a long and productive life with the disease.

12. People bent on suicide often kill others and not themselves. Jumping off buildings, ingesting poison while pregnant, and driving into another car are just some of the myriad methods that can lead to this bizarre result. The prosecutor would argue that the defendant actually has a desire that (his) death will occur (though not that of others), and that he is therefore guilty of purposeful murder. Moreover, since the defendant premeditated his own death, the prosecution could contend that this was first degree. What about the doctrine of transferred intent (see Chapter 4)? Defense counsel, on the other hand, would contend that suicide is no longer a crime. Since the defendant did not intend any other person's death, there was no transferred intent because there was no *criminal* intent to begin with. In addition, it is hard to see how the defendant, who wished to kill only himself, demonstrated a common law "depraved heart" or MPC "extreme recklessness." It is also possible that the defense counsel may argue some form of mental instability or incapacity; see Chapter 17.

    In the case on which this example is based (in which, fortunately, no one died), the court found the judge guilty of reckless endangerment. *People v. Feingold*, 852 N.E.2d 1163 (N.Y. 2006).

13a. This incident occurred in San Francisco on March 29, 2012, and the cyclist was subsequently charged with felony vehicular manslaughter based upon reckless diving of a vehicle (yes, a bicycle is a vehicle for these purposes). See www.articles.latimes.com/2012/jun/16/local/la-me-sf-bikes-20120616. Whether Albert is reckless or not, of course, will depend on the facts as they develop. But if he has had several "near hits" on prior occasions, he's going to find it hard to convince a jury that he didn't "consciously disregard" a significant risk that he could hit a pedestrian. And going down those streets on Nob Hill at those speeds is certainly likely to result in serious injury or death. There is—as always—another side to some of these issues. It appears that bicyclists have been injured so often by cars (and sometimes pedestrians) that some are now wearing video cameras to provide evidence of how a collision occurred. See Nick Wingfield, A "Black Box" on a Biker, N.Y. Times, July 21, 2012, p. B1.

13b. Since the charge involves recklessness, the prosecution will have to show that there was serious risk of serious bodily harm or death. This evidence will therefore be admissible. Two questions, however, will remain: (1) does this level of injury per year, in a city of several million people, amount to a "substantial" risk of death of serious bodily injury? and (2) would it be prejudicial to introduce this evidence unless the prosecutor can also show that Albert was aware of this statistical danger? As the text suggests, "substantial risk" is really more a normative than an empirical judgment, and the evidence would be probative on at least the first issue.

14. Under the common law, Janet will likely be charged with second-degree murder. There is a legitimate question as to whether Janet acted with "malice aforethought." There is no evidence that Janet truly wanted to kill her husband; arguably, the fact that she stabbed him in the leg—as opposed to the chest or stomach—corroborates her story that she only intended to harm him. However, recall that the common law presumes that an actor acts with malice when killing with a deadly weapon. Here, such an inference may be a reasonable one. Moreover, without any evidence that Janet premediated the murder, a prosecutor would likely not charge her with first degree felony. Another possibility under the common law is manslaughter, since Janet did not have the intent to establish a first or second degree murder and this likely qualifies as an "accidental" killing.

    Under the MPC, Janet would likely be charged with some type of homicide; but the question of which type is a close one. Janet did not deliberately kill her husband, so she did not act purposely or knowingly. However, stabbing someone with a knife is arguably reckless under circumstances manifesting indifference to the value of human life. This would be the prosecutor's best argument to support a charge of murder. Recall, however, that the Code's definition of "reckless" requires that the actor *subjectively* recognize the risk of death. If Janet can successfully show that she honestly believed there was no risk of death in stabbing someone in the leg with a small pocket knife, then she may escape liability for murder. However, the prosecutor may have an argument that Janet was criminally negligent, and so, liable for manslaughter (or negligent homicide under the MPC). This will likely come down to whether the jury finds that a reasonable person should have recognized the potential threat to life in stabbing someone as Janet did (see below for further discussion on the "reasonable person" standard in this context).

FELONY MURDER

Introduction

Although murder in the common law generally required "malice aforethought," two kinds of slaying were labeled murder even without such a mens rea. One, the killing of an officer in resisting arrest, will not be discussed in these materials. The other is an infamous rule called the "felony murder" rule. Of dubious origin, the felony murder rule, as usually stated in its broadest possible form, declares:

Any death occurring during the course of a felony is murder.

The broad language of this rule traditionally has two components. First, "it imposes murder liability for any death caused, even if entirely accidentally, in the course of the attempt, commission, or flight from a felony."[12] Second, the rule "holds accomplices in the felony to be accomplices in the murder, whether or not they aided the killing specifically, and even if the killing was performed by a nonfelon (such as the felony's victim, or a responding police officer).[13] These components may be subject to several exceptions that will be discussed below.

The rule in this broad form has been called "a monstrous doctrine," 3 J. Stephen, History of the Criminal Law of England 75 (1883), and Thomas Jefferson, while Governor of Virginia during the Revolution, proposed

12. Paul H. Robinson, Shima Baradaran Baughman, and Michael T. Cahill, Criminal Law: Case Studies and Controversies, 212 (New York: Wolters Kluwer, 2017)
13. Id.

the abolition of the doctrine (however, the bill did not pass because the British seized Richmond). It is "difficult to find a jurisdiction outside the United States—even in the English-speaking world—that still applies the rule." Fletcher, The Nature and Function of Criminal Theory, 88 Cal. L. Rev. 687, 694 (2000). The doctrine imposes liability (and perhaps capital punishment) for murder whether a felon kills intentionally, recklessly, negligently, or even non-negligently. It is in fact a form of strict liability.

One explanation for this harsh rule is the notion of "transferred intent"—the defendant's intent to engage in the felony is "transferred" to the death. This use of the transferred intent doctrine, however, is problematic at best, since it usually refers to transferring an established intent from one victim to another (*A* intends to kill B, but the bullet misses and kills C, *A*'s closest friend). Perhaps when all felonies were capitally punishable, transferring one's intent to commit one capital felony to another capital felony might have made some sense. This explanation, however, is no longer applicable, since the penalty for all nonhomicidal felonies is less than death.[14] This is NOT a version of the "greater crime" theory we saw in Chapter 6—there, the defendant was usually guilty of a higher degree of the *same crime*—e.g., grand larceny rather than petty larceny. Here, the intent to commit crime A is sufficient to find the defendant guilty not only of crime A, but of the entirely different crime B (murder).

The primary philosophical explanation given for the rule is that it will deter felonies. However, even Justice Holmes, a prime believer in deterrence, declared that threatening to hang at random one chicken thief out of every thousand would carry more deterrence and be just as sensible. O.W. Holmes, The Common Law 58 (1881). Moreover, it is difficult to understand how such a rule "deters" negligent homicides which, by definition, the defendant is not contemplating.

The only effect of the felony murder doctrine is to relieve the prosecutor of proving mens rea ("malice aforethought") with regard to death. Even if a defendant cannot be convicted of felony murder, there is still the possibility of a "straight" murder conviction.

Restrictions on the Doctrine: "Cause" Questions

Most courts have shared the view that the doctrine is too broad and have found ways to limit its application.

As originally understood, the felony murder doctrine applied to "any" death that "occurred" during the felony. This obviously clashed with

14. *Kennedy v. Louisiana*, 554 U.S. 407 (2008) (death penalty cannot be imposed upon any rapist of a child).

notions of causation (discussed in detail in Chapter 7). The difficult cases arise where, while *D* is committing a felony (e.g., a robbery), the actual victim is killed by someone other than the *D* or his accomplice. Thus, in the classic cases, *D* and *C* attempt to hold up a grocery store and

1. *V* (the intended robbery victim) or *P* (a police officer responding to the crime) kills *D*'s accomplice, *C*;
2. *V* or *P* kills an innocent bystander (*IB*);
3. *D* grabs *IB* and uses her as a "shield," during which *V* or *P* kills *IB*.

Obviously, *D* is "a" cause of the death: "But for" the attempted robbery, *C* or *IB* would be alive. However, not even tort law rests liability on mere but-for causation. There is always the issue of proximate cause. In the context of felony murder, the courts have used different approaches, although ultimately the results are similar. In most states, *D* is liable only in Case 3, and possibly not even then.

The "Proximate Cause" Theory

As indicated in Chapter 7, courts have wrestled with whether criminal liability should *ever* be predicated on tort causation concepts. Although some courts attempted to apply the tort notion of "proximate cause" to the situations discussed here, that effort has proven largely frustrating and unfruitful. First, the elusive quality of "foreseeability" raises serious questions itself. Second, the use of an objective standard in assessing criminal *guilt* seems undesirable. In a famous series of decisions,[15] the Pennsylvania Supreme Court first adopted and then rejected the "proximate cause" approach, although it is still used in some jurisdictions.

The "In Furtherance" ("Agency") and "Provocative Act" Theories

Courts alternatively have required that the killing be "in furtherance" of the felony. See, e.g., *People v. Washington*, 402 P.2d 130 (Cal. 1965). This obviously eliminates Case 1, where *D*'s accomplice is killed, thus making it more difficult to accomplish the felony. A similar notion is the "agency theory," which draws its theoretical base from accomplice doctrine (discussed in Chapter 14). A person is responsible only for his own actions or those who are acting with him in the felony and who are, therefore, his

15. *Commonwealth v. Almeida*, 362 Pa. 596 (1949); *Commonwealth v. Redline*, 391 Pa. 486 (1958); *Commonwealth ex rel. Smith v. Meyers*, 438 Pa. 218 (1970).

"agents." If *C* had killed *IB*, *D* would be liable because *C* is *D*'s agent. But neither *V* nor *P* is *D*'s agent. Although these two approaches usually come to the same conclusion, there is some possibility of a conflict in strange situations. Thus, if *IB* or *V* shoots an officer who is about to thwart the robbery, the killing may in fact further the criminal purpose, although IB is obviously not D's and or C's agent. The most obvious way around this tension is to say that while *IB*'s acts *did* further the crime, they were not *intended* to be "in furtherance thereof."

In other states, the result may depend on who fired the first shot. This may be a rational result on the basis of cause. After all, one who starts a gun battle may anticipate the likelihood that others will return fire and misaim. However, that explanation would also hold if *V* fires first: Store owners may reasonably react without waiting to see if they will be killed. A few courts have crystallized this latter idea by adopting a so-called "provocative act" notion of felony murder—if the defendant's crime "provoked" the killing or "created an atmosphere of malice," the defendant is guilty of felony murder even if *V* fired first.

Justified vs. Excused Killings

Still other courts have argued that *D* should not be liable for C's death because the policeman or the robbery victim was justified in killing C. *D* is liable, however, for the death of IB or *V* because that death is not justifiable but excusable (see Chapter 15). Thus, since C's death is *desirable*, D should not be held liable for it. But the death of IB or *V* is *not desirable*, and D should be held accountable.

This is a misunderstanding of the distinction between excuse and justification approaches. An act is justified depending not on its results but on the circumstances under which it occurred. Thus, when *V* shoots at *D* but hits *IB*, it is *V*'s *act* of shooting, not the result, that is either justified or excused, not the result. Whether the bullet hits *IB*, *C*, *D*, or *X* should be irrelevant.

The Shield Cases: Exception to an Exception to an Exception

However the courts decide these cases, they all seem to agree that in the "shield" case (Case 3 above), *D* is liable. Thus, in *State v. Canola*, 73 N.J. 206 (1977), the court, while holding that D could not be liable for the death of a co-felon by the intended victim of a robbery, declared in dictum that the result would be different if the deceased were used as a shield. This result can be easily explained on a "risk-generating" theory of mens rea.

Other Restrictions

In addition to resolving the issues of causation, American courts by the middle of the twentieth century had established other restrictions on the felony murder doctrine as well:

1. The killing must be done "during" the felony.
2. Neither person-endangering felonies nor "nondangerous" felonies can be the basis of a felony murder charge.

Duration of the Felony: Time Matters

The felony murder rule applies while a defendant is attempting a crime or escaping from the scene. Though courts have differed as to how long an "escape" may take, it is clear that a death occurring days after the felony takes place is not covered by the felony murder rule. Courts have often spoken of the felony "coming to rest" or the defendant having obtained "temporary respite" or having found a "safe haven."

Thus, if *A* robs a store and, while exiting the store, pushes *V1*, who dies from the fall, the death is said to occur "during" the felony. If, however, *A* returns to his house, sits an hour, and then, hearing the police come to the front door, runs through the back door, pushing *V2*, who dies from the fall, the death does not occur "during" the felony, and the homicide is not felony murder.[16]

Limitations on the Predicate Felony

Two limitations are placed upon which felonies can be the basis of the doctrine.

(1) "Merger" (or "Independent Felonious Purpose") Doctrine

This doctrine states that the *predicate felony must not be one involving personal injury* but have a purpose other than inflicting harm. The explanation for this limitation is easier to understand than to apply. If, for example, manslaughter could be used as a basis for the felony murder rule, there would be no more manslaughter convictions, since every such death would become a felony murder. Thus, in *People v. Smith*, 678 P.2d 886 (Cal. 1984), the court held that a mother who intentionally beat her child could not be held for

16. See Annotation, What Constitutes Termination of Felony for Purpose of Felony-Murder Rule, 58 A.L.R.3d 851.

the resulting unintended death *under the felony murder doctrine.*[17] The application of this doctrine becomes more difficult when the underlying felonies are less clearly life-threatening. Most courts agree that if the underlying felony is assault or mayhem, the merger occurs. In more difficult cases, the courts have been divided. For example, "burglary" was defined under the common law as the breaking and entering of a dwelling at night with intent to commit a felony therein. Usually, that felony is theft. But if the intended felony is a life-threatening one which would merge if the assault occurred on the street (*D* enters with the intent to assault *V*), some courts hold that the burglary merges and there is no felony murder charge. *People v. Sears*, 2 Cal. 3d 180 (1970). Only a few jurisdictions refuse to acknowledge the limitation at all. The merger doctrine has thwarted prosecutions based upon a felony murder theory for deaths resulting from child abuse,[18] but state legislatures have responded by passing specific statutes covering homicidal child abuse. See, e.g., Utah Crim. Code §76-56-208.

(2) "Inherently Dangerous Felony" Rule

By far, the most important limitation is the "inherently dangerous felony" rule, which states that the felony can only be used as the basis of a conviction if the defendant was engaged in a felony that created serious risk of death. American courts almost uniformly limited the reach of the felony murder doctrine to felonies involving violence, dangerousness, or both. Guyora Binder, The Origins of American Felony Murder Rules, 57 Stan. L. Rev. 59 (2004). Professor Binder has written extensively on the subject.[19] This limitation has two variations:

1. "dangerous" as defined *in the abstract* by the statute;
2. "dangerous" *as perpetrated.*

The first of these approaches looks only at how the felony in question is perpetrated "in most cases." If, most of the time, the felony is not dangerous to human life, then it is not considered dangerous "in the abstract," even if, on occasion, a defendant does commit it so as to endanger life. An infamous case is *People v. Phillips*, 64 Cal. 574 (1966), in which a chiropractor, knowing that his eight-year-old patient was dying of cancer of the eye, continued to deceive her parents that he could cure her. Upon her death, he was charged with (1) grand larceny and (2) felony murder. The Supreme

---

17. This does *not* mean that the mother could not be convicted of "depraved heart" murder.
18. See Stewart, Murder by Child Abuse, 26 Willamette L. Rev. 435, 440 (1990).
19. See Guyora Binder, Making the Best of Felony Murder, 91 B.U. L. Rev. 4032 (2011); Guyora Binder, The Culpability of Felony Murder, 83 Notre Dame L. Rev. 965 (2008).

Court of California held that only felonies "inherently dangerous in the abstract" could be used for this doctrine and that grand larceny "in the abstract" is not a dangerous felony. It could therefore not be the basis of a charge of felony murder.

This approach has several problems. First, since there is no evidence at trial to determine how a felony is perpetrated "normally," judges or juries may guess at the way in which "this crime" is usually perpetrated. Second, it can create major difficulties when the legislature combines multiple offenses in one statute. Thus, for example, in *People v. Patterson*, 49 Cal. 3d 15 (1984), the defendant furnished cocaine to a friend, who died of an overdose. Defendant's act violated a statute that prohibited "selling, transporting, administering or furnishing" nearly one hundred different dangerous controlled substances, including marijuana, heroin, and cocaine. The court had to decide what "the felony" was: (1) all 400 (or so) of these acts; (2) each specific kind of conduct with respect to all the listed drugs; (3) all acts with respect to a specific drug; (4) each act with regard to each drug. The court chose the last approach and asked whether *furnishing cocaine* was an inherently dangerous felony in the abstract.

The court then had to face the further problem of deciding what test should be used in deciding this question. The court rejected a standard that would have found furnishing cocaine "inherently dangerous" if there were a "substantial likelihood" of death. Instead, it selected a test requiring a "high probability" of death. The dissent argued (almost surely correctly) that if the majority's test is to be based on statistical probabilities, it essentially nullified the doctrine, since *no* felony carries with it the "high probability" of death as a side result.[20]

It may be difficult to determine whether even a "dangerous-sounding" crime can be a predicate. For example, is driving while intoxicated (DUI) a "dangerous" act? Statistically, the answer is no; although a substantial percentage of car deaths are caused by DUI drivers, of all DUI drivers, few actually cause death or even serious bodily harm; most actually make it home without an accident.

The alternative approach asks whether the felony was dangerous "as perpetrated." Thus, in *Phillips*, supra, the defendant clearly perpetrated the felony of grand larceny in a way to endanger the life of his patient, even if grand larceny usually does not endanger life. This approach makes the felony murder doctrine virtually superfluous. If the jurors find that the defendant perpetrated the felony in question in a dangerous way, they can surely

---

20. The United States Department of Justice Bureau of Justice statistics for 1994 show that of all violent crimes, only 20 percent resulted in any injury at all, and that only 1 percent of all victims required any hospitalization. In 1992, less than a third of robbery victims were injured, and only 3 percent required medical treatment. See Moran, FBI Scare Tactics, New York Times, May 7, 1996, at A23.

find that he was aware of this risk and acted recklessly and with a depraved heart. Such a finding establishes mens rea by itself and makes the felony murder rule unnecessary. Indeed, in *Phillips*, the defendant was reconvicted on retrial solely on the basis of depraved heart murder.

These two limitations together, or separately, narrowly restrict (some would say essentially abolish) the felony murder doctrine. When a defendant engages in a felony that is "dangerous in the abstract" (such as armed robbery, or rape, or burglary), a jury could easily find that he was reckless (or had a malignant heart) with regard to the risk of death. *People v. Wilson*, 1 Cal. 3d 431 (1969). And even if the felony is not one "dangerous in the abstract" but only "as perpetrated," the jury may well find the requisite mens rea for murder, as it did in the retrial of *Phillips*. See also *People v. Washington*, 62 Cal. 2d 777 (1965).

In a similar fashion, the combination of the "inherently dangerous" and "merger" rules severely restrict the ability of the prosecutor to use the felony murder approach. The former rule says that only person-endangering felonies can be used as a predicate, while the latter rule says that at least *some* person-endangering felonies may not be used as a predicate. See Gerber, The Felony Murder Rule: Conundrum Without Principle, 31 Ariz. St. L.J. 763 (1999).

Summary

In sum, the courts have generally been critical of the doctrine, and many limit its application to cases where the mens rea for murder could be found in any event. Only in the truly rare cases involving inherently dangerous felonies carried out in a nondangerous way is the full impact of the doctrine likely to be put to the test.

Despite the virtually unanimous criticism by legal scholars, and the willingness of courts to invent limitations upon its reach, however, the felony murder rule is still viable in all but a few states. A few legislatures have repealed it by statute, and one court[21] has judicially abandoned it. Even the Model Penal Code version (see below) has been adopted by only a few jurisdictions. The tenacity of the doctrine probably has several explanations. First, there is an intuition that persons engaged in felonies, particularly very risky felonies, should be held responsible if they commit a greater harm than they anticipated (see the discussion of the "greater crimes" theory in Chapter 6). Second, we are willing to place on the prosecution the burden of proving mens rea with regard to death when the defendant has not shown himself to be "criminal" or "evil" in some other way. We recognize that an erroneous

21. *People v. Aaron*, 409 Mich. 672 (1980).

conclusion would imprison a totally innocent person. However, when the defendant has already demonstrated a mens rea of ignoring mores and laws, we are less willing to cede that benefit of the doubt. See generally Tomkovicz, The Endurance of the Felony-Murder Rule: A Study of the Forces That Shape Our Criminal Law, 31 Wash. & Lee L. Rev. 1429 (1994).

Another way of looking at this question is to try to define the constitutional limits on a state legislature's ability to define crimes. Could a state legislature, for example, declare that any death occurring during jaywalking would be capitally punished? If not, then perhaps there is a constitutional limit to the crimes that can serve as predicates for a felony murder charge. And, most likely, these would be "inherently dangerous" felonies (however that term is defined). In recent years, numerous attacks have been leveled at the doctrine on the ground that the felony murder doctrine generally, and most specifically with regard to the statutory version, establishes an irrebuttable "presumption" of mens rea, which at least arguably violates the due process clause (see Chapter 15). Were the legislature expressly to apply the doctrine to an unquestionably non-inherently dangerous, non-person-endangering felony without the other limiting doctrines as well, the courts might confront a different, and more testing, constitutional problem.

Statutory Felony Murder: The Interplay of Courts and Legislatures

The picture is even more complex. In the United States, where murders are divided into "degrees," legislatures have typically listed a number of felonies that can serve as the predicate for "first-degree" murder. These usually include rape, kidnapping, robbery, arson, and burglary. Individual state statutes may include others as well. But what of "other" felony murders? Under the common law (and by inference therefore in most states), these are "murders." By default, since they are not included in the statutory provision, they are "second-degree" murders.

The Model Penal Code Approach

In accord with most judicial and academic criticism, §210.2 of the Model Penal Code severely limits the doctrine, allowing its application only in cases involving robbery, rape, arson, burglary, kidnapping, or felonious escape. Even then, the Code raises only a (rebuttable) *presumption* that the defendant was murderously reckless with regard to the possibility of death. Under the Code, once a defendant produces sufficient evidence to raise an issue on which there is a presumption, the prosecution must then prove the presumed fact (mens rea) beyond a reasonable doubt. It is fair to say that the Code effectively abolishes the doctrine in the vast majority of cases.

Most legislatures that have otherwise adopted the MPC have rejected its view here.

England, the originator of the rule, statutorily abolished it in 1957. Eng. Homicide Act, 1957, 5 & 6 Eliz. 2, c.11, §11. A few states, while not following the Code on this question, have limited the doctrine in other ways. See, e.g., N.Y. Penal Law §125.25(3), which has been adopted by several states.[22]

EXAMPLES

Examples

1a. Ashley walks into Mom-and-Pop's grocery with a gun and says "Give me your money." Pop refuses, and she shoots him six times at point-blank range. She is charged with murder. Is it?

1b. On her way to the grocery store, but several blocks before she gets there, Ashley trips and falls, the gun discharging and killing a pedestrian. Is this murder?

1c. Ashley attempts the hold-up, but Pop shoots first, killing Zuzu, a customer in the store. Murder?

1d. Pop shoots at Ashley and misses, whereupon Ashley takes Zuzu hostage, using her as a shield. Thereafter, (a) Pop or (b) a police officer responding to the call shoots at Ashley, killing Zuzu instead. Murder by Ashley? By Pop or the officer?

2. Russ, a bank teller, decides one day to embezzle $50,000 from the bank. As he walks unarmed out of the bank with the money in his briefcase, he non-negligently slips on a bank pen left on the floor by some customer and falls into Jezebel, the bank guard, whose gun discharges, killing her. Is Russ guilty of any level of homicide?

3. Go back to Chapter 4, page 96, Example 10. Is this now felony murder?

4. Zeke, a cocaine dealer, sells Gonzo, one of his regular purchasers, enough cocaine for six days. Gonzo takes the cocaine home and, in a

---

22. That statute provides that the defendant may plead an affirmative defense in a felony murder case if he can prove that he "(a) did not commit the homicidal act or in any way solicit, request, command, importune, cause or aid the commission thereof; and (b) was not armed with a deadly weapon, or any instrument, article or substance readily capable of causing death or serious physical injury and of a sort not ordinarily carried in public places by law abiding persons; and (c) had no reasonable ground to believe that any other participant was armed with such a weapon, instrument, article or substance; and (d) had no reasonable ground to believe that any other participant intended to engage in conduct likely to result in death or serious physical injury."

fit of depression or pique, consumes all six days' supply in one hit and dies. Will Zeke be guilty of murder?

5. Bernard Madoff perpetrates a massive securities fraud on thousands of people, inducing them to invest millions of dollars in areas he knows are speculative at best and fraudulent at worst. Two of these investors, having lost their life savings in this scam, commit suicide. Is Madoff a murderer?

6a. Larry burns down his house for the insurance money. Hortense, a firefighter called to the scene, is killed while fighting the fire. Has Larry murdered Hortense?

6b. Same facts, except that Hortense dies because she is negligent in fighting the fire.

7. Reconsider Chapter 6, page 152, Example 8. Is Marty guilty of felony murder?

8. At 12:40 a.m., Keith is in a rural area driving a Chevrolet Tahoe (an SUV) with no rear license plate. He is pulled over by a state trooper, but when the officer exits his cruiser, Keith takes off at speeds up to 90 mph, turning off his car's headlights, running two stop signs and a red light, and driving on the wrong side of the road. As the vehicles enter an urban area, the trooper stops the pursuit, fearing that the chase might cause an accident. One minute later, Keith runs another red light and collides with a car, killing the driver. A state statute (which we'll call §101) provides that it is a felony "(a) if a person flees or attempts to elude a pursuing peace officer . . . and the pursued vehicle is driven in willful or wanton disregard for the safety of persons or property. . . . (b) For purposes of this section, a willful or wanton disregard for the safety of persons or property includes, but is not limited to, driving while fleeing or attempting to elude a pursuing peace officer during which time three or more violations that are assigned a traffic violation point count . . . occur." By another statute, among the violations that are assigned points (in addition to reckless and dangerous driving) are (1) driving an unregistered vehicle owned by the driver, (2) driving with a suspended license, (3) driving on a highway at any speed more than 55 miles per hour when a higher speed limit has not been posted, (4) failing to come to a complete stop at a stop sign, and (5) making a right turn without signaling for 100 feet before turning. Did Keith commit felony murder?

9. Dave sees an SUV sitting outside a convenience store, with the motor running. He jumps in and throws the car into reverse. At that moment, a woman runs out screaming: "You can have the car, just let me have my son." Dave then notices, for the first time, that there is a five-year-old

in a car seat in the back. The woman tries to take the child, but the child becomes entangled in the seat belt. Dave hits the gas, and the car speeds forward, the child hanging halfway out of the car, and the woman running alongside yelling. When the car finally stops, and Dave runs out, the child is dead. Has Dave committed murder?

10. John and Henry conspire to embezzle money from the corporation for which they work by taking monies that should be used to pay for proper disposal of hazardous wastes, instead dumping the wastes into a river. Allyson is killed by the wastes. Assuming that the dumping is not a felony, are John and Henry murderers?

11. Mehta and Saul burglarized Sarah's house, but Sarah walked in on them and called the police. They leaped in their car and took off. As Mehta drove, Saul took several shots at a pursuing police car but injured no one. The police then stopped the car, and Mehta surrendered. The police handcuffed him and threw him into the police cruiser. As they were handcuffing Saul, however, he broke free, ran back to the car, and sped off. Five minutes later, he fired one shot at the pursuing car of Police Officer Joshua Aleman. The shot killed Aleman. The state wishes to try Mehta for Aleman's death, using a felony murder charge. What result?

12. Arabella, an executive vice president of CityBanc, is in desperate need of money. She decides to go to the bank on a quiet Sunday afternoon and take a few hundred thousand dollars in cash from the bank vault. She brings a large, wheeled suitcase and stuffs it with cash, as well as with jewels from safety deposit boxes in the bank. As she is leaving, George Guard comes around the corner, pulls his revolver, and says, "Freeze." Arabella, panicked, rolls the suitcase toward George and runs through the fire exit before he can shoot. The suitcase hits George, who is standing at the top of a steep flight of stairs, and pushes him down. He dies from the fall. Charged with his homicide, Arabella wishes to plead self-defense. Can she?

13. Brenda commutes 30 minutes to work every day. For the past year, the only freeway leading to her destination has been under construction, to her great dismay. Large signs notifying drivers of the construction—and the accompanying 45-mile speed limit—are displayed miles in advance. One morning, Brenda is running very late for work. She grabs her morning thermos of coffee, dashes into her car, and speeds off. As she approaches the construction on the freeway, the roads are relatively clear. Staring at the clock, she speeds through the construction zone at 90 miles an hour. Suddenly, Brenda spills steaming hot coffee on her legs and subsequently loses control of the wheel.

She barrels into the construction zone, injuring several construction workers and killing one. Brenda later learns that in her jurisdiction, driving 40 miles or more over than the speed limit is a felony. Is Brenda liable for felony murder?

EXPLANATIONS

Explanations

1a. This is the most obvious use of the felony murder doctrine. Ashley is clearly involved in an inherently dangerous felony, the killing is "in furtherance" of the felony, and it occurs during its perpetration. It is also causally linked to the felony. In most jurisdictions this will be a first-degree murder because it is a felony listed in the first-degree murder provision. But we don't need the felony murder doctrine here. Ashley has killed with premeditation (common law) and purposely (MPC).

1b. Ashley may be liable because she killed a pedestrian as she was on her way to commit a robbery. This, however, stretches the limits of the duration doctrine, since the danger here comes simply from Ashley's carrying a weapon; the robbery has not yet "begun" in that sense. That is, suppose that Ashley were not intending to rob the store, but merely carrying an illegal gun, and killed a pedestrian in the same way, because of tripping. Is carrying the gun in a public place sufficiently dangerous to warrant *murder* liability when the gun unexpectedly discharges? Moreover, Ashley's accidental discharge of the weapon was clearly not in furtherance of the robbery. If her jurisdiction has this agency requirement, she will likely escape liability for felony murder.

1c. The difficult question here is that someone *other than the felon* killed someone else. As to this type of scenario, the courts are mixed. Ashley's culpability for murder will depend on what factors courts in her jurisdiction examine to determine whether Ashley "caused" the customer's death. The shooting here is not in furtherance of the felony, and it is justified (a term which means it was not a crime for Pop, or the officer, to shoot at Ashley; see Chapter 16). However, Pop would not have fired his weapon—and in turn, the customer would not have been killed—had Ashley not been in the midst of robbing the store. The possibility that someone would be shot during the robbery is arguably foreseeable, so under a proximate cause approach, this may be enough to show causation.

1d. Recall our earlier discussion regarding felonious actors using third parties as shields from harm. Under this scenario, virtually all the courts, either in holdings or dicta, are in agreement that Ashley may be held responsible. The Model Penal Code would address the problem as one of cause, not of felony murder (see Chapter 7).

2. This is intended to demonstrate the clearly contrasting case to Example 1a. The typical kind of horrible hypothetical raised by opponents, it employs the broadest statement of the felony murder doctrine to demonstrate its irrationality. The death has occurred "during" the perpetration of "a" felony. The felony is causally related to the death. If the doctrine were not limited in some way, opponents argue, Russ would be guilty not only of embezzlement but of murder. Thus, "the inherently dangerous" requirement is imposed, and embezzlement is not inherently dangerous. Without this requirement, Russ might be liable for murder even though he was totally non-negligent with regard to any risk that death would occur. Despite the fact that critics have used such "horribles" in attacking the doctrine, they have not pointed to a single appellate reported opinion in which the courts have applied the doctrine to such a situation. Under the MPC, felony murder doctrine, Russ is not liable for the death. Only a few felonies will even serve as a possible predicate for felony murder, and embezzlement is not among them.

3. In Chapter 4, we concluded that Helen had no mens rea with regard to Harry's death. Now, however, we add the doctrine of felony murder. Helen has arguably committed felony murder. Burglary is one of those felonies that most courts have held to be "inherently dangerous" *in the abstract*. Thus, even though she is unarmed and has been extraordinarily careful not to endanger life in committing burglary *as perpetrated*, Helen may be found guilty of felony murder. It is possible to argue that the death here was not "in furtherance" of the felony, and therefore the application of the felony murder rule is inapt. Under the MPC, there is a presumption in any burglary that the defendant acted with reckless indifference to the value of human life. But the presumption is rebuttable, and Helen would have no difficulty here rebutting that presumption.

4. Zeke may be liable for felony murder in some jurisdictions, which have declared drug transactions (or sales of specific drugs) "inherently dangerous" in the abstract. This is a difficult result to accept, since hundreds of thousands of sales are consummated every day with relatively few deaths. Courts have reached differing conclusions. Most find that drug transactions are not, per se, inherently dangerous. Some find no causal relation between the sale and the overdose unless the seller (a) helps administer the fix or (b) watches while the victim administers the fix. But in those situations, the act is not "really" the sale, but the administering or encouraging the administration of the drug. Moreover, this

seems to be applying the "as perpetrated" approach rather than the "in the abstract" approach, and may not need the felony murder doctrine at all to convict. Again, if Zeke knows that Gonzo has overdosed before, Zeke's transfer of so much cocaine at one time might be found by a jury to reflect "a conscious disregard of a risk . . . etc." under the Model Penal Code or the common law, qualifying Zeke for either manslaughter or murder but not "felony murder."

5. Madoff is probably not guilty of felony murder and probably not even of murder. The felony is not "inherently dangerous," either in the abstract or as perpetrated. *Even* if a suicide were "foreseeable," the risk is not so great that Madoff should be held criminally responsible (civil liability might be another question). And even if all these limitations were somehow avoided, it is hard to see how the deaths are "in furtherance of" the felony. Finally, unless the suicide occurred immediately after the victims lost their money, it is possible that the "duration" requirement of the doctrine might not be met. Madoff may be a scoundrel but he is not a murderer, at least under the felony murder doctrine.

6a The first problem here is defining what the underlying felony might be. Is it "arson" (almost surely an inherently dangerous felony and a statutorily enunciated basis for first degree felony murder in most states) or is it "insurance fraud" (almost certainly not inherently dangerous in the abstract)? If arson, then under the common law, Larry may be guilty of murder and possibly first-degree murder. Larry's best argument is that the felony has ended, but if the felony is still continuing, he is responsible for the causally related death. Under the MPC, if the predicate crime is arson, a presumption of recklessness would be established, but Larry could probably rebut that easily unless he knew that the fire would be more dangerous than anyone might expect. See Chapter 7 for a discussion of the causation questions here. Another consideration is whether the death was "in furtherance" of the crime. Under these facts, it would be difficult to argue that it was.

6b. In common law and under the MPC, the victim's negligence is relatively unimportant in any crime and particularly in a felony murder. The only opportunity for Larry here is to argue lack of causation (see Chapter 7).

7. No, not unless the state applies the harshest possible version of the felony murder rule. First, larceny or theft is not inherently dangerous. Even as carried out here, the theft itself was not dangerous to anyone. Second, the theft itself is over. Marty is "home" and "safe." Mary Lou's death is a tragedy, but it's not felony murder.

8. Surprise! (Or not. You know the answer must be bizarre; we wouldn't include it here if it were the obvious one.) The California Supreme Court, in *People v. Howard*, 34 Cal. 4th 1129, (2005), held that this could not be felony murder. California uses the "inherently dangerous in the abstract" test to determine whether a crime can be the predicate for felony murder. The court held that although Keith's driving was clearly inherently dangerous, he *could* have violated §101 by nonviolent means (the ones listed at the end of the example). Therefore, since not all ways of violating §101 are "inherently dangerous in the abstract,"§101 could not be the predicate for a felony murder count. The court combined the number of ways in which §101 could be violated, concluded that some of them were nondangerous, and therefore held that the statute *could* be violated "in the abstract" in a nondangerous way. This methodology seems to be in direct conflict with the one used by the same court in *Patterson*, discussed on page 224.

   In view of these results, it would be hard to argue with a layman's conclusion that this is an absurd result. After all, how could killing someone with *that* vehicle after *that* kind of car chase, at *that* speed, not be murder? But consider that (1) the prosecutor could easily have charged Keith with "depraved heart" murder and almost assuredly convicted (after all, the officer recognized that the chase was dangerous); and (2) many courts are generally hostile to the felony murder rule, preferring that the prosecutor prove mens rea as to the deaths.

9. This tragic scene actually occurred in Missouri several years ago. First—is Dave guilty of "straight" murder? He certainly did not "premeditate" the death of the child, and therefore would probably not be guilty of first-degree murder in most states. Moreover, he probably did not have "universal malice," or a "depraved mind" (under the common law) or "recklessness under circumstances manifesting extreme indifference" (under the MPC) unless he recognized a real risk to the child. This could be argued either way, but it is at least possible that the entire situation was so confusing at that point that Dave's actions would fall short of this standard.

   Can he then be guilty of felony murder? What felony has Dave committed? Perhaps kidnapping, but many states require that the taking be for ransom, which is not the case here. Perhaps robbery: It could be the taking of property by force or threat of force. That is surely an "inherently dangerous" felony and many states statutorily list it as a predicate for first degree murder. Carjacking is an even more likely predicate. Legislatures enacted carjacking statutes when the penalty for robbery was seen as too lenient. So it may be an "inherently dangerous" felony. However, many of these same legislatures, while creating this new felony, did not list it as a predicate for first degree murder. So if the prosecutor uses that statute, it may only be second-degree murder. Let's consider that—a felony which has a harsher sentence than robbery can't be the basis of a first degree murder charge while robbery, with a "lighter" sentence, could be. Is this any way to run a criminal code?[23]

10. This question raises, again, defining "the" felony involved. Is the "predicate felony" (a) embezzlement? (b) conspiracy to embezzle? (c) dumping wastes? The first two are almost surely not "inherently dangerous." But the last one might be, depending on the precise wording of the statute. (For example, if the statutory violation is "dumping hazardous wastes without a permit," it would not be inherently dangerous, for one could safely dump, but still not have a permit. If the statute prohibited "dangerous dumping of hazardous wastes" or "dumping of hazardous materials into aquifers or other sources of drinking water," however, it might be a predicate felony.) Since none of these felonies is specifically articulated in §210.2 of the MPC, the prosecutor will not be able to rely on the felony murder doctrine at all in an MPC jurisdiction.

11. The issue, of course, is whether Mehta's arrest and custody means that the felony has "come to a rest." Clearly it has for him, but not for Saul. The courts are actually divided three ways on this. Some say arrest terminates liability for the arrestee, whatever his cohorts do. See, e.g., *State v. Milam*, 108 Ohio App. 254 (1959). A second group says the felony continues until everyone is arrested (or comes to rest in some other way). E.g., *State v. Hitchcock*, 350 P.2d 681 (Ariz. 1960). A third group emphasizes the particular facts of capture, surrender, or arrest. *Auman v. People*, 109 P.3d 647 (Colo. 2005). Many of these decisions rely on statutory wording (although none of the statutes is explicit on this point). On the one hand, a rule requiring the arrest of all co-felons emphasizes the potential danger that any felon generates when working with others. On the other hand, accomplice liability generally requires that the risk of death be "reasonably foreseeable" by the defendant, and many states require that the defendant actually foresee the risk of death, or possibly intend that death occur (see Chapter 14). In the example as given, Mehta knows that Saul is armed—maybe he should have

23. In the real case, the defendant was convicted of first degree murder, not on the basis of felony murder, but on the basis that the defendant dragged the boy for almost four-and-a-half miles, and a jury could conclude that during that time he deliberated. *State v. Davis*, 107 S.W.3d 410 (Mo. App. 2003).

warned the police (perhaps the police in the first cruiser didn't warn Aleman). As a general matter, whether the felony has "come to rest" is an issue of fact for the jury. *State v. Lee*, 969 S.W.2d 414 (Tenn. Crim. App. 1997).

12. The general rule is that a participant in a felony cannot claim self-defense if he committed the homicidal act during the course of the felony. *Street v. Warden*, 423 F. Supp. 611, 613-614 (D. Md. 1976); *State v. Celaya*, 135 Ariz. 248 (1983). But in most of the cases so stated, the defendant was involved in a violent felony (usually robbery) and used deadly force. Here, neither of those predicates is true—larceny is not an "inherently dangerous felony" in the abstract nor as committed here, and Arabella did not use deadly force. (If the Example had said that she picked up a nearby pistol and shot George, that might raise a different question entirely.)

13. Brenda's actions fall within the standard common-law definition of felony murder (i.e., a death occurred during the course of a felony). However, we then must examine whether any exceptions to the rule may give Brenda relief from liability. Brenda's strongest argument would be that the death certainly was not "in furtherance" of the felony. If Brenda's jurisdiction places this restriction on felony murder, then Brenda will likely escape liability.

    Brenda may also argue that the felony of speeding is not "inherently dangerous," and so cannot be the basis of a felony murder charge. The strength of this argument will undoubtedly rely on the way the court defines "dangerous"—in the abstract or as perpetrated. The circumstances of Brenda's crime—specifically, speeding at such a high rate through a construction zone, where it is known that construction workers will be vulnerable—would likely be deemed inherently dangerous. Therefore, Brenda's best hope is if the court examines dangerousness in the abstract. She will argue that people speed on a regular basis and that, statistically, few incidents of speeding actually result in a crash or death. The prosecutor will counter that the court should not examine the dangerousness of speeding generally, but specifically speeding at rates over 40 miles per hour over the speed limit. Certainly, such reckless driving is inherently dangerous even in the abstract.

    The answer to this question is simple under the MPC. Since the predicate felony of speeding is not under the category of robbery, rape, arson, burglary, kidnapping, or felonious escape, Brenda would not be liable for felony murder.

MANSLAUGHTER

Manslaughter is usually defined as "an unlawful homicide without malice aforethought." This is then subdivided between "voluntary" and "involuntary" manslaughter:

1. Voluntary manslaughter is a killing done "on a sudden" in the "heat of passion" after "adequate provocation."
2. Involuntary manslaughter is either "merely" reckless (but not the result of a "depraved mind") or "criminally negligent" killing.

Voluntary Manslaughter

The Rules of Voluntary Manslaughter

By the middle of the nineteenth century, most American courts had come to the conclusion that *only* a killing

1. engendered by an act recognized as "legally adequate provocation" and
2. actually done suddenly, in the heat of passion

would be reduced to a category of homicide called "voluntary manslaughter," for which the punishment was significantly less than murder.

Unfortunately, the courts were unclear as to why these killings were "reduced." As Justice Holmes said, "the life of the law has not been logic; it has been experience." The Common Law 1 (1881). Manslaughter was a category of homicide created by the judiciary as a way of limiting capital punishment; it was not based on carefully thought-out doctrine.[24] When they did make such an attempt, the courts articulated two conflicting themes:

1. Voluntary manslaughter was indeed a murder but because of the law's "regard for the frailty of mankind," the punishment was reduced.
2. The defendant killed "in a frenzy" brought on by "sudden provocation" at a time when "reason was dethroned," so there was no mens rea.

The tension in these two explanations is obvious. Under the first, the defendant is a murderer because he has intentionally or with a depraved

24. This explains why provocation affects only murder liability. If *D* is "adequately provoked" by *V* but only breaks his leg, the provocation is irrelevant.

heart taken human life. Under the second, because the defendant had no mens rea, he is *not* a murderer; indeed, if he truly had no mens rea, he should perhaps be exonerated.[25] This tension has never been resolved.

This failure to explain the rationale of manslaughter has other implications. Thus, even today scholars are unable to agree on whether manslaughter is a "partially excused" or "partially justified" homicide (see Chapter 16). In addition, this ambiguity creates problems when the defendant, while acting "in the heat of passion," kills the wrong person, either because the actual provoker ducks or because the defendant is mistaken as to who provoked him. If the basis of the reduced liability is that the killing is "partially justified" because the victim in some sense "asked for it" or "had it coming," this rationale clearly is inapplicable to the innocent victim or the mistaken defendant. If, on the other hand, the rationale is that the defendant's actions are "understandable" because of his loss of control, and therefore "partially excused," the rationale would appear to cover even such a "misaim" case.

"Legally Adequate Provocation"

People are angered by many things. During that anger they sometimes (a) flail out in despair or (b) take intentional action against the persons they believe responsible for that event. Although the early decisions appeared willing to reduce the punishment of any such killing, by the middle of the nineteenth century, courts had limited the kinds of events that would generate such a reduction to the following:[26]

1. a battery, mutual combat, or aggravated assault
2. adultery
3. illegal arrest.

---

25. For example, Neb. Rev. Stat. §28-305 provides that "A person commits manslaughter if he kills another without malice . . . upon a sudden quarrel," and California similarly provides that manslaughter is "the unlawful killing of human being, without malice. . . ." Cal. Penal Code §192 but Judge Stephen argued that "Homicide, which would otherwise be murder, is not murder, but manslaughter if the act is done in the heat of passion . . . ," J. Stephen, A Digest of the Criminal Law (1877), and the Model Penal Code a century later uses almost exactly the same formula, defining manslaughter as "a homicide which would otherwise be murder [if] committed under the influence of extreme mental or emotional disturbance."

26. One of the authors of this book has attempted to show that the common law decisions did not in fact so restrict the juries but treatise writers misconstrued the decisions, and courts began following those writers rather than the much more liberal, and subjective, decisions. See Richard Singer, The Resurgence of Mens Rea I: Provocation, Emotional Disturbance, and the Model Penal Code, 27 B.C. L. Rev. 243 (1986).

We will not speak here of the last of these categories. The first, however, is interesting because of its interplay with the doctrines of self-defense. Initially, the writers and courts spoke of a "tweak on the nose" as being sufficient provocation to warrant reduced punishment if killing ensued: Honor, and not physical disabling, was at stake.[27] A second subcategory involved cases of "mutual combat" undertaken in "chance (or "*chaud*"—hot) medley." If Jim and John got into a heated barroom debate that escalated from words to fists to weapons, the one who killed the other was held to be a manslaughterer rather than a murderer because the killing was done "on a sudden passion" during a "chance" (or *chaud*) occasion. If, however, during the same encounter, Jim tried to "retreat" from the argument and the use of deadly force but found himself pursued by John, whom he then killed, Jim might be acquitted of any homicide because the killing was "*se defendendo*" (see Chapter 16).

The second category, adultery, is the most interesting (and controversial). The doctrine was easily stated: If the defendant found his (the defendant was always male) spouse *in flagrante delicto* and killed either the spouse or the lover, or both, the killing was manslaughter. Although this might appear to be a case of "infidelity," the leading, early English case described adultery with the defendant's wife as the "highest invasion of [his] property."[28] Although no case appears to have actually involved a spouse who walked in on the spouse and lover naked in bed but not actually *in flagrante delicto*, some courts came nervously close to restricting the exception to such a case. See, e.g., *State v. John*, 30 N.C. (8 Iredell) 330 (1848), where the husband saw *V* climbing out of the bedroom window and pursued him. The court rejected the claim of manslaughter: "to extenuate the offense, the husband must find the deceased in the very act of adultery with his wife." The reason for the restriction may be clear; courts did not wish to encourage precipitous action by unduly jealous husbands. However, the restriction was also irrational: Jealous husbands who, for example, see their wives in "semi-undress" in the (undressed) presence of another man may in fact become enraged. To require them to wait until adultery actually occurs seems both unrealistic and unnecessary in assessing the level of their guilt.

At the other extreme of the "adequate provocation" doctrine was an unequivocal rule that words alone could never constitute adequate legal provocation.[29] Some courts, however, appear to have created an exception to this exception: If the words spoken by the victim informed the defendant of an event that, had the defendant witnessed it, would be legally provocative,

27. Jeremy Horder, Provocation and Responsibility (1993).

28. *R. v. Mawgridge*, (1706) Kelyng, J. 119.

29. One of this book's authors, however, reviewing the cases, has concluded that "there is no basis in the early cases for the doctrine." Singer, *supra* n. 22, 27 B.C. L. Rev. 243, 256 (1986), even if the doctrine were restricted to "insults."

the words might qualify. However, other courts held that not even a confession of adultery would suffice. Thus, in *State v. Grugin*, 147 Mo. 39, 47 S.W. 1058 (1898), the defendant father expressly sought out the victim, whom he had been told had had sexual relations with the father's minor daughter. The victim declared, "I'll do as I damn well please about it." The father killed the rapist, and the court reversed a second-degree murder conviction, holding that the words could amount to legal provocation. A century ago, the Harvard Law Review declared that "words which . . . are a mere vehicle to convey intelligence of the fact which actuates the crime were not included in the original rule. . . ." Note, 27 Harv. L. Rev. 89 (1913). Nevertheless, many American courts continue to follow the "rule," e.g., *Sheppard v. State*, 243 Ala. 498, 10 So. 2d 822 (1942).

"Heat of Passion and Cooling Off"

The corollary of a requirement that the killing be done in the "heat" of passion is logically that if the defendant has cooled off, he cannot claim the reduction. Before the middle of the nineteenth century, the issue was not whether the defendant had, in fact, cooled off, but whether "enough" time had elapsed to allow him to cool off. This issue was seen as question of law, to be decided by the judge—if the judge decided that there was sufficient time then, at least in legal theory, the jury should never hear of the actions that provoked the defendant into killing the victim. This doctrine severely penalized "brooders," such as Hamlet. Thus, if D finds his wife and her lover in bed and kills them instantly, it is manslaughter. But if D does not kill instantly, but broods about the event for several hours (or days) and then lashes out, the law did not allow a defense. This is questionable, since it appears to be "rewarding" the person who does not try to control himself, while penalizing one who tries, but fails, to avoid lashing out.

Twentieth-Century Changes in the Doctrines

These restrictive doctrines were criticized as inconsistent and too restrictive. Gradually the courts loosened the rules.[30]

(1) The "Reasonable Man" Test

Adequate legal provocation became anything that could cause the "reasonable man" (now the RPP) to act in passion. Quickly, however, this

30. Other countries have also "subjectivized" the doctrine. Michal Gilad, Provocation and Multiculturalism, 46 Crim. L. Bull 1097, 1113 (2010) (Ireland, South Africa and Israel); S. Yeo, Unrestrained Killings and the Law (1998) (India).

change led to allowing other events to act as provocation, since reasonable people become angry over events other than those listed above. Today, even words may be sufficient. Thus, confessions of adultery or taunts relating to sexual potency or competency may suffice as provocation. *People v. Berry*, 556 P.2d 777 (Cal. 1976). The law with regard to racial epithets also seems to be changing, although this has been rather slow, at least in jurisdictions that have not adopted the Model Penal Code's approach (see below).

In many jurisdictions the RPP now has many of the physical characteristics and experiences of the defendant. Thus, courts have allowed juries to consider, as part of the reasonable person's makeup, the defendant's age, gender, physical stature, physical disabilities, lack of sleep, and other such factors. Most courts refuse to consider any of the defendant's "psychological" characteristics, fearing that this would allow "hotheads" who do not attempt to control their anger a reduction based on their failure to improve their character. This explanation, however, is unconvincing. Even a hotheaded defendant, after all, will be convicted of manslaughter and be punished for that crime; it may seem excessive to punish the defendant for murder just because he has failed to sufficiently alter his hotheaded nature.[31]

(2) The Cooling-Off Period Cools Off

Both as part of the adoption of the RPP test, and as part of a general individualization of the criminal law, the law with regard to the "cooling-off" period has also changed. First, whether the defendant has cooled off or had time to do so is now a question of fact for the jury to resolve. Second, more courts have spoken as well of the "cooled-off person" who has been "rekindled" either by the sight of the victim (initial provoker) or by words, informational or otherwise, spoken by the victim regarding the initial provocation. Thus, if *V* sodomizes D and escapes, only to be seen by D some days, weeks, or even months later, whereupon D immediately kills *V*, there is a greater likelihood today that D will be found guilty of manslaughter rather than murder. Finally, at least some jurisdictions appear to allow "brooders," whose anger *increases* over time, to plead provocation to reduce the offense to manslaughter.

---

31. Even if the theory here is that D has been reckless with regard to whether he might kill, that should require some showing that D has either killed, or come close to killing, at earlier times. This would require evidence of the extent of his anger and loss of control.

(3) Cumulative Provocation and Time Framing

Courts have been divided on whether the jury may consider "cumulative provocation" in determining a defendant's guilt.[32] In battered spouse cases, for example, which are also discussed in Chapter 16, it may be that the "straw that broke the camel's back" would not suffice to meet a test of legal provocation, but that an ordinary (or reasonable) spouse, having been subjected to humiliation or worse over a period of years, might "snap" in response to what would otherwise be a "trivial" action on the part of the provoker.

In a larger sense, this is a question of "time framing"—whether to allow the defendant to introduce evidence of recent (but not immediate) provocations and acts by the victim, or whether to focus exclusively on the moments immediately prior to the shooting. We will visit this question again, when considering justifications and excuses, and the extent to which earlier decisions by the defendant will affect his ability to raise a claim.

THE MODEL PENAL CODE APPROACH

Consistent with its general embrace of subjective liability, the Code rejects the rigidity of the common law on heat-of-passion killings. It provides that a "killing which would otherwise be murder" is manslaughter if it is done

> under extreme emotional or mental disturbance [EED] for which there is a reasonable explanation.

Several things should be noted about this provision. First, by declaring that the killing would "otherwise" be murder, the Code implicitly adopts the theory that a reduction to manslaughter is not a matter of right, that is, that the defendant's reason was *not* "dethroned" and that he acted "purposefully, knowingly or recklessly" "under circumstances manifesting extreme indifference to the value of human life" with regard to death. Second, there is no "time limit" or "cooling-off" period. Third, the Code does not require "provocation" at all—if the defendant became emotionally disturbed over an event such as 9/11, it is possible that he would qualify for an EED claim. Fourth, *any* impetus for the disturbance is sufficient. Thus, for example, not only informational words but highly inflammatory taunts (racial, ethnic,

32. For example, "Continuing strain in a marriage" may constitute sufficient provocation in New Jersey, *State v. Erazo*, 126 N.J. 112 (1991) and Wisconsin, *State v. Felton* 110 Wis.2d 485 (1983), but in Illinois, a history of marital discord "undermines, rather than supports, such a claim." *People v. Chevalier*, 131 Ill. 2d 66 (1989).

or gender epithets), once explicitly excluded from the doctrine of heat of passion, might be covered by the MPC approach. Twenty years ago, a rioter in Los Angeles, outraged by a verdict of acquittal for several white police officers who had beaten a black defendant, chose a white trucker at random and hit him in the head several times with a brick. Had the victim died (which, fortunately, he did not), it is plausible that the Code would have allowed the rioter to claim EED; it is clear that the common law would not have allowed such a claim. However, a disturbance must still be "extreme"; an event of everyday life would probably not be sufficient.

Ironically, the language of EED, which was expected by the Code drafters to liberate the jury from the rigors of the common law and send all these cases to the jury, has been interpreted by many courts to require expert witnesses, usually psychiatrists or psychologists, to testify to an "emotional or mental disturbance." Eric Drogin, To the Brink of Insanity: "Extreme Emotional Disturbance" in Kentucky Law, 26 N. Ky. L. Rev. 99 (1999) ("Successive waves of judicial interpretation have effectively transformed Kentucky's EED doctrine into an insanity defense . . ."). Thus, if a defendant is unable (due to any cause, including lack of funds) to put on such evidence, these courts preclude reference in jury instructions to this Code section.

Furthermore, the Code appears to re-inject an objective standard by requiring that the explanation for the disturbance be "reasonable." However, the next sentence of the Code's provision declares that "[t]he reasonableness of such explanation of excuse shall be determined from the viewpoint of a person in the actor's situation under the circumstances as he believes them to be." Thus, the Code both subjectivizes and objectivizes the standard for the reduction to manslaughter. The commentary to the Code *explicitly* refuses to explain what factors (e.g., age, gender, impotency) should be considered as part of the "actor's situation," preferring to leave to the courts the development of that definition.

Direct Attacks on the Concept of "Heat of Passion"

Both the increasing "subjectivization" of heat of passion and the very notion that anger should be relevant in assessing guilt have been attacked in the past two decades by many commentators and some legislatures as both sexist and too tolerant. Writers began to argue that the doctrine was clearly created to indulge male hierarchies,[33] and far too often applied to reduce

33. Gender Equality, Social Values and Provocation Law in the United States, Canada and Australia, 14 Am. U.J. Gender, Soc. Pol'y & L. 27 (2006); Victoria Nourse, Passion's Progress: Modern Law Reform and the Provocation Defense, 106 Yale L.J. 1331 (19997); Suzanne D. Rozelle, Controlling Passion: Adultery and the Provocation Defense, 37 Rutgers L.J. 197 (2005).

the penalties for men who killed women (often their spouses or lovers) out of jealous rage. The notion that insults to honor would partially excuse a killing was also seen as pandering to male pride (similar to dueling).[34] Finally, modern cases where (male) defendants claimed their homophobia should mitigate their killings of gays or lesbians generated much debate; while courts usually rejected such claims, these critics joined the movement for repeal or severe revamping of the defense.[35] These critiques in some ways took the law "back to the future," where judges, and not juries, decided what constitutes "adequate legal provocation." In addition, a series of English court decisions that appeared to embrace a virtually totally subjective approach[36] were rejected by a very high English court in 2005[37] and heavily criticized by academic commentators.[38]

These criticisms have been somewhat successful. In the United States, Texas has relegated the entire issue of heat of passion and provocation to the sentencing stage—a killing is a felony of the first degree, but is punished as a felony of the second degree if the defendant, at sentencing, shows by a preponderance that it was "under the immediate influence of sudden passion arising from an adequate cause." V.T.C.A. Penal Code, §19.02.[39] Maryland has overturned three centuries of common law by declaring that "[t]he discovery of one's spouse engaged in sexual intercourse with another" is not adequate provocation. Md. Code, Criminal Law §2-207.

---

34. Richard Holton and Stephen Shute, Self-Control in the Modern Provocation Defence, 27 Oxford J. Legal Stud. 49 (2007).

35. Joshua Dressler, When "Heterosexual" Men Kill "Homosexual" Men: Reflections on Provocation Law, Sexual Advance, and the "Reasonable Man" Standard, 85 J. Crim. L. & Criminology 726 (1995); Cynthia Lee, The Gay Panic Defense, 42 U.C. Davis L. Rev. 471 (2008); Robert Mison, Homophobia in Manslaughter: The Homosexual Advance as Insufficient Provocation, 80 Cal. L. Rev. 183 (1992).

36. For example, the defendant's addiction to glue sniffing was considered a characteristic of the RPP, at least when the provocation consisted of taunts about his addiction. *R v. Morhall* (1995) 3 W.L.R. 330. In *R. v. Doughy* (1986) 83 Cr. App. R. 319, the court considered the stress generated by no sleep when the defendant father almost inadvertently "silenced" his crying infant baby. In *R. v. Weller* (2004) 1 Cr. App. R. 1, the defendant's jealously and possessiveness were characteristics of the RRP. The height of subjectivity in England was *R. v. Smith (Morgan)* (2003) 3 W.L.R. 654 (House of Lords).

37. *Attorney General v. Holley* (2005) All. R. 371 (Privy council).

38. Sarah Christie, Provocation: Pushing the Reasonable Man Too Far?, 64 J. Crim. L. 409 (2000); Jesse Elvin, The Doctrine of Precedent and the Provocation Defence: A Comment on *R v. James*, 69 Mod. L. Rev. 819 (2006); Edward M. Hyland, *R. v. Thibert*: Are There Any Ordinary People Left?, 28 Ottawa L. Rev. 145 (1997).

39. The Texas story is extraordinary. Until the mid-1970s, the killing of a spouse (usually the wife) found in adultery was not merely partially excusable, and hence manslaughter, as under the common law and in the rest of the states, but justifiable, and hence noncriminal. See Bill Neal, Sex, Murder, and the Unwritten Law: Gender and Judicial Mayhem, Texas Style (2009). In the mid-1970s, Texas joined the majority of states in allowing the claim to reduce (but not justify) the crime of conviction. Now it is "merely" a sentencing consideration.

Minnesota, while expressly allowing "words or acts" to be considered as provocation, nevertheless singles out (probably in response to *Doughy*, mentioned in fn. 36 above) "the crying of a child" as inadequate provocation. Minn. Stat. §609.20. Several Australian states have abolished the defense entirely.[40] In England, Parliament, rejecting what was seen as the totally subjective approach adopted by the courts, legislatively replaced the claim with a "loss of control" criterion if the loss is caused by an adequate "trigger." A defendant's gender and age could be considered, as could characteristics of the defendant which were the target of the provoker, but clearly ruled out were matters of the defendant's "temperament." Sexual infidelity, is explicitly precluded as an "adequate trigger." Coroners and Justice Act 2009, §§54-56.[41]

The Rules of Involuntary Manslaughter

Reckless and Negligent Manslaughter

Early common law cases spoke of a defendant who, while committing an "unlawful" act, killed someone as being guilty of "involuntary" manslaughter. The term "unlawful" included not only crimes but torts. Thus, to use an old example, if a roofer in a crowded city throws a beam down to the street and, in doing so, kills someone, it is manslaughter. However, if the case occurs in a remote area, the death is not manslaughter. The courts and writers were unclear as to the explanation, but it is certainly appropriate to consider the first roofer, but not the second, "reckless," or "negligent."

Serious confusion, however, arose in this area because some courts suggested that the two roofers were (respectively) "negligent" and "non-negligent" in tortious terms. Thus, the notion grew that a tortiously negligent actor could become liable for manslaughter. This view, however, has been emphatically rejected by virtually all courts, which require a "higher degree of negligence" for criminal liability generally, see Chapter 4, and for homicidal liability in particular. *Fitzgerald v. State*, 112 Ala. 34 (1896); *State v. Weiner*, 41 N.J. 21 (1964).[42]

---

40. Carolyn B. Ramsey, Provoking Change: Comparative Insights on Feminist Homicide Law Reform, 100 J. Crim. L. & Crim. 33 (2010); Adrian Howe, Reforming Provocation (More or Less), 12 Austl. Feminist L.J. 127 (1999).

41. Anna Carline, Reforming Provocation: Perspectives from the Law Commission and the Government (2009), Web JCLI; http://webjcli.ncl.aac.uk/2009/issue2/carline2.html; C. Withey, Loss of Control, 174 Crim. L. & Justice Weekly 197 (April 3, 2010).

42. This may not be the case where the legislature has *explicitly* adopted tortious negligence as a possible predicate for liability. Compare the definition given in a British case: "All sober and reasonable people would inevitably have realised that the defendant's conduct must have

As in tort, once an "objective" standard is introduced as a benchmark, the question becomes the degree to which the standard is subjectivized. In criminal law, where the defendant's culpability is the main focus, that becomes critical. In many instances, the courts instill the RPP with at least some of the defendant's characteristics. Thus, in *People v. Strong*, 37 N.E. 2d 568 (1975), the defendant intentionally stabbed the victim with a hatchet and three knives. Based upon his prior experience and his religious beliefs, he truly believed that he could do so without harming the victim. The majority concluded that these characteristics should be a part of the jury's RPP standard and that the defendant might be liable only for criminally negligent homicide, rather than second-degree murder (as a person without such beliefs or experience surely would be). On the other hand, *State v. Williams*, 4 Wash. App. 908 (1971), discussed on pages 76-77, supra, held that the trial court, applying a state statute which appeared to employ a tortious negligence standard for manslaughter, properly refused to consider any of the defendant's characteristics; (1) poorly educated; (2) unaware that his child's tooth infection could lead to gangrene and death; (3) imbued with certain cultural beliefs and (4) fearful that reporting the child's illness to the authorities might result in having the child removed from the home permanently. (The state statute was altered soon after *Williams* to require a "criminal" negligence standard, but the legislature did not directly address the issue of whether any of the characteristics in *Williams* should be considered in that standard.)

Misdemeanor-Manslaughter

Accidental deaths that occur while the defendant is committing a misdemeanor are sometimes held to be manslaughter. This doctrine acts in the same way as does the felony murder rule. However, courts have not surrounded it with the same limitations and safeguards that they have used in dealing with the felony murder rule, perhaps because there is no possibility of the death penalty. Thus, even misdemeanors that are not "inherently dangerous" in any true sense of that term can be used as the predicate for a manslaughter charge.[43]

In non-EED cases, a killing that is "merely reckless" (done with a subjective awareness of the risk of death but not under circumstances manifesting extreme indifference to the value of human life) is manslaughter. If, on the other hand, the killing is done with "criminal negligence" (no actual awareness of the risk, but with a gross deviation from the standard of care of an RPP), it is "negligent homicide," which is punished less severely than manslaughter.

---

subjected the victim to some harm, regardless of whether the defendant realised that or not." *R v. A* (2005) All E.R. (D) 38 (Jul); *State v. Barnett*, 218 S.C. 415 (1951).

43. See, e.g., *Todd v. State*, 594 So. 2d 802 (Fla. 1991); *State v. McLaughlin*, 621 A.2d 170 (R.I. 1993).

8.1 Homicide Under the Common Law and the MPC

Common Law Category	INTENDED KILLINGS	NON-INTENDED KILLINGS
First-Degree Murder	PREMEDITATION, DELIBERATION, AND WILLFULNESS Purposely or Knowingly	STATUTORY PREDICATES OF FELONY MURDER
Second-Degree Murder	INTENTIONAL Purposely or Knowingly	DEPRAVED HEART FELONY MURDER Recklessly under circumstances manifesting extreme indifference to the value of human life
Manslaughter (Voluntary)	HEAT OF PASSION Extreme Emotional or Mental Disturbance (EED)	HEAT OF PASSION; RECKLESS CULPABLE NEGLIGENCE EED or Reckless
Manslaughter (Involuntary)		CULPABLE NEGLIGENCE Criminal Negligence

KEY: Common law is in capitals; Model Penal Code language is in upper/lowercase.

Finally, and not surprisingly in light of its views on the felony murder doctrine, the Code rejects entirely the misdemeanor-manslaughter analog.

One possible way to conceptualize the various tests, both common law and modern, with regard to homicides is shown in Table 8.1.

Examples

1a. Papa loved Mama, and Mama loved men (with apologies to Garth Brooks). Papa, a trucker, comes home unexpectedly one night and finds Mama and Neighbor in flagrante delicto. Papa kills Neighbor with the bottle of champagne he had brought to surprise Mama (as Brooks says, "If he was looking to surprise her, he was doing fine."). Manslaughter?

1b. As in the song, Papa finds the house deserted (except for his children) and heads downtown in his semi-tractor trailer truck. He gets to the local motel and, changing from first to fourth gear, plows through the room in which Mama and Neighbor are cavorting. One or both are killed. Murder or manslaughter?

1c. Same facts as 1b, except that Papa rams his truck into the wrong room, either because (a) the clerk gave him the wrong number, or (b) Papa misread the number on the room. What crime(s)?

1d. Papa, depressed by his discovery, and having no clue where Mama is, simply waits at home for her. When she arrives, he asks where she has been, and she responds "I've been with a real man, you chump," at which point Papa hits her with the champagne bottle, killing her.

1e. Suppose that, instead of having intercourse in the hotel room, Mama was having her foot massaged by her (obvious) boyfriend.

2. Mike Douglas, after a particularly hard day at the office, is driving home when he is caught in a traffic jam in mid-August. His air conditioning is out. He has been sitting in 106°F weather for one hour with no relief in sight. Just as he sees an opportunity to take an off-ramp, another car, driven by Donny DeVito, cuts him off. Furious and frustrated, Douglas shoots DeVito. Is Mike a murderer?

3a. Marie, an electrician, is called on Super Bowl Sunday, just an hour before kickoff, by Gus, a mechanically inept homeowner, who begs her to come to his house, which has experienced an outage. Expecting the job to take 15 minutes, Marie accepts it, but once there, determines that there is a more serious problem, which *could* result in a fire, although in her judgment the risk is low. Anxious to see the game, she puts in a temporary fix and tells Gus she'll be back tomorrow. Of course, the house burns down during the third quarter, and Gus is killed. Has Marie committed manslaughter?

3b. Same facts except that, in her anxiety over missing the game, Marie simply does not find the latent defect at all.

4. Glen does not know it, but both of his taillights are out. Because of this, Linda collides with his car from the rear, and kills Joshua, Glen's passenger. Driving without operative taillights is a strict liability misdemeanor. Is Glen guilty of manslaughter?

5. Hamlet's hunting license has, unknown to him, expired. Using all care, he shoots at a deer but nevertheless kills Polonius, whom he does not know is there. Hunting without a license is a misdemeanor. Manslaughter?

6. Paul was raised by a very religious family. At the age of eight, he attended church four nights a week. By 18, he was in seminary, and by

22, he was an ordained minister. His family always inveighed against abortion. For the first few years of his ministry, Paul preached against abortion on many occasions, but took no further action. As he grew older, however, he first joined, and then led, local and national anti-abortion groups. He participated in numerous sit-ins outside abortion clinics and was frequently arrested. After an abortion provider was killed in another state, Paul's fury intensified. He resigned the ministry and devoted himself full-time to anti-abortion activities. Finally, he decided that he could no longer stand on the sidelines. To him, abortion providers were committing murder. He purchased a gun and practiced with it every day. After two weeks, he determined to kill the local doctor who performed abortions. Knowing that this was done on Fridays, Paul positioned himself outside the clinic at 6 a.m. and waited. As he sat there, he was nagged by doubts about his course of action, but he convinced himself that it was necessary to save the lives of the unborn. He, himself, says: "I thought maybe I would feel, y'know, a lot of resolution and that kind of thing, but my stomach felt like literally a bottomless pit." When the doctor arrived, Paul shot him four times as he stepped from his car. Paul is charged with first-degree murder. What result?

7a. Harry takes Hillary out on a date. Intent on having intercourse with her, he obtains some GHB, a colorless, odorless drug that is known as the "date rape" drug. The drug can produce lassitude and a temporary euphoria, and sometimes hallucinations. Unknown to Harry, the drug can also produce unconsciousness if it is even slightly "impure." He asks the bartender, Henry, to put the GHB, which he tells Henry is a harmless substance, in Hillary's drink. If Hillary dies as a result of the drink, what homicidal crime has Harry and/or Henry committed?

7b. Same facts. Now suppose that the state legislature has recently declared GHB a controlled dangerous substance, whose possession or delivery is a felony. Is there any different answer?

8. On a Friday afternoon, Ruth Clark, a suicide bomber, kills herself and 10 other people in a downtown mall. On Monday, the police arrest Donald Poker, the person who persuaded Clark to commit the act. On Tuesday, as Poker is being arraigned, Richard Regnis, whose wife and three children were killed in the explosion and who is still clearly distraught, jumps out of a courtroom seat and shoots Poker five times, shouting at him, "You killed my family, you creator of mass destruction!" What will be the likely result if Regnis' attorney seeks to obtain a manslaughter instruction?

9a. Theresa, a model, was savagely attacked by her boyfriend, who threw acid in her face, resulting in her severe disfigurement. When she returned to work, virtually all of her co-workers were sympathetic. Maggie, however, greeted her with the comment "You look like you were run over by a lawn mower." Every day, for weeks, Maggie continued her barrage of insults and insensitive comments. As Theresa walked into the office one day, Maggie exclaimed, "Look, everyone, Scarface is back." Theresa killed Maggie on the spot. What is the likely result?

9b. Suppose, instead, that Margaret, a new worker who had never seen Theresa before, quietly whispered to Fran "Theresa looks like Scarface," but Theresa overheard that remark and killed Margaret on the spot.

10a. Bernice agrees to appear on a television talk show, believing that the purpose is to discuss her gardening prowess. As the show is being taped for future broadcast, the host suddenly announces, "Fooled you, Bernice. This show is not about gardening. In fact, this is about secret lovers. And here, now, is your secret lover, Barnaby." Barnaby comes out and describes, in graphic detail, his seven-year passion for Bernice. He grabs Bernice's hand and begs her to marry him immediately. Bernice has always detested Barnaby. She is deeply in love with another man, and she is extremely humiliated. She grabs a lamp on the set and hits Barnaby, killing him. With what level of homicide should she be charged?

10b. Now assume that the reason Bernice is upset is because Barnaby is of a different race than she. Any difference in the result?

11. Chester decides to rob the corner convenience store. His wife, Pauline, implores him, "No violence. No weapons. Just go in, take a few things, a little money, and leave." Chester agrees. As he walks into the shop, however, Chester screams at the owner, Apu, "It's you. I've been waiting 20 years for this." Chester grabs a nearby snow shovel for sale in the store and hits Apu. "You killed my daughter 20 years ago. Now you'll pay for it," says Chester. Chester hits Apu 30 more times, killing him. Chester then takes several food items and the money from the cash register, and leaves. Twenty years earlier, Apu had been (non-negligently) driving a car when Chester's daughter ran directly into its path. An investigation found that Apu had not committed any crime or tort. Chester had always thought Apu criminally responsible, but had moved away soon thereafter, and did not know that Apu was running the convenience store. For what level of homicide, if any, are Pauline and/or Chester guilty?

12. Harry, the sorcerer's apprentice, was working hard in his lab when his mentor, Dumbledore, came in and told him to take the rest of the day

off. Gleeful, Harry went to the florist to pick up a dozen roses, with which to surprise his new bride, Hermione. Well, he did surprise her. But he surprised Snape, too. Furious, Harry picked up the quidditch ball that he had brought back as a trophy for having won the latest tournament, and threw it at Snape. Snape, however, ducked, and the ball went out the window, where it killed Ron, Harry's best friend. Harry is charged with murder. Can he magically get the charge reduced?

13. Imam is a Sikh, whose religion requires him to wear a turban. Imam has been subjected to many outspoken abuse, and many people have addressed him as "towelhead." Among these folks is Imam's boss, Sarah. For the past two weeks, Imam has spent hours and overnights working on a major project. He is exhausted, but proud of his work. He hands the completed report to Sarah, who, taking one look at it, throws it at him, hitting him on the arm. As she does so, she says, "Do it again, Towelhead. Even you can't think this (expletive deleted) is sufficient." Imam picks up a tape dispenser and throws it at Sarah, killing her. What level of homicide?

14. In September 2010, Taylor jumped to his death from the George Washington Bridge, humiliated by the dissemination on MyTube and the Internet of a video taken by his roommate, Rave, showing Taylor and another man involved sexually. Is Rave criminally liable for Taylor's death?

15. Ludwig calls his girlfriend, Elise, on the phone. Although she answers, Elise says, "I can't talk now, I'm driving." Ludwig responds, "Don't be silly. You've got a hands-free phone. No prob." Elise agrees and continues to talk with him for five minutes, but the conversation is stopped short when she runs through a red light and crashes into a van, killing three people. (a) Is she liable for their deaths? How about Ludwig? (b) Would it make a difference if the state had a law, punishable by a $100 fine, precluding use of a handheld cell phone while driving? (c) Suppose instead the two were texting?

16. Gus and Lynn are devout Christian Scientists. When their three-year-old daughter is diagnosed with leukemia, they steadfastly refuse to allow any treatment, confident that God will save their child. Tragically, she dies. Have Gus and Lynn committed manslaughter?

17. Gary and Cindy are college students who have been best friends since middle school. Gary is generally aware that Cindy has a peanut allergy; she is always careful to mention such at restaurants and to friends who make her any sort of food. However, Gary has never seen Cindy actually ingest peanuts and is clueless as to the severity of her allergy. Having mild allergies himself, Gary is sure that peanuts would simply

give Cindy a rash, or a case of the hives at worst. Gary and Cindy are also huge jokesters and are always playing pranks on each other. One day, Gary decides to make Cindy a sandwich laced with a hint of peanut butter. He chuckles in his head as he imagines her confusion when she begins to feel itchy. Not wanting to cause serious discomfort to Cindy, he even stocks up on antihistamine medication. Unfortunately, Cindy's reaction is much worse than expected. Her throat constricts and, unable to find her epinephrine injector, she dies before Gary can find help. Is Gary guilty of manslaughter?

Explanations

1a. Papa is guilty of manslaughter. This is the classic case of "adequate legal provocation" even under the common law. But the facts as stated could hide an enormous amount of ambiguity. For example: Did Papa see Neighbor's car in the driveway? Did he hear heavy breathing as he approached the bedroom? Suppose Papa had to go to the refrigerator for the champagne, or to his truck for a tire iron? Most discussions of these events leave out the "ancillary" facts, but they might be enough to suggest either that (1) Papa was not as surprised as he claims; (2) Papa had "some" time to cool off before he killed.

1b. The Brooks song fails to tell us how Papa *knew* the room in which Mama was carrying on; if he had to ask the clerk for this information, there may be less opportunity for reduction. Moreover, Papa may have had time to cool off, either objectively or subjectively, while he was driving to the motel. Remember that under the common law, this was a question of law for the judge. Under modern common law, there is no "threshold" that the defendant must meet. Under the Model Penal Code, the passage of time, while one factor, is not determinative of a defendant's inability to have the slaying reduced to manslaughter, as long as he is still acting under the extreme disturbance.

1c. These are misaim cases, and the difference in the *reason* for the misaim would seem irrelevant. The question here is whether the law should mitigate Papa's conduct because of *his* mental state ("partial excuse") or preclude mitigation because the *victims* did not "ask for it" ("partial justification") (see Chapter 15). The issue here is whether the law should look solely at the mens rea of the defendant, without knowing the results of his actions, or whether the law should consider the fact that an innocent person was killed, EVEN IF the defendant was in a provoked, or otherwise extremely emotional, state. IF the issue is whether the defendant (or others like him) is morally culpable, then the law should consider whether the defendant had "lost control" and reduce the punishment accordingly. If, however, we consider the innocent victim, the calculus may be revised. Most courts will allow the defendant to claim heat of passion. Under the MPC, there is no requirement that the victim (or anyone) have "provoked" the defendant, and it goes to the jury. (Do you see a pattern here?)

1d. Under the original common law, Papa has no reduction because words alone are never adequate legal provocation. However, under more recent doctrine and under the Code, this will be a jury question.

1e. Movie buffs will recognize this crime. In *Pulp Fiction*, the boss had someone thrown out of a window for massaging his wife's feet. That crime is reported, but never seen. The answer under the common law is clear—nothing less than intercourse could be adequate legal provocation. Under the test of the "reasonable person," however, and certainly under the MPC approach, this question might go to the jury.

2. Most of us have been frustrated by such cutoffs, losses of parking spaces, and so on. Indeed, the phenomenon described here has become so common that, in both England and the United States, it has a label: "road rage." Under the common law, this is an easy case. Unless DeVito's car has hit Douglas's car (arguably the equivalent of battery), there is no adequate legal provocation. Thus, although Douglas is *really* irate, there is no reduction. This is also the likely result under the Model Penal Code. Even if there is "extreme" mental or emotional disturbance, it is probably not due to a "reasonable explanation" (but the question is closer). Still, no reported case reduces the killing from murder to manslaughter.

   Since the late 1990s, a wide variety of "rages" have been proffered by defendants to reduce homicide liability. Recall the "air flight rage" situation when a passenger, incensed about a delay in landing, attacked (fortunately nonfatally) an airline attendant. Or the "hockey rage" father who, apparently upset by what he considered to be "rough play" in his son's hockey practice, killed the person he thought was encouraging the aggressive play. (During the trial, the defendant claimed self-defense, not rage, but the episode is unfortunately typical of hotheaded parents at Little League games.) After the (involuntary manslaughter) verdict, the victim's son said the defendant "just lost it," and told the defendant, "I don't hate you. I forgive you." See N.Y. Times, Jan. 12, 2002. Again, this sentiment reflects the tension in these cases. People (mostly men?) do "lose it" at times; should they be convicted of murder, or are they less culpable than a "depraved heart" killer? Can the criminal law change behavior patterns, both of the actual defendants and others, by punishing those who do not train themselves *not* to "lose it"?

3a. Marie could be found guilty of manslaughter. Her action here might be characterized as "reckless" under the common law or the MPC, but it is almost certainly not "under circumstances manifesting extreme indifference to human life" or "with a depraved mind." Those tests might be met if Marie had not even put in a temporary fix but had rushed off with no regard for the risks at all. We told you football could be a dangerous game, Marie.

3b. Since Marie did not see the defect, she was not reckless; she did not subjectively perceive and disregard a risk. This is involuntary manslaughter under common law, and, at worst, "negligent homicide" under the Code. Under the Code, the question is whether her failure to see the defect is a "gross" deviation from what a reasonable electrician would see (if not pressured by the big game).

4. Under application of the misdemeanor-manslaughter rule, Glen is guilty of involuntary manslaughter, even if his failure to be aware of the dead taillights is not negligent. The Code rejects this rule and would require proof that Glen's failure to know of the situation was "grossly deviant" from the actions of an RPP.

5. This is not an easy case. Under a rigid application of the misdemeanor-manslaughter rule, Hamlet should be guilty. But unlike Example 4, the failure to have a license has little or no causal relation to the injury; Hamlet has been careful in his hunting. Thus, even under the common law, he should not be found culpable.

6. This is the true story of Paul Hill, who in 1994 shot and killed Dr. Bayard Barrett in Pensacola, Florida. See N.Y. Times, Sept. 24, 1995, sec. 4. Assuming that Paul has no claim of necessity (see Chapter 16), or insanity, or diminished capacity (see Chapter 17), he appears to be liable for first-degree murder. He premeditated the crime by purchasing the weapon in advance, practicing with it, and lying in wait for the victim. Under the common law, Paul has no other claims. However, under the Model Penal Code, he may argue that he is guilty only of manslaughter because his killing was committed under "extreme emotional or mental disturbance." The Code, unlike the common law, does not require provocation, much less adequate provocation. Its focus is on the mental state—or lack of it—of one who kills. Arguably, a person in Paul Hill's "situation," as the Code puts it, might gather that his conclusion was reasonable, even though he clearly knew that what he was doing was illegal. In fact, Florida has not adopted the MPC, and Paul Hill was found guilty of first-degree murder.

7a. Begin by asking whether Harry has committed murder. Harry may be a bad actor, and a potential rapist, but under the common law, it is unlikely that he had a "depraved heart" *with regard to death*. Thus, this is probably not murder. And if it were murder, it would not be first degree, since the death was not premeditated. The same result would obtain under the MPC: Harry is not purposeful or knowing *with regard to death*, and even if he knew that there was *some* risk of death, it would be hard to argue convincingly that he acted under "circumstances manifesting extreme indifference to the value of human life." Under the common law, then, Harry is, at worst, guilty of manslaughter, but not voluntary manslaughter, since this did not occur in the heat of passion brought on by adequate provocation. The common law and the MPC, in slightly different language, would require that Harry exhibit "gross negligence" or "recklessness" in his conduct, which might be appropriate here, depending on Harry's (or the reasonable person's) understanding of GHB's potency.

Henry, not knowing the kind of drug he was distributing, would probably not even be "grossly negligent."

Caveat. In legal theory, Harry and Henry have both committed battery upon Hillary, since they have knowingly caused her to be touched by a drug to which she did not consent. The battery is likely to be a misdemeanor (since no serious bodily harm occurred as a result of the mere touching). If the common law notion of "misdemeanor manslaughter" were applied here, both might be guilty of manslaughter.

This hypothetical is based upon a real case, in which a jury convicted two defendants of involuntary manslaughter. In the actual case, the young men who laced the drinks failed to call emergency help; instead, they argued about what to do when the victim passed out.

7b. Is this now a felony murder? The first question would be whether Harry or Henry has committed a felony under the statute. Harry knew that GHB was a drug. His failure to know that it was a legally proscribed drug is irrelevant (see Chapter 5 on mistake of law). Thus, he has committed a felony. But the felony is probably not "inherently dangerous," either in the abstract, as many courts have required, or even as perpetrated here. Thus no felony murder.

But Harry *might* be guilty of felony murder if his drugging of Hillary could be seen as an "attempt" to commit rape (or sexual assault) (see Chapter 9 for a discussion of why this could be rape). Most states provide by statute that a death that occurs during an attempt to commit rape will be first degree felony murder. The issue here would be whether Harry has moved sufficiently toward the target crime as to constitute an attempt. For a detailed analysis of that question, see Chapter 12. The short answer is that Harry is probably *not* guilty of attempt under most common law tests, but might well be guilty of attempt under the Model Penal Code. Under the Code, rape (or deviate sexual intercourse) is a predicate crime for which the rebuttable presumption of recklessness arises. Still, Harry can probably rebut that presumption fairly easily.

Henry will *probably* not even be guilty of the felony, since he did not know that he was dealing with a drug which *might* be legally proscribed. If, however, the statute is read as imposing strict liability, or if possessing or distributing any substance is a crime activating the "greater crime" theory (see Chapter 5), then Henry might be responsible for the felony possession. Even then, just as with Harry, this is probably insufficient to warrant felony murder liability.

8. Under the common law, Regnis will fail, for several reasons. First, although he may well have been provoked by Poker's homicidal acts, those acts were aimed not at him, but at others. Second, many courts would require that Regnis actually have *seen* the deaths of his family. Third, Regnis only acted 72 hours after his family's deaths, and 24 hours after Poker's arrest. Under the original common law, this would almost surely be held, as a matter of law, to be sufficient time to "cool off." Finally, Regnis sought out Poker, so the meeting is hardly "chance." Regnis premeditated the encounter and the killing; had Regnis simply been in the courthouse and inadvertently bumped into Poker, it might have been a situation of "rekindling" the cooled-off man. But this is not the case here.

   Under the MPC, the results are likely to be different. The Code does not require a provocation, nor does it preclude "brooders" from obtaining a possible manslaughter instruction. The question, rather, is whether a reasonable jury could find that Regnis was acting under "extreme mental or emotional disturbance." Surely a jury could so find, even though three days have passed since the bombing. Indeed, under the Code's formulation, which is much more subjective than the common law's, Regnis might obtain such an instruction three years after the event.

9a. This example has two problems. First, the provocation consists of "only" words, and not even informational words at that. Under the original common law, this would be sufficient to prevent Theresa from claiming heat of passion. At least some states today might recognize some insulting words as sufficiently provocative to raise a jury issue. But that's not the end of it. One insult, even as snide and dastardly as Maggie's, is unlikely to be sufficient provocation under the common law. Thus, Theresa is going to have to argue that the law should view the threats as "cumulative." As noted in the text, courts have been divided on whether to allow such evidence.[44] Given the persistence of

---

44. A classic case is *Freddo v. State*, 127 Tenn. 376 (1912), Defendant, a "quiet, peaceable, high-minded young man," had been raised to abhor profanity. A coworker, knowing of his sensitivity, taunted him by deliberately calling him a "son of a bitch" at every opportunity.

Maggie's nastiness (combined, her defense counsel would argue, with Theresa's agony over her condition), Theresa's reaction is "reasonable." Certainly, in the words of the MPC, it is the result of "extreme emotional distress." We considered (and you should, too) having the insults here be racial in nature: Is the victim of constant racial discrimination, who suddenly hears the "n" word one time too many, from someone he has never met, entitled to have the jury consider a reduction to manslaughter?

The Model Penal Code would be more likely both to allow evidence of the words *and* of the cumulative nature of Maggie's acts. Teresa would be much better off in England, where judicial decisions prior to 2009 had made clear that any physical characteristic (a permanent limp, kyphosis (having a humped back, etc.)) would be part of the reasonable person's characteristic. That basic premise has been codified in the new statute.

9b. This exacerbates the problem. If, in Example (a), Margaret might be said to have "asked for it" by riding Theresa day after day, that can surely not be said about Margaret. Even if Margaret had spoken these words directly to Theresa, it would stretch the notion of partial justification to say that Margaret's barb "asked for" Theresa's reaction. On the other hand, if the reduction is a partial excuse, then the focus should be more on Theresa and the effect that Margaret's remark had on her.

10a. Under traditional common law, Bernice cannot plead heat of passion. Barnaby's profession of love would be "words only" and would therefore not suffice. And although the words are "informational," they do not inform her of an act that, had she seen it, would qualify as provocation. Even under modern common law, the words are insufficient. Barnaby's touching her hand is a bit more problematic. Although early common law referred to an "assault" as sufficient provocation, and although assault is usually defined as a nonconsensual touching, the assaults that were contemplated were "insulting" touching, which "aggravated" a man's (?!) honor. The question is whether to view the touching from Barnaby's viewpoint, which would mean that the touching was not intended as an insult, or from Bernice's, which might qualify it as an insulting touching. The better judgment, however, is that the touching alone would not meet the common law requirements.

One day, Freddo "snapped" and killed the coworker. The appellate court, conceding that defendant was "in the heat of passion," nevertheless upheld a murder conviction, declaring that "the law regards no mere epithet or language, however violent or offensive, as sufficient provocation for taking life. . . ."

The result might be different under the Model Penal Code. The Code does not preclude words, informational or not, as the possible basis of a manslaughter mitigation. If Bernice was truly distraught, she might meet the "extreme emotional or mental disturbance" part of the Code's test. The crucial issue would be whether her reaction is "reasonable" for someone in her "position."

From a purely subjective viewpoint, Bernice has lost control. Both common law courts and the MPC have moved toward increasing subjectivism to recognize that persons who have actually lost control are less blameworthy (and possibly less deterrable) than those who have killed with a "depraved heart."

10b. This example takes the question one step further. Certainly, we wouldn't want to "validate" Bernice's racism by allowing it to mitigate her culpability. In recent years, several defendants have claimed "gay panic" when they killed someone who made a homosexual advance upon them. In fact, this example is based upon a real event in which a gay man announced, during the taping of a television show, his love for the male defendant, who then killed him, although the actual killing occurred several days after the taping of the show. The defendant was found guilty of second-degree murder. See *People v. Schmitz*, 586 N.W.2d 766 (Mich. App. 1998), but his conviction was reversed on other grounds. Although the courts have generally refused to allow a heat of passion (or EED) claim, the writers have been divided—some arguing that if the defendant truly was outraged, and had lost control, (s)he should not be lumped together with "depraved heart" killers. Others have argued that the law should not tolerate homophobia, even as a mitigation, and that the law should require the defendant to learn how to control his animosity toward others. Compare Bradfield, Provocation and Non-Violent Homosexual Advances: Lessons from Australia, 65 J. Crim. L. 76 (2001); Dressler, When "Heterosexual" Men Kill "Homosexual" Men: Reflections of Provocation Law, Sexual Advances, and the "Reasonable Man" Standard, 85 J. Crim. L. & Criminology 726 (1995). Lee, The Gay Panic Defense, 42 U.C. Davis L. Rev. 471 (2008).

11. Chester has killed Apu. But while it took at least several minutes to kill Apu, this will probably not be "premeditation," even in a jurisdiction where "premeditation may occur in a second." But it may be second-degree murder—malice aforethought homicide in the old common law. Chester will argue heat of passion but Chester had 20 years to cool off. That's more than enough time, certainly under the common law view that this was a question of law, not of fact. Under more modern views, however, the cooling-off question is for the jury—and Chester will argue that he was "rekindled" (although Apu did nothing

to remind him of the original grief). Under the Model Penal Code, the issue is always one for the jury—which might be sympathetic to Chester and conclude that a "reasonable person" in Chester's "situation" would experience "extreme mental and emotional disturbance."

What about felony murder? Certainly, Chester had larceny on his mind when he entered the store. And he committed larceny after he killed Apu. But there seems to be little connection between the larceny and the killing. Chester will argue that he did not kill Apu to facilitate the larceny—he was so enraged that he forgot the larceny. So, the killing was not "in furtherance of" his crime. He will then argue that, having killed Apu, he "remembered" the larceny and took the money, but that by that time Apu was dead so, once again, although the killing furthered the larceny (making it easier to steal the money), it was not in furtherance of the larceny. There are reported cases, for example, where *A*, in a rage, kills *B*, and then steals his money. Assuming that the idea of taking the money occurs AFTER the killing, courts have found no felony murder. This is a more difficult case, because Chester intended to steal before he saw Apu. But he will argue that there were two—or possibly even three—unconnected "events" in this scenario.

To the extent that Chester is culpable for Apu's murder, Pauline may be, as well. Recall that the felony murder rule imposes liability on accomplices in the felony for a felony murder, whether or not they actually aided in the killing. Here, Pauline would certainly be found to be Chester's accomplice in the predicate felony; her arguments against liability would then mirror Chester's.

12. This is difficult, because it raises the question of why the common law declared that acts in the "heat of passion" generated by "adequate legal provocation" reduced a killing to manslaughter. If the notion is that the provocateur somehow "deserved" his comeuppance because of his dastardly deeds, then Harry hasn't a chance—Ron certainly didn't deserve death just because he was passing by Harry's window. If, on the other hand, the argument is that Harry was transported by anger, then his ACT (and not its result) should be our focus, and Harry's act was surely provoked.

    This is also much easier under the Model Penal Code, which focuses exclusively on the defendant, and eschews the requirement that he be provoked by anyone, much less the deceased. If the jury could conclude (as surely it could) that Harry was reacting as many in his "situation" would, he will be convicted of manslaughter, not murder.

13. Under the common law, Imam is likely to be guilty of murder. It is very unlikely that he can successfully claim "heat of passion," for several reasons: (1) insulting words are never adequate legal provocation; (2) the

common law rarely recognized "cumulative provocation," so the fact that Sarah was constantly abusing him will not help him—indeed, it may undercut his claim, since he never reacted with deadly force before; and (3) the reasonable person of the common law probably is not a Sikh, and it is unlikely that a judge would tell a jury to assess Imam's actions as those of a "reasonable Sikh." The problem, of course, is that to a non-Sikh, "towelhead" does not demean or attack one's religious views. Imam has one possible claim—the file that hit him on the arm. Common law sometimes stated that "an assault" was sufficient provocation. But usually, the assault had to be more than a "mere" touching. But wait—Imam's not through—the "assaults" that counted in the common law were typically "insulting" touches. The writers and courts often wrote of a "mere fillip upon the nose" as being sufficient provocation, because the act insulted the defendant's dignity. It's not likely that this would be followed in the twenty-first century, but consider the possibility that a minor touching might qualify while the deepest verbal insults won't even get Imam to the jury.

Under the MPC, the case is entirely different. The Code does not require a provocation—merely that the defendant act under "extreme mental or emotional disturbance." Sarah's constant attacks on Imam, combined with his exhaustion, as well as her direct rejection of his work, might raise a jury issue here. Moreover, the MPC asks the jury to consider the actions from someone in the defendant's "situation." As the text suggests, this may not include hotheadedness—but Imam's longstanding toleration of these insults might demonstrate that he does NOT have a short fuse, and that the jury should consider all these factors as part of his "situation" and the "reasonableness" of his explanation.

14. This, of course, is the nationally publicized case of Tyler Clementi. Clementi's suicide was the latest in a series of such deaths that had, in one way or another, occurred after similar abuse. In another well-known incident, 13-year-old Megan Meier hanged herself fifteen minutes after she received a Myspace message, ostensibly from a 16-year-old neighbor boy, that declared, "The world would be a better place without you." In fact, the was message sent by a 49-year-old woman who believed Megan was spreading rumors about her daughter. At least six states have enacted statutes criminalizing abuse of the Internet and social media. Lyrissa Lidsky and Andrea Pinzon Garcia, How Not to Criminalize Cyberbullying, 77 Mo. L. Rev. 693 (2012).[45]

45. See generally http://www.cyberbullying.us/research.php; Ian Rivers et al., Bullying: a Handbook for Educators and Parents (2007); S. Hinduja, J.W. Patchin, School Climate 2.0: Preventing Cyberbullying and Sexting One Classroom at a Time (2012); J.W. Patchin, S. Hinduja, Cyberbullying Prevention and Response: Expert Perspectives (2012).

These statutes raise significant First Amendment issues and carry relatively small sentences.[46] The question for this chapter, however, is whether the roommate, or the mother in Meier's case, is criminally responsible for their victims' deaths. As we saw in Chapter 7, there are a few decisions where a victim's suicide has been held to be "caused" by the defendant, but these cases usually involved serious physical violence (or even attempted murder) by the perpetrator. Assuming that causation can be proven, demonstrating that the cyberbully is criminally negligent or reckless will be quite difficult. As horrifying as the action of the roommate or the mother is, the likelihood of suicide or some similar self-injury is low. Even though it is highly unlikely that any person seeking to torment another on the Internet has not heard of one or more of these tragic results, the statistical likelihood of suicide from such an event is incredibly low. One survey, for example, indicated that 35 percent of surveyed teens said that they had been the subject of "rude" or "nasty" or "threatening or aggressive" messages. See Lidsky and Garcia, supra, at n. 45 page 259. Yet the usual reaction is either anger or frustration, not self-loathing. This then raises the question whether the (mathematically low) risk of self-injury is so trivial that not even a reasonable person would consider it. The alternative interpretation is that whether a risk is "substantial" is not quantitative but normative, and that *any* possibility that death would result from this kind of activity is sufficient to make the defendant "criminally negligent" or possibly even reckless.

15. If the risks of cyberbullying are not well-known or are too small to result in a conclusion of negligence (or worse) (see Example 14 above), the same cannot be said for using cell phones while driving. And the data are crystal clear here—the dangers from hands-free cells are just as high as those from hand-held. Even if neither Elise nor Ludwig knows that, they "should" be aware of those facts. Moreover, since she is driving there could be an argument made that she is engaging in an inherently a dangerous activity (while on the phone), and thus Elise's actions might well be "grossly negligent" under the common law and "criminally negligent" under the MPC. That many (possibly even a majority of) people continue to use cell phones while driving could potentially make the action less likely to be criminally prosecuted; however,

46. Ravi was not charged with Clementi's death; instead, he was indicted for bias intimidation, invasion of privacy, hindering apprehension and tampering with evidence. Convicted on all counts, his ultimate sentence was thirty days in jail. The state prosecutor in the Meier case could find no basis on which to proceed, and a federal prosecutor "creatively" interpreted federal law to charge computer fraud and abuse. The jury found the mother guilty, but the trial court overturned the verdict. *United States v. Drew*, 259 F.R.D. 449 (C.D. Cal. 2009).

negligence is judged by the *reasonable* person, not the *ordinary* person. Of course, even if Elise is liable, Ludwig may well argue (lack of) causation—Elise could (and should) have terminated the conversation, and it was her failure to keep watch that was an intervening cause that resulted in the collision. Ludwig is not an accomplice (see Chapter 14) because he had no intention, nor purpose, that a collision occur.

15b. Ironically, the statute might make the duo *less* liable for the deaths. Even if the legislature has acted unreasonably (by not banning all cell phone use, handheld or hands-free, given the data), El and Lud can certainly argue that the legislature has implicitly said that hands-free is not as negligent as handheld. That the legislature might have made a "politically sound" rather than a "statistically sound" judgment is not likely to undermine their position.

15c. If cell phone use is dangerous, texting while driving is even more so. Fifteen states ban cell phone use while driving; Forty-seven ban texting. http://www.ghsa.org/state-laws/issues/distracted%20driving (last visited Jan. 25, 2018). A Car and Driver test showed that driving while texting is 20 times more dangerous than driving while inebriated. http://www.caranddriver.com/features/texting-while-driving-how-dangerous-is-it. There is a stronger case that Elise (at least) is criminally negligent. Whether she (or Ludwig) actually considered the possibility of a car accident is relevant under the MPC and probably under the common law as well if the prosecutor seeks to show "recklessness" or a "depraved heart." In a recent prosecution in Massachusetts, the texting driver was convicted of motor vehicle homicide and sentenced to 2.5 years in prison, with the last 18 months to be served on probation. http://www.usnews.msnbc.msn.com/_news/2012/06/06/12090348-massachusetts-teen-sentenced-to-prison-for-texting-while-driving?lite.

16. Every year there are news reports of such events, and prosecutors usually do not prosecute, either themselves infusing the RPP with the religious beliefs of the defendants, or assuming that at least one juror will do so if the case goes to trial. Even if the RPP should not be attributed with such a belief or trait, jurors often do so. Of course, there is, as well, the issue of whether a court could order life-saving treatment,[47] but that is a First Amendment, not a criminal, question. Some states

47. E.g., Utah Criminal Code, §76-5-109(4)(6). "A parent or legal guardian who provides a child with treatment by spiritual means alone through prayer, in lieu of medical treatment, in accordance with the tenets and practices of an established church or religious denomination of which the parent or legal guardian is a member or adherent shall not, for that reason alone, be considered to have committed (child abuse)."

deal expressly with the issue. On the other hand, if the parent has no religious reasons for failing to provide treatment, but just fails to do so, there is at least manslaughter or criminally negligent homicide.[48] The leading case is *Comm. v. Twitchell*, 416 Mass. 114 (1993). Allison Ciullo, Prosecution Without Persecution: the Inability of Courts to Recognize Christian Science Spiritual Healing and a Shift Towards Legislative Action, 42 New Eng. L. Rev. 155 (2007). Of course, if the neglect is not based on spiritual beliefs, the issue is entirely different. See, e.g., http://www.courttv.com/graphics/13th/shim.gif (second-degree murder where parent failed to provide insulin to an 11-year-old diabetic daughter).

17. It is unlikely that Gary would be liable for voluntary manslaughter under the common law. Gary clearly did not intend any serious harm or death to come to Cindy, so he had no "depraved mind." But Gary may be liable for involuntary manslaughter if a jury finds that he was reckless or criminally negligent. Gary's liability will depend on the reasonable person standard that the jury applies—and to what extent they take into account Gary's specific characteristics. The prosecutor will argue that a reasonable person should have known the risks of exposing someone to a known allergen—including the risk of death. Gary was well aware of Cindy's peanut allergy for years, and exploited this knowledge for his own entertainment. Gary will argue that a reasonable person in his shoes would have no reason to suspect that Cindy could die from exposure to peanuts, given that he had never seen such a reaction from her before and was never informed of the severity of her allergy.

    The analysis would be similar under the MPC, except we could more quickly dismiss the argument that Gary acted recklessly. As previously discussed, recklessness requires that an actor subjectively recognize the risk of death; here Gary did not have this subjective understanding.

48. See, e.g., Mass. G. L.: "A child shall not be deemed to be neglected or lack proper physical care for the sole reason that he is being provided remedial treatment by spiritual means alone in accordance with the tenets and practice of a recognized church or religious denomination by a duly accredited practitioner thereof." c. 273, §1 (1992 ed.).

CHAPTER 9

Rape

OVERVIEW

Rape is the taking of sexual intimacy with an unwilling person by force or without consent. Historically, rape was regarded as an offense that could be committed only against a woman not married to the defendant, and it was seen as both a crime of violence against her and a property crime against her husband or her father. Today, the law recognizes that rape can be committed against females and males, and it is viewed both as a crime of violence and as a violation of an individual's basic right to decide with whom to have sex.[1]

Probably no crime has been more sharply affected by contemporary society's rapidly changing attitudes. Influenced by the newly arrived voices of women in the law, legislatures have enacted sweeping changes in the statutory definitions of rape and the evidentiary rules for trying rape cases. That this law reform has been controversial is not surprising. It reflects shifting perceptions about our most intimate human activity, appropriate sexual behavior by males and females, the relative status and power of men and women in society, the proper balance between convicting the guilty but not the innocent, and the legal consequences of the marriage relationship.

1. See generally, Stephen J. Schulhofer, Unwanted Sex (1998); Susan Estrich, Real Rape (1987).

A discussion of how the law should define rape and establish procedures for trying rape cases can elicit intense emotional responses. Many people feel strongly that the common law treated women as chattel, keeping them in a subordinate social position. For example, under the common law, a wife could not accuse her husband of rape. Furthermore, any crime committed by a married woman (except killing her husband) was deemed to have been coerced by her husband, and she could not be punished for it. The common law essentially treated a married woman as totally passive and subject to the will of her husband. Though she may have received some modest advantage from her marriage status, the disadvantages she suffered under the law far outweighed any advantages.

Thus, many critics argue that retaining *any* remnants of the common law, especially the common law of rape, simply preserves women's profoundly disadvantaged legal status. Others, while perhaps agreeing with these criticisms, argue that the common law, including the common law of rape, had some good points that should not be discarded rashly in the process of revising rape laws. Proponents of keeping some common law principles express concern about possible harmful consequences of contemporary law reform, such as increasing the risk that innocent people will be convicted. The discussion is made more complicated by changing social contexts in which acts that are (or can be seen as) rape occur, especially "date rape"; by perceived tensions in the sexual relations between men and women; and by the pressures generated both by biology and culture.

Everyone will undoubtedly approach this subject in light of his or her individual characteristics, experiences, and attitudes. Nevertheless, we should each try to understand the complexity of the issues involved and the different viewpoints others may have.

THE COMMON LAW APPROACH

Definition

The common law defined rape tersely as "carnal knowledge of a woman forcibly and against her will."[2] Rape included only sexual intercourse; it did not include other sexual acts such as oral or anal sex or consensual sex with minors. Those acts were usually punished as other crimes. Because of the brevity of the common law rape definition, courts had to explain its terms in greater detail.

2. 4 William Blackstone, Commentaries on the Law of England 210 (1769).

Generally, the prosecution had to prove:

1. the defendant had *sexual intercourse* (penetration by the penis of the vulva);
2. with a *woman not his wife;*
3. using *physical force* or the *threat of force;* and
4. *without her consent.*

Rape was a felony at common law and there were no degrees. Like most other common law felonies, rape was punishable by death. The extreme consequences of a rape conviction may have affected both how the common law defined rape and how judges and juries applied that definition.

Spousal Immunity

At common law a man could not rape his wife.[3] Thus, under the doctrine of spousal immunity, a husband who forced his wife to have sexual intercourse could not be convicted of rape, regardless of how much force was used. Several arguments were put forth to justify this rule:

1. A wife was deemed to have "consented" by marriage to have sexual relations with her husband throughout the course of their marriage.[4]
2. A wife was considered to be the property of her husband.
3. After marriage, both the husband and wife became one person under the law, and neither one retained a separate legal existence.[5]

Force

A major issue courts faced was explaining the element of "force or threat of force" in the common law definition of rape. Though case law on the

3. This rule applied only to persons who were actually married. It did not apply to couples living together who were not married.

4. Matthew Hale, a seventeenth-century jurist, said: "But the husband cannot be guilty of a rape committed by himself upon his lawful wife, for by their mutual matrimonial consent and contract the wife has given up herself in this kind unto her husband which she cannot retract." 1 Matthew Hale, History of the Pleas of the Crown 629 (1778). This marital consent theory emerged in a time when marriage vows themselves (and the conjugal consent implied therefrom) were virtually irrevocable. It is outmoded in contemporary times when changing divorce laws make it much easier to end the marriage relationship.

5. *State v. Smith*, 401 So. 2d 1126 (Fla. 1981) (holding that the unity concept no longer applies in Florida). See also *State v. Smith*, 85 N.J. 193, 426 A.2d 38 (1981), for an excellent overview of this common law doctrine.

subject is sparse, "force" was generally considered to consist of physical compulsion or violence (beyond that involved in the act of intercourse itself) that effectively subdued the woman. Usually (though not always), such force would result in physical injury to the victim.

Many courts also required that the complainant *physically resisted* the defendant before a jury could find he used sufficient force to be convicted of rape. This approach seems to condone the use of force by males in obtaining sexual gratification until or unless the female physically resists. If the female does resist, *then* the male must stop. Moreover, requiring resistance converts what appears to be an element of rape focusing on the defendant's behavior, force, into an inquiry as to how the woman reacted. In these jurisdictions, a woman's refusal to have sex was protected by the law of rape only if she put up physical resistance.

The amount of required resistance varied. Though some courts expected the female to have "resisted to the utmost"[6] or "to follow the natural instinct of every proud female,"[7] most jurisdictions required only "reasonable resistance." Even in a jurisdiction that required only reasonable resistance, a woman who submitted when attacked by a stranger rather than risk death or serious injury often could not prove rape because she had not "resisted" her attacker. The common law afforded far too much protection for the rapist who could subdue his victim quickly or chose a less assertive victim.

While requiring substantial physical resistance makes the complainant's lack of consent abundantly clear to the defendant and provides compelling evidence that the sexual act was forced and nonconsensual, it also (1) puts the victim at greater risk of injury because her resistance may escalate the level of violence,[8] and (2) allows the use of force by the male until or unless the victim physically resists. Many victims describe an inability to resist when placed in the position, or fear that more harm will come to them if they resist.

Threat of Force

Courts generally did not require proof that the defendant actually used physical force or that the victim resisted if the defendant threatened the victim with serious harm. They did require, however, that the victim's fear

6. *State v. Dizon*, 47 Haw. 444, 452, 390 P.2d 759, 764 (1964) (applying a "relaxed" version of the utmost resistance rule).

7. See *State v. Rusk*, 289 Md. 230, 255, 424 A.2d 720 (1981) (Cole, J., dissenting).

8. Law Enforcement Assistance Administration, Battelle Memorial Institute Law and Justice Study Center, Forcible Rape 7 (Prosecutor's Volume 1977). But see Anderson, Reviving Resistance in Rape Law, 1998 U. Ill. L. Rev. 953 (1999).

of serious harm be reasonable. The threat usually had to be one of death or serious bodily injury to the victim or to a third person. Often the defendant was armed with a deadly weapon and used it to threaten the victim. Under such circumstances resistance would be futile.

Threats of economic harm, damage to reputation, or other nonviolent intimidation usually did not satisfy this element of rape, though the defendant may have committed another crime, like extortion. Thus, if a defendant threatened the victim with the loss of her home or damage to her reputation to obtain sexual intimacy, his threat would not satisfy the "threat of force" element of rape.

Consent

If the woman consented to sexual relations, then the defendant could not be convicted of rape. Consent was a factual question for the judge or jury to decide, and it was not always clear. Words or actions clearly manifesting a willingness to have sex were the most obvious means of expressing consent. Conversely, words or actions clearly manifesting a lack of willingness would normally be sufficient to establish that the woman did not consent. Some courts concluded that behavior short of physically fighting back, such as saying "no" or other actions expressing unwillingness to have sex, did not establish the absence of consent. In these cases the requirement of *nonconsent* is effectively transformed into a requirement that the victim *resist*. Defendants successfully argued that the victim had consented even in cases in which the defendant was a stranger or had used force, brutality, or otherwise harmed or intimidated the complainant.

Attacking the Credibility of the Complainant

Often, the only testimony on the question of consent is that of the complainant and the defendant. This is not surprising because sexual acts are usually done in private and, typically, there are no other witnesses. As a result, rape prosecutions often turn on the participants' testimony (which often is in conflict) and their credibility. In many cases, the defense counsel tries to persuade the jury that the complainant had consented by focusing attention on her character and credibility, usually by delving into her past sexual history. The common law generally allowed such cross-examination. Under the common law, women who claimed that they had been raped could expect to be questioned extensively at the trial on their sexual history. This inappropriate badgering is prohibited under the modern rules of evidence.

Legally Ineffective Consent

Over time, the common law expanded the definition of rape so that, in a few types of recurring situations, rape occurred even if no force was used. These cases generally involved victims who were considered incapable of giving legally effective consent because of age or incapacity.[9] For example, an early English statute punished intercourse with a female under age 10 as a felony; it did not require proof that it was without her consent. Subsequently, Coke relied on this statute to define rape to include "unlawful and carnal knowledge of . . . a woman child under the age of ten with her will or against her will."[10] The definition of rape was thus expanded to include such cases apparently on the ground that children of such tender years lacked the maturity necessary to comprehend the nature of the sexual act.

The definition of rape was also broadened to include intercourse with a woman who was unconscious or mentally incompetent. Because such individuals were not aware of what was occurring or did not sufficiently understand the significance of sexual intercourse, legally they could not consent to the act.

Fraud

Someone who obtained sexual intercourse by fraud was not a rapist under the common law, as long as the complainant understood that she was having sexual intercourse. Flattery, promises, or other attempts to manipulate or persuade the woman, even if deliberate and untrue, did not establish the crime of rape. These types of cases were considered "fraud in the inducement." This rule could be pressed to the extreme. Someone who shows up at a woman's house in the dark and passes himself off as her lover does not commit rape (even though she was mistaken as to his true identity) because the woman understood that she was having sexual intercourse. Though somewhat controversial, the majority rule today is still that fraud in the inducement does not constitute rape.[11]

If, however, the defendant deceived the woman about the nature of the act, he could be convicted of rape. This was considered "fraud in the *factum*." For example, if a gynecologist told a female patient he needed to

9. This concept is similar to the capacity to enter into a legally binding contract or to commit a crime or a tort. The law requires at least a minimal ability to comprehend the nature of the transaction or event and to understand its consequences.

10. 3 Coke, Institutes of the Law of England *60 (1597).

11. See *People v. Evans*, 85 Misc. 2d 1088, 379 N.Y.S.2d 912 (1975).

insert a medical instrument into her vagina as part of a medical exam, but inserted his penis instead, this would be fraud in the factum because the woman was deliberately misled about the nature of the act, and therefore he could be convicted of rape.[12] If, however, a man falsely pretended to be a doctor and told a woman she had a disease that could best be cured by having intercourse with an anonymous donor who had been injected with a special serum, he could not be convicted of rape because the woman understood that she was having sexual intercourse which is only fraud in the inducement.[13]

American Common Law

Early American statutes adopted the common law approach to rape, though they varied in their specific definitions. Statutes defined rape in various ways, such as "sexual intercourse" with a woman other than one's wife "forcibly," "against her will," or "without her consent." Most American statutes also treated all forms of rape as a single crime for grading purposes and punished them with the same severity.

In summary, the common law defined rape as (1) sexual intercourse by a man with a woman not his wife, (2) by force or threat of force, (3) without consent, or (4) with a victim who could not consent because she was unconscious, mentally disabled, or of a young age, or (5) by fraud in the *factum*.

THE ACTUS REUS OF RAPE

Rape requires a voluntary act by the defendant, though intentional intercourse is seldom in dispute. The prosecution must prove penetration. Occasionally, a defendant might raise the defense of impotence or intoxication. A claim of impotence is generally an evidentiary claim denying penetration, while intoxication usually is relevant to mens rea (did the defendant *know* the woman did not consent?) rather than to the actus reus of rape.

12. See *People v. Minkowski*, 204 Cal. App. 2d 832, 23 Cal. Rptr. 92 (1962), for a similar fact pattern.
13. *Boro v. Superior Court*, 163 Cal. App. 3d 1224, 210 Cal. Rptr. 122 (1985). But see Falk, Rape by Fraud and Rape by Coercion, 64 Brook. L. Rev. 39 (1998).

THE MENS REA OF RAPE

The common law did not specify the mens rea of rape. This caused numerous problems. The prosecutor had to prove the defendant *intentionally* had intercourse with a woman he *knew* was not his wife.[14] The prosecution also had to establish the defendant *intentionally* used force or threatened serious physical harm.

The more difficult issue for courts was defining the mens rea toward *consent*. Did the prosecution have to prove the defendant knew or, instead, only that he *should* have known that the woman had not consented? Even if he used force? Or must the woman also resist?

The 1976 *Morgan* case, decided in the House of Lords, finally resolved this uncertainty in England by requiring the prosecution to establish that the defendant *knew* that the woman had not consented.[15] According to the defendants in this case, the victim's husband convinced them to come to his house and have sex with his wife. He told them not to be surprised if she struggled because she was "kinky" and only enjoyed sex in this way. The defendants entered the husband's home and had sex with his wife even though she resisted them.

The House of Lords concluded that rape was a specific intent crime and that, consequently, intention applied to all of its elements: nonconsensual sexual intercourse. Therefore, it determined that a defendant's *belief* that the woman was consenting, even if unreasonable, negates knowledge of nonconsent. There is language in the *Morgan* opinion suggesting that "recklessness" is sufficient for conviction. The court said: "[T]he mental element [of rape] is and always has been the intention to commit that act [sexual intercourse] or the *equivalent intention of having intercourse willy-nilly not caring whether the victim consents or not* [emphasis added]."

Morgan is consistent with a criminal law jurisprudence that puts primary emphasis on punishing the mens rea of the defendant and only punishes someone severely if he knew that he was inflicting a serious harm on another person. It is conceivable that, in some cases of sexual activity, the male honestly but erroneously believes he is engaged in a mutually desired physical act, while the female does not desire to engage in a sexual act and is seriously harmed by it. If, however, the criminal law should be more protective of victims and focus primarily on the harm done rather than on the mens rea with which it was done, the *Morgan* case can be persuasively criticized as favoring fairness to defendants over preventing harm to victims.

---

14. A man who had intercourse with his wife's twin under the mistaken belief that she was his wife could not be convicted of rape.
15. *Regina v. Morgan*, [1976] A.C. 182.

The *Morgan* case caused a great deal of controversy because it appears to most observers that the defendants clearly knew that the victim had not consented. (The House of Lords affirmed the defendants' conviction on the ground that the judge's instructions were harmless error; that is, no miscarriage of justice had occurred because no jury could have concluded that the defendants honestly believed that the complainant had consented.) Critics argued that the case would permit a future defendant to claim his victim was willing to have sex with him, even when the defendant had used force and any reasonable observer would conclude that the victim had clearly manifested her lack of consent. Parliament subsequently enacted a new rape law that only required the prosecution to prove the defendant was *reckless* as to the victim's nonconsent.

THE MODEL PENAL CODE

The Model Penal Code's (MPC) definition of rape was instrumental in provoking rape law reform throughout the United States. The MPC recognizes that the common law definition of rape created difficult problems of meaning and proof and concludes that the law of rape must be modernized. However, it does not use sex-neutral terms for rape for either the defendant or the victim, and it retains marital immunity for husbands. It also requires prompt complaint and corroboration of the allegation[16] and provides a mistake of age defense.[17] Its underlying policy seems based on the view that claims of rape are often groundless[18] and that defendants need more protection, not less.[19] Because the MPC does not sufficiently embody the emerging consensus on how the law of rape should be reformed, most states have not adopted the MPC's proposed definitions for rape.

Nonetheless, the MPC breaks new ground in three important ways:

(1) *It expands the behavior that can constitute rape.* All forms of sexual penetration of the female by the male, including vaginal, oral, and anal penetration, are considered rape under the MPC.

16. MPC §213.6(4) & (5).

17. MPC §213.6(1).

18. However, a number of studies show that although the general public believes that false accusations frequently occur, a number of false reports is actually between 2-8% of all rape cases, which is comparable to the false report rate for other crimes. Julie Valentine, National Institute of Justice, National Institute of Justice (NIJ) Sexual Assault Nurse Examiners' (SANE) Toolkit Research Findings for Salt Lake County 8 (2013).

19. Leigh Bienen, Rape III—National Developments in Rape Reform Legislation, 6 Women's Rts. L. Rev. 170-213 (1980).

(2) *It provides for degrees of rape.* The MPC has both first- and second-degree rape and a new crime, "gross sexual imposition," to distinguish among the more serious and less serious harms. This approach permits both grading and punishment to reflect more accurately the culpability of the offender and the harm done to the victim.

(3) *It focuses on the actor's behavior rather than on his internal thought processes.* The MPC acknowledges the difficult task often faced by the prosecution in proving the actor knew that the complainant had not consented, especially when in most cases of rape, there were no witnesses to the event. The MPC's solution is to focus on objective criteria, specifically "upon the objective manifestations of aggression by the actor" rather than trying to decipher his *state of mind* concerning the complainant's *consent*. The essential element of rape in the MPC is the use of *force* or *threat* of serious physical harm by the defendant. *Nonconsent* and *resistance* by the victim *are not* elements of the crime. Thus, the prosecution does not have to prove the defendant *knew* his victim had *not consented* or that the victim had *resisted*. The victim's behavior has evidentiary significance only.

Though these MPC revisions are, by today's standards, woefully out of date, they were an improvement at the time they were promulgated. There is a push by the American Law Institute (author of the MPC) to revise the rape standards. This is a work in progress in 2018.[20]

Second-Degree Rape

Section 213.1(1) of the Model Penal Code provides that anyone who compels the victim to have sexual intercourse "by force or by threat of imminent death, serious bodily injury, extreme pain or kidnapping, to be inflicted on anyone" is guilty of rape. It is a felony of the second degree.

The MPC elements of rape are

1. *sexual intercourse* (broadly defined)
2. by *a man with a woman not his wife*
3. by *force*, or
4. by *threat* of serious physical harm or kidnapping to the victim or a third person.

Rape also includes cases where

1. without her knowledge the actor uses drugs or other means to substantially impair the woman's ability to appraise or control her conduct or to resist;

20. See http://www.prosecutorintegrity.org/sa/ali/ (last visited Jan. 25, 2018).

2. a male has intercourse with an unconscious female or with one who is under 10 years old.[21]

First-Degree Rape

Generally, rape is a second-degree felony (MPC §213.1(1)). However, if the actor satisfies the elements of rape and inflicts serious bodily harm on anyone or the complainant was not a "voluntary social companion of the actor . . . and had not previously permitted him sexual liberties," the crime is elevated to a felony of the first degree. This definition can make prosecution in "date rape" cases more difficult.

Gross Sexual Imposition

Finally, the Model Penal Code creates a new crime, "gross sexual imposition," which includes intercourse by a male with a female not his wife if he

1. compels her to submit by any threat that would prevent resistance by a woman of *ordinary* resolution; or
2. knows that she is so mentally impaired that she is incapable of appraising the nature of her conduct; or
3. knows that she is unaware that a sexual act is being committed upon her or that she mistakenly believes the actor is her husband.[22]

Element 1 breaks new ground by expanding the type of threat that will support criminal responsibility. Under the common law, the threat had to be one of physical violence. The MPC, however, includes nonviolent but nonetheless coercive threats, such as economic loss, provided that the threat would induce a woman of ordinary resolution not to resist. The drafters provided illustrations. Thus, threatening a woman with the loss of her job could support a conviction under this provision. In contrast, a policeman who tells a woman he will not give her a ticket if she has sex with him should not be convicted of gross sexual imposition. This threat is so trivial that a female of ordinary resolution would not be intimidated by it.[23]

---

21. MPC §213.1.
22. MPC §213.1(2).
23. The MPC also creates the crime of *deviate sexual intercourse by force or imposition*, which has virtually the same definitional scheme as rape except that it includes coerced sexual intercourse between an actor and victim of any sex. MPC §213.2.

MODERN RAPE STATUTES

A primary focus of contemporary law reform has been to change the definition of rape. Most modern rape laws, reflecting a concern for gender equality and recognizing that coercive sexual activity between individuals of the same gender occurs, are gender-neutral and reach most coerced sexual activity between individuals of the opposite or same gender. Many have also abandoned the "force" standard for rape to a consent one, or in requiring force, allow the sexual act alone to satisfy the definition of rape.

In many new statutes, the definition of prohibited conduct has been greatly expanded to encompass, in addition to sexual intercourse, a wider range of sexual acts, such as cunnilingus, fellatio, anal intercourse, and any other intrusion into the body, including those accomplished by the use of objects.[24] Many states have thus renamed the crime of "rape" as the crime of "criminal sexual conduct" or "sexual assault."[25]

A number of jurisdictions have eliminated the concept of nonconsent entirely from the definition of rape or restrict its use to an affirmative defense. Instead, the statutes in these jurisdictions use modern definitions of force or the threat of serious bodily harm as the essential definitional elements of rape. The use of these behavioral criteria is intended to shift the fact finders' focus from the internal thought processes of the defendant to his objective conduct.[26] In theory, they also put less emphasis on the complainant's behavior and character.

Though a few states retain spousal immunity in some form, many state laws have eliminated or restricted spousal immunity from the definition of rape.[27] Increasingly, legislatures have concluded that, though husbands and wives agree generally by their marriage to have sexual relations with each other, each still retains the right to decide whether to have sex on any particular occasion. Thus, a husband does not have a legal right to demand sex from his wife. More important, these new laws acknowledge that marriage

---

24. See, e.g., Mich. Comp. Laws Svc. §750.520a(r) (Supp. 2012) (criminal sexual conduct).

25. See, e.g., Mich. Comp. Laws Ann. §750.520b (West 2012); Tex. Penal Code Ann. §22.021 (West 2012) (aggravated sexual assault).

26. At least one state, Washington, may consider rape in the first and second degree and rape of a child to be *strict liability* offenses, requiring no mental state with respect to *any* of the elements. *State v. Brown*, 899 P.2d 34 (Wash. 1995); *State v. Chhom*, 911 P.2d 1014 (Wash. 1996).

27. Beginning in 1976, states began to dissolve their marital rape exemptions, and by 1993, spousal rape was a crime in all 50 states and the District of Columbia. However, that does not mean that spouses were not still given some immunity. Klarfeld, A Striking Disconnect: Marital Rape Laws Failure to Keep Up With Domestic Violence Law, 48 Am. Crim. L. Rev. 1819 (2011). See Anderson, Marital Immunity, Intimate Relationships, and Improper Inferences: A New Law on Sexual Offenses by Intimates, 54 Hastings L.J. 1465 (2003); Connerton, The Resurgence of the Marital Rape Exemption, 61 Alb. L. Rev. 237 (1997).

does not entitle the husband to use force or the threat of force against his wife to obtain sex.

Modern laws also reflect changing ideas about the nature of the harm done. Rape is now seen not only as a crime of violence but also as a crime that violates a person's most personal sphere of privacy, thereby inflicting severe and long-lasting psychological damage.[28]

Moreover, society's attitudes toward permissible sexual conduct have changed. In the past, the law was unduly protective of aggressive male sexual behavior, tolerating physical assertiveness unless and until the female made it very clear by physical resistance that she did not desire to have sex with the male. Now the law more readily acknowledges that males have no right to use compulsion in sexual relationships. True equality of genders means that the law must protect the right of both men and women to decide with whom they will share sexual intimacy.

Many states have also passed laws limiting the scope of permissible cross-examination of complainants to protect them from being humiliated and having their privacy invaded. For example, many states prohibit the defendant from asking about the complainants sexual history, with a few narrow exceptions. Reformers believe that these laws will encourage both the reporting and prosecution of rape cases.

Rape by Force or Threat of Serious Bodily Injury

Force

State statutes vary on how they define the "force" or "threat of force" element of rape. Some statutes do not define "force" at all, leaving it for case law to fill in an operational definition. Most modern laws, however, seek to define more precisely the level of force necessary for rape. In providing a more explicit definition for this element, some courts require the defendant to use physical force that restrains the victim or to threaten death or serious bodily harm to the victim or to a third person.

Additional Force

Most statutory definitions of force require the defendant to use additional force beyond that necessary to accomplish penetration. Several state laws

28. See, e.g., the California statute, which states: "The essential guilt of rape consists in the outrage to the person and feelings of the victim of the rape. Any sexual penetration, however slight, is sufficient to complete the crime." Cal. Penal Code Ann. §263 (West 2012).

use the term "forcible compulsion," which, though seemingly providing a consistent definition, can have different meanings. For example, New York law defines this term as the use of physical force or a threat of serious harm.[29] It does not take into account the complainant's behavior in determining whether the defendant used "forcible compulsion." Washington law, on the other hand, defines this term as the use of "physical force which overcomes resistance" or a threat of serious harm.[30] The Washington statute requires fact finders to focus on the behavior of *both* the defendant *and* the complainant.

Focus on the use of force by the defendant may not, as a practical matter, eliminate pressure on the complainant to physically fight back. In the controversial *Berkowitz* case, a Pennsylvania court concluded that a male college student who removed a female student's clothes without *additional* physical force or threats did not use "forcible compulsion," even though the woman said "no" throughout the sexual act.[31] The court held that her *verbal* resistance was relevant to consent but not to whether the defendant used forcible compulsion. Consequently, the court reversed his conviction for rape but reinstated a conviction for indecent assault.

In a somewhat similar case, however, a California court reached the opposite conclusion.[32] In the *Iniguez* case, the defendant had met the victim for the first time earlier that evening. Later, he awakened her while she was sleeping on the sofa in the living room at a friend's house, pulled her pants down, and inserted his penis into her vagina. She did not resist because she was afraid.

The court held that the defendant's conduct satisfied the statutory language of sexual intercourse "accomplished by means of force, violence or fear of immediate and unlawful bodily injury." The *fear* element was met because the woman's fear of bodily injury was reasonable under these circumstances. In California, a rape conviction can be obtained even in cases where the defendant does not use additional force and the victim does not resist, provided that the victim honestly and reasonably fears immediate and unlawful bodily injury.

---

29. See, e.g., N.Y. Penal Law §130.00(8) (West 2012). "Forcible compulsion means to compel by either . . . the use of physical force; or . . . a threat, express or implied, which places a person in fear of immediate death or physical injury to himself, herself, or another person, or in fear that he, she, or another person will immediately be kidnapped."

30. Wash. Rev. Code Ann. 9A.44.010(6) (West Supp. 2012). "Forcible compulsion means physical force *which overcomes resistance*, or a threat, express or implied, that places a person in fear of death or physical injury to herself or himself or another person, or in fear that she or he or another person will be kidnapped (emphasis added)." This definition requires the victim to resist physical force. *State v. Weisberg*, 65 Wash. App. 721, 829 P.2d 252 (1992).

31. *Commonwealth v. Berkowitz*, 641 A.2d 1161 (Pa. 1994).

32. *People v. Iniguez*, 7 Cal. 4th 847, 872 P.2d 1183, 30 Cal. Rptr. 2d 258 (1994).

Inherent Force

Some states do not require the defendant to use additional force beyond that necessary to accomplish the proscribed sexual act before he may be convicted of rape. In other words, force is established by the sexual act itself, not any additional physical contact.

In New Jersey, sexual assault could be committed by sexual penetration when the defendant "uses physical force or coercion, but the victim does not sustain severe personal injury."[33] In *State of New Jersey in the Interest of* M.T.S., the New Jersey Supreme Court held that "physical force" as used in its statute means "any unauthorized sexual penetration."[34] It does *not* require *additional* physical force.[35] Simply using the amount of force inherently necessary to accomplish sexual penetration is sufficient for conviction unless the defendant reasonably believed that the victim had "freely given *affirmative permission*." Moreover, the victim is under no obligation to express nonconsent or to have denied permission.

In reaching this conclusion, the court stressed that New Jersey sexual assault laws had been reformed to afford maximum protection for victims and to make it clear sexual assault should be seen primarily as a crime against personal autonomy rather than as a crime of violence.

Nonphysical Force

Some states by statute have broadened the concept of nonphysical force. California criminalizes sexual intercourse with a nonspouse if accomplished by "duress" or "menace."[36] Other states criminalize the use of coercion,[37] extortion,[38] or a "position of authority"[39] to achieve sexual intercourse. Pennsylvania prohibits the use of "physical, intellectual, moral, emotional or psychological force, either express or implied."[40] The respective ages and prior relationship of the defendant and the complainant can be considered.

Other states, however, limit force to a basic meaning of physical compulsion or threat of serious physical harm. In *State v. Thompson*, the court affirmed a trial court's dismissal of an indictment for sexual assault in a case where a high school principal allegedly intimidated a student to have sexual

33. N.J. Stat. Ann. 2C:14-2c(1) (West 2012).
34. 129 N.J. 422, 433, 609 A.2d 1266 (1992).
35. Id., 129 N.J. 422 at 444.
36. Cal. Penal Code Ann. §261(a)(2) (Supp. 2012).
37. N.J. Stat. Ann. §§2C: 14-1j and 2c(1) (West 1995 and Supp. 2012).
38. Del. Code Ann., tit. 11, §778(5) (West 2012).
39. Wyo. Stat. Ann. §6-2-303(a)(vi) (West 2012).
40. 18 Pa. C.S. §3121 (West 2012).

intercourse with him by threatening to prevent her graduation.[41] The court held that "force" must be interpreted as conveying its ordinary and normal meaning of physical compulsion.

Threat of Force

Even when the defendant does not actually use force, he still can be convicted of rape if he *threatens* death or serious bodily injury to the victim or to another person.

This element can be confusing. Does the intent of the *speaker* or the perception of the *listener* determine whether the words constitute such a threat? If the mens rea of the defendant is essential for rape, then he can be convicted only if he *intended* to frighten his victim. Some courts have required the prosecution to prove that the defendant intended his words as a threat.[42] However, if fear felt by the complainant is enough to establish the element, then the listener's understanding of his words controls. If that is the case, must her understanding be reasonable? Most courts require that the victim's fear be reasonable under the circumstances.[43]

Most states specify that the "threat of force" required for rape must be a threat of physical harm to the victim or a third person that is sufficient to create fear in a reasonable person.[44] But obtaining sex by using other types of threats, such as economic harm or damage to reputation, is often made criminal under state extortion or criminal coercion statutes instead of rape statutes.

Dispensing with the Force Requirement

Increasingly, state statutes define rape as nonconsensual intercourse even in the absence of force or threat of force. Thus, sexual intimacy without the *affirmative* manifestation of consent by words or actions is a crime. Usually it is a less serious degree of rape or sexual assault, and spousal immunity often applies.[45] Criminalizing sexual intimacy obtained without affirmative permission affords maximum protection to the right of individuals to decide when and with whom they will share sexual intimacy. This approach, according to some critics, may result in the conviction of some defendants

---

41. 243 Mont. 28, 792 P.2d 1103 (1990).

42. *People v. Evans*, 85 Misc. 2d 1088, 379 N.Y.S.2d 912 (1975).

43. See, e.g., *People v. Warren*, 113 Ill. App. 3d 1, 446 N.E.2d 591 (1983).

44. *State v. Rusk*, 289 Md. 230, 424 A.2d 720 (1981).

45. Wash. Rev. Code §9A.44.060 (West 2012) (third-degree rape).

who honestly (and perhaps even reasonably) thought the other person was willing to have sex with them. Though, cases of this are rare.

Resistance by the Victim

Less than half of the states, either by statute or by case law, no longer require the complainant to resist, though some states still do.[46] Eliminating resistance as an element of rape is seen as decreasing the risk that victims who fight back may suffer greater physical injury than if they remained passive. It also does not make the criminal responsibility of the defendant dependent on the willingness of his victim to offer physical resistance. Otherwise, some defendants might avoid responsibility if they happened to select non-aggressive victims. Additionally, it recognizes that many victims of rape do not physically resist for a variety of reasons—for example, a woman's lifetime socialization to be nice, her hesitation to cause a scene, embarrassment, or a "strategic decision not to resist in order to avoid a major injury."[47] Further, it recognizes that when a victim is confronted with a stressful situation, the body can react in a number different ways, what is commonly known as "fight or flight." However, studies have shown that some victims of rape experience one of two terror-induced altered states of consciousness called "dissociation" and "frozen fright."[48] Both responses render the victim totally passive.

As noted above, however, other states still require the complainant to offer some resistance unless threatened with death or serious bodily injury. This requirement raises the question of whether saying "no" satisfies the resistance element. The argument there is that our culture still teaches men that women are often ambivalent about whether to have sex and that, even when a woman is saying "no," she really means "yes." Based on this cultural conditioning, some men may *honestly* believe that a woman is not resisting when she says "no" or takes other evasive action. However, there has recently been a lot of education on this issue and the general consensus is that verbal resistance is resistance.

This controversy poses difficult policy choices for the criminal law. How should the criminal law treat the male who honestly believes that "no" really means "yes"? Should the criminal law punish someone who has no subjective awareness that he might be committing any crime, let alone

46. Anderson, Reviving Resistance in Rape Law, 1998 U. Ill. L. Rev. 953 (1999).

47. Kaarin Long, Caroline Palmer & Sara G. Thoome, A Distinction Without a Difference: Why the Minnesota Supreme Court Should Overrule Its Precedent Precluding the Admission of Helpful Expert Testimony in Adult Victim Sexual Assault Cases, 31 Hamline J. Pub. L. & Pol'y 569, 582-583 (2010). [Hereinafter Long et al.]; Schafran *supra* note 12.

48. Schafran supra note 12.

a serious crime that can result in a long prison term? (Indeed, until not too long ago, rape was a capital offense in many American states.) If so, should it punish him as severely as an actor who does know that his victim does not want to engage in sexual intimacy? The harm done to the victim who does not desire sexual intimacy may be the same in both cases. However, there is a significant difference in moral blameworthiness between someone who does not comprehend the other person is unwilling and one who does.

Others argue that the criminal law is an instrument for social change and that it should be used to help transform the culture. Thus, they argue a woman is raped when she says "no" and the man proceeds to have sex anyway—even if the defendant did not intend to commit rape. If the criminal law gets too far in front of the common social and cultural understanding, however, it runs the risk of using arguably morally blameless individuals solely as an instrument for the common good. This could violate Kant's command that no one should be used solely as a means to an end.

Consent

The modern trend is to eliminate nonconsent as an element in the statutory definition of rape. Nonetheless, consent is still a definitional component or an affirmative defense in a number of states.[49] A few statutes require the prosecution to prove that the defendant knew the complainant did not consent or was negligent as to her consent.

Most recent American cases permit a mistake defense but only if the defendant can show he honestly and *reasonably* believed the victim had consented.[50] Some states require proof of *recklessness* as to consent to convict the defendant of rape,[51] while a number of states have made sexual intercourse without obtaining *affirmative* consent a crime.[52] Some states provide for degrees of rape with different mental states required for nonconsent, while others have actually made nonconsent a strict liability element. In a strict liability state, the defendant may be convicted of rape if the victim did

49. See, e.g., Tex. Penal Code Ann. §22.021 (West 2012); *People v. Stull*, 127 Mich. App. 14, 338 N.W.2d 403 (1983) (consent is affirmative defense to rape); *Commonwealth v. Hill*, 377 Mass. 59, 385 N.E.2d 253 (1979) (lack of consent is an element of rape); *Goldberg v. State*, 41 Md. App. 58, 395 A.2d 1213 (1979) (consent is an element of rape). Note that the MPC would simply require the defendant to carry the burden of producing evidence on this issue. He would not carry the burden of persuasion. MPC §1.12.

50. See, e.g., *State v. Oliver*, 133 N.J. 141, 627 A.2d 144 (1993); *State v. Smith*, 210 Conn. 132, 554 A.2d 713 (1989); *People v. Mayberry*, 15 Cal. 3d 143, 542 P.2d 1337 (1975).

51. *Hess v. State*, 20 P.3d 1121 (Alaska 2001); *State v. Marchet*, 219 P.3d 75 (Utah 2009).

52. Anderson, All-American Rape, 70 St. John's L. Rev. 625 (2005).

not consent, even though he honestly and reasonably believed the victim had consented.[53] This is a minority rule, however.

Reformers argue that retaining consent as an element inappropriately focuses the jury's attention on the complainant's behavior rather than on the defendant's behavior. It also allows defendants to claim they believed the complainant had consented in almost any situation, making it too difficult to convict rapists. On the other hand, requiring the initiator of sexual conduct to obtain the unambiguous agreement of his or her partner ensures that physical intimacy is mutually desired, providing more protection to victims.

Deception

The general rule in most states is that sexual intimacy obtained by deception does not constitute rape.[54] This approach is consistent with the common law, which considered fraud in the factum to be rape, but not fraud in the inducement.

Rape in the First Degree

Many state statutes aggravate the crime of rape if, in addition to the use of force or the threat of force, an aggravating circumstance is present. Examples of such a circumstance are commission of another felony, use of a deadly weapon, or the infliction of serious injury on the victim.

Spousal Immunity

Although every state legislature has formally abolished its marital rape exemption, reminders of the exemption still remain in the statutory law of several states.[55] These additional hurdles are found in decreased sentences for the accused, proof of force or resistance, and shorter time frames for a woman to report a rape by her husband. These make spousal rape more difficult to prosecute. The modern trend is to eliminate or restrict marital status as a definitional element or as an affirmative defense. Increasingly,

53. *Commonwealth v. Lopez*, 745 N.E.2d 961 (Mass. 2001); *State v. Reed*, 479 A.2d 1291 (Me. 1984).
54. *People v. Evans*, 85 Misc. 2d 1088, 379 N.Y.S.2d 912 (1975). But see Cal. Penal Code Ann. §261(a)(4) (2012).
55. Klarfeld, A Striking Disconnect: Marital Rape Laws Failure to Keep Up with Domestic Violence Law, 48 Am. Crim. L. Rev. 1819 (2011).

legislatures and courts are recognizing that a woman does not give irrevocable consent to sexual intimacy to her husband solely by marriage nor does the marriage relationship entitle the husband to use force to obtain sexual intimacy.[56]

In some states that allow some form of spousal immunity, filing for divorce or living separately will eliminate any claim of spousal immunity,[57] though obtaining a protective order without more may not.

Rape Because No Legally Effective Consent

Most state statutes include within the definition of rape a situation where the defendant does not use force but where he knows, or in some states *should* have known, that the victim is incapable of giving legally effective consent because of physical or mental incapacity. Some states follow the MPC and consider a defendant's belief about the victim's capacity to give legally effective consent as relevant to the mens rea of rape. Others require the defendant to use the affirmative defense of mistake of fact. This approach requires the defendant to carry the burden of persuasion and also to establish that his belief was reasonable.

Intoxication

Some state statutes now provide that intoxication, even if voluntary, may preclude consent even when the victim consciously participates in sexual activity.[58] Courts have held that intoxication may impair the victim's judgment about the nature or harmfulness of the sexual behavior, thereby invalidating consent.[59] Defining and applying these standards to individual cases consistently and fairly to all participants in intimate sexual activity may be difficult.

Age

Nonforcible sexual intimacy with children is often called "statutory rape," though some states are now using more pejorative terms like "rape of a

---

56. *State v. Smith*, 401 So. 2d 1126 (Fla. 1981).

57. *Commonwealth v. Chretien*, 383 Mass. 123, 417 N.E.2d 1203 (1981) (conviction of husband for raping his wife after she had filed for divorce and obtained a judgment nisi upheld even though divorce had not yet become final).

58. Patricia J. Falk, Rape by Drugs: A Statutory Overview and Proposals for Reform, 44 Ariz. L. Rev. 131 (2002).

59. *People v. Giardino*, 82 Cal. App. 4th 454 (2000).

child."[60] The degree usually depends on the age of the victim and sometimes on the age of the defendant.

Summary

Most modern statutes define rape as (1) obtaining sexual intimacy with another (2) by force or threat of force or (3) without legally effective consent due to incapacity. Some states also include nonconsent as an element in the definition or allow the defendant to use a reasonable belief that the complainant consented as an affirmative defense. Rape will be aggravated to the first degree if another harmful act occurs, such as using a deadly weapon, seriously injuring the victim, or committing another felony. Spousal rape is criminalized in all states but how spousal rape is treated compared to nonmarital rape varies with each state.

EVIDENCE REFORMS

Rape Shield Laws

Until recently, it was common defense strategy in rape cases to attack the credibility of a female complainant by attacking her character.[61] Defense counsel would cross-examine a complainant concerning her past sexual history and reputation, implying that women who had sex outside of marriage were immoral and thus not believable. Defense counsel justified these tactics, arguing that the complainant's past behavior was relevant to determining her behavior during the alleged rape.

Today, many state laws, referred to as "rape shield laws," expressly forbid or severely limit such an inquiry.[62] For example, past consensual sex with the defendant is generally admissible on the issue of consent. Usually, judges must hold a hearing prior to trial to rule on whether inquiry by the defense into a complainant's sexual history is relevant and admissible.

These laws prevent people who file rape charges from having their privacy invaded and from being humiliated in court based on matters that are

---

60. Washington now uses this term instead of the term "statutory rape." Wash. Rev. Code 9A.44.073, 9A.44.076, 9A.44.079 (West 2012).

61. See *State ex rel. Pope v. Superior Court*, 113 Ariz. 22, 545 P.2d 946 (1976).

62. See Anderson, From Chastity Requirement to Sexuality License: Sexual Consent and a New Rape Shield Law, 70 Geo. Wash. L. Rev. 51 (2002); Berger, Man's Trial, Woman's Tribulation: Rape Cases in the Courtroom, 77 Colum. L. Rev. 1 (1997).

not relevant to their credibility or the issues. Protecting rape victims in this way, in turn, may encourage the reporting and prosecution of rape. On the other hand, critics are concerned that rape shield laws may deprive criminal defendants of their Sixth Amendment right of confrontation.[63] Some courts agree, ruling that rape shield laws are unconstitutional if they preclude the admission of relevant sexual history.[64]

Examples

1. Shortly after her husband left for work early in the morning, Sarah was startled to find Andrew, whom she did not know, in her bedroom where Sarah had just placed her one-year-old baby in the crib. Andrew, clearly agitated, walked over to the baby's crib and, pointing angrily at the baby, said: "You know what I want. Get on the bed and take off your clothes and no one will get hurt." Frightened and concerned for the safety of her baby, Sarah complied. When Andrew took off his clothes, Sarah, fearing Andrew might be HIV-positive, said to him: "Please use a condom. If you don't have one, I do." Andrew took the condom offered by Sarah and then had intercourse with her.

2. Jane and Tom meet for the first time at a bar and have some drinks. Tom offers to give Jane a ride home. On their way there Jane accepts Tom's invitation to come up to his apartment. After kissing Jane for a while on the couch, Tom starts unbuttoning her blouse:
   a. Jane tells Tom that she does not want to have sex with him. Tom pulls out a knife and says: "If you don't have sex with me, I could get angry." Jane, terrified, says nothing and lets Tom have intercourse with her.
   b. Jane tries to push Tom (who has no weapon) off and says: "I don't want to have sex with you." Tom, calling her a tease, pins her arms and manages to have intercourse with Jane.
   c. Jane, confused by this sudden turn of events, says nothing. Tom lies on top of her, while she does and says nothing, and has intercourse with Jane.
   d. Tom starts fondling her. Jane lies down and fondles him as he unbuttons her blouse. When Tom takes off his clothes, she takes off hers. Tom and Jane begin to have intercourse. Just as Tom is about to reach climax, Jane says, "I've changed my mind. I don't want to do this, and I want you to stop right now." Tom says, "I just need a few more minutes to finish." He remains on top of her for approximately two or three more minutes until he reaches climax.

63. See generally Tanford & Bocchino, Rape Victim Shield Laws and the Sixth Amendment, 128 U. Pa. L. Rev. 544 (1980).
64. See, e.g., *Commonwealth v. Spiewak*, 617 A.2d 696 (Pa. Super. 1992).

e. Jane says: "Stop, Tom. I don't want to have sex with you. We just met tonight." Tom replies: "You're right. You don't even know me. Don't you feel foolish coming up here? For all you know, I could be a serial sex killer who preys on women just like you." Though Tom does not intend to frighten Jane, she becomes very frightened after suddenly realizing that what Tom just said could well be true. She moves away from Tom and replies in a faltering voice: "God, you're right. You could be a maniac." Trying to calm the situation and reassure herself, Jane approaches and Tom puts her hands in his hands. Tom, thinking Jane has changed her mind, starts again to undress her. Jane, truly concerned that Tom may be another sex serial killer like Ted Bundy, says nothing while helping Tom take off her clothes. They then have sex.

f. Tom secretly puts a "roofie" into a drink and offers it to Jane, who wastes little time in finishing it. A "roofie" is the drug Rohypnol, which is a sedative and muscle relaxant that soon makes a person drowsy and disoriented. Jane feels dizzy, groggy, and unsure of what she is doing. Tom undresses her while she is mumbling words that don't make sense and they have intercourse without any resistance from Jane. When Jane wakes up the next day, she doesn't remember anything.

g. Jane says to Tom: "I believe you should only have sex with the one you love." Tom replies: "It was love at first sight for me, Jane. I think you are the girl I will marry." Jane, moved by Tom's earnestness, says: "Oh, Tom. I'm so glad you feel that way. Let's make love." They have intercourse and, as Tom leaves that night, he turns to Jane and says: "I don't want to see you again."

h. Jane and Tom go to Jane's apartment rather than to Tom's. After kissing Jane for a while on the couch, Tom starts unbuttoning her blouse. Jane says: "I want you to leave. I expect my boyfriend to come back from a business trip later tonight." Tom leaves. Jane leaves the door unlocked for her boyfriend and then, after turning out the light, goes back to sleep. One hour later, Tom enters the apartment, goes into Jane's bedroom, and whispers in her ear: "I can't wait to have sex with you." Thinking it is her boyfriend, Jane pulls him into bed without turning on the light and they have intercourse.

i. Jane and Tom go to Jane's apartment rather than to Tom's. After kissing Jane for a while on the couch, Tom starts unbuttoning her blouse. Jane says: "No. I want you to leave." Tom does. Jane goes to bed and falls asleep, forgetting to lock her apartment door. Several hours later, Tom enters Jane's bedroom and, seeing Jane asleep, lies on top of her. Jane awakens and is very frightened. Afraid, Jane says nothing and offers no resistance, while Tom has intercourse with her.

3. Richard, age 42, instructed 13-year-old Elizabeth, his daughter, that the Bible commanded a daughter to perform a mother's duties if the mother could not. Elizabeth believed devoutly in the Bible and accepted Richard's teaching on this subject. After several months of stressing her special responsibilities as a daughter to act when her mother could not, Richard went into Elizabeth's room one evening and told her that, because her mother would not have sex with him, Elizabeth must follow the Bible and take on those responsibilities. Without using any physical force other than normally used in the act, Richard undressed, and Elizabeth allowed him to have sexual intercourse with her.

4. Mary Kay, a high school history teacher, kept Jamie, a strapping, six-foot mature male 14-year-old student of hers, after school often during the spring semester. Having him serve as her paid student assistant, she groomed him with praise and responsibility. One day after all the other students had left, Mary Kay started to kiss Jamie and then to fondle him. Jamie responded, and they had intercourse. They continued the relationship for several months. Mary Kay became pregnant and these events became known. Jamie and Mary Kay insisted that they loved one another and wanted to get married.

5. Demi, a top computer executive, is attracted to Mike, her administrative assistant. Demi and Mike have been working late on a special project the past few weeks. One night, Demi asks Mike to have sex with her. Mike politely declines. Demi tells Mike she will fire him if he does not. Mike, who has just purchased a house and needs his salary, feels he cannot afford to lose his job. They have sex.

6. Dr. Brown, a gynecologist, is about to give his patient, Heather, a vaginal exam. Contrary to professional protocol, he suddenly tells his nurse to leave the examination room on the pretext of locating some test results. Pretending to put on a latex glove, Dr. Brown inserts his bare hand into Heather's vagina and touches it for his own sexual gratification rather than to conduct a proper exam.

7a. Max picks up Roberta, a prostitute, in his van and agrees with her to have sexual intercourse for $100. He gives her a counterfeit bill and has intercourse. The next day Roberta realizes the bill is phony.

7b. Max picks up Roberta, a prostitute, in his van and agrees to have sexual intercourse for $100. Just before having intercourse, Roberta tells Max she wants her money first or she won't have sex. Max, who does not have the $100 and had hoped to tell Roberta this after they had sex, says to Roberta: "I don't have any money." He then physically overpowers Roberta and has sexual intercourse with her.

8. Hector and José, corporate trainees, shared a room with single beds at a company retreat. After several drinks, Hector and José retired for the evening. José got into bed. Hector sat on the side of José's bed and started to rub his back. José said nothing. Hector then rolled José over, pulled down his pants, and fondled his penis, which became erect. José said nothing. Hector then sat anally on José's still erect penis and moved up and down. José, who froze at this point, said nothing. Did Hector commit rape?

9. Chris and Christine met at a college party. Both had several drinks while they were talking and dancing. Chris led Christine into a nearby bedroom, where they undressed, got into bed, and had intercourse. They then fell asleep. Upon waking, Christine called the police while Chris was still asleep and told them she had been raped. She said that, though she was conscious during intercourse, she did not really understand what she was doing with Chris because of her extreme intoxication. The police then took a blood sample from each of them. They both had a blood alcohol level of .08—the legal threshold for driving under the influence in the state. Can Chris be convicted under a statute that defines third-degree rape as "sexual penetration accomplished with any person if the victim is incapable of giving consent because of any intoxicating agent"?[65]

10. Jim, 51, signed onto an Internet chat room for preteens and conversed with young girls online. Jim initiated a conversation with Amy, who told Jim that she was 10 years old. Once Amy warmed up to him, Jim asked her to turn on her virtual camera, which was attached to her computer screen, so that he could see her. Jim then asked Amy to take off her shirt and slowly rub her chest. As she did what he asked, Jim watched from home on his computer screen and became sexually aroused. The next day Jim was arrested for sexual fondling in the first degree, defined as "touching a child under the age of 12 in a sexual manner for sexual gratification."

11. Jo Anne, a heavy crack cocaine user, could not afford to pay cash for her drugs. Instead, she would offer sex in exchange for drugs. Harry, a dealer who has not sold drugs to Jo Anne before but knows of Jo Anne's past sex-for-drugs dealings with other dealers, has sex with Jo Anne. Later, Jo Anne files a rape complaint, alleging Harry forcibly raped her. Harry claims Jo Anne is making a false claim of rape because he did not pay Jo Anne with cocaine for the sex as promised.
    a. At his trial, Harry's attorney wants to cross-examine Jo Anne about her past exchange of sex for drugs with other dealers.

---

65. See, e.g., SDCL 22-22-1(4) (West 2012).

b. At the end of the trial, Harry's lawyer argues that the only proof of rape is Jo Anne's testimony. He asks the judge either to dismiss the case for lack of corroboration or to instruct the jury that there must be evidence in addition to the complainant's testimony to establish the elements of rape.

12. Larry, 32 years old, was Marcia's junior high school history teacher. Marcia, who was 13, had a reputation of sleeping around. She was also barely maintaining the minimum grade point average necessary to stay in school. One day, Larry kept Marcia after school and told her he would give her a failing grade if she did not have sexual intercourse with him. Marcia agreed, and they had sex. A few weeks later, Marcia reported the incident to the police.

13. Sal and his wife, Carmen, needed a babysitter for their two small children. Carmen interviewed Pam, who, though only 14, looked and acted much older. Because of Pam's maturity, Carmen hired her to babysit the kids. One evening, Sal came home early from work and asked Pam to have sex with him. Pam eagerly agreed, and they had intercourse. A week later, Pam, angry because Sal would not sleep with her again, reported the incident to the police. Sal was shocked to learn Pam was only 14. She easily looked 18, and Carmen had never told him Pam's age.

14. Alex, 12, engaged in consensual sexual intercourse with his girlfriend, Faith also 12. Faith became pregnant and a criminal investigation followed. State law provides, in part, "Rape is an act of sexual penetration accomplished by any person if the victim is less than 13 years of age." The prosecutor wants to have Alex and Faith adjudicated as juvenile delinquents for an act that would have constituted first-degree rape if committed by an adult. Can both parties be adjudged juvenile delinquents?

15. One night, Ally is awoken to her roommate's boyfriend Joe on top of her. Joe was trying to remove Ally's pajamas, and Ally told him to stop. Joe did not listen and continued to undress Ally. Ally tried pushing Joe off of her but she was not strong enough. Joe then punched Ally in the face, and she stopped fighting back. Joe inserted his penis into Ally's vagina. Afterwards Ally left the room and went to the hospital. Joe was awoken by police arriving at the apartment. Joe was surprised to see that not only was he naked, but he was in Ally's bed. Joe has been diagnosed with sexsomnia, a disorder that involves engaging in sexual behavior while asleep. Joe argues that his sexsomnia is what caused him to have sex with Ally. If the jury believes Joe's defense, should he be convicted of rape?

Explanations

1. This is the paradigm case. Andrew has committed rape under the common law. He had intercourse with a woman not his wife forcibly and without her consent. Andrew could also be convicted of rape under modern statutes. Though he did not actually use physical force to subdue Sarah, he threatened serious physical harm to a third person, Sarah's one-year-old baby. This implied threat should be sufficient for conviction. In some states, the fact that Andrew committed a burglary by entering Sarah's house unlawfully to commit rape would aggravate the rape to first degree.

   If the jurisdiction required the victim to resist, Andrew might argue that he thought Sarah consented because she did not even say "no," let alone resist. He would also argue that Sarah's request that he use a condom was further evidence of consent.

   Andrew's defense should not succeed. In many states, a victim no longer has to resist the use of force by the defendant. Even states that do require the victim to meet physical force with physical force do not expect physical resistance from a victim who is confronted with a threat of serious physical injury to herself or to a third person. Though Andrew's words did not expressly threaten Sarah's baby, it is clear from the context (an uninvited stranger unlawfully enters a woman's home and points at a vulnerable child using words that demand compliance with sexual demands as the price of not harming the baby) that Andrew was threatening a person other than the victim with serious physical harm.

   Even in states that retain nonconsent as an element of rape, Sarah's acquiescence to intercourse under these facts is very similar to an acceptance of a contract offer under duress. Sarah had no real choice. If she refused, Andrew would seriously harm her young child. Nor would her request that Andrew use a condom establish that Sarah consented or that Andrew believed (or reasonably could have believed) that she had consented to intercourse. In contemporary society it is a reasonable precaution for everyone, especially rape victims who have no knowledge of the rapist's sexual history, to insist on precautions against the spread of serious diseases.

2a. Tom has committed rape. Jane clearly told Tom that she did not want to have sex. Rather than accept her decision about not sharing sexual intimacy with him, Tom threatened her with serious physical harm. Though the common law did, and some states still might, require Jane to physically resist Tom if he used physical force, most states no longer require the complainant to offer any resistance when confronted with a *threat* of serious physical harm on the view that resistance would be both futile and potentially dangerous.

Tom should not be able to avoid conviction by testifying that he thought Jane had consented to sex. Consent is not an element of rape in many states, and even if it were, his threat of serious physical harm and use of a deadly weapon are very strong evidence that he knew Jane did not consent.

In many states, the use of a deadly weapon would aggravate the rape from second degree to first degree because the harm done to the victim also includes fear that her life is in danger.

2b. Tom has committed rape. He has used force to have intercourse with Jane. Even in those states in which consent is an element, Jane has clearly stated that she does not consent to sex and, in addition, has physically resisted.

2c. This is a more difficult case. Some states require that the defendant use force that overcomes physical resistance or threatens the victim with serious physical harm.[66] Tom might not be convicted of rape under this approach because he has, arguably, used only that force normally involved in having intercourse and has not threatened Jane. Moreover, Jane offered no physical or verbal resistance.

Other states consider the defendant's act of nonconsensual sex *by itself* to be rape. Thus, even though Tom might argue that he has not used any force beyond that normally involved in sexual activity, his failure to obtain Jane's *affirmative assent* to sexual intimacy would be rape, though probably of a lesser degree.

If lack of consent is an element, the prosecutor might be able to prove that Tom knew or should have known that Jane did not consent. If consent is an affirmative defense, then Tom would have the burden of establishing that he reasonably believed that Jane had consented.[67]

2d. Jane initially consented to an act of intercourse. She sexually fondled Tom, took off her clothes, and joined in an act of intercourse. Whether Tom committed forcible rape depends on whether Jane can effectively withdraw her initial consent *during* intercourse and, if so, whether Tom continued the act against her will. Known as a "postpenetration" rape, this offense occurs when the victim (a) initially consents to intercourse, (b) withdraws consent during the intercourse, and (c) the perpetrator forcibly continues in what has become nonconsensual intercourse.

Some states, like California, hold that a sexual partner can withdraw consent anytime during sex and that, if he or she does, the other participant is not entitled a reasonable time to complete intercourse.

---

66. See, e.g., *State v. Weisberg*, 65 Wash. App. 721, 829 P.2d 252 (1992).

67. See, e.g., *State v. Camara*, 113 Wash. 2d 631, 781 P.2d 483 (1989) (consent is an affirmative defense to a charge of rape); *People v. Williams*, 841 P.2d 961 (Cal. 1992).

Instead, the other person must stop the act immediately. Other states reach a contrary conclusion. In California, Tom's argument that he had "passed the point of no return" and should not be expected to stop might be of no avail.[68] Other states have adopted this postpenetration rape standard.

2e. If Tom threatened Jane with death or serious physical injury to have sex with her, then he can be convicted of rape. But did Tom intend merely to state his perception of the obvious, or did he intend his words to intimidate Jane into having sex with him? In those states that define "threat" by the defendant's state of mind, Tom could not be convicted of rape (assuming he did not have this intent). In those states that define threat by whether the victim honestly and reasonably feared death or serious physical injury, Tom might be convicted of rape.

2f. Because of the drug (known on the street as a "date-rape drug"), Jane was incapable of consenting to sexual intimacy. Even though Tom did not use physical force or threaten force and Jane did not resist, she was not "conscious" for the purpose of legally consenting to intercourse. Tom knows this because he slipped the drug into her drink for this very reason. Thus, he can be convicted of rape.

2g. Tom has not used any force or threat. Tom has clearly lied to Jane and misrepresented both his affection for her and his future intentions. But this is not fraud in the factum; Tom has not deceived Jane as to the nature of the sexual act. It may be fraud in the inducement, but the law of rape does not criminalize obtaining sexual intimacy by deception. Jane was still able to make her own decision about sharing sexual intimacy. Thus, Tom has not committed rape. For better or worse, the law of rape does not protect humans from persuasion or seduction, even if it is deliberately dishonest and manipulative.

2h. In some states Tom has committed rape. To be more exact, this kind of rape is called fraud in the inducement. He has not used force or threats of physical harm nor was Jane unable, because of incapacity, to give consent. However, since he faked her partner's identity, Jane was induced to have sex based on fraud. Many states would not allow rape in this circumstance, however, since Jane fully understood that she was about to have sexual intercourse, and she gave legally effective consent.

2i. Tom has, arguably, used force or the threat of force by creating a situation in which Jane honestly and reasonably feared bodily harm. Thus, under these circumstances Tom has used an implied threat of force by entering a stranger's bedroom uninvited at night and engaging in

68. *In re John Z.*, 60 P.3d 183 (Cal. 2003).

intercourse. Many states would not require Jane to resist or even to say "no" in this perilous situation.[69]

3. Whether or not Richard's despicable behavior constitutes rape depends on the law of his state. Some courts have held that coercion is inherent in the parent-child relationship and, therefore, no physical force or threat of force is required to convict a parent of rape.[70] In addition, Richard is also likely to be guilty of statutory rape (nonforcible intercourse with a minor who, because of her age, cannot consent) and incest (intercourse with a close family member). Other courts, however, have held that if the complainant is over the age of majority, even a past pattern of incest will not, by itself, satisfy the force requirement.[71] Here the victim is not over the age of majority, so Richard could be convicted of rape.

4. Mary Kay has committed "statutory rape"—that is, nonforcible intercourse with a minor, who, because of age, cannot give legally effective consent. The degree will depend on the state's particular statute. Mary Kay has not used force, threat of physical harm, or fraud, and Jamie was a willing participant. Indeed, they now want to be married. Nonetheless, most states do not permit minors under the age of 15 to give legally effective consent to intercourse.

   Some state laws, following the lead of the MPC, define the crime of statutory rape and its degree by referring to the ages of the victim and of the defendant. In these states, consensual sex between individuals close in age is not a crime. This approach will not help Mary Kay; she is significantly older than Jamie.

   A few states, however, have statutory rape laws that protect only females. If Mary Kay and Jamie lived in such a state, Mary Kay could not be convicted of statutory rape. Indeed, when Jamie reaches the requisite age, they can be married.

5. Demi has not committed rape. In most (but not all) states, rape requires force or the threat of physical injury. Demi has threatened Mike with economic harm, which does not satisfy the force element of rape. However, she may have committed extortion and, in a few states, rape. This is also a clear case of sexual harassment.

   Under the MPC, a male might be convicted of "gross sexual imposition" under §213.1(2) if the prosecutor can persuade a jury that this threat of economic injury "would prevent resistance by a woman of ordinary resolution." Since Demi is not a male, however, she cannot be

---

69. *People v. Iniguez*, 7 Cal. 4th 847, 872 P.2d 1183, 30 Cal. Rptr. 258 (1994).

70. *State v. Eskridge*, 38 Ohio St. 3d 56, 526 N.E.2d 304 (1988).

71. *State v. Schaim*, 65 Ohio St. 3d 51, 600 N.E.2d 661 (1992); *Commonwealth v. Biggs*, 320 Pa. Super. 265, 467 A.2d 31 (1983).

convicted. This lack of gender equality is one reason the MPC has not been influential in shaping modern rape law reform. Does the MPC's open-ended standard sweep too broadly?

6. This scenario is based on the movie *The Hand That Rocks the Cradle*. Dr. Brown would not have committed rape under the common law because he did not have sexual intercourse with Heather. Whether he could be convicted of rape under contemporary statutes is problematic.

   Most modern statutes cover a broader range of areas protected against penetration (usually including the vagina, anus, and mouth) and the means used (usually including not only the penis but fingers and any other objects used for this purpose). Unlike the common law, modern statutes probably would include the act of digital penetration in the definition of conduct covered by rape.

   However, it would be difficult to convict Dr. Brown under a statute that requires the use of *force* because, arguably, he did not use any force greater than that necessary to accomplish the penetration. Dr. Brown might be convicted of a lesser degree of rape under a statute that only requires *nonconsent* for rape because he inserted his bare hand into Heather's vagina without her consent. Heather consented to a professional medical exam, not to an ungloved digital penetration of her vagina by Dr. Brown for his sexual gratification.

7a. Max has not committed rape even though he used fraud to obtain sexual intercourse. His use of counterfeit money may be considered fraud in the inducement because Roberta understood that she was having sexual intercourse for money. Max might have committed fraud or theft (as well as possessing and passing counterfeit money), but he did not commit rape.

7b. Max has committed rape. True, he had hoped to obtain sexual intercourse by fraud. However, when Roberta told him no money, no sex, she withdrew her consent to sexual intercourse. Max then used physical force to overpower her and have intercourse. The fact that the victim is a prostitute and has regularly exchanged sex for money does not change the nature of the crime. Even though her sexual activity might violate laws on prostitution, Roberta's sexual autonomy is still protected by the law of rape and should be.

8. Hector did not use force beyond the inherent force necessary to accomplish anal intercourse. The prosecutor would have a difficult time convicting the defendant of sexual assault in a jurisdiction that requires *extrinsic* force or threat of force as an element of the crime. If only *inherent* force—the force necessary to accomplish the sex act—is required, then the prosecutor could establish that element.

But what if the prosecutor must prove that the sex act was committed without the *consent* of the victim? If *words* indicating affirmative agreement to have sex are required to establish consent, then the prosecutor would probably prevail. He could show that José said nothing indicating assent to this act. If, however, *conduct* can constitute consent, the defense would claim that José's compliance and seeming enjoyment *are* behaviors manifesting affirmative assent.

If affirmative assent is not required to establish consent, the defense would argue that José did not even say "no" or do anything else, like moving away or pushing Hector away, to indicate that he was an unwilling participant. Thus, the *absence* of any *resistance*—verbal or physical—proves that José *did consent*.

It is entirely possible that Hector honestly and reasonably believed that José consented to have sex but that José, in fact, did not consent. Whether Hector will be convicted of a serious sex crime will then depend on whether consent is an element of the crime or an affirmative defense. If it is an element, the crucial issue becomes what, if any, culpability is required toward consent. If it is a strict liability element, then the only question for the jury is whether José consented; Hector's attitude toward his consent is irrelevant. If consent is an affirmative defense, Hector would have to convince the jury by a preponderance of the evidence that he made an honest and reasonable mistake about José's consent. Should mistake of fact be a defense for sex crimes? How did you analyze Example 2c?[72]

9. The prosecutor would argue that the law is clear. A victim is incapable of consenting to sex if she is too drunk to consent. Though conscious during the event, her extreme intoxication prevented Christine from having the ability to appreciate the nature and consequences of the act and, therefore, to give lawful consent. The law is clear on its face: The prosecution does not have to prove Chris *knew* (or even *should* have known) she was too drunk to consent. Nor does the prosecution have to prove that Chris or someone acting on his behalf was responsible for getting her drunk. Her blood alcohol level was so high that she was legally incapable of operating a motor vehicle. Surely, it prevented her from having the capacity to consent to sexual intercourse. Even if she voluntarily agreed to get drunk, she did not thereby voluntarily agree to have sex with a stranger. This enlightened law protects victims from themselves as it should. Excessive drinking is too often the cause of unwanted sex.

---

72. For a similar case see *R. v. R.J.S.*, [1994] 123 Nfld & P.E.I.R. 317.

The defense would counter that Christine undressed herself, voluntarily got into bed with Chris, and was conscious during the sexual act. At no time did Chris use force or threaten her, nor did Christine say "no" or otherwise indicate in any manner her lack of consent. To the contrary, she was fully conscious while having sex and her cooperative behavior was perfectly consistent with saying "yes." Even though Chris knew she had been drinking, there was nothing to indicate Christine was so drunk that she did not understand what she was doing. Moreover, to read the law as the prosecutor does would convert a crucial element of rape in this state—consent—into a strict liability offense because the prosecutor would not even have to prove Chris *should* have known Christine lacked the capacity to consent. Mutual intoxication in this case should not increase the defendant's risk of conviction, while at the same time relieving Christine of responsibility for her own actions.

How would you rule? Would you decide the case the same way if Chris had called the police and Christine had been charged with rape? Should rape be a strict liability crime in this situation?

10. The defense would argue that the prosecution could not establish a necessary element of the crime, that is, that he "touched" a child in a sexual manner for sexual gratification. Instead, Amy touched herself. Moreover, it would claim that this is a clear case of *factual impossibility* because he could not have touched her in the manner prohibited by the statute.

    The prosecutor would respond that Jim told Amy to partially undress and touch herself in a sexually explicit manner for his own sexual gratification. Thus, Jim caused an *innocent agent* (a young child who did not understand the sexual nature of her behavior) to engage in the conduct prohibited by the statute and that his purpose, sexual gratification, is clearly established by his arousal. The prosecutor may well prevail in this age of "virtual crimes" committed over the Internet, even though Jim never physically touched Amy himself.

11a. This is a close case under most rape shield laws. This evidence would seriously damage the credibility of the complaining witness by showing that she had engaged in sex for drugs in the past. However, it is relevant to defendant's claim that the complainant consented to have sex and also sheds light on the complainant's motive—that is, she may be filing a rape charge in retaliation for Harry not paying her as promised. This evidence would probably be admitted.[73]

73. *Johnson v. State*, 332 Md. 456, 632 A.2d 152 (1993).

11b. Most states now consider the testimony of a rape victim to be legally sufficient to prove rape and do not require additional corroboration evidence. The jury will be instructed that the prosecution must prove its case beyond a reasonable doubt and will have to decide who is telling the truth.

12. The prosecutor might bring a rape charge if his state is one of the minority jurisdictions that permit nonphysical threats (such as Larry's threat to give Marcia a failing grade) to satisfy the threat of force element. Since Larry's threat did not involve one of physical violence, most jurisdictions would not consider this a case of rape.

    However, the prosecutor could readily bring a statutory rape charge (also called "rape of child" in a few states) because Marcia was clearly under the age of consent, set by many states today at 16 years old. The degree of the charge would depend on Marcia's age and in some states on Larry's age. The law simply considers children and young adolescents as legally incapable of giving consent. Thus, even if Larry might argue that Marcia voluntarily agreed to have sex with him, a statutory rape charge will succeed. In some states this type of threat might also constitute extortion.

13. Sal can be charged with statutory rape. Though Pam was a willing partner, the law protects young people from sexual exploitation by adults. In some states, Sal might have a defense of reasonable mistake of fact because his belief that Pam was 18 appears to be reasonable. However, many states do not permit this defense to a charge of statutory rape, while others limit it to cases involving victims of a certain minimum age. Some states provide for degrees depending on the age of the victim.

14. The prosecutor would argue that the clear language and plain meaning of the state statute apply to the conduct of both Alex and Faith. Each engaged in an act of sexual intercourse with someone who was under the age of 13. The legislature unmistakably intended to punish this type of behavior in order to prevent sexual victimization of young children even if the offender is another child. If the legislature had intended to exclude responsibility when the perpetrators are of the same age or close in age, it could easily have done so by requiring an age differential between perpetrator and victim as many states do. It did not. In this case, an adjudication of juvenile delinquency only results in commitment to a state agency for supervision and rehabilitation until each reaches the age of 21.

    Even with that, there may not be a prosecutor willing to prosecute two 12-year-old kids for having intercourse. And at a minimum, defense counsel would argue that, though the prosecutor is correct in her literal reading of the statute, this result is absurd and contrary to public policy. This law was intended to protect juveniles, not to ensnare them as perpetrators when they simply engage in consensual sex with another child of the same age. An adjudication of juvenile delinquency would stigmatize them, possibly for life. He would note that both children might have to register as sex offenders in this or another state well past the age of 21. Rehabilitation in such circumstances will be difficult. Moreover, if this joint adjudication is allowed, there would be nothing to prevent future prosecutors from seeking to prosecute future under-age sexual partners as adults in a criminal court (see Chapter 17) where the penalties are much more severe.

As a judge, would you allow the adjudication of delinquency or dismiss the petition?

15. No, it is unlikely that Joe will be responsible for the rape. While it appears that all of the elements of rape have been satisfied, there is one key element missing. If Joe truly suffers from sexsomnia, then the actus reus is not satisfied because there was no voluntary act. A defendant cannot be convicted if he acted without both the actus reus and mens rea. Also, if Joe was asleep at the time of his conduct, he likely would not have the requisite mens rea to commit rape. Therefore, if the jury believes Joe's defense, he cannot be convicted for raping Ally.

    However, if it is discovered that Joe knows he suffers from sexsomnia and did not take the proper precautions, then it is likely that he could still be found to have committed a rape in this instance.

    Do you think this is the correct outcome?

CHAPTER 10

Theft

OVERVIEW

Some people always want what the other person has. And they'll do anything to get it: take it, trick the owner into giving it up, hide it, perhaps even destroy the property if they can't have it.

These unhappy facts of life have given rise to one of the most arcane areas of criminal law: property offenses. The doctrines of the various crimes that constitute property offenses—larceny, embezzlement, taking under false pretenses, extortion, and others—are laced with rules and a host of exceptions to those rules. Courts have created fictional devices to reach the "right results" when the rules would not allow such a result. The doctrines also reflect tension between courts and legislatures about the reach of the criminal law and the impact of the death penalty.

There are three "major" property offenses: *larceny*, *embezzlement*, and *taking under false pretenses*. At the risk of grossly oversimplifying, one might say that the characteristics that distinguish these crimes from each other are as follows:

1. *Larceny* is a taking of the *possession* of another.
2. *Embezzlement* is the *conversion* to the defendant's use of another's property lawfully obtained.
3. *False pretenses*—unlike the previous two, which are offenses against *possession*—is a taking of *title* by *deceit*.

These simplifications hide a vast array of interlocking and overlapping requirements and fact patterns. The ingenuity of persons who want someone else's property is vast and unlikely to be hemmed in by specific differences among the "elements" of various crimes. Nevertheless, it may help if you keep your eye on these skeletal definitions.

THE IMPACT OF HISTORY

The Death Penalty

Prior to the common law,[1] most legal systems, including both Greek and Roman law, treated most infringements against property as torts, with damages as the only remedy.[2] In sharp contrast, the common law punished larceny as it punished all felonies, with death, until the early part of the nineteenth century.[3] Many judges, however, gave restrictive readings of the "elements" of larceny to avoid imposing the death penalty in opposition to either the penalty itself or to its imposition for "mere" invasions of property. In the eighteenth century, as the death penalty became more discretionary, the need to restrict the reach of property offenses ebbed, and courts upheld liability in larceny (most notably in *Pear's Case*, infra). And when in the nineteenth century the death penalty was removed as a possible penalty for most property offenses unconnected with potential physical violence, courts gave increasingly broad readings to the elements of larceny. Similarly, legislatures enacted a wide range of new statutes proscribing other interferences with property, but not punishable by death.

1. No group of crimes so reflects the various tensions in the centuries during which they were developed as do property offenses. For an extraordinary in-depth analysis of the historical development, see J. Hall, Theft, Law and Society (1952).

2. There were some exceptions: Stealing a bather's clothes and theft of livestock were criminally punishable in Rome. Housebreaking and theft at night, which indirectly involved the potential threat to persons, were also treated criminally (under the common law scheme, they would be dealt with as burglary).

3. There is some suggestion that "larceny" was initially (1000-1250 A.D.) limited to forcible takings (what we now call robbery), but the history is somewhat cloudy.

LARCENY

The "elements" of larceny are easily stated:

1. There must be a *trespassory*
2. *taking*
3. and *asportation*
4. of the *personal property*
5. *of another*
6. with the *intent*
7. to deprive him of it *permanently* (or *for a long period of time*).

Trespass

The first element of larceny limits the crime to acts that violate possession of an item. If the defendant has already obtained lawful possession of the property, his later use or conversion cannot be a "trespass" and he has not committed larceny. Thus, if George, with Ralph's permission, borrows Ralph's Maserati, and decides later that he loves the car too much to return it, George may be a dastardly evildoer, but he is not guilty of common law larceny because his initial taking was not a trespass.

That limitation, however, conflicted with the need to protect trade in mid-Renaissance England. In *The Carrier's Case, Anon. v. The Sheriff of London*, 64 Seld. Soc. 30 (1473), a London dealer (call him Henry) had hired the defendant (Jerry) to take some goods from London to Southampton. The goods were inside packages. Jerry got about halfway, broke open the packages, and hid the contents. In a prosecution for larceny, Jerry argued that he had obtained possession of the goods lawfully and consensually and therefore was not guilty of the crime because there was no trespass. Jerry *was* right, but he lost anyway. The court announced a new fiction. Jerry, it said, had possession of the packages *qua* (as) packages. Had he simply sold those packages, he would not have "trespassed" on the goods. But since he had *"broken bulk"* of the packages (removed the items from the pakages), he had trespassed on the goods inside and hence was guilty of larceny.

The fiction of "breaking bulk" was only the first of many such fictions that the common law courts would create, some favorable to the defendant, some not, in trying to square specific acts with the definition of larceny. A second judicially created fiction was *constructive possession*, which elaborated on the distinction between "custody" and "possession." Usually, we think of anyone who has "dominion" over an item as "possessing" it. However, the courts concluded that a person who had only temporary and extremely limited authorization to use the property had only custody and not possession. This was said to be the case with employees[4] and bailees but not with carriers, apparently because they had authority for longer periods of time than did bailees or employees. Constructive possession remained with the owner, such that a taking by an employee was trespassory.

The doctrine of constructive possession was also used in the case of persons finding lost items. Even if the owner did not know where the item was, he was said to have constructive possession of the item. Then, if the finder, F, knew, or could suspect, who the owner was and intended at the time of finding to convert the item, the finding became trespassory.

The constructive possession fiction did not apply to the merchant deliverer situation nor to a host of other similar (but not identical) relationships. For example, if *A* gives B her first edition of Shakespeare, believing B to be C, an antiques dealer, B has obtained possession voluntarily, and his later conversion of the book is not larceny. Similarly, if D owes E $10 but gives him $100 in error, E has not committed larceny of the $90 excess because he obtained it nontrespassorily. *Cooper v. Commonwealth*, 110 Ky. 123 (1901). Now the courts *could* have found B and E to be "bailees" or, alternatively, could have concluded that *A* and D retained "constructive possession" as well. But they did not, and it was left up to legislatures to deal with these situations.

One such exception to the general involuntariness requirement *was* created by the courts, relatively late, in the infamous *Pear's Case*. *R. v. Pear*, 168 Eng. Rep. 208 (1779). Pear rented a horse from Victim, intending all the while to take the horse and sell it. Pear argued that his initial taking of the horse was consensual and not trespassory. The court responded by finding that his intent at the initial rental to take the horse vitiated the consensual aspect of the rental and created "larceny by trick." Had Pear formed the intent to take the horse *after* he rented it, it would not be larceny (but *might* be embezzlement) (see infra).

This muddle of rules as to when a trespass does (or does not) occur baffled both courts and prosecutors. And when courts required that the prosecutor indict for the precise crime committed, and prove *that* offense or lose, the stakes were substantial.

Asportation and Taking

Although "taking" and "asportation" seem to describe the same actions, the common law distinguished between them. *Asportation* (a sufficiently clumsy

4. The common law could not be quite so rule-bound. If the employee had "significant" authority, he obtained possession and not mere custody. See *Morgan v. Commonwealth*, 47 S.W.2d 543 (Ky. 1932).

word to justify vilification of the common law courts) occurred only if the defendant actually "moved" the property. Where the property is incapable of being "carried away," such as a house or a heavy object, it may not be the subject of asportation. See Annot., 70 A.L.R.3d 1202 (1976).

The movement need not be far; there are cases holding that even a change of position of two or three inches is sufficient. However, if the item is not moved at all, there is no asportation and hence no larceny. Of course, the courts were always ready to create a fiction if justice required it. Suppose that George "sells" Jamal that red Maserati of Ralph's. George gives Jamal convincing fake copies of title, and Jamal, after depositing $50,000 in George's hand, drives the car away. Even if George has never entered the car, he has "asported" it. The fiction of *innocent agency* turned Jamal into George's "agent," so that when Jamal took the car, it was "really" George driving it away.[5]

Taking, on the other hand, required "caption," defined as exercising *control and dominion* over the property. If the property was not *capable* of being taken, a mere asportation was insufficient. For example, if a clothing store attached a coat to a mannequin by a chain, even if the defendant "moved" (and therefore asported) the coat, his conduct was not a "taking," since the coat could not (short of a blow torch) be removed.

Personal Property

Larceny never applied to real property (possibly because it could never be asported). However, with regard to items that are "fixtures" on the land, the common law really outdid itself in creating confusion. If Mary Ann trespassed on Celia's land one day, cut down eight cedar trees, and immediately removed the lumber, there was no larceny because the act was seen as affecting not personal property but real property. If, however, Mary Ann got tired after the hewing, went home to relax for an hour or two, and then returned, her subsequent asportation of the downed lumber was *now* larceny, since the trees had become Celia's personal property.[6]

Documents representing either real property or causes of action were not the subject of larceny. The fiction upon which this result rested, that the documents "merged" into the things they represented, may have been helpful in other branches of the law but was a hindrance in criminal law. On the other hand, some *incorporeal* items, such as electricity, *could* be the

5. Not all courts agreed. See *Smith v. State*, 11 Ga. App. 197 (1912) (asportation and hence larceny); *State v. Labrode*, 202 La. 59 (1942) (no larceny). See Annots., 19 A.L.R. 724 (1922); 144 A.L.R. 1383 (1943).

6. It is sometimes explained that if the "trees" are laid on the owner's ground, the "lumber" becomes his property, and the taking is thus from his possession.

subject of larceny while others, such as ideas, could not. Thus, when David Ellsberg stole papers from the Pentagon, photocopied them, and publicized them, he was guilty under the common law (if at all) only of the larceny of the value of the paper. The ideas were not items that could be "stolen" under common law larceny.

The common law also held that theft of *services* (as opposed to property) did not constitute larceny. Thus, if Basil hires Joanne to fix his car and then takes off in the repaired auto without paying, Basil has not committed larceny because services are not property and, hence, their "taking" is not criminal.

Finally, the common law distinguished among animals. Not surprisingly, wild animals (*ferrae naturae*) that merely "lived" on a victim's land were not "his," and hence could not be personal property, the subject of larceny. But the law went further: Cows *could* be stolen, but domesticated dogs could not because, while not wild, pets were "base" animals below the law's cognition.

Of Another

It would seem obvious that you cannot "steal" your own property. However, the obvious is never necessarily the legal. Since larceny is a crime *against possession, not ownership*, if Ben loans Greg his putter for a week but then decides in the middle of the week that he wants it back, and simply takes it from Greg's golf bag, Ben can be guilty of the larceny of "his" putter. Similarly, if Greg had a lien on the putter, Ben could be guilty of larceny. You can also steal from a thief; although he obviously does not have "title" to his goods, he does have "possession" such that removing his property, albeit stolen, constitutes larceny.[7]

One aspect of this rule is the effect of a so-called *claim of right*. If George wrongly believes that Stan owes him Stan's red Maserati (for whatever reason) and takes it, George is not guilty of larceny. One way of expressing this rule is to say that a claim of right negates the "specific intent" of larceny. However, as we have already seen (in Chapter 4), the specific-general intent distinction is tenuous at best. The better analysis is simply to say that the defendant acting under a claim of right does not "know" that the property belongs to "another," and hence does not meet the culpability requirements with respect to the material elements of the offense. Moreover, consistent

7. One suggestion is that this deters thieves from stealing from other thieves. But that would be true only if the second thief *knew* that the possessor was a thief. This seems a stretched explanation.

with other "specific intent" crimes, any mistake (either of fact or law), no matter how unreasonable, will "negate" liability for larceny.

When the taker has some interest in the property but does not have "full" possession, the common law concluded that a co-owner (partner, spouse, tenant in common) cannot commit larceny from another co-owner. When, however, the partners are in the process of dissolving their relationship, this rule may not always apply.

With Intent

Get ready for another great Latin phrase, *animus furandi*. Under this phrase, the defendant had to "intend" to "deprive" the possessor "permanently" of the item. Suppose that George intends to take what he knows to be Ralph's car but intends to return it within a day or a week. Here the law was somewhat haphazard. If George intended to return the exact same car, then usually there was no larceny. If, however, the property was otherwise fungible (such as money), many courts found there *was* larceny, even though Ralph would get "the equivalent" money returned. George had in fact deprived Ralph of the "very" paper that he had taken. That, said the criminal law, was sufficient.

Moreover, George's liability in each instance would depend in part not only on his intent to return the item but on the *reasonableness of his belief that he could do so*. If George was merely wishfully thinking that he could return the same car or even the same amount, it is larceny. Thus, if George intends to use Ralph's car in a demolition derby or even in a stock car race, his ability to return the car in the same condition he takes it is so small that he will be guilty of larceny *even though* his "subjective intent" was not to deprive Ralph of it permanently. In a sense, if George was "reckless" as to his ability to return the property, that was a sufficient basis for liability. Similarly, even in those jurisdictions that would allow George a defense if he intended to return the equivalent amount, if George intended to use the money to gamble on a horse (even a "sure winner"), he would be guilty of larceny because he was "reckless" as to whether he would actually get that money back in order to return it to Ralph. On the other hand, an objectively plausible intent to return the property prevents liability even if some unexpected obstacle prevents an actual return. *Schenectady Varnish Co. v. Automobile Ins. Co.*, 127 Misc. 751 (Sup. Ct. 1926). For example, if George only intended to drive Ralph's car around the block, a relatively safe block with very little traffic, before returning it, and as he was turning the last corner a car ran a red light and collided with him, George would not be guilty of larceny.

To Deprive

The mens rea of larceny is *animus furandi* (intent to steal), not *lucri causa* (because of gain). Although most thieves take property so that they can use the stolen item, that is not required by the definition of larceny. The focus is on *the loss to the possessor*, not the gain to the defendant. Thus, if George, jealous of Stan, takes the Maserati and has it destroyed, it is larceny even though George never expected to retain the car.

Permanently

As already suggested, if George takes Stan's car but only intends to make Stan walk to work for a week and then to return the car, most courts would find that the taking was not larcenous because the intended deprivation was not "permanent." Thus, "borrowing" an item was almost never enough for larceny. Suppose, however, that the defendant knows that the owner needs the item during the time it will be missing? Greg, intending to return it immediately after the tournament is over, takes Ben's favorite putter the night before Ben is to participate in the Masters, or Sheila takes Madeleine's stocks and bonds for a week, knowing that Madeleine will have to declare bankruptcy without them. Some courts began to include in the definition of larceny an intent to deprive of "important" or "economically significant" possession, even if the taker had the purpose to return the property after this usefulness was exhausted.

Injury to aesthetic interests, however, was never included within larceny. If Tom removes Mary's Monets from the wall of her summer house for the one month during which Mary will be there, intending to replace them as soon as Mary leaves, Tom has not committed larceny, even though he has inflicted harm on Mary, because Mary's only harm was aesthetic. Again, suppose that Tom has removed the Monets not to upset Mary but to use as collateral in obtaining a loan. Since Tom's (reasonably achievable) intent is to return these very paintings, it is not larceny.

Contemporaneity

As if all these factors weren't enough to cause apoplexy, the courts further required that the mens rea and the actus reus coincide. Only if, at the time of the taking, *D* had the requisite mens rea did the taking constitute larceny. Thus, if Greg takes Ben's putter out of his golf bag without Ben's knowledge with every purpose of returning it after ten minutes' practice, but then decides to keep it, Greg has not committed larceny because his intent at the time of the taking was not to deprive Ben of the putter permanently. His later conversion may be immoral, unethical, and even not nice, but it's not larceny.

Here again, however, the common law created new fictions to cover egregious cases. In this instance, courts developed the fiction of *continuing trespass*. Since Greg's original taking was trespassory, the courts concluded that the trespassory nature "continued" as long as Greg had the putter. Therefore, at the time Greg decided to keep it, there was a coincidence of mens rea and actus reus, and Greg could be guilty of larceny. But even here, things were complicated. Some courts limited the application of this fictional doctrine to cases where the original taking was not only "trespassory" but done with an immoral, even if not criminal, mens rea. Thus if, when he picked it up, Greg thought that the putter was his, the taking, though objectively a trespass,[8] was held *not* to be "continuing"; hence, when he later converted it to his own use, the conversion did not transform the original taking into larceny.

Finders

Assume that Alice mislays, or loses, her treasured collection of classic minicars, and John finds them and takes them home. Is this larceny? At first blush, John's taking does not seem to be trespassory, but the common law established early on a fiction that lost or mislaid property was still in the constructive possession of the owner. Thus, John's taking was trespassory. However, the law still would not convict John unless:

1. The property bore some indication that it belonged to someone (although it was not necessary that the specific possessor be indicated).
2. At the time of the finding, John expected and intended to keep it.

Thus, if John finds the cars, and there is no indication of ownership, he is not guilty of larceny. Even if there is such indication (the owner's mailing label would be nice), it is not larceny if John takes them, intending to return them to Alice, but only later decides to enjoy the cars himself (the contemporaneity requirement).

Hasn't this trip through larceny been fun? Every time it looks as though we've got a firm "rule," it turns out squishy. Rules gave way to exceptions, which then became qualified by sub-exceptions, which in turn were

8. In tort, mistake of fact is not a defense to a claim of trespass. It may negate mens rea, but it does not negate the trespassory nature of the taking.

changed by fictions to reach a "right" result. And that, as Justice Holmes put it, has been the life of the law. Super clear, right?

EMBEZZLEMENT

Not even all the fictions and exceptions to the general requirements of larceny could meet the needs of society nor the ingenuity of bad-minded folk. Suppose, for example, that Marvin is a bank teller, and Laurel, a depositor, gives him money to deposit for her account. If Marvin puts the money into the till and then removes it for his trip to Rio, he would be guilty of larceny from the bank since the money would first go into possession of the bank (the till), and his later taking would be trespassory. However, if Marvin immediately puts the money in his pocket planning an immediate trip to Rio, it is not larceny. Since Laurel has voluntarily parted with her money, Marvin's initial "taking" is not trespassory from her. And since he has not "tricked" her into giving up her money, *Pear's Case* and the doctrine of larceny by trick are not applicable. Moreover, the bank never possessed the money so there can be no trespass against it. Thus, Marvin is not guilty of larceny.

It made little sense to hold Marvin guilty of a crime depending on whether the money physically went into the till. Yet this was exactly the result in the (in)famous *Bazeley's Case*, 168 Eng. Rep. 517 (1799), where Bazeley was acquitted of a larceny charge. Of course, the courts could have established yet another "fiction," for example, that the money remained in the depositor's "constructive possession" until put into the till, but it chose not to do so. The legislature quickly filled this gap by creating the statutory misdemeanor of *embezzlement*.[9] The elements of embezzlement then became

1. a *fraudulent*
2. *conversion*
3. of *property*
4. of *another*
5. by one who is *already in lawful possession* (not mere custody) of it.[10]

---

9. It has been suggested that common law courts were not prepared to treat as larceners, and thus subject to the death penalty, employees who simply misappropriated property that they received on behalf of their employers. But this seems unlikely, since those same courts treated disloyal employees as guilty of larceny if they misappropriated property given to them by their employers, and indeed erected the new fiction of constructive possession to explain it.

10. The initial statute against embezzlement was limited to bank tellers, but subsequent additions to the idea were eventually generalized to include any person who had been "entrusted" with the property in question.

The key differences between embezzlement and larceny are (1) an actual conversion must occur; and (2) the original taking must *not* be trespassory—that is, the conversion here is *against ownership and not possession*. (Note that it is still necessary to distinguish between "title" and "ownership"; if *title* is misappropriated, it is false pretenses, discussed next.)

Conversion

Conversion requires that the defendant "seriously interfere" with the property—unlike larceny, in which even a movement of a few inches is sufficient to qualify.[11] Like larceny, however, embezzlement does not require that the conversion be for the benefit of the defendant. It can benefit another or in some cases result in little or no gain to anyone, but merely a loss to the owner. Indeed, as in larceny, the focus is on the loss of the owner, not the gain of the thief.

In Lawful Possession

As we have seen, the crime of embezzlement was statutorily enacted to fill the gap in larceny law where possession was initially obtained lawfully; lawful possession is usually the issue in deciding whether the defendant committed larceny or embezzlement. Given the fictions that common law courts previously created to fill *other* gaps in larceny law, there can be confusion. Thus, an employee may either have possession of property given to him by his employer (and hence be guilty of embezzlement if he converts it) or be only in custody (since his employer retains "constructive possession") and hence be guilty of larceny if he "takes" the property. For example, if Jim gives John (his employee) $500 in cash, and John heads for Rio, it is fairly clear that this is larceny and not embezzlement, for the "constructive possession" fiction applies. Suppose, however, that Jim gives John a check for $500 and John cashes it, but then takes the proceeds and heads for Rio. Did Jim ever have possession of "the cash," such that John has committed larceny? Or is this a case of embezzlement? Courts differ.

Fraud

The requirement that the conversion be "fraudulent" is somewhat misleading, at least if we think of "fraud" in the normal usage of that term, which

11. In this sense, larceny, which requires only an "intent to deprive" and not an actual deprivation, can be seen as an inchoate offense, while embezzlement is a "result" offense.

suggests that at the time he actually got the property, John (a) intended to convert it to his own use and/or (b) induced the owner to part with it on the basis of deceit. The term, at least as used in embezzlement statutes, does not necessarily suggest either of these.

As with larceny, embezzlement is said to be a "specific intent" crime, so a person who converts property under a mistaken claim of right, or with the intent to return the very property he takes, is not guilty of the crime. Also as with larceny, the intent to return the equivalent property is a defense. However, in contrast to larceny, where an intent to return equivalent property that is offered for sale *may* be a defense, embezzlement occurs even with such an intent.

FALSE PRETENSES

The common law defined larceny as an offense against possession, and embezzlement as an offense against ownership-possession. Thus, if George persuades Stan to loan him his Maserati for a day, and then converts it to his own use, it is embezzlement even if the initial taking was not trespassory. It's larceny by trick if George always intended to convert it. But if the defendant obtained not merely possession of the item but *title* as well, the common law courts held that this was neither larceny nor embezzlement. Thus, if George persuades Stan to *give* him the Maserati so that George can allegedly donate it to a charity, or on the false representation that George needs to sell the car to save his dying mother, George has committed neither of these two crimes. Since, in almost all cases of title passing, possession also passes, the common law courts surely could have held that larceny covered the offense. However, because courts hesitated, for some unclear reason, to create another common law property offense,[12] Parliament stepped in by enacting a statute to plug this loophole and prohibit *obtaining property by false pretenses*. As explained by case law, the offense requires:

1. a *representation*
2. of a *material present or past fact*
3. which the *defendant knows to be false*
4. and which he *intends* will and
5. does *cause the victim*

12. It might be remembered that *Pear's Case*, which created the crime of "larceny by trick," was decided 30 years after the false pretense statute was enacted. Ten years after *Pear's Case*, the courts refused to bring embezzlement with the common law larceny crime, thereby impelling Parliament to enact embezzlement statutes.

6. to pass *title*
7. of his property.

While the requirements of causation and "property" seem to be fairly straightforward elements, the other elements have created difficulties for the courts.

Representation

The misrepresentation has to be affirmative. The failure to disclose a fact does not constitute common law false pretenses, unless there is a preexisting fiduciary duty between the parties. Thus, if John sells Joe a book labeled "Modern Tax Law," knowing that Joe believes it to be current whereas John knows that the book deals with a repealed Code, John has not obtained the money by false pretenses unless he *affirmatively* tells Joe that the book is "current." His failure to correct Joe's misunderstanding is insufficient.

Present or Past Fact

Although the statutory language contained not even a hint of the limitation, common law courts quickly held that only the representation of a *present or past fact* could be the basis of a conviction of this new crime. If the defendant fraudulently pays the seller with counterfeit money, this is false pretenses because the representation is that the money is valid. If, however, the defendant fraudulently promises the seller that he will pay tomorrow, and does not, this is not false pretenses because the misrepresentation regards the defendant's future intent or acts, and that is a "false promise," not a present fact.

This distinction is often hard to make. A defendant's (intentionally false) statement that he "will" pay tomorrow could be construed as a misstatement about a present fact, his current state of mind. Moreover, although one hears echoes of the common law's refusal to protect fools, it is not clear why persons who rely on promises about the future are "bigger fools" than those who do not ascertain the accuracy of representations as to present or past facts.[13] (Or, to put it another way, why persons who deceive using present facts are more dangerous, or more blameworthy, than those who deceive by making promises.)

---

13. Although there apparently was some authority that the lie had to be one calculated to deceive a reasonable man (see *Commonwealth v. Norton*, 93 Mass. 266 (1865)), the modern rule is that the victim's failure to act reasonably is irrelevant.

Supporters of the distinction argue that it is necessary to protect legitimate business deals. Virtually all contracts concern themselves with promises to be performed in the future. Persons often contract with one another with the full expectation of performing in the future. If every failure to perform a contract could be construed as obtaining by false pretenses, business agreements would be undermined. One cannot be sure whether a borrower who has defaulted made a false promise or simply changed his mind about the use of borrowed money (or was unable to pay it back). If criminal liability were this likely, contracts would become far less prevalent, and commerce would surely decline.

Those who think that it should be possible to convict on the basis of false promises argue that juries are as capable of deciding this mens rea as they are in other cases. And empirically there appears to be no flood of "bad" prosecutions in jurisdictions that recognize false promises as bases for false pretenses.

Title

The distinguishing factor between false pretenses and the other two offenses we have considered is that *title must pass* at some point to the defendant, whereas in the other two it does not. In many instances, it is clear whether title passes, but some cases are not obvious. Thus, suppose that only part of the title passes, such as when there is a conditional sale induced by false representation. Although full title does not pass until the sale is complete, courts usually conclude that "enough" indices of title have passed to warrant a conviction of false pretenses. On the other hand, if a defendant induces a victim to depart with property for a specific purpose (e.g., to buy a piece of nonexistent land; to give a (fictitious) bribe to a third party), it is held that this is not false pretenses but larceny by trick because title would only pass if the purported goal were actually achieved.

Mens Rea, Knowledge, and Intent to Defraud

Since this crime is limited to representations regarding present or past facts, the prosecution must show not only that the representation was false,[14] but

14. For some reason, if the defendant believes the representation to be false but it turns out (much to the chagrin of the defendant) to be true, the crime has not been committed. It is *possible* that such a defendant could be convicted of attempting to obtain property by false pretenses, but since there was never a possibility that the fact would be false, such a conclusion is problematic at best. See the discussion of impossibility in Chapter 12.

that the defendant knew the falsity of her representation when she made it. Although on principle, one might be willing to convict a defendant who states facts recklessly, the majority view seemed to be that this was not sufficient for liability.

In addition to knowing that the statements she makes are false, the defendant must "intend to defraud." As in larceny and embezzlement, therefore, this "specific intent" requirement is not present if the defendant is acting under a claim of right or intends to return the property.

CONFUSION

All of these conflicting doctrines, exceptions, fine-edged distinctions, and springing fictions gave both courts and prosecutors headaches, particularly in light of the view, held at least by most courts through the early part of the twentieth century, that the prosecutor could allege only one such crime in an indictment. If the wrong crime were alleged, there was no remedy except to retry the defendant for the "other" crime. Thus, if George were convicted of larceny by trick, he could successfully appeal by arguing that he had not intended to convert at the time that he obtained the property. If he were then retried for embezzlement, he could argue that the evidence showed that he *did* intend to convert then, and that he could therefore not be guilty of embezzlement. These flimsy lines between larceny and embezzlement, and between false pretenses and larceny by trick, generated severe displeasure with "the system."

During the middle part of the twentieth century, state legislatures began attacking these problems, but the attacks were often piecemeal, such as adding a line or two to the larceny statute or embezzlement statute that tried to reach all the various possibilities. Some statutes provided that one who commits embezzlement or false pretenses "shall be deemed guilty of larceny." Still other states allowed the prosecuting attorney to join several counts in one indictment, thus potentially leaving to the jury the job of determining the exact crime committed by the defendant. However, there was the danger that the jurors would not agree on the crime or, if they did, that an appellate court would find that they had selected the wrong one.

Moreover, a number of these statutes seemed wildly untamed. For example, some statutes penalized as embezzlement a breach of faith, even if there was no expropriation. Other states altered the kinds of property that could be the subject of these crimes, varied the requirements for lost or mislaid property, and so on. In short, there was little uniformity among the statutes.

The Model Penal Code has sought to bring some uniformity to the states. Even here, however, notions of past precedent, ambiguity in statutes, and the ingenuity of defendants still plague the courts. Until and unless we find a way to either be more precise with our language or allow more flexibility in the process of charging and convicting of crime, the dead hand of the past will continue to govern much of the doctrine of property offenses.

GRADING

When larceny was punishable by death, Parliament (and later the states) enacted statutes providing that really trivial (petit) larcenies be exempted from that punishment. This method used was to assess the value of the goods taken: If the amount was less than 30 pence (the value of one sheep), death was not an available penalty.[15]

Even after the abolition of the death penalty for larceny, American jurisdictions have continued to use the value of goods taken as the demarcation between "grand" and "petty" larceny, with the former obviously being punished more severely. Some states have three or four degrees of larceny, depending on the amount taken. Whether this is a sensible approach is not clear, particularly in cases where the defendant is mistaken as to the amount he intends to take (or risks taking). As discussed in the materials on mistake (Chapter 5), there are instances where such a mistake might be relevant, particularly under the Model Penal Code. Thus, if the defendant *thinks* he is stealing a nickel but the nickel is a valuable coin worth thousands, most jurisdictions would hold that the defendant takes the risk that his crime is greater than he believes (see the discussion in Chapter 6 of the "greater crime" theory). The MPC, however, would make the defendant liable only for the amount he *thought* he was taking. Of course, if the defendant decides to simply take a pocketbook, he takes the risk that it will contain the Hope Diamond because that defendant has no knowledge as to the amount he is taking.

Measuring the value of the goods, is not always easy, particularly where the value of goods changes drastically and quickly, as in futures or works of art. Usually the market value as of the day the item is stolen is used,

15. The animosity of English juries to the death penalty is reflected in 1 L. Radzinowicz, History of English Criminal Law and Its Administration (1948), which recites numerous jury verdicts finding the value of goods taken as one pence less than the "death amount." In an intriguing reversion to that time, the current New Jersey statute explicitly provides that the amount of the value of the goods taken shall be fixed by the trier of fact; no guidance is provided by the statute. See N.J. Stat. Ann. 2c:20-2(b)(4).

but there are problems involved in determining both market value and the "time" at which the item was "stolen," particularly in cases of "continuing trespass," which require a "conversion" that occurs principally in the defendant's mind. Problems also occur if the defendant takes several items over a period of time (e.g., a bank teller who embezzles $500 a week for ten weeks), but the courts generally allow aggregation of these amounts if they are from the same victim and appear to be part of a "single" plot.[16]

THE MODEL PENAL CODE

Although several states preceded it, the Model Penal Code (MPC) is the leader in the current movement for statutory reform and consolidation of theft crimes. The MPC provides for one crime of "theft," which can be committed in a variety of ways, including larceny, or embezzlement, or false pretenses (the MPC also includes extortion, receiving stolen goods, and similar offenses in its general sections on theft). The fine distinctions between crimes based on the intention of the parties and crimes based on the victim's understanding and intent have been eliminated; the MPC takes the position, reaffirmed by most other modern statutes, that thieves are equally dangerous or culpable and the harm of such crimes equally serious, no matter how caused.

It is important to note the provision that the prosecution will not be thwarted if its evidence at trial suggests a different "method" of committing theft than was pled in the indictment; a charge of "theft," without more, will suffice for conviction as long as the actual proof shows that the conduct violated a specific statutory prohibition.

Because it combines all thefts, the MPC does not require a "taking" or an "asportation." The MPC calls "criminologically insignificant" the question of whether the item has been "moved" or not. Instead, the MPC requires that the defendant "unlawfully take or exercise unlawful control over" movable property or "unlawfully transfer" immovable property. As the MPC Commentary puts it: "[T]he critical inquiry is twofold: whether the actor had control of the property, no matter how he got it, and whether the actor's acquisition or use of the property was authorized."

The MPC does not require that the defendant intend to "permanently" deprive, as the common law did, but it does focus on the deprivation of "economic" value, thereby ignoring the aesthetic or psychological value

16. This problem is not unique to theft, of course. If a drug pusher sells ten bags of 1 gram each to a single customer, has he sold 10 grams, or committed ten sales of 1 gram each, assuming that there is a punishment difference?

of items, such as Ben's putter or Mary's Monets. Indeed, since the MPC requires that the defendant deprive the victim of the "major portion of the economic value" of the putter, it is not even clear that taking the putter for one golf tournament (even if it is *the* golf tournament) would be sufficient.

Additionally, a trespass is not needed, and all property, both movable and immovable, is a proper subject of theft. The MPC also abolishes the "property" limitations erected by the common law, providing that "anything of value, including real estate, tangible and intangible personal property, contract rights, choses-in-action and other interests in or claims to wealth, admission or transportation tickets, captured or domestic animals, food and drink, electric or other power," are possible subjects of theft.

Unlike the common law, the MPC emphasizes the gain to the defendant rather than the loss to the victim. Actions designed to destroy or damage the tangible property of another are dealt with as "criminal mischief" rather than as theft under the MPC. As the commentary puts it: "The provisions against theft contemplate cases where the actor uses the property for his own purposes."

Whether the defendant had the intent at the time of "taking," or formed that intent afterward, is likewise not relevant to the defendant's liability under the MPC. Not surprisingly, the MPC does not limit "deceptive" takings to representations about "past or present facts," and includes all promises as to future action, if not actually fulfilled, as potential grounds of liability. However, reflecting the fear that many good intentions often go awry, the text of the MPC expressly warns that a person's intention to deceive shall not be inferred "from the fact *alone*" that he did not fulfill the promise. Finally, the MPC allows false promises to be the basis of a charge of theft by deception but continues the common law's reluctance to criminalize those who merely capitalize on others' misimpressions, unless they helped create those impressions or had a fiduciary duty to dispel them.

The MPC also rejects the common law rule that one cannot steal from one's spouse, although it does not criminalize the taking of items generally shared, unless the couple has separated.

The MPC has a specific provision that broadens the claim of right defense to all theft crimes and focuses on the way in which a claim negates culpability. The MPC also recognizes a claim of right based defense based on a mistake of law, as well as establishes a defense that the property was for sale as long as the defendant either intended to pay for it promptly or reasonably believed that the owner, if present, would have consented.

Section 223.0 of the MPC sets three levels of "theft"—petty misdemeanor (under $50 and as long as there was no threat or breach of a fiduciary obligation), misdemeanor ($50-$500), and third-degree felony (over $500)—and distinguishes punishment on the basis of the types of items stolen.

Examples

A hint on how to analyze theft questions: First determine which of the three kinds of common law theft the crime may be before deciding whether it meets all of the sub-rules. Probably the best way to do this is to decide what the crime is not. Thus:

A. Did the victim intend to give title? Or only possession?

If the former, it can only be false pretenses. If the latter, it can only be either larceny or embezzlement. To decide which of the latter it might be, ask:

B. Did the defendant come into the property lawfully (usually by consent)?

If so, then the offense can only be embezzlement. If not, then it can only be larceny. (*Caveat:* If the consent was obtained by deceit, it can be larceny by trick.)

C. Once you have determined which of the three major offenses it could be, *then* explore the intricacies of that offense.

1a. Harry buys the *National Enquirer* every week from Joe, the neighborhood grocer. This week, discovering to his chagrin that he did not have enough money, Harry took the paper without telling Joe, but intending to pay Joe the next time he visited the store. Has Harry committed any property crime with regard to the paper?

1b. Suppose Harry tells Joe that he's taking the paper, and Joe nods. Afterward, Harry decides to stiff Joe unless Joe "reminds" him to pay for it.

1c. Same facts, except that Harry knew at the time he took the paper he would not pay for it.

2. Larry asks his neighbor Joan if he can borrow her lawn mower, intending at the time to sell it. He does so.

3. Evelyn and John have been married 15 years. Evelyn has lost $10,000 in a miscalculated investment in Bitcoin. To pay for her losses, she takes John's Rolex watch and sells it.

4. Jessie, tired and impoverished, but driving a Maserati, pulls into the Hampton Inn, where she signs in. She is not required to give a credit card deposit. The next morning, she leaves the Hampton Inn without paying as she had intended to do all along.

5a. Alexander strolls into Pop's bookstore one day. Picking up the classic Agatha Christie (*Murder on the Orient Express*), he browses through it. Finding it intriguing enough, he decides to steal it. As he makes his way toward the door, however, he spots Jeremy, who works for the store, looking at him. Fearful that Jeremy has seen him take the book, Alexander replaces it on the shelf, exactly where it was at the start.

5b. Same facts, except that Alexander went to the bookstore with the purpose of taking the Christie book.

6. Melinda goes to the bank and receives change for her $10 bill. In the middle of the $1 bills, however, there is a $1,000 dollar bill. Melinda keeps the $1,000 bill.

7a. Happy Hennigan, the used car man, knows that the car he is selling Juanita has a defective motor block and will probably run only 500 miles before dying. Assuming that he makes no representations of the fitness of the car, even when asked by Juanita, of what crime is he guilty when he takes her money?

7b. Happy sells Juanita the car above. She knows at the time she buys it, but he does not, that it is a very rare antique auto that, even with a cracked block, is worth $50,000. Has she "stolen" the car and, if so, under what rubric?

8. Martin Miner knows that Billingsley Buyer believes that Miner's mine is valuable. Miner, however, knows it is dry. What offense, if any, if Miner sells it to Buyer?

9a. Bernard, a lawyer, believes that a certain stock will quickly rise in value. He takes several bonds belonging to clients and secures $10,000 from the First National Bank, using the bonds as collateral. He buys the stock, which goes up. He makes a $20,000 profit, pays the bank its $10,000, and returns the bonds. Has Bernard committed any property offense?

9b. Same facts, but Bernard leaves an envelope, to be opened in a week if he does not return the money and bonds, explaining his whole scheme and asking for forgiveness. He actually returns both items. What offense?

10. Lloyd, a car mechanic, fixed Bobby's car, for which Bobby has yet to pay him. Bobby has removed the car from Lloyd's garage. One day, Lloyd spots Bobby's new thoroughbred dog. He picks up the dog and sells it to the nearest Poodle Palace, netting $500, which he applies toward Bobby's bill. What crime has Lloyd committed?

11. James has spent all day conversing with Johnnie Walker Black and by now is severely drunk. He fantasizes that Ralph's Maserati belongs to him, and he takes it for a very long drive, never intending to return it. Neither the police nor Ralph thinks this is funny. Has James committed larceny?

12a. Vince is late for a racquetball match, but his car is in the garage. He knows that his neighbor, Jeff, is away in Europe, and will not return for another week. Vince hotwires Jeff's car, drives it ten miles to the courts, plays his match, and returns the car, filling the gas tank. He also slides a $50.00 bill into Jeff's glove compartment to pay for the wear and tear on the car. Vince's arch nemesis, Rick, has seen all that transpires and tells the police, who charge Vince with larceny. Is Vince guilty?

12b. Suppose that months ago, Jeff allowed Vince to drive his car to another match, giving him a key, and that Vince and Jeff both forgot, so that Vince retains the key. If Vince used that same key to take the car, is it still larceny?

12c. Suppose the reason that Vince took the car was not to go to a racquetball match, but to take his 11-year-old son, who had just cracked his head on a cement floor, to the hospital. Is it larceny now?

13. Rosita's rapid transit system charges $2.00 per ride, but you can purchase a monthly ticket for $60 and use it as often as you wish. The card explicitly declares that it is "not transferable." Rosita buys a monthly card on the first of the month. Thereafter, she stands next to the turnstile of the train, and swipes her card for anyone who wishes, charging them $1.00 for each ride. Rosita is charged with larceny from the transit system. What result?

14. A college student, Bryan, was the sole lifetime beneficiary under a large trust administered by Paul. Bryan received a large monthly distribution from the trust, and whenever he ran short, he simply called Paul for extra money, because the trust provided that Bryan was to receive whatever he needed. Bryan's roommate, Anthony, found out about the trust arrangement and decided to see if he could make it pay off for him. Anthony sent an email to Paul, which appeared to be from Bryan, and which asked for several thousand dollars to cover medical expenses. The email further stated that, since he was in the hospital, Bryan would send Anthony to pick up the money. The next day, Anthony showed up at Paul's office and received the money on the promise that he would take it to Bryan in the hospital. The roommate left town with the funds. What offense?

Explanations

1a. First, which kind of crime is this "potentially"? Since Joe didn't know of the taking, he did not intend title to pass. Thus, it cannot be false pretenses. Moreover, since Joe didn't "entrust" the paper to Harry, it is not embezzlement. Thus, if anything, it is larceny.

But Harry has probably *not* committed larceny. Because the item was for sale, and Harry did intend to pay for it, he did not have the "animus furandi" required by the law. (This is the American rule: English courts generally see this case as larceny.)

The Model Penal Code has a subsection that deals expressly with items of property "exposed for sale." The section adopts the American view and provides that if a defendant took such an item, "intending to purchase and pay for it promptly, or reasonably believing that the owner, if present, would have consented," there is no theft.

1b. Now we seem to have title pass when Joe allows Harry to take the paper. Joe does not expect to see the paper again, so this appears to be a case of false pretenses, if anything. But it is probably not anything. Why? Because at the time he took the paper, Harry lacked the proper mens rea: He didn't intend to deceive Joe.

This might seem to be a case of larceny by trick, as in *Pear's Case.* Here, however, the possession was not trespassory as it was there; Harry did not have the intent to take the paper when he removed it from Joe's store.

Assuming that the "exposure for sale" provision did not exculpate Harry, the MPC would find Harry guilty of unlawful control of the paper without regard to when the "proper mens rea" occurred to Harry.

1c. Since title to the paper passed to Harry with Joe's blessing, this could only be false pretenses—Harry got title by inducing Joe to give him the paper. Under the common law, however, Harry's false promise as to his future payment is insufficient. The (mis)representation must be as to present facts. This would be true even if Harry had the money in his pocket to pay for the newspaper; unless he says, "I don't have enough money, Joe. I'll pay you tomorrow," Harry has committed no common law offense.

Under the Code, a false promise can be sufficient to convict of theft by deceit, so that Harry's precise mental state would be important here.

2. This is not false pretenses since Joan never expected title to pass, nor embezzlement because Larry's intent effectively makes his initial taking trespassory, much as in *Pear's Case.* Thus, this is larceny by trick and not embezzlement.

Under the MPC, however, the common law distinctions are unimportant. Whether title passed (or was intended to) is irrelevant. Larry's taking is "by deception," and his control is therefore "theft" under the Code.

3. Since Evelyn took the watch without John's permission, it is not a "title" crime. It might be either embezzlement or larceny, but we need not bother with the distinctions between those crimes here since both agreed that spousally owned property could not be the subject of either offense.

The MPC expressly abolishes the "spousal exception." However, "household belongings or personal effects, or other property normally accessible to both spouses" still cannot be the subject of theft as long as the parties are living together. The watch is a "personal effect" and is "normally accessible to both spouses." Thus, while taking some items from a spouse may now be theft under the Code, Evelyn is probably not going to the slammer.

4. This is obviously not false pretense. There is nothing to which title has passed. Neither is it embezzlement or larceny, since intangible property can't be the basis of these crimes under common law. This has changed in modern statutes and in the MPC, which has a specific provision (§223.7) dealing with "theft of services."

5a. This is not false pretenses since title never passed. Nor can Alexander be guilty of embezzlement. Even if one were to argue that he had lawful possession when he decided to keep the book, that decision is not sufficient: There must a significant interference with ownership (conversion), which is absent here. Has Alexander committed larceny? He has taken and asported the book, although not off the premises of the store. That would suffice for that part of the crime. But did he have the requisite intent when the taking occurred? If not, he is not guilty of larceny. But could he be convicted of *attempted* larceny? See Chapter 12.

    Under the Code, Alexander exercised illegal control over the book as soon as he formed an intent to deprive the bookstore of it, even if it never left the premises. No express requirement of asportation or "taking" is present in the Code, although it is usually difficult to exercise "control" over property unless some physical movement occurs with regard to it.

5b. This *is* larceny; the taking and intent coincide. Larceny in this aspect is really an inchoate crime. Alexander's *intent*, not the actual loss, is the gravamen of the crime.

    Similarly, under the MPC, there is not even a minimum requirement of taking or asportation, and Alexander clearly exercised some unlawful dominion or control over the book.

6. This is not false pretenses because the bank did not intend for title to the $1,000 bill to pass. Nor is it trespassory since Melinda did not know at the time she received the package of bills that there was a $1,000 bill inside. It might be "embezzlement" under current statutes but not under the common law since the common law usually required an "entrusting" of the property, and there was no reliance by the bank on Melinda here.

    Some common law courts might find that the $1,000 was still in the "constructive possession" of the bank, although this fiction was usually restricted to employer-employee situations.

Under the MPC, Melinda exercised unlawful control once she realized that she had the $1,000 bill and did not return it to the bank. This is theft by unlawful taking.

7a. Under the common law, Happy's happy. Obviously, Juanita consented to pass title to her money so this could only be false pretenses. But it is not false pretenses because the common law required an affirmative misleading; passive nondisclosure, in the absence of a fiduciary duty, would not suffice. Under modern statutes, however, this may be theft. Even here, however, the question is close. Section 223.3 of the Model Penal Code, for example, requires that the defendant "reinforce" a false impression, and there is no reinforcing here. The only exceptions involve fiduciaries or those who have previously set the false impression.

7b. Again, since Hennigan wished title to the car to pass, unless Juanita has affirmatively represented that she knows that the car is an "old heap" and repressed her expert qualifications, there are no false pretenses. (Of course, if Hennigan wished to replevin the car, he *might* have trouble under *Sherwood v. Walker*, 66 Mich. 568, 33 N.W. 919 (1887), the classic contracts case.)

8. Since title to the mine passed, it can only be false pretenses and not larceny or embezzlement. However, this is not false pretenses under the common law unless Miner has created or reinforced in an affirmative way Buyer's impression: As long as Miner stays silent, it is not illegal.

   Even under the MPC, there may be no crime here since Miner has not "created or reinforced" Buyer's impression and does not stand in a fiduciary relationship to Buyer.

9a. As to the bonds, Bernard is not guilty of false pretenses since he never "assumed" title to the bonds. And the possession is not trespassory, unless you consider the constructive possession fiction, which generally required that the employer give the employee the specific property and not merely authority. However, Bernard is guilty of embezzlement; while he didn't take title, he converted the property of which he was lawfully possessed. Even if he didn't personally continue to exercise dominion over the property, his acts were a severe interference with the property rights of the bond owners.

   As to the bank loan, Bernard is guilty of false pretenses since he took title to the money. Even though he returned the monies and the bonds, this is not relevant. Similarly, Bernard took the monies under false pretenses; that he returned them may mitigate his sentence but not his basic culpability.

9b. Bernard is still guilty of the crimes above. Although he hoped that he would be able to return the items, he took a serious risk that the owners of each of the items, respectively, would lose them. This is sufficient for liability.

10. Lloyd is probably not guilty of larceny under the common law for two reasons. First, dogs are "base animals" and cannot be the subject of larceny. Just as important, however, Lloyd has a "claim of right" against Bobby's property. While Lloyd probably does not, under law, have a lien against Bobby's dog, any belief, however unreasonable, that he does so "negates" Lloyd's specific intent (animus furandi) and exculpates him from larceny liability.

    The MPC abolishes the "base animals" limitation of the common law, but it continues the "claim of right" defense. However, under the wording of the Code, the defendant must have an "honest claim of right to the property or service involved." If Lloyd had taken Bobby's car and sold it, the Code would clearly exculpate. But it is not clear whether the claim of right can exist against "equivalent" property. However, the commentary would strongly suggest that an honest belief that he can take any property, not just the original property involved in generating the belief, would exculpate.

11. There are two ways of explaining why James has not committed larceny. First, he was truly unaware that the property belonged to Ralph and therefore did not have the requisite mens rea. In that unfortunate jargon of the common law, he lacked the "specific intent" required for larceny. The other explanation, which is the same explanation in different words, is that his "claim of right," however misguided, is a "defense" to the charge of larceny. In either event, James is exonerated.

    The MPC reaches the same result under either the claim of right provision or under the general definitions of culpability. As the commentary to the Code puts it, "The claim-of-right defense . . . can thus be regarded as redundant." However, the Code includes a special section on the claim of right to underscore the point about culpability.

12a. Most likely. Larceny is the taking of property; returning it doesn't negate the taking. Whether Jeff suffers a permanent loss or not, the property was taken and "asported," as the old common law would require. Vince may argue that he did not "intend" to "deprive" Jeff of the property and was "only borrowing" it. But even if Vince left Jeff a note to that effect (not part of the facts given here), he has deprived Jeff of that property. Just suppose Jeff had returned from his vacation early or promised the car to someone else. That's sufficient deprivation to constitute larceny. However, Vince can make the argument that he never intended to permanently deprive Jeff of the property and he always intended to return it. This would likely not fly under most state statutory schemes because this "permanently" language is not used as often in today's statutes.

12b. You bet. Jeff's earlier acquiescence was only for that one trip and match. Unless Jeff expressly permitted Vince to "use the car any time you need to get to a match," there was no consent to the most recent taking of the car. Vince can again make the argument (likely unsuccessful) that he never intended to permanently deprive Jeff of the car.

12c. This is a trick question. Vince has still committed larceny. Whether his taking of the car is justified such that he will not be convicted, or punished, depends on many other factors. For example, could he have called an ambulance? Could he have hailed a passing car? Was there public transportation? For discussion of *these* issues, see Chapter 16.

13. Rosita will walk and live to ride again. Larceny is the taking of the property of another. But Rosita has not deprived the transit system of any property it ever owned. She has deprived the system of money it *would have had*, but not money it ever possessed. Under the common law, depriving someone of services was not larceny—that's why legislatures had to enact statutes making "larceny of services" criminal. Under modern statutes, Rosita would be charged with "theft" and the difference between larceny and theft of services would be irrelevant. See *People v. Hightower*, 18 N.Y.3d 249 (2011).

14. Anthony committed larceny by trick because Paul's consent to Anthony's taking of trust money was induced by the misrepresentation that Anthony would take the money to Bryan. Larceny consists of a taking and carrying away of tangible personal property of another by trespass, with intent to permanently deprive the person of his interest in the property. If the person in possession of property has not consented to the taking of it by the defendant, the taking is trespassory. However, if the victim consents to the defendant's taking possession of the property, but such consent has been induced by a misrepresentation, the consent is not valid. This type of larceny is larceny by trick. Here, the roommate obtained the money from the banker on the promise that he would take it to Bryan. This misrepresentation induced Paul to give possession of the money to Anthony. Anthony then proceeded to take the money and carry it away, intending all the while to permanently deprive Bryan of the money. Thus, all of the elements of larceny are satisfied.

    In this case, Paul intended only to convey possession of the money to Anthony so that he could give the money to Bryan. Paul did not intend to convey title. Because Anthony did not obtain title by means of his misrepresentation but simply obtained possession, the offense of false pretenses was not committed.

CHAPTER 11

Solicitation

OVERVIEW

Some people always want someone else to do the dirty work. As with many things in life, this is also true with crime. Some people would rather get others to commit a crime rather than do it themselves.

Solicitation punishes anyone who deliberately encourages someone else to commit a crime. Though in most cases the solicitor will be the one who first thinks of committing a crime, he doesn't have to be. A person is also guilty of solicitation if he encourages someone who has already decided to commit a crime.

In theory, the ability to punish solicitors is a useful law enforcement device. As with attempt, police can prevent the commission of a more serious crime by arresting the initiator as soon as he has acted with the necessary mens rea to commit a crime. Unlike attempt, however, proximity to the ultimate harm intended is irrelevant. Thus, it makes no difference whether the effort to persuade has been successful or whether the person solicited ever begins to commit the desired crime. Even criminal encouragement doomed to fail from the outset (such as offering money to an undercover police officer to kill someone) will establish solicitation.

Solicitation adheres to the basic principle of the criminal law requiring a person to act. Solicitation permits the arrest of people who have shown themselves to be dangerous because they have *acted* with the purpose to cause the commission of a crime. True, the criminal law does not punish for thoughts alone, but solicitors have *spoken* words or engaged in other conduct designed to implement their criminal intent.

Because it can reach so far back in time and space from the crime solicited and because it sets the threshold of crime without *any* concern for prospects for its success, solicitation is the most *inchoate* of *inchoate* crimes. (Who said Latin was a dead language!) Perhaps setting this threshold so early can be justified by the fear that solicitation may give rise to cooperative criminal effort and its special dangers. (Indeed, solicitation has been thought of as an attempt to conspire.) In addition, a solicitor may be a more intelligent and more dangerous criminal because he works through others. However, one can also argue that mere encouragement without agreement by anyone else is not socially dangerous because the resisting will of an independent moral agent stands between the solicitor and the commission of the intended crime. Additionally, a solicitor may not be dangerous precisely because she has shown she is unwilling to commit the crime herself or at least alone. She may really be a reluctant lawbreaker. In any event, several purposes of the criminal law, including retribution, rehabilitation, and incapacitation, can be served by convicting solicitors.

Like attempt, solicitation is a relatively recent creation of the common law. It was developed during the nineteenth century and covered only solicitation to commit felonies or serious misdemeanors. Generally, solicitation was punished as a misdemeanor. Today, some states limit the crime of solicitation to serious felonies only. Others provide for degrees of solicitation, the various degrees depending on the seriousness of the crime solicited.

The Model Penal Code, however, does not limit the crimes that can be the object of solicitation. Rather, it is an offense to solicit *any* crime, but soliciting someone to commit a "violation" is *not* punishable. In addition, the MPC punishes solicitation as severely as the crime solicited except that the solicitation of a capital offense or first-degree felony is punished as a second-degree felony. (MPC §5.05(1).) This is consistent with the MPC's primary focus on the dangerousness of an offender rather than on how close he actually comes to committing the intended crime.

There are several interesting wrinkles to solicitation, but they are best discussed later.

DEFINITION

The Common Law

The common law defined solicitation in general terms. The defendant must have acted with the specific intent that another person commit a crime and she must have enticed, advised, incited, ordered, or otherwise encouraged the person to commit a crime. It was not necessary for the person solicited to agree to commit the crime, let alone that the solicited crime be attempted or committed.

Because solicitation sets the threshold of criminality so early, some state statutes require corroboration of the testimony of the person claiming he was solicited. This evidentiary safeguard helps prevent convicting someone based on a misunderstanding or on a false accusation.

The Model Penal Code

Under §5.02 of the MPC, a person is guilty of solicitation if, "with the *purpose* of promoting or facilitating its commission he *commands, encourages* or *requests* another person to engage in *specific conduct* that would constitute such crime or an *attempt* to commit such crime or would establish his *complicity* in its commission or attempted commission" (emphasis added). The MPC definition has been influential in shaping state solicitation laws.

The MPC definition is similar to the common law but applies to the solicitation of any crime, not just felonies or serious misdemeanors. Also, unlike the common law, which only applied to the solicitation of another to act as a principal in the first degree (see Chapter 14), the MPC also includes any encouragement that would generate responsibility as an accomplice.

Thus, a typical common law case of solicitation might involve the solicitor asking a hired gunman to kill a particular victim. Here the defendant would be an accomplice (accessory in the second degree) and the gunman would be the principal in the first degree. Under the MPC, the defendant would also be guilty of solicitation. However, under the MPC, the defendant could also commit solicitation if he encouraged the gunman to sell him a weapon with which the defendant himself could kill the victim. This would constitute solicitation under the MPC because the defendant has encouraged the gunman to become an accomplice.

Another Version of Solicitation

Some states have adopted a different definitional approach to solicitation. Under this approach, a defendant must not only encourage another to commit a crime; he must also offer him something of value. This requirement (somewhat similar to the requirement of consideration in contracts) ensures that the defendant is serious about his criminal purpose. It also identifies those cases in which there is an increased probability that the crime solicited will be committed because human nature responds more readily to money than it does to mere cheerleading.

THE MENS REA OF SOLICITATION

The Common Law

Like attempt, solicitation is a specific intent crime. The defendant must *intend* that the individual solicited commit a crime. The defendant must be serious about encouraging another person to actually commit the solicited crime. If he is merely thinking out loud about the possibility or joking about it, he does not have the mens rea necessary to commit solicitation. As in attempt (see Chapter 12), the defendant must have specific intent as to the conduct, results, and circumstances, even if the crime solicited is a strict liability offense.

The Model Penal Code

Under the MPC, solicitation also requires the highest possible mens rea—purpose. MPC §5.02. Thus, the defendant must desire to encourage all conduct and result elements of the crime solicited and must know or believe that all circumstance elements will be satisfied. (MPC §2.02(2)(a)(ii).) The defendant must also fulfill any additional mens rea elements of the solicited crime.

THE ACTUS REUS OF SOLICITATION

The Common Law

Through words or other conduct the defendant must entice, advise, incite, order, or otherwise encourage another person to commit a felony or serious misdemeanor. Speaking is the most common form of actus reus for this crime, but it could also take other forms, such as simply being present and applauding or cheering.

If the defendant's "encouraging words" did not, in fact, reach the individual he hoped to encourage, in some jurisdictions he could only be convicted of *attempted* solicitation (pushing the threshold of criminality back even farther).

The Model Penal Code

The defendant must command, encourage, or request another to (a) commit a crime, (b) attempt to commit a crime, or (c) become an accomplice in the commission or attempted commission of a crime. MPC §5.02(1). As mentioned earlier, the MPC specifically does not require the person solicited to act as a principal. The MPC also punishes as solicitation criminal encouragement that does not actually reach the person solicited, provided it was designed to be communicated. (MPC §5.02(2).)

THE RELATIONSHIP BETWEEN SOLICITATION AND CONSPIRACY

Solicitation is defined solely by the actor's intent and conduct. The response of the person solicited is irrelevant to the crime. In this sense, solicitation is similar to an "offer" in contracts. Whether an offer has been made does not depend on whether there has been an acceptance.

But what if the person solicited does respond to the act of solicitation and agrees to commit the crime solicited? Then, both individuals have entered into a *conspiracy*. (See Chapter 13.) Just as an acceptance to an offer forms a contract, so does acceptance of a solicitation form a conspiracy. (A person, however, cannot be convicted of both solicitation and conspiracy because the solicitation merges into conspiracy.)

RESPONSIBILITY FOR CRIME SOLICITED

Under the general principles of accessorial liability, a solicitor will be responsible for any solicited crime that is committed or attempted by the person he solicited. The common law would treat the solicitor as an accessory before the fact. Under modern principles he would be considered an accomplice. (See Chapter 14.)

In states where the statutory definition of solicitation does not cover certain crimes, a defendant who solicits another person to commit one of these crimes might be charged with an attempt. (Keep in mind that the defendant has not committed solicitation because the solicitation statute does not include the crime he solicited.) It is not clear, however, whether mere solicitation can constitute an attempt; some courts[1] (and the MPC)[2] hold that it cannot, while others hold that it can.[3] In any event, a defendant cannot be punished both for solicitation and attempt based on the same conduct.

SOLICITATION AND IMMUNITY FOR CRIME SOLICITED

Generally speaking, the prosecutor cannot use solicitation to convict someone who could not be convicted of the crime solicited. In other words, if a person could not be charged had they personally done the conduct they were soliciting, they cannot be charged with solicitation. Thus, a customer who seeks the services of a prostitute cannot be convicted of *soliciting* prostitution if the prostitution statute only punishes the prostitute's behavior. The law assumes that the legislature did not intend to punish the customer's conduct. To permit the customer's conviction under a general solicitation statute would undermine the public policy clearly reflected in the prostitution statute.

However, there are cases that require an exception to this general policy. For example, at common law a husband could not rape his wife. (See Chapter 9.) If, however, he encouraged another person to rape his wife, the husband could be convicted of solicitation even though he could not have committed rape as a principal in the first degree.

SOLICITATION AND INNOCENT AGENTS

Sometimes a defendant may trick an innocent agent into committing a crime. For example, a daughter might substitute poison for the medicine her mother is supposed to take and ask a home caregiver who is ignorant of the switch to administer the fatal "medicine." This is not a case of solicitation because the defendant does not intend that another person knowingly commit a crime. Instead, she is using an innocent agent (i.e., someone who,

1. *Gervin v. State*, 212 Tenn. 653, 371 S.W.2d 449 (1963).

2. Model Penal Code and Commentaries, Comment to §5.02 at 369 (1985).

3. *Ashford v. Commonwealth*, 626 S.E.2d 464 (Va. App. 2006); *United States v. May*, 625 F.2d 186 (8th Cir. 1980).

through no fault of her own, is unaware of the nature of her conduct and who does not intend to commit a crime) as the means to commit murder.

A defendant who activates an innocent agent has committed an *attempt* rather than *solicitation* because she has done her "last act," which was designed to commit the crime. If the innocent agent actually does what the defendant wants her to do, then the defendant is guilty of the crime as a *principal*. (See Chapter 14.)

IMPOSSIBILITY

The Common Law

Legal Impossibility

Common law, true legal impossibility is a defense to a charge of solicitation. A person does not commit solicitation by encouraging another to do something that is not a crime. Thus, an individual, who erroneously believes that it is a crime to dispense birth control information on public school property and encourages another person to engage in that conduct, has not committed solicitation because she has not encouraged another person to do anything that is a crime. (See our discussion of legal impossibility for attempt in Chapter 12. The same rules apply here.)

Factual Impossibility

Factual impossibility will seldom occur in cases involving solicitation because the threshold of criminality is set so early that the offense is complete once the defendant has purposefully encouraged another to commit a crime. The law is usually not concerned with how the crime was to be committed or whether it could be committed successfully.

Occasionally in real life (and more frequently in criminal law exams), however, the solicitor is very particular about how he wants the crime committed. And, it turns out, due to facts or conditions unknown to the solicitor, the crime cannot be committed.

The Model Penal Code

As we shall see with attempt (in Chapter 12), the MPC looks unkindly on impossibility. The MPC would not convict the defendant only in cases of true legal impossibility—that is, where there is no law prohibiting the conduct solicited. In that situation, the prosecutor would not be able to prove that the defendant encouraged another person to commit any particular crime. She could only prove that the defendant had shown a willingness to break the law but not a particular law.

In cases of factual impossibility, the MPC simply assesses the defendant's responsibility based on what he thought the facts were. Recall that the MPC is more concerned with the dangerous attitude of the offender and the need to prevent future crime than actually seeing how close an offender comes to causing harm.

ABANDONMENT

It is unclear whether the common law permitted a change of heart on the solicitor's part to avoid criminal responsibility.[4] At the very least, the solicitor would probably have to communicate his change of heart to the person solicited and perhaps even ensure that the crime was not committed. On the other hand, the common law did not permit the defense of abandonment (renunciation) to an attempt charge, so it might not favor using abandonment as a defense to solicitation.

The MPC expressly provides for the affirmative defense of abandonment to a charge of solicitation. MPC §5.02(3). There are two requirements. First, as in conspiracy (see Chapter 13), the defendant must either persuade the person solicited not to commit the crime or else prevent its commission. Second, his renunciation must be "*complete* and *voluntary*." As in attempt, renunciation must be due to a sincere change of heart rather than a discovery that the offense is more difficult to commit than anticipated or that detection is more likely. These are the same requirements for renunciation of an attempt, except that, because another person is involved, the defendant must take steps to prevent that person from committing the offense, thereby stopping what the defendant has put in motion.

From a policy perspective, permitting the defense of renunciation may encourage criminals to break off their planned criminal activity, thereby preventing harm to both the victim and society. The defendant may also not be as dangerous as initially thought if he is willing to change his mind for the right reasons. Several states have adopted the defense of voluntary renunciation by statute.[5]

4. Evidently, no appellate court has ruled on this question. W. La Fave, Criminal Law 575 (4th ed. 2003).
5. W. La Fave, Criminal Law 575 (4th ed. 2003).

SOLICITATION AND LAW ENFORCEMENT

The police often catch criminals by providing them with the opportunity to commit crimes, particularly "victimless crimes" such as drugs, prostitution, and gambling. Thus, undercover officers may solicit prostitutes or try to buy or sell drugs. Much of what law enforcement officers do would be criminal solicitation if done by ordinary citizens. Usually, statutes specifically authorize police officers to engage in conduct that would otherwise constitute solicitation in the interests of detecting criminal activity and arresting criminals. Even in the absence of such a statute, the officers could argue justification for their conduct. (See Chapters 15 and 16.)

Such police activity, however, is not without controversy. Some argue that the police should detect crime, not manufacture it. As we shall see later, defendants often raise the defense of entrapment when caught by this type of police activity. (See Chapter 17.)

PUNISHMENT

The Model Penal Code frowns on cumulative punishment of essentially the same conduct. Thus, though a solicitor will be liable as an accomplice for the crimes committed by the person solicited (assuming the person solicited commits these crimes), the solicitor cannot be punished both for solicitation and (1) the crime solicited; (2) an attempt by the person solicited; and (3) conspiracy with the person solicited to commit that offense. (MPC §§1.07(1)(a), 1.07(4)(b), and 5.05(3).) Solicitation is a lesser included offense to the crime solicited. (MPC §1.07.) Moreover, a person can be convicted of only one Article 5 offense—attempt, solicitation, *or* conspiracy—for conduct designed to culminate in the commission of the *same* offense.

EXAMPLES

Examples

1. It's the final game of the World Series, with bases loaded in the bottom of the ninth inning, two outs, and the Los Angeles Dodgers leading the Chicago Cubs 3-2. The last Cubs batter is up, and the count is three balls and two strikes. The Dodger pitcher glares at the batter, goes into his windup, and throws a pitch that to most observers is clearly a ball. But the umpire raises his right hand, calls, "Strike 3, you're out," and the Dodgers win the series. A livid Cubs fan yells at the top of his voice: "Kill the umpire!" Can he be charged with solicitation?

2. In the motion picture *Becket*, Henry II, upset with Thomas à Becket's opposition to his expansion of royal jurisdiction, cries out in a drunken stupor: "Will no one rid me of this man?" Subsequently, one of the listeners in fact kills Becket. Did Henry solicit the murder of Thomas à Becket under the common law or the MPC?

3. Liz, a nondrinker, joins Jen, Stephanie, and Megan on the patio of a bar and grill for happy hour. The others each have a couple of drinks. Sipping only water, Liz says: "It would be so easy to 'dine and ditch'—this place is packed." Jen replies: "I have no problem with you all taking off, but I will quietly leave what I owe on the table." After Jen does that, they all get up and casually stroll out to the sidewalk and leave without paying. Can Liz or Jen be charged with any crime?

4. Professor Zoey, an academic in New Jersey, angry at Professor Nerd in Illinois for some unforgivable academic put-down, contacted Mad Max the mad bomber on the Internet, asking him to send one of his infamous fatal explosive devices to Dr. Nerd. Unknown to Professor Zoey, Mad Max had already been arrested and sent to prison for mailing such a device to someone else. Only the police read Professor Zoey's message. Can Professor Zoey be charged with any crime?

5. Amy desperately wanted the job of her boss, Rebecca. Her only hope was getting Rebecca fired. Amy asked Sam, a seriously mentally ill individual who did not know the difference between right and wrong, to injure Rebecca so that Rebecca could no longer work, and her position would need to be filled (hopefully by Amy). Sam listened to Amy, then got on a bus and left town. Can Amy be convicted of any offense?

6. Fred was drinking at the Spar Tavern with José. José leaned over to Fred and said, "I've taken enough trash talk from Wilson, who is standing over there at the bar. I'm going right over there now and hit him upside his head and teach him not to 'dis' me anymore." Fred replied, "That's a great idea. I think Wilson deserves it. Go ahead and unload on him!" José got up, went over to Wilson, and taking another look at just how big Wilson really was, decided not to punch him after all. Has Fred committed any crime?

7. Angry because her red Tesla was stolen recently and because it was not insured against theft, Harriet asked Ozzie to steal the red Tesla she saw every day being charged in the Safeway parking lot far across town. Rather than steal that car, Ozzie, who had already been charged with several car thefts, struck a deal with the police and told them about Harriet. Harriet was arrested. Upon further investigation, it turned out that, unknown to her, the car she wanted Ozzie to steal was actually

Harriet's own previously stolen red Tesla. Can Harriet be charged with any crime?

8. Yvonne works in a fashionable dress shop in a suburban shopping mall. She craves a great dress in the window but knows she will probably be caught if she takes it without paying for it. So Yvonne asked her good friend Yolanda to shoplift it for her and told her how to do it without getting caught. Yolanda agreed to snatch the dress during the busy Saturday afternoon shopping period.

   Thursday evening Yvonne changed her mind out of true remorse. She called Yolanda to tell her that she did not want Yolanda to go through with the shoplifting plan. Yolanda was not home, however, so Yvonne left a voicemail message to this effect on Yolanda's phone. Unfortunately, Yolanda never checks her voicemails and was arrested while trying to steal the dress that Saturday. Would you charge Yvonne?

9. Billy, a struggling college student, decided to sell marijuana over the weekend to make enough money to pay the rest of his tuition due Monday. Lisa, Billy's best friend, knew that Billy had been stressed about money and wanted to take his mind off of his problems. Lisa told Billy about a party happening Saturday night. At first, Billy was hesitant about going to the party because he knew he needed to sell the marijuana over the weekend. Lisa encouraged Billy to go by telling him, "There will be a lot of people there having fun and letting loose. It will do everyone some good to have some drinks and maybe even smoke some weed." Billy realized that this would be an excellent setting for him to sell marijuana. Lisa was right; there were lots of people drinking and smoking at the party. In fact, Billy was able to make enough to pay his tuition and have a little left over for his textbooks. Could Lisa be charged with solicitation? Would your answer change if Lisa knew that Billy had been planning on selling marijuana over the weekend?

Explanations

1. If the Cubs fan actually intended to encourage someone else to kill the umpire, then he could be convicted of solicitation—even if no one actually acted on his encouragement. In some states he would be punished just as severely as the individual who actually did kill the umpire. Under the MPC, solicitation of a capital offense or a felony in the first degree would be punished as a felony in the second degree. In the context of American sports, however, it is extremely unlikely that any jury (especially a Chicago jury!) would conclude that the defendant actually spoke those words with the intent of encouraging someone to kill the umpire.

(For a discussion of the fan's liability if someone actually does kill the umpire as a result of the shout, see Chapter 14.)

2. Because solicitation was not fully developed until the nineteenth century, Henry could not be convicted of solicitation. (Sorry, but we wanted to make sure that you were also paying attention to the history!)

   However, under both late common law and the MPC, the analysis would essentially be the same. Did Henry act with the necessary mens rea for solicitation? Did he speak with the *specific intent* or *purpose* of encouraging someone to murder Becket? If he did, then at that moment he committed solicitation even if none of his listeners accepted the challenge. Upon commission of the murder, Henry would also become an accessory before the fact under common law or an accomplice under the MPC and would be criminally responsible for murder along with the person solicited. (This assumes that there would be a sheriff foolish enough to arrest and charge Henry!)

3. Liz's statement may have been only an observation made without the aim of encouraging her friends to commit theft. However, since the group acted on her statement and Liz raised no objection, a jury could conclude that her words were said with the *purpose* of encouraging her friends to commit this crime even though Liz, herself, owed nothing and did not commit theft. Jen may argue that she paid her portion of the bill and that this demonstrates she did not approve of such conduct. Furthermore, Jen will argue that Liz came up with the idea and that Liz and Stephanie had already formed their intent to commit the crime. But a jury could find that Jen's words were spoken with the intent to reinforce Liz's, Megan's, and Stephanie's decision to leave the bar without paying. The prosecution's case against Liz seems stronger than against Jen.

4. Under the common law, Professor Zoey has committed attempted solicitation. In states that only require the solicitor to try to encourage someone else to commit a crime by communications designed to reach that person, Professor Zoey has committed solicitation.

   Under the MPC, Professor Zoey has committed solicitation because his communication was sent with the purpose of encouraging Mad Max to send his fatal explosive device to Dr. Nerd, and it was designed to reach Max. Professor Zoey would be punished just as severely as the crime he solicited (probably arson or murder), even though he did not come close to causing either of these serious harms and even though an intervening moral agent (okay, it was only Mad Max) with free will would have had to choose to commit a crime. The MPC is concerned with individuals who have demonstrated their dangerous attitude, if not their skill. This is also one of the few times when the criminal law *does* impose responsibility for conduct beyond the last responsible human being.

Professor Zoey might try to argue factual impossibility because Max never received his message and, in any event, was otherwise indisposed. This would fail under both the common law and the MPC because Professor Zoey's responsibility would be assessed based on the facts as he *believed* them to be.

5. Amy deliberately encouraged Sam to commit a serious assault. However, because Sam is legally insane (see Chapter 17), he is not a responsible agent and could not be convicted of the offense solicited (had he committed it). Because Amy has used an "innocent agent," she is guilty of attempted assault under the common law. In effect she has committed her "last act."

   Under the MPC, Amy has probably committed solicitation. The MPC focuses on the defendant's attitude rather than on the legal responsibility of the person solicited.

6. When Fred spoke these words with the purpose of reinforcing José's resolve to commit the assault, Fred solicited José to commit an assault on Wilson under both the common law and the MPC. This is true even though José had already formed the intent to commit the assault and even though José did not, in fact, commit the solicited crime. A person can commit solicitation even if he does not come up with the idea initially and even if the person solicited changes his mind and never commits the crime.

7. Under both the common law and the MPC, Harriet could probably be convicted of solicitation in this case because she encouraged another to engage in conduct with the intent of having him commit a crime. The crime is complete as of that moment. How it was to be done is not the concern under solicitation.

   Harriet might raise the defense of legal impossibility, claiming she could not solicit anyone to steal *her own* property. However, this is really a case of factual impossibility because there is a law against stealing cars. Thus, Harriet's criminal responsibility is determined by the facts as she *believed* them to be.

8. The common law probably did not provide the defense of abandonment so Yvonne has committed the crime of solicitation even though she changed her mind for the right reasons.

   The MPC does authorize the affirmative defense of renunciation, provided that the defendant's decision is voluntary and complete and provided that the defendant either persuades the person solicited not to commit the crime or otherwise prevents the commission of the crime.

Unfortunately, Yvonne did neither and therefore could be convicted of solicitation. Unlike an attempt to persuade that can establish solicitation, an attempt to "unpersuade" is not effective in establishing renunciation. Yvonne could have taken other measures such as telling the store owner, but she did not (undoubtedly because she knew she would be fired).

When Yolanda agreed to steal the dress and Yvonne told Yolanda how to accomplish the theft, Yvonne and Yolanda also committed conspiracy. (See Chapter 13.) When Yolanda attempted to commit the theft of the dress, Yvonne was also responsible for that crime as an accessory before the fact under common law and as an accomplice under the MPC. However, the MPC prevents cumulative punishment for solicitation, conspiracy, and attempt based on essentially the same conduct.

9. As seen in Example 6, a person can commit solicitation even if they do not originally come up with the idea. However, Lisa still needed to have the requisite mens rea for solicitation. Did Lisa speak with the *specific intent* or *purpose* of encouraging Billy to sell marijuana at the party? Regardless of whether Lisa knew of Billy's plan to sell marijuana over the weekend, Lisa's statements were not made with the intent or purpose for encouraging Billy to sell marijuana at the party. Lisa simply encouraged Billy to go to the party to take his mind off of his money troubles. Because Lisa did not have the requisite mens rea, she cannot be charged with solicitation.

CHAPTER 12

Attempt

OVERVIEW

Not every criminal succeeds at crime. Some try their best but fail; others change their mind and stop short of their initial goal. Some are even caught before they can complete their crime. *Attempt* punishes offenders who intend to commit a crime (referred to here as the "target" crime) and act to implement that intent, but do not achieve their goal.

Attempt is an important law enforcement tool. Police can prevent crime by arresting an offender before he actually commits his target crime. (This is why attempt is sometimes called an *inchoate* or uncompleted crime.) Attempt also enables the criminal justice system to punish individuals who have acted on their criminal intentions and are dangerous.

Attempt is a crime of recent origin in the common law. Initially, it was usually a misdemeanor. Today, the seriousness of an attempt and its punishment generally depend on the seriousness of the crime attempted. Attempt often carries a lighter penalty than the target crime because the offender has done less harm than a successful criminal. However, except for capital offenses and felonies of the first degree, the Model Penal Code punishes attempt just as severely as the crime attempted because it considers an unsuccessful criminal just as dangerous as a successful one.

If an offender successfully completes the target offense, he cannot also be convicted of an attempt. Attempt is a lesser included offense of the crime attempted and will merge if the prosecution proves the completed offense.

DEFINITION

In general, attempt punishes a defendant because he intended to commit a particular crime and took a significant step to commit it. Most jurisdictions have a single attempt statute phrased in general language that is used to prosecute all attempt crimes. (Otherwise, the legislature would have to enact a separate attempt provision for each substantive crime, creating a much larger and more cumbersome criminal law.) Because this single statutory definition of attempt must be used for so many target crimes, legislatures usually use very broad and abstract language. As a result, many state statutes do not define attempt very carefully, and often courts must interpret these laws to provide a more useful legal definition.

Some state laws make what would ordinarily be considered an attempt into a completed offense. For example, burglary is a form of inchoate crime because it punishes conduct that is preliminary to the commission of the real criminal goal. Thus, a typical burglary statute proscribes "*entering a building* with intent to commit a crime against a person or property therein." Many states push the threshold of criminality back even farther. They prohibit the mere possession of burglar tools, even though the defendant has not used the tools to enter a building, let alone commit a crime against people or property inside. Other statutes define assault as "an attempted battery." Thus, trying to punch someone and missing may be punished as a completed assault rather than an attempted battery.

The Mens Rea of Attempt

The mental state is the intent to commit the target crime. Because attempt does not require successful completion of a crime, the mens rea of attempt is usually more demanding than the mens rea of the crime attempted.

The Actus Reus of Attempt

Criminals often think about committing a crime. They may even take some preparatory steps that will make it easier to commit a crime sometime in the future. Finally, they may actually implement their criminal purpose and begin to commit a crime.

The criminal law does not punish for thoughts alone. (See Chapter 3.) When, however, does a person cross the dividing line between thinking and preparation on the one side, and actually committing an attempt on the other? The definition of the actus reus of attempt draws the line between noncriminal and criminal behavior. Drawing this line early may prevent more crimes and catch more dangerous people, but it may also increase the risk of convicting people who would change their mind. The common law generally drew this line quite late; the MPC draws it much earlier.

THE COMMON LAW

Mens Rea

The defendant must have the same state of mind required for conviction of the target offense. Because attempt is a specific intent crime at common law, the defendant must also *intend*

1. to *do the act*
2. to *accomplish the result*
3. *under the same circumstances*

that would be required for conviction of the target offense.

Intend the Act

This specific intent requirement means that a person cannot commit an attempt recklessly or negligently. He must, at the very least, intend the act. Some cases suggest, however, that it is possible to attempt a crime that only requires an act done with recklessness or even negligence. Thus, a person who knows that his car brakes do not work might commit attempted reckless driving if he gets into his parked car and starts it, intending to drive it on the streets. However, because he does not actually drive the car, he cannot be convicted of reckless driving.

Intend the Result

To be convicted of attempting a crime that has a result element, the defendant must intend the result. A defendant who drives his car so dangerously that he kills someone may be convicted of murder or vehicular homicide because his risk-creating behavior has resulted in death. If, however, the same defendant struck the victim while driving in the same reckless way but did not kill him, he cannot be convicted of attempted murder or attempted vehicular homicide because he did not intend the death.

Intend the Circumstances

Likewise, the defendant must know the circumstances of the target offense—even if strict liability applies. Thus, an adult, who had intercourse with a juvenile under the age of 16 erroneously believing she was 18, could be convicted of statutory rape. If, however, the same adult were arrested moments before having intercourse with this juvenile, he could not be convicted of attempted statutory rape because he did not *intend* the juvenile to be under 16.

Actus Reus

Common law definitions of actus reus varied, but generally they required behavior that provided strong evidence of a criminal intent and that came quite close to completing the target offense.

Last Act

The "last act" test is very favorable to the defendant. He must have taken the very last step within his power to commit the target offense.[1] Only after the actor had taken the last step and events were out of his control could the law punish him for attempt. This approach preserves a maximum opportunity for the actor to change his mind (often called *locus penitentiae* or "opportunity to repent"), while also requiring very strong evidence of criminal intent. A professional killer who shoots at his victim intending to kill him has committed the last act. Whether he succeeds is now out of his control.

When the "last act" has occurred, the attempt is considered a "complete attempt."[2] This means that the actor completed all steps required for the crime to take place, but, for whatever reason, the result did not happen. Completed attempts are easier to identify than "incomplete attempts." The following tests analyze incomplete attempts and draw lines between incomplete attempts and mere preparation.

The Equivocality Test

Some courts and commentators have argued that the actus reus of attempt should *by itself* unquestionably show that the actor is trying to commit a crime.[3] Otherwise, the defendant's behavior is merely "equivocal"—that is, it is consistent with *either* innocent or criminal purpose. This can also be referred to as the *res ipsa loquitur* test—Latin for "the thing speaks for

---

1. *R. v. Eagleton*, 169 E.R. 826 (1855).
2. Paul H. Robinson, Shima Baradaran Baughman, & Michael T. Cahill, Criminal Law: Case Studies and Controversies, 335-336 (New York: Wolters Kluwer, 4th ed., 2017).
3. *The King v. Barker*, [1924] N.Z.L.R. 865. See also Wis. Stat. Ann. 939.32(3) (West 2006).

itself."[4] This test is also quite favorable to defendants. Under this approach the prosecutor may not use any other evidence, such as a confession, a diary, or other statements, to demonstrate that the actor was implementing a criminal design. (This has sometimes been called the "manifest criminality" approach.[5]) Thus, someone who lights a pipe with a match and then drops the match in a haystack in a barn may be simply careless or trying to set the barn on fire. Without additional evidence, it is not clear if he was trying to commit a crime. The equivocality test can be very difficult for the prosecution to satisfy.

Supporters argue that this test maximizes the sphere of liberty in which an individual is free from government interference. Critics claim it damages effective law enforcement and permits dangerous individuals to remain at large because the police can only arrest the actor at the last possible moment because virtually no preparatory act is unequivocal.

Proximity Test

Still other courts used a more flexible definition of actus reus known as the "proximity test." It did not require the defendant to take the last step or to do an unequivocal act before an attempt had been committed. Instead, it allowed the jury to weigh several factors, including the seriousness of the offense, community resentment, and closeness in space and time to completing the crime.[6] This test provided flexibility but also created uncertainty about when an attempt occurred. Some courts required the actor to get physically close to the intended victim or to set in motion a chain of events that created a high probability that the crime would be completed. Other courts have permitted conviction on behavior more remote from the result.

Probable Desistance

Some courts have used the "probable desistance" test. Only an act that would normally be sufficient to result in the commission of a crime "but for" the intervention of some outside person or event is sufficient for the actus reus of attempt.[7] This definition considers whether an ordinary, law-abiding person would probably have changed his mind and broken off from the criminal course of conduct. A terrorist who checked a bag armed with a sophisticated

---

4. Paul H. Robinson, Shima Baradaran Baughman, & Michael T. Cahill, Criminal Law: Case Studies and Controversies, 336 (New York: Wolters Kluwer, 4th ed., 2017).
5. G. Fletcher, Rethinking Criminal Law (1978).
6. *Commonwealth v. Peaslee*, 177 Mass. 267, 59 N.E. 55 (1901); *People v. Rizzo*, 246 N.Y. 334, 158 N.E. 888 (1927).
7. *Comer v. Bloomeld*, 55 Crim. App. 305 (1971) (Eng.).

explosive device designed to explode when an airplane reaches 30,000 feet has probably satisfied this test. Although he could still change his mind after checking the bag and warn the authorities, it is unlikely, given the preparation required and his motivation, that he would reconsider.

This test has been criticized because it encourages speculation. How should a jury decide if most law-abiding people would have had a twinge of conscience and stopped? More to the point, a law-abiding citizen does not commit crimes!

In sum, the common law generally required the defendant to engage in behavior that provided strong evidence of his criminal intention and also came close to the commission of the target offense before his conduct satisfied the actus reus requirement of attempt.

THE MODEL PENAL CODE

Definition

The Model Penal Code definition of attempt is, in sharp contrast to the common law, very specific but also very long and complex. (MPC §5.01.) In general terms, a person commits an attempt under the MPC if, acting with the same state of mind otherwise required for commission of the target offense, he *purposely* does an *act* and *purposely* causes (or believes he will cause) the *result* under the same *circumstances* required by the target offense and he takes a *substantial step* to commit the crime. A "substantial step" is conduct that is "strongly corroborative of [a defendant's] criminal purpose."

Mens Rea

The MPC takes the following approach to the mens rea (i.e., culpability) required for attempt:

Conduct

The MPC requires that the defendant must *purposely* engage in all elements of conduct made criminal by the crime attempted. (§5.01(1)(a).)

Result

The MPC expands the mens rea of attempt slightly beyond the common law approach where causing a particular result is an element of the crime attempted. The MPC permits conviction for attempt if the defendant acted with the purpose or *belief* that his act would cause a particular result. (§5.01.1(1)(b).)

Circumstance

The MPC approach to circumstance is different than that of the common law. Unlike the common law, which required that the defendant *know* the circumstances of the target offense, the MPC provides that, for these elements, the mens rea of the target offense controls. Thus, whatever mens rea toward circumstances is required by the target crime will also be required for an attempt under the MPC. Though the language of the MPC is not as clear as it could be on this point, the commentaries state that the drafters intended this approach.

The statutory rape example given above for the common law would have a different result under the MPC. An adult who intended to have intercourse with a 16-year-old female, erroneously believing she was 18, could be prosecuted for committing attempted statutory rape if arrested just before the act because age is a strict liability circumstance element of the target offense.

Actus Reus

The MPC requires that the actor take a *substantial step* before she can be convicted of an attempt. A "substantial step" must be "*strongly corroborative* of the actor's criminal purpose." (MPC §5.01(2).) The MPC emphasizes the dangerousness of the offender based on her criminal determination rather than on how close she is to committing the target offense.

The MPC lists several types of behavior that are *legally sufficient* to prove a substantial step.[8] These include searching for the victim, reconnoitering the crime scene, unlawfully entering a building where the defendant contemplates committing the crime, possessing tools or instruments necessary for committing the crime near the crime scene, or soliciting an innocent agent to do an element of the crime. Unlike the common law, the MPC definition focuses on what the defendant has done rather than what remains to be done. The prosecution also can use evidence other than the substantial step to prove mens rea, including confessions, diaries, and other proof relevant to the actor's state of mind.

---

8. This means that a jury *could* find that the defendant took a substantial step based only on this evidence.

In contrast to the common law, the MPC does not require much of an actus reus before a defendant may be convicted of an attempt. Thus, it sets the line between preparation and attempt quite early and expands the authority of the police to nip crime in the bud.

The MPC definition of a "substantial step" has been very influential, and many states have adopted it. Even when the federal or state statutes have not defined the actus reus requirement for attempt, courts often use the MPC approach to interpret the attempt statute in their jurisdiction.[9]

SUMMARY

Mens Rea

Analyze the defendant's mens rea using the following steps:

1. Did she act with the same mens rea required by the crime attempted?
2. *Common law*: Did she also *intend* to commit the *act* and to cause the *result* and intend the same *circumstances* as required by the crime attempted?
3. MPC: Did she have
   a. the purpose to do all the *conduct* elements of the target offense?
   b. the purpose to cause the *result* (or believe she would cause the result) of the target offense?
   c. the same mens rea toward the circumstance elements as required by the target offense?

Actus Reus

Analyze the defendant's actus reus using the following steps:

1. *Common law*: Did the defendant's act satisfy the applicable test:
   a. *last act*—did the defendant do everything that he could do and is the result now beyond his control?
   b. *"equivocality test"*—would reasonable people, observing only the defendant's conduct, necessarily conclude that he was trying to commit a crime?
   c. *"proximity test"*—in light of the seriousness of the offense and the scope of possible harm, did the defendant come close in space and time to completing the offense?

9. *United States v. Jackson*, 560 F.2d 112 (2d Cir. 1977); *United States v. Buffington*, 815 F.2d 1292 (9th Cir. 1987).

d. *"probable desistance"*—did the defendant's conduct start a chain of causation sufficient to result in the commission of the completed offense unless another person or event would prevent it? Would a law-abiding person likely have changed his mind?

2. *MPC*: Did the defendant's behavior *strongly corroborate* his criminal purpose? If he searched for his victim, familiarized himself with the crime scene, unlawfully entered a building where he thought he might commit the crime, had special tools essential for committing the crime, or solicited an innocent agent to commit the crime, a jury *could* (but is not required to) find him guilty of an attempt.

ABANDONMENT

The Common Law

The common law did not allow the defense of abandonment. Once a defendant had crossed the line dividing preparation from implementation and had committed an attempt, he could not go back. Of course, if the actus reus test used requires the defendant to be so close to completion before an attempt has occurred, there will probably be no appreciable time left in which to abandon. If, for example, the defendant is guilty of an attempt only after he has pulled the trigger (the last act in his control), he has only a nanosecond to abandon and shout a warning to the victim.

Some states, however, allow a defendant to prove that, though he actually committed an attempt, he subsequently *abandoned* his criminal purpose. The defense is available only if the defendant changed his mind through genuine remorse and not because the risk of arrest or difficulty of committing the crime was greater than anticipated. Though arguably permitting the acquittal of someone who has demonstrated a willingness to engage in criminal conduct, the defense may encourage criminals to change their mind and not complete the crime, saving both the victim and society from more serious harm. Generally, abandonment is an affirmative defense that the defendant must establish by a preponderance of the evidence.

The Model Penal Code

Under the concept of "renunciation," the MPC permits the defendant to introduce evidence that he "abandoned his effort to commit the crime or otherwise prevented its commission, under circumstances manifesting a complete and voluntary renunciation of his criminal purpose." (MPC

§5.01(4).) Thus, the defendant must give up his criminal goal or prevent its successful commission. The use of renunciation is strictly limited.

First, the defense is available only when the target offense has a *result* (§5.01(2)) or *circumstance* (§5.01(3)) as a material element. It is not available when *conduct* is the only material element of the target offense because, once the defendant has completed the criminal conduct, the harm has been done and there is nothing for him to abandon. Only outside forces have prevented successful completion of the target offense.

Second, it must be *voluntary*. The defendant must *not* have changed his mind because it was *more difficult* to commit the crime than he originally anticipated.

Third, it must be *complete*. Basically, the defendant must not have decided to wait for a better time or opportunity.

The Code's adoption of an abandonment claim is almost surely the quid pro quo for moving the time frame of attempt back earlier than the common law tests allowed. Thus, if the defendant intends to rob a bank in one month and reconnoiters it today, he could be convicted of an attempt under the Code (but not under the common law). If we want the defendant to abandon his intent between now and next month, we must provide him with some inducement for doing so. The Code's provision does so.

See Table 12.1 for a summary of the law of attempt.

IMPOSSIBILITY: LEGAL, FACTUAL, AND INHERENT

Despite their best efforts and for reasons beyond their control, criminals sometimes do not commit the crime they set out to commit because—it turns out—it is *impossible* to commit the crime. What, if anything, should the criminal law do in such cases? Consider these examples. An individual smuggles a prescription drug into the country thinking it is against the law, but there is no criminal law forbidding the importation of this particular drug. A pickpocket tries to pick someone's pocket, but there is nothing in the victim's pocket. A hunter shoots at a stuffed deer out of hunting season. In *some* cases, the criminal law uses *attempt* to punish the offender. In other cases, using the doctrine of *impossibility*, the criminal law does not punish the actor.[10]

10. One might argue with both logic and irony that *every* attempt is a case of impossibility because—for whatever reason—the defendant did not succeed. The concept of impossibility is built into attempt. Many commentators argue that impossibility is of little practical significance in the criminal law. However, other scholars and even some criminal law

The Common Law

At common law, there were two kinds of impossibility: factual and legal. Legal impossibility was a defense; factual impossibility was not. This means a law student must know the difference. Unfortunately, impossibility is a very complex and confusing area.

Legal Impossibility

Consider a defendant who engages in conduct (such as smuggling a new abortion pill into the United States), thinking it is a crime when, in fact, there is no law making it a crime. This is a case of true legal impossibility under the common law, and the defendant could not be convicted of an attempt. Though the defendant has shown himself willing to break *the* law, he has not broken any *particular* law. Thus, he could not have the mens rea required to attempt a particular offense.

As we saw earlier in the mistake of law section, a belief that conduct is not against the law usually does not excuse behavior if it is a crime. (See Chapter 5.) In legal impossibility, a belief that conduct *is* against the law does not make the conduct criminal if there is no law prohibiting that conduct.

Factual Impossibility

Factual impossibility occurs when the defendant, despite his intentions, could not complete his intended crime because of facts or conditions unknown to him or beyond his control. Thus, a defendant can be convicted of attempt even though it was factually impossible for him to accomplish his goal.

Consider a defendant who, in violation of a specific statute, tries to sell foreign abortion pills to an undercover police officer and is arrested in a sting operation. After the pills are tested, it turns out that, although the defendant *thought* he was selling the foreign abortion pills, he had been duped by his supplier and had *actually sold* sugar pills. This would be a case of *factual* impossibility. Because of facts unknown to the defendant (the pills were sugar), he did not succeed in selling foreign abortion pills. However, he could be convicted of an *attempt* to sell the proscribed pills.

---

students find the doctrine a fascinating opportunity to explore the doctrinal logic and policy choices of the criminal law. See Symposium, 5 J. Contemp. Legal Issues 1-398 (1994).

12.1 The Material Elements of Attempt

ATTEMPT — COMMON LAW

Thinking **MENS REA**	**Preparing**			**Doing** **ACTUS REUS**			
1. Same mens rea as target offense ± 2. Intent to i) do the same act ii) accomplish same result iii) know the same circumstances as target crime	**C R I M I N A L**	**"Proximity Test"** (close in space and time *or* set forces in motion with high probability of completion)	**"Probable Desistance"** (law-abiding person would have broken off)	**"Unequivocal Act"** (clearly manifests criminal purpose)	**"Last Act"** (beyond's *D*'s control)	**Abandonment Not Permitted**	**T A R G E T**

ATTEMPT — MPC

CULPABILITY		**SUBSTANTIAL STEP**		
1. Same culpability as target crime ± 2. Purposefully engages in conduct ± 3. Purposefully causes result *or* believes result will ensure ± 4. Same culpability toward circumstances as target offense	**T H R E S H O L D**	1. "Strongly corroborates" criminal purpose	**Abandonment Permitted If** 1. Volutary renunciation and 2. Complete renunciation	**C R I M E**

Analysis

Unfortunately, it is not always easy to tell whether a case is one of legal or factual impossibility, and sometimes courts reach different results in similar cases.

People v. Jaffe[11] is a well-known example of a court's confusion and reluctance to convict someone for trying to commit a crime although, through no fault of his own, he did not succeed. The police, running a "sting" operation, had sold the defendant goods that had at one time been stolen but had since been recovered. The defendant *believed* he was purchasing stolen property. Charged with buying or receiving "any stolen property *knowing* the same to have been stolen" (emphasis added), the defendant was convicted of an *attempt* to commit that crime.

New York's highest court reversed the conviction. It concluded that the defendant could not *know* the property he possessed was stolen if, in fact, it was *no longer* stolen. The court essentially said that the defendant could not *know* something that was not true (even though he *believed* it to be true). Because the defendant could not be prosecuted for *knowingly* "buying or receiving stolen property," the court held that the defense of *legal* impossibility prevented his conviction for *attempted* buying or receiving property knowing it was stolen.

This case and the reasoning supporting its conclusion have been much criticized. The majority characterized this as a case of *legal* rather than *factual* impossibility because the defendant was mistaken about the legal status of the property; that is, it was no longer stolen. To convict the defendant of the target offense, the prosecution would have to establish that the property was stolen. Thus, this "legal fact" (see Chapter 5) is a circumstance element of the target crime, and the court should have characterized this as a case of factual impossibility.

The confusion generated by the doctrine of impossibility has been made worse by some commentators and some court opinions that determine what an actor *intended* by what he *did*. Consider a defendant who shoots at a human silhouette behind a window shade intending to kill the person he thinks is standing there. It turns out that there is only a mannequin placed there by the police to create the illusion of a human body. Some commentators (and even some courts) conclude that what the defendant *did* in fact—shoot at a mannequin rather than at a human—is what he *intended* to do. This is a very unusual interpretation of what "intent" means in the criminal law. It equates mens rea with actus reus (he intended what he did) rather than trying to determine what mental activity was occurring in the actor's mind when he performed the actus reus.

---

11. 185 N.Y. 497, 78 N.E. 169 (1906).

The current trend in the criminal law is to focus on what the defendant *thought* he was doing rather than on what it turns out he actually did. If there is no law making what the defendant intended to accomplish a crime, then it will be a case of legal impossibility. Otherwise, most cases of this sort will involve factual impossibility, which is not a defense to attempt. The only question remaining then is whether the defendant's conduct satisfies the actus reus requirement of attempt.

Inherent Impossibility

What, if anything, should be done with an individual who wants to kill her rival for a loved one's affections but uses means that are inherently unlikely to accomplish the intended result—say, sticking pins into a voodoo doll? Though the defendant clearly has a dangerous attitude and has acted to implement her criminal intent, she may seem to some so hopelessly inept as to be more worthy of pity than condemnation and imprisonment. Nonetheless, inherent impossibility was not a defense at common law. Such a defendant's best hope was the common law's demanding actus reus definitions. Many steps taken by a bungling individual might not satisfy them.

The Model Penal Code

Legal Impossibility

The MPC does not explicitly provide a defense of legal impossibility. Instead, §5.01 requires the *prosecutor* to prove that there is a criminal statute punishing what the defendant intended to accomplish. Thus, a person who engages in behavior he *thinks* is a crime, but is not, cannot be convicted of an attempt. (Of course, the effect is the same as if the MPC *did* provide this defense!)

Factual Impossibility

Under the MPC, factual impossibility is not a defense to attempt. (§5.01.) A defendant is guilty of an attempt if he would have committed the target offense had the facts or conditions been as he *believed* them to be. Thus, in the *Jaffe* case, the defendant could have been convicted of an attempt to purchase or receive stolen property because he *believed* the property to be stolen, and he would have committed the target offense if his belief were true. Likewise, a defendant, who *believed* his victim to be alive and shot at him to kill, can be convicted of attempted murder even though the victim had already died.[12]

Inherent Impossibility

The MPC does not allow a defense of inherent impossibility. However, it does permit the court to dismiss a prosecution if the defendant's conduct was so "inherently unlikely to culminate in the commission of a crime that neither such conduct nor the actor presents a public danger." (§5.05(2).) Most such cases are probably disposed of by the prosecutor's exercise of discretion not to prosecute.

Thankfully, the MPC has simplified what had been a very confusing area of the law and the modern trend is to follow the MPC. Remember, however, that the doctrines of legal and factual impossibility occasionally bedevil prosecutors, defense lawyers, judges, and, yes, law students (especially on criminal law exams!), even today.

Stalking

Legislatures sometimes criminally punish conduct that may appear harmless to most observers. Stalking is a contemporary example of this type of crime. It punishes an actor for repetitive behavior and/or for credible threats that cause the victim to reasonably fear serious bodily harm. Stalking may reach conduct that would not qualify as an attempt. Thus, it permits even earlier intervention by the criminal law. It is similar to "attempt" in stopping preliminary conduct from escalating into more serious violence against the target.

Supporters believe this new crime is necessary because many victims, especially women, are stalked by former spouses, friends, and even strangers who, too often, kill or seriously injure their victims. Fifteen percent of women and six percent of men are reportedly victims of stalking at some time in their lives.[13] In 2011, it was estimated that there could be as many as 7.5 million people stalked in the United States (per year? or people who have ever been stalked?).[14] Reportedly, 90 percent of all women killed by their

12. *People v. Dlugash*, 41 N.Y.2d 725, 363 N.E.2d 1155 (1977).

13. http://victimsofcrime.org/our-programs/stalking-resource-center/stalking-information/stalking-statistics (last visited January 26, 2018).

14. Prevalence and Characteristics of Sexual Violence, Stalking, and Intimate Partner Violence Victimization — National Intimate Partner and Sexual Violence Survey, United States, 2011.

husbands or boyfriends were stalked by them before the fatal attack.[15] Other remedies, such as prosecutions for attempt and civil protection orders, have proven ineffective in preventing behavior that creates significant fear and can lead to death or serious injury. Critics are concerned that these laws are too vague (see Chapter 1) or that they punish conduct that is constitutionally protected, including speech.

These statutes punish deliberate and repeated conduct involving visual or physical proximity to the victim (such as following or visually surveilling) or threats that would cause a reasonable person to fear for her safety. Today every state has a stalking law. Most statutes define stalking as the willful, malicious, and repeated following or harassing of another person. Some require the defendant to exhibit threatening behavior *intended* to place the victim in reasonable fear of her safety. This approach allows conviction even if the victim did not feel threatened. Others only require the prosecution to prove that the defendant knew, or *should have known*, that his intentional course of conduct would cause fear of death or serious bodily injury in a reasonable person. This approach allows conviction for *negligence* as to result; that is, even if the defendant did *not intend* to cause such fear. Some stalking statutes exclude behavior that has a legitimate purpose or is constitutionally protected. More recently, these laws have been used to prosecute "cyberstalking," stalking, involving e-mail communications or web postings.

Stalking laws enable law enforcement to protect victims from ongoing intimidation. They also codify a specific "inchoate" offense in order to prevent a preliminary course of action from accelerating into more serious injury to the victim.[16]

Examples

1. Suzy, tired of her marriage, decided to kill her husband, Bob, and collect his life insurance. She purchased a .38 caliber pistol, took shooting lessons, and put the gun in the drawer next to her side of the bed. Pretending she heard a burglar late one evening, she induced Bob to go outside their house to investigate.

---

15. Antistalking Proposals: Hearing on Combating [sic] Stalking and Family Violence Before the Senate Comm. on the Judiciary, 103d Cong., 1st Sess. 3 (1993) (Statement of Sen. Joseph R. Biden, Chairman) at 10. (Statement of Sen. William S. Cohen). Not all stalking is romantically motivated. Some stalkers are persecutory [This seems a troublesome distinction—all stalking is persecutory]; that is, they feel their targets have harmed them, either physically or financially. Revenge is their primary motivation. Ronnie B. Harmon et al., Sex and Violence in a Forensic Population of Obsessional Harassers, 4 Psych., Pub. Pol'y & L. 236 (1998).

16. Kathleen G. McAnaney et al., From Imprudence to Crime: Anti-Stalking Law, 68 Notre Dame L. Rev. 819 (1993).

a. Suzy shot Bob in the head, later telling the police she thought he was a burglar. Bob did not die but lived on in a vegetative state.
b. Suzy loaded her .38 caliber pistol, sneaked out the back door, and, unknown to Bob, with finger on the trigger, aimed directly at his heart. She fired but the gun only made a loud noise. Unknown to Suzy, she had loaded the gun with blanks, thinking they were real bullets.
c. Suzy loaded her .38 caliber pistol with real bullets, sneaked out the back door, and, unknown to Bob, with her finger on the trigger, aimed directly at his heart. Suddenly, Suzy became upset. She sneaked back inside without being detected, put her gun away, and awaited Bob's return.

2. Jim fired nine rounds from an assault-style semi-automatic rifle at the White House from a speeding car about 750 yards from the target—about the maximum effective range for this weapon. One bullet struck a bulletproof window in the first family's residential quarters, cracking it and then falling to the ground outside. Another round was found on the lawn. Unknown to Jim, the president and his wife were out of town at the time. Jim has been charged with attempted assassination of the president. Can he be convicted?

3. Max wanted to collect fire insurance on an old tenement building he owns, which contains 25 apartments. Late one evening, he spilled gasoline in the basement and set a time-delayed fuse, which erupted into flame at 3:00 a.m. By some miracle most of the tenants escaped the resulting fire without serious harm; however, two tenants were horribly burned and almost died. He is charged with attempted murder.

4. Connor, a gang member, is selling drugs to a customer on his street corner. As Raphael, a rival gang member, saunters toward him, Connor uses a stolen gun to fire a warning shot over Raphael's head to scare him out of Connor's turf.
   a. Raphael is struck in the head by the bullet and almost dies.
   b. Raphael is struck in the head by the bullet and dies.
   c. What if Connor intends to kill Raphael, but the bullet only grazes Raphael and he dies anyway from a heart attack partially induced by "ecstasy," a street drug Raphael had just taken?

5a. Following a fight with Tong, a member of the Aces, a rival gang, Paulo, a member of the Spades, drove by the scene an hour later and fired a single shot at a group of six members of the Aces, shouting, "I'm going to kill one of you #*!#!" Fortunately, no one was injured.

5b. An hour after a fight with Tong, a member of the Aces, a rival gang, Paulo drove by the scene and threw a grenade at Tong, who was standing right next to six other members of his gang, shouting, "I'm going to kill you, Tong!" Fortunately, no one was killed even though the grenade exploded, injuring Tong and several other gang members.

6. During the course of a drug deal in New York City, Paula, thinking Reuben was trying to rip her off by selling her harmless powder as crack cocaine, shot at Reuben intending to kill him. Reuben almost died but eventually recovered. Unknown to Paula, Reuben was an undercover state narcotics officer who was selling her real crack in a "sting" operation in order to then arrest her. In New York, first-degree murder includes acting "with intent to cause the death of another person, . . . caus[ing] the death of such person; and . . . the person was a police officer . . . killed in the course of performing his official duties." Is Paula guilty of attempted first-degree murder?

7a. Last week, Terrence, a law student about to graduate, told Dennis that he is going to "hack" into Sallie Mae's computer system and erase all of his own student loan records so he would not have to repay his humongous debt. That same day, Terrence visited websites describing basic hacking techniques (including how to penetrate computer security systems and erase files) and downloaded this information. Has Terrence committed an attempt?

7b. Yesterday, Terrence wrote a program that would penetrate Sallie Mae's website security system and obtained the remote access telephone number that would provide him entry into the site. Now?

7c. Earlier today, Terrence loaded the hacking program he had written into his computer and dialed the remote access number for Sallie Mae's website. He was met by an unexpected firewall. The system denied Terrence access to his files because he was not using a predesignated computer to access the site. The system posted: "Unauthorized attempt to access system. Please contact administrator" and listed an 800 number for assistance. Terrence quickly exited the system. Now?

8. At lunch in a bar, Joe, an undercover cop, inquired if Sam could sell him some cocaine. Sam said he would call his suppliers and made several telephone calls. Sam then told Joe he would have a pound of cocaine to sell him at the same bar at 6:00 p.m. that evening. He instructed Joe to return alone at that time with cash. Joe agreed and left the bar. While picking up cocaine from his supplier, Sam was told of a rumor that the FBI was in town with undercover agents trying to set up cocaine buys. Sam gave the cocaine back to his supplier and did not go back to the bar that evening. Sam was arrested three days later and charged with attempted sale of drugs.

9. Noreen needed money for a down payment on a new house. She decided to collect insurance on her wedding ring, a family heirloom insured for $8,000 against theft. She drove to a distant city and sold the ring to a jeweler. Two days later she broke her window from the outside and ransacked her bedroom where she had previously kept the ring. She then called her insurance company and asked what steps she had to take to be paid for the theft of her ring under the policy. The company said it would pay her the $8,000 if she filed a police report and then submitted a claim. Noreen reported to the police that the ring had been stolen.
   a. A few days later, overwhelmed by guilt, she confessed to the police.
   b. The jeweler to whom she sold the ring called her and said he had received a police bulletin describing her ring as stolen property and that he intended to report it to the police. Noreen immediately notified the insurance company that she would not be submitting an insurance claim.

10. Julie, an explosives expert who is angry over Dave's decision to break off their relationship, sneaked over to Dave's house and wired his car so that it would explode when Dave started it the next morning. Later that evening, Dave died of a heart attack. Upon learning of Dave's sudden demise, Julie sneaked over to the car the next evening and removed the explosives.

11a. Chauncey knew that he had the Zika virus and that having unprotected sex exposed his partners to a significant risk of contracting Zika. He also knew that most people who have Zika can have babies who contract a disease that makes them unlikely to survive. Nonetheless, he continued to have extensive unprotected sex with various partners, lying about his condition. Chauncey has been charged with attempted murder after impregnating one of his partners.

11b. Chase, a convict who knew that he was HIV positive, spat at a prison guard, screaming: "Now you will get AIDS and die, just like me!" In fact, AIDS seldom develops in human saliva, and there is a very low probability of transmitting AIDS by saliva. Fortunately, the guard has remained HIV free. Chase has been charged with attempted murder.

12. Trevor and Gloria, college freshmen, met briefly during Greek Week. When Trevor asked Gloria for a date, she firmly declined. Trevor then acquired her e-mail address:
   a. The love-struck Trevor sent Gloria three e-mails, professing his undying love. The first stated that he thought of her constantly and could not get her out of his mind. The second stated that he would do anything to have her. The final one stated that, as he watched her

walking to class, he realized she was the only one for him. Gloria, fearful of Trevor's obsession with her and his secret observation, became very fearful of what he might do next. Nervous and apprehensive, Gloria became very jittery and constantly looked over her shoulder whenever she left her room. Has Trevor committed a stalking offense?

b. When Gloria did not react favorably to his "nice" e-mails, Trevor became angry and decided to send some intimidating messages to Gloria as payback. Trevor sent her two anonymous e-mails. One contained lyrics from a contemporary rap song which were sexually explicit and graphically violent. The other contained lyrics about constantly watching a woman who was unaware of the surveillance. Gloria trashed them, thinking a quirky friend with deficient social skills had sent them to her as a joke.

c. After receiving more e-mails, Gloria obtained a restraining order against Trevor ordering him to refrain from all contact with her. Karl, a mutual friend, told Trevor that Gloria was so upset that she had gone to her parents' house, a two-hour drive from campus. Trevor looked up her parents' address and drove to her parents' home with the intention of seriously frightening her. As he approached the house, he circled the block a couple of times and then drove away because he did not want to violate the order. Gloria did not see him. Attempted stalking? Abandonment?

13. Sebastian, 45, sent a follow request on Instagram to "Amanda," a teenage girl he found in the search feature, in hopes that she would have sex with him. Amanda accepted Sebastian's follow request and told him she was 14 and wanted to have sex with an older man. Amanda was actually a female FBI agent, Barbara, who was on the prowl for people like Sebastian. After exchanging several direct messages, Sebastian and Amanda agreed to have sex at a motel near Amanda's home. Sebastian checked into the room, and Amanda called him from the lobby as planned. When Sebastian opened the door, he was immediately arrested and charged with attempted sexual assault of a minor.

14. Quentin loves Cuban cigars. He thinks their importation into the United States should not be a crime. He purchased several high-priced cigars in Colombia while on a business trip, thinking they were Cuban cigars, and hid them in a secret compartment in his suitcase. A customs inspector discovered the cigars at the airport in Miami.

    a. There is a law forbidding the importation of Cuban cigars, but, it turns out, these cigars are from Santo Domingo.
    b. These cigars are Cuban, but there is no criminal law forbidding their importation.

c. There is a law forbidding the importation of Cuban cigars, but, unknown to Quentin, these cigars actually are 100 percent marijuana.

15. Judge Smith sentences John to 40 years for minor offenses. John plans to put a death hex on Judge Smith. John asks his brother, Lonny, to call Judge Smith's house keeper, Emma, to get some personal items of Judge Smith's, a hair brush and an old picture. Lonny agrees to assist John and contacts Emma. Lonny offers to pay Emma for the personal items of Judge Smith. Emma works with authorities in a sting operation to stop the voodoo murder.[17]

Explanations

1a. Suzy's purpose was to kill Bob. Because she acted with the purpose to achieve the result element of the target crime, causing the death of another human being, and did the last act necessary to accomplish that result (or took a substantial step under the MPC), Suzy committed attempted murder even though she did not achieve the intended result.

1b. Suzy had the necessary mens rea to commit murder. She intended to kill another human being. She also acted on that criminal purpose by purchasing a gun, becoming proficient in its use, and luring her victim to a scene where she could establish a good cover story explaining the murder as an accident.

Under the common law, she took the last step; she actually pulled the trigger of what she thought was a loaded pistol while aiming it at Bob's heart. In addition, her behavior probably satisfies the equivocality test because her course of conduct seems consistent only with a planned murder. (However, because the jury cannot consider any evidence other than her conduct, it could conclude that her behavior was consistent with law-abiding conduct; i.e., she was looking for a burglar and was simply mistaken as to Bob's identity.) Under both the proximity test and probable desistance test, Suzy has committed the actus reus of attempt. She has come very close in time and space to causing the result (proximity test), and she did not break off her criminal course of conduct (probable desistance test).

Under the MPC, Suzy took a substantial step that was strongly corroborative of her criminal purpose. She obtained a gun, learned how to use it, lured the victim to the contemplated crime scene, aimed the gun at a vital part of Bob's body, and pulled the trigger.

---

17. This is a real case! See Paul H. Robinson, Shima Baradaran Baughman, & Michael T. Cahill, Criminal Law: Case Studies and Controversies, 362 (New York: Wolters Kluwer, 4th ed., 2017).

Suzy might argue impossibility. However, this is simply a case of factual impossibility (unknown to Suzy, the shells were blanks, not bullets), not legal impossibility (there is a law against unlawfully killing another human being). Factual impossibility is no defense at common law. Under the MPC, had the facts been as Suzy believed them to be (i.e., the gun was loaded with bullets, not blanks), Suzy would have committed the target crime (assuming a good aim). Thus, she is guilty of an attempt. The MPC focuses on the defendant's attitude more than on how close she came to actually causing harm.

1c. The same general analysis for mens rea and actus reus used in Example 1b applies here. However, Suzy has not taken the last step (there is still an opportunity to repent and she did), nor is it clear that her conduct satisfies the equivocality test (she could have been looking for a burglar). The prosecution would have a better chance under the proximity test (she stalked her victim and almost pulled the trigger) or probable desistance test (though Suzy did break off her criminal conduct and change her mind, most citizens would not have gone as far as she did). Because murder is a serious crime and most law-abiding citizens would not go through such an elaborate scheme, a jury could convict her under all of these tests except the last-step test. Note how the common law requires the defendant to come very close to actually committing the target offense and also requires strong evidence of criminal intentions.

The MPC, however, is more concerned with preventing harm and apprehending dangerous individuals; it is less concerned with waiting until the last possible moment to see if a defendant will actually commit the target offense.

Under the common law, there is no defense of abandonment, so Suzy cannot claim she has changed her mind. Under the MPC, Suzy can present evidence that she renounced her criminal scheme and did not have the firmness of criminal intention. She also might argue that her renunciation was complete and voluntary because she could easily have carried out the murder as planned. There were no unexpected facts making it more difficult. Suzy would argue that she was filled with remorse and should not be convicted. Her change of heart shows she is not really dangerous. This will be a jury question.

2. The prosecution would claim that Jim intentionally aimed and fired a high-powered rifle at the White House. One round struck a window in the residential area of the White House. Though stopped by bulletproof glass, these facts clearly demonstrate that Jim intended to fire lethal rounds into a place where the president lives. Surely, Jim intended the natural and probable consequences of his action—killing the President. The jury may infer this intent based on the

defendant's conduct. Since Jim intended to accomplish this result, he has the *mens rea* required by the common law for an attempted murder of the President. Jim also committed the "last act" under his control to achieve this result; there was no longer an opportunity to desist. This easily satisfies the actus reus or conduct element of the crime. Though bulletproof glass prevented the bullet from entering the residential quarters and the intended victim was not physically present, Jim cannot argue factual impossibility. It is not recognized as a defense at common law.

Under the MPC, the prosecution can prove that Jim purposely fired several high-powered rounds at the president's living quarters. The prosecution must also prove that the defendant acted with the purpose or *belief* that his act would cause the proscribed result—the president's death. Jim fired at the White House *believing* he would kill him. Why else would he use such a powerful weapon and fire so many rounds? Jim also committed a substantial step that strongly corroborates this criminal purpose. He did more than simply possess a deadly weapon near the White House—legally sufficient to prove a substantial step under the MPC. He actually shot the weapon at his intended target.

Defense counsel would note that there is no evidence of intent other than Jim's discharge of the weapon at great distance in the general direction of the White House from a speeding car. Though conceding that his client has committed some crime, perhaps unlawful discharge of a weapon, there is insufficient evidence that he intended to kill the president. If anything, his incompetent and inept plan for the shooting indicates a clear absence of this goal. Jim's act was equivocal as to result. At most, Jim committed a reckless act that created a substantial risk that someone might be struck by a bullet from his weapon and could die. But under the common law, attempt requires the prosecution to prove that the defendant intended to achieve that result.

Under the MPC, the prosecution must prove that the defendant acted with the purpose or belief that his act would cause this result. Surely Jim did not believe he could kill the president from such a long distance from a speeding car. Nor does his conduct establish that he acted with the criminal purpose or belief as to this result. Though conceding that inherent impossibility is not recognized as a defense under the MPC, the long range, shooting from a speeding car with its inevitable inaccuracy, and the known security of the building, all indicate that Jim did not intend to kill anyone. Rather, this was bizarre behavior that is a less serious crime.

3. Max did not attempt murder even though he acted recklessly with extreme indifference to human life. His purpose was to destroy the building, not to kill people.

Under the common law, he did not act with the specific intent as to result—that is, he did not intend to take human life. Thus, he cannot be convicted of attempted murder.

Under the MPC, Max also cannot be convicted of attempted murder because he did not act with the purpose of taking human life. (This explanation assumes that Max did not *believe* that people would die. Under the MPC, such a belief would satisfy the mens rea for result required for an attempt.)

If a human being had died in the fire, Max could have been convicted of murder under either of two theories: intentional risk creation or felony murder. (See Chapter 8.) However, to convict someone of attempted murder, most jurisdictions and the MPC require that the defendant have acted with the purpose or intent of achieving the result element—that is, taking human life. Even if Max had knowledge that his conduct created a high probability that someone would be killed, he did not commit attempted murder.

Contrary to this clear majority rule, a few jurisdictions have held that a defendant can be convicted of "attempted reckless manslaughter"[18] or "attempted extreme indifference to life murder"[19] even if he did not intend to kill. This minority approach eliminates the traditional requirement for attempt that the defendant must act with the purpose of causing the result element of the target offense. It is sufficient if he intentionally or purposefully does an act either recklessly or with extreme indifference to human life. The rationale is that, when the defendant does an intentional act knowing that it may come very close to killing an innocent victim, he is both blameworthy and dangerous; consequently, attempt liability is appropriate. The facts of this example demonstrate why courts might be persuaded to adopt this approach.

4a. Connor did not commit attempted murder. Even though Raphael almost died as a result of Connor's intentional act, Connor did not act with the *purpose* of killing him. His purpose was to cause his rival to leave Connor's "territory." Thus, under both the common law and the MPC, Connor did not commit attempted murder. Of course, we have posited that Connor's mental state is known. Without such evidence, however, a jury is free to conclude that Connor "intended" the result that he almost caused and to convict him of attempted murder.

4b. Because Connor proximately caused the death of another human being who was not a co-felon during the commission of a felony (the drug sale), Connor could be convicted of felony murder even though he did not intend to cause Raphael's death. Unlike attempt, which focuses on

---

18. *People v. Thomas*, 729 P.2d 972 (Colo. 1986).

19. *People v. Castro*, 657 P.2d 932 (Colo. 1983).

the actor's mental state or attitude toward causing a particular result, the felony murder rule imposes homicidal responsibility based primarily on the harm the defendant proximately causes during the commission of a serious crime. (See Chapter 8.)

4c. This is a close one and could go either way. The jury might decide that "ecstasy," the drug voluntarily ingested by Raphael, proximately caused his death and that it was an independent intervening cause. (See Chapter 7.) If so, then Connor can be convicted only of *attempted* murder because, even though his purpose was to kill Raphael, he did not cause that result. While the fright caused by Connor's warning shot may have contributed somewhat to Raphael's death, his death was caused primarily by his own voluntary conduct. Thus, the felony murder rule would probably not snare Connor. The moral? Don't forget to analyze *both* mens rea and causation on those tricky law school exams!

5a. The prosecutor would argue that Paulo is guilty of a single count of attempted premeditated murder because, as his words clearly show, he acted with the purpose of killing at least one member of the rival gang and took both the "last step" (under common law) and a "substantial step" (under the MPC) to accomplish that result by discharging a deadly weapon at a group of people. Attempt does not require the government to prove which specific individual Paulo wanted to kill, but only that he intended to kill *someone*.

The defendant would argue that attempt is a specific intent crime, requiring the prosecution to prove that he intended to kill a *specific* human being. Paulo clearly did not have a specific target or victim in mind when he shot at the group. At most, Paulo engaged in very dangerous conduct that created a significant risk of death, but, in fact, no one died. Thus, he may have committed the crime of reckless endangerment or even assault with a deadly weapon, but not attempted murder.

The government would probably succeed in obtaining a conviction of attempted murder. Paulo did not care which individual he killed, but he certainly purposed the death of at least *one* of the persons in the group and tried to achieve that result. Thus, he has satisfied the mens rea and actus reus of attempt.

5b. The prosecutor would argue that Paulo is guilty of seven counts of attempted premeditated murder; one count for each member of the group. She would point out that Paulo clearly admitted that he intended to kill Tong; thus, there is no disputing his mens rea or culpability as to that victim. Surely, throwing a grenade that exploded in close proximity to the specifically targeted victim (Tong) satisfies all actus reus tests. She would further argue that a jury could readily infer that Paulo intended to kill the other members of the gang (despite the absence of words manifesting that intent) because he used a weapon that could readily kill *everyone* in the immediate vicinity of the intended victim (called the "kill zone" by some courts).

The defense would argue that Paulo only intended to kill Tong. Thus, he did not act with the premeditated objective of killing the other gang members. Thus, he can only be convicted of a single count of attempted premeditated murder and, perhaps, six counts of reckless endangerment or assault with a deadly weapon.

California would allow convictions under the prosecutor's theories in both of these examples. *People v. Stone*, 46 Cal. 4th 131, 205 P.3d 272 (2009).

6. This is a tough one! Paula clearly intended to cause Reuben's death and took a substantial step (and the last step) toward accomplishing her goal. Thus, she can surely be convicted of at least attempted second-degree murder.

   But must the prosecution prove that Paula also intended to kill a police officer in the course of performing his official duties? The prosecution probably could not prove this because Paula would not have knowingly bought drugs from a police officer, nor do any facts indicate that Paula knew Reuben was an undercover police officer.

   Under common law, Paula must know all circumstances of the target crime. Because she did not intend to kill a police officer while he was performing his duties, she could not be convicted of attempted first-degree murder even if this circumstance is a strict liability element in the target offense.

   Under the MPC, however, the mens rea toward circumstances of the target offense determines her guilt. If the circumstance that Reuben was a police officer performing his official duties is a strict liability element, then Paula would be guilty of attempted first-degree murder. (Under the MPC, however, it will be a material element.) If, on the other hand, the mens rea of "purpose" or "knowledge" also applies to this circumstance, then she would not be.

7a. Terrence clearly has the mens rea to commit several crimes, including contemporary crimes that prohibit computer hacking and the destruction of computer information, as well as traditional crimes like fraud and theft (by not repaying his student loans). His criminal intention can be established by his statement to Dennis and by his gathering information on hacking techniques.

   The more difficult question is whether Terrence is simply in the "preparation" phase or has actually put his plan into "action" by engaging in conduct sufficient to make him guilty of attempt. Under the common law, Terrence has surely not yet taken the "last step" since he would have to do much more to accomplish his goal. And his behavior so far (without looking at any other evidence like his remark to Dennis) does not plainly demonstrate that he is going to commit a crime. Thus, it does not satisfy the "equivocality" test.

Even under the proximity test, Terrence has probably not committed an attempt because he has not come close in space or time to actually committing the unauthorized computer entry (let alone destruction of computer information). Under the probable desistance test, he still can change his mind since there are still actions he must take to accomplish his goal. Thus, Terrence has not committed an attempt.

Under the MPC, has Terrence taken a "substantial" step? Probably not. His actions appear to be only preparation, acquiring the information necessary to commit the crime at some future time.

7b. Terrence's mens rea is the same as in Example 7a. Under the common law, he has probably not satisfied the following tests: last step, equivocality, or probable desistance. However, the facts are stronger for the prosecution than in Example 7a. Terrence would argue that even though he has assembled the "tools and instruments" necessary for committing the crimes on his computer and the computer would be used to carry them out, this location may not be sufficiently "near" the crime scene. However, the prosecutor might argue that Terrence custom-designed his "hacking" program to commit these crimes and that the program has no lawful use. Thus, under the MPC, he has committed a "substantial step." Ultimately, the jury must determine if this conduct "strongly corroborates a criminal purpose."

7c. Terrence has committed an attempt! He had the necessary mens rea. His actus reus in trying to enter a secure computer site has satisfied all of the common law tests except the "last step" and, perhaps, the equivocality test. Terrence's action would clearly constitute a "substantial step" under the MPC because it confirms his criminal purpose. He used a hacking program, a custom-designed criminal instrument, and went (in cyberspace) to the scene of the contemplated crime, a secure computer system, by dialing the remote access number and trying to gain entry.

Under the MPC, Terrence might raise the defense of renunciation, arguing that he decided not to commit the offense after all. However, Terrence changed his mind about committing the crime only because he was having difficulty in succeeding and because the chances of being detected had become much higher. He was probably postponing the crime until he could determine how to breach the firewall. Thus, his renunciation is not voluntary and complete. Poor Terrence: criminal punishment and student loans!

8. Sam has the mens rea necessary for conviction of the target offense because he has the purpose of selling drugs to Joe. Under the common law, Sam has not taken the last step (though Sam has actually located and bought the drugs, he still must return to the bar to complete the sale). It is also not clear that he has satisfied the proximity test; he is not close in space or time to bringing the drugs to the bar where the sale to Joe would take place. However, his conduct probably satisfies the probable desistance test and, arguably, even the equivocality test, because locating and buying illegal drugs are not consistent with innocent behavior. Thus, under some common law tests, Sam has committed an attempt. Under others, he has not and his conduct is still only preparation.

   Under the MPC, Sam has probably taken a substantial step and has committed an attempt. He actually located a supplier and arranged to pick up and pay for the drugs that he would resell to Joe. This demonstrates that Sam is firm about committing the crime.[20]

   Sam might argue, however, that he never came close to actually selling the drugs to Joe. In addition, Sam might argue that, even if he did commit an attempt, he subsequently renounced his plans. The first defense is essentially a denial that he committed the necessary actus reus; it would probably not succeed under some tests. The second defense does not satisfy the elements of renunciation because the only reason Sam decided not to complete the crime is the rumor that Joe might be an undercover officer. Sam has not changed his mind for the right reasons and is simply waiting for a better opportunity.

9a. Noreen has probably not committed attempted fraud (though she may be convicted of filing a false police report). Although she intended to file a false claim of theft, she only engaged in preparatory conduct.

   Under the common law, she has not taken the last step; she must still submit the claim to the insurance company. Nor is she proximately close to committing fraud. She has ample opportunity to change her mind and has not yet set in motion a chain of events that would lead to her being paid by the insurance company for the "loss" of her ring.

   Even under the MPC, it is unlikely she has taken a substantial step. Because she needed to actually file the claim before she would collect any money, she could still change her mind and, in fact, she did. Even if she has attempted under the Code, she has abandoned her plan.

9b. Just as in Example 9a, Noreen has not committed an attempt. True, she changed her mind only because the chances of succeeding were almost zero. However, her actions would still probably be considered preparation rather than implementation under the analysis in Example 9a.

---

20. *United States v. Mandujano*, 499 F.2d 370 (5th Cir. 1974).

10. Julie has committed attempted murder. She purposefully wired Dave's car in order to kill him.

    Under the common law, she took the last step (though it could be argued that events were not yet beyond her control since she, in fact, did disarm the bomb). Her behavior may also have satisfied the equivocality test because planting a car bomb manifests criminal intent. Under the proximity test, a jury could well find her guilty because she has come close in time and space to committing the target crime, and this is a very serious offense likely to arouse strong community resentment. Though she did change her mind, it was not for the same reasons that would motivate a law-abiding person.

    Under the MPC, Julie has surely taken a substantial step; planting a car bomb so it would explode when someone started the engine is strongly corroborative of a criminal purpose to kill.

    Can Julie raise the defense of impossibility because she could not possibly have killed Dave, who had died during the night? This is not a case of legal impossibility. If the facts had been as Julie thought they were, Dave would have been alive and her plan to kill him would be a crime. Thus, Julie can be convicted of attempted murder.

    Julie cannot raise the defense of renunciation. Even though she unwired the car so that no one else would be killed and she probably would not try to kill anyone else, she did not change her mind for the right reasons as required by the MPC. So sorry, Julie!

11a. Chauncey has engaged in conduct that poses a serious risk that he will infect one or more of his partners with Zika, which can lead to Zika in an unborn child and in due course to death. The prosecutor could argue that by deliberately engaging in this very high-risk behavior, Chauncey intended to kill his partner's unborn child. But the only evidence of mens rea here is the conduct that creates risk. Without better evidence that Chauncey acted with the purpose of killing his partner's unborn child rather than with extreme indifference to the possibility of infection and death of a future child, the prosecutor will probably fail to prove attempted murder. One court has upheld multiple convictions for attempted murder for HIV cases, which are slightly different, on the finding that a jury could conclude beyond a reasonable doubt that the defendant intended to kill his victims or cause them serious bodily injury.[21] Thus, conduct that creates a serious risk of death can support an inference that the actor *intended* that result.

11b. Chase has engaged in conduct that poses a much lower risk of infecting the guard with HIV, which can lead to AIDS and death. Yet, there is

21. *State v. Hinkhouse*, 139 Or. App. 446, 912 P.2d 921 (1996).

much better evidence (his own words) that Chase acted with the purpose of killing the guard. Thus, the prosecutor has a stronger case for proving the mental state or culpability required for attempted murder. Note how attempt focuses more on the actor's intentions than on his proximity to succeeding in his goal.

The defense could argue Chase's attempt to infect the guard with HIV by spitting on the guard is so inherently unlikely to result in AIDS and death that the court should dismiss the case. Keep in mind, however, the MPC does not recognize inherent impossibility as a defense.

12a. Even though Trevor's three e-mails were willful, they were not malicious and probably not harassing. In addition, Trevor did not intend to place Gloria in fear. Rather, it could be argued his purpose was to convey his heartfelt emotions. Nonetheless, Gloria became fearful for her physical safety because of the obsessive tone of these unwelcome e-mails. If the state stalking statute defines stalking as repeated behavior *intended* to cause fear of death or serious physical harm, then Trevor did not commit a stalking offense. His intention was not to create such fear; rather, it was to express his feelings for Gloria. If, however, the state law defines stalking as intentional conduct that the individual *should have known* places a reasonable person in fear of death or serious bodily injury, then Trevor (despite his nonthreatening intentions), has committed a stalking offense if Gloria's fearful reactions of serious bodily injury were reasonable.

12b. Gloria is not fearful for her physical safety, but Trevor intended to intimidate and harass her and to put her in fear of serious physical harm. Thus, he would clearly be guilty of stalking under a statute that focused on the culpability or attitude of the actor—repeated threatening behavior *intended* to put the victim in fear. However, he might not be guilty under a law that focused on the harm done—intentional conduct the actor knew or *should have known* would cause fear of serious physical harm in a reasonable person—because Gloria was not frightened and, arguably, neither would a reasonable person. If the statute required *both* that the actor intended his conduct to cause fear of serious physical safety and that it did cause such fear, Trevor could not be convicted of stalking.

12c. Trevor seemingly had the mens rea to commit a stalking offense. He located her parents' address and drove to her parents' home with the intent to frighten Gloria. Can he be convicted of attempted stalking? Under the common law, Trevor did not take the last step since he did not actually try to contact Gloria; moreover, he changed his mind about intimidating Gloria. But, under the equivocality and proximity tests, he might be convicted of attempted stalking. Likewise, under the MPC,

Trevor could be convicted of attempted stalking. He took a substantial step that strongly corroborated his criminal purpose. He located his victim and drove two hours to come into close proximity to her. Has he renounced his criminal purpose? This is a close case because he broke off his course of conduct to avoid violating the court order, not because of a sincere change of heart. What do you think? Notice how moving back the threshold of criminality in a codified offense such as stalking may allow an "attempt" to occur even earlier.

13. Sebastian would argue that it was impossible for the prosecution to prove he *could* have committed sexual assault of a minor. "Amanda" was not underage; thus, it was *legally* impossible for him to attempt this crime.

    The prosecution would counter that, if the facts were as Sebastian believed them to be—if Amanda were 14—he could have committed this crime. Thus, this is a case of *factual* impossibility: Sebastian intended to have sex with an underage girl. Thus, Sebastian is guilty of attempt.

    The age of his sexual partner is a "circumstance" element of the crime; thus, this a case of *factual* impossibility. Most jurisdictions would agree with the prosecutor and convict Sebastian of attempt. Only if a court took the approach in the *Jaffe* case and construed Sebastian's intention to be what actually happened in the real world, rather than what he expected to happen, would Sebastian have a chance of acquittal under the doctrine of legal impossibility.

    The MPC would also convict Sebastian. It does not allow the defense of impossibility. Here, Sebastian believed that Amanda was 14, and he would have committed a crime if she were that age. Thus, he attempted to sexually assault a minor. Notice once again that the MPC focuses primarily on the actor's attitudes rather than on whether he came close to causing harm.

14a. Quentin clearly had the mens rea to commit an attempt, and he took a substantial step to implement that attempt (hiding the cigars in a secret compartment and not declaring them at customs). His actions also satisfy all of the common law tests. Unknown to Quentin, the cigars were not Cuban and could lawfully be imported into the United States.

    Under the common law, this is a case of factual impossibility, not legal impossibility. There is a law forbidding importation of Cuban cigars into the United States. Quentin intended to engage in conduct that would violate that law, and he took significant action to implement that intent. Though these cigars are not Cuban, Quentin thought they were. Thus, most courts would conclude that Quentin had the purpose to import Cuban cigars and would not allow the defense. However, a minority of courts might conclude that Quentin intended to do what, in fact, he did—import Santo Domingan cigars. This analysis misapprehends the meaning of intent and also equates mens rea with actus rea.

The MPC would also convict Quentin of attempt. It provides that the mens rea toward circumstances required by the target offense will be the mens rea required for an attempt. In this case, Quentin has acted with the purpose of importing Cuban cigars. Because this is the highest culpability, it will satisfy whatever mens rea is required by the target offense.

14b. This is a case of true legal impossibility under the common law. There is no statute forbidding the importation of Cuban cigars into the United States. Quentin has shown he is willing to commit a crime and has acted on that willingness, but what he tried to do is not criminal. A belief that one is breaking the law, even when coupled with action to implement that belief, cannot generate criminal responsibility.

Quentin could not be convicted under the MPC either, because there is no statute punishing the importation of Cuban cigars.

14c. Quentin can be convicted of attempted importation of Cuban cigars. The analysis of mens rea and actus reus is the same as in Example 14a. This would be a case of factual impossibility under the common law and it would not be a defense. Under the MPC, Quentin is also guilty of an attempt because he acted with the same mens rea toward circumstances as required by the target offense.

Whether Quentin can be convicted of possession and/or importation of marijuana depends on whether the applicable statute requires the defendant to know that the substance he possesses or imports is marijuana or whether it is a strict liability element. If it is not a strict liability element, Quentin could raise the defense of mistake of fact under the common law. Under the MPC, he could present evidence of his belief to negate the culpability element of the offense. If it is a strict liability element, Quentin is in real trouble!

15. John had the mens rea required under common law. He intended to carry out a death hex to cause the death of Judge Smith. John has not yet committed the "last act" of his offense, because the authorities stepped in. The prosecution would have a better chance of convicting John under the probable desistance test. John showed no indication of ceasing his attempt to put a death hex on Judge Smith, and if Emma had not alerted the authorities, John likely would have continued in his efforts.

Under the MPC, John also satisfied the mens rea requirement. It is likely John also satisfied the actus reus requirement. John solicited his brother to help with the crime by instructing Lonny to obtain specific objects needed for the death hex from Judge Smith's housekeeper. He was in the process of obtaining the "tools" he needed to complete the voodoo and kill the Judge. These activities strongly corroborate John's purpose.

The defense could argue impossibility. On one hand, this could be a case of legal impossibility because there is no law against voodoo. However, because John *thought* he was going to accomplish the murder of Judge Smith, which is a crime, it may be a case of factual impossibility. Finally, the defense could contend that killing the judge by way of a voodoo death hex is so inherently unlikely to result in the death of Judge Smith that the court should dismiss the case. Are John and Lonny subject to conspiracy liability as well?

CHAPTER 13

Conspiracy

OVERVIEW

Sometimes you can get things done more efficiently by working with others. Criminals have found this form of organization works for them too.

Conspiracy punishes individuals who agree to commit a crime (often called the "target" or "object" crime). Conspiracy, then, responds to the special dangers created by *group criminality*: division of labor, expanded scope of potential harm, mutual encouragement, and greater likelihood the agreed-upon crime—or even future crimes not yet determined or contemplated—will be committed.

Conspiracy is an *inchoate* or unfinished crime because it permits the police to arrest those who have agreed to commit a crime long before they actually carry out their agreement. In fact, conspiracy sets the threshold of criminality much earlier than does attempt.

The early common law did not have a separate crime of conspiracy. It first appeared in a narrow statutory form in the early part of the fourteenth century. By the end of the eighteenth century, it had become a common law misdemeanor. Today, every state and the federal government have a conspiracy statute. As both criminal activity and criminal organizations have become more complex and sophisticated in modern society, conspiracy has become a more important law enforcement tool. Federal prosecutors in particular rely on conspiracy to prosecute crimes (such as drug smuggling, transportation of illegal aliens, and more recently terrorism) that require planning and complex coordination of many individuals or groups.

Conspiracy is a powerful weapon for prosecutors. It allows them to take advantage of special procedural and evidentiary rules that increase their prospects for obtaining convictions. Moreover, in many jurisdictions, defendants can be punished *both* for conspiracy and for crimes committed in furtherance of the conspiracy. This threat of increased punishment gives prosecutors tremendous leverage in obtaining plea bargains from defendants charged with conspiracy.[1]

Critics complain that the definition of conspiracy is too vague. Historically, there was a great deal of merit to this criticism because common law definitions were very broad. However, law reforms during the second half of the nineteenth century have provided narrower and clearer definitions for this crime.[2]

Because the essence of conspiracy is criminal agreement, many definitions of the crime only require an agreement to commit a crime. Critics maintain that contemporary conspiracy definitions set the threshold of crime too early, essentially punishing thoughts rather than conduct. Supporters retort that the early threshold of criminality set by conspiracy is necessary to meet the special dangers posed by collective criminal action.

DEFINITION

At common law and until recently in many states, conspiracy was defined as an agreement of two or more individuals to commit a criminal or unlawful act or a lawful act by unlawful means.[3] No conduct other than the agreement itself was required. (Remember that words alone are a type of conduct that can satisfy the actus reus requirement for a crime. See Chapter 3.) Today many (but not all) statutory definitions of conspiracy do require that at least one conspirator take an *overt act* in furtherance of the conspiracy before the crime is committed.[4] Some states require that one conspirator

1. Statistics indicate that conspiracy is one of the most commonly charged crimes in the federal system, though it appears not to be used frequently by state prosecutors. Marcus, Conspiracy: The Criminal Agreement in Theory and Practice, 65 Geo. L.J. 925, 947-948 (1977).

2. See Johnson, The Unnecessary Crime of Conspiracy, 61 Cal. L. Rev. 1137 (1973).

3. A husband and wife could not commit a conspiracy at common law because a married couple was considered to be one person under the law. This is no longer the law in most jurisdictions.

4. The general federal conspiracy statute, 18 U.S.C. 371, expressly requires proof of an overt act. But the Supreme Court held in *United States v. Shabani*, 513 U.S. 10 (1994), that 21 U.S.C. 846, the federal drug conspiracy statute, which is silent about an overt act, does not require one. The Court concluded that congressional silence concerning an overt act indicates that Congress intended to adopt the common law definition of conspiracy for drug conspiracies.

take a "substantial act" in furtherance of the conspiracy, pushing the threshold of criminality much closer to the target offense. The Model Penal Code requires an overt act *unless* the object crimes are serious felonies.[5]

The Common Law

The common law and early statutory definitions of conspiracy did not limit the object of the agreement to *crimes*. Rather, they included any act that was *unlawful* or *against public policy* or even *lawful* acts committed by *unlawful means*. These open-ended definitions created uncertainty in the criminal law. Criminal responsibility could attach for agreeing to do something with another (such as charging usurious rates of interest[6] or agreeing to bargain for wages as a group[7]) that, if done alone, would not be a crime. In short, common law conspiracy permits conviction for acts that are not expressly made criminal, creating serious risk of ex post facto punishment.

Thus, in the English case *Shaw v. Director of Public Prosecutions*,[8] the defendant's conviction for "conspiracy to corrupt public morals" for agreeing with others to publish a directory for prostitutes was upheld by the House of Lords even though prostitution was not a crime. A statute containing such a broad definitional term would probably be found unconstitutional in the United States as void for vagueness. (See Chapter 1.)

The Model Penal Code

The Model Penal Code, troubled by the expansive definition of conspiracy provided by the common law and by many early-twentieth-century American state statutes, requires that the object of the agreement must be a *crime* for conspiracy to be committed. Most states, though not necessarily using the specific language of the MPC, have followed its policy choice and require that the object of the agreement be a crime.

But beware! Some states still define conspiracy in the old-fashioned sweeping manner. California, for example, defines conspiracy as an agreement of two or more people "[t]o commit any act injurious to the public health, to public morals. . . ." Cal. Penal Code §182(a)(5).

---

5. MPC §5.03(5).

6. *Commonwealth v. Donoghue*, 250 Ky. 343, 63 S.W.2d 3, 89 A.L.R. 819 (1933).

7. *People v. Fisher*, 14 Wend. 2 (N.Y. 1835) (union members who organized to raise wages and refused to work until an employee working below union wages was discharged were found guilty of conspiracy against trade and commerce).

8. [1962] A.C. 220 (Eng.).

PUNISHMENT AND GRADING

The Common Law

At common law, conspiracy, like attempt, merged into the completed substantive offense. Consequently, conspirators could not be punished both for conspiracy and the target offense.

Today, however, in most jurisdictions conspiracy is a *separate* substantive offense. Unlike solicitation and attempt, conspiracy does not merge with the object crimes. The rationale supporting this antimerger rule is straightforward. Conspiracy criminalizes the act of agreeing to commit a crime and beginning to actually implement that agreement; the target offense punishes the separate behavior of actually committing the offense agreed upon. Thus, generally speaking, conspirators can be (1) convicted of *both* the crime of conspiracy and of target crimes actually committed in furtherance of the conspiracy, and (2) sentenced to consecutive (rather than concurrent) sentences for *both* conspiracy and the target offense.[9]

Conspiracy once was commonly punished with a fixed term without regard to the seriousness of the crime the conspirators planned to commit. Today, however, most jurisdictions either set the punishment at some term less than the object crime or follow the MPC.

The Model Penal Code

The Model Penal Code sets the punishment for conspiracy at the same grade and degree as the most serious object crime, except that a conspiracy to commit a capital offense or a felony of the first degree is punished as a felony of the second degree. MPC §5.05(1). The MPC considers a criminal group to be especially dangerous. Consequently, the deterrent impact of punishment must be harsh to be effective.[10] Critics of this approach argue that, if the conspirators have been arrested *before* they have accomplished

9. See *Callanan v. United States*, 364 U.S. 587 (1961) (upholding *consecutive* twelve-year sentences *each* for obstructing commerce by extortion and for conspiracy to commit the same offenses). There is some evidence, however, that defendants convicted of both conspiracy and the target offense are seldom punished for both. Marcus, supra n. 1, at 938.

10. Weschler, Jones & Korn, The Treatment of Inchoate Crimes in the Model Penal Code of the American Law Institute: Attempt, Solicitation, and Conspiracy, 61 Colum. L. Rev. 957 (1961). The authors argue that, to the extent that sentencing should focus on the offender's antisocial disposition and the demonstrated need for correction, there is little difference in the required sentences depending on the accomplishment or failure of the plan. Thus, there is no reason to treat conspiracy differently than the completed target offense. However, once sentences

their criminal goal, they should be punished *less severely* because they have not done as much harm.

The MPC does not permit conviction for both conspiracy and the target crime except in rare cases. Thus, in effect, conspiracy does merge into the target crime under the MPC. MPC §1.07(1)(b). It takes the view that, once a criminal group has committed the object crime, the group's dangerousness should be measured by the same punishment as provided for the object offense. However, a defendant may be convicted of as many target offenses as are committed in furtherance of the conspiracy whether as perpetrator or accomplice.

In unusual situations, however, the MPC does permit punishment for both conspiracy and target offenses. If the conspiracy had a goal of committing unspecified future crimes, the MPC permits the government to convict and punish its members for both the conspiracy and any object crimes committed or attempted. MPC §1.07(1)(b). (Note, however, that the MPC does not permit conviction for both conspiracy and an attempt to commit the target crime. MPC §5.05(3).)

THE SPECIAL ADVANTAGES OF CONSPIRACY FOR PROSECUTORS

Conspiracy affords prosecutors a number of significant advantages in trying criminal cases. Some of the more important ones are discussed below.

Choice of Venue

The Sixth Amendment to the Constitution provides that an accused has the right to trial "by an impartial jury of the state and district wherein the crime shall have been committed." This important constitutional protection requires the prosecutor to file charges and to try the case where the crime was committed.

The crime of conspiracy, however, is deemed to have been committed in any jurisdiction (or in the federal system in any district) in which any member of the conspiracy committed an act in furtherance of the conspiracy—even an act that was not itself a crime. This rule gives prosecutors, particularly federal prosecutors who often are dealing with conspiracies that they allege span several states, a tremendous tactical advantage. Frequently,

reach a certain level, the effectiveness of deterrence declines, so lesser punishment for the most serious crimes (like first-degree crimes) is more economical.

there will be more than one such venue where an act connected to the crime has allegedly been committed and where, consequently, the case can be tried.

Joint Trials

Because all members of the conspiracy are considered to have committed the same crime, co-conspirators may be tried together in a single trial. This is far more efficient than having to select a new jury and have a new trial for each defendant. However, joint trials can create serious problems, including "guilt by association." As Justice Jackson said in *Krulewitch v. United States*: "A co-defendant in a conspiracy trial occupies an uneasy seat. There generally will be evidence of wrongdoing by somebody. It is difficult for the individual to make his own case stand on its own merits in the minds of jurors who are ready to believe that birds of a feather are flocked together."[11]

Use of Hearsay Evidence

Hearsay evidence is a statement made by someone who is not actually testifying but is repeated by a testifying witness and offered as stating the truth. Subject to a number of exceptions (many of which you will puzzle over in a course on evidence), the use of "hearsay" to prove something is generally prohibited because the person who made the original statement was not under oath when he made it and cannot be cross-examined in the courtroom. Thus, the truthfulness of the person who actually made the statement cannot be tested adequately.

Under the law of conspiracy, however, each co-conspirator is deemed to have authorized other members of the conspiracy to act and speak on her behalf. Thus, statements that co-conspirators make in furtherance of the conspiracy can be admitted later at trial to prove the defendant entered into a conspiracy. This is an exception to the hearsay rule.

The logical dilemma posed by this rule is clear: Evidence that is admissible only if a conspiracy exists will be admitted to prove that a conspiracy exists! This is a classic case of "bootstrapping."

Should courts first require the prosecutor to use nonhearsay evidence to prove beyond a reasonable doubt that a conspiracy exists before admitting hearsay testimony under the conspiracy exception? This approach, though preserving the logical premise that hearsay is admissible only if there is a conspiracy, might seriously hamper prosecutors' effective use of conspiracy. It can also disrupt the presentation of evidence in a coherent chronological sequence.

---

11. 336 U.S. 440, 454 (1949).

The Supreme Court resolved this question for the federal courts in *Bourjaily v. United States.*[12] The Court decided that the use of the co-conspirator hearsay exception is a question of evidence to be decided by a judge under the Federal Rules of Evidence. A hearsay statement by a co-conspirator is admissible if the prosecutor, using both nonhearsay evidence *and* hearsay evidence, first proves to the judge's satisfaction by a preponderance of the evidence that a conspiracy exists. The jury may then use the hearsay evidence in determining whether a conspiracy existed. Thus, the jury will usually hear the hearsay evidence before its admissibility is determined. If the judge concludes that the prosecutor has not proven the existence of a conspiracy, the jury will be instructed to disregard this evidence. (This may be like asking the jury not to look at the elephants sitting quietly in the corner!) Otherwise, jurors may use the hearsay statement in reaching their verdict.

Responsibility for Crimes Committed by Co-Conspirators

The Common Law

Under the "*Pinkerton* rule" (so-called because it was confirmed by the Supreme Court in *Pinkerton v. United States*[13]), each co-conspirator is responsible for

1. any *reasonably foreseeable* crime committed by a co-conspirator
2. in furtherance of the conspiracy.

This rule is an extremely powerful tool in prosecutors' hands.

First, it essentially establishes vicarious liability for every member of a conspiracy for all foreseeable crimes without requiring the government to establish accessorial liability. (See Chapter 14.) The prosecutor does not have to prove that the defendant *intended* to aid and abet or otherwise facilitate or encourage the commission of these crimes; she only has to prove that they were *foreseeable*. Under the *Pinkerton* rule, each conspirator, by entering into the conspiratorial agreement, authorizes other members of the conspiracy to act as his agent to commit crimes necessary to implement their criminal objective. In turn, each conspirator is responsible for these crimes. The *Pinkerton* rule works like a kind of automatic "cash register" that rings up added punishment for each member of a conspiracy even when, as in the *Pinkerton* case itself, the defendant probably did not know of many of the crimes committed by his co-conspirator and certainly could not have assisted him because the defendant was in prison!

12. 483 U.S. 171 (1987).
13. 328 U.S. 640 (1946).

Second, the *Pinkerton* rule establishes vicarious liability based on *negligence*, which is the lowest level of culpability. The prosecutor does not have to prove that the defendant knew or recklessly disregarded the fact that his co-conspirator might commit specific crimes in furtherance of the conspiracy. She need only prove that the crimes were *reasonably foreseeable*—that is, that the defendant *should* have anticipated their possible commission. Under the *Pinkerton* rule, a conspirator may be convicted on a lower degree of culpability, negligence, than that often required to convict the person who commits the object offense. (See Chapter 4.)

Supporters argue that this rule is necessary so that the masterminds who organize and control sophisticated criminal conspiracies are held responsible for crimes committed by their foot soldiers. Without it, these "generals" would usually be insulated from any criminal responsibility for these target crimes. Critics of the rule assert that guilt is personal under our criminal justice system. Imposing punishment for substantive crimes in which the defendant did not participate or assist in some way runs contrary to that fundamental premise.

The *Pinkerton* doctrine can sweep broadly, making members of a conspiracy responsible for serious crimes "not within the originally intended scope of the conspiracy." An example is *United States v. Alvarez.*[14] Here the court affirmed the murder conviction of several members of a drug conspiracy for the death of a federal undercover agent after a proposed drug sale erupted into a gun fight in which the defendants were not personally involved. The court held that, though the murder "was not within the originally intended scope of the conspiracy," it was reasonably foreseeable by the defendants because the deal involved a large volume of drugs with a high value. Relying on this fact, the court concluded that the defendants "*must* have been aware of the *likelihood* that (1) at least some of their number would be carrying weapons, and (2) that deadly force would be used, if necessary, to protect the conspirators' interests" (emphasis added). Moreover, each of the defendants played a significant part in the transaction, such as acting as a lookout; introducing the principals and being present during some of the negotiations; or letting the participants use a motel room and translating during some of the negotiations.

The *Pinkerton* rule imposes criminal responsibility on co-conspirators for contingent crimes to which they did not agree but which, under the circumstances, might well be necessary. Thus, the specific terms of the agreement do not set the limit for each member's criminal responsibility. The *Pinkerton* rule, however, is not retroactive. A person who joins a conspiracy is not responsible for crimes *already* committed by co-conspirators.

---

14. 755 F.2d 830 (11th Cir. 1985).

The Model Penal Code

The MPC rejects the *Pinkerton* rule because the scope of vicarious responsibility theoretically possible under this rule is too broad. Consequently, a co-conspirator must satisfy the MPC elements for accessorial liability (set forth in §2.06), which are more narrow than the common law (see Chapter 14). This means that conspiracy by itself is not a basis for establishing complicity for all reasonably foreseeable substantive offenses committed in furtherance of the conspiracy. Instead, the MPC asks "whether the defendant *solicited* commission of the particular offense or *aided*, or *agreed* or *attempted* to *aid*, in its commission" (emphasis added).[15] A number of states, including New York, follow the MPC in rejecting the *Pinkerton* rule.[16]

DURATION

How long does a conspiracy last? By its very nature, conspiracy is an ongoing offense; that is, the parties agree to commit a crime, and then usually they must take steps over a period of time to accomplish their criminal objective. The statute of limitations does not begin to run until the conspiracy terminates.

The Common Law

A conspiracy usually terminates when all of its objectives have been achieved or when all of its members have abandoned all of its objectives.

Extending the Life of a Conspiracy

Prosecutors have been resourceful in trying to extend the life of a conspiracy beyond the accomplishment of its criminal objectives, usually to make full use of the special prosecutorial advantages we discussed earlier. (See pages 377-379, supra.) In *Krulewitch v. United States*,[17] for example, the government argued that conspirators always agree, at least implicitly, to conceal their

15. Model Penal Code and Commentaries, Comment to §2.06(3), at 307 (1985). Under the MPC, the act of conspiracy may be used as *evidence* of solicitation or aiding and abetting, but it cannot establish vicarious responsibility as a *matter of law*. Id. at 309.
16. *People v. McGee*, 49 N.Y.2d 48, 399 N.E.2d 1177 (1979).
17. 336 U.S. 440 (1949).

conspiracy even after they have accomplished its objectives. Relying on the conspiracy hearsay exception, the prosecutors sought to introduce against one conspirator the statement of another conspirator made several months *after* the target offense of the conspiracy had been completed.

The Supreme Court held that such testimony was inadmissible because the conspiracy in this case had terminated once the object crime had been committed. Subsequent case law permits the government to use hearsay testimony made after the normal end of a conspiracy only if it can prove an *express* agreement to conceal the conspiracy or if it can show that ongoing concealment was essential to the conspiracy's success. This type of proof is usually very difficult.[18]

The Model Penal Code

The Model Penal Code considers conspiracy to be a "continuing" crime, beginning when the conspiracy is formed (see the Overview to this chapter) and ending when its criminal objective has been committed or when the agreement has been abandoned by the defendant and those with whom he has conspired. MPC §5.03(7)(a). (Remember, however, that a conspiracy can be charged and prosecuted *immediately* once an agreement and, under some conspiracy statutes, an overt act have been committed. See pages 374-375, supra.) The MPC also presumes abandonment if no conspirator does an overt act in furtherance of the conspiracy during the applicable statute of limitations.

A conspiracy is terminated for an individual defendant if he abandons the conspiracy by advising his co-conspirators of his abandonment or informing law enforcement of the conspiracy's existence and his participation in it. MPC §5.03(7)(c). (See pages 399-400, infra, for a more complete discussion of this topic.)

Consequences of Termination

As we saw earlier (see pages 377-379, supra), conspiracy affords prosecutors enormous evidentiary, procedural, and substantive advantages, including choice of venue, joint trials, hearsay exceptions, and responsibility for substantive offenses. How fully prosecutors can exploit these advantages and avoid other legal constraints, such as the statute of limitations, depends in part on how long the conspiracy exists.

18. See *State v. Rivenbark*, 311 Md. 147, 533 A.2d 271 (1987), and cases cited therein.

THE MENS REA OF CONSPIRACY

The Common Law

Conspiracy is a "specific intent" crime at common law. First, the defendant must *intend* to agree with someone else. Merely approving of or seeking another's participation in a criminal purpose does not satisfy the mental state for conspiracy (though it may trigger criminal responsibility for solicitation (see Chapter 11) or as an accomplice (see Chapter 14)). Second, the defendant must *intend* to commit the offense that is the object of the conspiracy. Thus, the defendant must intend that the group, or at least one member of the group, will commit all elements of the crime agreed on (or, in jurisdictions that have the broader definition of conspiracy, all elements of the acts that are unlawful or against public policy).

Act and Result

Because conspiracy is a specific intent crime, it can require a *higher* mens rea than the crime the parties agree to commit. Recall Example 3 from the Attempt materials (see page 355). Change the facts slightly so that Max and Mollie agree to burn down the apartment building in order to collect the insurance, hoping that no one will be injured. If Mollie subsequently sets the time-delayed fuse *and* causes a fire that both destroys the building and causes the death of a tenant, both Max and Mollie could be found guilty of conspiracy to commit arson and guilty of murder under either extreme risk creation or felony murder. Neither, however, is guilty of conspiracy to commit murder because, when they agreed, they did not have the specific intent to cause the death of another human being. Thus, the mens rea requirement for conspiracy can be higher than the mens rea of the crime that is committed as a result of the agreement. If, however, both Max and Mollie had agreed to kill an occupant of the building by setting fire to it, they could be convicted of conspiring to commit murder.

Circumstances

Another interesting question is whether the specific intent requirement of conspiracy includes the circumstance elements of the target crime. Put differently, must the government prove that the defendants intended the circumstance elements of the target crime or must it only prove the same mens rea toward a circumstance element for conspiracy as that required for conviction of the target offense?

This question was raised in *United States v. Feola*.[19] In that case, several defendants agreed to sell heroin to prospective purchasers. Being overly ambitious (and perhaps a little lazy), they planned to pass off powdered sugar (no kidding!) as heroin, hoping to "rip off" the purchasers. If the purchasers discovered that the "heroin" was fake, the defendants had agreed to simply take their money by armed force.

Unfortunately for the defendants and unknown to them, their naive "buyers" were actually undercover federal narcotics officers. During the course of this bungled sale, one of the defendants assaulted one of the buyers without knowing he was a federal officer. Subsequently, all the defendants were charged with and convicted of both assault on a federal officer and of *conspiring* to assault a federal officer while engaged in the performance of his official duties.

The Second Circuit reversed the conspiracy convictions, holding that, although the substantive offense did not require intent as to the victim's status as a federal law officer, the federal conspiracy statute did.[20] The court held that the government must prove that the conspirators *intended* to assault a person they knew was a federal officer while engaged in the performance of his official duties because conspiracy is a specific intent offense. Failure to require such proof would expand the terms of their original agreement beyond those agreed to by the conspirators. Because the defendants did not know that their victims were federal officers, they could not intend to assault them while they were performing their official duties.

The Supreme Court reversed and affirmed the conspiracy convictions, holding that the federal conspiracy statute only requires the prosecutor to establish the same mens rea toward this circumstance element (i.e., the victim was a federal officer performing his official duties) as that required for conviction of the substantive crime.[21] By disregarding the generally accepted understanding that conspiracy is a "specific intent" crime, this case establishes that the federal conspiracy statute does not require any higher proof toward a circumstance element of the agreed-upon crime than that required for conviction of that crime.

The Model Penal Code

The MPC is not as precise on the mens rea or culpability elements as one might expect. Section 5.03 states only that the agreement must have been

19. 420 U.S. 671 (1975).

20. *United States v. Alsondo*, 486 F.2d 1339 (2d Cir. 1973).

21. *United States v. Feola*, 420 U.S. 671 (1975). A good argument can be made that the federal status of the officers is not a circumstance element of the offense but only a jurisdictional element. See Chapter 4.

made "with the purpose of promoting or facilitating" the commission of a crime.

Conduct and Result

However, the Commentaries to §5.03 state that the MPC requires *purpose* as to the conduct and result elements to establish conspiracy *regardless* of what the substantive crime requires. Thus, if the target offense is the sale of narcotics, the defendant must act with the purpose of promoting or facilitating the sale of narcotics. Likewise, the Commentaries state that if the target offense is defined in terms of a prohibited result (such as homicide, which requires the death of a human being), the MPC requires that the defendant must act with the purpose of promoting or facilitating that result.

However, consider the following case. Suppose that a defendant conspires to sell what he thinks is heroin but is actually crack cocaine. The sale of heroin is punishable by a five-year sentence, and the sale of crack cocaine is punishable by a ten-year sentence. Conspiracy is punishable by a term one-half as long as the target offense of the conspiracy. If the defendant is arrested and convicted of conspiracy, what is his sentence?

Under *Feola*, whether the defendant could be punished for conspiring to sell crack cocaine would depend on whether the substantive offense required him to act with the purpose of selling crack cocaine. Obviously, he could not have this purpose on these facts because he thought he was selling heroin.

According to the MPC Commentaries, however, the prosecution would have to prove that the defendant acted with the purpose of conspiring to sell crack cocaine regardless of what the target offense required. This approach in effect requires the prosecution to prove "specific intent" for conspiracy even though it might not be required for the target offense.

Circumstances

Section 5.03 is also silent concerning what culpability toward circumstances is required. The Commentaries add that the conspiracy provision "does not attempt to solve the problem by explicit formulation."[22] Rather, the MPC concluded that the matter was best resolved by the courts.

If "purpose" toward circumstances is required to convict for conspiracy, then under §2.02(2)(a)(ii), knowledge or belief that the circumstance exists is sufficient. This is so because §2.02(2)(a)(ii), the general culpability provision in the MPC, provides that "purposely" with respect to

22. Model Penal Code and Commentaries, Comment to §5.03, at 413 (1985).

circumstances is satisfied if the defendant "is aware of the existence of such circumstances or he believes or hopes they exist."

Purpose or Knowledge When Providing Goods and Services

A special mens rea problem occurs when one of the alleged parties to the conspiracy provides goods and services, such as a telephone answering service for prostitutes or ingredients for the manufacture of illegal goods. Can the supplier be convicted of conspiracy solely because he *knows* his goods or services are being used for a criminal goal? Or must the prosecutor prove that the defendant provided the goods or services with the *purpose* to advance the criminal object? Cases reach contrary conclusions, but the majority rule appears to be that purpose is required for a conspiracy conviction.

Case Law

In *People v. Lauria*[23] the government charged the owner of a telephone answering service and three prostitutes with conspiracy to commit prostitution. Lauria, the owner of the answering service, readily admitted that he knew some of his customers used his answering service for prostitution. However, he denied that he intended to further their criminal business. The court held that the government must prove intent; mere knowledge was insufficient. The court went on to explain that a jury may infer intent from knowledge, especially where the defendant has a "stake in the venture." A stake in the venture, in turn, may be established by showing that (1) the defendant charged excessive prices; (2) there is no legitimate use for the goods or services (e.g., selling gambling equipment in a state that does not allow gambling); or (3) the volume of defendant's business with the buyer is grossly disproportionate to any legitimate demand for his goods or services or constitutes a substantial percentage of the defendant's business.[24]

In *People v. Roy*, a companion case with facts very similar to *Lauria*, the court upheld liability because there was evidence the answering service operator actively participated in the prostitution business by arranging the sharing of customers by two prostitutes who used the service. The court concluded that this constituted "promotion of a criminal enterprise."[25]

Requiring *purpose* rather than *knowledge* maximizes the freedom of businesses to pursue their individual economic gain rather than imposing a

23. 251 Cal. App. 2d 471, 59 Cal. Rptr. 628 (Cal. Ct. App. 1967).
24. *Direct Sales Co. v. United States*, 319 U.S. 703 (1943).
25. 59 Cal. Rptr. 636, 641 (1967).

more demanding duty on them to prevent their products or services from being used to commit crime. It is also consistent with the criminal law's general policy to not look beyond the last responsible moral agent. The purchaser of the goods and services must still decide whether she will use them to commit a crime.

On the other hand, some courts consider knowledge that another will use the provider's goods or services to commit a crime sufficient to impose criminal liability for conspiracy, especially when a serious crime, such as a felony, is involved. Even the *Lauria* court, in dictum, indicated it might hold that knowledge rather than purpose is sufficient to convict of conspiracy when a serious crime such as kidnapping or the distribution of heroin is involved.[26] Critics respond that this rule is too burdensome on businesses and that, in most cases, the purchaser will simply obtain the goods or services from someone else who will not know of their intended use. Others argue that causation—simply being a link in a chain of events that enables someone to commit a serious crime—is not the gravamen of conspiracy. Rather, conspiracy requires a purposeful union of wills with the intent to accomplish a crime.

The Model Penal Code

The Model Penal Code requires that a provider of goods or services must have "the *purpose* of promoting or facilitating" the commission of the crime. Mere knowledge that his services or goods are being used by another to commit a crime will not satisfy this culpability requirement. MPC §5.03.[27]

Note: Whether a person who provides goods or services to someone he knows will use them to commit a crime can be convicted as an accomplice or for criminal facilitation under the MPC raises the same general issue! See Chapter 14.

THE ACTUS REUS OF CONSPIRACY

Agreement

The Common Law

The actus reus of conspiracy at common law was an *agreement* between *two or more parties* to commit a criminal or an unlawful act or a lawful act by

26. 251 Cal. App. 2d 471, 480, 59 Cal. Rptr. 628 (1967).

27. Model Penal Code and Commentaries, Comment to §5.03, at 404 (1985).

unlawful means. Historically, an "overt act" in furtherance of the conspiracy was *not* required. However, it is important to remember that modern common law jurisdictions typically require an overt act.

Though a conspiracy may involve an express agreement, perhaps verbal or written, in which the parties explicitly communicate their accord, it can also be indirect. What is required is a shared determination to accomplish a goal that is punishable by the applicable conspiracy statute. The parties do not have to know all of its details, but they do have to know its basic purpose.

A person can become a party to a conspiracy without knowing the exact identity of all of its members or without having direct dealings with them. One can also join a conspiracy *after* its initial formation. However, the late-arriver, though guilty of conspiracy, is not responsible for substantive offenses committed by her co-conspirators in furtherance of the conspiracy *before* she joined. Thus, the *Pinkerton* rule is not retroactive.[28] (See pages 379-381, supra.)

The difficult question is not *what* must be proven—an agreement—but *how* it can be proven. Parties to a conspiracy might well discuss their plans in some detail and orally agree to the important points. Typically, however, when three people decide to rob a bank, they usually do not sign a "Bank Robbery Contract" and have it notarized—perhaps because they can't write or, more likely, because they fear such incriminating evidence may come back to haunt them at trial. Thus, prosecutors are unlikely to obtain a written document that embodies the terms of the agreement or its signatories. Unless one of the conspirators later turns state's evidence and becomes a witness for the prosecution or, better yet, law enforcement has the good fortune of obtaining a warrant and placing an electronic recording device where the parties entered into their agreement, it is usually difficult for the prosecution to present direct evidence of the agreement.

The law accommodates this difficulty by letting prosecutors use indirect evidence to prove the existence of a conspiracy. This evidence often consists of aiding and abetting or coordinated action by the parties from which the jury is asked to *infer* a *prior* agreement. The logic of such evidence is that group conduct is usually the result of a previous agreement. Neither aiding and abetting nor concerted action, however, necessarily establishes a prior agreement because one can assist another in committing a crime without such an agreement. (See *State v. Tally*, page 390, infra.) Moreover, proving an earlier agreement from a later criminal act runs the risk of collapsing the substantive offense into the prior criminal agreement.

Permitting proof of an agreement by circumstantial evidence, though necessary, requires careful implementation so that it does not seriously

28. *United States v. Blackmon*, 839 F.2d 900 (2d Cir. 1988).

weaken the due process protection afforded criminal defendants. As one commentator has cautioned: "[I]n their zeal to emphasize that the agreement need not be proved directly, the courts sometimes neglect to say that it need be proved at all."[29] Ensuring that the prosecution establishes the agreement by sufficient probative evidence is especially important because the "conspiracy doctrine comes closest to making a state of mind the occasion for preventive action against those who threaten society but who have come nowhere near carrying out the threat."[30]

In some cases, the evidence of agreement is quite minimal. For example, in *United States v. Alvarez*,[31] government undercover agents agreed to purchase from two conspirators marijuana to be flown into Florida from South America. Speaking in Spanish near the proposed off-loading site, the agents asked the two about Alvarez, the person driving their truck. They replied that he would be at the site when the marijuana would be off-loaded. One agent turned to Alvarez and asked if he would be at the site to help off-load. Alvarez nodded his head indicating "yes," smiled, and asked the DEA agent if he was going to be on the plane when it arrived to unload the marijuana. After some further conversation with the original two conspirators concerning the details of the plane's arrival and unloading, they and Alvarez were arrested and charged with conspiracy to import drugs into the United States.

A three-judge panel initially reversed Alvarez's conviction for conspiracy, holding that this evidence was insufficient to establish that the defendant had joined in an agreement to import drugs. The court noted that a defendant "does not join in a conspiracy merely by participating in a substantive offense, or by association with persons who are members of the conspiracy."[32] The court was concerned that Alvarez's expressed willingness to assist in the commission of the conspiracy's target offense was also used to establish that he had previously joined the agreement to commit that offense.

Subsequently, an en banc decision[33] of the Fifth Circuit reversed the panel decision and affirmed the conviction. It noted that a conspirator can join a conspiracy after its initial inception. Moreover, Alvarez knew criminal activity was planned and that a conspiracy had been formed to import drugs and unload them at this site. There was also direct evidence that Alvarez planned to help unload the drugs; a jury could infer from this fact that he must have agreed at an earlier time to help unload. Alternatively, in

---

29. Note, Developments in the Law—Criminal Conspiracy, 72 Harv. L. Rev. 920, 933 (1959).

30. Goldstein, Conspiracy to Defraud the United States, 68 Yale L.J. 405, 406 (1959).

31. 610 F.2d 1250 (5th Cir. 1980), conviction aff'd, 625 F.2d 1196 (1980) (en banc).

32. 610 F.2d at 1255.

33. An en banc opinion is one in which all sitting members of the Circuit Court of Appeals for the particular circuit participate. In the initial *Alvarez* decision, three judges participated.

assuring the others that he would help unload, a jury could find that Alvarez was doing an act to further the conspiracy. Consequently, there was sufficient evidence from which a jury could find that Alvarez had intentionally joined the conspiracy.

The Model Penal Code

The Model Penal Code takes the same basic approach as the common law; agreement is the core concept of conspiracy. The MPC provides a more thorough definition to include two types of agreement: (1) the defendant or another co-conspirator will commit, attempt to commit, or solicit a crime, or (2) the defendant agrees with another to aid him in the planning or commission of a crime, an attempt to commit it, or its solicitation. Under the MPC, a person is guilty of conspiracy if he agrees (a) with other persons that any one of them will commit, attempt, or solicit a crime, or (b) to be an accessory to the crime by facilitating its commission. MPC §5.03(1)(a)(b). Note, however, that aid *without agreement* does not constitute conspiracy under the MPC.

In *State v. Tally*,[34] the defendant tried to aid murderers by preventing the delivery of a warning telegram to the victim. He would not be guilty of committing conspiracy under the MPC because there was no agreement or concert of action between Tally and the others. Tally could be convicted of aiding and abetting but not conspiracy. Otherwise, anyone who aided and abetted could be convicted of conspiracy and subjected to the broad vicarious liability and additional punishment for conspiracy. Most states have adopted this approach.

Overt Act

In General

Unlike the common law, which required only an agreement for the actus reus of conspiracy, most modern statutes also require that *one member* of the conspiracy commit an *overt act* in furtherance of the conspiracy for the crime to be committed.[35] The overt act demonstrates that the conspiracy has

---

34. 102 Ala. 25, 15 So. 722 (1894). See Chapter 14 for a more detailed account of this case.

35. Sometimes conspiracy statutes can vary within a jurisdiction. The general federal conspiracy statute, 18 U.S.C. 371, expressly requires an overt act. However, 21 U.S.C. 846, the federal drug conspiracy statute, does not. *United States v. Shabani*, 513 U.S. 10 (1994). See also *Whitfield v. United States*, 543 U.S. 209 (2005). If a federal statute is silent, no overt act element should be read into it. A settled principle of statutory construction is that, absent a contrary indication, Congress intended to adopt the common-law definition of statutory terms (in this case "conspiracy").

gone beyond the purely "mental state" and has reached the implementation stage. However, the overt act can be an act that, by itself, would be lawful and innocent such as renting a van or buying a ladder. It does not have to be an act that would come anywhere near satisfying the actus reus of attempt, such as an "unequivocal act" or a "substantial step." A few states do require that at least one member of the conspiracy must take a "substantial step" in furtherance of the conspiracy.[36] This usually has the same meaning as it does in attempt—an act that "strongly corroborates the actor's criminal purpose." (See Chapter 12.)

The Model Penal Code

The Model Penal Code only requires that the defendant or any other party to the conspiracy must commit an overt act if the substantive offense is relatively minor—that is, a felony of the third degree or a misdemeanor. If the substantive offense is serious, a felony of the first or second degree, no overt act in furtherance of the conspiracy is required. MPC §5.03(5). When a serious crime is the object of the agreement, the MPC essentially adopts the common law actus reus requirement that the act of agreeing is itself the actus reus of conspiracy. The MPC concludes that the act of agreeing is "concrete and unambiguous." Thus, there is much less danger of incorrectly interpreting innocent or equivocal behavior as criminal conduct. Also, the act of combining wills makes it more likely, both psychologically and practically, that the target offense will be committed.[37]

THE SCOPE OF THE AGREEMENT OR HOW MANY CONSPIRACIES?

Perhaps the two most perplexing questions to be resolved in conspiracy cases are (1) how many conspiracies are there? and (2) who is a party to which conspiracy? The answers to these two questions are extremely important because they determine a number of other significant legal issues, including choice of venue, propriety of a joint trial, admissibility of hearsay testimony, satisfaction of the overt act requirement, and liability for any substantive offense committed in furtherance of the conspiracy.

However, setting forth the black letter law is much easier than applying it, as the case law makes clear. The law of conspiracy permits the fact finder

36. See, e.g., Wash. Rev. Code Ann. §9A.28.040 (West 2012).

37. Model Penal Code and Commentaries, Comment to §5.03, at 388 (1985).

to convict only those individuals who have entered into the same agreement. Yet, as we saw earlier, there is seldom tidy evidence available clearly establishing who those parties are. To the contrary, there is often a large cast of characters involved in committing a number of similar crimes. Often, individual members of the cast deal directly with some characters but not with others. Unfortunately, the case law has developed some rather primitive analytic approaches to ascertaining who is a member of a particular conspiracy.

Single Agreement with Multiple Criminal Objectives

One agreement establishes one conspiracy, even though there may be several criminal objectives of that agreement.[38] Thus, if *A*, *B*, and *C* agree to rob one bank each day for the next five days, there is only one conspiracy—even though the conspirators have agreed to commit five robberies. If there are multiple agreements, however, then there are multiple conspiracies even if each has only a single criminal objective. So if *A*, *B*, and *C* agree to rob a bank and do so and then, elated with their success, agree to rob another bank, there are two conspiracies.

Single or Multiple Agreements?

The Wheel and Spokes Approach

In *Kotteakos v. United States*,[39] the government charged and convicted 32 defendants of participating in a *single* conspiracy with Simon Brown. The evidence showed that over a period of time, each of the defendants and Brown had fraudulently obtained loans to be insured by a federal agency. The defendants, on the other hand, claimed that each of them had formed a separate conspiracy with Brown but not with each other. Thus, there were a number of distinct conspiracies rather than one large one.[40]

Needless to say, all the defendants had a tremendous stake in how this question was resolved. Under the government's view, each of the 32 defendants could be punished under the *Pinkerton* rule for each of the fraudulent loans obtained by the others. Under the defendants' view, Brown could be found guilty on 32 separate counts of conspiracy, each with one co-conspirator.

---

38. *Braverman v. United States*, 317 U.S. 49 (1942).

39. 328 U.S. 750 (1946).

40. "As the Government puts it, the pattern was 'that of separate spokes meeting at a common center' though, we may add, without the rim of the wheel to enclose the spokes." Id. at 755.

The Supreme Court determined that, though these defendants committed similar crimes with the same individual, Brown, there was no connection or relationship between the defendants. The pattern of their behavior looked like many spokes of a wheel with a common center (Brown) but without a common rim. Thus, the Court held that there were a number of conspiracies rather than a single conspiracy.

Therefore, committing the same type of crime with a common participant is not necessarily sufficient to establish a single agreement. In *Kotteakos,* there was no interdependence or even communication among the defendants; they did not depend on one another for their individual success. Nor was there any division of labor or other cooperation that facilitated a common goal.

Contrast *Kotteakos* with *Interstate Circuit, Inc. v. United States.*[41] A manager of Interstate, a chain of theaters, sent a letter to each of eight movie distributors (who together controlled 75 percent of the first-run film market in the country), with copies to the others, demanding that theaters charge a minimum price and not permit first-run movies to be shown on a double feature with another feature film as a condition of Interstate's continued showing of their movies. Subsequently, each distributor complied with Interstate's terms.

The trial court found that the distributors had agreed with one another and with Interstate to fix prices in violation of the Sherman Antitrust Act because each of the distributors knew that the others had received the letter and because concerted action of all was necessary for the price-fixing to be effective. The Supreme Court upheld the convictions, concluding: "It is elementary that an unlawful conspiracy may be and often is formed without simultaneous action or *agreement* on the part of the conspirators" (emphasis added).[42]

This case comes perilously close to *dispensing* with the need to prove an agreement rather than letting the government use circumstantial evidence to establish an agreement. It also demonstrates how the loose definition of conspiracy often applied in antitrust cases poses the risk of being applied in more traditional criminal cases. Finally, the case establishes that co-conspirators can enter into a criminal agreement by concerted action alone if they have the necessary knowledge.

The Chain Approach

Blumenthal v. United States[43] involved a scheme whereby an unknown owner sent shipments of liquor to Weiss and Goldsmith. In turn, Weiss and Goldsmith

41. 306 U.S. 208 (1939).
42. Id. at 227.
43. 332 U.S. 539 (1947).

agreed with three other defendants (Feigenbaum, Blumenthal, and Abel) that these three would sell the liquor to various taverns at prices exceeding the ceiling set by law. There was no evidence that these three defendants knew of the unknown owner or of his part in the plan. Nonetheless, the Supreme Court affirmed the trial court's finding there was only one conspiracy including all six individuals.

The Court concluded the case was not like *Kotteakos*, saying:

> The scheme was in fact the same scheme; the salesmen knew or must have known that others unknown to them were sharing in so large a project; and it hardly can be sufficient to relieve them [of responsibility] that they did not know, when they joined the scheme, who those people were or exactly the parts they were playing in carrying out the common design and object of all. By their separate agreements, if such they were, they became parties to the larger common plan, joined together by their knowledge of its essential features and broad scope, though not of its exact limits, and by their common single goal [emphasis added].[44]

The Court analogized each of the defendants as links in a common chain, each essential to the ultimate task of selling the liquor at illegal prices. Where there is a common objective that, because of complexity, magnitude, or other factors, requires the attributes of collective criminal behavior, courts are more likely to find a single conspiracy rather than a number of conspiracies.

However, not all behavior that initially looks like the result of a single agreement will support that finding. In the Woody Allen movie *Take the Money and Run*, two groups of would-be bank robbers enter a bank at the same time, each trying to rob it. An observer seeing this scene might well conclude that, because all of the robbers enter the bank and start to rob it simultaneously, everyone is a party to the same agreement and, therefore, there is one conspiracy. However, the two groups soon start arguing with each other about who was there first and which one has the "right" to rob the bank. As unrealistic and farcical as this example is, this additional evidence establishes that there were two conspiracies at work here, each with a different membership.

Wheel and Chain Conspiracies

United States v. Bruno concerned a complicated drug-smuggling operation involving four groups.[45] One group imported the drugs into the country and sold them to middlemen, who in turn distributed them to two

---

44. Id. at 558.

45. 105 F.2d 921 (2d Cir.), rev'd on other grounds, 308 U.S. 287 (1939).

groups of retailers, one in New York and one in Louisiana. The government charged them all with one conspiracy. The defendants claimed that there were at least three conspiracies: one between the importers and the middlemen; another between the middlemen and the New York retailers; and a third between the middlemen and the Louisiana retailers. Though there was no evidence of communication or cooperation between the two retail groups in New York and Louisiana or between these groups and the importers, the court affirmed the finding of a single conspiracy involving all four groups. It found that the importers knew that the middlemen must in turn sell to retailers and, conversely, the retailers must have known their distributor bought from an importer. Thus, everyone could be found to have embarked on a common venture whose success depended on the participation of all.

The Model Penal Code

In General

Under the Model Penal Code, the identity and scope of a conspiracy are determined by the combined operation of §5.03(1), (2), and (3). The MPC adopts a *unilateral* approach to conspiracy. It looks at each individual defendant and asks *with whom did she agree* to commit a *common criminal objective*. MPC §5.03(1). If the defendant knows that a person with whom she has conspired to commit a crime has also agreed with a third person to commit the *same* crime, then the defendant has agreed with both of them. MPC §5.03(2). Thus, the MPC determines the scope of a conspiracy for *each* defendant by asking with whom each defendant agreed to commit the same target offense. This approach, based on personal culpability and shared criminal objectives, can result in different conclusions for each defendant.

The MPC also provides that each person has entered into a single conspiracy even if there are multiple criminal objectives as long as the "crimes are the object of the same agreement or continuous conspiratorial relationship." MPC §5.03(3).

The Wheel and Chain Approach

The MPC would require a different analytic approach in the *Bruno* case and could produce a different result. In that case there were two distinct crimes: importing drugs and selling drugs. As to each defendant, the MPC asks whether and with whom did he conspire to commit *each* of these crimes? Only if *both* of these crimes were the object of the same agreement or conspiratorial relationship among *all* parties would there be a single conspiracy. As the Commentaries note, "it would be possible to find . . . that the smugglers conspired to commit the illegal sales of the retailers, but that the retailers did not conspire to commit the importing of the smugglers."[46]

When applying the MPC, look at each possible conspirator *individually*. Decide with whom she has agreed to commit a specific crime or crimes. This will determine what conspiracy charge may be brought against her.

Whatever the applicable law, you will find it very useful to actually outline the relationship of the various actors in analyzing both a real life situation and a criminal law exam question. Simply characterizing the group as a "wheel with (or without) a rim" or as a "chain" does not necessarily provide the correct answer, though this will help provide a picture of the actors and their roles. Instead, keep in mind this fundamental question: Who agreed to carry out the common criminal goal? This question, in turn, is often answered by a functional analysis of the group. Even if they did not know of each other's identity, did each know of the others' existence? Was each person useful in accomplishing a common goal? Did the success of the venture depend on each of them carrying out their task successfully? Was there communication and cooperation between or among the parties? Were the other characteristics of group criminality present: a division of labor, specialization, reinforcement of wills?

PARTIES TO A CONSPIRACY

The Common Law's Bilateral Approach

The common law required an agreement between two or more guilty persons. This approach has been called the "bilateral approach" to conspiracy. The logic of requiring at least two guilty parties for a conspiracy (sometimes called the "plurality" requirement) is inherent in the meaning of agreement. Usually, it takes two people to "agree."

Thus, at common law, if a defendant agreed to commit a crime with a legally insane person or with an undercover police officer who did not intend to commit the substantive offense, there was no agreement between two or more guilty individuals, and, thus, no conspiracy. Though prosecutors have occasionally tried to convict the defendant of attempted conspiracy in such cases, most courts have not been very sympathetic. In their view, solicitation is the proper charge. (See Chapter 11.) The federal courts have adopted the bilateral approach to conspiracy.[47]

Contemporary statutes that adopt the bilateral approach will often use definitional terms like those used by California. Its statute begins with "If

46. Model Penal Code and Commentaries, Comment to §5.03, at 427-428 (1985).
47. *United States v. Escobar de Bright*, 742 F.2d 1196 (9th Cir. 1984).

two or more persons conspire. . . ."[48] Be on the lookout for definitional terms that require at least two persons to agree or to conspire, because they often indicate the jurisdiction has adopted the bilateral approach.

The bilateral approach to conspiracy makes sense if conspiracy is viewed primarily as a charge that strikes at bona fide group criminal activity. If the defendant has agreed with an undercover police officer to commit a crime, there is no genuine criminal collaboration at work and the special dangers of a group are not present. (Indeed, in such a case, law enforcement is well positioned to ensure that the criminal objective is *never* going to be achieved.) However, the plurality requirement can be overly broad. A defendant who agrees with a mentally disabled individual to commit a crime has formed a genuine collaborative criminal effort. Though the mentally disabled individual might subsequently be found "not guilty by reason of insanity," he could still contribute significant intelligence, effort, and encouragement to achieving the criminal objective of the agreement.

In jurisdictions that have adopted the bilateral approach, the prosecutor must prove that two or more persons have agreed to commit a crime. Under the common law rule requiring consistency in a verdict, if all but one of the charged conspirators are acquitted in the same trial, the conviction of the remaining conspirator must be reversed. The rationale is that because the common law requires at least two guilty parties, if the jury verdict establishes that there was only one guilty party to the conspiracy—that conviction must be reversed. If, however, one of the alleged co-conspirators has fled the jurisdiction and cannot be brought to trial, the prosecutor can still convict the remaining co-conspirator, provided he proves there was an agreement between two or more persons to commit a crime.

The bilateral approach can be criticized when considering conspiracy as an *inchoate* crime. Police cannot intervene early and convict someone of conspiracy unless there are two or more culpable individuals. This is true even though an individual has clearly demonstrated her dangerousness and might subsequently find a truly willing and able partner in crime. Instead, the police can arrest her for solicitation, which has a relatively light punishment (see Chapter 11). Or, they can wait until the defendant has moved much closer to the target offense and actually committed an attempt. The bilateral approach thus seems to conflict with the inchoate *rationale* of conspiracy—to prevent crime at its earliest stages.

The Model Penal Code's Unilateral Approach

The Model Penal Code departs from the bilateral approach of the common law. Instead, it permits conviction of any person who "agrees" with another

48. Cal. Penal Code tit. 7, ch. 8, §182(a) (West 2012).

person to commit a crime. MPC §5.03(1)(a) and (b). Thus, the MPC would convict a defendant who has agreed to commit a crime with someone who could not be convicted, such as a diplomat or a legally insane individual, or with someone who has no real intention to commit a crime, such as an undercover police officer. In this sense, the MPC imposes responsibility on a defendant who *believes* he has agreed with another person to commit a crime. A defendant who agreed with another to commit a murder could be convicted of conspiracy to commit murder even if the evidence showed that his co-conspirator never intended to participate in the murder but merely feigned agreement while cooperating with the police.[49]

Under the inchoate or unfinished crime part of conspiracy's rationale, the MPC assesses each individual's culpability based on his individual mental state and conduct. Its definition of conspiracy does not require an agreement between at least two guilty parties. MPC §5.03(1). Consequently, the MPC does not require the same "answer" for each party; indeed, it accepts that its analytic approach may generate a different result for each party, depending on his individual culpability and conduct.

Section 5.04(1)(b) explicitly states that it is no defense that the person with whom the defendant conspired is irresponsible or has immunity from conviction. Under the MPC, the result is the same in the case of a co-conspirator who does not really intend to commit the crime, such as an undercover police officer. The MPC is not concerned with whether a truly criminal group forms or whether it has a good chance of succeeding. Rather, it is concerned with convicting a culpable individual who has provided "unequivocal evidence of a firm purpose to commit a crime."[50]

Critics of the MPC argue that its unilateral approach (1) departs without justification from the well-settled law of conspiracy and its group crime rationale, which requires actual collaborative effort; (2) invites police to "manufacture" crime by encouraging police agents to enter into unilateral conspiracies; and (3) is unnecessary because solicitation and attempt are adequate to protect the public from the perceived dangerousness of a unilateral conspirator, at least when an undercover police agent is the only other party.[51]

Some commentators support the MPC's unilateral approach. By way of a contracts analogy, they argue that a mental reservation by one party to an express acceptance of an offer (such as an undercover police officer would surely have in agreeing to commit a crime) should not prevent a judge or jury from finding an "agreement." Rather, the court *should* find that there is an agreement in such cases, and then decide whether the police agent

49. *State v. St. Christopher*, 305 Minn. 226, 232 N.W.2d 798 (1975).

50. Model Penal Code and Commentaries, Comment to §5.04, at 400 (1985).

51. Burgman, Unilateral Conspiracy: Three Critical Perspectives, 29 DePaul L. Rev. 75 (1979).

has a valid defense to the charge, such as statutory privilege or necessity, or whether the defendant has a defense of entrapment (see Chapter 17). Making police officers run the risk of being found to be co-conspirators if they do not have a valid defense or of having entrapped the defendant might make them think more carefully about their proper role in detecting crime.

ABANDONMENT

The Common Law

The common law does not allow the defense of abandonment to conspiracy. The crime of conspiracy is complete with the agreement and no subsequent act can exonerate the actors. As in attempt, once the actors have crossed the threshold of criminality, they cannot go back.

The Model Penal Code

The Model Penal Code does allow this defense to conspiracy and calls it "renunciation." It is a limited affirmative defense and there are two stringent requirements: (1) the defendant must have "thwarted the success of the conspiracy," *and* (2) the abandonment must be "complete and voluntary." MPC §5.03(6). (Remember that under the MPC, the defendant has the burden of producing evidence to support an affirmative defense, but the prosecution has the burden of persuasion. MPC §1.12.) Ordinarily, informing law enforcement officials in a timely manner is considered sufficient; simply withdrawing from the conspiracy is not. However, if such notice fails to thwart the success of the conspiracy because it is too late or because the police simply fail, then the defense of renunciation will not prevail. It will, however, start the running of the statute of limitations under §5.03(7)(c) for that defendant.[52]

Also, as in attempt (see Chapter 12), the defendant must have made his decision for the "right" reasons. It is ineffective if he changed his mind

52. Model Penal Code and Commentaries, Comment to §5.03, at 458 (1985). Contrary to the position taken by the MPC Commentaries, some states will permit the defense of renunciation if the actor has given timely notice but the police, nonetheless, fail to prevent the conspiracy from succeeding. Id. at 459. See, e.g., Ark. Code Ann. §5-3-405(2)(B) (Michie 1987); Haw. Rev. Stat. tit. 37, §705-530(3).

because the chances of detection became greater or he wanted to wait for a more opportune time or place.

The MPC permits this defense because (a) effective renunciation demonstrates a lack of firm criminal determination and thus of dangerousness, and (b) the law should create incentives for individuals to call off their criminal plans.

Most recent state criminal law revisions have followed the MPC in creating the defense of renunciation. A majority of those states that have adopted the renunciation defense place the burden of proving it on the defendant.

WITHDRAWAL

The Common Law

This defense is available to co-conspirators in a number of jurisdictions.[53] Giving reasonably adequate notice to *all* co-conspirators that one no longer intends to take part in the criminal plan in time for the other conspirators to abandon the conspiracy is usually sufficient to establish withdrawal. This defense permits a conspirator to avoid criminal responsibility for *future* crimes. Unlike the MPC defense of renunciation, the common law defense of withdrawal does not "undo" the offense of conspiracy or the withdrawing conspirator's responsibility for any substantive crimes *already* committed. However, withdrawal does start the running of the statute of limitations and limits the admissibility of co-conspirator statements and actions occurring after withdrawal.

The Model Penal Code

The MPC also provides this defense. MPC §5.03(7)(c). To be effective, the actor must either advise his co-conspirators that he is no longer involved or inform law enforcement of the conspiracy and his involvement in it.[54]

For a comparison of conspiracy under the common law and the MPC, see Table 13.1.

53. See, e.g., *Hyde v. United States*, 225 U.S. 347 (1912).

54. Federal courts also permit the defense of withdrawal. It is generally established if the defendant takes affirmative acts inconsistent with the conspiracy's goal and takes reasonable steps to communicate his abandonment to his co-conspirators. *United States v. United States Gypsum Co.*, 438 U.S. 422, 464-465 (1978).

13.1 Comparison of Conspiracy Under the Common Law and the Model Penal Code

Common Law	Model Penal Code
Rationale:Inchoate crime and group liability	*Rationale*: Treated *solely* as inchoate crime
"Unlawful act" may be object of conspiracy	Only a "crime" may be object of conspiracy
No overt act required historically (modern common law jurisdictions typically require an overt act)	Overt act required except for first- and second-degree felonies
Does *not* merge with target offense	Merges with target offense unless criminal objectives go beyond particular offenses
Specific intent required for all *material* elements	"Purpose" required for *conduct* and *result* elements; unclear if "purpose" required for *circumstance* elements
Pinkerton rule adopted	*Pinkerton* rule rejected; accomplice liability required
Bilateral requirement that *both* conspirators *must* agree	Agreement can be unilateral
No renunciation (no abandonment)	Renunciation permitted
Withdrawal permitted	Withdrawal permitted

IMPOSSIBILITY

Impossibility in conspiracy cases does not occur very often. However, just in case a clever law professor thinks it should occur on your exam, here is an explanation!

Legal Impossibility

If the parties agree to commit an act they *believe* is a crime or is covered by the applicable conspiracy statute but is not, they cannot be convicted of conspiracy. Just as in attempt (see Chapter 12), the actors' belief that they are breaking the law cannot generate criminal responsibility when there is no law proscribing their conduct. Though the group has shown themselves willing to break *the* law, they have not managed to plan behavior that breaks a *specific* law. The principle of legality limits the power of the state to punish in such cases.

Moreover, the group does not pose any special danger to socially protected interests, though it may be argued that the group may eventually shift its aim to conduct covered by the law of conspiracy, and corrective action is appropriate. However, this is a general problem in cases of legal impossibility and probably should be dealt with on a uniform and consistent basis rather than being adjusted on a crime-specific basis.

Factual Impossibility

Factual impossibility in an attempt case is where the defendant tried to implement her criminal mens rea but, for some reason beyond her control, could not. In conspiracy, however, the crime is completed at the moment there is an agreement or, in some jurisdictions, when any member of the conspiracy commits an overt act in furtherance of the conspiracy. Thus, it is still possible that the substantive offense could be committed.

Consider this case. *A* and B agree to kill C while C sleeps, and *A* buys a gun in furtherance of that agreement. Two days later, unknown to *A* and B, C dies in his sleep of a heart attack several hours before B shoots to kill C as he apparently sleeps. *A* and B can be convicted of *conspiracy to murder* C even though (a) in some jurisdictions shooting at C would be considered a case of *legal impossibility* and, therefore, B would not be guilty of attempted murder; (b) under the MPC and in those jurisdictions that consider this *factual impossibility*, B would only be guilty of *attempted murder* because he *thought* C was still alive. *A* and B cannot use the impossibility of accomplishing the goal of their conspiracy as a defense to the charge of conspiracy to commit murder. Both have demonstrated their dangerousness by entering into an agreement and acting on it. Even if C died right after *A* and B committed the crime of conspiracy, and *A* and B took no further acts because they learned of C's death, *A* and B could be convicted of conspiracy to murder C.

The only tricky case arises when parties agree to commit a crime in a particular way and, on those facts, the substantive offense could not be accomplished. Suppose Jody and Jenny agree to steal the red Tesla in the Safeway parking lot but are then arrested. Can they be convicted of conspiracy when the car they agreed to steal was actually Jody's car? This is the strongest case for a claim of impossibility. However, the trend today, particularly under the MPC, is to assess the actors' culpability based on the facts as they believed them to be. In all probability, both Jody and Jenny would be convicted of conspiracy to commit theft.

WHARTON'S RULE

The Common Law

Some crimes logically require the participation of two individuals. Common law crimes such as adultery or dueling, for example, require two participants, as do some contemporary crimes. For example, the sale of drugs requires both a seller and a buyer. When the substantive offense requires concert of action between two people to accomplish a common criminal goal, it necessarily requires agreement. Wharton's rule (named after a legal scholar who analyzed this problem) says that conspiracy cannot be used to criminalize the agreement that is a logically required component of the substantive offense.

The rule, generally accepted by most courts, prevents the use of conspiracy to pile up more punishment on conduct that is already punished by the substantive offense. Moreover, when only the two necessary parties are involved, there is no additional threat posed by this particular group that is not already anticipated and punished by the substantive offense.

On the other hand, the rule defeats the use of conspiracy to punish conduct that has not yet resulted in the commission of the target crime. Consequently, only attempt may be used. Attempt requires the parties to come closer to committing the offense than does the crime of conspiracy. By eliminating the availability of conspiracy when two parties are logically required for commission of the target offense, Wharton's rule decreases the usefulness of conspiracy as a preventive measure to reach inchoate or unfinished crimes.

There are exceptions to this rule. The "third party" exception provides that conspiracy may be used when *more* than the two parties logically required to commit the target offense are involved. The rationale is that the addition of a third (or more) person does, in fact, enhance the dangers of group criminal activity. This type of line drawing can be criticized as highly formalistic and perhaps even unrealistic. However, it does provide a "bright line" for courts and prosecutors and may also serve as a deterrent to keep the size of criminal groups to the number of individuals necessarily required to commit the substantive offense.

In *Iannelli v. United States*,[55] the Supreme Court treated Wharton's rule as a presumption to be applied by courts in the absence of contrary legislative intent. When legislative intent does indicate that conspiracy may also be charged in addition to the substantive offense, Wharton's rule does not bar its use.[56]

55. 420 U.S. 770 (1975).

56. Comment, An Analysis of Wharton's Rule, 71 Nw. U. L. Rev. 547 (1977).

Some courts also hold that Wharton's rule is inapplicable when the substantive offense requires the participation of two culpable parties but does not specify any punishment for one of them.[57] For example, Wharton's rule would not preclude a charge of conspiracy to sell intoxicating liquor when the law punished only the seller but not the buyer.[58]

The Model Penal Code

The MPC rejects Wharton's rule. Instead, it provides that a person who could not be convicted of the substantive offense or as an accomplice to the substantive offense may not be convicted of conspiracy to commit that offense. MPC §5.04(2). Under the MPC's unilateral approach to conspiracy, immunity for one defendant under this section does not prevent conviction of another co-conspirator.

IMMUNITY FOR SUBSTANTIVE OFFENSE

The Common Law

Another common law rule, based on inferred legislative intent, prevents the prosecutor from using conspiracy to punish the conduct of an individual whose participation in the substantive offense is logically required but whose behavior is not made criminal by that offense. In *Gebardi v. United States*,[59] the Supreme Court reversed a woman's conviction for conspiracy to violate the Mann Act. This statute prohibited the transportation of a woman across state lines for immoral purposes. However, it punished only the individual who transported the woman; it did not punish *her* conduct. To permit the use of conspiracy to punish the agreement of the woman who is necessarily included in the proscribed act but whom the legislature decided not to punish would undermine the public policy of the statute.

The Model Penal Code

The Model Penal Code states that, unless otherwise provided in a criminal statute, a person cannot be convicted of conspiracy if she could not be

57. *United States v. Previte*, 648 F.2d 73 (1st Cir. 1981).
58. *Vannata v. United States*, 289 F. 424, 428 (2d Cir. 1923).
59. 287 U.S. 112 (1932).

guilty of the substantive offense either (a) under the definition of the substantive offense, or (b) as an accomplice to its commission under the MPC's definition of accomplice. MPC §5.04(2) (incorporating by reference MPC §2.06(5) and 2.06(6)(a)). Under the MPC's accomplice section, an individual cannot be convicted as an accomplice if she is the victim of the conduct or if her participation is "inevitably incident to its commission." The *Gebardi* case would come out the same way under the MPC for the woman, but not for the man. Remember the MPC adopts a unilateral approach to conspiracy. It does not require two guilty parties. The prostitute's conduct is "inevitably incident" to a violation of the Mann Act. Similarly, in a statutory rape case, the prosecutor cannot use conspiracy to convict the underage participant, because the substantive offense considers her to be the "victim" protected by the statute. To permit a conspiracy conviction in such cases would undermine the legislature's intent and the public policy of the specific criminal law.

Examples

EXAMPLES

1a. Heather and Penelope are having lunch at the Brass Rail, a posh watering hole for the upscale and trendy. Bemoaning the high price of the cocaine they consume in rather large quantities and the resulting crimp in their lifestyle, Heather turns to Penelope and says: "Why don't we sell the stuff ourselves? That way we can make enough money to buy and use as much as we want and have enough money left over to indulge ourselves." Penelope, sipping her champagne slowly, finally says: "That is a great idea. Let's do it! I know where we can get crack cocaine in volume and on credit. I will call my friend tomorrow and make the arrangements. We are on our way to coke independence!" Heather and Penelope then lift their glasses to toast their arrangement, saying in unison: "To our new business!"

1b. The next day, Penelope calls Rachel, her cocaine supplier, on the telephone to arrange for the purchase of a large amount of cocaine on credit, but Rachel does not answer.

1c. It turns out Heather is an undercover police officer who, after telling her superior officers, arrests Penelope. Penelope utters the immortal words: "Et tu, Heather?"

1d. Heather is *not* a police informant. Two days later, Penelope reaches Rachel, her supplier, and tells Rachel: "My friend and I want to purchase a large amount of cocaine on credit in order to sell it at retail."

Rachel, having earned her undergraduate degree in economics at a famous midwestern urban school, is always looking to expand her market share. She decides this is a great idea and tells Penelope she will furnish Penelope with two kilos on credit and that Penelope can get another two kilos from her under the same terms after Penelope has paid for the first two kilos. The next day, Rachel delivers the cocaine to Penelope's apartment after telling Penelope how much she owes and when she expects both Penelope and "her friend" to repay her.

Over the next two weeks Penelope sells most of the cocaine in five separate sales while Heather is away on vacation. Unfortunately for Penelope, the last sale she makes is to Pat, an undercover police officer. Pat tries to arrest Penelope, who pulls a gun and shoots and wounds Pat. Other officers arrive almost immediately and subdue and arrest Penelope.

Heather, Penelope, and Rachel are all arrested. The prosecutor charges all three of them with a single conspiracy, four counts of selling drugs, one count of an attempted sale, and one count of assaulting a police officer while in performance of her duties. Heather and Rachel's lawyers object.

How many conspiracies are there and who are parties?

What charges can be brought as a result of Penelope's shooting Pat, the federal undercover police officer?

1e. In prosecuting Heather, Penelope, and Rachel for conspiracy, the prosecution seeks to introduce the statement of Penelope to Rachel ("My friend and I want to purchase a large amount of cocaine on credit in order to sell it at retail") to establish that Heather was a member of the conspiracy. Assuming for the moment that Rachel is prepared to testify as to what Penelope told her, is this statement admissible to establish that Penelope and Heather had entered into a conspiracy to purchase and sell drugs?

2. Susan, Kelly, and Cathy have smuggled cocaine into Florida from various Caribbean islands using the same modus operandi: They charter a small plane at rates well above market, use different disguises during each trip, fly at night, fly low to avoid detection, and depart from destinations known to be drug sources.

   Recently, they chartered a small plane owned and piloted by Norm to fly them to the islands and then to fly them back to Florida. Although they did not explicitly tell Norm that they were using these trips to transport drugs into the United States, they told Norm all the other details of their previous trips. In addition, they paid Norm $3,000 more than his normal fee and used obvious disguises for each trip. On the fifth flight, Norm and the ladies were arrested in Florida and charged with a conspiracy to smuggle drugs into the USA.

   a. Can Norm be convicted of conspiring with Susan, Kelly, and Cathy to illegally transport cocaine into the United States?

b. If so, can Norm be convicted on the smuggling counts for the trips the ladies made prior to his involvement?

3a. Jay is being held in an old rural county jail. Late one afternoon, Rhonda, his girlfriend, visits Jay and tells him that she and Joe, his best friend, are going to bust him out that night. (Rhonda does not tell him they do not intend to leave any witnesses.) Jay says: "Great! I knew I could count on both of you." At about 3:00 a.m. the next morning, Rhonda and Joe ring the jail's night bell and are admitted by Doug, the night jailer. While Joe distracts the guards, Rhonda walks up behind Doug and kills him. Unfortunately, Rhonda and Joe cannot find the keys to Jay's cell, so they flee. The next day they are both apprehended. Is Jay responsible for the murder of Doug?

3b. Same facts, except as Joe and Rhonda enter the jail, Jay sees Rhonda pointing a gun at Doug's head. Jay screams to her: "Put the gun down. Don't shoot him!" Rhonda ignores Jay and kills Doug.

4. José was arrested after flying into JFK International Airport in New York on a flight from Afghanistan. The U.S. Attorney charged him with conspiracy to commit terrorism, including future acts of murder and kidnapping people in a foreign country and planting explosive devices in the United States. At trial, the prosecutor introduced a signed application form José filled out to attend a training camp run by Al Qaeda in Afghanistan. Can José be convicted of conspiracy to commit terrorism on this evidence?

   What if the prosecutor could also show that José actually completed the training camp?

5. Stan told Gary, a federal undercover narcotics agent, that Stan's friend, Stella, occasionally drives to Mexico, purchases heroin, and smuggles it into California where she resells it. He also told Gary that he thought Stella would probably drive with Gary to Mexico where they could pick up heroin and bring it back to California for resale at a hefty profit. Gary contacted Stella and they decided to drive to Mexico together, buy the heroin, and bring it back to California. They were stopped while driving back across the border. Can Stan *and* Stella be convicted of conspiracy to transport heroin into the United States?

6. Al Falfa, a retail seller of farm chemicals, sold several large batches of ammonium nitrate, a fertilizer generally known to be a key ingredient in homemade terrorist bombs, to Jed, a young man in his 20s with very short hair and dressed in an army surplus camouflage uniform. Al Falfa knew Jed did not own a farm but did own a very small house with a small yard. He also knew that Jed belonged to a militant "people's militia" that advocated extreme antigovernment views. After the first

sale, Al Falfa said to Jed: "You know this is far too much to use on your lawn. If you use all of it, you'll surely kill it." Jed replied: "I am not going to use it on my lawn. As a former army explosives expert I know how to use this stuff in some unusual ways. It's not the lawn I'm going to kill. It's time we showed those government folks we mean business!" Jed loaded the fertilizer onto his large pick-up truck and left. Jed subsequently returned to make several more large purchases. Al Falfa, content with making more than half of his annual sales of this product to a single customer at his usual price, did not take any further action.

One week later, a huge explosion destroyed the federal building in a nearby city killing over 20 children in an on-site day care center and over 50 federal workers. Jed was arrested shortly thereafter and experts have determined that he used the fertilizer that he purchased from Al Falfa to make the bomb. Can the government convict Al Falfa of entering into a conspiracy with Jed?

7. Tom and Dave run into Linda at a bar. They have a few drinks and then decide to walk to a different bar nearby. While they walk along, Tom suggests a short-cut through an alley. Linda and Dave agree. Once they are in the alley, Tom grabs Linda and rapes her. While Tom is raping Linda, Dave pulls a garbage can in front of them so that no one can see from the street what Tom is doing. Did Tom and Dave conspire to rape Linda?

8. Sherrie and Bill Green agreed with Dr. Feelgood to exchange stolen goods for amphetamines. The Greens would steal household goods and bring them to Dr. Feelgood, who would then write them a prescription for amphetamines. Eventually, the Greens and Dr. Feelgood were arrested and charged with conspiracy to unlawfully dispense controlled substances. Dr. Feelgood's lawyer argued that laypersons cannot conspire to illegally dispense prescription drugs because laypersons are not authorized to prescribe them. Is Dr. Feelgood's lawyer correct?

9. Lisa, Jane, and Mark learn that Lisa's elderly uncle keeps his life savings under his mattress. They agree to break into his home, kill him, and take the money. Lisa buys a gun and delivers it to Mark.
   a. Lisa, on the way to meet Mark and Jane at her uncle's home, is overcome by guilt and fond memories of her uncle. She decides she cannot go through with the plan. Instead, she catches a plane to San Francisco. Shortly thereafter, Mark and Jane break into the uncle's house, kill him, and steal his money.
   b. Lisa meets Mark and Jane at her uncle's house as planned. Overcome by guilt and fond memories of her uncle, she turns to Jane and Mark and says: "I can't go through with this. I want nothing more to do with this crazy idea." She then leaves Mark and Jane who, nonetheless, break into her uncle's house, kill him, and steal his money.

c. Overcome by guilt and fond memories while on the way to meet Mark and Jane at her uncle's house, Lisa calls her uncle to warn him of the impending crimes. Unfortunately, his telephone is busy. Mark and Jane break into the uncle's house, kill him, and steal his money.
d. Overcome by guilt and fond memories while on the way to meet Mark and Jane at her uncle's house, Lisa calls the police and tells them of the planned crime. The police dispatch a patrol car, which arrives in time to arrest Mark and Jane before they can break into the uncle's house.

10a. Remember the facts of John and Lonny and their plan to hex Judge Smith in Chapter 12, Example 15, page 359. Analyze those facts to consider a potential conspiracy.

10b. Now suppose John is convicted by a jury of conspiracy, but not Lonny. Are there any implications?

10c. Consider now that John does not involve Lonny, but directly contacts Emma himself. Emma agrees to help John, but unknown to John, Emma is working with the police and does not intend to participate in the murder of Judge Smith. What result now?

11. Courtney learns she can make a small fortune dealing prescription drugs. Courtney's sister Anna works as a medical assistant at a doctor's office. Courtney asks Anna to steal a doctor's prescription pad so that Courtney can write forged prescriptions. Courtney promises Anna twenty percent of the profits made through this drug dealing venture if Anna succeeds in obtaining the prescription pads. Anna agrees to Courtney's plan and obtains a prescription pad. However, before turning the prescription pad over to Courtney, Anna decides she could keep all of the profits if she continues on alone. Anna never gives Courtney the prescription pad.

Explanations

EXPLANATIONS

1a. Heather and Penelope agreed to commit at least two crimes, (1) the purchase and (2) the subsequent sale of drugs. Under the common law and the MPC (because the substantive crimes that are the object of the agreement are serious felonies), Heather and Penelope committed one conspiracy once they entered into the criminal agreement (even though it had two target crimes). In many jurisdictions, however, one of the parties must commit an overt act in furtherance of the conspiracy in addition to the agreement before the elements of conspiracy are satisfied. In these jurisdictions, Heather and Penelope have not committed conspiracy until one of them does an overt act to implement their agreement.

1b. Even in those jurisdictions that require an overt act, both Heather and Penelope can be convicted of conspiracy because Penelope acted to implement their criminal agreement by calling her supplier in an attempt to secure drugs on credit. Even though it is an innocent act that does not provide strong evidence of criminal intent and even though it did not move the conspiracy any further along the path of implementation, making the telephone call at least demonstrates that the conspiracy has moved beyond intention to action. The defendants will argue that, because Penelope did not actually talk to Rachel, the telephone call should not be considered an "overt act in furtherance of the conspiracy." This argument will probably not succeed. Unlike attempt, there is no requirement that the overt act come close to committing the target offense or even strongly corroborate the actors' criminal purpose. Thus, both Heather and Penelope can be convicted of conspiracy.

This particular example illustrates that the "overt act" requirement for conspiracy often does not provide very strong evidence establishing either firmness of criminal intention or significant implementation of the criminal plan.

1c. In this example, Heather does not have the mens rea necessary to commit conspiracy because she is a police officer. In those states that have retained the common law's bilateral theory of conspiracy, Penelope could not be convicted of conspiracy because the crime requires at least two culpable parties. Because Heather is a police officer, there is no true collaborative criminal enterprise at work and the special dangers of a criminal group are not present. The prosecutor might consider charging Penelope with solicitation; however, Heather, not Penelope, originated the criminal scheme. Thus, Penelope cannot be convicted of encouraging Heather to commit a crime. Nor will attempted conspiracy succeed; to permit this strategy to work would undercut the bilateral theory of conspiracy and its plurality requirement. Finally, Penelope cannot be convicted either of attempted possession or sale of cocaine. The bad news? Penelope has lost a good friend! The good news? Penelope probably cannot be convicted of any crime.

Under the MPC, however, Penelope *could* be convicted of conspiracy. She did agree with Heather to commit a crime; under the unilateral theory of conspiracy adopted by the MPC, she is guilty of this crime. The MPC focuses on the culpability and conduct of each individual and her dangerousness. It does not require that a genuine criminal group be actually at work.

1d. *Number of conspiracies and parties.* Rachel, the supplier, will argue that she agreed to sell cocaine to Penelope and did so. Thus, in her view she can be convicted only of the sale, not of agreeing to sell. She will claim that

Wharton's rule precludes her conviction when the participation of two parties is necessary to commit the crime (as in the sale of drugs that require a seller and a buyer). The government will respond that, even if Wharton's rule might normally apply, Rachel knew that there was a third party involved because Penelope told her about her friend. Thus, the *third-party exception* would defeat Wharton's rule, and Rachel can be convicted for both the prior criminal agreement and committing the crime that is the object of that agreement.

The government will also argue that this is a "chain" conspiracy. Though Rachel did not know who Penelope's friend was, she knew there was a friend who would help sell the cocaine and be jointly responsible for paying for it. Thus, she knew the essential elements of the scheme. Finally, the government will argue that Rachel had a "stake in Heather's and Penelope's venture" to sell crack cocaine because Rachel sold the drugs on credit and also entered into an ongoing business relationship, promising to sell additional drugs on the same favorable terms. Unless Heather and Penelope succeeded in selling the cocaine, Rachel might not get paid. The government will probably succeed in charging and proving a single conspiracy.

If it does, then Rachel is responsible under the *Pinkerton* rule for all of the retail sales Penelope made because they were foreseeable crimes. Heather is also responsible for these sales under the *Pinkerton* rule even though she was on vacation when Penelope made the sales and did not aid and abet those crimes. The *Pinkerton* rule effectively attributes criminal responsibility for foreseeable crimes in furtherance of the conspiracy committed by other co-conspirators without requiring proof that would satisfy the elements of accomplice liability.

The MPC focuses on each individual and analyzes with whom each agreed and to what purpose. The government might still succeed in establishing that this is a single conspiracy with three parties. Heather did not know who Rachel was, but she did know that Penelope had a friend who would supply the cocaine on credit. Thus, Heather has arguably authorized Penelope to enter into an agreement with Rachel on her behalf. Likewise, Rachel knows that Penelope has a "friend" (though she does not know her identity) and that the friend will help Penelope sell the drugs and be responsible for paying for them.

Unlike the *Pinkerton* rule, however, both Rachel and Heather might not be responsible under the MPC for the five retail sales that Penelope made since the government will have a difficult time establishing the elements of accomplice liability (especially "purpose" rather than "knowledge") as required by the MPC.

The assault on Pat. Penelope is clearly guilty of assaulting Pat, an undercover police officer, while in the performance of her duties. The more difficult question is whether Heather and Rachel can be charged with this crime by virtue of being co-conspirators with Penelope. On these facts, neither Heather nor Rachel expressly agreed that Penelope should use deadly force if necessary to resist arrest. Nor is there any indication that Heather or Rachel knew, or should have known, that Penelope was armed or would use deadly force to resist arrest. The amount and value of the cocaine involved in the sale were not large. Neither Heather nor Rachel was present during the sale or played a major role in the attempted sale. Thus, it is unlikely that a jury would conclude that, under these circumstances, Heather or Rachel should have foreseen that Penelope would use deadly force to resist arrest.

1e. Under the conspiracy exception to the hearsay rule, a statement by one conspirator implicating another conspirator is admissible in federal courts, provided the prosecutor proves by a preponderance of the evidence (including the contested statement itself) that a conspiracy involving these individuals exist. If the judge so finds, Penelope's statement to Rachel about her "friend" is admissible.

2. A jury could infer that, though Norm did not actually know he was transporting cocaine into the United States, he nonetheless knew he was participating with others in illegal drug smuggling and that he intended to join and participate in the conspiracy. Norm was paid more than his usual fee, made several trips at night while flying low to and from destinations known as sources for drugs, and knew his clients used various disguises. He also knew that they had done this before. A conspirator does not have to know all the details of a conspiracy as long as he knows its essentials and intends to participate in the conspiracy.

   Though Norm may have joined a conspiracy "in progress," so to speak, he is not liable for any substantive offense committed by his co-conspirators *prior* to his becoming a co-conspirator. The *Pinkerton* rule does not impose responsibility for foreseeable crimes committed before a co-conspirator joins the conspiracy.

3a. Rhonda and Joe obviously formed a conspiracy to break Jay out of jail and each of them is responsible for the murder committed by Rhonda because they had expressly agreed to kill all witnesses. Even under the MPC, Joe would be responsible for the guard's death because he aided Rhonda by distracting Doug.

   The prosecutor would argue that Jay joined the conspiracy the afternoon Rhonda visited him and outlined the general plan. But did Jay agree to kill the guard? Can he be held accountable for Doug's murder when he did not know of the planned killing and was a completely passive agent unable to control the behavior of either Rhonda or Joe?

The prosecutor will argue that Jay is also responsible for these murders under the *Pinkerton* rule because it was reasonably foreseeable that deadly force might be necessary to accomplish the general plan. Consequently, Jay can be charged with Doug's murder. Under the MPC, the prosecutor must prove that Jay is an accessory to the murder because he solicited this *particular* crime, or aided, or agreed to aid, or attempted to aid in its commission. Without more evidence, this will be difficult—but not impossible—to prove.

3b. Under these facts, Jay might still be responsible for Doug's murder under the *Pinkerton* rule. Though he tried to prevent Doug's murder, the prosecutor could still try to establish that this crime was foreseeable and in furtherance of the conspiracy. Under the MPC, it will be very difficult to prove that Jay, who was confined to a cell, is responsible for the murder. Not only did he not assist or try to assist in any way; he actually tried to prevent the crime. Thus, he is not an accessory to Doug's murder.

4. The prosecutor would argue that the application form clearly establishes that José has intentionally joined a well-known terrorist group, Al Qaeda, which has as its only goal committing criminal acts of terrorism against citizens of the United States and other countries here and abroad. By signing this application, he has effectively become a member of an on-going conspiracy and, under well-settled case law, is responsible not only for the criminal act of conspiracy itself, but also for all reasonably foreseeable crimes committed by other co-conspirators in furtherance of the conspiracy after he became a member. Under a bilateral conspiracy approach, José has accepted an offer from Al Qaeda to join its ranks and participate in terrorist training. By signing the agreement he has not only signaled that he is joining this criminal conspiracy, but that he will become proficient in carrying out acts of terrorism. Any requirement of an additional act is easily satisfied by any of the daily acts of terrorism committed by other members of the Al Qaeda conspiracy, his co-conspirators. In either case, José can be convicted of conspiracy to commit terrorism and will be responsible for all foreseeable acts of terrorism committed by his partners in crime in the future, even those unknown to him . This responsibility attaches even if he is in custody unless he withdraws from the conspiracy.

   Defense counsel would claim that, at worst, José simply indicated he might join the terrorist group at some time in the future. Under the common law, he has not agreed with another person or organization to commit a criminal act. Nor did he form a unilateral conspiracy since he had no present intention to join any criminal conspiracy. Certainly he did not commit any overt act in furtherance of the conspiracy. The government is using flimsy evidence of possible future criminal conduct to impose expansive criminal responsibility on José.

Of course, presenting evidence that José participated in the terrorist training camp would strengthen the government's case immensely. The government would argue that defense counsel can no longer claim that José only indicated a possible willingness to join the conspiracy at some time in the future; he actually became an active member. The defense counsel would argue that mere preparation is not a criminal agreement, but that argument is very weak.

5. Without additional evidence, it would be difficult to prove that Stella and Stan had previously agreed to transport heroin into the United States. It seems more likely that Stan was simply telling Gary about Stella's past drug smuggling. This is particularly true since it was Gary who contacted Stella and made specific arrangements. Thus, it would be very difficult to convict Stan and Stella of conspiring together to transport heroin into the United States.

   Whether Stella can be convicted of conspiracy to transport heroin into the United States depends on whether the federal law embraces the unilateral or bilateral theory of conspiracy. The prevailing view is that it adopts the bilateral theory; thus, Stella cannot be convicted of conspiring with Gary, an undercover federal drug agent, who did not have the necessary mens rea to commit the object crime. Stella can be convicted of an attempt to transport heroin into the United States, but she cannot be convicted of conspiracy.

6. Most cases require the government to prove a provider of goods or services acted with the *purpose* of furthering the criminal objective; mere *knowledge* is not enough. The cases hold, however, that a vendor can be convicted of conspiracy if he has a "stake in the criminal venture." The first question is whether Al Falfa knew that Jed was going to use the fertilizer for a criminal purpose. This is a close question. Given events like the bombings of the World Trade Center in New York City and the Federal Building in Oklahoma City, most sellers of this type of fertilizer probably know it can be used to make powerful homemade bombs. Assuming that Al Falfa did know that Jed would use the fertilizer to make a bomb, can the government prove purpose? Al Falfa sold more than half of his supply to this customer who did not appear to use it for its intended use. He also knew that Jed was a former army explosives expert and a member of a group whose political views were very extreme. However, he did not sell the product at an inflated price and it is possible that Jed did have some legitimate use for the purchase unknown to Al Falfa. It will be a jury question whether Al Falfa had a "stake in the venture" and acted with the purpose of furthering the

criminal objective. The facts of this example may be less persuasive than the facts in Example 2 in establishing that a vendor of goods or services acted with the "purpose" of furthering the criminal objective and thereby entered into a conspiracy.

Should "knowledge" suffice, at least when the harm to be avoided is so serious? Some commentators argue that knowledge should suffice—at least in cases like this. They would use the criminal law to impose a duty on a seller of goods or services to take rather modest measures (such as not selling) in order to prevent such serious harm. Though some jurisdictions would convict if the seller of goods or services had *knowledge* of the purchaser's criminal objective (particularly if a serious crime is involved), the MPC requires the government to prove that Al Falfa acted with *purpose*.

7. Probably not. To find a conspiracy, there must be evidence of a prior agreement that reflects a shared criminal purpose. An agreement does not require an express act of communication; a jury may infer the existence of a prior agreement from concerted activity. Nonetheless, on these facts, it appears that Tom's rape of Linda was a spur of the moment decision, and that it was not the result of a prior agreement with Dave. Obviously, Tom can be convicted of rape. Because Dave has seemingly acted with the purpose of facilitating Tom's crime, Dave has aided and abetted the rape and can therefore be convicted and punished as an accomplice. It is likely that neither Tom nor Dave would be convicted and punished for the separate crime of conspiracy.

8. This argument is clever but will fail. This is a variation of a defense of "legal impossibility." However, a person can be guilty of conspiring to commit a crime even if he could not commit the substantive crime himself. It is sufficient where persons knowingly participate in a conspiracy to have one conspirator who is capable of committing the offense do so. This is also not a case where an individual who is immune from conviction for committing the substantive offense is being convicted by the use of conspiracy.

9a. *The common law*. The common law does not recognize the defense of *abandonment*. Thus, Lisa is guilty of conspiracy. Just as in attempt, a defendant who crosses the "threshold of criminality" cannot go back under the common law.

However, the common law does permit a conspirator to *withdraw* from a conspiracy by clearly indicating to all of her co-conspirators that she is no longer associated with the conspiracy. This communication must be made in a manner that would inform a reasonable person of her intent to withdraw and must be made in time for all co-conspirators to abandon the conspiracy. Because Lisa merely did not show up at the intended crime scene, she did not meet the requirements for withdrawal. She can be convicted of conspiracy and, under the *Pinkerton* rule, of the target offenses because she did not communicate her withdrawal to all of her co-conspirators in a timely manner.

The Model Penal Code. The MPC does permit the defense of *renunciation.* To be effective, the defendant must have "thwarted the success of the conspiracy" and must have completely and voluntarily renounced the criminal purpose. Lisa has not satisfied either of these two elements. She did not inform her co-conspirators of her firm intention to renounce the conspiracy, nor has she tried to prevent the commission of the target crimes. Thus, she can be convicted of conspiracy.

Lisa has also not satisfied the MPC's requirements for *withdrawal.* She neither advised her co-conspirators of her intention to abandon the conspiracy nor did she inform law enforcement authorities of the conspiracy or her involvement in it. MPC §5.03(7)(c). Thus, Lisa can also be convicted of the substantive offenses. She obtained the murder weapon with the purpose of its being used in the crime. Consequently, she is an accomplice of the target offenses.

9b. *The common law.* Because the common law does not permit the defense of abandonment, the analysis here results in the same answer as in Example 9a. Lisa can be convicted of conspiracy even though she has communicated her intention not to participate any further in the criminal conduct.

However, the common law does permit a co-conspirator to withdraw from a conspiracy, thereby terminating her liability for any crimes committed by her co-conspirators after her withdrawal. Because she has conveyed to all of her co-conspirators her intention to withdraw from the conspiracy in time for them to abandon the target offenses, Lisa will not be responsible under the *Pinkerton* rule for the subsequent murder, burglary, and theft committed by Mark and Jane.

The Model Penal Code. Under the MPC, Lisa has successfully withdrawn from the conspiracy because she has advised all of her co-conspirators that she will have no further involvement in the criminal plan and leaves them. Thus, Lisa is not responsible for crimes committed *after* her withdrawal.

However, Lisa has not met the tough requirements for renunciation under the MPC. She has not thwarted the success of conspiracy as required by §5.03(6). Consequently, she may be convicted of conspiracy but not of the target offenses.

9c. *The common law.* Under the common law, Lisa cannot abandon the conspiracy; thus, she is guilty of conspiracy. In this hypothetical, Lisa has not communicated to her co-conspirators her firm intention to withdraw from the conspiracy. Thus, her vain attempt to thwart the target offense is of no benefit to her. She can also be convicted of the target offenses.

The Model Penal Code. Under the MPC, the result is the same. Lisa neither communicated her intention to withdraw nor thwarted the success of the conspiracy. Too little, too late!

9d. *The common law.* Again, under the common law, there is no defense of abandonment to conspiracy. Lisa can be convicted of conspiracy.

It is not clear that she has withdrawn under the common law because she did not communicate to her co-conspirators her firm intention to withdraw in a timely manner. Timely police intervention prevented Mark and Jane from committing the target offenses; however, depending on the facts, they may have attempted the substantive offenses. Lisa may be responsible for any attempt but not for the target offenses that were not committed.

The Model Penal Code. Under the MPC, Lisa has successfully thwarted the commission of the target offenses in a manner that reflects a complete and voluntary renunciation of criminal purpose. Thus, she may succeed in using the defense of renunciation, thus cutting off liability *both* for the conspiracy and for any attempts.

10a. Lonny agreed to help John in the murder of Judge Smith. Under the MPC, because murder is a serious crime (a first or second degree felony), the agreement is enough convict the brothers, and an overt act is not required. Even so, an overt act was made when Lonny contacted Emma and offered to pay for the judge's personal items. So whether the jurisdiction requires an overt act or not, both brothers can be convicted of conspiracy to commit murder.

10b. In the common law, there must be consistency among the verdicts of the defendants convicted of conspiracy, meaning at least two defendants must be convicted of a conspiracy to satisfy the bilateral agreement requirement. Because Lonny was not convicted, John's conviction must be reversed in a jurisdiction applying the common law or the bilateral approach. However, the MPC does not follow the bilateral approach. The MPC imposes liability on an individual who believes they have agreed with another person to commit a crime. So even if the jury finds Lonny not guilty on a charge of conspiracy, John could still be convicted for conspiracy.

10c. John could still be convicted of conspiracy under the MPC, even though there was never a bilateral agreement. John believed he agreed with Emma to commit the murder of the judge, and that is enough under the MPC. Under the common law, John could not be convicted due to the bilateral theory of conspiracy. For attempt analysis of this example see Example 16 in Chapter 12.

11. Even though Courtney cannot complete the crime of selling prescription drugs because Anna did not follow through, Courtney can still be charged with conspiracy. Courtney planned and agreed with Anna to commit this crime. The focus in a conspiracy analysis is the agreement, not whether both parties followed through as agreed, or whether the crime was completed.

    No defenses will be available to Courtney. Common law does not allow for the defense of abandonment. The MPC does allow a defense of renunciation, but Courtney has not renounced the crime. She did not voluntarily abandon her objectives; rather, Anna excluded Courtney from achieving her objective. Further, Courtney never withdrew from the crime. She intended to complete the crime, but again, Anna excluded Courtney from this venture. So the defense of withdrawal under both common law and the MPC will not be available to Courtney.

CHAPTER 14

Complicity

OVERVIEW

A leading actor or actress often has a supporting cast who assist in one way or another in the leading player's performance. Likewise, criminals are often assisted by others in the commission of crime.

Complicity is a broad doctrine that imposes criminal responsibility on individuals for a crime committed by someone else, usually because these secondary actors have intentionally helped or encouraged the primary actor to commit the crime. Complicity can also impose responsibility based on other criminal law doctrines such as conspiracy.

In this chapter, we will focus on a form of complicity called *accessorial* or *accomplice* liability. In general, individuals who help another person to commit a crime are *accessories* or *accomplices* to that crime and are also responsible for its commission. Frequently, statutes and case law will use terms like "aid, abet, encourage, assist, advise, solicit, or procure" to describe the various kinds of conduct that can generate accomplice liability. (Note that complicity, including accomplice liability, is usually not a separate crime with its own punishment. It is simply one way of committing a crime.) Throughout this chapter, we will call individuals who help another to commit a crime through such activities "accomplices."

There are two ways of helping someone else commit a crime:

1. *Physical Aid*. The defendant can physically help another person commit a crime. For example, he might obtain the gun used by the primary actor in

the bank robbery. Or he may be present at the crime and help with its commission, perhaps by acting as a lookout or by driving the getaway car.
2. *Psychological Aid*. The defendant can encourage or reinforce the primary actor's decision to commit a crime. For example, she may urge a fellow gang member to shoot a rival gang member who has shown her disrespect.

Note two interesting aspects of accomplice liability. First, it is a form of *group criminality*. It will necessarily involve at least two individuals: a primary actor (P) and a secondary actor, the accomplice (*A*), who is helping or encouraging P. Second, although the accomplice is held accountable because of his own voluntary act and mens rea, his guilt is based on the commission of a crime by P. Thus, *A*'s guilt is *derivative*: *A*'s liability is dependent on P committing a crime or a criminal act.[1] The accomplice will usually be guilty of the same crime committed by the primary actor. Conversely, if P does *not* commit a crime, the accomplice cannot be convicted at common law because of the absence of a "guilty principal." (As we shall see, the Model Penal Code does not require a guilty principal.)

Complicity can actually be a very expansive doctrine, making individuals responsible for crimes committed by others that they did not expressly aid or encourage. As we saw in Chapter 13, the *Pinkerton* rule in conspiracy makes every co-conspirator responsible for all reasonably foreseeable crimes committed by other members in furtherance of the conspiracy. This is a very broad type of complicity. It does not require any co-conspirator to aid or encourage the specific crime committed by a co-conspirator. Likewise, felony murder makes all members of the joint venture responsible for a murder committed by a joint venturer in furtherance of the felony even though they might not have helped commit the murder or encouraged another to commit it.

In this chapter, we will focus on the more narrow type of complicity that requires the individual to actually encourage or help with P's crime.

THE RATIONALE OF ACCOMPLICE LIABILITY

As we saw in Chapter 7, the criminal law usually does not look beyond the last responsible human agent in determining causation.[2] Thus, the person who pulls the trigger in a homicide is normally responsible for the crime of murder.

1. Kadish, Complicity, Cause and Blame: A Study in the Interpretation of Doctrine, 73 Cal. L. Rev. 323, 337-338 (1985).
2. *Stephenson v. State*, 205 Ind. 141, 179 N.E. 633 (1932).

Should other individuals who helped with the crime, perhaps by providing the murder weapon or encouraging the shooter to kill the victim, also be held responsible for the murder? If so, why? After all, the shooter has free will; he could have decided *not* to pull the trigger. Moreover, *A* did not engage in the conduct that actually constituted the crime of homicide. Why hold him responsible for what someone else did?

Causation is not the basis of accomplice liability. Though *A* may influence P to act, the law assumes that P's criminal act is volitional and not physically caused by *A*'s encouragement or assistance.[3] Indeed, *A* may have played a very minor role in helping P commit the crime, and P may have committed the crime even if *A* had not encouraged him. Thus, one may be found guilty as an accomplice even though his actions do not satisfy "but for" causation.

Accomplice liability differs from the law's general approach to human causation. Accomplice liability *does* look beyond the last responsible human agent and makes others also responsible for P's criminal act. This extended reach of accomplice liability is justified because *A*, by her actions and her state of mind, has chosen to *adopt* P's criminal act as her own. By encouraging or helping another commit a crime, she has extended her will to embrace the actions of another.[4] P's criminal act is now also *her* criminal act. Moreover, in intentionally helping another to commit a crime, she has demonstrated by her own state of mind and by her own action that she is a socially dangerous individual.

In making *A* also responsible for the crime committed by P, accomplice liability might appear to contradict the general assumption in our criminal system that guilt must be personal. However, accomplice liability still requires proof of mens rea and a voluntary act for *A*. Thus, *A*'s guilt *is* personal.

Accomplice liability has been criticized on several grounds. First, it may extend the net of criminal responsibility too widely, punishing truly peripheral actors who did not play a significant role in causing harm. Second, it may punish a defendant more for her attitude than for the significance of her actions. Third, because the modern trend is to punish accessories just as harshly as principals, punishment may not be proportional to the defendant's moral guilt. All accessories, including those who play very minor roles or whose help or encouragement may not have been needed, will be *punished the same* as those who commit the object offense. In short, standby actors can be treated as if they played leading roles.

---

3. Kadish, supra n. 1, 73 Cal. L. Rev. 323 (1985).
4. Id. at 355.

DEFINITIONS

The Common Law

The common law used fairly precise terms to describe individuals who could be responsible for crimes committed by others.[5]

Principals and Accessories

Principal in the first degree (P-1) is the individual who (1) personally commits the crime or (2) uses an innocent agent to commit a crime. Thus, the professional killer who commits homicide by shooting and killing the victim is a P-1. An individual can also be guilty as a P-1 if he uses an innocent agent to commit a crime.

Innocent agent is someone who (1) commits a criminal act but (2) lacks capacity to commit a crime or the mens rea for the crime and (3) is fooled or forced into committing the criminal act. An innocent agent is usually a person, but it can also be an animal or an inanimate object (such as a computer programmed to destroy files). A drug dealer who deceives a teenager into delivering drugs by telling him it is medicine has used an innocent agent to commit a crime. Or a dolphin trained to attach a magnetic explosive device to a boat that then explodes and kills the passengers would be an innocent agent. Both have committed a criminal act, but neither would be considered to have committed a crime.

The actus reus of the person delivering the drugs will be combined with the dealer's mens rea to impose liability on the dealer as P-1 for the crime of delivering drugs. Likewise, the actus reus of the dolphin will be combined with the mens rea of P-1 to impose liability on P-1 for murder. Similarly, someone who is forced by another at gunpoint to commit a crime is an innocent agent; the coercer is guilty as a P-1.

Note that when someone uses an innocent agent to commit a crime, the law considers him a principal in the first degree and not an accomplice. The act of an innocent agent is not considered the act of the agent but rather the principal's act.

Principal in the second degree (P-2) is the individual who intentionally helps or encourages P-1 to commit the crime and is either present at the crime scene or constructively present (i.e., near enough to assist P-1 if needed). P-2 could be the lookout who alerts the shooter to the victim's imminent arrival or the driver of the getaway car.

---

5. We have modified the basic definitional terms provided by Blackstone at 4 Blackstone, Commentaries, ch. 3, 33-39.

Accessory before the fact (*A-BTF*) is someone who intentionally helps P-1 *beforehand*, perhaps by obtaining the murder weapon or by encouraging P-1 to commit the murder, but is *not present* or *nearby* when P-1 commits the crime.

Accessory after the fact (*A-ATF*) is someone who, though not part of the planning or commission of the crime committed by P-1, intentionally renders aid *after* the crime. For example, he may furnish plane tickets to help P-1 escape or destroy evidence or hide the fruits of the crime. An *A-ATF* obstructs justice by making it more difficult to apprehend and convict the other parties to the crime. At common law, husbands and wives could not be *A-ATF*s. Because of the marital relationship, they were expected to aid each other and therefore had an excuse if they did.

Misprision of Felony

Individuals who, knowing that a felony had been committed, did not report it to authorities, could be convicted of misprision of felony at common law. A federal law enacted in 1908, 18 U.S.C. §4, makes misprision of a felony a crime. However, it has been interpreted to require active concealment. A person cannot be convicted for simply not reporting the crime.[6]

Only a few states recognize misprision of a felony, while a few states impose a general duty to report any known felony. Many states, however, impose a statutory duty on eyewitnesses to specified crimes to report them.[7] And all states impose a duty on specified professionals (teachers or doctors, for example) to report suspected cases of child or sexual abuse.

Treason

All parties to treason were treated as principals.

Misdemeanors

All parties to a misdemeanor were treated as principals, though it was not a crime to be an *A-ATF* to a misdemeanor.

The Model Penal Code

Principals and Accessories Before the Fact

The MPC abandons the common law's definitions of principals and accessories. It considers *all* actors, except those involved *after* the commission of

6. *United States v. Johnson*, 546 F.2d 1225 (5th Cir. 1977).

7. Ciociola, Misprision of Felony and Its Progeny, 41 Brandeis L.J. 697 (2003).

the crime, as equals. Thus, §2.06 spells out the responsibility of principals in the first and second degree as well as accessories before the fact. The MPC provides a separate crime to cover the conduct of accessories after the fact.[8]

Section 2.06(1) provides that a defendant is guilty of any offense "committed by his own conduct"—that is, by his own voluntary act and mens rea. An actor is also guilty of offenses "committed by the conduct of another for which he is legally accountable."

Under §2.06(2), an actor is "legally accountable" for the conduct of another when:

(a) P uses an "innocent agent" or "irresponsible person" (e.g., a legally insane agent[9]) to engage in the criminal conduct. For example, P could deceive or force someone else to steal property.

(b) The legislature has enacted a special law making one person liable for the conduct of another. For example, some jurisdictions have enacted vicarious liability statutes based on an employer-employee relationship. This MPC provision allows the legislature to enact broader rules of responsibility for the conduct of another beyond that allowed in subsection (c).

(c) The actor is an *accomplice* of another. Accomplice liability is the basis for imposing criminal responsibility for the conduct of another in most cases.

Section 2.06(3) then spells out when someone is an accomplice:

(i) If the defendant *solicits* another to commit a crime, then the defendant is also responsible for the crime committed by the person solicited.[10]

(ii) If the person "aids or agrees or *attempts* to aid" another in planning or committing a crime, he is responsible for the crime committed by the other person. Note that this section makes an *attempt* to aid (but not an attempt to solicit under (i) above) just as culpable as successfully aiding. The MPC thus expands liability for accomplice liability beyond what the common law would impose.

(iii) If the person has a duty to prevent P's crime but fails to act, then he is responsible for the crime committed by P.

Accessories After the Fact

The MPC does not use the common law term "accomplice after the fact." Section 242.3 (Hindering Apprehension or Prosecution) is the primary offense covering the conduct of those previously considered *A-ATFs*.

For a summary of terms and definitions used by both the common law and the MPC to describe accomplice liability, see Table 14.1.

8. See offenses provided in MPC Article 242.
9. For more on legal insanity, see Chapter 17.
10. For more on solicitation, see Chapter 11.

14.1 Accomplice Liability

COMMON LAW

T-1 **Before Target Crime** **Accessory Before the Fact (A-BTF)**	T-2 **During Target Crime** **Principal in First Degree (P-1)**	T-3 **After Target Crime** **Accessory After the Fact (A-ATF)**
1. Helps or encourages *P-1* to commit Target Crime *BUT* 2. Is not present at or near crime scene	1. Personally commits Target Crime *OR* 2. Uses Innocent Agent to commit Target Crime **Innocent Agent** 1. Commits criminal act; but 2. Lacks capacity or mens rea for crime; and 3. Is fooled or forced to commit criminal act **Principal in Second Degree (P-2)** 1. Helps or encourages *P-1* to commit Target Crime *AND* 2. Is at or near crime scene	1. Helps *P-1*, *P-2*, or *A-BTF after* Target Crime

MODEL PENAL CODE

T-1 **Before Target Crime** **Principal**	T-2 **During Target Crime** **Principal**	T-3 **After Target Crime**
1. Solicits another to commit a crime, which is then committed by person solicited *OR* 2. Aids, agrees, or attempts to aid another in planning a crime who then commits the crime *OR* 3. Having a legal duty to prevent the commission of the crime, fails to do so	1. Personally commits Target Crime *OR* 2. Uses Innocent or Irresponsible Person **Principal** 1. Aids, agrees, or attempts to aid another in committing a crime	1. Hinders apprehension or prosecution; see MPC §242.3

PROCEDURAL CONSEQUENCES OF CLASSIFICATION

The Common Law

Venue

At common law, P-1 and P-2 could only be tried in the jurisdiction where the crime was committed. *A-BTF* could only be tried in a jurisdiction where she provided assistance.

Pleadings and Proof

A defendant charged as a P-1 could still be convicted even if the evidence established that she was actually a P-2. The converse was also true; a defendant charged as a P-2 could be convicted if the evidence established that she was actually a P-1.

However, if a defendant was charged as either a P-1 or P-2, but the evidence established that she was an *A-BTF* or vice versa, a variance between the pleading and the proof was not allowed, and the defendant could not be convicted.

The Requirement of a Guilty Principal

Even though an *A-BTF* and a P-1 could be tried together, *A-BTF* could not be convicted unless P-1 was convicted first. A formal finding of P-1's guilt had to be made before the guilt of *A-BTF* could be considered. This stringent rule, designed in part to limit the death penalty, was applied even in those cases where P-1 was guilty but could not be prosecuted for reasons unrelated to guilt or innocence—for example, because P-1 enjoyed diplomatic immunity.

This approach was not followed in prosecutions of P-1 and P-2. They could be prosecuted in any sequence and an acquittal of one did not affect the guilt of the other.

The Model Penal Code

The MPC, as well as most jurisdictions today, does not have the complex procedural rules that the common law had.

Venue

Section 1.03(d) of the MPC provides that an accomplice can be prosecuted in the same place where P committed the offense or where the accomplice provided aid.

Pleadings and Proof

The MPC does not cover variance between the pleadings and proof. The generally applicable procedural rules would apply, and there are no special rules for each specific type of accomplice.

The Requirement of a Guilty Principal

Section 2.06(7) does not require the prior conviction of P. The evidence must only prove that an offense was committed by P and that *A* was an accomplice to that crime; what happened to P is simply not relevant to *A*'s guilt.

CONTEMPORARY LAW

Most jurisdictions treat *P-1*, *P-2*, and *A-BTF* by statute as "principals." Thus, they are all considered equally responsible for the crime committed by *P-1*. Only *A-ATF* is treated differently.

Principals and Accessories

Most states now call all parties who committed the crime or provided assistance either before or during its commission *principals*. (Note, however, that many courts and commentators still use the term "principal" to describe the primary actor (*P-1*) and "accomplice" or "accessory" to describe the supporting actors (*P-2* and *A-BTF*). These terms help clarify the respective roles the actors played in the crime, but they generally do not affect their legal responsibility.) We also will continue to use the terms "principal" (*P*) to describe the primary actor and "accomplice" (*A*) to describe the secondary or supporting actor.

Generally, the procedural consequences of the common law classifications have also been abolished. Thus, for example, an accomplice can be tried and convicted even though the primary actor has fled the jurisdiction or has died. Nonetheless, some states still retain the old common law definitions and some of the procedural consequences.

Accessories After the Fact

Most states now treat individuals who provide aid *after* the commission of a crime less harshly than those involved in its planning or commission. These after-the-fact helpers are usually convicted of a different crime, often called "rendering criminal assistance," "criminal facilitation," or some variation.

ELEMENTS OF ACCESSORIAL RESPONSIBILITY

Mens Rea

There are two kinds of mens rea generally required for accomplice responsibility.

The Mens Rea of the Crime Aided

The Common Law

A must act with at least the same mens rea or culpability required for conviction of the offense committed by P.[11] If the object offense requires a specific intent, *A* must act with that same intent. If the object crime requires only recklessness or negligence as to result, it is sufficient if *A* acts with the same mens rea toward result as is required by the object offense.

The Model Penal Code

The MPC would also require that *A* act with at least the same culpability or mens rea of the crime being aided.

The Mens Rea to Be an Accomplice: Purpose or Intent to Aid the Principal's Criminal Action

The Common Law

In addition, an accomplice must want to help someone else commit a crime.

Conduct. Most jurisdictions require the accomplice to act with the *purpose* or *intent* to encourage or assist in the conduct element of a crime. Suppose *A* yelled the following at *V*, who was about to be shot by P: "Take off your hat and die like a man." P, understanding these words as encouragement to kill *V*, shoots and kills *V*. Though *A*'s words may have had the *effect* of encouraging P to shoot *V*, *A* would not be guilty under accomplice liability unless he spoke those words with the *intent* of encouraging P to engage in that conduct.[12] Likewise, unintentional assistance does not result in responsibility as an accomplice.

---

11. Kadish, supra n. 1, at 349.
12. *Hicks v. United States*, 150 U.S. 442 (1893).

Requiring the highest level of mens rea or culpability for conduct makes sense because, as we saw, the actus reus of accomplice liability can be quite minimal; that is, one does not have to provide very much help or encouragement to become an accomplice. In this sense, accessorial liability may punish more for bad attitude than for bad behavior!

Recklessness or Negligence as to Result. Though cases are split, the general rule is that *A* must act with the same mens rea toward result as is required to convict P of the object crime. Consider *A* who aids P in the commission of stealing a car, perhaps standing lookout while P hot-wires the car, and then jumps into the car while P, the driver, speeds away. What if P hits and seriously injures a victim? If P may be convicted of the crime of vehicular assault based on proof of recklessness toward injuring another, then *A* also may be convicted of being an accomplice to that offense if the prosecution can show *A* also acted with recklessness toward this result.

Strict Liability. If *A* assists P in committing a strict liability offense, can *A* be convicted as an accomplice? In theory, the answer should be yes. After all, *A* acted with the purpose of aiding P engage in conduct that constituted the offense.

However, most courts find the reach of strict liability through the doctrine of complicity to be unfair. In *Johnson v. Youden*, [1950] 1 K.B. 544, the court affirmed the dismissal of an indictment against solicitors (English lawyers), charging them with aiding their client in selling a house at an unlawful price, which was a strict liability offense. The court concluded that *A* could not be convicted as an accomplice to a strict liability offense unless he "knows the facts that constitute an offense." Because the defendants did not know all of the facts, they could not be convicted.

The Model Penal Code

To be an accomplice, the actor must act with the "purpose of promoting or facilitating the commission of an offense." §2.06(3)(a). This rule needs careful analysis.

Conduct. The accomplice must have as her *purpose* that P will engage in the conduct elements of the object crime. Knowledge as to P's conduct is an insufficient basis for responsibility under the MPC.

Circumstances. Though it is not clear from the language of the MPC itself, the Commentaries indicate that the drafters intended to let the courts decide whether purpose as to circumstances is required for conviction or simply the same *culpability or mens rea* toward circumstances as is required for the object crime.[13] Courts that demand *purpose* as to circumstances may require a *higher* culpability for the accomplice than might be required for P.

Result. The MPC requires the same culpability or mens rea toward result as would be required for conviction of P for the object offense. §2.06(4).

Knowledge That Another Intends to Commit a Crime

Some courts hold that furnishing assistance to someone that the defendant knows is intending to commit a crime is sufficient for accomplice responsibility, particularly if the object crime is very serious. Thus, in *United States v. Fountain,*[14] a prison inmate who furnished a knife to another inmate knowing it would be used to attack a guard was convicted of aiding and abetting murder. Judge Posner concluded that the use of the criminal law to deter individuals from helping others they *know* intend to commit *serious* crimes is justified. Nonetheless, many courts take the MPC approach and require purpose or intent rather than knowledge for accomplice responsibility.

Providers of Goods and Services

As we saw in conspiracy,[15] a troublesome question of mens rea arises when someone provides innocuous goods and services to another she knows will use them to commit a crime. Can someone who provides large quantities of sugar at prices higher than usual to another she knows will use it to make illegal liquor be convicted as an accomplice?

The Common Law

Some earlier cases held that providing goods or services with knowledge that another intended to use them to commit a crime established accomplice liability.[16] However, most jurisdictions permit conviction only if the prosecutor can prove that the defendant acted with a *purpose* to aid.[17] The

13. Model Penal Code and Commentaries, Comment to §2.06, at 311 n. 37 (1985). "There is deliberate ambiguity as to whether the purpose requirement extends to circumstance elements of the contemplated offense or whether, as in the case of attempts, the policy of the substantive offense on this point should control. . . . The result, therefore, is that the actor must have a purpose with respect to the proscribed conduct or the proscribed result, with his attitude towards the circumstances to be left to resolution by the courts."
14. 768 F.2d 790 (7th Cir. 1985).
15. See Chapter 13.
16. *Jindra v. United States*, 69 F.2d 429 (5th Cir. 1934).
17. *United States v. Peoni*, 100 F.2d 401 (2d Cir. 1938).

prosecutor has to demonstrate that the defendant had a "stake in the venture"—for example, the provider's success or profits depended on helping P successfully commit the object offense or the provider has a psychological involvement in P's success. This analysis focuses both on the materiality of the aid provided to P as well as the profit the provider realizes. Many jurisdictions permit the jury to use the defendant's knowledge that P intends to commit a crime, together with other evidence such as excess volume or profits, to find that *A* acted with the requisite purpose.

The Model Penal Code

The Model Penal Code also requires the prosecution to prove that the actor had the "purpose of promoting or facilitating" the commission of the crime. §2.06(3).

Some commentators argue that those who supply legitimate goods and services in normal quantities and at market price have no duty to intervene to prevent the harm P intends to commit. In their view, the criminal law only requires each of us not to personally harm others. Absent a specific legal duty in civil law, we have no duty in the course of our everyday lives to prevent someone else from committing a harmful act.[18] This analysis turns on characterizing furnishing goods with knowledge as an "omission" rather than as a voluntary act. (See Chapter 3.)

Some states have responded to this difficult question by statutorily creating the less serious crime of criminal facilitation. These laws punish someone who *knowingly* provides another with significant aid used to commit a serious crime. The punishment provided is usually less than that provided for the crime committed by P. Purpose to aid is still required to convict D as an accomplice. Under a criminal facilitation statute, the defendant in *Fountain*, supra, could only be found guilty of criminal facilitation rather than accomplice liability.

Liability for Unintended Crimes Committed by the Principal

The Common Law

In theory, the mens rea element of accomplice liability clearly suggests that an accomplice should only be held responsible for the *specific acts* of P that he intended to aid. This approach, used in early cases, would limit *A*'s responsibility to those crimes he had, through the mens rea of intent, adopted as his own acts. This limiting principle made sense because, as we just saw,

18. G. Fletcher, Rethinking Criminal Law 676 (1978).

accomplice liability is very broad and can be extended to very minor actors who may not even satisfy "but for" causation.

A number of recent cases, however, have expanded *A*'s liability beyond this limit to include those acts that *A* should have "reasonably foreseen" or that were a "natural and probable consequence" of the offense that *A* intended to aid. This approach is very similar to the rule in conspiracy that all co-conspirators are liable for all reasonably foreseeable crimes committed by other co-conspirators in furtherance of the conspiracy.[19]

Imposing liability on *A* for "reasonably foreseeable" crimes committed by P may make sense in cases where there is a high probability of an additional crime being committed. But how is such probability determined? *A* helps P enter a residence at night so P can steal jewelry. P, while inside, assaults the homeowner who has come to investigate the noise. Should *A* be held responsible for P's assault? Both *A* and P were undoubtedly hoping there would be no assault. Thus, it is hard to conclude that *A* intended to assist or encouraged P to commit an assault. Is P's assault "a natural and probable consequence" of committing a residential burglary in the evening? On what basis should a jury decide this issue?

More recently, courts have supported an even broader extension of accomplice liability to encompass those crimes committed by P that *A* has "naturally, probably and foreseeably put in motion."[20] This approach has been used to impose liability when P killed *V* rather than roughing him up to get information (as *A* expressly told him), thereby defeating *A*'s goal.[21] It has also been used even when *A* tried to stop P from killing someone because *V* was not their intended victim.[22]

Justifications for holding *A* responsible not only for the crime *A* intended to aid, but also for any other reasonably foreseeable crime committed by P, are based on *A*'s causal role in bringing about these crimes. However, this overlooks the fact that accomplice liability does not require that *A*'s assistance be very significant before liability attaches. Indeed, the MPC includes "attempts" at aiding as sufficient. Thus, even an unsuccessful role in causing another to commit a crime will trigger accomplice liability. This expansive approach to accomplice liability primarily punishes attitude rather than acts that cause harm.

Just as in conspiracy, then, some jurisdictions are imposing criminal responsibility on accomplices if P commits an unintended or unplanned crime, including one clearly not sought by *A*, provided that it was reasonably foreseeable.[23] This approach essentially makes the accomplice

---

19. See Chapter 13.

20. *People v. Luparello*, 187 Cal. App. 3d 410, 439, 231 Cal. Rptr. 832, 849 (1986).

21. Id.

22. *People v. Brigham*, 216 Cal. App. 3d 1039, 265 Cal. Rptr. 486 (1989).

23. See, e.g., *People v. Luparello*, supra n. 20; Me. Rev. Stat., tit. 17-A, §57(3)(A) (Supp. 2007).

responsible for his *negligence*—that is, he *should* have foreseen that P may have committed crimes other than those *A* intended to aid. Convicting *A* on this low mens rea is ironic in that the prosecution may have to prove a higher degree of culpability to convict P. It also inflicts punishment that is disproportionate to *A*'s mental state.

Courts that enlarge accomplice liability based on foreseeability may be using a *causal* analysis to expand the mens rea of accessorial liability. Or, to put it differently, what P *does* is what *A should have been aware* might happen. There is also the risk that tort law's concept of reasonable foreseeability may be imported into the criminal law.

The Model Penal Code

The MPC does not permit responsibility to be imposed on *A* because of negligence toward unanticipated crimes committed by P. Thus, *A* cannot be convicted of crimes that were the "natural and probable consequence" of the crime *A* did intend to assist. Instead, the MPC's culpability requirements for the conduct and result elements (discussed above) must be met.

Actus Reus

The actus reus element of accomplice responsibility includes a broad range of conduct. Descriptive words such as "aid, abet, counsel," and so on that are used in various statutes to describe the actus reus of accessorial liability can be broken down into the following general categories of conduct.

Actual Assistance

In general, there are two primary kinds of conduct that will satisfy this requirement: helping in a *physical* sense (providing the murder weapon, acting as lookout, or driving the getaway car) or assisting in a *psychological* sense by reinforcing the will of P (encouraging P to commit the crime either before or during its commission).

Usually, it will not be too difficult to establish this actus reus element. If *A* holds the victim while P punches him or steadies the ladder while P climbs in the second story of the home, there will be strong evidence of actus reus. So, too, if *A* yells at P while P is assaulting *V*: "Kick him again; he's still moving!"

But what if *A* is simply present while P commits an offense? Is the mere act of "being there" sufficient to constitute the actus reus for accomplice liability? This conduct is ambiguous. Nonetheless, presence during the commission of a crime by another *is* legally sufficient to constitute the actus reus provided P *knows* *A* is there to render encouragement or to help if necessary. If, however, P does not understand that *A* will assist if needed, then a person's mere presence with knowledge that P is committing a crime does not satisfy the actus reus requirement. In addition, yelling words of encouragement at P is insufficient if P does not hear them.[24] (But note that the MPC would consider an attempt at aiding and abetting sufficient for responsibility.)

Omission

The Common Law

The actus reus requirement can also be satisfied by an omission, provided *A* has a legal duty to act. Thus, a police officer who stands by and watches P attack and rape *V* in a bar has satisfied the actus reus requirement. This is a classic case of a failure to act when there is a legal duty to act generating criminal responsibility.

The Model Penal Code

The Model Penal Code also takes this approach. A person who has a legal duty to prevent the commission of the offense is responsible for that offense if he "fails to make proper effort" to prevent it. MPC §2.06(3)(a)(iii). The passive police officer observing a rape would also be liable under the MPC.

How Much Aid Is Enough?

Perhaps the most difficult question is how much aid is enough to become an accomplice? Short answer: any aid! This compact summary obviously needs some explanation.

The Common Law

There can be instances in which *A* renders aid to P, but it really is not very helpful. Nonetheless, courts generally will find *A* guilty if his help was useful in any way to P. Thus, in *Wilcox v. Jeffery*, the defendant was found guilty of aiding and abetting an American jazz musician play unlawfully in England because *A* attended a concert along with hundreds of others in the

24. Kadish, supra n. 1, at 358-359.

audience and later wrote about the concert in a magazine.[25] Of course, the musician would have performed whether or not *A* was present or wrote about his concert. Here, there is accomplice liability without *any* meaningful causal connection between *A*'s presence and P's crime.

In *State ex rel. Attorney General v. Tally*, the court impeached Judge Tally for sending a telegram trying to prevent the delivery of another telegram sent earlier that warned the intended murder victim of his peril. In considering when the action of an accomplice will impose responsibility, the court said: "If the aid in homicide can be shown to have put the deceased at a disadvantage, to have deprived him of a *single chance* of life, but for which he would have had, he who furnishes such aid is guilty though it cannot be known or shown that the dead man, in the absence thereof, would have availed himself of the chance."[26] Note that it is not necessary for P to know that *A* is assisting him before *A* can be found guilty of accessorial responsibility. In the *Tally* case, the principals did not know that the judge had sent the telegram in order to help them kill their victim. Nonetheless, *A* will still be guilty as long as his aid had some minimal effect on P's being able to commit the crime.

In some cases, the offered assistance will have no impact at all on P's commission of the crime. Suppose that in the *Tally* case the telegram operator had simply delivered the warning telegram while tearing up Tally's telegram. Or if *A* shouts words of encouragement to P to commit a crime, but P is deaf and cannot hear *A*. As long as the aid is completely ineffective or P does not know that any encouragement is being given (thus leaving P unaware that anyone is encouraging him to commit the crime), most courts will probably not find accomplice liability.

The Model Penal Code

The Model Penal Code takes a broader approach. It considers any effort at aiding, even if ineffective or unknown to P, as satisfying the actus reus requirement of accessorial liability. The MPC does this by providing that a person is an accomplice of another if she "aids or agrees or *attempts* to aid such other person in planning or committing" the crime. MPC §2.06(3)(a)(ii) (emphasis added). Thus, an "attempt" at providing aid is sufficient for accomplice responsibility even if it is unsuccessful. The term "attempt" most likely has the same meaning here as it does under §5.01. And, as you recall from our discussion of attempt in Chapter 12, the MPC requires

25. *Wilcox v. Jeffery*, King's Bench Division, [1951] 1 All E.R. 464.

26. *State ex. rel. Attorney General v. Tally, Judge*, 102 Ala. 25, 15 So. 722, 739 (1894) (emphasis added).

that the actor's conduct "strongly corroborate the actor's criminal purpose" (§5.01(2)).

The MPC thus converts the question of how much aid is enough from a substantive element into an evidentiary element—that is, has the accomplice done enough to persuade a jury that he acted with the *purpose* of aiding in the commission of the crime, even if he wasn't helpful at all?

Immunity from Conviction

The Common Law

Accomplice liability cannot be used to convict an individual whose behavior is not punished by the substantive law. For example, statutory rape laws make it a crime to have sexual intercourse with a minor because minors lack the maturity necessary to give legally effective consent.[27] A prosecutor cannot charge a minor who encouraged the defendant to have sexual intercourse with her with liability as an accomplice to statutory rape. Because she is a victim in need of protection, the substantive law of statutory rape does not punish the minor. Permitting her to be convicted as an accomplice would undermine the legislative policy expressed in the substantive offense. (This same limitation applies to conspiracy. *Gebardi v. United States*, 287 U.S. 112 (1932). See Chapter 13.)

The Model Penal Code

The MPC takes the same approach. Under §2.06(6)(a) a person cannot be an accomplice if he is "a victim of that offense." Thus, an underage minor could not be convicted under the MPC of being an accomplice to a principal charged with statutory rape.

Conduct Necessarily Part of the Crime

What if the legislature has only punished one party to a criminal transaction that necessarily involves another person? Can the other party be convicted as an accomplice?

The Common Law

Courts generally have said no. Again, using accomplice liability in such cases would undermine the policy of the substantive offense. Thus, a customer who hires a prostitute cannot be convicted as an accomplice

27. See Chapter 9.

to prostitution if the substantive law of prostitution does not punish his behavior. Prostitution necessarily involves a customer and a provider. If the legislature had wanted to punish both parties, it readily could have done so.

The Model Penal Code

Section 2.06(6)(b) provides the same result. An individual cannot be convicted of being an accomplice if "the offense is so defined that *his conduct* is *inevitably incident* to its commission" (emphasis added).

Legal Incapacity to Commit Substantive Crime

Occasionally, only an individual with certain attributes can commit a crime. Under common law, a husband could not rape his wife,[28] but he could be guilty of raping his wife if he acted as an accomplice.

In *Regina v. Cogan and Leak*, [1976] 1 Q.B. 217 (Eng.), Leak, the husband, persuaded Cogan to have sexual intercourse with Leak's wife by incorrectly telling him that his wife consented to have sex with him. Cogan was acquitted of rape, based on *Morgan*, because he did not intend to have intercourse without consent. Leak argued that *he* could not be convicted because he was the victim's *husband*. The court disagreed, concluding that Leak had used Cogan as an innocent agent. Therefore, while Leak could not be convicted as aider and abettor to Cogan as originally charged, his guilt as a principal had been clearly established and his conviction was upheld. This case demonstrates that courts will not allow individuals to hide behind their own legal incapacity to commit a crime if they use others to accomplish it.

The Common Law

In the infamous *Morgan* case,[29] for example, the husband could have been convicted as an accomplice to rape either for encouraging others to rape his wife or (if you believed the defendants) for using innocent agents to rape her. The husband would be held liable even though *he* could not have been guilty as P if he had forcibly had sexual intercourse with his wife.

The Model Penal Code

The MPC follows this approach also. Under §2.06(5), a defendant who was herself legally incapable of committing a particular crime may become an accomplice if she helps someone who is legally capable of committing the offense.

---

28. See Chapter 9.

29. *Regina v. Morgan*, House of Lords, [1976] A.C. 182. See discussion of this case in Chapter 9.

THE RELATIONSHIP BETWEEN PRINCIPAL AND ACCESSORIES

The Common Law

The Requirement of a Guilty Principal

As noted at the outset, accomplice responsibility is *derivative*. *A* is legally responsible for the crimes committed by P that *A* aided or (in some jurisdictions) that were a natural and probable consequence of the crime *A* aided. Thus, complicity is a means of attributing the criminal responsibility of P to *A*. This means that there *must* be a guilty P; without a guilty P, there can be no guilty *A*. (Of course, if P is convicted of an *attempt* rather than the completed offense, *A* can be convicted of being an accomplice to that attempt.)

At common law, the acquittal of P, for whatever reason, precluded the conviction of *A* as a principal in the second degree or as an accomplice. (There is an occasional exception to this principle. See our discussion of *Cogan*, supra.) Even if P did commit the crime and *A* fully intended to aid P in its commission, *A* could not be convicted if P was acquitted. This was true even if P's defense was personal, such as diplomatic immunity, or if P had an excuse, such as legal insanity. The requirement of a guilty P can benefit *A* in fortuitous ways that are unrelated to *A*'s moral culpability. Nonetheless, some jurisdictions still retain the requirement of a guilty principal.

The Pretending Principal

Can *A* be convicted if P does not have the mens rea necessary for conviction? No. Thus, in *State v. Hayes*,[30] P, related to the store owner, entered the store in an apparent burglary. However, P had no intention of stealing the goods inside. He only went through with this charade to secure *A*'s conviction. Because P was acting as a citizen decoy, he did not have the mens rea necessary for burglary and larceny. Consequently, *A*'s conviction as an accomplice on these charges had to be reversed for lack of a "guilty principal" even though *A*'s moral culpability and need for punishment were apparent.

Some courts and commentators, however, have indicated their dislike for this rule.[31] In *Vaden v. State*,[32] the Alaska Supreme Court upheld the conviction of a pilot for aiding an undercover agent to shoot foxes illegally from the pilot's airplane. The majority held that the undercover agent's

30. 105 Mo. 76, 16 S.W. 514 (1891).

31. Kadish, supra n. 1, at 381; Fletcher, supra n. 18, at 664-667.

32. 768 P.2d 1102 (Alaska 1989).

actions were not justified under a public authority defense. Thus, there was a "guilty" (though unprosecuted) P. The majority also said in dicta that, even if the defense were valid, it was *personal* to P, and *A* could therefore be convicted. This approach is inconsistent with traditional common law rules. The acquittal of P, even under a personal defense, would have precluded the conviction of *A* at common law.

Differences in Degree of Culpability Between Principal and Accomplice

There is no clear consensus among jurisdictions as to whether *A* can only be convicted of the same crime as P was convicted or whether *A* could be convicted of a *greater* offense. Put differently, does the level of P's responsibility establish the upper limit of *A*'s responsibility?

Consider a case in which Iago (*A*) with cool deliberation provokes Othello (P), through false information, to kill *V*. P might be able to prove that he did not premeditate or that he acted in the heat of passion. *A*, on the other hand, could not. Can *A* be convicted of a more serious crime than P? Or consider the *Richards* case in which a wife hired two men to beat her husband severely enough to be hospitalized; they, however, merely roughed him up without serious injury. Can *A*, the wife, be guilty of a more serious assault charge than either P?[33]

At common law, *A* was convicted of the same offense as P unless the crime was homicide. Because murder and manslaughter were considered different forms of the same offense,[34] *A* in the homicide case above could be convicted of murder even though P had been convicted of manslaughter. In the *Richards* case, however, the court held that the accomplice could not be convicted of a more serious assault charge than that for which the Ps were convicted.

Today, some jurisdictions have changed the common law approach and permit *A* to be convicted of a more serious offense than P.[35] This approach allows the law to assess the moral culpability of each party according to his or her *individual* mens rea.

Withdrawal of Aid

Under the common law, *A* could avoid criminal responsibility if she withdrew her aid before P committed the offense. As in withdrawal from

33. *Regina v. Richards*, [1974] Q.B. 776.

34. See Chapter 8.

35. *Regina v. Howe*, [1987] 1 All E.R. 771, 799. However, the House of Lords in dicta indicated that *Regina v. Richards*, supra n. 33, was wrongly decided.

conspiracy,[36] *A* must (1) inform P not to commit the offense and (2) do everything possible to render ineffective any aid she has already given.

If *A* had encouraged P to commit the crime, she must try to discourage P. If *A* had provided physical assistance of some sort, she must try to render it useless. *A* must take these steps in sufficient time to prevent P from committing the crime. *A*'s efforts can satisfy the required elements of withdrawal even if P independently decides to commit the crime anyway without *A*'s help.

The Model Penal Code

The Requirement of a Guilty Principal

The MPC *seemingly* does not require the conviction of P for *A* to be guilty, *provided* P has engaged in the *conduct* required by the commission of the object crime or by an attempt to commit it. This is true regardless of the basis of P's acquittal.

This is the result reached if "conduct" in §2.06(1) refers *only* to *A* assisting P to engage in conduct sufficient to constitute the offense (or an attempt) and does *not* refer to the mens rea with which P engaged in the conduct or to P's guilt for having engaged in the conduct. Put more simply, §2.06(1) makes *A* responsible for P's conduct and for *A*'s mens rea or culpability. This reading is consistent with the MPC's focus on each individual's moral culpability. A contrary reading of this section is possible, however. If a court did not accept the approach we outline, it might well require a guilty P before *A* could be convicted.

There is a more difficult question. What, if any, responsibility does *A* have if *A* "aids" P to commit a crime, but P does not engage in conduct sufficient to constitute the crime or even an attempt to commit the crime? Section 5.01(3) or 5.03(1)(b) covers this situation. *A*'s conduct would be an "attempt" to commit the object crime (not *attempted* aiding and abetting) or conspiracy, if there was preconcert of action.

The Pretending Principal

For the reasons explained in the previous section, a pretending P does not affect responsibility under the MPC. Thus, an *A* who assists a P who cannot be convicted (because he lacks mens rea or has a personal excuse, for example) can still be convicted under §2.06(1).

---

36. See Chapter 13.

Differences in Degree of Culpability Between Principal and Accomplice

Under the MPC, an accomplice is graded based on the *conduct* committed by P and the *culpability* of *A*. Thus, the MPC readily allows differential punishment for P and *A*.

Withdrawal of Aid

Section 2.06(6)(c) permits an accomplice to withdraw previously provided assistance and thereby avoid criminal responsibility already incurred. To accomplish an effective withdrawal, *A* must terminate his complicity before P commits the offense and do any one of the following: (i) completely deprive the aid of its effectiveness, or (ii) give timely warning to the police, or (iii) otherwise make a "proper effort to prevent the commission of the crime."

Examples

Whom would you charge? With what crime? Why? Who is an accomplice, principal, or accessory?

1a. Linda robs a bank while Brad drives the getaway car.

1b. Linda enters a bank to rob it. She turns to Clara, a kindly elderly lady, and says: "Would you deliver this note to my boyfriend? He is the teller behind that first window. I don't want to get him in trouble for conducting personal business during banking hours." Clara gladly delivered the folded note to the teller. The teller opened and read it: "I have a gun and will use it. Put all the money in a bag and have this lady give it to me." He complied and gave the bag to Clara, asking her to return it to the person who gave her the note. Clara, not suspecting anything, took the bag and gave it to Linda, who promptly left the bank with the cash.

1c. Linda enters the bank to rob it and points her gun at Olga, a bank customer, saying: "Get all the cash from the tellers and put it in a bag for me or else you're dead!" Olga does this and hands Linda the bag with all the cash in it. Linda then runs out the door with the cash.

1d. Same facts as Example 1c except that after Olga hands Linda the bag, Linda hits the bank guard over the head with her gun to immobilize him. Two days later the guard dies from massive internal bleeding in the brain.

1e. Linda and Brad are married. Unknown to Brad, Linda robs a bank by herself and comes home with a lot of money. She tells Brad of her accomplishment and asks him to throw the gun she used in the robbery in a deep lake. Brad gladly disposes of the gun as requested.

2. Dan tells Laura, his wife, that he is going out to rob a grocery store on the other side of town. Laura shouts out as Dan is leaving: "Be sure to bring back some milk while you are at it." Dan robs the grocery store and brings back a half-gallon of milk.

3. While driving along the highway with Tara in the passenger seat, Jennifer spotted Bob, her fiancé, several car lengths ahead of her. She speeded up to wave at him. Bob, recognizing Jennifer in the car behind him, waited until she almost caught up to him and then sped away. Jennifer then increased her speed so she could catch up to Bob once more. Again, Bob, smiling, waited until Jennifer almost caught up to him and then increased his speed even more. This game of "cat and mouse" continued as each car increased their respective speeds. Bob and Jennifer were both laughing out loud when, suddenly, Jennifer, traveling well above the speed limit, lost control and hit a tree. Tara died instantly. Jennifer was charged with vehicular homicide. Is Bob liable as an accomplice? (Remember this scenario from Chapter 7?)

4. Frank and Mark went to an ATM to get cash. Frank used his ATM card to withdraw $40. After Frank inadvertently pushed the "Enter" button a second time, the machine gave him $80, but his account only reflected a $40 deduction. Frank said: "WOW! Two for one! I asked for $40 and got $80 and my account is down only $40. You can't beat that. I mistakenly pushed the 'enter' button a second time." Mark, until then unaware of what had happened, inserted his card and, instead of withdrawing $50 as planned, withdrew $400. He pushed the "Enter" button a second time. The machine gave him $800, while his account only reflected a $400 deduction. Frank and Mark then returned to their dormitory and told Chris all about this magical machine. Chris went to the ATM and withdrew $1,000. It gave him $2,000, while his account only reflected a $1,000 deduction. Is Frank, Mark, or Chris responsible for any crimes committed by each other?

5a. Lydia covets a painting at the local museum. She persuades Bruno, a guard at the museum, to leave a window in the ladies' room unlocked so that she can enter the museum during the night and steal the painting. That evening, Bruno leaves the window unlocked. While on her way to the window, Lydia discovers that a door has been inadvertently left open by a museum employee. Lydia enters through the door, steals the painting, and leaves.

5b. Bruno was angry at the museum for making him stand up during his day shift. One day he saw Anthony creeping slowly toward a famous small painting on display at the museum. Strongly suspecting that Anthony intended to steal the picture and hoping to get back at his boss, Bruno took an unscheduled "coffee break" to make it easier for Anthony. Anthony, unaware that Bruno had left the room, took the painting from the wall and quickly left the museum.

6. Eric and Ian are students at Columbia, a large suburban high school. They sell drugs to a number of students. Pat, a friend, often buys drugs from them. Eric and Ian know that Pat's father is an avid gun collector and that Pat has access to his father's large gun collection. Eric and Ian have frequently told Pat that they want to get their hands on guns like those his father owns so they can kill all the "jocks" and "punks" at their school. One day Eric and Ian offer Pat a very large amount of cocaine in exchange for borrowing several semi-automatic guns and a lot of ammunition from Pat. Pat knows something is brewing because Eric and Ian never make deals—they always make him pay top dollar for his drugs. Nevertheless, Pat agrees to loan them the guns and ammo in exchange for the drugs because he is not worried for his safety—after all, he is not a jock nor a punk. To be extra safe, Pat decides he won't go to school until the guns are returned. The next day Eric and Ian open fire in the school cafeteria with the guns and ammo they borrowed from Pat. Ten students are killed and many more are wounded. Is Pat guilty as an accomplice of these murders and attempted murders?

7. Sister of Fortune magazine, compiled and published solely by Amanda Ashwood, recently ran an advertisement in its classified ad section that read: "Do you need help PERMANENTLY ridding your life of battering boyfriends? Just call Tammy the Terminator at 1-800-MRCNARRY." One week later the body of a battering boyfriend was found. Two weeks later Tammy confessed to this murder-for-hire homicide, telling the police that Leslie, her client, found her and hired her through this ad. The prosecutor wants your advice (ignoring any constitutional law or corporate law issues) on whether she can prosecute Amanda as an accomplice. Please advise.

8. Pedro's wife, Maria, recently left him for José. Pedro, upset and angry, discussed his situation with his close friend, Al. Pedro told Al he was so mad, he could kill José. Al replied: "The man who stole Maria deserves to die. Your honor will be upheld and you will feel much better. If you are a real man, you must do it."
   a. That evening Pedro grabs his pistol from his closet but cannot bring himself to leave his house. Nothing further happens.
   b. Same facts, except that Pedro leaves his house and kills José.

c. Same facts, except that Pedro leaves his house and kills José and Maria.
d. Same facts, except that Al gives Pedro a loaded gun and says: "Here, my friend. This is for your honor." That evening Pedro kills José and Maria.
e. Same facts as in Example 8d except that later that afternoon Al decides that killing José is wrong. Al calls Pedro and tells him in strong language that killing José is wrong and will not solve anything. Pedro says he will think it over. Later that night Pedro uses the gun Al gave him and kills José.
f. Pedro uses his own gun to kill José and later goes to Al's house (who does not know that Maria has left Pedro to run off with José) and says: "I have just killed the man who stole my wife with this gun. Get rid of it immediately." Al has already heard news reports that say that Pedro is the prime suspect but that the murder will probably not be solved unless the murder weapon is recovered. Al takes the gun Pedro gave him to a garbage dump where it is soon covered over with several tons of new garbage.
g. Same facts as in the first paragraph of this Example except that Pedro tells Al that he has placed a bomb in José home set to explode at 9:00 p.m. Al replies that Maria and José will be at a movie at that time. Pedro says: "I know that. I just want to scare them. Maybe Maria will come back to me." Al decides that scaring Maria and José is not enough. At 8:30 p.m., Al calls José at the movie theater and tells him his house has been broken into. José and Maria immediately leave the theater and return to José's house. The bomb explodes while they are there, killing both of them.

9. "Sharkie" specializes in lending money at illegal interest rates to individuals with terrible credit records. He tells Thug, one of his collection agents, to "do what you have to do to collect the money from Sam but, remember, I want my money." Thug, not being terribly bright, uses his fists a bit too liberally on Sam trying to persuade Sam to pay the money he owes Sharkie. Sam dies from the beating.

10. Tiny regularly visits an exotic dancing club. The local prostitution law makes it a criminal offense for exotic dancers to make physical contact with a customer in exchange for money.

    One evening Tiny becomes extremely frustrated with the law and offers Candy, a dancer, $100 for a lap dance. Candy agrees and does a lap dance while seated on Tiny's lap. An undercover police officer immediately arrests both. Subsequently, the prosecutor charges Tiny as an accomplice to Candy's act of prostitution.

Explanations

1a. Brad intentionally provided assistance to Linda while she committed the bank robbery. Thus, Brad is an accomplice and could be held liable as such for the crime of bank robbery committed by Linda. At common law, Brad would be a principal in the second degree because he was present and rendering assistance while Linda, the principal in the first degree, was committing a crime.

Under the MPC, and most modern statutes, Brad would be considered a principal and would be convicted as such for the crime of bank robbery because he purposefully rendered aid to one he knew was committing this crime.

1b. Although Clara assisted Linda in robbing the bank by delivering the note to the teller and then delivering the cash to Linda, Clara had no intention to assist Linda in the commission of a crime. Clara is an "innocent agent" who, while trying to be helpful, has been deceived as to what she is doing.

1c. Olga assisted Linda to commit the bank robbery by gathering up the cash and putting it in a bag for her. However, Olga did so only because she was threatened with imminent deadly force. Olga would have a successful defense of duress (see Chapter 16) and, thus, would be an innocent agent. She could not be convicted as an accomplice.

1d. Linda could be convicted under a felony murder/murder charge in most states. Olga also may be in trouble unless this jurisdiction allows the defense of duress to a murder charge, including felony murder. Most jurisdictions would probably allow Olga to use this defense. If not, then Olga might be held liable under the law as an accomplice.

The point here is that liability as an accomplice can depend on other legal doctrines such as duress. If the alleged accomplice has a defense in cases where she intentionally rendered aid, then she cannot be held guilty as an accomplice. If that defense fails, however, she then may be convicted as an accomplice. (*Note:* A really clever defense attorney might argue that Olga did not act with "purpose" to take the money by threat of deadly force. But that evidence may be relevant only to "motive.")

1e. At common law, Brad would not be liable as an accessory after the fact. Both husband and wife were expected to help each other avoid conviction if a spouse committed a crime.

In most jurisdictions today, Brad would be convicted of rendering criminal assistance or criminal facilitation. There is no defense for a spouse or relative who knowingly helps someone who has committed a crime avoid apprehension or conviction. Some jurisdictions, however, will reduce the degree of the offense if a spouse or relative is involved and only provides certain kinds of assistance.

2. The general rule is that *any* encouragement is sufficient even though the principal would have committed the crime anyway. If the jury finds that Laura's statement was intended to encourage Dan to commit the crime and had any impact on the principal, it would be legally sufficient to convict Laura as an accomplice. See *State v. Helmenstein*, 163 N.W.2d 85 (N.D. 1968).

3. Jennifer is clearly a principal in the first degree at common law and is a principal under the MPC.

   In many jurisdictions, Bob could be charged as an accomplice in the vehicular homicide of Tara for intentionally encouraging Jennifer to drive well over the speed limit by initiating and continuing to play this dangerous game. Granted, Bob did not verbally communicate with Jennifer to egg her on, and Jennifer was the last responsible moral agent who could have slowed down at any time and avoided this tragedy. However, the law of accomplice liability does not require significant encouragement nor does it require "but for" causation as required elements for liability. Thus, Bob can be convicted as an accomplice and could receive the same sentence as Jennifer.

4. Frank, Mark, and Chris are each responsible for their own withdrawal and each may face a criminal charge of theft if they do not return the extra cash or tell the bank. (See Chapter 10.) Frank and Mark were both present when the other obtained the extra cash. Generally, being present with the knowledge that someone else is committing a crime is not sufficient for accomplice liability unless the individual is there for the *purpose* of encouraging a crime or unless the principal knows that the individual is willing to help if necessary. Here Mark did not know what Frank had done until after Frank had obtained the extra cash. Thus, Mark is clearly not responsible for any crime Frank may have committed. Frank, however, told Mark what happened and provided Mark with essential knowledge about how to obtain extra cash. Mark, relying on that information, increased his withdrawal significantly and also received a double payment. But did Frank tell Mark what happened and provide him with vital information on how to obtain an extra payout with the *intent* to encourage Mark to commit a crime? If the prosecution can prove that Frank did have this purpose, then Frank could be convicted as an accomplice and would also be responsible for Mark's crime. In most jurisdictions, merely providing useful information without intent to encourage another person's committing a crime does not suffice for accomplice responsibility. The MPC also requires *purpose*. This will be a close case. The same analysis applies to Frank's and

Mark's responsibility for Chris's crime. It may be easier for the prosecution to prove that they did act with the purpose of encouraging Chris to commit a crime because they sought him out and provided the information necessary to improperly obtain extra cash. What do you think the result should be?

5a. Bruno would argue that his aid to Lydia—leaving the window unlocked—was completely ineffective; consequently, he cannot be convicted of being an accomplice. This argument would probably be successful. The prosecutor may have a fallback theory, however. By telling Lydia he would leave the window open, Bruno may have encouraged Lydia to commit the burglary and theft. Thus, these words by themselves might be considered legally sufficient assistance to convict Bruno of being an accomplice.

At common law, doing something that did not help P-1 in any way to commit the offense was an insufficient actus reus for accomplice liability. Under the MPC, however, Bruno has clearly "attempted" to render assistance; consequently, under §2.06(3)(a)(i) he can be convicted as a principal even though he did not provide any useful assistance. (This assumes that leaving the window open meets the MPC's definition of "substantial step" by "strongly corroborating" the actor's criminal purpose.) The MPC focuses more on the actor's attitude rather than on whether his help was useful.

Of course, the prosecutor may also be able to establish a conspiracy to commit burglary and theft if she can show that Bruno and Lydia had entered into an agreement to commit a crime and one of them took an overt act in furtherance of the conspiracy. If this argument proves successful, Bruno would be liable for the crimes of burglary and theft committed by Lydia in a jurisdiction that follows the *Pinkerton* rule.

5b. Bruno can be convicted of being an accomplice to Anthony's theft of the painting. This is a case of omission or failure to act when there is a legal duty to prevent another person from committing a crime. As a security guard, Bruno had a civil legal duty by virtue of his employment contract to take reasonable steps within his power to prevent the theft of the picture. Instead, Bruno left the room with the purpose of making it easier for Anthony to commit the crime.

Note that Bruno is an accomplice even though Anthony did not realize that he was being assisted in committing the crime. There is no requirement that the principal know he is being assisted to commit the object offense, though this is generally the case.

6. This example is based loosely on the Littleton, Colorado high-school massacre. The tragedy really makes one think about what culpability should be required for accomplice liability.

Pat loaned his father's semi-automatic weapons and a large amount of ammunition to Eric and Ian. The prosecutor could probably prove Pat *knew* they intended to use them to kill fellow students at their high school. Eric and Ian had often told Pat they wanted to use his father's guns to kill certain students. Pat also knew something big was up because Eric and Ian had never let him swap for drugs; they always insisted on cold cash. Finally, Pat avoided the crime scene precisely because of what he expected would happen.

Nonetheless, without additional evidence, it would be difficult to prove that Pat loaned his father's automatic weapons with the *purpose* of assisting or encouraging their crimes. Pat would argue that his purpose was simply to obtain drugs and that he was indifferent as to what Eric and Ian did with the weapons and ammunition. Because Pat was able to obtain a large amount of drugs without paying for them—only by loaning these dangerous items—the prosecutor could argue that Pat had a "stake in the venture" and thus did act with purpose to assist Eric and Ian. The MPC and a number of jurisdictions would not convict Pat as an accomplice unless the prosecutor could prove Pat acted with such purpose.

Other jurisdictions, however, would convict Pat if he had had *knowledge* that the guns and ammunition he loaned his friends would be used to commit a *serious* crime. Criminal conviction and punishment of such "enablers" is necessary to deter them and others like them from providing such aid. A much stronger case can be made that Pat had such knowledge.

In some states, Pat could be convicted of criminal facilitation because he knowingly provided significant aid, the weapons and ammunition, to someone he knew (or, in some states, had reason to know) intended to commit a serious crime. In this case, Pat would be punished less severely than Eric and Ian.

7. Amanda provided vital information about how to hire a professional killer to interested consumers. Most jurisdictions and the MPC would require the prosecution to prove that Amanda acted with the *purpose* of assisting another person to commit a crime. Some courts would hold an actor guilty as an accomplice if she provided assistance to someone she *knows* intends to commit a *serious* crime. (See the *Fountain* case, supra.) The prosecutor would point out that this information could only be used to assist someone in committing a serious crime; it had no lawful purpose. Moreover, the language in the advertisement was very clear about the ultimate criminal purpose for which Tammy would be hired. Amanda would counter that she did not know that Tammy, let alone Leslie, presently intended to commit a crime. Thus, she could not have acted with the necessary mens rea. What would you tell the prosecutor?

8a. Because Pedro has not committed any crime, there is no guilty principal. At common law, Al could not be convicted as an accomplice. Under the MPC, the result is the same; Al cannot be convicted as an accomplice because Pedro has not engaged in the conduct required to commit the object crime or an attempt to commit it.

8b. Al is guilty as an accomplice because he has provided psychological reinforcement to Pedro to commit murder and the principal committed that very crime. Because there is a guilty principal, Al would be convicted under both the common law and the MPC.

An interesting question here is whether Al might be guilty of a greater crime than the principal. Pedro might have a heat of passion or related defense (though unlikely); Al would not. If Pedro is convicted of manslaughter, can Al be convicted of premeditated murder? At common law the accomplice's liability is generally limited by that of the principal's unless the crime is murder. Thus, Al can be convicted of a more serious offense than Pedro. If a crime other than homicide were involved, such as assault, the general rule is that the accomplice cannot be convicted of a more serious crime than the principal.

Under the MPC, and the law of some jurisdictions, the liability of the accomplice is measured by *his* culpability together with the conduct of the principal. Consequently, Al could be convicted of a more serious degree of homicide. This is true even for less serious crimes than homicide.

8c. This is a tricky one. Al encouraged Pedro to kill only José; he did not encourage him to kill Maria. Thus, Al did not intend to assist Pedro in the particular criminal action of killing his wife. The MPC and many jurisdictions would require that the accomplice act with the purpose or intent of encouraging the specific criminal conduct of the principal. Negligence toward other crimes committed by the principal is not a sufficient basis for accomplice liability. Thus, Al would not be guilty as an accomplice for Pedro's murder of Maria in these jurisdictions.

However, some jurisdictions are expanding accomplice liability to include crimes committed by the principal that were a "natural or probable consequence" of the offense the accomplice intended to aid or that should have been "reasonably foreseen." A prosecutor could argue that Al should have foreseen that a jealous husband might well kill his wife as well as her lover. (Unfortunately, this argument may reinforce the law's acceptance that male violence in intimate relationships is understandable and should be condoned or at least partially excused.) Or a prosecutor could argue that the accomplice has set in motion forces that might readily lead to this particular consequence. Convicting Al as an accomplice for the murder of Maria would be possible in these jurisdictions.

8d. The only difference here is that Al provided physical assistance as well as psychological reinforcement. The analysis of Al's criminal responsibility here is the same as in Explanations 8b and 8c above. Evidence of the actus reus required for assistance is stronger here.

8e. By calling Pedro and telling him not to kill José, Al has clearly withdrawn the psychological encouragement to commit murder he had given Pedro earlier in the day. Thus, his call to Pedro is an effective withdrawal of aid previously furnished. However, Al also gave Pedro a loaded gun to use in killing José. Al has not rendered *that* aid ineffective. Thus, under common law, Al would still be liable as an accomplice.

The MPC is also very demanding before withdrawal will be legally effective. Al has not completely removed the effectiveness of his aid (providing the loaded gun). Al should have gone to Pedro's home and taken back the gun. Nor did Al call the police. A jury might conclude that Al has made a "proper effort" to prevent the commission of the crime, but more likely Al will be convicted because he did not take sufficient steps to prevent the commission of the crime.

8f. Al is clearly an accomplice after the fact at common law because he has intentionally disposed of a weapon that he knows has been used in a homicide, making it difficult, if not impossible, for the police to gather essential evidence for investigation and prosecution.

Under the MPC, and many modern statutes, Al would be guilty of criminal facilitation or rendering criminal assistance. The degree of punishment often depends on the severity of the crime committed by the principal. The liability of the person rendering aid after the crime has been committed usually is not affected by the subsequent acquittal of the principal. The essence of this crime is obstructing justice by aiding flight, preventing apprehension, or destroying or concealing evidence.

8g. This is an extremely difficult problem (even for us, if that is any consolation). Pedro only intended to scare José and Maria; he did not intend to kill them. Al did not intend to help Pedro accomplish that goal. Instead, Al decided to kill José and Maria. Thus, Al is a principal in a homicide charge. Granted that Pedro might be liable as a principal under a separate felony murder theory, is he guilty as an accomplice to Al's murder? Probably not because Pedro did not act with the purpose to assist Al commit a homicide. Indeed, Pedro did not know that Al intended to commit any crime.

9. Thug is surely guilty of homicide, either "serious bodily injury" murder or manslaughter in the first or second degree. But is Sharkie also guilty as an accomplice? Sharkie did not want Sam killed because Sam's death means Sharkie will *not* get his money back. Thus, Sharkie did not

intend that Thug engage in the criminal action that caused Sam's death. Because Sharkie did not have this necessary mens rea, many jurisdictions, including those that follow the MPC, would not convict Sharkie as an accomplice to Thug's crime of manslaughter.

Some courts, however, are now holding the accomplice responsible for crimes committed by the principal if P's crime was reasonably foreseeable or if *A* has set in motion a chain of events and P's crime was a "natural and probable result" of this chain. In these jurisdictions, Sharkie might be convicted as an accomplice to Thug's crime of manslaughter.

10. The criminal law in this jurisdiction prohibits exotic dancers from making physical contact with patrons in exchange for money. It does not punish the customer who pays for the dance. By doing a lap dance in exchange for money, Candy has clearly violated the law.

    Can the prosecutor convict Tiny as an accomplice? After all, he initiated Candy's crime and gave very strong encouragement to her by paying her $100. Nonetheless, the charge should be dismissed. The substantive law here punishes only the conduct of one party even though the crime necessarily requires participation by two parties. A court will conclude that the legislature, in not punishing the conduct of one party essential to the commission of the crime, did not intend to impose criminal responsibility on that party. To permit a prosecutor to use accomplice liability to punish that very same conduct will subvert legislative intent.

CHAPTER 15

Defenses: An Initial Survey

OVERVIEW

The materials in this chapter concern two procedural hurdles that defendants may confront at trial. We will first discuss presumptions, which are far less prevalent in criminal practice now than several decades ago. Our attention for the remainder of the chapter, and indeed of the book, will be almost exclusively on the place of "defenses" in the criminal law. These are unsettled areas of the law. The notion that defenses can be categorized as either excuse or justification, which is the primary topic in this chapter, is new to Anglo-Saxon jurisprudence. The distinction, however, is hardly academic; it has many practical, as well as theoretical, implications.

This chapter investigates what we mean when we say that *D* has a "defense." Does a defense relate to an element of the crime? If so, how? May the state require the defendant to carry the burden of proof on a "defense"? And by what procedural mechanisms or labels may it do that? Chapters 16 and 17 investigate specific kinds of defensive claims. Chapter 16 looks at many claims that may be classified as "justifications," while Chapter 17 considers claims of "excuse." Throughout those two chapters, however, we will refer back to the issues raised in this chapter. They are all of the same cloth.

PRESUMPTIONS

One procedural device by which the state may attempt to shift the burden of proof (or production) to the defendant is a *presumption*. Civil law employs many kinds of presumptions. Some are "conclusive"—no matter what proof the opposing party wishes to present, the law will "presume" the fact against her. For example, the common law presumed that a child born to a married woman was the child of the husband. No contrary facts, such as that the husband was infertile or that he had been absent for one year (or even ten), were admissible to rebut the presumption. This was a policy decision. The courts did not wish to inquire into the private lives of married couples, nor did they wish unnecessarily to label children as "illegitimate."

Other presumptions are established for different reasons. Some are based on common sense and experience. For example, the law presumes that a letter dropped in a government mailbox was delivered because, in the vast majority of cases, when a letter is sent, it actually arrives. By applying this "presumption," we move the litigation forward. Since, in our common experience, most letters are delivered, once the plaintiff has shown that he put the letter in a mailbox, the defendant must show that our common experience should not be applied to the specific facts of this specific case. It would be needlessly time-consuming to require the plaintiff to show that the letter was delivered. On the other hand, if the defendant wishes to demonstrate that the letter did not arrive, he may be allowed to rebut the presumption. He might, for example, show that the mailbox into which the letter was placed was thereafter robbed, or that, as a normal business matter, the defendant records every incoming piece of mail and that there is no such recording of the plaintiff's letter.

Finally, some presumptions, such as res ipsa loquitur, seem to be devices by which we "smoke out" the opposing party (usually the defendant), to get him to tell us what he knows about the event. These presumptions were first applied when there was little or no discovery and a defendant, merely by stonewalling, could effectively prevent the plaintiff from proving his case. *Byrne v. Boadle*, 159 Eng. Rep. 299 (1863).

We usually speak of this process as *presuming* fact B (delivery of the letter) from the *basic* (or *predicate*) fact A (posting of the letter), and require that there be some connection between facts A and B. This may be graphically illustrated as follows:

$$\text{(Predicate) A} \rightarrow \text{B (Presumed)}$$

Thus, if the jury finds fact A by the proper standard, it may conclude that the presumed fact (B) is also proved.

There is considerable uncertainty, even in civil cases, as to the procedural importance of presumptions. Although some presumptions based on policy decisions are irrebuttable, such as the child-father rule mentioned above, most presumptions are rebuttable. The question contested is who must rebut them, and to what degree. Some argue that a presumption should always shift the burden of (dis)proof to the opposing party (whom we will refer to as the defendant, since it is usually the plaintiff who seeks to use a presumption). E. Morgan, Basic Problems of Evidence (1963). Others argue that most presumptions are simply "smoking out" devices and should disappear entirely if the defendant comes forward with as much evidence as he has. J. Thayer, A Preliminary Treatise on Evidence at the Common Law (1898).

These rules may be more easily understood as they are applied. If you see puddles in the street after you've been in a building for hours, you are likely to conclude that it has rained, although you didn't see it rain. Why? Because "in the vast majority of cases" puddles in the streets come from rain. A presumption that "puddles on the street implies rain" is probably commonsensical: Proof of the predicate fact A (puddles) leads to the conclusion B (that it has rained). You may later learn that the water was from some other source (e.g., a street cleaner or an overturned water truck), but you start from the premise, based on common experience, that if there are puddles, it is highly *likely* that it rained. Indeed, in the absence of other suggestions, you are likely to conclude beyond a reasonable doubt that it rained.

These same empirical considerations may apply to criminal cases. Suppose, for example, that statutes prohibit the possession of certain drugs *only* if they have been imported into the United States. An instruction to the jury that if the prosecution proves the drug to be heroin, it can be presumed that it was imported, unless the defendant brings some evidence to the contrary, is constitutional because virtually no heroin is produced in the United States. On the other hand, that same instruction applied to marijuana is probably invalid because much marijuana (even if not over 50 percent) is homegrown. See *Leary v. United States*, 395 U.S. 6 (1969).

In earlier centuries, the criminal law employed many such presumptions. A defendant was "presumed" sane. A person who used a deadly weapon in killing another was "presumed" to have "malice aforethought" (or, in a variation of this presumption, to "intend" the death). More broadly, defendants were "presumed" to "intend the natural and probable consequences of their acts." Some of these presumptions were established not only because they might be commonsensical, but also because defendants were precluded from testifying. Thus, mens rea "had to be" presumed from facts proved by the prosecution. Whether these presumptions are valid today, when defendants have a constitutional right not to testify and to not have their silence construed against them, is highly doubtful.

Constitutional Aspects of Presumptions

Presumptions concerning the elements of the crime in criminal cases are subject to constitutional scrutiny. Establishing a "conclusive" presumption against the defendant would obviously conflict with the requirement that the prosecution carry the burden of proving every element. *In re Winship*, 397 U.S. 358 (1970) (see Chapter 1). But what about lesser "rebuttable" presumptions? And what of those presumptions that try to "smoke out" the defendant, or that don't require but merely "allow" the jury to reach certain conclusions?

In *Allen v. Ulster County Court*, 442 U.S. 140 (1979), and *Sandstrom v. Montana*, 442 U.S. 510 (1979), the Supreme Court divided such devices into "mandatory" presumptions and "permissive" inferences. Presumptions that actually shift the burden of proof on such elements—or could be misconstrued by the jury as doing so—are unconstitutional. Devices that only shift the burden of going forward on an element are constitutional, if there is a sufficient connection between A (the predicate fact) and B (the presumed fact).

The *degree* of relation between A and B—mandatory presumption or permissive inference— depends on the exact instructions given by the judge to the jury.

Mandatory Presumption: The judge instructs the jurors that if they find A, the defendant has the burden of going forward on B. → The connection between A and B must be *beyond a reasonable doubt*.

Permissive Inference: The judge does not instruct the jury on the matter, simply allowing the prosecutor to make the case to the jury, *or* is very clear that the inference is permissive, and does not require rebuttal by the defendant. → The connection between A and B must be merely *more likely than not*.

The thrust of these cases is that presumptions are on weak ground, and that they are likely to be valid only if (1) the link between A and B is very strong and (2) the judge's instructions so weaken the "mandatory" nature of the "presumption" and make it so fact-specific to the case at hand that it is no longer an abstract proposition.

The Model Penal Code

The Code does not recognize mandatory presumptions, preferring that when the legislature wishes to require the defendant to carry the burden of production or persuasion, it say so explicitly. (As already noted, the Code itself establishes only a small handful of such claims.) On the other hand, §1.12(b) allows the court to instruct the jury that it *may* (not *must*) use a permissive inference on its way to finding the presumed fact.

"AFFIRMATIVE" DEFENSES

Not everything a defendant says in an adversarial setting is a "defense." If a defendant in a tort case denies an allegation of negligence by saying that the light was green when he went through it, he is not raising a "defense" but challenging the very heart of the plaintiff's case. On the other hand, there are (affirmative) defenses in civil law. For example, demonstrating that the case was not brought within the time allowed by the statute of limitations is an affirmative defense for which the defendant carries the burden.[1]

In criminal cases, some claims that we initially think of as defenses actually go to the heart of the prosecution's case. Just as with the stoplight color issue above, a criminal defendant who claims that he was in Cleveland when the killing occurred in Poughkeepsie is not raising a defense. He is challenging a critical aspect of the prosecutor's case: that it was *D* who was present at the crime. We call this kind of claim a failure of proof or an element negation defense because it argues that the prosecution has failed to prove even its prima facie case. Robinson, Criminal Law Defenses: A Systematic Analysis, 82 Colum. L. Rev. 190 (1982).

Are all defenses "element negations"? Surely in the early common law that argument could be made. Virtually all defenses concerned whether the defendant should be punished as an "immoral actor" (traditional mens rea) and, if so, how severely. In that sense, all defenses were element negations.

Most modern criminal law analysts, however, would reject that approach. They would argue that, based on *Winship*, the prosecution must prove beyond a doubt only "every fact necessary to constitute the crime." This language seems equivalent to the term "material element" as used in both the common law and the Model Penal Code (see Chapter 4). These analysts would then argue that some affirmative defenses, at least, do not negate such elements or facts. The basic "rule," which is nevertheless very difficult to apply, seems to be that the legislature may require the defendant to carry the burden of proof on whatever the common law recognized as an "affirmative defense," BUT that if the legislation "copies" or is "similar to" a common law offense, the government must "disprove" such a defense. History, therefore, matters a great deal. The problem is that history is not

1. This is not a problem in England. In *D.P.P. v. Woolmington*, [1935] A.C. 481, the House of Lords declared that the prosecution held the burden of proof in all aspects of the case. But see Tanovich, The Unravelling of the Golden Thread: The Supreme Court's Compromise of the Presumption of Innocence, [1993] Crim. L.Q. 194. The International Criminal Code also requires all defenses to be rebutted by the prosecutor once properly raised. See Rome Statute of the International Criminal Court, art. 31-33 (adoption July 17, 1998; entry into force, July 1, 2002), available at http://www.icc-cpi.int/NR/rdonlyres/EA9AEFF7-5752-4F84-BE94-0A655EB30E16/0/Rome_Statute_ English.pdf at art. 67(1)(i).

necessarily clear. First, common law courts did not distinguish between "burdens of production" and "burdens of proof" as courts do today.[2] Second, the common law was fluid—judicial positions changed throughout the nineteenth century, raising questions of the date a court should use in deciding what the "common law" rule was. Students of constitutional law will not be surprised to find that even the Justices of the Supreme Court choose different approaches: (1) originalist (1776 or 1789); (2) originalist plus (1865, when the Fourteenth Amendment was adopted); (3) "recent history" ("in the last fifty or so years"). The problem is made more complex by the alleged distinction, discussed below, between justifications and excuses. In 2006, the Supreme Court appeared to hold that there was no federal constitutional barrier to requiring the defendant to prove those defenses called "excuses." We will discuss those decisions—*Dixon v. United States* and *Clark v. Arizona*—in detail later in this chapter, and even more extensively in Chapters 16 and 17.

Legislative Clarity and the Offense-Defense Distinction

Let's begin with the "easy" case. Consider the following two statutes:

1. Unauthorized possession of A is a crime.
2. Possession of A, unless authorized, is a crime.

Obviously, authorization (or its absence) is relevant. In which of these statutes, however, must the state prove that the defendant "lacked" authority? In which may the state require that the defendant establish that he acted "with" authority? Does either statute clearly tell us?

Common law courts relied on maxims of statutory construction to resolve these issues. But as we have already seen in other contexts, none of these maxims solves the conundrum. Professor Robinson has argued that "whether a defense is a failure of proof defense or an offense modification may depend on the form in which it is drafted." Robinson, supra, at 203. But Professor Williams has responded that this is a purely verbal and formal distinction: "The definitional elements are those that we choose to pick out from all the elements expressed in the rules relating to the offense." Williams, Offences and Defenses, 2 Legal Stud. 23 (1982); Williams, The Logic of "Exceptions," 47 Cambridge L.J. 261 (1988).

Williams' point is essentially that legislatures have an obligation to be clear (see the discussion of the legality principle in Chapter 1) and the

2. Fletcher, Two Kinds of Legal Rules: A Comparative Study of Burden-of-Persuasion Practices in Criminal Cases, 77 Yale L.J. 880 (1968).

legislature could have made the statute clearer on this point. If the legislature wished the defendant to carry the burden of demonstrating authorization, the statute could have been written as follows:

3. Possession of A is a crime. If the defendant proves by a preponderance of the evidence that he had authorization for the possession, there is no criminal liability.

There will always be a way in which the legislature could have phrased a statute to clarify on whom it intended to place the burden of proving an issue. In accordance with the rule of lenity (see Chapter 1), an ambiguous statute should be construed to narrow the reach of the criminal law, thus requiring legislatures to reenact the statute in a clearer way. Therefore, a salutary rule of interpreting criminal statutes might be, "Unless the legislation expressly uses the form 'X is a defense that must be proved by the defendant,' all claims relevant to guilt must be proved by the prosecution." Unfortunately, courts do not adopt such easy rules. And they may apply different approaches to interpreting two apparently similar statutes (see the discussion of the Supreme Court's decisions in *Dean* and *Flores-Figueroa*, supra, pages 145, 146). The answer, then, is that some courts would require the prosecution to prove non-authorization in both statutes, while some would require the defendant to carry the burden of proving authorization, at least in statute #2.

The Constitution and Affirmative Defenses

If the common law was uncertain as to which defenses were "affirmative"—under which the defendant could be required to carry the burden of proof—there is no greater clarity regarding the constitutionality of such legislation. In *Mullaney v. Wilbur*, 421 U.S. 684 (1975), the Court held that a defendant could not be required to prove the "affirmative defense" of "heat of passion" because that defense negated an element of the crime of murder (malice aforethought). Two years later, the Court upheld as constitutional a New York statute that put upon the defendant the burden of proving the "affirmative defense" of "extreme emotional or mental disturbance," concluding that claim did NOT negate an element of the crime of murder. *Patterson v. New York*, 432 U.S. 197 (1977). There are ways to attempt to reconcile *Mullaney* and *Patterson*. First, the statute in *Patterson* was written clearly, while the law in *Mullaney* was not. Second, the history of the common law regarding the relation of "heat of passion" and "malice aforethought" seemed to put the burden on the state, whereas the New York statute, which was enacted only in the 1960s, had no such history. Third, the New York statute, which was obviously copied from the MPC, provided a defendant with much more opportunity than did the common law to have his homicide reduced to manslaughter (see Chapter 8 for a broader discussion). Thus, New York was giving the defendant a "bonus" beyond that which the common law recognized, and the state could, as a quid pro quo for that "bonus," constitutionally place upon the defendant the burden of showing that he deserved the "bonus." The literature on these cases and their progeny is voluminous and still very contentious. Suffice it to say that, 40 years later, there is no single "fulfilling" reconciliation between these two opinions, much less clear explanation in other cases.

The Common Law and Affirmative Defenses

The aspect of statutory interpretation described above, where a statute establishes both a rule and an exception to the rule in the same text, is known as the exception problem. But most "defenses" were established in the common law, long before the lenity rule of statutory interpretation was applicable. The problem begins where these "defenses" are raised. Healy, Proof and Policy: No Golden Threads, [1987] Crim. L. Rev. 355.

There is substantial disagreement as to the relation between defenses and the elements of a crime. For example, does a claim that the defendant was under duress challenge the mens rea (or actus reus) of the crime? Or is such a claim irrelevant to either of these two elements? Some would argue that no "insane" person can have mens rea, even if he can "intend" his acts and those acts' consequences. Others would argue that many, if not all, insane persons intend their acts and therefore are guilty of crime, even if they are insane. Perhaps when mens rea entailed moral as well as legal guilt (see Chapter 4), it could have been suggested that these claims demonstrated lack of moral culpability and hence denied guilt. The argument is much harder to make now since statutes have adopted "mental state" words (statutory mens rea) that do not, on their face, entail an additional moral culpability (traditional mens rea).

Yet all commentators and courts agree that there is a need for some generic defenses, if only because no legislation could possibly list all the factual circumstances under which an intentional crime would not and should not be punished. The Sixth Commandment, after all, is "Thou shalt not kill," not "Thou shalt not kill except in self-defense, or under duress, or in necessitous circumstances."[3] Even if the legislature were to adopt the

3. Some linguists argue that the original Hebrew uses the word "murder" rather than "kill." But that only postpones the problem; if the distinction between "kill" and "murder" is self-defense, duress, necessity, and so on, we still need to define those terms.

latter language, those terms would still have to be defined (and refined). The issue, then, is under what circumstances a defendant who appears prima facie to meet the elements of a crime should not be found guilty. We explore specific pleas such as insanity and self-defense (among others) in the next two chapters; here the inquiry is a broader one.

EXCUSE AND JUSTIFICATION: THE DEBATE AND CONFUSION

The Distinction Drawn

The early common law recognized the difference between excuse and justification, at least in instances of self-defense.[4] A justified act totally exonerated the defendant; an excused act exempted him from criminal punishment (i.e., the gallows), but resulted in forfeiture of all his personal and real property. Since forfeiture was prohibited in America, the distinction disappeared, and when England abolished forfeiture in 1838, it became less important there, also—all defendants proving either justification or excuse were simply not convicted. The distinction remained unexamined until Professor George Fletcher reintroduced it to American law professors 30 years ago.[5] For example, suppose Schmidlap has purposely parked next to a fire hydrant near a hospital. When asked why he did so, he replies either

1. "I had to. I was taking my injured baby to the hospital to save his life."

or

2. "I had to. The Martians told me to do it."

In the first response, Schmidlap is said to be *justifying* his action. He is claiming that although the act appears to be illegal, he violated the law in order to achieve a greater social good: saving the life of his child. His claim is that his act is not wrongful; some violations of statutes are not wrongful if

4. The literature on this topic is voluminous. For a smattering of some recent writings, see Gardner, The Gist of Excuses, 1 Buff. Crim. L. Rev. 575 (1998); Finkelstein, Excuses and Dispositions in Criminal Law, 6 Buff. Crim. L. Rev. 317 (2002); Berman, Justification and Excuse, Law and Morality, 53 Duke L.J. 1 (2003); Baron, Justifications and Excuses, 2 Ohio St. J. Crim. L. 387 (2005); Nourse, Reconceptualizing Criminal Law Defenses, 151 U. Pa. L. Rev. 1691 (2003).

5. G. Fletcher, Rethinking Criminal Law (1978).

a greater good is thereby served. His decision to violate the law should be seen as praiseworthy.

In the second response, Schmidlap is obviously irrational. His claim is that although he should never have done what he did (it was wrong), because of some personal disability (in this case, what the law calls insanity) he should not be punished for that wrongful act. His claim is not one of justification but of *excuse*. It is often said that justification focuses on the act, whereas excuse focuses on the actor.

In some cases, it is clear that the defendant is claiming only justification. If Martha, the state executioner, premeditatedly injects George with a lethal dose of poison, her killing is not merely excused but justified. The state wanted—indeed, ordered—her to carry out the killing. Killings in war are similarly said to be justified.

The problem is very likely "academic." As one commentator has noted, "[T]here is much better reason to distinguish excuse and insanity and duress from the justifications of necessity and self-defense than there is to classify mistaken necessity and mistaken self-defense as excuses and distinguish them in that way from actual necessity and actual self-defense." Michael Louis Corrado, Self-Defense, Moral Acceptability, and Compensation: A Response to Professor Fontaine 47 Am. Crim. L. Rev. 91, 92 (2010).

The Distinction Questioned

Some courts and writers argue that many, indeed most, acts sought to be excused or justified are sufficiently morally problematic as to not be "clearly" justified or "clearly" excused. Consider, for example, the following hypothetical:[6] Gary sees Ingrid, a two-year-old, pointing a gun (which Gary knows has a hair trigger) directly at the temple of Henrietta. Gary concludes that the only way to save Henrietta's life is to shoot Ingrid. He does so, killing Ingrid. It is difficult to claim that Gary's act was morally praiseworthy and hence justified. On the other hand, the act was not "wrong," and he should not be blamed for it under the circumstances. He did, after all, save the life of an innocent person, although he also took an innocent life. To excuse Gary suggests that he did something wrong, for which he would usually be blamed, if not punished. At best it was a tragic choice, which we should tolerate.

Critics of the distinction also argue that if academics cannot resolve difficult cases, juries may also be unable to do so. There would be no benefit in asking them to decide whether, for example, Gary's shooting was

---

6. Dressler, New Thoughts About the Concept of Justification in the Criminal Law: A Critique of Fletcher's Thinking and Rethinking, 32 UCLA L. Rev. 61, 84-85 (1984).

justified or excused, so long as all agreed that he should not be punished. In response to the argument that a verdict should reflect jurors' moral resolution of this issue so that it "sends a message," critics ask: What happens if the jury splits 8-4 on which of these explanations is the "better" one? Neither the proponents of the "message" theory nor courts have yet answered that question.

The Problems with Explaining Justification

As noted earlier, it is often said that justification focuses on the act whereas excuse focuses on the actor. But it's not that simple. In Chapters 3 and 4, we saw that there is an ambiguity in the term "act"—whether it means solely conduct, or whether it also includes the result. We saw that the Model Penal Code resolves that issue by distinguishing conduct from result. American academics are divided as to how to approach justifications. Some, arguing that the core requirement is an actual social benefit, focus on the results of the entire event, without considering the mental state of the actor. This school is referred to as the "deeds" school.[7] Another view is that the focus should be on the defendant's mental state. This school is referred to as the "reasons" school. The impact of these two different views will be explored below. At the moment, and in large part because the division is relatively new, these differing approaches have not had much impact on judicial decisions; it is likely, however, that courts will increasingly accept one view or the other as persons who have been exposed to the excuse-justification debate in law school argue cases before judges and then become judges themselves. It is also likely that even if judges haven't yet grappled with the different schools, your professor will expect you to do so.

Mistake and Justification

Jane pulls out a gun and aims it at Joe, who then kills her.

Case 1: Jane actually intended to kill Joe.
Case 2: Jane did not intend to kill Joe, but Joe reasonably believed that she did.
Case 3: Jane did not intend to kill Joe, and Joe's belief that she so intended was honest but unreasonable (Jane had a water pistol).

---

7. Because the commentators use this term, we will use it here. A better term, perhaps, would be the "results" school, since these writers are concerned only with the result of a defendant's actions, and ignore the reasons for the actions.

In case 1, Jane is an actual aggressor intending to kill Joe, so some social benefit has arguably occurred from Jane's death—either because we wish to protect the life and autonomy of an innocent person, or because Jane has forfeited her right not to be killed. The deeds and the reasons schools agree here that Joe was *justified*. For the deeds school, a social benefit was achieved (dastardly Jane is dead). For the reasons school, Joe's reasons—self-preservation—were sufficient in themselves to warrant his conduct.

In case 2, Jane is at worst a practical joker who deceived Joe into believing her purported deadly threat. Jane's death is not a social gain (unless we think practical jokers should be killed). It is almost assuredly better for Joe to have been scared than for Jane to be killed. Those in the deeds school, who believe that an act is justified only if actual social benefit results, deny that Joe's act is justified (though as we will see below, they may excuse Joe); this school views Joe's act "ex post"—after the results are known. Those in the reasons school, on the other hand, assess Joe's *conduct (not the result)* and ask whether, *under the facts known to him at the time he shot Jane,* he was justified "ex ante"—before we know the result or the true facts. From that perspective, Joe was justified, because under the facts as he (and we) saw them, he was doing a social good—dispatching an apparent killer and saving an innocent life. The focus is on Joe's conduct, not on the results of that conduct.

Mistake: Honest or Reasonable?

Case 3 raises problems we have seen elsewhere, particularly in provocation doctrine (see Chapter 8).

If Joe's belief was unreasonable—if no one in the world but Joe would have believed Jane had a real pistol—should Joe lose his claim of justification and be held fully liable? Or does his mistake reduce what would otherwise be a justifiable act to a wrongful (but excused) one? The "deeds" school has no trouble here. Since only the factually justified actor is justified, the mistakenly justified actor cannot be. And he should be excused if, and only if, his mistake was reasonable. Since the unreasonably mistaken actor is "worse" and "more dangerous" than the reasonably mistaken one, the unreasonably but honestly mistaken actor is neither justified nor excused, and he should be treated as a fully culpable shooter. For the "reasons" school, however, the dilemma is greater. For them, the truly justified actor and the reasonably mistaken one are equally entitled to exoneration. The dilemma associated with that approach is whether the unreasonable actor should be (1) excused (and hence treated no worse than the actually justified actor), (2) only partially excused, or (3) not excused at all, and thus made to undergo the same punishment as a fully culpable shooter.

As we will see in more detail in the discussion of specific claims, most courts hold that a *reasonable* mistake as to justification will still exonerate the actor. But where the mistake is *unreasonable*, some hold the defendant to a reduced liability, such as criminal negligence, while others rule out any reduction and hold the defendant liable for the result of what was intentional conduct.[8]

Unknowing Justification: The *Dadson* Problem

A conundrum surrounding justification is whether the actor who is objectively justified must know that he is justified in order to claim justification. The issue arose in a real case, *R. v. Dadson*, [1850] 4 Cox C.C. 358. The defendant, D, seeing *V* fleeing from a house with a bundle in his hand, shot *V*. Under the common law, this was a crime because deadly force could not be used to prevent a misdemeanor. As it turned out, however, unknown to D, *V* had already been twice convicted of similar acts, and thus his third (misdemeanor) try was *by law* a felony. Under the then-existing common law, using deadly force to prevent a felony was justified. This meant, in turn, that D's shooting was objectively justified. Nevertheless, the court held that D was culpable if he did not know the facts (i.e., *V*'s prior two misdemeanor convictions), which would otherwise have justified his using deadly force.

The theoretical problem generated by this decision and situation is provocative. Under the "deeds" theory of justification, the act is justified if, on balance, D did the "right" thing—that is, he prevented more social harm than he caused. Dadson satisfied this condition—the law viewed the death of a felon-thief as better than the loss of the property he was taking. Therefore, no crime occurred. But the "reasons" school argues that a defendant who believes he is committing a crime should be punished because he has demonstrated (1) a bad character and (2) a criminal choice. The analogs in other areas—impossible attempts, for example (see Chapter 12)—are manifest. Unfortunately, the law is no more settled here than it is there.[9]

---

8. Price, Faultless Mistake of Fact: Justification or Excuse?, 12 Crim. Just. Ethics 14 (1993); Larry Alexander, Inculpatory and Exculpatory Mistakes and the Fact/Law Distinction: An Essay in Memory of Mike Bayles, 12 Law & Phil. 33 (1993); Byrd, Wrongdoing and Attribution: Implications Beyond the Justification-Excuse Distinction, 33 Wayne L. Rev. 1289 (1987).

9. For a review of the problem, see Christopher, Unknowing Justification and the Logical Necessity of the *Dadson* Principle in Self-Defense, 15 Ox. J. Legal Stud. 229 (1995) (cataloging the position of courts and academics). One of the hypotheticals used in discussing this problem involves D, who is a patient in a hospital. D has decided to kill N, her nurse, the next time he comes in. Unknown to D, N has decided to kill D by injecting D with poison. If D shoots N before N can inject D with a poison, is D's act justified since it turns out that N was about to use illegal deadly force? The hypothetical divided academics for years, but Christopher makes the (now self-evident) point that both actors are in exactly the same posture, and that the puzzle was created only because the question was always framed from D's point of view. Christopher points out that N is being threatened (unknown to him) by deadly force from D. Because two people cannot both be justified in a setting, and because the two people here are

The debate over these matters goes to the heart of the purposes of the criminal sanction. As we go through each defense claim in Chapters 16 and 17, keep in mind these generic issues. Here is a quick summary:

	Reasons	**Deeds**
D is reasonable, and not mistaken; the result is socially desirable[10]	Justified	Justified
D is reasonable, but mistaken, and the result is not socially desirable[11]	Justified	Not Justified; Possibly Excused
D is unreasonable, but honest in her mistake; the result, nevertheless, turns out to be socially desirable[12]	Not Justified, But Possibly Excused	Justified
D is unreasonable, but honest in her mistake; the result is not socially desirable[13]	Not Justified, But Possibly Excused	Not Justified, Nor Excused
D intends to commit a crime but actually prevents harm[14]	Neither Justified Nor Excused	Justified

The Problem with Explaining Excuses

If the focus of *justification* is "the act" (ambiguous as that phrase is), the focus of *excuse* is said to be "the actor." Beyond that, however, the articulation of the explanation breaks down. Some writers, for example, argue that the defendant is excused because he suffers from some "disability." This is easily seen in the paradigm case—insanity—but it is not a helpful distinction when applied to a normal, sane actor who, at the point of a gun, commits a crime. On the other hand, a different explanation as to why the coerced

---

in exactly the same situation, Christopher argues that no person can be unknowingly justified in a self-defense setting. Even if that conclusion is sound, however, it is unclear whether this would bar a Dadson, who is not in a reciprocal setting, from being justified.

10. Medea honestly, reasonably, and accurately believes a firewall is necessary to stop a fire from consuming the town. She burns down Jason's house. The town is saved.

11. Medea, honestly and reasonably, but inaccurately, believes it is necessary to burn down Jason's house. The fire turns out not to be as strong as she (reasonably) believed, and it burns itself out before reaching Jason's house, much less the town.

12. Medea, at the time she burns down Jason's house, unreasonably believes the fire will reach the town. Unknown to her or anyone else, there was a strong wind that would have pushed the fire to the town, but the firebreak works to stop the fire from spreading.

13. Medea's honest belief turns out to be absolutely wrong, and there was no need to burn down Jason's house.

14. Medea sets a torch to Jason's house, gleefully crying, "Arson." But the fire serves as a firebreak; otherwise, the entire town would have been destroyed.

actor is excused—that he was in an emergency situation—does not seem to apply well to the insane actor.

Another explanation of excuses is that the actor had "no choice" but to do what she did. But that is not really true; as Sir James Stephens argued regarding the claim of duress, a defendant who is threatened with death unless she commits a crime always has the choice to die. Although that is indeed a hard choice, Stephens contends that the actor should choose that path rather than break the criminal law. H.L.A. Hart, recognizing the cogency of Stephens' remark, has countered that excused defendants have no "real" choice or "fair opportunity" to choose. The vagueness of that standard, however, has itself engendered criticism.

A third possible explanation of excuses is the utilitarian view that the excused defendant will not (or cannot) be deterred, and therefore, there is no point in punishing him. But while it may be true that the self-defender who is insane, under duress, or unreasonably mistaken will not be deterred, it is perfectly possible that defendants who would seek to have their acts falsely excused would not commit those acts if there were no excuse. (If Dwight thinks he can fake insanity, he may kill Chauncey if insanity is an excuse; but he is less likely to commit homicide if even the insane killer is customarily executed or otherwise punished.)

A fourth possible explanation of excuses is based on the so-called character theory of excuses. When Mother Teresa commits what would appear to be serial murder, we just don't believe it—it is so "out of character" for her to act that way that we are convinced that she must have had some explanation. Even if she admits that she acted in cold blood (first-degree murder), we are likely to look for some "excusing condition"—if not to exonerate, then at least to mitigate her guilt (and her punishment).

Procedural Implications of the Distinctions

These debates as to whether a claim is an excuse or a justification may appear to be academic in the pejorative sense: the musings of tweed-coated law professors with nothing better to do after having pummeled and confused first-year law students. Yet these distinctions may have critical practical impacts: (1) The allocation of the burden of proof could depend on whether a claim goes to justification or excuse; (2) If an excuse does not "affect" an element of the crime, the legislature could simply abolish that excuse, which it could not do with a justification; (3) Since justified acts are "right," they cannot be resisted by others; excused acts, however, are wrong and can be resisted; (4) One may assist a justified actor but not an excused one.

The Burden of Proof Problem

In re Winship, 397 U.S. 358 (1970), held that the prosecution had the burden of proof on "all facts necessary to constitute the crime." No matter how narrowly one reads *Winship*, due process requires the state to show that a crime has been committed. A claim of justification essentially denies that a crime has been committed. Under this analysis, the prosecution must disprove any justificatory claim. On the other hand, an excuse claim appears to acknowledge that a crime has been committed but argues that the defendant should not be punished because of something unique to her. If so, then the prosecution has proved a crime, and the state may require the defendant to show that she should not be punished for that crime.[15]

In 2006, the Supreme Court concluded that duress (*Dixon v. United States*, 548 U.S. 1 (2006)) and insanity (*Arizona v. Clark*, 548 U.S. 735 (2006)) were both excuses. Although each case can be narrowly construed, a fair reading of the two decisions is that the state may constitutionally place upon the defendant the burden of proving, by a preponderance of the evidence, that an excuse existed. There is no similarly clear decision, however, on justification and burden of proof. In *Martin v. Ohio*, 480 U.S. 228 (1987), the Court held that the state may put on the defendant the burden of proving he killed in self-defense (usually viewed as a justification; see Chapter 16), but the Court's opinion made no distinction (as did *Dixon* and *Clark*) between excuses and justifications. While this probably settles the question, it can still be argued that when the defendant raises a justification, and not an excuse, he may put the burden on the state of disproving that claim.

The Abolition Problem

A claim that does not go to whether a crime has been committed could simply be ignored by the state altogether. Thus, as discussed in Chapter 17, all "excuses" could theoretically be abolished by the legislature. Indeed, several state legislatures have abolished the "special defense" of insanity. If insanity is an excuse, this legislation would appear to be constitutional.

The Assistance and Resistance Problem

It seems self-evident that George (a condemned criminal) could not kill Martha (the executioner) and claim self-defense. The doctrinal explanation is that Martha's act was justified and hence cannot be resisted. Nor can Alexander help George, since George's act was unjustified. But Andrew can help Martha resist George's escape attempt because her act was justified. These conclusions

15. As noted earlier, England puts the burden on the state to disprove any defensive claim once it has been properly and sufficiently raised.

have led most writers to suggest that only one act (or actor) may be justified in a situation. This position, however, can create problems. Suppose Gene, during a heated debate with Roy about baseball, screams, "You'll never make that mistake again, buster!" and reaches into his inside jacket pocket. Reasonably believing that Gene is reaching for a gun, Roy kills Gene with his ever-present machete. It turns out that Gene was reaching for his baseball almanac. For the "deeds" adherent, it's an easy resolution: Roy is not justified, because a greater good has not been achieved. Gene is dead and no social good has been achieved (unless we wish to deter people from reaching into their jacket pockets). For the "reasons" analyst, however, Roy's act is justified because of his (reasonable) belief. Now assume that Roy misses Gene, and Gene thereupon kills Roy with a handy beer bottle. If Roy's act was justified, then according to the "incompatible justifications" approach, Gene's cannot be. From this vantage, Gene is either "excused" (in which case, the law says that his act of reaching into his pocket was wrongful) or has no claim at all and will go to prison. Yet that seems wrong; Gene is really the innocent person here. To call his action merely excused is to imply that he has done something wrong. This has led many to contest the view that two actors cannot simultaneously be justified.[16]

On the other hand, Schmidlap's insanity defense (see page 462, supra) does not make his act "right"; it merely establishes a reason for not punishing him. If Hermione assisted him in parking, and assuming she is not similarly obeying Martian instructions, she has no insanity claim. If she knows that Schmidlap is insane, she cannot claim an excuse either directly or derivatively. If, however, she is unaware of Schmidlap's insanity, and (reasonably?) believes he is justified because he is trying to save his child, Hermione may be either justified or excused. Similarly, if Gregory, a passerby, tried to force Schmidlap out of the space and injured him, Gregory's acts are acceptable because Schmidlap's act was not justified.

THE MODEL PENAL CODE

With a few very clearly enunciated exceptions, the Code puts on the prosecution the burden of proving any element and disproving all excuses and justifications. Section 1.12(2)(a) provides that the prosecutor need not disprove an affirmative defense "unless there is evidence supporting such defense." When there is such evidence, the prosecution must bear the burden. Section 1.13(9)(c) of the Code provides that an element includes any

16. Dressler, New Thoughts About the Concept of Justification in the Criminal Law: A Critique of Fletcher's Thinking and Rethinking, 32 UCLA L. Rev. 61 at 87-91 (1984); Greenawalt, The Perplexing Borders of Justification and Excuse, 84 Colum. L. Rev. 1897 at 1921-1925 (1984); Dolinko, Note, 26 UCLA L. Rev. 1126, 1177-1181 (1979).

factors or explanations that "negatives an excuse or justification" for the defendant's act. Neither "excuse" nor "justification," however, is defined in the Code. The prosecution will carry the burden on all issues, except those explicitly left to the defendant. See, e.g., MPC §2.13 (entrapment); MPC §2.04(3)(b) (reasonable reliance on official advice).

Examples

EXAMPLES

1. On a very hot summer night Alan, a homeless person, breaks into the house of Beatrice, who he knows is away for the week. He is prosecuted for burglary, which is defined as "the breaking and entering of the dwelling house of another" and is punishable by a mandatory five years in prison. The statute further provides, however, that if the defendant proves he did not intend to commit a felony inside the house, the penalty shall be no more than two years in prison. Alan claims that he only wanted to sleep in an air-conditioned place, and there is no evidence that he took, or even attempted to take, any items in the house. Can the state make Alan bear this burden?

2. Ronald kills his mother, who is dying of terminal cancer and has asked him to assist her to die. He is prosecuted for first-degree capital murder, but the statute provides that "whoever proves, beyond a reasonable doubt, that he has committed murder in order to alleviate the pain and suffering of a person within two degrees of consanguinity shall be guilty of merciful murder, punishable by 25 years." Can the state make Ronald prove these facts?

3. Lionel lends his car to Hampton. Six weeks later, Lionel receives in the mail a ticket with a $500 fine for parking near a fire hydrant on the day Hampton borrowed the car. The statute, after defining "illegal parking," provides that "the owner of an illegally parked car is responsible for the fine, unless he can prove that he was not driving it that day, and otherwise did not exercise control over it." May the state make Lionel prove such "noncontrol"?

4a. Claudius Hamlet's checkbook showed he had balance of $5,000. Just before leaving with his wife, Gertrude, on a six-month vacation to Nepal, he wrote a check for $3,500 as payment to a roofer. Unknown to him, Gertrude had written another check on the same account for $1,800. As they stepped off the plane six months later, they were arrested for fraud. The relevant statute provides that anyone "who overdraws on his bank account" is presumed to intend to defraud the payee. In their mailbox are three notices from the bank indicating the overdraft. At the trial, the judge instructs the jury of the statutory presumption. Can Claudius and Gertrude successfully attack this instruction if they are convicted?

4b. Same facts and question as in Example 4a, except that the statute provides that "intent to defraud is presumed if the overdrawn check is not made good within 30 days after the payor has been notified by the bank of the overdraft."

4c. Same facts and question as in Example 4a, except that the Hamlets are prosecuted under a statute providing that "writing a check on an account with insufficient funds is a felony, unless the defendant proves that he was unaware of the insufficiency."

5. Derek, having decided to kill Ronald, his enemy of many years, comes upon Ronald bending over a package and shoots him three times in the head at point-blank range. It turns out that Ronald was about to detonate a bomb that would have killed roughly five hundred people. Derek claims his killing was justified. Is he correct?

6. Mike suffers from paranoid schizophrenia—the belief that everyone is out to kill him. Nurse Ratchet, who works in the mental hospital where Mike is detained, knows this. One day, Mike sees Jack Nichols, and shouts, "He's going to kill me. Someone give me a knife." Ratchet, who has always detested Nichols, provides the weapon to Mike, who kills Jack. Who's responsible for the death?

7. While fleeing a police officer attempting to pull him over for a traffic stop, Rob runs a red light, hitting a pickup truck in the intersection and killing its driver. Rob is charged with manslaughter. At Rob's trial, the judge does not instruct the jury concerning justification or excuse in homicide charges. Is the court in error? Does this instruction matter in regard to a manslaughter offense as opposed to a homicide offense? Does Rob have a right to the instruction even if the facts aren't concerned with justification or excuse?

Explanations

1. This is difficult. Under the common law, burglary was defined as requiring the intent to commit a felony in the house. It thus appears that the legislature has taken one of the elements of this common law offense and turned it into a "defense." The legislature cannot alter the common law rules by turning a common law "element" into a defense. The statute is unconstitutional. The state, however, would argue that the issue should be one of proportionality, not history. Five years in prison, it would contend, would not be constitutionally disproportionate to the offense of breaking and entering a dwelling house. Thus, the state is giving Alan a break by reducing his exposure by three years, and thus can place the burden upon Alan to prove lack of (ulterior) intent.

The MPC would not allow the state to put the burden on the defendant of any "excuse" or "justification." Problem solved. But would five years in prison be constitutionally disproportionate to the mere offense of breaking and entering a dwelling home, if there was no intent to commit a felony there? The example could be made even more difficult if the penalty for burglary were one to five years in prison so that even a real burglar could be punished less than Alan. Then the state would be giving Alan a break by reducing his exposure by three years, but not necessarily treating him as less dangerous than a "real" burglar.

2. Certainly. Ronald has premeditated the killing and hence has committed first-degree murder under the statute. Notwithstanding the arguments that one who kills in such circumstances lacks the mens rea necessary for murder (or even manslaughter), the common law has rejected such arguments. Thus, the state here has given Ronald a "bonus" beyond that which the common law would allow. The state may circumscribe such a defense by placing upon the defendant the burden of proving it. Under the Code, such "exceptions" seem like excuses that, pursuant to §1.13(9), must be "disproved" by the state once reasonably raised by the defendant.

3. This problem raises yet another possible argument about affirmative defenses—that the state may require a defendant to prove a "defense" in cases where it need not provide the defense at all. The alleged reason is that the "greater includes the lesser." Since the state could abolish the defense of "noncontrol," it can place the burden of its proof upon the defendant. This, of course, assumes that the state can constitutionally prohibit such parking without requiring any showing of actus reus or mens rea. Since this is a "malum prohibitum" offense (see Chapter 6), the state probably could enact such a statute. Thus, it probably can put the burden on the defendant to show noncontrol.

4a. This is a trick question. It may well depend on what else the jury was told. After *Allen* and *Sandstrom*, the complete instructions to the jury are critical. And it would appear that the instruction established a "mandatory presumption" which the jury could interpret as shifting either the burden of proof or the burden of production. If the jury understood the instruction as shifting the burden of proof, then it violates *Sandstrom*. But even if the jury understood the instruction as only shifting the burden of production, Claudius and Gertrude are probably safe. After all, many people make "innocent" mistakes involving their checkbook balances, whether for large or small amounts. It is not even a case of "more likely than not," much less "beyond a reasonable doubt," that such people intend to defraud their payees. The presumption is therefore empirically invalid. Under the MPC, the answer is again very simple—no presumption, no matter how "commonsensical," can shift the burden of proof. Problem solved.

4b. This change in the statutory language may have dire consequences for the Hamlets. Surely it is the case that many people who innocently write such a check, after being informed of the overdraft, make up the difference immediately. And the statute goes further: it allows a 30-day grace period, just in case (as here) there was an error in the keeping of the accounts. Thus, the presumed fact (fraudulent intent) does seem to flow from the predicate fact (failure to make up the deficit within 30 days) in many cases. This may be sufficient to meet the "beyond a reasonable doubt" test enunciated in *Allen*. Although in the way we have worded the question it may seem that the Hamlets are "innocent," a jury could certainly infer negligence, or even recklessness, from their failure to provide measures to take care of such matters should they arise while they were away. Of course, the Hamlets may in fact rebut the statutory presumption by producing evidence of nonculpability. "Fraud" generally requires "specific intent," so that even recklessness would be insufficient as a predicate for the crime.

4c. We have now moved from presumptions to "affirmative defenses." Does this change the analysis? There is at least some suggestion in *Patterson* that it might. After all, if the legislature could punish mere "overdrafting" (and it probably could), then it would seem within its powers to make "lack of fraudulent intent" a defense. This demonstrates the fragility of the line, which seems to be drawn by the cases, between presumptions and affirmative defenses. Since, as suggested in the text, there appear to be few limits (under a theory of proportionality) to the state's ability to punish almost any act with almost any penalty, drafting this statute as an affirmative defense may abolish the possible constitutionality when it was cast as a presumption.

5. The answer to this example is "murky." As noted in the text, some courts and writers (the "deeds" school) focus on the act, arguing that if the outcome of the act was socially beneficial, then Derek, who is otherwise a scumbag, should nevertheless not be punished. Others (the "reasons" school) focus on the actor and claim that actors, not acts, are justified because of their mental state. If Derek was not aware of the justifying circumstances, they argue, he cannot be justified, even if his action resulted in a social benefit. The controversy here began in two law review articles. Compare Robinson, A Theory of Justification: Social Harm as a Prerequisite for Criminal Liability, 23 UCLA L. Rev. 266 (1975) with Fletcher, The Right Deed for the Wrong Reason: A Reply to Mr. Robinson, 23 UCLA L. Rev. 293 (1975).

6. We will discuss insanity in detail in Chapter 17, but you already know (from life, if not from a criminal law casebook) that an insane person is excused for his crimes. But Ratchet is not insane (jealousy usually does not qualify). And since Mike's actions are not justified, but "merely" excused, Ratchet is guilty of the crime of homicide. A person who understands that an act is not justified is guilty if she helps an excused person commit that act. The criminal law may be crazy, but it's not insane.

7. A Florida Appeals Court thought so. In *Burford v. State*, 77 So. 3d 917 (Fla. Dist. Ct. App. 2012), where this fact pattern occurred, the state argued that failure to give the instruction was not a fundamental error, because the facts did not support a finding of excusable homicide. The Court disagreed, citing precedent that held, "It matters not whether any view of the evidence could support a finding of either excusable or justifiable homicide." Id. at 919. Manslaughter is a derivative offense of homicide, and justifiable and excusable homicide were excluded from this crime. Therefore, the Appeals Court held, the trial judge should have included an instruction that justifiable and excusable homicide were excluded from this crime.

CHAPTER 16

Acts in Emergency: Justification vs. Excuse

OVERVIEW

Donald, charged by a raging bull, hits it with Victoria's Ming vase, destroying the vase but diverting the bull. Is Donald guilty of intentional damage to Victoria's property? Martina tells Ken that unless Ken steals Joan's lawn mower, Martina will kill him. If Ken does so, is he guilty of larceny? Suppose the threat is not to kill Ken but to destroy his Mercedes. What then? Finally, Ebenezer sees Marley coming at him with what appears to Ebenezer to be a machine gun. May Ebenezer pull out a pistol and shoot Marley, or must he wait until Marley himself actually shoots?

In each of these situations, the defendant is faced with a situation in which a decision must be made instantly. Rather than labeling all three such acts as "emergency decisions" and treating them similarly, the common law created separate doctrines that, while similar, have been treated differently with somewhat different rules. Thus, Donald would have to argue that he acted in "necessity" (choosing the lesser of two evils). Ken, in either of the examples, would have to argue "duress." Finally, Ebenezer would claim neither of these defenses but "self-defense." In assessing these doctrines do not lose sight that each of them involves action taken in dire, emergency conditions.[1]

1. Elliott, Necessity, Duress and Self-Defense, [1989] Crim. L. Rev. 611; Colvin, Exculpatory Defenses in Criminal Law, 10 Ox. J. Legal Stud. 381 (1990). Arguing strongly that it is the "crisis" aspect of these defenses that distinguishes them from other claims, see William Wilson, The Filtering Role of Crisis in the Constitution of Criminal Excuses, 17 Can. J.L. & Juris. 387 (2004). Consider, also, the analog to provocation, discussed in Chapter 8.

COMMON REQUIREMENTS, COMMON PROBLEMS

The *essence* of these three claims is that the defendant

a. is acting under *extraordinary pressure*,
b. from which there is (or appears to him to be) no *reasonable escape*,
c. to do something that *involves injury to his or another's person or property*, and that, in the absence of the emergency, would clearly be criminal (although the defendant may not recognize or know that).

Actus Reus, Mens Rea, or Both? Or Neither?

Actus Reus

Some theorists argue that the defendant who acts under such pressure does not meet even the primary requirement for criminal responsibility—a voluntary act (see Chapter 3). One who kills another while a gun is aimed at his own head is not "really" acting voluntarily, the argument goes. As is often said, the defendant may be faced with a hard choice, but it is a choice nonetheless. The contention considered in the last chapter, that a defendant in an emergency has no "fair" choice, while more appealing, does not deny the choice—merely the inculpatory nature of the choice. The law has rejected this nonvoluntary act argument.

Mens Rea

Somewhat more plausibly, a defendant who "chooses" to kill when faced with such dangers may be argued to have no mens rea. After all, who has a "mens" at all when a gun is aimed at his temple or that of his spouse or child? The argument is that the defendant's mind is "blank," not only metaphorically but literally. This argument is more persuasive if one adopts the broad (traditional) sense of mens rea (see Chapter 4) that the defendant must act in a culpable, blameworthy way. Even if one uses the narrow (statutory) meaning of mens rea (see Chapter 4), there are at least some instances when a plausible argument can be made that the defendant did not "intend" or "purpose" death. The mountain climber who cuts the rope below him to save himself from being plunged into the canyon, thereby sending a fellow climber into a deep abyss, may hope and pray that his falling colleague is saved. And a person who, trembling, shoots another in self-defense, all the while saying, "Please just go away—don't make me shoot you," might well argue that it was not his "conscious object to cause death." Nor does a bank teller who hands over money at the point of a gun necessarily have the mens rea for larceny/robbery, that is, to intend to permanently deprive the owner of his money; he probably hopes the robber will be caught instantly. Indeed, in some emergency situations, it is plausible that the defendant is not even *reckless* with regard to the risk of criminal harm. Simply put, he never subjectively thought about this risk because he was consumed only by a concern for his own safety. In such a case, the defendant really is arguing that there was no mens rea, even in the narrow sense, as to the result. In such a case, the defendant is arguing an "element negation."

The argument is less tenable in other factual settings. The defendant who, under duress, destroys a car or severely assaults an innocent victim may not "want" to inflict the injury but surely foresees the unlikelihood of putting things back together again later on. Far too often the use of generic terms, such as "intent" or "mens rea," conceals important factual differences within the assumed scenarios each writer or court tacitly posits when discussing these issues. Thus, it is more accurate to say that *some* persons in extremis have statutory mens rea, while others do not.

Why Punish?

Whether actors who see themselves as acting in necessity can be deterred is uncertain. Most persons thrust into a situation in which death seems imminent are unlikely to be intimidated by a threat of later punishment (including death) if they survive. Perhaps the only deterrent effect here is to reduce precipitous action—that is, to require the defendants to hold off until the "very last minute."[2] However, the dilemma is that almost every defendant in such situations believes that "the final minute" has arrived.

A retributivist would argue that anyone who succumbs in these terrifying situations is not morally blameworthy for doing so and should not be punished. Many utilitarians might agree in this result, claiming that most individuals will inevitably succumb to the terror of the moment rather than worry about criminal punishment in the future. Consequently, punishment in such cases would be futile.[3]

2. One therefore might explain the opinion in *Dudley and Stephens*, infra, as arguing that taking the life of an innocent is never justified because it is never actually necessary. As Justice Cardozo put it, "Who shall know when the masts and sails of rescue may emerge out of the fog?" B. Cardozo, Law and Literature 113 (1931). Indeed, one could argue in *Dudley* itself that the four should have waited until one of them died. This argument would then turn on whether the men believed that, if they had waited, the remaining three (whoever they were) would have been so weakened as to make nourishment unavailing. If this were then the case, one could analyze it as a mistake as to a justification, discussed in the text below.

3. On the other hand, Sir James Stephen, a prominent utilitarian, argued that it is exactly when human nature is most vulnerable to the almost irresistible threat of death that the law

DURESS

The common law normally does not expect most of us to be heroes—that is, to die willingly or to suffer serious bodily harm—if we can avoid this fate by doing what someone else demands of us, even if that means committing what would otherwise be a crime. So long as the pressure was great and there was no obvious escape, a defendant who acted under duress from another human being was exculpated.[4] The one exception, discussed in more detail below, is homicide. Not even the threat of immediate death will allow (justify or excuse) the killing of a person the duressed person knows to be "innocent." Instead, the duressed person is required to sacrifice her own life.

The Doctrines of Duress

As a general matter, the common law required the following elements for a claim of duress:

1. a *well-founded fear*, generated by
2. a *threat from a human being* of
3. an *imminent* (or "immediate")
4. *serious bodily harm or death*
5. to *himself* (or sometimes to a near relative)
6. *not of his own doing*.

Personal Injury

Under this restriction, no threat to property, no matter how severe when compared to the injury threatened, will sustain a duress claim. For example, if Bob helps Alex embezzle $1,000 from Bob's employer because Alex threatens to destroy the *Mona Lisa* or a $10 million building unless Bob helps him, Bob cannot claim duress. If he has any useful claim at all, it may be one of "necessity" rather than duress (see below).

---

should be least forgiving. It is precisely in such situations, he argued, that a counterbalancing motivation for not committing a crime is most needed.

4. Aristotle says that actions performed under duress are ones "under pressure which overstrains human nature and which no one could withstand." Aristotle, Nicomachean Ethics, in The Collected Works of Aristotle, §1110(A)(25) (Jonathan Barnes ed., 1984). Spanish law characterizes duress as a defense of "insurmountable fear." Daniel Varona Gómez, Duress and the Antcolony's Ethic: Reflections on the Foundations of the Defense and Its Limits, 11 New Crim. L. Rev. 615 (2008).

Source of the Threat

The requirement that the threat emanate from a human being is hardly controversial, although, as discussed below in the prison escape cases, it sometimes turned out to be a difficulty.

"Imminence"

The common law requirement that the threat be one of "imminent" harm seems uncontroversial, at least in the paradigm case where *A* puts a gun to B's head and tells B to steal the Hope Diamond NOW "or else." But some threats are equally effective if vague: "Sometime when you least expect it" can be almost as frightening as "I'll break your arm now." In *State v. Toscano*, 74 N.J. 421, 378 A.2d 755 (1977), the defendant chiropractor had agreed with others to file false medical claims. He contended that, when he balked at participating, one of his "co-defendants" had declared, "Remember, you just moved into a place that has a very dark entrance and you live there with your wife. . . . You and your wife are going to jump at shadows when you leave that dark entrance." The court explicitly noted that "defendant described the exit from his office as a 'very, very pitch black alleyway' on the side of the building." The court allowed the claim of duress to go to the jury, even though the co-defendant had not actually threatened to harm Toscano and his wife "immediately."

An argument can be made that the defendant should have gone to the police. Had he done so, the police would have protected him and the fraud could have been stopped. This contention certainly has an appeal—why let someone force another to commit a crime if the "duressed" person could have avoided the threatened harm by going to the police? Nonetheless, requiring the threat to be imminent raises other serious questions (as we will see again shortly in self-defense cases, especially involving the battered spouse defense). For example: (1) to what extent should the trial investigate the actual ability of the police to protect someone like the defendant? (2) should the defendant's liability depend on whether his belief that he would not be protected was (a) reasonable or (b) merely honest, even if unreasonable? *Toscano* and similar cases would put the issue to the jury, rather than resolving it as a matter of law.

This requirement has been tested by the "drug mule" cases, where persons caught attempting to smuggle narcotics into the United States have claimed that drug lords have threatened their families. Although requiring these defendants to tell their arresting authorities in the United States about the threats will do little to protect their families in their home countries, courts almost uniformly refuse to allow the defendant to even raise the claim.[5]

---

5. See, e.g, *United States v. Vasquez-Landaver*, 527 F.3d 798 (9th Cir. 2008); *United States v. Ibarra-Pino*, 657 F.3d 1000 (9th Cir. 2011).

Reasonableness of Fear

The common law generally provides an answer in the above scheme. (Well, at last!!!!) Under the common law, only a reasonable fear is sufficient to sustain a claim of duress. Thus, if Hans pointed at Stephi what Stephi unreasonably believes is a real gun, but what is obviously a water pistol and threatened to kill her "instantly" unless she stole *V*'s wallet, Stephi has no claim of duress to a charge of theft because the threat is not well grounded and the fear is unreasonable. As with all other instances of objectivization, however, this requirement has the undesirable effect of criminalizing a person who, in the maelstrom of circumstances, acts unreasonably but does not intend to act criminally. Again, the question of which characteristics of the defendant are relevant arises here—a threat to break a finger made to a pianist may be much more oppressive than the same threat made to a law professor.

To "Himself"

The common law appears initially to have limited duress to cases where the defendant personally was threatened. Threats to strangers, and even to spouse and children, were insufficient. These limits have now been discarded by most states and most states would allow the claim where any person's life or bodily harm is threatened by the duressor.

Creating Conditions of Duress

Another restriction on the availability of the claim is that the defendant must not have been "responsible" for the threat. If *D* knowingly joins a violent gang and later commits a crime under threat of immediate death from fellow gang members, he will not be permitted to claim duress.

Of course, the law may seek to deter people from joining such gangs, but a good case can be made that disallowing duress in such a case is disproportionate to the defendant's blameworthiness. One may wish to punish someone for his knowing membership in the gang, but to punish him for a serious crime when he actually was duressed may be unfair. At the very least, there should be a causal link between *D*'s joining the gang and *D*'s crime. If *D* had actually heard of other inductees being required to commit criminal acts in order to be accepted and joined the gang anyway, then disallowing duress would be logically related to the defendant's moral culpability.

Duress and Homicide

Under the common law, a defendant could not claim duress if he killed a victim. Instead, he was required to sacrifice himself to the threatener.[6] Besides the uneasiness exhibited in these cases, critics of the rule argue that it is unfair to the duressed actor to be categorically denied the defense in this one crime, since many reasonable persons would kill another rather than die themselves (or have significant others killed).

Termination of the Threat

Once the threat has ceased, the defendant must cease his criminality. In a series of cases in the 1970s involving prisoners who claimed they "escaped" from prison after they were threatened with rape, the courts, culminating in *Bailey v. United States*, 444 U.S 394 (1980), held that even if the escape was warranted, escape was a "continuing offense." If the escapee did not turn himself into authorities as soon as he was sufficiently far from the prison, he lost the claim as a matter of law. Some courts have held that this requirement is limited to prison escape cases. See *United States v. Solano*, 10 F.3d 682 (9th Cir. 1993) (so long as a defendant—in a non-prison-escape case—continued to fear a threat, it was a jury question whether he was duressed, even if he could have gone to the police).

The Guilt of the Duressor: A Note

Just in case you're wondering (or forgot about the innocent pawn doctrine), the person who threatens the defendant in a case of duress is always going to be guilty of the crime, whether or not the actual perpetrator has a duress claim. The criminal law may be weird, but it's not stupid. See Chapter 14.

The Rationale of Duress

There is no agreement on the rationale of duress. Until recently, one of the leading criminal law Hornbooks took the view that duress was a justification but in the most recent editions labeled it an "excuse." The argument that it is (or was) a justification is fairly straightforward. Under the

6. The English House of Lords, in two cases in the 1970s, appeared to reconsider the rule, distinguishing between those who (under threat of death) actually killed the victim and those who merely aided in the killing. See *Director of Public Prosecutions v. Lynch*, [1975] 2 W.L.R. 641 and *Abbott v. Queen*, [1977] 3 W.L.R. 462. The House ultimately concluded that this distinction was illogical, and inconsistent with history, and reinstated the old common law rule barring the use of duress to anyone involved in a killing. In 2003, the Law Commission, A New Homicide Act for England and Wales, urged that duress be allowed as a defense to murder.

common law, only a threat of death or serious bodily harm would sustain a claim of duress. Since duress was not allowed in homicide cases, under the common law, the defendant's act was almost surely less harmful than the harm with which he was threatened. Put simply, the defense will generally result in choosing the lesser harm, which is the essence of a justification.

In *Dixon v. United States*, 548 U.S. 1 (2006), the Supreme Court held that, at least for purposes of federal criminal law, duress is an excuse. Although that decision is certainly not binding on the states, it will likely be followed in many jurisdictions, thus perhaps bringing some closure to that question. The Court's view in *Dixon* that duress is an excuse is now widely accepted, although there are some dissenters.[7]

In deciding in *Dixon* that duress was an excuse, the Court also concluded that the defendant could be made to carry the burden of proof that he was under duress. This is consistent with the general analysis in Chapter 15 that an excuse concedes the defendant's wrongdoing, but contends that he should not be punished because he is not blameworthy.

If duress were available in homicide cases and not restricted to cases in which the actor was threatened with death or serious bodily harm, it would more clearly be an excuse. Such an expansion would recognize that defendants who act in such situations lack moral culpability. Simply put, people threatened with what they perceive as serious threats simply do not have the "vicious will" that criminal penalties require. By expanding duress in this manner, however, we would occasionally exonerate individuals who inflict more harm than they prevent.

The Model Penal Code

The Model Penal Code, §2.09, retains the common law requirement that the threat be one of personal injury rather than property damage. But the MPC allows a threat of "unlawful force" to support duress, thus allowing the threat of minor physical harm.

The Code has changed the common law of duress in several ways. It subtly varies the common law's requirement of reasonableness by requiring that the threat involved would have similarly affected a "person of reasonable firmness *in the defendant's situation*" (emphasis added). For example, if the defendant is unusually vulnerable (e.g., a hemophiliac) or has a particular fear of a particular injury (e.g., an ice skater who fears someone breaking

---

7. See Westen & Mangiafico, The Criminal Defense of Duress: A Justification, Not an Excuse—and Why It Matters, 6 Buff. Crim. L. Rev. 833 (2003). But see Huigens, Duress Is Not a Justification, 2 Ohio St. J. Crim. L. 303 (2004). And see Kahan & Nussbaum, Two Conceptions of Emotion in Criminal Law, 96 Colum. L. Rev. 269, 333-334 (1996) (duress is neither wholly a justification nor wholly an excuse).

her knees), this may be part of the "situation." Whether other factors such as extreme cowardice would qualify is less clear. Thus, as in §2.10 on manslaughter (see Chapter 8), the Code takes a much more subjective view of the possible claims the defendant might raise.

The MPC rejects most of the specific limitations imposed by the common law. Thus, (1) duress is a valid claim in all prosecutions, including homicide;[8] (2) there is no restriction to "imminent harm"; (3) the threat may be to any person, not solely a relative, or even an acquaintance, of the defendant.

Like the common law, the Code disallows the defense if the defendant *recklessly* placed himself in a position where he could be placed under duress. Thus, if he joined a gang of known terrorists, the defendant cannot claim duress even if he is charged with a crime requiring knowledge or purpose. In contrast, if he was only negligent in joining the gang, he has a claim of duress except to a charge requiring negligence. This is in clear contrast to the requirements of necessity discussed below.

NECESSITY

The Doctrines of Necessity

The defense of necessity is available in roughly half of all jurisdictions in the United States.[9] The claim of necessity and the restrictions on it essentially replicate the claim of duress.[10] There must be

1. a *threat* (usually from a natural source) of
2. *imminent injury* to the person or property

8. Only eight states allow duress as a full exculpation in homicide cases; a few others allow the claim to mitigate the killing to manslaughter. Cara Cookson, Confronting Our Fear: Legislating Beyond Battered Woman Syndrome and the Law of Self-Defense in Vermont, 34 Vt. L. Rev. 415, 444 (2009).

9. Paul H. Robinson, Shima Baradaran Baughman, & Michael T Cahill, Criminal Law: Case Studies and Controversies 546 (New York: Wolters Kluwer, 4th ed., 2017).

10. It is unclear how many states recognize a necessity claim. Compare Michael H. Hoffheimer, Codifying Necessity: Legislative Resistance to Enacting Choice-of-Evils Defenses to Criminal Liability, 82 Tul. L. Rev. 1291 (2007), asserting that less than a majority of states have statutorily enacted a necessity defense, and only two of those have followed the precise wording of the Model Penal Code with Elizabeth O'Connor Tomlinson, Proof of Necessity Defense in a Criminal Case, 115 Am. Jr. Proof of Facts 3d 309 (listing at least 24 states that have codified a necessity of choice-of-evils defense, many modeled on the MPC). Other states may have judicially adopted the concept.

3. for which there are *no (reasonable) alternatives* except the commission of the crime;
4. the *defendant's acts must prevent an equal or more serious harm;*
5. the defendant *must not have created the conditions of his own dilemma.*

Source of the Threat

First, the target of the threat must be a legally protected interest.[11] In contrast to duress, the source of the threat in necessity was always a "teleological" (natural) force, such as an avalanche, starvation (as in *Dudley and Stephens*), fire, or a similarly natural force. Again, this did not usually constitute a problem but did in the prison escape cases. Arcane though it might be, this qualification on necessity was followed by some courts in the "prison escape" cases mentioned earlier. Here, inmate Brutus would threaten inmate Wally with rape. Wally would jump the wall. When caught and charged with escape, he would claim duress or necessity. But duress was unavailable because Brutus didn't order Wally to escape (indeed, that was the last thing that Brutus wanted). And necessity was unavailable because the source of the threat was human, not a force of nature (although rapists might sometimes metaphorically be so labeled). Thankfully, the courts ultimately jettisoned the restrictions of the two doctrines, at least in these cases.[12]

Necessity and Homicide

As already discussed, duress was simply not allowed as a claim when the duressed person had killed a person he knew to be innocent, no matter how severe the conditions under which the killing occurred. It is not as clear whether necessity could be asserted in homicide cases. In the movie *Seven Beauties*, the protagonist is incarcerated in a concentration camp. The commander hands him a gun and orders him to shoot his best friend and five others. If he refuses, the commander says, he will kill everyone in the barracks. The friend acquiesces in his own death. The protagonist would not have a claim of duress under the common law, but he might have a claim of necessity, since he saved more lives than he took. However, the most famous necessity case involving such a claim seemed to establish that, at least in English law, a defendant in this situation could not claim necessity either.

---

11. Paul H. Robinson, Shima Baradaran Baughman, & Michael T Cahill, Criminal Law: Case Studies and Controversies 547 (New York: Wolters Kluwer, 4th ed., 2017).

12. See Gardner, The Defense of Necessity and the Right to Escape from Prison: A Step Towards Incarceration Free from Sexual Assault, 49 S. Cal. L. Rev. 110 (1975).

In *Regina v. Dudley and Stephens*, 14 Q.B.D. 273 (1884), four men were cast adrift in a lifeboat in the Atlantic Ocean when their ship sank. After 19 days of subsisting on two small cans of turnips and a small turtle, the two defendants killed one of the other two (Richard Parker), whom they selected because he was (a) the youngest; (b) the only one without family; and (c) the weakest/sickest. (The fourth seaman refused to participate in the killing.) The three survived by eating the corpse.

The court, while acknowledging that it was establishing a moral rule that no one could follow, refused to allow the two defendants the claim of necessity. It concluded that knowingly taking innocent life could never be allowed by the law. In this sense, the *Dudley and Stephens* limitation replicates that initially placed on duress.

However, the limitation may not hold where it is "fate" that decides the victim. In *Dudley*, the victim was apparently chosen because he was the youngest, had no family, and was the weakest. On the other hand, in *United States v. Holmes*, 26 F. Cas. 360 (C.C.E.D. Pa. 1842), an almost identical case, an American court had suggested that, if lots were chosen to select the victim, the claim might be recognized.[13] Similarly, in a hypothetical often used by law professors, if several mountaineers suddenly find themselves hanging over a crevasse, with the rope threatening to break from the excessive load, the topmost may cut the rope holding the ones below, since fate decided the "obvious" victims. Of course, a perverse law professor might ask, particularly on an exam, how it was that *D* became the "topmost." If *D* determined the order in which the mountaineers were linked, it is arguable that he, and not fate, decided who would be the "lowermost." Or consider this case: If in order to save 100 houses and their occupants from a flooding river, someone breaks a dike and causes the destruction of three houses and the death of their five occupants, the principle of necessity would appear to apply.

A tragic event in England in 2001 raised the question of necessity in dramatic form. Doctors sought permission from a court to separate conjoined twins, although they acknowledged that this operation would mean the death of one twin. If, as one interpretation of *Dudley and Stephens* would argue, necessity cannot be pled to allow the taking of an innocent life, the operation could not be justified as necessary. Moreover, since doctors agreed that the twins could live conjoined for a significant period of time,

13. In dictum, Lord Coleridge, in *Dudley*, rejected the suggestion that casting lots would change the verdict. The casting of lots is at least as old as Jonah and as "modern" as Walt Whitman, who wrote, "I observe sailors casting lots who shall be killed to preserve the lives of the rest. . . . See, hear and am silent." Whitman, I Sit and Look Out. Mark Twain wrote a short story in which a group of politicians, stranded on a snowbound train, vie for the "honor" of being voted best orator, and therefore the first to be sacrificed by their peers.

the threat to the one twin was not "imminent." Nevertheless, a court authorized the operation.[14]

The Problem of Imminence

Many of the problems discussed in the duress section apply here as well. For example, it is not clear what "imminent" means in this context. Similarly, the question of what alternatives are relevant and must be considered (thereby rendering the threatened harm "nonimminent") is uncertain. Blackstone argued that a starving person could not claim necessity for stealing bread because in eighteenth-century England there was always help and food for the starving. Judge Cardozo once suggested that no act is ever "necessary" at the time it is committed, because relief might come the very second after the act is done: "Who shall know when the masts and sails of rescue may emerge out of the fog?"[15] In short, one can never be completely sure of the future, and therefore one cannot justify actions based on speculation about the future. Not surprisingly, the issue here (and in self-defense) splits the "deeds" and "reasons" schools (see Chapter 15). To the first group, if no rescue occurs until a substantial number of days after Parker is killed, the homicide is justified because the facts demonstrate that without the killing, the three would not have survived; if, however, just as the knife slits Parker's throat (or the mountaineer's rope), a ship (or a tow truck) arrives, the act was not "necessary" and hence not justifiable. The "deeds" school would not necessarily punish the defendant; if he was reasonable, his act would excuse him. For the "reasons" school, if D's decision was reasonable, even if mistaken, the act is *justified*. Again, *D* is exonerated, but on different rationales. The "deeds" school would not justify the unreasonably but honestly mistaken actor, while the "reasons" school would excuse him.

Choice of Evils and Alternatives

"Necessity" is also referred to as a "choice of evils" claim. Someone (usually the defendant) is threatened with serious harm and chooses (to the extent that one chooses in such a situation) to inflict harm in a way that would otherwise be deemed criminal. If the harm the defendant inflicts is less (or, in some versions, not greater) than that which would have occurred had he not acted, a social benefit has occurred, notwithstanding that the harm inflicted would otherwise be criminally proscribed. He has chosen

14. Re A, [2001] WLR 480, [2001] 4 All ER 961. See Bohlander, Of Shipwrecked Sailors, Unborn Children, Conjoined Twins and Hijacked Airplanes—Taking Human Life and the Defense of Necessity, 2006 J. Crim. L. 147.

15. B. Cardozo, Law and Literature 113 (1931).

the "lesser evil." (However, if the "lesser evil" does nothing to actually prevent the harm, then there is no necessity.)[16]

Thus, if Elvira purposely burns down Josh's barn to act as a firebreak, which prevents the fire from destroying the town, the town has a net benefit. What would otherwise be arson is no longer criminal. One problem with viewing necessity as limited to "lesser evil" cases is that when two innocents confront each other, neither can claim necessity in killing the other. The chestnut case is John and Jim, two innocent passengers of a capsized ship, each swimming toward a plank that can hold only one. If John kills Jim by pushing him off the board, he cannot meet the strict test of self-defense, which requires that the force against which the defender acts be "unlawful" (see infra). And if necessity requires a "lesser" evil, the death of neither is a "lesser" evil than the death of the other. This conundrum also occurs if Jim is an infant, mentally disturbed, acting under duress, or otherwise excused. Yet it seems outrageous to punish John for his actions.[17]

What constitutes a "lesser evil" is largely based on community standards.[18] An individual defendant might conclude for herself that her criminal conduct is a lesser evil, but, ultimately, it is for the jury to decide whether the crime was sufficiently proportional.[19]

Creating Conditions of Necessity

As with duress, if the defendant "created the conditions of his own necessity," the common law denied the claim. The point is just as ambiguous here as it was there. For example, in *Dudley and Stephens*, it is not clear why the yacht sank, although there is some indication that alterations to the ship, which had been a racing vessel and not meant for ocean duty, were insufficient and that the ship, unknown to Tom Dudley (the captain), was of dubious seaworthiness. Suppose, however, that Dudley or Stephens had been negligent (or worse) in navigating the ship. Should that alone preclude the claim for a much different event that occurred much later in time? On the other hand, suppose that the starving condition of the lifeboat occupants was due to reckless consumption of the foodstuffs they had. What if, for example, on the first day in the lifeboat they had eaten four large hams, which otherwise could have been used to feed them for three weeks? (Does

---

16. Paul H. Robinson, Shima Baradaran Baughman, & Michael T. Cahill, Criminal Law: Case Studies and Controversies 549 (New York: Wolters Kluwer, 4th ed., 2017).

17. See Marshall, Life or Death on a Plank—Ripstein and Kant, 2 Ohio St. J. Crim. L. 435 (2005).

18. Paul H. Robinson, Shima Baradaran Baughman, & Michael T. Cahill, Criminal Law: Case Studies and Controversies 550 (New York: Wolters Kluwer, 4th ed., 2017).

19. Paul H. Robinson, Shima Baradaran Baughman, & Michael T. Cahill, Criminal Law: Case Studies and Controversies 550 (New York: Wolters Kluwer, 4th ed., 2017).

this sound familiar? Does the term "proximate cause" spring to mind? If not, see Chapter 3. If so, see it anyway.)

Excuse or Justification?

As with duress, the question arises whether necessity is an "excuse" or a "justification." The court in *Dudley and Stephens* framed it only as a justification, but the Canadian Supreme Court held that necessity could only be an excuse and never a justification.[20] The answer may be that it can be either. That is the answer that some foreign legal systems have given.[21]

Neither the question nor the answer is academic. A justificatory claim would have to demonstrate that the defendant achieved, or intended to achieve, a "greater good" (or lesser harm) than he committed. In contrast, an excuse claim would argue that the defendant was not morally blameworthy in choosing, in extremely severe and pressing circumstances, a path that at the time looked reasonable, even if it (a) was not in fact reasonable and (b) did not result in a "greater good." This debate, in part, reflects the same debate between the "deeds" and "reasons" approaches to the general issue of defenses discussed in Chapter 15.

The justificatory analysis may be construed to support a quantification approach. Thus, in *Dudley*, Lord Coleridge resisted a quantification analysis because it would allow Dudley and Stephens to claim necessity if they later killed Brooks (the fourth passenger) and then allow Dudley to kill Stephens (or vice versa). Calculating net gain (or loss) in this manner would, according to Coleridge, allow one survivor to justify the killing of three other people. Consequently, Coleridge rejected the plea of necessity.

Coleridge, however, was wrong on two grounds. First, the surviving sailor of the four would claim not that he killed three to save one, but that he killed three rather than allow all four to die. Second, such manipulation of the quantification approach is undesirable. The real question should be whether a person acting under such extreme pressure can be held morally culpable if he "capitulates" to those pressures.[22] That's why we have juries.

The quantification limitation is exemplified by the "trolley" case. Don is a conductor on a trolley, which loses its brakes. Down the track, five people are asleep in a train. The trolley must hit and kill them unless Don turns the trolley down a spur line, on which there are two people, asleep, who

20. *Perka v. The Queen*, 13 D.L.R. (4th) 1 (1984).

21. German Penal Code §§34 & 35 (1975); Swedish Penal Code ch. 24, §§4 & 5 (1963).

22. Extraordinarily, W.S. Gilbert (Sullivan's cohort) wrote a poem in which a mariner discloses to a listener that he is the captain and the mate and the cook and the bo'sun, and indeed, the entire crew of the *Nancy Bell*, a distressed ship, having serially committed cannibalism on each of those members. The poem was considered so upsetting that the magazine PUNCH refused to publish it, for being "too cannibalistic."

also are certain to be killed. If Don does nothing, and the five are killed, his inaction will probably not be criminal, unless he owed a duty to any of the people on the track. (See Chapter 3 and the discussion of omissions.) If there was such a duty, and if necessity is "quantified," then his failure to act will not be justified. (He killed five to save two.) On the other hand, if he acts affirmatively to go down the spur, his action is justified, because he killed two to save five. Aside from other consideration, quantifying human life seems distasteful, and perhaps a bit ghoulish. Judith Jarvis Thomson, The Trolley Problem, 94 Yale L.J. 1395 (1985).

Duress vs. Necessity

Necessity does not require a threat of death or serious bodily harm. As long as the defendant inflicts less harm than he was threatened with, the claim of necessity can be made. Thus, if Trump lashes his $500,000 yacht to a dock in a fierce storm, thereby doing $500 worth of damage to the dock, he has a defense to the criminal charge of intentional destruction of property.[23]

This means that necessity may serve as a "default" claim for some cases where duress cannot apply. Thus, Bob, who helped Alex embezzle money from Bob's employer rather than have Alex destroy the *Mona Lisa*, has no claim of duress. But he might have a claim of necessity, depending on how the jury balances the employer's money against the loss of a valuable piece of art.

The Problem of Democracy

Another problem, though not unique to necessity situations, occurs more frequently there than in duress situations: The legislature may have already addressed the balancing of harms, even if indirectly. Texas has taken this approach one step forward, by providing that a defendant has a claim of justification if "the legislative purpose to exclude the justification claimed for the conduct does not otherwise plainly appear."[24] Many recent attempts to invoke necessity have involved civil disobedience in one form or another. For example, sit-in demonstrators at nuclear plants or abortion clinics, patients using prohibited drugs to ease the pain or to stop the progress of a disease,[25] or public health advocates distributing clean needles to drug

---

23. Of course, as every torts student knows, Trump may still have to pay the dock owner damages for the loss. See *Vincent v. Lake Erie Transp. Co.*, 109 Minn. 456 (1910).

24. Tex. Penal Code §9.22.

25. As of 2018, a total of 29 states, the District of Columbia, Guam and Puerto Rico now allow for comprehensive public medical marijuana usage. See http://www.ncsl.org/research/health/state-medical-marijuana-laws.aspx. But in *Gonzales v. Raich*, 545 U.S. 1 (2005),

addicts in an effort to prevent the spread of AIDS[26] have claimed necessity when charged with crimes arising out of their acts of civil disobedience. Some juries have acquitted in these cases. Appellate courts, however, have almost unanimously rejected the claims on two grounds: (1) the threatened injury (suffering AIDS or death) was not "imminent" enough or (2) the legislature (or in the abortion cases, the Constitution) had already weighed the conflicting policies and resolved them against the disobedients. The defendants could have participated in the political process to alter public policy but chose not to (or previously lost the issue in the legislature). Consequently, their claim that breaking the law to protest public policy was justified by necessity was rejected. As one commentator has put it: "[T]he necessity defense attacks the very foundation of American capitalist and democratic structures."[27]

Jury nullification can undermine the rationale adopted by courts. Appellate courts have generally held that it is not reversible error to preclude evidence of defendants' beliefs from being introduced at trial, thereby reducing the possibility of nullification on such claims.

Most of these cases involve civil disobedience, where the "dissenters" see themselves as taking the moral high ground—protesting against racially discriminatory laws, or abortions (which they see as murder), or the operation of nuclear power plants (which they see as endangering thousands of lives). They contend that the political (or judicial) process has been corrupted and they therefore have "no choice" but to take direct action against the current law. Scholars—but not courts—often distinguish between "direct" civil disobedience, where the law that is violated is the "direct" target of the protest (sit-ins at restaurants to protest segregationist serving laws; distribution of clean needles to addicts), and "indirect" civil disobedience, where the law violated is not the target (a sit-in to protest the war in Vietnam).

---

the Court (6-3, with Stevens writing for the majority) held that even seriously ill patients who use locally grown marijuana, under a doctor's order and pursuant to state law, may nevertheless be prosecuted for violating federal law. However, the Rohrabacher-Farr amendment (also referred to as the Rohrabacher-Blumenauer amendment) is legislation that passed the house in 2014 prohibiting the Justice Department from spending federal funds to interfere with the implementation of state medical marijuana laws. See https://www.congress.gov/amendment/113th-congress/house-amendment/748. The amendment does not change the legal status of cannabis however, and must be renewed each fiscal year in order to remain in effect. It also passed in 2015, 2016 and 2017.

26. As of 2007, all states had programs for such needle exchanges or allowed individual local governments to establish such programs.

27. Shaun P. Martin, The Radical Necessity Defense, 73 U. Cin. L. Rev. 1527 (2005).

The Model Penal Code

The Code recognizes a claim of necessity or "lesser evils."[28] D must believe that his conduct is necessary to avoid harm to himself or others and that the harm inflicted by committing a "criminal" act is less serious than that sought to be avoided by the criminal law. The Code rejects most common law restrictions on the claim. Thus, the Code's provision (a) does not require that the actual infliction of the harm be "imminent"; (b) does not distinguish between threats from human versus nonhuman forces; (c) does not restrict the claim to instances involving a threat of death or serious bodily harm; and (d) does not preclude the defense in a homicide. The Code appears to resolve the "democracy" problem by requiring that the claim be allowed only if the harm "sought to be prevented" *outweighs* the harm that the law broken seeks to prevent. The decision as to this balance is apparently one of law to be made by the judge, who will ostensibly consider the political apparatus available in cases of civil disobedience.

In contrast to its section on duress, which made that claim unavailable if the defendant had recklessly created the conditions of the threat, the Code provides that if the defendant has been reckless or negligent in placing himself in the position where the necessity occurred, he may still raise the claim in all instances where he is charged with a purposeful or knowing crime. However, he may be prosecuted for a reckless or negligent crime. Thus, a defendant will be treated differently under the Code depending on whether he has a claim of duress or necessity. Someone who has been reckless in creating a duress situation will be guilty of murder, while a defendant who has been reckless in creating a necessitous homicide situation will be guilty only of manslaughter.[29]

Finally, to make clear the relation between necessity and duress, the *duress* section of the Code explicitly provides that §2.09 does not, by negative implication, limit any defense that would be available under §3.02.[30]

It is unclear whether federal law generally would recognize a necessity defense. The Supreme Court has suggested (but not held) that it is available only if a statute expressly permits the claim.[31]

---

28. MPC §3.02.

29. MPC §3.02(2). See DeGirolami, Culpability in Creating the Choice of Evils, 60 Ala. L. Rev. 597 (2009); Robinson, Causing the Conditions of One's Own Defense: A Study in the Limits of Theory in Criminal Law Doctrine, 71 Va. L. Rev. 1 (1985).

30. See §2.09(4).

31. *United States v. Oakland Cannabis Buyers' Cop.*, 532 U.S. 483 (2001) See Stephen Schwartz, Is There a Common Law Necessity Defense in Federal Criminal Law? 75 U. Chi. L. Rev. 1259 (2009).

EXAMPLES

Examples

In which of the following can the defendant(s) claim a justification or excuse of duress or necessity?

1a. Boris and his wife Natasha are sitting in their car at a traffic light when they are suddenly confronted by six men wearing ski masks and armed with machine guns who "hijack" the car. Three miles later, the men kidnap a police officer and handcuff him. They then force Natasha to drive to a remote spot, where they order Natasha to hold the officer still while Boris shoots him in the head. The men threaten to kill Boris, Natasha, and their two children (who are not in the car) unless the two comply. Natasha holds the officer, but Boris, after firing three wild shots, faints. The men then order Natasha to shoot the officer while they hold him. She does so.

1b. Suppose, instead, that Boris and Natasha are kidnapped and told to help rob a bank by holding open the bags into which the money is put. During the robbery, one of the original robbers accidentally shoots and kills a teller.

2. Alvin tells Van Cliburn (a famous concert pianist) that unless Van helps him extort money from Sylvia, Alvin will break his fingers so that Cliburn can never play the piano again. Van helps Alvin and is charged as an accomplice.

3. Three days after 9/11, Carla, a devout Sunni Muslim wearing hijab, is driving her car non-negligently in an area known to be highly indignant about the terrorist attack, when Jimbo, a 4-year-old white child, runs right in front of her car and is hit. Carla immediately calls an ambulance on her cell phone. A crowd gathers and recognizes the hijab as Islamic attire. Carla then departs. During her trial for leaving the scene of that accident, she tries to introduce evidence that (1) someone in the crowd shouted, "She's a terrorist," and (2) a resident of the neighborhood, whom she knew well, said to her, "You'd better get out of here now. This crowd is getting nasty." The trial judge refused to allow this testimony. Was the judge right in doing so?

4a. Darrell, a bank executive, has spent the last 20 years of his life writing his version of the great American novel. He has only one hard copy of the manuscript, which is now 98 percent complete. Douglas steals the one existing hard copy of the manuscript and erases the original from the hard drive. He tells Darrell that he will destroy the piece unless Darrell gives Doug the combination to the bank vault. Darrell, after much agony, complies and is charged with theft.

4b. Suppose, instead of threatening to destroy the manuscript, Douglas threatens to kill Shadow, Darrell's five-year-old golden retriever, whom Darrell rescued as a pup and has cared for ever since.

5. Jonathan, the head of a dedicated right-to-life organization known for using violence, tells Bruce, the secretary of an abortion provider, that unless Bruce gives Jonathan the key to the office so that Jonathan can destroy the equipment in the office, he will kill Bruce "when he least expects it, sometime in the next month, or the next year, or whenever." Bruce complies.

6. Horace, a nurse at the local hospital, has spent the last three years ministering to those in the last stages of AIDS. Distraught by what he has seen, he steals hypodermics and syringes from the hospital and distributes them to heroin and cocaine addicts in an attempt to reduce the spread of AIDS. He is prosecuted for (1) larceny; (2) distribution of drug paraphernalia.

7. Despite adverse weather predictions and warnings from several knowledgeable climbers, Edmund Hillary tries to scale K2, a mountain in the Himalayas, with a crew of four. All are tied together, with Hillary at one end. The weather is indeed terrible (even worse than forecast), and the five fall into a crevasse. Hillary cuts the rope that holds three of the other four, and they die.

8. While driving down the street at a legal rate of speed, Clara is suddenly beset by a mob screaming at her and clearly intending serious bodily harm. The streets are blocked, and she drives on the sidewalk, in desperation, seeking an avenue of escape. She is arrested and charged with driving on a sidewalk.

9. Gottfried is driving to Pittsburgh in a car that has failed to pass environmental and safety inspection four times. In the middle of this drive, he stops at a rest stop. As he gets back into the car, Himmelfarb, an escaped convict, comes up, points a gun to his head, and says, "Drive to Pittsburgh." Gottfried complies. He is charged with (1) driving an unsafe car; (2) assisting Himmelfarb's escape.

10. Jack, an accountant, is ordered by Gertrude, his boss, to fraudulently increase the billings for customers by 30 percent; she tells him he will be fired unless he complies. Unknown to Gertrude, Jack has a daughter who will die unless she obtains a liver transplant in the next week. If Jack is fired, he will not have sufficient funds to pay for the transplant. Jack complies. Has Jack committed fraud?

11. Reread the case of Paul Hill in Chapter 8, Example 6, on page 253. Consider that case in the context of this chapter.

12a. Paul, a licensed doctor, believes that the medical profession should help those who are truly terminal and who have made what appears to be a rational decision to die, and do so with the most dignity possible. He makes his views well known, and over a period of several years assists several people in committing suicide, after interviewing them extensively to assure himself that they are not clinically depressed or otherwise unable to make such a decision. He then tapes one such death and puts it on national television. If he is prosecuted for his actions, will he claim excuse or justification?

12b. Paul's father is dying of terminal cancer. He is in the hospital, in severe pain. The doctors say that he could continue to live for several years, but that he will not improve. His son comes to the hospital several times a week for several months. One night, he finds a way to deceive the nurse into leaving the hospital room, pulls out a gun, and shoots his father four times. He waits for the police, and explains that he killed his father to end his suffering. If he is prosecuted for his actions, will he claim excuse or justification?

13. Enrico and Mario are employees of Brinks Armored cars. They have just picked up $1,000,000 in cash when Aloysius approaches Enrico and says, "I've got your child, Christopho. Put the money in this bag now, or else Georgina will kill him." Enrico starts putting the money in the bag. Mario, who cannot escape, but who also is not directly threatened by Aloysius, helps Enrico. Enrico and Mario are later charged with robbery. What result?

14. Darth and his 15-year-old son Luke walk into a bar. Darth orders two scotch and sodas, but Carrie, the server, refuses to give one to Luke, who is obviously under the legal age for drinking. "He's my son," says Darth. "I can serve him anything I want." "Not here," replies Carrie. Darth demands to see the owner-manager, Han, who reaffirms Carrie's decision. At that point:
    a. Darth pulls out a badge, which shows that he is with the Alcohol Beverage Commission. "If you don't serve my son right now, I'll close you down for six months. See how that helps your business in this economy." After that the liquor flows freely for both customers.
    b. Darth pulls out the same badge and says, "If you don't serve my son today, I'll be sure to revisit you within two weeks. And you'd better not have any violations, or I'll close you down for six months." The liquor flows freely again.
    c. Darth pulls out a light saber and destroys one of the wine bottles on the bar's shelf. "Want to see how much damage this can do? And it doesn't just destroy bottles, either," he says. The liquor flows freely for both Darth and Luke.

Carrie and Han want to plead duress when charged with serving alcohol to a minor. Will they be successful?

15. George Estate went out riding on his snowmobile on a bright sunny day. He took a trail, which he knew was near a national park, but thought nothing of that because he had been on the trail many times without getting into the park. Suddenly, however, there arose a "ground blizzard," which blinded George. His snowmobile soon failed. He built himself a snow cave and was rescued from there 24 hours later, suffering from frostbite. He is later prosecuted for violating 16 U.S.C. §551, which prohibits using a motor vehicle on national park land without permission. At his trial, the trial judge instructed the jury that he carried the burden of proving necessity. George appeals his conviction on the ground that the government had to carry the burden. Who's right?

16. Jean Val Jean steals two loaves of bread to feed his starving family. Necessity?

17. Reginald is a pizza delivery guy. While out on delivery one night, he knocks on a door and is confronted by two armed men, who immediately insist he comes inside. Afraid for his life, Reginald complies. It turns out the two men are criminals and they want to use Reginald to drop off some drugs for them. They hand him a brick of cocaine and tell him to walk to the 7-Eleven down the block and wait there for a man in a red jacket. They tell him if he fails to do comply with their instructions they will "carve him up with a butcher knife." Reginald is terrified. He takes the brick of cocaine and goes to the 7-Eleven. A man in a red jacket approaches him and asks if he "has it." Without a word, Reginald hands the cocaine over and then runs. Moments later he is stopped and arrested by a police officer that had watched the whole exchange. Reginald is booked and charged with distributing drugs. Does he have a defense?

Explanations

1a. The threat here is obviously serious enough to constitute duress: It is a threat of death or serious bodily harm that would make any person reasonably fear that it will be carried out in the immediate future. The threat to the children, however, might not be "imminent" enough under common law. If the threat had only been to the children, the original doctrine of the common law *might* have barred the use of the threat at all, as it sometimes required that the threat be to the defendant personally. Most courts, however, would now allow a jury to consider the threat. Nevertheless, under the common law, neither Boris nor

Natasha would be able to assert the issue since they are charged with homicide. The Model Penal Code would allow both to claim duress. Some states have found a "compromise" position by allowing defendants to reduce their liability to manslaughter.[32]

There is one other possibility. Since the threat was to kill four people, and only one was killed, Boris and Natasha might have a choice-of-evils (necessity) claim. This depends on whether the common law would have allowed the claim in a homicide case, notwithstanding *Dudley and Stephens* (remember—there, three were saved, although one was killed). Moreover (although this is an arcane rule), some courts still restrict necessity to those cases in which a force of nature posed the threat. Since the threat here is human, that doctrinal restriction would have been sufficient to preclude a claim of necessity.

1b. This death falls under the felony murder rule. (Go back to Chapter 8 if this sounds only vaguely familiar.) Can duress be a defense to *felony* murder, even if not to "regular" murder? Most courts have said yes. Whether this would be true if it were one of the duressed who accidentally killed the teller is unclear.

2. There are two issues here. First, is this "serious bodily harm"? If not, then under the common law, which only allowed the claim if the threat was one of "serious bodily harm or death," a claim of duress would not be viable. Bodily injury is a risk but what is the meaning of the word "serious"? (This doesn't mean that broken fingers don't hurt, but if the word means anything, surely this is a dubious application.) Under the MPC, however, the threat need only be "unlawful force." Second, if we assume that this is serious bodily harm, would a person of "reasonable firmness" have resisted the threat and accepted the broken fingers? This is obviously a difficult question. That is what juries are for.

   Assume, however, that a jury would conclude that a "usual" person would prefer broken fingers to having Sylvia suffer extortion. What, then, of the Model Penal Code's restriction that the defendant's "situation" must be considered? Is the fact that Van Cliburn is a concert pianist whose career will be ended part of his "situation"? Again, the issue is difficult. And we can make it more difficult. Assume, for the moment, that a concert pianist of reasonable firmness would not help the extortion. Or change the threat to Sylvia from extortion to rape. How does one balance these interests and assess these threats and interests?

3. According to the court in *Knight v. State*, 601 So. 2d 403 (Miss. 1992), no. Carla's claim of necessity depended on why she left the scene. Since

32. E.g., N.J. Stat. Ann. 2C:2-9.

the purpose of the statute—to assure assistance to Jimbo—had been achieved by the presence of the crowd and the calling of the ambulance, Carla's continued presence was not required, and if she feared for her life, it is at least possible that the jury might have found her departure both reasonable and necessary. (The *Knight* cases actually involved a 48-year-old black defendant who hit a 5-year-old white child riding a "Big Wheel" toy into the car's path.)

4a. Even if a reasonable person in Darrell's position would give the key to Douglas, the common law would not allow Darrell a claim of duress to a charge of being an accomplice, since the threat is not one of serious bodily harm or death. The Model Penal Code would similarly disallow a duress claim and for the same reason. Poor Darrell. We told you to always have a backup copy.

4b. While we dog lovers may become deeply emotionally attached to our pets, Shadow is only "property" under the law, and a threat to her life is insufficient to raise a question of duress, even under the Model Penal Code.

Wait, Darrell! Don't pack for prison yet! Even if you don't have a claim of duress, you might have a claim, at least under the MPC and possibly even under common law, of necessity. If the jury felt that your decision was the "right" one—that is, balancing all the interests, the lesser of two evils—you might be exonerated.

5. Under the common law, the threat must be one of "imminent" violence if the defendant is to be able to use the plea. A vague threat such as the one here has divided the courts over whether there is such a plea. In *State v. Toscano*, 74 N.J. 421 (1977), a case of threats of unspecified future injury, the Court adopted the rationale of the Model Penal Code that duress was a question of fact for the jury rather than a question of law for the judge.

6. The claim here must be one of necessity. Yet the threat of death to the addicts is surely remote for most of those who received the needles: Even if some of them were to become afflicted with the disease, their deaths are not "imminent."[33] Moreover, from an objective viewpoint, Horace has alternatives, including those of the usual political process. Therefore, Horace should be admonished to use those processes. On the other hand, Horace may seek to assert an "excuse" version of necessity; given his personal anguish over the plight of those with AIDS, he was subjectively unable to weigh carefully such arguments and honestly believed he was doing the "right thing." But will this defense

33. *Comm. v. Leno*, 616 N.E.2d 453 (Mass. 1993).

work for the theft? Probably not, since Horace had an alternative—he could have bought the syringes. The case also asks whether, in assessing the weight of the defendant's actions against the crime committed, one should weigh the crime "in the abstract" (larceny) or in the context of the facts (larceny of needles from a hospital with distribution in mind). Horace will not have a defense under the common law but would have a possible defense under the Model Penal Code.[34] In the past 20 years, all states have adopted, either by statute or administratively, some programs of needle distribution, which might dilute Horace's claim of necessity. He may think the statutory process is too narrow, but his claim that the political process is unyielding will be harder to make in 2018 than it would have been in 1990.

7. Under the common law, if *Dudley and Stephens* is the rule, Hillary would have no defense to a homicide. Even if *Dudley* is not the clear rule, she has (at least) negligently placed herself in the situation of peril and loses all claim of necessity. Under the Model Penal Code, however, Hillary would have a defense to prosecutions for purposeful and knowing murder, and possibly even reckless murder, but almost surely not for reckless manslaughter or negligent homicide.

8. This case poses the same dilemma as that of the prison escape cases. Clara has no claim of duress, since the mob did not want her to escape. On the other hand, under the earlier common law, she has no claim of necessity since the force is not a teleological one. Some courts have created a claim that they have called "duress of circumstance" to reach this case, while others have simply left the case to the jury on the issue of "responsibility." Some writers have urged rejection of any such "situational duress" claim, lest it swallow all concepts of free will and moral culpability; yet, this may show a lack of faith in the jury's ability to weigh these intricate and difficult moral issues.

9. If Gottfried were charged with aiding Himmelfarb's escape, he could easily claim duress (or necessity). He has been threatened with serious bodily harm or death, he has no route of escape, and his choice to drive the car is clearly the lesser of the two evils. But what if he is charged with driving an unsafe vehicle? It is not clear that Himmelfarb's threat induced him to drive to Pittsburgh; he was already on the way.

34. Another possible way to confront the issues in Example 5 is to avoid them, to argue that in all cases of civil disobedience the only proper "claim" that a defendant has is to accept the consequences of his intentional conduct. He must suffer the criminal penalties in order to demonstrate the immorality of the regime or the law to which he objects. Thus, those who sit in to protest civil rights infringements, or abortions, or the proliferation of nuclear power plants could be denied the claim of necessity/justification solely as a definitional matter.

Moreover, even if that were not a problem, it is not clear that duress or necessity *could* be used as a claim in what may be a strict liability crime. If it goes to mens rea, duress is probably *not* allowable since strict liability offenses do not require mens rea.

10. This problem raises the issue of immediacy since it is *possible* that the hospital would perform the operation in any event. Even though the question says Jack's daughter "will" die, nothing in the future is certain. Jack's daughter *might* undergo a spontaneous remission, or another hospital might perform the operation for free. But, as the court suggested in *Toscano* (page 479), a believable threat of harm "in the future" should still form the basis of a jury question. But leaving that aside, the problem really raises the issue of whether the duressor has to know that her threat endangers life. If Jack did not have a dying daughter, he would be unable to claim duress since the threat of losing one's job has not been recognized by the law in a duress context. However, here *he* knows that the threat is one to life but Gertrude does not. Does the threat then meet the common law's requirements of "death or serious bodily harm"? All the policy reasons for allowing a claim suggest that it should be so considered. But the common law was often very restrictive and hewed closely to doctrine. On the other hand, Jack may be able to claim necessity in any event. Any reasonable person would have chosen to have committed fraud rather than see his daughter die. At the very least, whether he chose the "lesser evil" would constitute a jury question.

11. In the actual case, Hill was precluded by the court, as a matter of law, from raising the plea of necessity. The court concluded that under the United States Constitution fetuses were not "human beings," and Hill could not therefore argue that his shooting was justified by the need to save lives. Had the doctor been planning to kill "human beings," Hill might have had a claim of necessity. But even then he would face two further hurdles: (1) whether their deaths were "imminent" since Dr. Brittan had not even entered the clinic; (2) whether a killer can claim necessity. The Second Circuit reached the same conclusion as to necessity in killing abortion providers in *United States v. Kopp*, 562 F.3d 141 (2d Cir. 2009).

    Notice that these problems exist as well under the MPC, which requires not only that the defendant believe his act is necessary but that the court determine that a jury could find that he has in fact (and law) done the "right thing." If this were not the case, all terrorists might successfully plead necessity. Indeed, in *Dudley*, Lord Chief Justice Coleridge quotes from Milton's *Paradise Lost* that the devil, in explaining his temptation of Eve, claimed necessity—"the tyrant's plea." On the other hand, Paul Hill is, in his own eyes, not acting immorally. And he is certainly not the "bad actor" that a paid assassin is. How should the law differentiate between these two?

12a. This is a (very) shortened version of the facts involving Dr. Jack Kervorkian, sometimes referred to as "Dr. Death," who conducted a national crusade in the 1980s and 90s to call attention to this issue. He was prosecuted several times, all of them unsuccessfully, except the last one, which resulted in his conviction for second-degree murder. Kervorkian was clearly claiming a justification—that while the law prohibited taking life, either directly or indirectly, in a premeditated manner, there were some situations where taking life outweighed the suffering that continued life would bring to the patient. He argued that, as a doctor, his first duty was to relieve his patients of pain.

12b. These facts are typical of euthanasia cases and track those of *State v. Forrest*, 362 S.E.2d 252 (N.C. 1987). While Paul could, like Kervorkian, claim justification (ending his father's pain was a greater good than having his father continue to suffer in pain for years), he could also claim, which Kervorkian could not, that his killing was excused. He would argue that his personal anguish and the great emotional stress placed upon him by seeing his father in this condition simply overwhelmed him and that while he killed premeditatedly, he simply had no "real choice." Under the common law, this claim would not be heard, but under the Model Penal Code, it is at least arguable that the killing might be seen as done in "extreme emotional or mental disturbance" and reduced to manslaughter. Many—perhaps most—of these cases are never prosecuted and, quite often, the grand jury refuses to indict, or the trial jury acquits.

13. Under the *very* early common law, Enrico might not have a defense of duress, which required that the threat be made against *him*, not even a close relative. But under "modern" common law, that claim is extended to include at least threats against family members. Mario would not fare so well—only in a Model Penal Code jurisdiction, which allows a threat of bodily harm against any person, even unrelated persons, would he have a real chance of a successful claim.

14a. No. Threats of an economic nature cannot be a basis for a duress claim. Even if Han believes that his business would go bankrupt, he has no duress claim.

14b. No. In addition to the economic nature of the threat, this example concerns a "non-imminent" threat. Han, at least in theory, could prevent the closing or could appeal it.

14c. No. The destruction of the bottle, while immediate, is still only economic. Carrie and Han have a plausible, but still weak, argument that they feared that Darth would turn the laser on them. But Darth's words are ambiguous, and there is nothing in the Example, as worded, that would lead to a reasonable belief that he would harm them. If there were such facts, the issue might then go to a jury. But note—under the common law, both Carrie and Han must claim that they feared that Darth would harm the person claiming duress. If the threat to Han, for example, was to harm Carrie, Han would not have had a claim of duress—the harm has to be to oneself (or, later, to a family member).

The MPC would give the same answer in (a) and (b)—economic threat is not a basis for a duress claim. However, the Code does not require that the threat be imminent—merely that a person of reasonable firmness might capitulate. In (c), however, the Code allows the claim if any person (not necessarily the duressed person) is threatened. Carrie and Han would therefore have that argument, but, again, only if Darth's words were construed as threatening personal injury.

Caveat. This question was phrased only in terms of a "duress" defense. If Carrie and Han had a creative attorney, they could also raise a "lesser evils" argument. While the common law often required that the source of a necessity threat be human, many common law courts, as well as the MPC, have rejected that as a separate element. And neither the common law nor the Code precluded the lesser evils argument if the threat was economic. But it might be hard to persuade a jury that loss of a liquor license is a greater evil than serving an underage customer. Their best bet is to persuade the jury that serving the defendant's *son* is not a greater evil, because the defendant is the one who wanted his son served.

15. The judge. First, there is the possibility that this is a strict liability "public welfare offense," in which case no mens rea is required for guilt (see Chapter 6). If so, there is some question as to whether *any* defense is available. Second, even if that were not the case, the Supreme Court has questioned whether a claim of necessity can be raised under a federal statute unless Congress has specifically permitted it. Third, even if the claim may be raised, it is arguable (though certainly not clear) that as in duress (see the *Dixon* case cited in the text), the government may require the defendant to carry the burden of proof. The contrary argument is that necessity is a justification, while duress is an excuse, and that it may be that the two are different for purposes of burdens of proof. See page 488-489. See also *United States v. Unser*, 165 F.3d 755 (10th Cir. 1999).

16. This, of course, is Les Miserables. In the *Dudley* opinion, Lord Coleridge addressed this precise question, saying that theft of food would not be justified because England provided relief for the poor. But what if the government could not provide relief? During Hurricane Katrina, many people stole food because government relief was unable to provide all

of the needed food. Was this justified? In similar situations, some have argued that the defendants are in a "state of nature" and no longer governed by the laws of man.[35] Six states actually have anti-looting statutes, and it is unclear whether the actions of defendants even in Katrina would be protected. Ironically, Louisiana had enacted an anti-looting statute "during the existence of a state of emergency," which became effective exactly two weeks before Katrina hit. One woman was arrested for stealing sausage because she lived across from the police station; the view was that she could have asked the police for food. (The charges were ultimately dropped.) On the other hand, three defendants who took liquor, beer, and a case of wine coolers were sentenced to fifteen years in prison.[36]

17. Under the elements of duress, Reginald would not likely have a defense. Initially, there was certainly a real and immediate threat of bodily harm or death. The two men were armed with firearms and apparently were capable of disposing of Reginald. Even under the more stringent, objective test that requires that a "reasonably firm-willed" person would have complied, Reginald would have a good argument; however, Reginald's defense may fail because he could have escaped. He could argue he was still under duress when he left the house because the two men had told him they would be watching him, but Reginald had not seen anyone. The prosecution could argue that a person of a "reasonably firm-will" would have chosen to go to the police as soon as he or she got to a public space and called the police instead of carrying out the drug deal.

SELF-DEFENSE

The claim of self-defense was one of the first recognized by the common law. Definitions and restrictions on its use were slow in coming, and over the centuries there has been much confusion in its application. Although courts and scholars are unanimous that self-defense should be recognized as a claim, there is substantial uncertainty about why this is so. From these disagreements come disagreements on the conditions under which

35. See Lon L. Fuller, The Case of the Speluncean Explorers, 62 Harv. L. Rev. 616 (1949).
36. See Stephanie J. Hamrick, Is Looting Ever Justified?: An Analysis of Looting Laws and the Applicability of the Necessity Defense During Natural Disasters and States of Emergency, 7 Nev. L.J. 182 (2006).

self-defense may properly be claimed, and the degree to which the law should use a subjective standard to judge such claims.

A utilitarian might argue that failure to recognize a claim of self-defense would be pointless, since, as with other acts done under threat of death, the law's threat of punishment in the future is unlikely to deter an actor who believes he must act or die now. As Justice Holmes once said, "Detached reflection cannot be expected in the presence of an uplifted knife." Other utilitarian explanations, sounding in partial or total justification, would posit that (a) the defendant-slayer did the right thing, and (b) by initiating an aggressive (or deadly) attack, the aggressor "asked for" the response and lost his right not to be injured or killed. In addition, allowing victims of aggressive attacks to respond with proportionate force may deter future aggression.

A retributivist would argue that innocent victims of aggressive attacks are not immoral actors and cannot be seen as "blameworthy" when they respond to such attacks. Moreover, people who are or believe they are suddenly threatened by death may not think clearly. Unlike Holmes, who argued that a threat of punishment *could not* change a human response to a threat of death, the retributivist would care only that the defendant *did not* reflect, even if others could be made to do so. To paraphrase Holmes (supra), "Detached reflection *is usually not present* in the presence of an uplifted knife," or more particularly, "This defendant did not reflect in the presence of an uplifted knife, and that is not morally blameworthy."

Still another, morally based, explanation is that the defendant has a right to autonomy, which she cannot be made to surrender even if she must kill to enforce that right. Thus, even if the defendant could avoid injury to the aggressor by retreating, we authenticate her right not to have her "space" and autonomy infringed.

THE RULES OF SELF-DEFENSE

Self-defense mimics other in extremis claims, requiring

1. a *threat* of
2. "*imminent,*"
3. *unlawful,*
4. *(serious) bodily harm,*[37]

37. The defendant must use proportionate force. Thus, if *A* threatens to slap B, B may not kill *A*, even if that is the only way to avoid the slap. In general, the rules regarding the use of nondeadly force parallel those for the use of deadly force. The text focuses on the use of deadly force.

5. to which there are, or appear to be, *no available alternatives* to the defendant except the use of force.

Some courts add a sixth requirement:

6. *nonculpability* on the part of the defendant in *bringing about the situation.*[38]

Imminence; No Alternatives

The essence of self-defense is that it "sounds in necessity." Like that claim, self-defense usually demands that the defendant take any and all escape routes available before taking human life. The one exception—the "no retreat" rule—will be examined later.

Preemptive Strikes

In most states a claim of self-defense requires that the harm threatened be "imminent." If Mike threatens to kill Harry "the next time I see your ugly face," or tells Harry to "get out of town by sundown or else," Harry has alternatives to killing Mike. As with necessity, this can be articulated by the requirement that there be no (nonviolent) response possible. He can leave the territory, obtain police protection, try to persuade Mike to recant, or hope that Mike will reconsider (or die). However, some jurisdictions recognize that those who engage in "preemptive strikes" may be acting properly or at least excusably in some circumstances.[39]

In one sense, this phrasing is misleading—every act of self-defense is "preemptive."[40] Even Darth Vader, brandishing a light saber at an unarmed Obi-Wan Kenobi, *might* change his mind and walk away. But Obi-Wan need not wait until Darth Vader actually "fires" his weapon; if Obi-Wan can

---

38. This is most clearly the case when *A* assaults B with deadly force, then attempts to retreat, but B (not seeing *A*'s attempted retreat) uses deadly force, after which *A* kills B. See generally Paul Robinson, Causing the Conditions of One's Own Defense, 71 Va. L. Rev. 1 (1985).

39. *Carico v. Commonwealth*, 70 Ky. 124 (1870). For careful looks at the issue of preemption, both in self-defense law and in other contexts, see A. Dershowitz, Preemption: A Knife That Cuts Both Ways (2006); Ferzan, Defending Imminence: From Battered Women to Iraq, 46 Ariz. L. Rev. 213 (2004); Wallace, Beyond Imminence: Evolving International Law and Battered Women's Right to Self-Defense, 71 U. Chi. L. Rev. 1749 (2004) (listing as factors (a) probability, (b) availability of alternative recourses, and (c) magnitude of harm); Kaufman, Self-Defense, Imminence, and the Battered Woman, 10 New Crim. L. Rev. 342 (2007).

40. As one judge noted nearly six hundred years ago, "I am not bound to wait while the other fellow lands blow for perchance it will be too late." Y.B. Mich. 2 Hen. 6, f. 8, pl. 40 (1414) (Cokeyn, J.).

miraculously find some method of protection (including the use of deadly force), he may use it. As we shall see later, the real question is whether his decision has to be "reasonable."

To Retreat or Not to Retreat, That Is the Dilemma

The common law of the eighteenth century recognized two kinds of claims that we now combine under the heading of self-defense: (1) prevention of felony and (2) homicide *se defendendo*. The distinction worked as follows: If John Mouse, while walking peacefully down the street, was suddenly affronted by a "murderous assault" by Jim Godzilla ("your money or your life"), Mouse's killing of Godzilla was a justifiable *prevention of felony*. If, on the other hand, Mouse and Godzilla were engaged in a friendly argument that escalated into mutual combat, during which Mouse killed Godzilla on the spot, Mouse was guilty of manslaughter "in chaud [chance] medley" (see Chapter 8). If, however, Mouse "retreated" from the site of the dispute and ran "to the wall," with Godzilla pursuing, and only then killed Godzilla, the killing was "*se defendendo*," and Mouse was "excused" (not justified). In one sense, this looked like a "prevention of felony" killing. However, since Mouse had played a part in creating the situation in which deadly force became "necessary," the state leveled a severe "civil sanction," the forfeiture of all Mouse's property to the state.

The retreat requirement applied only to homicides *se defendendo* and not to "prevention of felony" slayings. In the mid-nineteenth century, however, American courts, possibly because of the abolition of the forfeiture sanction, jumbled the requirement, applying it either to *all* killings or to none. Thus, in some states retreat was *always* required, even of the obviously innocent victim of an aggressive, murderous attack, while in other states it was said that "no true man" (the actual language of some courts) would ever retreat in the face of an attack, even if he had helped create that situation.

A full "retreat" or "no retreat" rule would have at least established a bright line. However, in those states that *did* require retreat, exceptions were soon created. The courts held that the slayer need not retreat in, or from, his own home (no doubt a residue of the "home as castle" view). Unable, however, to articulate why this exception applied only to homes, some courts then expanded the exception to places "like" homes, in which a person *should* feel, and should be able to feel, secure—offices, private clubs, cars, and so on. At the same time, other courts, uncomfortable with the doctrine that allowed the (by hypothesis) otherwise unnecessary taking of life, restricted the application of the exception by severely redefining "home" to include (a) only the curtilage and not the entire residential "lot"; (b) only the house and not even the curtilage; (c) only the interior of the actual house and not even the porch.[41] Other problems occur: must a co-tenant or co-owner retreat if the aggressor is the other tenant/owner? What relationships might apply here? In the past ten years, several states, spurred by the battered spouse issue, have, either judicially or legislatively, eliminated the requirement that a co-owner retreat.[42]

"Stand Your Ground" Laws

Beginning in Florida in 2005,[43] a number of states (approximately 24[44]) enacted so-called "stand your ground" laws. Although the statutes differ at least marginally, Florida's provides as follows:

1. **No requirement of retreat, whether in the house or "in a place where he or she has a right to be."** Although this provision changed the law in Florida (and in several other states which adopted it thereafter),[45] the rule requiring retreat was, even at that time, a minority rule. Even the Model Penal Code, which purports to require retreat, does so only if the defendant knew that she could retreat with "complete" safety.
2. **A presumption that a person using deadly force while in his dwelling or vehicle had a reasonable fear of imminent death.** This presumption appears to be irrebuttable. While there are exceptions to it, this presumption alone makes successful prosecution of a home-dwelling killer very difficult. If the presumption is irrebuttable, as the legislative history suggests,[46] a home-dwelling killer will effectively be free from prosecution.

---

41. *State v. Bonano*, 284 A.2d 345 (N.J. 1971).
42. See Suk, The True Woman: Scenes from the Law of Self Defense, 31 Harv. J.L. & Gender, 237, 252-259 (2008).
43. Fla. Stat. Ann. §§776.012; 776.013; 776.031
44. See Zachary L. Weaver, Florida's "Stand Your Ground" Law: The Actual Effects and the Need for Clarification, 63 U. Miami L. Rev. 395, 397 (2008). See also States that Have Stand Your Ground Laws, available at http://criminal.findlaw.com/criminal-law-basics/states-that-have-stand-your-ground-laws.html (last visited December 8, 2017).
45. Denise M. Drake, The Castle Doctrine: An Expanding Right to Stand Your Ground, 39 St. Mary's L.J. 573 (2008) (Texas statute). On the other hand, Georgia's statute merely codified its common law "no retreat" rule." Daniel Merrett, Defenses to Criminal Prosecutions: Provide That Person Who Is Attacked Has No Duty to Retreat; Provide Immunity from Prosecution, 23 Ga. St. U. L. Rev. 227 (2006).
46. Elizabeth B. Meagle, Deadly Combinations: How Self-Defense Laws Pairing Immunity with a Presumption of Fear Allow Criminals to "Get Away with Murder," 34 Am. J. Trial Advoc. 105 (2010). See *People v. Heckman*, 993 So. 2d 12004 (Fla. App. 2007): Note, Florida Legislation: The Controversy over Florida's New "Stand Your Ground" Law: Fla. Stat. §776.013 (2005), 33

3. **A presumption that a stranger forcibly and unlawfully entering a dwelling intends to commit an unlawful act involving force or violence.**
4. **A ban on arresting the killer unless law enforcement "determines that there is probable cause that the force that was used was unlawful."**
5. **"Immunity" from both civil and criminal prosecution if he is justified in using such force.** Florida courts have interpreted the statute as requiring a hearing, at which the defendant carries the burden of persuasion by a preponderance of the evidence, that he did act properly under the statute(s). The trial judge is to weigh the credibility of the witnesses;[47] if immunity is granted, there is no further prosecution and the case never goes to trial.[48] Of course, if the judge does not grant immunity, the prosecution will have to prove, beyond a reasonable doubt, at trial that the defendant did not have a reasonable fear of death or serious bodily harm and therefore did not act in self-defense.

The Trayvon Martin Case

These provisions of the Florida law (and other laws like them) were thrown into deep controversy in 2012 when Trayvon Martin, a seventeen-year-old African American visiting his father's fiancée in her community was killed by George Zimmerman, a Hispanic resident of the community who had been involved with Neighborhood Watch programs (but was not so involved at the time). While many of the facts have been controverted, at this point these appear to be the basic facts: Martin was unarmed, carrying only a bag of candy and a cell phone. Zimmerman, in a car, had followed Martin for several blocks as he walked through the neighborhood. Calling Martin's actions "suspicious," Zimmerman phoned the police, who told

---

Fla. St. U. L. Rev. 351, 354 (Fall 2005). The creation of §776.013 eliminated the burden of proving that the defender had a reasonable belief that deadly force was necessary by providing a conclusive presumption of such. Fla. S. Comm. on Judiciary, CS for SB 436 (2005) Staff Analysis 5-6 (Feb. 25, 2005). See also Note 43 Florida's Protection of Perons Bill, 43 Harv. J. On Legis. 199, 201 (2006), citing Florida Senate Committee Report. Accord, Weaver, supra, n. 22 at 403-404. The Texas law's presumption appears to be rebuttable. See Denise Dennis Drake, The Castle Doctrine: An Expanding Right to Stand Your Ground, 39 St. Mary's L.J. 573, 590 (2008). There is no case law on either question as of this writing.

47. This, of course, should be contrasted with the usual process when there is a motion to dismiss, which should be denied if the judge determines that there are issues of fact to be determined by the jury. Some Florida trial courts had applied that concept, but the *Dennis* decision overruled them.

48. *Dennis v. State*, 51 So. 3d 456 (Fla. 2010).

him to stay in the car, but he left the car and confronted Martin. It appears that he told the police who arrived on the scene after the shooting that Martin assaulted him and was beating him on the ground, at which point he pulled his gun and shot Martin. Although Martin was clearly unarmed, the police accepted Zimmerman's claim of self-defense, and did not arrest him, although they took him to police headquarters for several hours.

Many characterized the police's failure to arrest Zimmerman as racist, and a national outcry ensued. The statute, however, actually precludes even an arrest unless the police "determine that there is probable cause that the force that was used was unlawful."[49] As the Martin case showed, in self-defense cases there are often no (or at least no apparent) witnesses when the police arrive, and the only tale they hear is from the killer.[50] After the case generated national publicity, a number of persons who heard (but did not see) parts of the event were discovered. Thereafter, a new prosecutor was named, who then obtained an indictment against Zimmerman for second degree murder. On July 13, 2013, Zimmerman was found not guilty of second degree murder and acquitted of manslaughter.[51] The jury was in deliberation for over sixteen hours before concluding that Zimmerman was justified in killing Martin.[52]

Right to Carry Laws. Although not directly involved in self-defense doctrine, it is important to note that a strong majority of states (42)[53] have now adopted so-called "right to carry" laws, which provide that a licensed gun owner may seek a permit to carry a firearm, concealed, in public.[54] When some places (churches, bars, educational institutions) forbade the

---

49. As one writer has put it, "[L]aw enforcement must not only establish probable cause that a crime has occurred, but also seek to rule out an affirmative defense (self-defense) to determine entitlement to immunity. . . . It goes beyond figuring out whether a crime occurred; the statute requires police to make the defendant's case and then disprove it beyond a reasonable doubt." Elizabeth B. Megale, Deadly Combinations: How Self-Defense Laws Pairing Immunity with a Presumption of Fear Allow Criminals to "Get Away with Murder," 34 Am. J. Trial Advoc. 105, 120, n. 92 (2010).

50. See Weaver, supra n. 22 at 420. "If police rely solely on the user of force's claim and do not perform a more thorough investigation into whether there is other evidence that the force used was unreasonable, then there is too great an opportunity for injustice."

51. Lizette Alvarez and Cara Buckley, *Zimmerman Is Acquitted In Trayvon Martin Killing*, N.Y. Times (July 13, 2013), http://www.nytimes.com/2013/07/14/us/george-zimmerman-verdict-trayvon-martin.html.

52. Lizette Alvarez and Cara Buckley, *Zimmerman Is Acquitted in Trayvon Martin Killing*, N.Y. Times (July 13, 2013), http://www.nytimes.com/2013/07/14/us/george-zimmerman-verdict-trayvon-martin.html.

53. States that Allow Concealed Carry, https://americanconcealed.com/articles/second-amendment/states-that-allow-concealed-carry (last visited January 26, 2018).

54. Note, Public Endangerment or Personal Liberty? North Carolina Enacts a Liberalized Concealed Handgun Statute, 74 N.C. L. Rev. 214 (1996).

carrying of such weapons therein, some states specifically enacted legislation allowing for the right to carry in such places. This book is not the place to debate the efficacy of gun control laws, but combined with the movement to "stand your ground," these statutes arguably make shootings (ostensibly in self-defense) more likely and more likely to result in acquittals of the shooters.

Proportionality and Subjectivity

Consistent with an attempt to limit the use of deadly force, self-defense doctrine has generally required that the defendant use no more force than "necessary" to repel the aggressor. Whether deadly force is "necessary," however, depends on a number of factors relating to the victim and the defendant. If, for example, Maury (the defendant) is 5 feet 3 inches and weighs 120 pounds, and Rocky (the threatener-aggressor) is 6 feet 4 inches and weighs 240 pounds, it may be "necessary" for Maury to use deadly force to prevent Rocky from carrying out a threat to "beat Maury to a pulp." If, however, the sizes are reversed, Maury's claim to self-defense, much less to the use of deadly force, is suspect. Thus, while the muscular Maury might use "some" force to push away the diminutive Rocky, he cannot use force that is disproportionate not only to the threatened harm, but also to the force necessary to avoid that harm.

Similarly, in a jurisdiction requiring retreat, the respective ability of each actor to escape may be relevant. If Egmont the track star is accosted by Theodore in an open street, he may be required to try to outrun Theodore to a point of safety. If, however, the threat occurs in a moving train, the relative running talents of the two are less important. ("You can run, but you can't hide" in a train.)

This raises the general issue, already discussed in many other contexts, of the extent to which the characteristics of the defendant or victim are relevant in the case. As in other areas, the decisions are mixed.

In *State v. Wanrow*, 559 P.2d 548 (Wash. 1976), the defendant was a 5 feet 4 inch woman on crutches who shot and killed an unarmed, drunk 6 feet 2 inch man who had not overtly threatened her, but who she ostensibly believed had threatened to molest her child, who was asleep only a few feet away. Outside the house, but only a few steps away, were two men in the family, each carrying a baseball bat. The relative size, weight, and mobility of the defendant and the victim were clearly relevant facts under existing law. *Wanrow* broke new ground, however, by holding that a jury could find that women, as a group, are socialized *not* to use intermediate force against aggressors, particularly aggressor males. Thus, if Sid hit Wally in the nose, Wally "would probably" react by hitting Sid back or wrestling Sid to the ground. But if Sid hit Henrietta in the nose, Henrietta (the court implied) would only either submit (to further force) or employ deadly force. Thus, proportionality had to be assessed from the viewpoint of a defendant with the characteristics, at least the gender characteristics, of the defendant. At the same time, the court suggested, but did not hold, that the concept was not limited to gender. If a male defendant could demonstrate that he, individually or as a member of a culture, had not been taught how to use intermediate force, the claim would be similarly available.[55]

The problem here, as in other areas where the law begins to "subjectivize" an objective standard, is finding the stopping point. Courts had long recognized, as suggested above, that the respective sizes of the defendant and the victim were relevant. Similar problems arise when considering defendant's habits (does he watch violent TV shows, such as "Criminal Minds," "CSI" (and its several hundred progeny and reruns), and "Narcos"?), his own past experiences (suppose the defendant has been assaulted before), or his understanding of others' experiences (suppose he knows someone who has been assaulted or has read about people who have been). In the (in)famous case of the "subway shooter," Bernhard Goetz, the New York Court of Appeals, while saying it adhered to an objective standard, held that most of these latter characteristics should be considered by the jury in assessing the reasonableness of Goetz's reaction when confronted in the subway by several youths who appeared to him to be threatening to rob him.[56]

Many courts, following the lead of the Model Penal Code, discussed below, allow the jury to consider specific aspects of the defendant's character. A few appear to embrace virtually full "subjectivization" of the "reasonably prudent person" (RPP) test,[57] whereas others do not allow the jury to consider the defendant's "courage" (or lack thereof). As with provocation and claims of "cultural defense" (see Chapter 8), the question is whether the defendant's failure to meet "objective" standards of conduct should result in full, partial, or no exculpation. The issue is complicated by the debate over whether he is justified or excused. One writer, seeking to jump this hurdle, has argued that self-defense, even when "necessary," should always be explained as an excuse rather than a justification.[58]

---

55. *Wanrow* is difficult to interpret. The trial court had precluded evidence that the defendant's Native American culture also militated against the use of deadly force. The Washington Supreme Court said only that it could not hold that this was an abuse of discretion. This certainly implies that it would have been within the discretion of the judge to admit such evidence. If so, then the implication is that *any* source that led the defendant (even a male) generically to abandon the use of intermediate force would be relevant and admissible.

56. *People v. Goetz*, 497 N.E.2d 41 (N.Y. 1986). One writer has warned about the "already porous, progressively more subjective" standards now being suggested. Stacy Caplow, The Gaelic Goetz: A Case of Self Defense in Ireland, 17 Cardozo J. Int'l & Comp. L. 1 (2009).

57. *State v. Leidholm*, 334 N.W.2d 811 (N.D. 1983).

58. Finkelstein, Self-Defense as a Rational Excuse, 57 U. Pitt. L. Rev. 621 (2006).

These questions are often played out in evidentiary rulings. Thus, virtually all courts hold that evidence of a victim's prior violent acts is admissible if the defendant was aware of these acts (or rumors of them) on the grounds that this evidence goes to the reasonableness of the defendant's fear. And a significant number of courts allow the evidence to be admitted, even if the defendant was unaware of these acts, for the purpose of showing that the victim may have been the aggressor.[59] As with those other areas, there is no easy resolution of these questions. The cases are very fact-specific, and while it is probably true that there is a trend toward allowing subjectivization, it would depend on specific jurisdictions and specific facts. The best approach here is simply to be aware of the issue in every case—particularly one that might appear on an exam.

Mistake and Reasonableness

We have already seen that the law puzzles over the effect of mistake in any allegedly necessitous situation. In self-defense cases, the defendant could be mistaken in his belief that he is about to be attacked, or about the need to use deadly force to repel the attack, or in his belief that retreat is not likely to be successful. Suppose, however, that (1) his belief is wrong; (2) his belief is not only wrong but unreasonable. The traditional classroom hypothetical is one where B and C become involved in a heated argument over the respective lifetime batting averages of Ty Cobb and Pete Rose, leading B to shout, "I've had enough of your lying, you SOB; I'll make sure you don't make that mistake anymore," while reaching into his coat pocket. C, fearing that B will pull out a gun, kills B instantly. Inside B's coat pocket is the encyclopedia of baseball but no weapon.

The early common law appeared to allow the mistake defense to any person who honestly believed that he was the victim of an aggressive attack even if that belief was unreasonable.[60] Therefore, C in the above hypothetical would be exculpated. In the mid-nineteenth century, however, many American courts adopted the rule that a defendant who killed in the mistaken belief that he was the victim of a deadly attack would entirely lose the defense if the mistake was unreasonable. This "all or nothing" approach appears to be the current rule in the majority of jurisdictions. Its advo-

59. See, e.g., *Commonwealth v. Adjutant*, 433 Mass. 649, N.E.2d (2005).

60. See Singer, The Resurgence of Mens Rea II: Honest but Unreasonable Mistake of Fact in Self-Defense, 28 B.C. L. Rev. 459 (1987). Cf. Giles, Self-Defense and Mistake: A Way Forward, 53 Mod. L. Rev. 187 (1990); Richard Anthony Simester, Mistakes in Defence, 12 Ox. J. Leg. Stud. 295 (1991). See Annot., Standard for Determination of Reasonableness of Criminal Defendant's Belief, for Purposes of Self Defense Claim, That Physical Force Is Necessary, 73 A.L.R.4th 993.

cates argue that defendants who act unreasonably should not be exculpated. Moreover, they contend, this rule will make persons who are or perceive themselves to be threatened act more cautiously before using any deadly force.

These arguments are misguided. If a defendant honestly believes she is threatened now with death, she is certainly unlikely to be deterred from self-defense by the threat of future state punishment. Moreover, even if she is negligent in not taking more time to assess the situation, it seems excessive to punish her equally with a killer who makes no such exculpatory claim at all. The harshness of the "all or nothing" approach has led many courts to create an intermediate position dubbed "imperfect self-defense,"[61] under which an unreasonable but honestly held belief would reduce the killing to manslaughter.

Another problem, never addressed by the courts who used the reasonableness standard, is that unless jurors are instructed to the contrary, it is at least possible that they will assume that the term "reasonableness" reflects the normal "tort" standard of the reasonable person. Thus, although the courts have struggled to make clear that criminal negligence is "more than" mere tort negligence (see Chapter 4), the objective standard may sneak in through the back door of defenses relying on reasonableness.

A particularly difficult version of this problem arises when police kill someone who turns out to be innocent and even unarmed. On the one hand, police officers are trained not to act precipitously and should be held to a higher standard of "reasonableness" than other citizens.[62] On the other hand, police are also trained to be cautious all the time; unlike most of us, they may be the target of a deadly attack by a complete stranger. And their very profession will bring them into contact with more people who are likely to be dangerous. The issue becomes even more difficult, and more controversial, when (as is often the case) the race of the victim and that of the police officer are different. Although the law should not embrace a "reasonable bigot" standard[63] (that is the point of the debate over racial profiling), the issue in a criminal prosecution, when self-defense is raised,

---

61. Be careful! Some states, such as North Carolina, use this same term differently, thereby adding confusion to any generalized discussion of this (and other topics). See, e.g., *State v. Norman*, 378 S.E.2d 8 (N.C. 1989). A substantial number of states allow manslaughter verdicts in imperfect self-defense cases. See *People v. Mejia-Lenares*, 135 Cal. App. 4th 1437 (2006) (collecting cases). England has a fully subjective view: so long as D honestly believed he was under attack, he is fully exculpated so long as he did not use force that would be excessive given the force he believed (mistakenly) he was facing. UK St. 2008 c. 4, Pt. 5, sec. 76 Self defence; *R. v. Williams* (Gladstone) 3 All E.R. 411 (1984). See Caplow, The Gaelic Goetz: A Case of Self-Defense in Ireland, 17 Cardozo J. Int'l & Comp. L.1 (2009).

62. Of course here, as in tort, this can be rephrased to require the "ordinary" care used by a person with "extraordinary" skills. The point is the same, however worded.

63. Stephen Garvey, Self-Defense and the Mistaken Racist, 11 New Crim. L. Rev. 119 (2008).

is whether this defendant overreacted, given all his life experiences, and should be criminally punished for doing so. However conceptualized, it is a thorny question.

The Position of the "Aggressor": Withdrawal

The rules articulated above apply to the innocent victim of an aggressive attack. The aggressor cannot claim his protection as *long as the initial aggression has not ended*. Thus, if *A* attacks B with deadly force, and B responds with similar force, *A* cannot claim self-defense when he injures or kills B, since *A* began the "episode." However, if *A* makes clear to B that he "withdraws" from the initial aggression, the right to self-defense returns to *A*, and B is now the "aggressor." *A* can make his withdrawal clear by (1) stating that he is withdrawing and/or (2) physically removing himself from the immediate area. This position reflects the common law, described above, which required retreat during a "chance medley" that had escalated to the use of deadly force. The retreat itself was surely evidence that the retreater wished to "withdraw" from the fight.

Suppose the initial aggressor changes his mind, but the putative victim then kills him. Does the victim kill in self-defense? In large part, the courts have said this depends on (a) the obviousness of the aggressor's decision to abandon the fight and (b) the original victim's perception of that abandonment. In other words, if the initial victim simply doesn't understand that the aggressor has withdrawn, or has become too frightened to perceive that, or simply thinks the aggressor is stalling for time, the victim may claim self-defense. (This may also hinge on the reasonableness of the victim's perception. If Polonius waves a gun at Claudius, who then pulls his Uzi, at which point Polonius drops his gun and tries desperately to flee, Claudius' use of the Uzi may well be seen as revenge, rather than self-defense. If, however, Claudius claims that others around the scene did not believe Polonius' acts were sincere, he may succeed on his self-defense claim.)

It is often hard to determine who the "aggressor" was or when an "episode" started or stopped. When B is walking peacefully down the street and *A* comes at him with a machete, it's a cakewalk. But in a barroom dispute that escalates from words to shouts to dares to threats to use of "some" force, it is not easy.[64] Suppose Linda picks up a (full) bottle of Lafitte Rothschild in the midst of an intense verbal dispute with Reina. Is

64. Ariz. Rev. Stat., §13-404(B) does not allow a self-defense claim when "verbal provocation alone" triggered the violent response. But in most instances, it is not words "alone" that are involved.

that deadly force? If she lifts it? If she swings it? At what point does one of them become the "aggressor"?

In some cases, the courts have held that *A* may have so disoriented or terrified B that B's failure to comprehend *A*'s attempt to stop the fight is *A*'s "fault," and therefore *A* cannot avail himself of the self-defense claim. Similarly, if B believes that *A*'s withdrawal is merely a ploy, and not seriously undertaken, B has an obvious right to continue to use defensive force, thus making *A*'s claim less potent.

The "Not Unlawful" Aggressor

Another way of articulating this aspect of self-defense is to say that defensive force can only be used against "unlawful" force. Suppose, however, that the "aggressor's" force is not "unlawful," although wrong? For example, suppose that Henrietta, loping down the sidewalk, suddenly sees Mary's car coming at her? Mary is having a seizure (see the *Decina* case in Chapter 3), and hence is not acting "unlawfully"; indeed, she is not even acting. Can Henrietta use force—including deadly force—to prevent the car from hitting her? Or suppose that she is attacked by Bugs, whom she knows to be insane? If Bugs were to kill Henrietta, his use of force would be excused (trust us; see Chapter 17). Does that mean that it is not "unlawful," such that Henrietta cannot defend herself? These questions keep academics awake at night debating whether Henrietta is (1) justified or (2) merely excused. The courts, using common sense, allow Henrietta to defend herself, often without even using the terms "excuse" or "justification."

Time Frames

In discussing provocation (Chapter 8), we mentioned briefly the issue of "cumulative provocation." The issue of time framing is raised by all claims of justification and excuse. In a necessity case, for example, we consider whether the defendant has "created his own conditions" of a claim (see, e.g., the example of Hillary on page 493). In self-defense cases, that question is even more germane. If we simply ask whether Pat was acting in self-defense when, at 5:05 p.m., he killed Vanna, who was coming down the street in his direction, apparently unarmed, the answer seems fairly clear. But if Pat is allowed to introduce evidence that Vanna has beaten him badly three times in the past, requiring hospitalizations each time, and that she threatened to kill Pat if she saw him after 5:00 p.m., and that Vanna is known to carry a firearm, Pat's actions may become a bit more "reasonable." Defendants will almost always wish to cast the time frame backward as far as possible to give their actions "context," while prosecutors will want to focus on the immediate moments before the shooting. In the *Wanrow* case, supra, page 509, the defendant shot the unarmed victim in the living room of a friend's house. The defendant believed that (a) the victim had molested children in the past and (b) the victim had attempted to molest another child on the afternoon preceding the shooting. The state said those beliefs, even if true, were irrelevant—the only question was whether shooting an unarmed man could be self-defense (or defense of others). The court held that the state's position too severely limited the jury's ability to consider "all the evidence."

The Battered Wives Cases: A Challenge to the Doctrines

Virtually every aspect of the claim to self-defense has been challenged in cases involving battered wives[65] who have killed their husbands in what are called "nonconfrontational" settings.[66] The challenging fact pattern often involves a husband who, over many years, has continuously beaten and abused his wife. He beats her again and falls asleep. Often, he threatens her with resumptions of the beating when he awakes; in other cases, she believes (reasonably?) that the beating will resume, even though he has said nothing in particular about this. She kills him while he sleeps. The issues raised in these cases have required courts to rethink the rules of self-defense. Even where the decisions have not altered these rules, the process of examination itself has proved illuminating.

The major doctrinal issue posed by the sleeping spouse cases is the meaning of "imminent." This, in turn, has two doctrinal components. First, if the husband is asleep, it may be hard to see any threat to injure the wife when he awakes as constituting an "imminent" threat such that the spouse has "no" alternatives left. Second, it may be argued that his sleeping puts an end to the entire episode. Several courts have held, often in the face of vigorous dissent, that when the abusive husband goes to sleep, the battering episode has terminated.[67] Thus, even if the battered wife *reasonably* believes that the battering will continue when the husband awakes, *she* becomes the "aggressor" against the sleeping husband in a new "encounter" and

---

65. This term will be used generically here. It includes battered women who are *not* married to the batterer at the time of the killing (although many were married to him at an earlier time) *and* battered children. It also includes battered husbands and battered partners in same-sex relationships.

66. Most cases involving battered wives involve actual confrontation and are thus governed by "normal" self-defense rules. Maguigan, Battered Women and Self-Defense: Myths and Misconceptions in Current Reform Proposals, 140 U. Pa. L. Rev. 379 (1991).

67. See *State v. Norman*, 324 N.C. 253 (1989); *State v. Stewart*, 763 P.2d 572 (Kan. 1988).

cannot avail herself of the self-defense claim at all. In short, these killings are perceived as preemptive strikes and, no matter how "reasonable," are disallowed.[68]

Prosecutors in these cases contend that the threat was not imminent because the defendants could simply leave their house, or their husbands, or both. These defendants have sought to explain why they did not do so. In effect, they seek to enlarge the time frame by pointing to past beatings (and past "recaptures" by their husbands) to demonstrate what they believed (in their view, reasonably) to be the futility of "leaving." They often point out that when in the past they have left, their spouses have simply followed them, beaten them, and "recaptured" them. This, of course, does not explain why they did not *then* leave.

To meet this issue, battered wives have relied on what has been termed "battered wife syndrome," a cycle of "learned helplessness" aggravated by the so-called Cinderella complex. The "learned helplessness" factor argues that, over a period of cycles involving beatings, reconciliation, and growing tension, the wives have come to believe that there *is* no escape. The Cinderella complex is said to convince the wives that it is they, not the husbands, who are to blame for the beatings; if they were simply better wives, the husbands would not beat them. Thus, a mixture of fear and guilt persuades these women to submit to intolerable abuse.

Forty years ago, evidence of battered wife syndrome was inadmissible in virtually all courts. Today, all courts admit evidence of the syndrome, and some state statutes now explicitly provide that this evidence is admissible, although there may be differences as to the precise point(s) as to which the evidence is permitted.[69]

In arguing that there were no realistic alternatives to the killing, battered wives often point to a history of inadequate protection by police and other governmental agencies.[70] Two objections to such evidence are raised:

---

68. In addition, the issue of whether the wife has to retreat has hung in the background because, unlike the aggressor who pursues the defendant to her home, *both* parties in this case have a claim not to retreat. Although as a matter of logic this should be irrelevant (since the husband has no right to use illegal force against his wife, even in the home), it appears to have bothered some courts. Moriarty, "While Dangers Gather": The Bush Preemption Doctrine, Battered Women, Imminence, and Anticipatory Self-Defense, 30 N.Y.U. Rev. L. & Soc. Change 1 (2005).

69. See, e.g., Cal. Evid. Code §1107 (Deering 2008). See generally, Annot., 57 A.L.R.5th 315; Annot., 58 A.L.R.5th 749.

70. The term "police" here is used generically to characterize all governmental response. For example, battered women often argue that there are few governmental shelters to which they can retreat, and that their spouses have often ignored, without penalty, court orders forbidding further contact. The statistics on these matters, while in dispute in any given jurisdiction, certainly have borne out the complaints that at least in the past, governmental response to fears, and even beatings, of wives has been slow and sporadic at best. Thus, among other

(1) it may distract the jury from the killing at hand to the *general* question of police response; (2) no matter how accurate a picture of governmental response the evidence may cast, it cannot generate a justification for the wife, who "should have" tried those avenues (or retreated) once more before taking life. The surrebuttal to the first point is that if the system has in fact failed to protect a person who has, by default, taken the law into her own hands, it *should* be subjected to such scrutiny. Fairness to the defendant, the argument goes, demands no less, and the community as a whole should be made aware of these failings. As to the second objection, it merely restates the subjective-objective question of necessity. Clearly, if the battering and the "syndrome" are part of the reasonable person's background, then the test is one of the reasonably battered woman who suffers from learned helplessness.

Even academics who conclude that a battered wife who kills in a nonconfrontational setting should be acquitted disagree whether her action is justified or excused. Because the traditional rules of self-defense seem to preclude viewing her action as justified, many writers have argued that it is better to analyze the slayer as seeking to excuse her conduct; indeed, defendants in early cases often sought to raise an "excuse" of either diminished capacity or insanity. Others respond that because excuse requires a "disability," this path improperly treats the women as victims whose mental ability is suspect. They argue that the death of the batterer is a social gain and should be seen as justified or that the woman's choice was reasonable, under all the circumstances.[71] Others argue that a new "syndrome"—*active survivor theory*—better captures the experience of battered women.[72] At least one commentator has suggested that people who kill their sleeping spouses could use a defense of duress (and not necessity or self-defense), at least under the Model Penal Code's language.[73] Many of those who believe

---

changes, most governments now fund safe houses for battered wives (and their children), provide for protective orders against battering spouses, have created special units in police departments, and may require arrest and/or prosecution of the spouse even if the wife/victim refuses to testify. Moreover, it is now a federal crime for a person to cross state lines with an intent to batter another and/or to possess a firearm if he has been convicted of a battering offense, or made subject to a state restraining order. While governmental authorities now seem to be much more sensitive to such concerns, there is still good reason to believe that the system has much left to do. See Tracy Chapman's song, "Behind the Wall."

71. Gerber, The Felony Murder Rule: Conundrum Without Principle, 31 Ariz. St. L.J. 763 (1999). C. Gillespie, Justifiable Homicide: Battered Women, Self-Defense, and the Law (1989); Kinports, Defending Battered Women's Self-Defense Claims, 67 Or. L. Rev. 393 (1988).

72. See E. Gondolf and E. Fisher, Battered Women as Survivors: An Alternative to Treating Learned Helplessness (1988).

73. Joshua Dressler, Battered Women and Sleeping Abusers: Some Reflections, 3 Ohio St. J. Crim. L. 1 (2006) (noting that the duress provision does not require imminence, or even a nonimminent threat).

that a battered spouse in a nonconfrontational setting does not have a full self-defense claim may agree that her killing constitutes "imperfect" self-defense, thus reducing her liability to manslaughter. In 2009, while altering its statutes regarding provocation (see the discussion, supra, Chapter 8), England also provided that a killing due to loss of control spurred by fear (as opposed to anger) would establish a partial defense reducing the killing to manslaughter, a concept expressly intended to allow some mitigation to battered wives who kill in a nonconfrontational situation.

The contentiousness reflected in these various views often hides the general consensus that, whatever the explanation, these spouses should not be criminally punished. Some writers argue that the rules of self-defense, as with provocation, were written by men, and were designed to deal with situations in which men typically used deadly force: stranger-on-stranger or at least acquaintance-on-acquaintance confrontations. Where the relationship is longstanding and intimate, they argue, the need for examination of the rules of self-defense is evident. Attempts to "shoehorn" these claims into an existing category of defense, or to deny the claims entirely, suggest that they may be right.

DOCTRINAL PROBLEMS OF SELF-DEFENSE

The Mens Rea of Self-Defense

Kant and Bentham become involved in a heated discussion about retribution and utilitarianism. Bentham grabs a bottle of beer, breaks it, and walks menacingly toward Kant, saying "I'll kill you, you retributivist, you." Kant pulls out a knife and says, "Don't come any closer. Just let me be. I don't want to be hurt." Bentham lunges at Kant, who stabs Bentham. Bentham dies.

We normally think of this typical scenario of self-defense as demonstrating an intentional death that *A* wishes to explain by referring to self-defense. But it can be argued that the killing was not intentional. Rather, Kant's *intent* (purpose) was to escape, without any clear reference to the possibility of killing Bentham. Catholic doctrine, for example, uses the so-called double effect analysis to explain self-defense.[74] More difficult is the issue of whether *A* was highly *reckless* ("under circumstance manifesting extreme indifference to the value of human life" in the words of the MPC, or manifesting a "depraved heart" in the common law language) as to B's

74. F. Spinagle, The Catechism Explained 388 (1961).

death. A jury could surely find that a person in *A*'s position *did* consciously disregard such a risk, but it could just as easily find that *A* did not consciously think about the consequences to B at all.

The issue here is whether a claim of self-defense is really a claim negating the mens rea of the crime. If so, then the prosecution must carry the burden of proof on this issue, once properly raised (see Chapter 15).[75] At one level, the question goes to what we have already called "statutory mens rea." At another level, however, the question involves what we have called "traditional" mens rea. (See Chapter 4 for both these terms.) Thus, even if a jury concludes that Kant "intended" or was "reckless" as to Bentham's death or serious bodily harm, it might well find that Kant was not "evil" or "malevolent" because of the exigent circumstances under which Kant operated. As already discussed, this sense of mens rea has somewhat disappeared from criminal law, but analysis should consider its impact.[76]

Defense of Others

If Yitzhak sees Yassir "beating up" Clyde and comes to Clyde's defense, Yitzhak may use force to defend Clyde to the same extent that he may use force to protect himself. This result can be understood by many of the explanations surrounding self-defense. For example, Yassir, the aggressor, has "given up" his right not to be assaulted.

But suppose Yitzhak is mistaken, and Yassir is (a) responding—legitimately—to Clyde's initial aggression or (b) a police officer arresting Clyde. Should Yitzhak be liable for assault on Yassir? States are divided on what result should obtain. On the one hand, we applaud Yitzhak's humanitarianism. On the other, Yitzhak has been an "officious intermeddler"—indeed, a vigilante. Early common law punished Yitzhak on the ground that he could use only as much force as Clyde could. This was known as the "alter ego" rule. Most courts—and the Model Penal Code—have now decided to encourage reasonable intervention and would exculpate Yitzhak.

---

75. Virtually all states place on the prosecution the burden of proof in self-defense. In *Martin v. Ohio*, 480 U.S. 228 (1987), however, the Supreme Court held that placing the burden of proof on the defendant did not violate the United States Constitution. The Court's opinion did not consider the question of whether self-defense is "usually" a justification, as many academic analysts have suggested. Nor did the Court refer to, much less discuss, the historic difference between excused and justified self-defense. Colorado has distinguished between charges of intentional or knowing homicide (where the state must disprove self-defense) and reckless or criminally negligent homicides (where the burden may be placed on the defendant). *State v. Pickering*, 2011 WL 4014400 (Colo.)

76. See Pilsbury, The Meaning of Deserved Punishment: An Essay on Choice, Character, and Responsibility, 67 Ind. L.J. 719 (1992).

THE MODEL PENAL CODE

The Code adopts many of the changes wrought by American courts in the nineteenth and twentieth centuries. Under §3.04, retreat is required before deadly force may be used except at D's home or office, but only where the defendant "*knows* he may retreat in *complete* safety"[77] (emphasis added). This may totally undercut the retreat requirement; in an age of guns and other such weapons, it is the rare case where the defendant "knows" (in contrast to believes or hopes) that he may retreat in "complete" safety. The Code, however, broadens the notion of "imminence" and also enlarges the notion of when an "occasion" occurs or ends. The Code also changes the aggressor rule slightly—a person is considered the initial aggressor if he had the purpose of causing death or serious bodily harm. The aggressor may regain the use of force in self-defense if he does not use it in the same "part of the encounter" in which he was the provoker. This seems, first, to narrow the definition of "initial aggressor" and then to allow "recapture" of the right to use force a bit more readily than the common law allowed.

Beware, the Code's initial sections on self-defense consistently describe the defendant's honest belief as sufficient to allow the claim. Section 3.09, however, dilutes this view by allowing prosecution for manslaughter or negligent homicide if the defendant has been reckless or negligent, respectively, in reaching a mistaken belief. Thus, on this issue, the Code is much more subjective than those courts adopting the "all or nothing" approach with regard to the self-defense claim, but only slightly more subjective than those endorsing the "imperfect self-defense" doctrine.

Examples

EXAMPLES

In which of the following can the defendant(s) claim self-defense?

1a. Hubert is walking down the street when he is confronted by Lyndon, who pulls a knife, drags Hubert into an alley and demands money. Hubert pulls out an Uzi and kills Lyndon.

1b. Same facts, except that Hubert has no Uzi and instead wrestles the knife away from Lyndon and then stabs him to death.

2. Quincy is mowing his lawn one day when his neighbor, Ralph, comes over, shovel in hand. "Your dog has ruined my azaleas again, Quincy," he shouts, and swings the shovel madly at Quincy. Quincy drops the mower, grabs a pitchfork, and kills Ralph.

77. The word "complete" is important—in *State v. Anderson*, 227 Conn. 518, 631 A.2d 1149 (1993), the trial court's omission of the word "complete" required reversal of a conviction.

3a. Jack, a famous movie actor, is driving on a major road when Bert's car pulls in front. Enraged because he believes he has been "cut off," Jack follows Bert's car to the next intersection, where both cars stop for a red light. Jack leaps out of his car with a golf club in his hand, and begins screaming at Bert, "I'll kill you, you S.O.B." He then begins smashing Bert's car. Bert jumps out of his car and wrestles Jack to the ground, breaking two of Jack's fingers.

3b. Bert also grabs the golf club and flings it into nearby bushes, hits Jack, runs to his car, and attempts to lock the door. Jack pulls Bert out and hits him several times in the face with his fists.

3c. Bert thereupon pulls out a knife and confronts Jack with it. Jack backs up and runs for his car. Bert follows. Jack finds another golf club and hits Bert once, killing him.

4. Jules and Jacques have lived in neighboring apartments for nearly 40 years. They were close friends until ten years ago, when they got into an argument about cable television lines. Since then, they have yelled at each other and verbally threatened each other with death. Indeed, one time, Jacques stabbed Jules with a small knife, inflicting a minor wound. One night, they are yelling at each other through their common wall when Jules pulls out an iron pipe and smashes the wall, making an indentation that Jacques can see. Jacques runs out of his apartment, and Jules opens his apartment door, standing in his doorway. Jacques comes nose to nose with Jules, declares "I'm going to kill you," and reaches into his pocket. Jules, still standing in his doorway, hits Jacques with the pipe, killing him. Self-defense?

5. Lyle, 14 years old, has been beaten by his father at least once every two months since the time he was seven. One night, three days before his junior high school graduation, Lyle and his father have another run-in, but his father is on the way to work. "You won't live to see graduation," says his father as he leaves. That night Lyle is unable to sleep. The next morning he goes to school but leaves at 11 a.m. to return home, where he picks up his father's shotgun and loads it. At 3 p.m. that afternoon, his father walks through the front door, and Lyle empties both barrels, killing him instantly.

6. Iran has stated that it supports the extinction of Israel, and it considers the United States a great evil and its primary enemy. Iran has not expressly said that it would bomb either country; indeed, it insists that it wants to develop nuclear power only for peaceful purposes. If Israel, or the United States, were preemptively to bomb the Iranian facilities before that country had a nuclear weapon, would its actions be justified? Excused? What if a new president of Pakistan (which already has nuclear weapons) were to make similar statements?

7. Leonard, 5 foot 3 inches and 135 pounds, is walking down a dark street at 2 a.m. Suddenly, as he turns a corner, he is confronted by a man who asks him for a light. As Leonard fumbles for a match, the stranger says "Well, maybe you can help me with something else," and puts his hand inside his pocket. Leonard draws his concealed handgun and shoots the man instantly. At trial, the prosecutor shows that the stranger was reaching for a street map. Leonard seeks to introduce evidence that (a) five years ago he was attacked by a stranger and severely beaten; (b) his best friend was recently mugged in this same area; (c) the stranger vaguely resembled the drawing, which had appeared in a number of local newspapers and which Leonard had seen at least five times, of a suspected robber, whose robberies, however, had occurred in another section of the city. Leonard also seeks to introduce evidence that (d) the victim was 6 foot 6 inches, weighed 268 pounds, and was redheaded; (e) defendant has always had a dread fear of redheaded men; (f) the stranger was wearing a raincoat but it had not rained for three days and the temperature at the time of their encounter was 65°F. Which, if any, of these pieces of evidence bears on a defendant's liability and is therefore admissible?

8a. Metropolis, population 150, is threatened with annihilation by a flooding stream. Shakir tries justifiably to divert the flood onto Nelson's farm, knowing that Nelson will be drowned as a result. Nelson runs out of his farmhouse and shoots Shakir before he can divert the stream. Is Nelson guilty of any crime?

8b. What if Shakir has a court order allowing him to divert the stream?

9. Fran, 90 years old, uses a walker to help her move around. One day, while playing bridge with three friends at the nursing home, she becomes enraged when Retief improperly plays a trump and claims the hand. Fran shouts, "I've had enough of your cheating!" She swings at Retief with her knitting needle. Retief, a 70-year-old former pro golfer who carries a walking stick crafted from the five iron with which he won the U.S. Open, immediately hits Fran and kills her. Retief is charged with second-degree murder. What result?

10. Samantha and James meet in a bar and go to James' apartment, where they spend the night "Netflix and chilling." The next morning, they are awakened by Jennifer, James' ex-girlfriend, who has a key to the apartment. Jennifer throws a book at James, knocking him out. She and Samantha then get in a fight, at which point Samantha sees a gun on James' coffee table. She picks it up and aims it at Jennifer, who runs into the bedroom and closes the door. Samantha aims the gun at the door and pulls the trigger once. Jennifer is killed instantly. Samantha claims self-defense. Will she succeed?

11. Yitzhak has invited his good friend Raisha to stay in his home while Raisha is touring the city. Four days into the stay, Yitzhak goes to work, leaving Raisha with a key in case he wants to see the sights. Instead, Raisha decides to sleep in. Two hours later, he hears the sound of glass and sees a figure coming through the porch door. Raisha is standing by the front door and could easily leave. Instead, he grabs a nearby rifle and shoots the figure, killing her.
    a. The figure is a burglar, intent on stealing Yitzhak's priceless violin.
    b. The figure is Helen, Yitzhak's girlfriend, who had forgotten her key and was desperate to enter the house and surprise Yitzhak.

12. For 20 years, Mortimer has abused his wife, Sheila, with some regularity. He has broken her arm twice, thrown her down stairs numerous times, and frequently threatened to kill her. She has left him several times, but each time he has persuaded her to return, pleading that he loves her. The typical cycle of atonement, slow buildup, and then battering has occurred continuously over the years. Tonight Mort said to Sheila, "Tomorrow's the day. I'm not taking any more. You are dead." Then he left the house. Sheila went to her next-door neighbor, Laurie, and told her, "I think he really means it this time. Give me your gun." Laurie hesitated, but finally acquiesced. When Mort returned that night, Sheila shot him five times as he came through the doorway. Sheila and Laurie are charged with murder. What result?

13. Marian, a private security guard who is licensed to carry a gun, is off duty enjoying her third glass of Chateau LaFitte Rothschild at the Dew Drop Inn while watching the New York Yankees lose (again) to the Boston Red Sox. She is delighted as A-Rod strikes out for the fourth time in the game. "I always said that no-good (ethnic slur) wasn't worth the money they paid him," she shouts. A patron at the other end of the bar walks up to her and declares, "A-Rod and I are personal friends. No one speaks about him like that when I'm around, particularly some chick. Someday, when you least expect it, I'm going to send you to that ballpark in the sky." He opens his coat, revealing a gun, which he does not touch. Discuss the potential self-defense claims if:
    a. The stranger starts to walk away, but Marian pulls out her revolver and shoots him dead.
    b. As the stranger walks away, the bartender says: "Do you know who that was? That's Don Giovanni—the top hit man for the mob. You've got real trouble." Marian runs after Don, who is out the door and 100 feet away, and shoots him dead.

14. Trent Hatfield and Jack McCoy have been bitter enemies for years. One day, as Jack is walking with his three-year-old son, Real, Trent grabs the child, puts a gun to his head and says: "You think you've suffered?

Watch this." He then kills Real. Jack whips out his Colt .45 (legally carried) and shoots at Hatfield, but the bullets go far wide of their mark and kill Saw Waterston, Jack's dearest friend, who just happens to come around the corner at that moment. Charged with Waterston's *murder*, Jack pleads heat of passion. What result?

15. Chris and Frank got into a heated argument outside Frank's trailer. Chris threatened to "take Frank's head off," and swung at Frank but missed. Chris then walked quickly to his truck, which was parked about 50 feet away, turned it around, and slowly went past Frank, with the driver's window down. Just as the truck passed, Frank "felt something whiz by" his head. He reached down, picked up his ever-present Winchester rifle and shot twice at the truck, which was moving away slowly. The second bullet hit Chris in the neck, killing him. There was no weapon in Chris's truck, and neither the alleged bullet Frank "felt" nor its source were ever found. At his trial for second degree murder, Frank sought instruction on (1) self-defense; (2) provocation. Lilith, the prosecutor, argued that the two concepts were incompatible—self-defense requires a reasonable fear of injury, while heat of passion showed no "reason" at all. If you were the trial judge, what would you do? (Sorry—recusal is not an option.)

16. Jedidiah is walking down the street when his arch rival Archie comes running at him with a gun in his hand, screaming "I've had it with you, J. Today's the day you meet your maker!" Jedidiah pulls out his (legally possessed) magnum .357 and kills Archie. The state statute follows the "stand your ground" Florida law, and provides that the person who uses defensive force cannot be "engaged in an unlawful activity." It turns out that Jedidiah has two (unsmoked) marijuana joints on him. Has Jedidiah's claim of self-defense gone up in (non)smoke?

17. Twelve people, including George Prado and Joan Miro, all quite intoxicated, become entangled in a fight outside a bar. By the end of the fight, Miro has been fatally stabbed by Prado. Prado asserts that Miro came at him, punched him twice and shouted, "Tonight you die." None of the other ten saw the struggle nor heard any words. Prado moves to dismiss the indictment, under a "stand your ground" statute which provides "immunity" from prosecution unless the state can establish, prior to trial, "probable cause" to disbelieve his claim. What result?

18. Joe is peacefully walking down the street when Jim steps out of an alley, raises his fist and says, "Give me that Rolex or I'll break your nose." Joe quickly reaches into his pocket, pulls out a switchblade and swings at Jim, missing him. Discuss the potential self-defense claims if: (a) Jim pushes Joe lightly, but Joe falls and cracks his skull on the cement; (b) Jim pulls out his own switchblade and stabs Joe, killing him.

19. Zephyr and Magnus are brothers. Since they were young, they have had a tense relationship; Magnus, the older of the two, used to physically and emotionally abuse Zephyr. The two brothers had a falling out when Zephyr stood up to Magnus's bullying one day. Years later, Magnus divorced his first wife with whom he has four kids. Magnus has continuously failed to pay child support since he divorced his wife. He expressed to Zephyr that he wanted nothing to do with his kids, even after his ex-wife died of breast cancer. Zephyr thought this was unacceptable since the four kids would be separated in the foster care system, so he told Magnus not to worry—he would adopt the kids. Magnus, thinking that Zephyr was after the child support money, threatened his brother, telling him that if he adopted the kids, Magnus would "shoot [him] in the head." Magnus thought the threat had been enough to convince Zephyr to change his mind, but a few months later he heard that his brother had, in fact, adopted his kids. In a fit of rage, Magnus drives to his brother's home in the middle of the night to teach him a lesson. Zephyr is awoken by the headlights shining into his home and looks outside to see his brother. Zephyr knows that Magnus is a big gun enthusiast with dozens of rifles and handguns and believes that Magnus is there to shoot him in the head like he threatened, so he fetches his revolver from the closet. Zephyr tells his wife and kids, who are now awake, to stay inside. He walks outside onto his porch and sees Magnus walking toward him. Yelling, "Stay back—I will shoot you!" Zephyr points the revolver at Magnus. Magnus, who is unarmed, runs back to his vehicle, where he grabs his own revolver from the glove compartment. Magnus fires two shots at Zephyr, missing both times. Zephyr returns fire, striking Magnus three times in the chest. Magnus dies instantly.
    a. Does Zephyr have a claim of self-defense?
    b. Now imagine that instead of missing, Magnus shot Zephyr, killing him. Does Magnus have a claim of self-defense?

Explanations

1a. This is the classic case of self-defense. Hubert is the innocent victim of an unprovoked felonious attack. He is clearly justified in killing Lyndon. Even in a jurisdiction requiring retreat, there is no apparent way for Hubert to retreat safely. Deadly force can respond to deadly force—even an Uzi to a knife.

1b. Now the facts have changed. Hubert *was* under deadly attack. But when he wrestles the knife away from Lyndon, the situation may be different than in Example 1a. Since Hubert now has the knife, it is at least arguable that he could have retreated. On the other hand, Hubert might reasonably conclude (particularly in emergency conditions) that Lyndon would continue the pursuit, perhaps with another deadly weapon, unless Hubert stopped him now.

2. Even in a jurisdiction that requires retreat, Quincy is on his own property, thereby apparently nullifying the requirement. Some courts, however, have restricted the "castle" exception to the house. Since Quincy is not in his house, he might lose the exception. If he could have ducked into the house, he may be required to do so in these jurisdictions. If Ralph had not swung the shovel at Quincy, we would have the issue of whether Ralph intended to hurt Quincy (as opposed to his dog) and also whether Quincy's perception that Ralph was threatening him was reasonable. See the next example.

3a. These facts show the ambiguity in many altercations. Although Jack's words carry a threat of serious bodily harm or death, his actions belie them. He has used force against Bert's property but not against Bert. Yet he has threatened Bert's person. If Bert used deadly force, it might be deemed excessive. On the other hand, it is not clear whether the force that Bert used could be characterized as deadly force. Whether Bert could *reasonably* fear serious bodily harm may be one for the jury.

3b. Since Jack was the initial aggressor, he cannot respond to Bert's use of force. Moreover, it appears that Bert has attempted to withdraw. Jack has no claim of self-defense.

3c. Bert's use of a knife may change this into a new encounter. Even though Jack used his golf club on Bert's car, he did not aim for Bert's head or other vital parts. Therefore, Jack was not threatening or using deadly force. Bert's reaction, however, does constitute deadly force, and Jack may respond to it accordingly. In a jurisdiction generally requiring retreat, however, Jack may have to retreat, since Bert may not have the ability to pursue, catch, and stab Jack if he runs away. These factual questions and whether Jack's assessment of his chance of successful retreat was reasonable will be for the jury to decide.

4. We couldn't make this up. These are the actual facts of *People v. Aiken*, 4 N.Y.3d 324 (2005). The New York Court of Appeals, declaring that the "castle doctrine" should be severely restricted because it allowed people to (otherwise unnecessarily) take life where they could retreat, upheld the trial court's refusal to grant a self-defense instruction. Even if Jules "reasonably feared" that Jacques was reaching for a knife and would stab him, said the court, he had a duty to retreat to his apartment—and the doorway was *not* his apartment. Therefore, as a matter of law, he was not entitled to a self-defense instruction.

5. These facts are very close to those of an actual case, *State v. Janes*, 64 Wash. App. 134 (1992). The questions raised include whether the father's words constituted an "imminent threat" of serious bodily harm or death, whether Lyle had alternatives other than killing, and whether he could reasonably believe those alternatives to be futile. All these issues could be used to determine whether the killing was "justified" self-defense. Still another issue that might be raised is whether Lyle had to retreat even if his father intended to beat him. Although he lives in the house, it is not, as a matter of property law, "his" house.

   Assuming for a moment that the killing is not justified, one other issue is whether Lyle could be excused: whether, notwithstanding the "intentionality" of Lyle's acts, the obvious stress under which he operated suggests that he is not as blameworthy as other "intentional" killers. If not, he might have his liability reduced to manslaughter. See Chapter 8.

6. Interceding in Iran to prevent that country from building a nuclear weapon would almost surely be premature, even if one recognizes the "preemptive strike" doctrine. There are still many steps required before Iran can build such a weapon. Experts disagree on how many years it will be before Iran has that capacity. On the other hand, we know that Pakistan has nuclear weapons. Whether it has the capability to deliver these weapons by an air strike on either Israel or the United States is unclear, since there is always the fear that such a bomb could be packaged in a suitcase or some other container and shipped to a target country.[78]

7. The question deals with the extent to which the reasonable man has characteristics of the defendant. As suggested in the example, these questions usually arise during evidentiary rulings. If the jurisdiction allows the comparison, then the evidence is admissible; if not, then the evidence is excluded. The stranger's resemblance to the robber is likely to be admissible even in a jurisdiction using the objective test, since a "reasonable person" might be aware of the drawings and therefore might be more justifiably afraid of someone with this resemblance. The dress of the victim is likely to be admissible because it goes to whether Leonard's fears were reasonable (contrast cases involving a person wearing a three-piece suit and one where the stranger is wearing a leather jacket and a set of brass knuckles). The two crime incidents are unlikely to be admitted in many jurisdictions because they do not go to what the "reasonable man" (as opposed to Leonard) might draw from

78. Onder Bakirgioglu, The Right to Self-Defence in National and International Law: The Role of the Imminence Requirements, 19 Ind. Int'l & Comp. L. Rev. 1 (2009).

them. Leonard's paranoia about redheads is also likely to be excluded, and therefore, the fact that the defendant was redheaded.[79] The long-standing paranoia is almost certainly not admissible since "reasonable people" are not paranoid. All the information is admissible in a jurisdiction that allows a claim if the defendant "honestly" believed himself to be in danger.

8a. This is tricky. Nelson may claim self-defense, but self-defense is, as a general matter, defined as a justified use of force against "unlawful" force. Shakir, as explained in the text, is justified in diverting the stream, and is thus not using unlawful force. Nelson therefore cannot be justified. Can he be excused? Usually, it is said that self-defense "sounds in" justification; can it also, on occasions like this, sound in excuse? There are at least two arguments for saying yes. First, in the case of an unreasonably mistaken self-defender, some jurisdictions allow a reduction to manslaughter, thus clearly recognizing that the slayer's acts, though not justified, could still be partially excused. Second, to the extent that we are interested in results, and only secondarily in explaining those results, there is surely no reason for treating Nelson as a murderer, cold-blooded or otherwise. On the other hand, he is *not* mistaken, unlike the putative self-defender. Could Nelson claim necessity? Not if necessity requires that he achieve a greater good relative to the harm he has inflicted. As it is, Nelson kills one to save one (himself). This demonstrates, again, the difficulty the common law had with analyzing one-on-one situations, where neither party was initially culpable. Of course, it could be argued that Nelson is killing 151. If so, even if Nelson killed Shakir to save Nelson's entire family (15 people), a quantification approach to necessity would deny him a defense.

8b. These circumstances make it clear that Shakir is justified in his act. But merely because he is justified does not mean that we should ignore Nelson's personal tragedy. Even if he were not justified, viewing him as excused seems correct.

9. Retief may be playing his last rounds in prison. First, although Fran "threatened" force, it is hard to see that she was threatening deadly force—while it might be deadly in the hands of a 25-year-old, a knitting needle is probably not deadly when swung by an elderly person. Thus, Retief is not allowed to use deadly force to respond to non-deadly force. Even if the needle is deadly force, however, Retief has

79. But see Garvey, Self-Defense and the Mistaken Racist, 11 New Crim. L. Rev. 199 (2008) (arguing, provocatively, that even a defendant's racism should be admissible, and allowed as excuse, because he is, at best, guilty of being a racist (which is not a crime), or of having failed to rid himself of racism (which, thus far, is also not a crime)).

two options: (1) he could almost surely disarm Fran rather than kill her; (2) he could retreat. After all, he is more spry than Fran, who probably would have only one chance (at most) even to hit Retief. It may be that the jury could conclude that Retief couldn't move faster than Fran (and that would be a jury question), BUT he could just use nondeadly force (pushing her over), which would surely allow him to escape.

10. Unlikely. Jennifer used force, but not deadly force, so Samantha's use of deadly force was probably excessive. Even if Jennifer had used deadly force, however, it is arguable that her race to the bedroom constituted withdrawal, thus nullifying Samantha's claim. If that weren't enough, Samantha probably will have to retreat—although she's James' guest, most states would probably not allow her to avail herself of the "castle" doctrine.[80] However, this decision was rendered prior to the "Stand Your Ground" Act in Florida, quoted in the text. Under that statute, even though Samantha cannot claim the "castle" doctrine, she can claim that she had a "right" to be in the apartment, and therefore did not have to retreat.

11a. The question is whether Raisha has to retreat. In virtually every state, including those that would otherwise require retreat, Yitzhak, the owner of the house, could clearly kill the burglar—an owner's home, after all, is his castle. But is a guest's temporary "home" *his* castle? The courts are split. Some say that the guest stands in the shoes of the owner. Others argue that the "no retreat" rule should be narrowly applied, since it allows the (by hypothesis, unnecessary) taking of life. Note: The length of Raisha's stay would be irrelevant to either of these schools of thought; if Raisha had been there only one hour, he still either "stands in Yitzhak's shoes" or he doesn't.

11b. Here the issue is whether, assuming that Raisha did not otherwise have to retreat, he had to wait to see if the intruder was threatening deadly force. The answer is generally NO. So long as the shooter made a reasonable mistake (and not waiting for the intruder to actually threaten to use deadly force is hardly unreasonable), Raisha's off the hook.

12. This is really complicated. The first question is whether Sheila will have a self-defense claim. This may depend on whether the jurisdiction allows an expert to testify about battered spouse syndrome, but virtually all do today, so Sheila will be judged by the "reasonable battered spouse." On the other hand, Mort was not threatening her at the

80. See *State v. James*, 867 So.2d 414 (Fla. App. 2003).

very moment she shot him. This nonconfrontational case raises all the issues generated by a long-time, simmering, and explosive relationship, and is not well handled by black letter self-defense law. Sheila will at least get her case to the jury.

Under the Model Penal Code, Sheila has a stronger claim. The common law required "imminency" for a claim of self-defense. The Code, instead, substitutes the phrase "immediately necessary on the present occasion." The Code is not concerned with the timing of the possible attack, but with the necessity to use force. As in the hypothetical, the question of imminence is most vividly raised by the "sleeping husband" cases, e.g., *State v. Norman*, 378 S.E.2d 8 (N.C. 1989).

Laurie's case is even more difficult, and her defense may depend on how Sheila's acts are characterized. If the jury finds that Sheila was *justified*, then Laurie's assistance will also be allowed. If, however, the jury concludes that Sheila was merely *excused* under current doctrine, a nonexcused or justified person cannot aid a person who is merely excused—because she does not share the actor's "disability." On the other hand, Laurie will raise a second claim—that she gave Sheila the gun only to be used if Mort actually attacked her, not when Mort walked in the door. Was Laurie unreasonable—or even reckless—in her belief that Sheila would not use the gun in a nonconfrontational situation? Under current accomplice law, discussed in Chapter 14, Laurie will not be an accomplice to Mort's death unless she "intended" that death or, in some jurisdictions, unless she was reckless (not merely negligent) as to whether her assistance would result in a crime. This is obviously a jury question—and a close one that might depend on more facts than a mere hypothetical can offer.

13a. The question raised is whether the threat is "imminent." Given the facts, it is not even debatable that Don's threatened acts are "imminent." Even under the Model Penal Code, it would be hard for Marian to give credence at all to Don's threat, much less believe that it was necessary for her to use force "immediately . . . on the present occasion." Marian's days as a security guard are history.

13b. NOW the threat is actually plausible—if the bartender is correct, Marian might become Don's latest notch. But again, the very words Don uttered make it clear that he was not going to use deadly force now. And his departure from the bar makes it extremely unlikely that he will return. Moreover, Marian could retreat, either by finding another exit, or simply by outwaiting Don. She certainly continued the quarrel by going after him.

On the other hand, under the Model Penal Code, Marian may well have feared not only that the threat was real, but that using alternatives (informing the police, for example) would be futile and that this force was necessary in the "immediate" occasion. She would have a claim of self-defense to a charge of murder, but if the jury concluded that her decision was either negligent or reckless, she could be convicted of the corresponding level of homicide.

14. This should depend on how and why we think a heat of passion/provoked killing should be mitigated. If the basis is that the victim (partially) "asked for it," then this is certainly not true of Sam, who was totally innocent. If the basis is that the *result* was (partially) justified, then this is also not the case. We do not have even a partially good result here; a totally innocent person has been killed. But if the question is whether Jack's *act* was partially *excused*, then the *result* becomes irrelevant, and Jack should be able to reduce his conviction to manslaughter because of his extreme "disability." It is also possible to argue that Jack should be able to claim "transferred justification (or excuse)." After all, if intent can follow the bullet, then why can't passion?

15. The self-defense claim is on thin ice. After all, Frank did not *see* Chris shoot at him. Indeed, it may have been a figment of Frank's imagination. Moreover, Chris was driving away, so it may be difficult for Frank to claim "defense" as opposed to "revenge." Nevertheless, a jury might conclude that Frank had a reasonable fear that Chris would return, or even throw the truck in reverse (contrast the case if Chris had driven at a high rate of speed after the "bullet" whizzed by Frank). If the jury rejects the self-defense claim, however, there is still some evidence that would allow them to find that, believing himself to have been a victim of a shooting, Frank was "provoked" by Chris, and had no time to "cool off" (even under the common law). If, additionally, the jurisdiction recognizes not merely anger, but fear, as a possible impetus to action, the claim of heat of passion might be sustainable. It was so held in *Howell v. State*, 917 P. 2d 1201 (Alaska App. 1996).

16. One would think not. After all, the whole point of the "stand your ground" statute would seem to be to protect a non-aggressive party, and Jedidiah meets that definition. One could argue that the provision against "unlawful" behavior was to deal with aggressors. But possession of marijuana is a crime. In *Dawkins v. State*, 252 P.3d 214 (Okla. Crim. App. 2011), the court held, under a similar statute, that possessing an illegal weapon deprived the defendant of the "stand your ground" protection. In dictum, the court further suggested that "current crimes (which would exclude the statute) include . . . possession of illegal drugs. . . ." Oops.

17. Although the facts were much more complicated than this in *Lemons v. Com.* S.W.3d, 2012 WL 2360131 (Ky. App. 2012), the court held

that the indictment should be dismissed because there were simply no actual witnesses to the stabbing to dispute the defendant's claim. Potential witnesses who might have testified otherwise were too intoxicated to provide substantial credible testimony to amount to probable cause (statute "dramatically changed the practice of criminal law in Kentucky").

18. (a) Joe had a right to defend himself and his property—but not by the use of deadly force. He may only use force proportionate to that threatened by Jim, and Jim has not threatened death or serious bodily injury. Even though he was the original aggressor, Jim may now respond to Joe's escalation by using equivalent force. Here, he has not used deadly force, but only non-deadly force, which, unhappily, resulted in Joe's death.
(b) Even here, Jim has the right to defend himself from the excessive force that Joe attempted by the use of deadly force (the knife). Test this by putting the robbery out of the picture, and assume that Jim "merely" wanted to punch Joe without taking any property. Note that this is not a "withdrawal" question—had Jim threatened deadly force, taken the watch and then left, after which Joe followed him using deadly force, Jim would be entitled to use deadly force only if his departure was an "obvious" withdrawal from the initial fray. But here the question is one of escalation, not of withdrawal.

19a. First, there is an issue of whether Zephyr reasonably believed he was in danger. Zephyr will argue that his response to Magnus was reasonable, both objectively and subjectively, particularly because Zephyr did not shoot until Magnus fired at him. Zephyr will want to introduce evidence of the brothers' strained relationship, especially how Magnus used to abuse him physically. This is similar to the "battered wife" argument, but with some meaningful differences: The brothers were largely estranged from each other; there was no cycle of abuse taking place. Still, Zephyr has a good argument for self-defense. He will argue that Magnus's past treatment of Zephyr, combined with Magnus's threat to shoot him if Zephyr adopted his kids (which he did) and the fact that Magnus has the means to do so—i.e. multiple different firearms—shows that he was reasonable to believe that Magnus presented a serious, even potentially lethal threat to him. Perhaps shooting at Magnus right away would have been unreasonable, but Zephyr waited; he warned Magnus, telling him to "stay back," and refrained from shooting until Magnus fired at him. But was Zephyr really reasonable? Sure, Magnus had threatened him and he owned firearms, but Magnus and Zephyr are brothers. Is it reasonable to believe your brother would murder you, even if he had physically abused you in the past?

The prosecution will make a number of additional arguments that Zephyr cannot claim he acted in self-defense: (1) Zephyr could have retreated, (2) Zephyr had an alternative option to using force and, by confronting Magnus on the porch, Zephyr contributed to the creation of the dangerous situation that compelled him to shoot Magnus.

First, the prosecution will argue that Zephyr could have retreated, even though he was on his porch. Some states do not require retreating where it is into the home or curtilage (like a porch); however, if it is a minority jurisdiction that requires defendants to retreat even from their curtilage into the home, the prosecution may have a strong argument.

If the jurisdiction has adopted a "stand your ground" law, this argument will not go far. Under a "stand your ground" law, like the one found in Florida, there is no requirement to retreat from a location where the defendant has a right to be. Zephyr will argue that he has as much right to be on his porch as he does to be in his home.

Second, the State will argue is that Zephyr is not entitled to a claim of self-defense because he had other options and was culpable in bringing about the situation that resulted in Magnus's death. Zephyr created the dangerous situation when he saw Magnus outside his home and, instead of calling the police and/or simply ensuring his doors were locked, he chose to leave the confines of his home and confront Magnus with a firearm. This is likely the State's strongest argument.

Zephyr could argue that perhaps he was not reasonable to believe Magnus would kill but he was reasonable to believe that Magnus would cause him serious bodily harm because of his history of physically abusing Zephyr. Still, Zephyr will run into an obstacle when trying to explain away why he chose to confront Magnus instead of calling the police. Even if the jurisdiction does not apply the fifth element requiring the defendant to not have been culpable for creating the dangerous situation, Zephyr will be hard-pressed to prove he had no other alternative than using force. Does it matter that he did not fire his revolver until Magnus fired at him?

19b. Magnus could claim that he acted in self-defense by shooting Zephyr. He could assert that when Zephyr pointed his revolver at him, Magnus reasonably believed his life was in danger. However, this may be a hard sell. Zephyr had shouted he would kill Magnus but he also shouted, "Stay back," implying that shooting Magnus was conditional on him continuing forward toward Zephyr. The prosecution will argue that this shows that Magnus had another option, that he could have retreated safely, and that his decision to shoot Zephyr was unreasonable. Additionally, the prosecution will argue that Magnus did not act in self-defense because he was the aggressor and as the aggressor, he has no right to a defense of self-defense. Magnus had threatened Zephyr months prior and upon hearing that his brother had adopted his kids, Magnus drove to Zephyr's house to "teach him a lesson." Still, this is not as clean cut as it could be; who is the aggressor here? Is it really Magnus? Is it Zephyr?

PROVOCATION — EXCUSE OR JUSTIFICATION?

One more instance where the actor is (usually) acting "suddenly" is provocation (heat of passion). As with the other three claims discussed here, there is fierce academic debate[81] over whether this is a partial excuse or a partial justification (since the claim only reduces the killer's culpability, rather than exonerates him, no one has argued that it is "total"). Those who argue partial justification[82] point out while that the *anger* is justified (the victim did something that would upset a reasonable person) and therefore is partially justified, the *conduct*—actually using deadly force—is excessive and cannot be justified, the defendant is excused. The other camp contends that anyone acting in a heat of passion is, by definition, "not himself" and should be partially excused[83] because he is "similar to," but not identical to, one claiming diminished responsibility or insanity. The Model Penal Code's "extreme emotional disturbance" provision weakens the justification contention, since the MPC does not require that the victim (or someone else) provoke the defendant; it is enough that he's acting under EED. Moreover, if the claim is "only" an excuse, it is conceivable that it could be eliminated entirely (as several jurisdictions have done). (See Chapter 8 for more discussion.)

81. The literature is voluminous. See Marcia Baron, The Provocation Defense and the Nature of Justification, 43 U. Mich. J.L. Rev. 117 (2009); Vera Bergelson, Justification or Excuse? Exploring the Meaning of Provocation, 42 Tex. Tech. L. Rev. 307 (2009); Reid Griffith Fontaine, Adequate (Non)Provocation and Heat of Passion as Excuse Not Justification, 43 U. Mich. J.L. Reform 27 (2009); Mitchell N. Berman, Ian P. Farrell, Provocation Manslaughter as Partial Justification and Partial Excuse, 52 Wm. & Mary L. Rev. 1027 (2011). See also Gabriel J. Chin, Unjustified: The Practical Irrelevance of the Justification/Excuse Distinction, 43 U. Mich. J.L. Reform 79 (2009)

82. E.g. Susan D. Rozelle, Controlling Passion: Adultery and the Provocation Defense, 37 Rutgers L.J. 197 (2005)

83. E.g. Baron, supra, n. 48.

DEFENSE OF PROPERTY AND HABITAT

Most people work hard to acquire their property and want to keep it safe from others. We have laws, such as those against theft, to help safeguard our property, but the law also allows people to use force if necessary to prevent others from taking or destroying their property.

Even more important, most people want to be safe in their homes. The maxim, "A man's home is his castle," though sexist by contemporary standards, recognizes that threats to our physical safety while we are in our homes commonly cause fear and fierce resentment. That is why we have laws against burglary and trespass. Again, however, the law also allows people the use of force, including deadly force in some cases, to defend themselves in their homes if they reasonably appear to be threatened.

Using force can involve harming those who want to take our property or harm us in our homes. It can also create a risk that innocent people will be hurt. Thus, the law must balance the need to forcibly defend property and personal security, on the one hand, and the need to protect lives and safety, on the other. The law prefers the value of human life (including that of the thief) to that of property. It does this by only permitting the use of nondeadly force to defend property, thereby ensuring that human life is not taken merely to save property. However, the law also prefers the value of innocent human life over the lives of aggressors who threaten innocent life. Thus, the law permits the use of deadly force in some cases to defend habitation.

Use of force to defend property or habitation is justified under the law because the owner's superior claims to possession and personal security are considered more important than the aggressor's bodily safety. Because the individual must act under tremendous pressure in an emergency situation, the law permits him to resort to self-help by using force against thieves and aggressors.

The Common Law

A defendant has a legal right to use nondeadly force when he has an honest and reasonable belief that it is necessary to protect real or personal property in his possession from imminent unlawful taking, damage, dispossession, or trespass. He may also use nondeadly force to reenter real property or to recover personal property immediately after it has been taken. However, as described below, there are limits on this right to use nondeadly force.

Other Lawful Means Available

Force may not be used if there is time to take other lawful measures, such as calling the police. Consistent with other defenses and excuses grounded in necessity, this rule avoids the possibility of physical harm to someone unless it is really required.

Warning

If he can do so without risk to himself or his property, an individual must warn the aggressor to stop unless it is clear the warning would be useless.

Deadly Force Not Permitted

A person may not use deadly force solely to protect property. This rule is based on the value judgment that human life is worth more than property.

Personal Property

An individual may use *nondeadly* force to protect personal property from imminent unlawful taking or destruction. If the property owner is then met with what reasonably appears to be deadly force by the thief, the owner may respond with deadly force in self-defense. The thief's resort to deadly force has changed the situation from the defense of property to the defense of human life, and the rules of self-defense now apply.

Conversely, if the property owner uses *deadly* force when the thief does not appear to be using it, the thief then has the right to use deadly force in self-defense because the property owner has exceeded his legal privilege to use force. (See the discussion of self-defense above at page 518.)

Real Property

In contrast to the rules governing the use of force to defend personal property, the common law is somewhat more permissive in authorizing the use of deadly force to defend real property.

Defense of Dwelling. One early English case held that deadly force could be used to prevent forcible entry into a dwelling, provided a warning had been given not to enter. Most jurisdictions, however, no longer follow this rule.

Today most jurisdictions allow the use of deadly force to prevent forcible entry into a dwelling only if the occupant has a reasonable belief that the intruder intends to commit a felony inside. The occupant can use deadly force in these circumstances because the balance of interests has changed dramatically. Now there is a threat of imminent harm both to property and to human life.

Several states have recently enacted laws that expand the right to use deadly force in self-defense in the home. Dubbed "castle laws" or "stand your ground" laws, they effectively allow residents to use deadly force against intruders entering a dwelling (and, in some cases, an occupied vehicle) unlawfully and forcefully.[84] Residents are presumed to have a reasonable fear of death or great bodily injury; they no longer need to determine the intent of aggressors using force to intrude into their homes, nor do they need to retreat. (See discussion at page 520.)

Mechanical Devices. Most jurisdictions do not permit the use of deadly mechanical devices, such as spring guns, to protect property. These devices operate automatically even when the occupant is not there. They pose serious risk of harm to innocent people, such as firefighters, and also activate deadly force when the occupant's life is not in jeopardy.

A few jurisdictions permit the use of these deadly devices, but only if the defendant would have been privileged to use deadly force if he were there. If a firefighter responding to an alarm at the dwelling is killed or injured, the occupant is strictly liable for the unlawful use of deadly force.

Some jurisdictions will permit the use of *nondeadly* devices, such as electric fences, provided proper warning is posted.

Mistakes. Most jurisdictions allow the use of force, including deadly force, if the occupant reasonably believes that the elements of the privilege exist. If, however, the defendant is *negligent* in forming his belief, his use of force is unlawful.

The Model Penal Code

The MPC also permits the use of nondeadly force to defend real or personal property.

Initial Aggression

Section 3.06(1)(a) permits a person to use nondeadly force (i) to defend against an entry into, or trespass against, her real property, or (ii) to prevent

84. Florida, for example, presumes that a person has a reasonable fear of imminent death or great bodily injury if she "had reason to believe that an unlawful and forcible entry . . . was occurring or had occurred." Fla. Stat. Ann. §776.013 (West 2012).

another from taking her personal property when she believes it is immediately required to prevent it. The actor must believe the land or personal property is in her possession or in another's possession for whom she is acting. Section 3.06(2) defines "possession."

Retaking Property

Section 3.06(1)(b) allows individuals to forcibly reenter land or retake personal property taken by another. The actor must believe that the other person does not have lawful title to the property and that she (or the person for whom she is acting) is entitled to possession.

The actor must also satisfy either of two additional requirements: (i) she uses force immediately or in "fresh pursuit," or (ii) the actor believes she is using force against someone who has no claim of right to possession and that, in cases involving real property, it would impose an exceptional hardship to wait for a court order before reentry.

Use of Force

Somewhat begrudgingly, the MPC authorizes the use of force to defend or retake property. The balance of §3.06 imposes limitations on the use of force otherwise authorized by that section. Some of the more important limitations are indicated below.

Request to Desist

The actor must first request the aggressor to stop, unless the actor believes that the request would be useless or dangerous or that substantial harm will be done to the property before the request can be made.

Risk of Serious Bodily Injury

Force, even if otherwise justified, cannot be used if the actor knows it may expose the aggressor to serious bodily injury.

Use of Deadly Force

The actor can use deadly force only if (a) she believes she is defending her dwelling against someone with no claim of right to possession, or (b) the aggressor is committing a serious crime and has used or threatened deadly force, or (c) the actor's use of nondeadly force would expose her (or someone else in her presence) to substantial danger of serious bodily injury.

Use of Mechanical Devices

Use of mechanical devices to protect property is permitted, provided they do not threaten death or serious bodily harm, are reasonable, and either are customarily used or a warning is given.

Examples

1. Maria Rodriguez owns a holiday condominium in Kansas City. She stays at the condo periodically and keeps her irreplaceable collection of twelfth- and thirteenth-century Mayan and Aztec jewelry from Latin America there. Last year, two attempts were made to break in; they almost succeeded. The condo cannot be made more resistant to break-ins and the jewelry cannot be insured. One night, Maria wakes up and hears someone in the kitchen. She grabs the .38 pistol under her pillow, quietly enters the kitchen, and shoots the intruder, killing him. Was Maria's use of deadly force lawful?

2a. Afraid to leave her invaluable jewelry at the condo without effective protection, Maria wants to use a deadly cobra snake as a "watch dog." She would place it in a very secure box that could be released electronically only if a door or window to her condo is opened. Advise Maria.

2b. Would your advice be different if Maria said she would post easily recognized warnings — "Do Not Enter Without Permission: Deadly Cobra Inside" — on the outside of her condo?

3. Finally, Maria decides she must put her rare jewelry in a bank safe-deposit box. She loads it into her large purse and drives downtown. While walking to the bank, a large man tries to snatch her purse by grabbing onto it and trying to pull it from her. Maria desperately hangs on. The man yells, "Let go. I'm not going to hurt you. All I want is your purse." With her free hand Maria manages to free her .38 pistol from her pocket and shoots the purse-snatcher, killing him instantly. As prosecutor, would you charge Maria with murder?

4. Jorge had a running feud with his Orlando neighbor, Julio. For several weeks, Jorge had complained to local authorities that Julio consistently placed four garbage cans out for collection every week, when only two were allowed. Julio, upset by Jorge's actions, went to his front door and knocked loudly. Jorge opened the door. Julio yelled at Jorge to "mind his own business." Jorge said, "Go to hell!" and started to close the door. Julio put his foot in the door and tried to open it. Jorge shot Julio with a pistol, wounding him. Did Jorge assault Julio or act in lawful self-defense?

5. Dani and Jon recently went through an ugly break-up. Before they met, Dani had adopted three pugs, one of which had died—a fact that had been instrumental in Dani and Jon getting together. While they were together, Jon developed a strong affection for Rhaegal, the bigger of the two remaining pugs, but when he and Dani split up, Dani refused to let him visit Rhaegal. One day while Dani was away, Jon broke into her apartment. As Jon sneaked down the hall he was suddenly struck by a dart from Dani's mechanical, home-defense device that flings darts at intruders. Fortunately, he had kept close to the wall and a single dart had struck his shoulder, causing only a flesh wound. Had he been closer to the middle of the hallway, the darts would have struck him in the chest, almost certainly killing him. Jon finally found and took Rhaegal. While walking to his car, Dani drove up and started yelling at him, but he jumped in his car and sped away. Dani followed Jon to his apartment and into his front room. Jon kept yelling for her to leave. Dani refused and attempted to retrieve Rhaegal from Jon. He moved away to stop her, so Dani sprayed her pepper spray in Jon's face. As Jon writhed on the floor, clawing at his face furiously, Dani left with Rhaegal. Discuss.

Explanations

1. As an occupant in lawful possession of a dwelling, Maria may use deadly force against an aggressor only if she reasonably believes he intends to commit a felony against person or property therein. The difficulty here is that there are no facts indicating what the dead aggressor intended once inside. The defense will argue that a homeowner should not have to make further inquiry to ascertain the intruder's intentions because that would only put Maria at greater disadvantage and increase her danger. Moreover, it is reasonable to infer that the intruder had a felonious purpose in mind when entering Maria's condo.

   Though this is a close case, a jury would probably find Maria was justified in using deadly force to defend herself and her dwelling from the intruder.

   The MPC takes substantially the same approach as the common law. Maria would have to persuade the jury that she reasonably believed the aggressor was committing a serious crime or that, without recourse to deadly force, she risked serious bodily injury. Again, the jury would probably agree with her.

   Under recently enacted "castle laws," Maria would have a much stronger case of self-defense. These laws effectively presume that an intruder who forcibly and unlawfully enters a residence intends to kill or do great bodily injury to anyone inside. Residents are presumed to have a reasonable fear for their lives and can use deadly force in self-defense without any duty to retreat. Shoot, Maria! Shoot!

2a. Hopefully, you immediately told Maria that she may be criminally liable for using a deadly cobra as a mechanical watch dog. Neither the common law nor the MPC authorizes the use of deadly devices to defend property, including a dwelling. The fact that this deadly device is also defending extremely valuable personal property does not make a difference. Human life, even that of a criminal, is considered more valuable than property. Thus, tell Maria to immediately take her killer cobra back to the pet store for a refund. Otherwise, she may be charged with a serious crime such as homicide or assault if the cobra is released during a break-in. You might also point out that her slinky sleuth also presents serious risk to innocent people like firefighters or caretakers who might be forced to enter the condo in an emergency.

2b. Posting warning signs would not relieve Maria of criminal responsibility. Neither the common law nor the MPC permits the use of deadly force to protect unoccupied dwellings or personal property located there. The MPC permits the use of unusual mechanical devices to protect real or personal property if adequate notice is given, but only if they do not pose a substantial risk of serious bodily harm.

Posting warnings does not relieve Maria of responsibility for using a *deadly* mechanical device to defend her property. Most jurisdictions prohibit the use of such devices. The MPC allows the use of non-deadly devices if they are customary (like razor-sharp wire around a warehouse) or if notice is posted. It does not allow the use of deadly mechanical devices under any circumstances.

3. Maria is not entitled to use deadly force to defend her personal property from a thief even though it is very valuable and, in this case, is not insured. Thus, she is guilty of homicide. Maria might claim that she reasonably feared death or great bodily harm at the hands of the thief, but he was unarmed and told her he would not hurt her and that he only wanted to steal her property.

4. In many states, Jorge would be charged with assault with a deadly weapon. A homeowner generally cannot use deadly force to defend his property. There was no reason to believe Julio was armed or threatened Jorge with death or serious bodily injury. In some states, however, a homeowner can use deadly force if he reasonably believes an intruder intends to commit a felony in the home. This might not help Jorge because Julio wanted to continue the argument. In states such as Florida, however, which have passed "castle laws," Jorge might successfully argue legitimate self-defense. A resident is presumed to reasonably fear for his life if an intruder unlawfully and forcibly enters

the dwelling of another; the homeowner can stand his ground. The prosecution could argue that Jorge knew that Julio was unarmed and only wanted to talk to him about the garbage cans. In a very similar case, prosecutors in Florida declined to prosecute.[85]

5. Dani will probably be charged with assault for setting up the dart trap that injured Jon. Under the common law, setting up automatic mechanical devices that seriously injure or kill intruders or emergency responders indiscriminately is illegal. In some jurisdictions, the use of nondeadly devices is permitted so long as there is a warning. The dart trap likely does not fall into that category since Jon likely would have died if he had not been hugging the wall and had been hit with the full force of the darts in a more vulnerable part of his body. There was no warning—such was the purpose of the device, after all: to catch an intruder unaware. Thus, Dani will not be able to assert defense against property for her assault against Jon via the dart trap.

   Many jurisdictions do not permit a defense of property defense where other lawful means of protecting the property are available. Under this rule, Dani probably acted criminally by following Jon home and trespassing on his property to retrieve the pug (under the law, pets are considered property). Instead of following Jon to his apartment, trespassing and assaulting him, Dani could have contacted the police to have Rhaegal returned to her.

   If the jurisdiction has adopted the MPC, Dani may fare better. The MPC permits a party to enter another's land to retrieve her personal property if it has been stolen. The party must be in fresh pursuit OR obtaining a court order to enter would impose an exceptional hardship on her. Here, Dani was in fresh pursuit, following Jon from the "scene of the crime" to his apartment where she immediately followed him into his apartment. She likely satisfies the MPC here; however, the remaining question is whether her use of force was lawful.

   The MPC permits the use of force if the party tells the other to stop (unless that would give rise to a risk of substantial harm to the property). Dani had yelled at Jon to not take Rhaegal when she drove up. She likely satisfies this requirement. The second requirement under the MPC is that the party not use force if she knows it would cause serious bodily injury. Dani could argue that the use of pepper spray against Jon, while painful, did not cause serious bodily injury to him.

85. 15 States Expand Victims' Rights on Self-Defense, N.Y. Times, Aug. 7, 2006, at A1.

USE OF FORCE

Trained police forces are a modern development. Before they were established, citizens often had to make arrests and bring those suspected of committing crimes to the public authorities. The common law developed special rules governing the use of force by peace officers and citizens to apprehend criminal suspects and prevent their escape.

Because citizens, as well as police, may need to prevent others from committing crime, the law authorizes both police officers and citizens to use force to stop crime. Again, the common law distinguishes between the use of *nondeadly force* and *deadly force* and between the authority of *police* and of *citizens* to use either kind of force.

To complicate matters, both police and citizens can be mistaken about whether a crime has been committed and whether the person they suspect has indeed committed it. Police and citizens may also be mistaken about whether a crime is in progress or whether the person they suspect is *attempting* to commit it. Thus, the law must strike a delicate balance between allowing police and citizens to arrest criminals and prevent crimes, while also protecting innocent people who may be mistakenly suspected of committing crimes.

Arrest

The Common Law

The common law permits both peace officers and citizens to use force, including deadly force in certain cases, to arrest individuals suspected of committing a crime. The common law distinguishes between the use of force by the police and by private citizens and between the use of nondeadly and deadly force. Not surprisingly, the common law provides broader authority for peace officers to use force than it does for citizens.

Police Authority to Arrest

At common law, police can arrest a suspect if they have a warrant for his arrest. They may arrest someone without a warrant if they have reasonable grounds to believe that the suspect has committed a felony or if the suspect commits a misdemeanor in their presence. Today most jurisdictions have enacted statutes that explicitly confer this same scope of arrest authority on police officers.

Nondeadly Force. Police can use nondeadly force when they reasonably believe it necessary to make a lawful arrest for any crime, including a felony or a misdemeanor. Apprehension of criminal suspects is considered more important than the risk of bodily injury that can occur when nondeadly force is used to make an arrest or prevent escape. Note that the police need only have reasonable grounds for believing that the suspect committed a crime. Their use of force under these circumstances is permitted even if it turns out that no crime was committed or that the suspect did not commit it.

Deadly Force. Police can use deadly force if they reasonably believe it necessary to prevent a felon from escaping arrest. Deadly force cannot be used to prevent the escape of a misdemeanant.

Some jurisdictions impose more restrictive limits on the use of deadly force, authorizing it only when police reasonably believe that the felon trying to escape arrest is dangerous. The officer must reasonably believe the fleeing felon is armed or has committed a serious crime dangerous to life, such as murder. This approach limits the possible taking of life to cases in which the felon, if not apprehended, may pose a future risk to human life.

Constitutional Limits. The Supreme Court has narrowed the common law authority of police to apprehend criminal suspects. The Court held that it is an unreasonable seizure of a person in violation of the Fourth Amendment for police to use deadly force to apprehend a fleeing felon unless (i) deadly force is necessary to prevent escape; (ii) if practical, a warning is given; and (iii) the officer has probable cause (essentially the same as "reasonable grounds" at common law) to believe the felon poses a serious threat of death or serious bodily injury to others if he is not apprehended.[86] Risking the life of a dangerous felony suspect is justified in this situation in order to prevent risking the loss of innocent life.

There are sound reasons for not allowing police to use deadly force to apprehend a criminal suspect who is not reasonably believed to be dangerous to human life. Killing a non-dangerous, unarmed suspect effectively deprives him of his due process right to a trial to determine his guilt or innocence and to be punished according to law. The police officer, in effect, becomes prosecutor, judge, and jury. Moreover, killing the suspect imposes a much harsher punishment than could be imposed for the crime he is suspected of committing unless it is a capital offense.

Self-Defense. If met with forcible resistance while trying to apprehend a criminal suspect, police are entitled to use force in self-defense, including deadly force, if they reasonably fear imminent death or serious bodily injury. (See pages 478-481.)

---

86. *Tennessee v. Garner*, 471 U.S. 1 (1985).

Private Citizens

The common law gives citizens authority to make arrests for any felony or for a misdemeanor involving breach of the peace occurring in their presence, provided (i) the offense was committed and (ii) the citizen reasonably believes the suspect committed the felony. The actual commission of the offense is a strict liability element. If no crime occurred, then a citizen who uses force to arrest or prevent flight of a criminal suspect is criminally responsible even if her belief was reasonable.

Thus, while a police officer may use force even when no crime has been committed provided he has probable cause to believe it has occurred, a private citizen will be criminally liable for the use of force in such circumstances.

Assisting the Police. A private citizen asked to help police officers stands in their shoes. The citizen can assert any defense that the officer can assert, including nondeadly or deadly force.

Nondeadly Force. Private citizens acting on their own may use nondeadly force only when they reasonably believe it necessary to arrest someone for a felony that was actually committed. If the felony was not committed, the private citizen is strictly liable for her use of force.

Deadly Force. The authority of a private citizen acting alone to use deadly force to apprehend a felon is narrower than that of a police officer. A citizen may use deadly force when she reasonably believes it necessary to arrest a person who has actually committed a felony (and perhaps only a dangerous felony). If the person did not commit the felony, a private citizen using deadly force is strictly liable. Thus, unlike a police officer, a private citizen uses deadly force to apprehend a felon at her own peril.

The Model Penal Code

Use of Force in Law Enforcement

Section 3.07 authorizes the use of force when the actor is making (or assisting in making) an arrest and believes it immediately necessary to effect a lawful arrest.

Limitations

This section limits the privilege as follows:

Nondeadly Force. Force is not justified unless the actor informs the person, if feasible, why he is being arrested and, if the arrest is made under a warrant, the warrant is valid or believed to be valid.

Deadly Force. Deadly force is not justified in making an arrest unless (a) the arrest is for a felony; (b) the person is a peace officer or assisting someone she believes is a peace officer; (c) the actor believes there is no substantial risk to innocent people; and (d) the actor believes the suspect committed a crime involving the use or threat of deadly force or there is a substantial risk the person will cause death or serious bodily injury if apprehension is delayed.

Note that (1) *all* four elements must be satisfied before deadly force can be used, and (2) a *private citizen* cannot use deadly force to arrest a felony suspect unless she believes she is assisting a police officer. Note also that §3.09(2) of the MPC allows an actor to be prosecuted for an offense requiring proof of recklessness or negligence if she was reckless or negligent in forming the beliefs required for justification under §§3.03 to 3.08. Thus, if the actor was reckless or negligent in forming the beliefs set forth in (b), (c), or (d) above, she can be prosecuted for any applicable offense requiring those culpability states.

Preventing Crime

The Common Law

Nondeadly Force

Individuals may use nondeadly force if they reasonably believe a misdemeanor is being committed. Deadly force is never permitted to prevent a misdemeanor. Preventing a minor crime is simply not worth the loss of human life that can occur when deadly force is used.

Deadly Force

There are two views on the lawful use of deadly force to prevent commission of felony.

Any Felony. Some jurisdictions allow both police officers and private citizens to use deadly force when they reasonably believe it is necessary to prevent the commission of *any* felony. Because it includes *all* felonies, this broad rule accepts the possible loss of life that deadly force may cause in order to prevent crimes that, though serious, do not necessarily pose danger to human life.

The balance of interests struck by this rule is even more remarkable because a *reasonable belief* is sufficient to justify the use of deadly force. Thus, human life may be taken even though the person killed may not actually have intended to commit any offense. For example, a citizen who shoots and kills a stranger he reasonably mistakes to be stealing the citizen's expensive mountain bike could not be convicted of homicide.

Dangerous Felony. Some jurisdictions only allow the use of deadly force to prevent the commission of felonies dangerous to human life. This appears to be the modern approach.

The Model Penal Code

Section 3.07(5) authorizes the use of force when the actor believes it is immediately necessary to prevent suicide or serious self-injury, a crime involving or threatening bodily harm, damage to property, or a breach of the peace subject to these two limitations contained in §3.05(a)(i) and (ii):

a. Other limitations on the use of force contained in the MPC apply even though the person against whom force is used is committing a crime.
b. *Deadly* force is not justified unless the actor believes: (a) there is a substantial risk the person will cause death or serious bodily injury to another if he is not prevented from committing the crime and there is no substantial risk of injuring innocent people; or (b) use of deadly force is necessary to suppress a riot or mutiny after the rioters (or mutineers) have been ordered to disperse and warned that deadly force will be used if they do not.

Examples

EXAMPLES

1. Rex is working alone at the grocery store late Friday evening. He notices Ruth, a suspicious woman who is quite small and wearing a long coat, loitering in the corner. He sees that a plainclothes police officer buying some milk has also noticed her. Suddenly, Ruth pulls a rifle out from under her long coat and, though having a great deal of trouble holding the weapon steady, points it in Rex's direction, saying, "Give me all the money in the cash register." The plainclothes officer, realizing what is going on, moves carefully toward her. Seconds after Rex has given Ruth all the money in the register, the officer lunges at the woman, knocking the rifle from her hands. She escapes his grasp and runs out into the parking lot.
   a. Rex picks up her rifle, aims it at Ruth and shoots, killing her instantly.
   b. The plainclothes officer aims his service revolver at the legs of the fleeing suspect in order to wound her and fires. Unfortunately, the bullet strikes Ruth in the head, killing her instantly.

As prosecutor, would you conclude that either Rex or the officer were justified in using deadly force?

2. Several young boys are playing basketball on a Saturday afternoon in an apartment complex. Julio thinks they are making too much noise, so he takes the basketball away from them and takes it to his apartment. Eric, one of the boys, runs to his dad, Hector, and tells him what Julio did. Hector starts walking toward Julio's apartment. Julio, seeing Hector coming, closes his front door. Rather than knocking, Hector simply opens the unlocked front door and walks into Julio's apartment intending to discuss the incident with him. Julio shoots Hector in the chest with a double-barrel shotgun, killing him instantly as he enters the apartment. Murder or a justified killing? Your call, district attorney.

3. Juan is driving a truck loaded with immigrants on a highway near San Diego. Officers Smith and Wesson spot the truck and suspect Juan is violating immigration laws. They turn on the siren and pursue Juan. Juan speeds up. After a very dangerous chase at high speeds, Juan pulls over and stops the truck. Most of the occupants (all immigrants whom Juan was smuggling into the country) flee. Officers Smith and Wesson pull up and see Juan running away from the truck and give chase. Smith yells, "Stop! Police!" Juan ignores the warning and continues to flee. Smith finally catches Juan and tackles him. Juan is sitting passively on the ground when Officer Wesson arrives on the scene and starts beating Juan severely about the head and shoulders with his baton. Can Officer Wesson be charged with assault?

4. River is walking home from work one winter night when he sees a homeless man fussing with the door of a red Lamborghini. The man is heavily clothed in dirty winter garb, with an unkempt beard, and combat boots. River walks toward him to see what the man is doing and notices that he is attempting to pick the lock of the car with a wire. Immediately, River becomes enraged, thinking the man is trying to steal the car. Only last month, River's car was stolen and found wrecked on the side of the road. River yells at the man to stop and starts walking toward him. The man turns, looking alarmed and afraid. "That doesn't belong to you, buddy!" River shouts, closing in on the man. Before the man can respond, River punches him in the face and proceeds beat him to a pulp. Soon the police arrive, intervening. It turns out that the man, despite his disheveled appearance, is the owner of the expensive vehicle. The man had lost his keys when he dropped them on the ground and ruined his nice clothing while searching through for them in the snow for hours . . . until he gave up and decided to try to pick his own lock. River is charged with assault. Does he have a defense?

Explanations

1a. Rex is not preventing a crime. The suspect has broken off her criminal enterprise and is fleeing. Thus, Rex's privilege to use deadly force must be analyzed under the law of arrest, not crime prevention.

Under the common law, a private person can use deadly force to apprehend a fleeing felon, provided a felony was committed. Here, Rex shot at someone who had, in fact, committed a felony. Thus, his use of deadly force to apprehend the woman is justified and he may not be convicted of any crime.

The MPC does not allow a private person acting alone to use deadly force to apprehend a felon, even one who might pose a danger to life if not apprehended. Was Rex acting alone? Or can he persuade the fact finder that he was actually assisting a police officer? Did the police officer ask for assistance? Ruth was committing a felony, so that element is met. But Rex must also show (1) he believed there was no substantial risk to innocent people; (2) the suspect committed a crime involving the threat of deadly force; and (3) the suspect is dangerous if not apprehended. He could probably prove the first two elements. But was Ruth dangerous if not apprehended? This is a close case on the facts and could go either way.

1b. Under the common law, a police officer may also use deadly force to apprehend someone he has reasonable grounds to believe committed a felony. Because he may act on "reasonable grounds," a police officer has more authority to use deadly force than a private citizen who acts at his peril that a felony has been committed.

The MPC limits police use of *deadly force* to arrest in the same manner as it limits private actors. Thus, the same analysis applies to the undercover police officer as we applied to Rex (except, of course, there is no dispute that the officer is a "peace officer" within the meaning of the MPC).

Tennessee v. Garner, 471 U.S. 1 (1985), imposes more stringent limits on the use of deadly force by police officers to arrest a fleeing suspect than the common law did. Police officers cannot use deadly force to apprehend a fleeing felon unless (1) deadly force is necessary to prevent the escape, (2) the officer has probable cause to believe that the person has committed a felony, and (3) is dangerous to human life if not apprehended.

This is a close case. Could the officer have run after the fleeing suspect and used nondeadly force to prevent her escape, or was deadly force necessary? Does the officer have probable cause to believe the suspect poses a danger to human life if not apprehended? True, Ruth used deadly force in an attempt to commit a felony, and the officer saw this with his own eyes. But the suspect could barely lift the weapon and use it effectively. Moreover, the rifle was knocked from her arms; thus, she was no longer armed. Would a reasonable police officer believe the suspect is dangerous if not apprehended immediately?

2. Julio will claim that the common law allows him to use deadly force to prevent the commission of *any* felony. Julio will argue that Hector, by entering Julio's dwelling without permission, was committing the felony of first-degree criminal trespass and that Julio was justified in killing Hector. The prosecution will counter that the felony was complete and that Julio was no longer justified in using deadly force to *prevent* the felony. Julio will respond that he shot Hector as Hector was committing the felony by entering his apartment without permission. Interesting issue!

   In those jurisdictions that have adopted the broad common law rule governing the use of deadly force to prevent the commission of *any* felony, Julio will probably prevail unless the jury concludes the felony was already over when Julio shot Hector.

   Ironically, this common law rule governing the use of deadly force to prevent felonies provides broader authority than does the law of self-defense. It is unlikely that Julio would be able to succeed with a claim of self-defense because he did not reasonably fear imminent death or serious bodily harm. To take a human life merely to prevent such a minor felony seems uncivilized in modern times. Because so many felonies were capital offenses at early common law, the rule did not seem so harsh then.

   If, however, the jurisdiction limits the use of deadly force to prevent the commission only of felonies that are dangerous to human life, Julio may not be privileged to use deadly force to prevent the commission of felonious trespass. Under the majority view today, Julio would not be privileged to use deadly force to prevent this nondangerous felony.

   Under the MPC, Julio would not be authorized to use deadly force because he did not believe he was preventing the commission of a felony that posed serious risk to human life.

3. Under the common law, police officers may use nondeadly force when they reasonably believe it necessary to make a lawful arrest for any crime. Under the MPC and under *Tennessee v. Garner*, police may use nondeadly force to apprehend someone they reasonably suspect of committing a crime after giving a warning (if feasible).

   Here Officer Smith's tackling Juan was lawful because Smith had reason to believe that Juan had committed a crime and Juan would not surrender even after being warned to stop and surrender. Officer Wesson's beating of Juan, however, is not lawful. Juan was already in police custody when Wesson arrived on the scene. Wesson's use of the police baton to beat Juan was probably intended as retaliation for fleeing and causing risk of death or injury during the police chase.

Officer Wesson is in deep trouble, especially if a local TV news helicopter catches the whole incident on tape and broadcasts it.

4. On one hand, River could argue that he reasonably believed that a felony was being committed by the man and thus he was justified in his use of force. Under common law, a private citizen may use up to deadly force to prevent a felony, so long as the belief that a felony is taking place is reasonable. River could argue that because the man appeared homeless—giving rise to a reasonable (but incorrect) inference that he could not own such an expensive car—and was trying to pick the lock, River's belief that he was attempting to carjack the Lamborghini was reasonable.

   However, River will be out of luck if he is in a jurisdiction that either applies strict liability or only shields citizens who attempt to prevent felonies that will cause serious bodily harm or death. In a jurisdiction that applies strict liability, even a reasonable mistake as to whether a felony is taking place is not sufficient.

CHAPTER 17

Defenses Based on Individual Characteristics

OVERVIEW

The criminal law generally assumes that most people have mental and psychological capabilities sufficient to hold them responsible for the crimes they commit. But the criminal law does provide limited opportunities for a defendant to avoid or lessen his responsibility by demonstrating that one or more of his important human capacities was significantly impaired when he committed the criminal act.

Defenses such as insanity, infancy, intoxication, and diminished capacity are among the more important of these opportunities. These doctrines permit a defendant to claim that it would be unjust to punish him at all or as severely as a normal person because of his unusual limitations. They are fundamentally different from defenses like self-defense or necessity, which claim the defendant did the "right thing" in the situation. The defenses discussed in this chapter acknowledge that the defendant did not do the "right thing" but that, nonetheless, other policy considerations require that he be treated differently. For this reason, many courts and scholars describe these defenses as "excuses" rather than "justifications." Included among these excuses is the defense of entrapment.

Entrapment differs from the other excuses detailed in this chapter. The defense of entrapment is somewhat unusual. It claims that the defendant did not "really" act with the same bad attitude as a criminal. In large part, the defense of entrapment is distinguishable because its purpose is different. It is aimed at making sure the police do not "manufacture" crime by inducing the defendant to act.

INSANITY

As we saw earlier, the criminal law assumes people know the law and have free will.[1] Their abilities to know and to choose (or, put in psychological terms, their cognitive and volitional capacities) are bedrock premises of criminal responsibility and underlie all philosophical theories of punishment.[2] Utilitarians expect the threat of punishment to influence behavior because people know they will be punished for breaking the law and will decide not to in order to avoid that punishment. Retributivists punish because defendants have chosen to commit a criminal act and have thereby earned their just deserts.[3]

Consequently, the criminal law generally does not ask whether a defendant knows if his conduct violates the law or finds it difficult to obey the law. Criminal law doctrine condones cognitive or volitional failure as an excuse in only a very few and well-defined instances.

For example, mistake of law is one situation in which the law may excuse the defendant if her belief about an act's legality was incorrect. However, that is a very narrow exception and difficult to establish. The common law did not permit the defense at all, and the MPC permits it only under stringent conditions. Likewise, duress is an example of when an individual will be excused because he does not make a free choice to commit a crime. But, again, the elements for a successful duress defense are quite demanding (see Chapter 16).

Legal insanity is an excuse that also permits inquiry into a defendant's capacity to know the law or to exercise free will. It focuses on the individual's personal characteristics rather than the situation in which she acts. There are two primary insanity defenses used by various jurisdictions in the United States: the *M'Naghten* test[4] and the Model Penal Code test.[5] Depending on the applicable legal test, a person is legally insane and not responsible for a crime if, as a result of mental illness, her cognitive or volitional capacity was seriously impaired when she committed the offense.

The rationale of the insanity defense is complex. Most supporters argue that it is vital to maintaining the moral foundation of criminal law.[6] Punishing a seriously disturbed person, who through no fault of her own, is simply unable to comprehend the immorality of her conduct or to obey the law, is pointless and cruel. These individuals can be sent to a secure

---

1. See *United State v. Barker*, 514 F.2d 208 (D.C. Cir. 1975) (Bazelon, J., dissenting).
2. J. Feinberg, What Is So Special About Mental Illness, in Doing and Deserving: Essays in the Theory of Responsibility (1970).
3. Hart, The Aims of the Criminal Law, 23 Law & Contemp. Problems 401 (1958).
4. *M'Naghten's Case*, 101 Cl. & F. 200, 8 Eng. Rep. 718 (H.L. 1843).
5. See §401 (Mental Disease or Defect Excluding Responsibility).
6. Bonnie, The Moral Basis of the Insanity Defense, 69 A.B.A.J. 194 (1983).

mental health facility to be treated. When they are no longer mentally ill or dangerous, they will be released.

The insanity test rests on three crucial assumptions. First, mental illness (sometimes called "mental disorder") exists and is beyond the control of the afflicted person. Second, this illness interferes with important psychological functions. Third, this impaired functioning significantly impairs an individual's ability to understand and direct her behavior. In sum, the insanity defense assumes there is a causal connection between the existence of mental illness and the individual's criminal conduct.

Though the insanity defense has been recognized since the early 1500s,[7] today it is extremely controversial. As we shall see, high-profile cases involving the insanity defense receive broad media coverage. Insanity acquittals often provoke public outrage and evoke powerful agitation for the reform or abolition of the defense and for changing the manner in which the insanity test is litigated.[8] Legal insanity sharply focuses the tension in the criminal law between ensuring community safety and doing justice to the individual.

The Relevance of Mental Illness in the Criminal Justice System

The mental illness of a defendant is relevant for different purposes in the criminal justice system. Before considering the insanity defense in depth, it is important to note the relevance of mental illness in several other situations.

Competency to Stand Trial

Our adversarial system of criminal justice assumes a contest between two parties: a prosecutor seeking to obtain a conviction and a self-interested defendant seeking to obtain an acquittal. Because the defendant is often the primary source of useful information for his own defense and because he has a constitutional right to make many significant decisions in the criminal justice system, including whether to plead guilty, to conduct his own defense, or to assert an insanity defense, he must be capable of meaningful participation in his own defense. Competency to stand trial ensures that a defendant can perform these vital roles and that the system will work as intended.

---

7. N. Walker, Crime and Insanity in England 24-26 (1968).

8. See J. Q. La Fond & Mary L. Durham, Back to the Asylum: The Future of Mental Health Law and Policy in the United States (1992).

Both the common law and the Constitution require that a criminal defendant be competent to stand trial.[9] The Supreme Court has stated the test of competency to stand trial as follows: "[T]he test must be whether [the defendant] has sufficient present ability to consult with his lawyer with a reasonable degree of rational understanding—and whether he has a rational as well as factual understanding of the proceedings against him."[10]

The MPC also requires that a defendant is competent before he can be tried. Section 4.04 states: "No person who as a result of mental disease or defect lacks the capacity to understand the proceedings against him or to assist in his own defense shall be tried, convicted or sentenced for the commission of an offense so long as such incapacity endures."

In assessing the competency of a criminal defendant to stand trial, the relevant time frame is his *current* mental status at the time of trial. Mental health professionals must evaluate the defendant and determine if he suffers from a mental illness that prevents him from understanding the significance of a criminal trial, including the role of the prosecutor, judge, jury, and defense counsel, and from being helpful in his own defense.

Burden of Proof

The common law assumed a criminal defendant was competent to stand trial unless some evidence indicated he was not. Historical analysis of British and American common law does not firmly establish whether the prosecution or the defendant carried the burden of persuasion on the defendant's competency to stand trial.[11] The Supreme Court has held that it is constitutional to impose this burden of proof on a defendant by a preponderance of the evidence,[12] but not by clear and convincing evidence.[13]

Disposition of an Incompetent Defendant

If a defendant is so mentally ill that he does not understand what a criminal trial is and cannot assist in his own defense, he may not be tried. Instead, the government may release him if he is charged with a minor offense or commit him to a mental health facility where he may be treated to restore his competency to stand trial. Different states have enacted statutes specifying how long a person may be committed before he must be released if not brought to trial. However, the Constitution requires that if it becomes clear

9. *Medina v. California*, 505 U.S. 437 (1992).
10. *Dusky v. United States*, 362 U.S. 402 (1960).
11. *Medina v. California*, 505 U.S. 437 (1992).
12. *Medina v. California*, 505 U.S. 437 (1992).
13. *Cooper v. Oklahoma*, 517 U.S. 348 (1996).

the defendant will *never* become competent to stand trial, he must be civilly committed under other commitment laws or be released.[14]

Transfer from Prison to a Psychiatric Hospital

Some convicted defendants may become mentally ill while serving their prison terms. The state may transfer them to a mental health facility for appropriate treatment, but the inmate must be provided adequate procedural due process to determine if he is presently mentally ill.[15]

Release from Confinement

A person found not guilty by reason of insanity (NGRI) may be committed to a secure mental health facility indefinitely, even beyond the maximum term for which she could have been sentenced if found guilty.[16] The rationale behind this is that, though innocent, dangerous and insane defendants present a danger and the government has a legitimate interest in protecting the public from them.[17] The government may use commitment standards and procedures that are somewhat different from those used to civilly commit mentally ill individuals. A defendant initially found NGRI must be released if she is no longer mentally ill or dangerous.[18]

Execution Pursuant to a Sentence of Death

Both the common law and the Constitution prohibit the execution of an individual sentenced to death if, at the time the death sentence is to be carried out, he is mentally ill and does not comprehend why he will be executed. This ensures that the individual understands the retributive purpose of his execution and will not view his death as pointless and cruel. It also ensures that he can assist in any appellate proceedings.[19]

The Insanity Defense

The defense of insanity is litigated at the criminal trial. The relevant time frame for the inquiry is the defendant's mental status at the time of the alleged offense. Thus, the assessment is retrospective.

14. *Jackson v. Indiana*, 406 U.S. 715 (1972).
15. *Vitek v. Jones*, 445 U.S. 480 (1980).
16. *Jones v. United States*, 463 U.S. 354 (1983).
17. Paul H. Robinson, Shima Baradaran Baughman, & Michael T. Cahill, Criminal Law: Case Studies and Controversies 732 (New York: Wolters Kluwer, 4th ed., 2017).
18. *Foucha v. Louisiana*, 504 U.S. 71 (1992).
19. *Ford v. Wainwright*, 477 U.S. 399 (1986).

In preparing for the trial, a mental health expert representing the government and one representing the defense may evaluate the defendant. Based on a wide variety of information, such as the defendant's mental health history, his account of the crime, the facts and circumstances surrounding the crime, and psychological and medical testing, these experts will form an opinion as to the defendant's mental status at the time of the crime and whether it satisfies the elements of the insanity test used in their jurisdiction.

The *M'Naghten* Test

First announced by the House of Lords in 1843, the *M'Naghten* test excuses a defendant from criminal responsibility if, at the time of the crime, he was "labouring under such a defect of reason, from disease of the mind, as not to know the nature and quality of the act he was doing; or, if he did know it, that he did not know he was doing what was wrong."[20] In modern times, the test has been slightly modified; it no longer requires a "defect of reason."[21] Under the *M'Naghten* test, a criminal defendant cannot be convicted if, as a result of mental illness at the time of the crime, he did not know what he was doing or that it was wrong.

In sum, mental illness must have virtually nullified the actor's cognitive capacity so that he was unable to exercise the moral understanding of normal persons. Without a rational ability to recognize and evaluate the moral issues raised by his behavior, the criminal law could not influence him.

In 2006, the Supreme Court concluded that due process does not require a state to use *both* prongs of the *M'Naghten* defense.[22] Ten states, including Arizona, limit their *M'Naghten* test to people who did not know their criminal act was wrong. The Court noted that four states do not even provide an insanity defense; thus, states that do afford it have broad authority on how to define the test. One way a defendant could show he did not know his conduct was wrong under the Arizona law was to prove that he did not know what he was doing when he acted. Thus, no evidence relevant to criminal responsibility was excluded at trial.

This case shows the continuing reluctance of the Supreme Court to constitutionalize and federalize the substantive criminal law, especially when defenses are at issue. States can decide if they want to provide the defense of insanity at all, and if they do provide it, they can define it however they choose.

---

20. *M'Naghten's Case*, 101 Cl. & F. 200, 8 Eng. Rep. 718 (H.L. 1843).
21. See H. Fingarette, The Meaning of Criminal Insanity (1972).
22. *Clark v. Arizona*, 548 U.S. 735 (2006).

The Meaning of Mental Illness

Most mental health professionals have interpreted the *M'Naghten* test as requiring the defendant to be out of touch with reality and not accurately perceiving the world around him.[23] For example, he may be hearing voices that command him to commit harmful acts. Or he may be acting under a delusional belief system, such as a belief that secret agents are out to kill him or that he is a significant historical person like Christ. These impairments can make it very difficult for the defendant to comprehend reality accurately and to evaluate the appropriateness of his conduct. Consequently, individuals with these impairments may engage in inappropriate and even criminal behavior.

The Meaning of "Wrong"

A major controversy surrounding the *M'Naghten* test is whether the term "wrong" refers to awareness of an act's criminality or immortality. And, if it means "morally wrong," should the defendant's personal moral beliefs or society's morality control? A mentally ill person may know that an act is against the law and even that society considers the act wrong. However, should he be punished for committing an act that, according to his own delusional sense of morality, is not wrong? Arguably, this person is not deserving of punishment because he did not choose to do wrong as he saw things. Nor could he be deterred if he thought he was doing the right thing.

American courts are split on this question. Some will hold a mentally ill defendant responsible if he knew his actions were against the law. This approach is consistent with the general rule that ignorance of the law is no excuse. However, it may ignore the serious and pronounced difficulty the defendant has in rationally taking that knowledge into account in deciding whether to act. Some states will excuse a defendant if, because of serious mental illness, he believed he had received a direct command from God to commit the harmful act.[24]

The Irresistible Impulse Test

A few jurisdictions added to the *M'Naghten* test by also permitting legal insanity to apply to cases in which mental illness produced an "irresistible impulse" to act. The irresistible impulse test complements the insanity

---

23. Many mental health professionals would probably require an individual to suffer from an axis 1 diagnosis under the Diagnostic and Statistical Manual of Mental Disorders-IV-TR (4th ed. 2000).

24. *State v. Cameron*, 100 Wash. 2d 520, 674 P.2d 650 (1983).

defense, which addresses a defendant's cognitive ability to perceive his or her actions meaningfully (both in terms of reality and morality) by focusing on the defendant's ability to choose.[25] The irresistible impulse test is appropriate where a defendant's ability to choose is inhibited by mental illness.[26] Under this test, the defendant could achieve an insanity defense if:

> (1) by reason of the duress of such mental disease, she had so far lost the power to choose between the right and wrong, and to avoid doing the action question, as that her free agency was at the times destroyed; (2) and if, at the same time, the alleged crime was so connected with such mental disease, in the relation of cause and effect, as to have been the product of it solely.[27]

This component, which adds severe volitional impairment to the insanity test, is generally satisfied if the defendant persuades a judge or jury that she would have committed the crime even if a policeman were at her side at the time.[28] Needless to say, it is a difficult test to satisfy. Roughly 30 percent of jurisdictions have adopted the "irresistible impulse" test.[29]

The Model Penal Code Test

During the 1950s, the *M'Naghten* test was severely criticized by psychiatrists, judges, and legal scholars because it excused only those individuals who lacked cognitive ability. These experts argued that legal insanity should also excuse those who could not control their behavior. In addition, the *M'Naghten* test required *total* impairment. Finally, it did not take into account new psychiatric knowledge about human behavior.[30]

Influenced by these criticisms and the emergence of rehabilitation as the primary goal of the criminal justice system, the American Law Institute proposed a new insanity test in the Model Penal Code, sometimes called the "Substantial Capacity Test." It provides in part that

---

25. Paul H. Robinson, Shima Baradaran Baughman, & Michael T. Cahill, Criminal Law: Case Studies and Controversies 726 (New York: Wolters Kluwer, 4th ed., 2017).
26. Paul H. Robinson, Shima Baradaran Baughman, & Michael T. Cahill, Criminal Law: Case Studies and Controversies 726 (New York: Wolters Kluwer, 4th ed., 2017).
27. Paul H. Robinson, Shima Baradaran Baughman, & Michael T. Cahill, Criminal Law: Case Studies and Controversies 726 (New York: Wolters Kluwer, 4th ed., 2017) (quoting *Parsons v. State*, 2 Sp. 854 (Ala. 1887).
28. See *United States v. Kunak*, 17 C.M.R. 346 (Ct. Mil. App. 1954).
29. Paul H. Robinson, Shima Baradaran Baughman, & Michael T. Cahill, Criminal Law: Case Studies and Controversies 729 (New York: Wolters Kluwer, 4th ed., 2017) (quoting *Parsons v. State*, 2 Sp. 854 (Ala. 1887).
30. For a thorough judicial critique of the *M'Naghten* test, see *United States v. Freeman*, 357 F.2d 606, 618-622 (1966).

> (1) [a] person is not responsible for criminal conduct if at the time of such conduct as a result of mental disease or defect he lacks substantial capacity either to appreciate the criminality [wrongfulness] of his conduct or to conform his conduct to the requirements of law.[31]

The MPC test expands the test of legal insanity significantly. First, it expands the kinds of psychological impairments that can excuse a defendant; now, *volitional* (as well as *cognitive*) disability qualifies. Second, the MPC test does not require *total* impairment; instead, if a person "lacks *substantial* capacity," he may be excused. Third, it expands the scope of relevant testimony by mental health professionals. Some psychiatrists had criticized the *M'Naghten* test because it required them to commit professional "perjury" in the courtroom in order to present evidence they considered relevant to criminal responsibility.[32]

This test is considered "modern" in that it is more in keeping with supposedly new knowledge about human behavior. Unlike *M'Naghten*, it accepts that some mentally ill individuals may understand that their conduct is wrong but cannot control their behavior. Thus, they cannot be deterred nor have they chosen to do wrong.

The Meaning of Mental Disease or Defect

The MPC does not define "mental disease or defect" other than to provide that these terms "do not include an abnormality manifested only by repeated criminal or otherwise antisocial conduct." This caveat was added to ensure that someone could not claim he was mentally ill just because he had an extensive criminal history. Therefore, it excludes psychopathic or sociopathic personalities as such disorders were generally known when the MPC was adopted.[33]

At trial, it is not for medical experts to decide whether the defendant has a mental disease or defect.[34] Rather, the term is a "legal concept," and the jury is vested with responsibility to find a mental disease or defect; however, the jury may consider a witness's medical expertise in making this decision.[35]

---

31. MPC §4.01 (Mental Disease or Defect Excluding Responsibility).
32. Diamond, Criminal Responsibility of the Mentally Ill, 14 Stan. L. Rev. 59, 60-61 (1961).
33. Today this definition would probably exclude individuals with an "antisocial personality disorder," a diagnosis based primarily on an extensive history of getting into trouble with the law. Diagnostic and Statistical Manual of Mental Disorders-IV-TR 701-706 (2000).
34. Paul H. Robinson, Shima Baradaran Baughman, & Michael T. Cahill, Criminal Law: Case Studies and Controversies 725 (New York: Wolters Kluwer, 4th ed., 2017).
35. Paul H. Robinson, Shima Baradaran Baughman, & Michael T. Cahill, Criminal Law: Case Studies and Controversies 725 (New York: Wolters Kluwer, 4th ed., 2017).

Expanding the Meaning of Mental Illness

Many mental health professionals have applied the MPC terms more broadly to include recently recognized diagnoses of mental disorder, particularly those that identify volitional impairment. Thus, as new mental disorders are recognized as appropriate for treatment, the MPC test permits them to be used to establish legal insanity.

The Meaning of "Appreciate"

The MPC test's use of "appreciate" rather than "know" suggests that a mere statement that the defendant has knowledge that an act is wrong will not suffice to find a defendant legally sane. Rather, the defendant must have a deeper understanding of its wrongfulness. The MPC and Commentaries said: "The use of 'appreciate' rather than 'know' conveys a broader sense of understanding than simple cognition."[36] Unfortunately, the Commentaries do not suggest just what that "broader sense" means.

The Meaning of "Substantial"

The MPC test does not require complete inability to know or to choose. Instead, a person may be legally insane if his impairment is "substantial." This determination may require the fact finder to make a value judgment in light of the evidence.

Criticisms

There are two primary objections to the MPC test. First, it may provide too much room for experts to recognize new kinds of mental illness that can excuse individuals from criminal responsibility. Second, many critics claim that mental health experts cannot determine with reasonable accuracy an individual's capacity for self-control or measure the extent of that impairment. As the American Psychiatric Association noted in recommending the adoption of a more restrictive version of the *M'Naghten* test for legal insanity, "the line between an irresistible impulse and an impulse not resisted is probably no sharper than that between twilight and dusk."[37]

---

36. Model Penal Code and Commentaries, vol. 2 at 169 (1985).

37. American Psychiatric Association Statement on the Insanity Defense 11 (Washington, D.C., 1982).

The Federal Insanity Test

Before John Hinckley tried to assassinate President Reagan in 1981, all but one federal court of appeal used the MPC test for legal insanity. In 1984, after Hinckley's subsequent acquittal by reason of insanity, Congress enacted a new insanity test that must be used in all federal prosecutions. In part 18 U.S.C. provides:

> **Section 17. Insanity Defense**
>
> (a) Affirmative Defense. It is an affirmative defense to a prosecution under any federal statute that, at the time of the commission of the acts constituting the offense, the defendant, as a result of a severe mental disease or defect, was unable to appreciate the nature and quality or the wrongfulness of his acts. Mental disease or defect does not otherwise constitute a defense.[38]

This new insanity test is arguably tougher than even the *M'Naghten* test adopted more than a century ago. The defendant must now suffer from a "severe" mental disease or defect. The federal test also does away with the "irresistible impulse" component of the insanity defense.[39]

Reform of the Insanity Defense

Substantive Changes

Before John Hinckley's acquittal by reason of insanity, every jurisdiction in the United States provided the defense of legal insanity. All but one federal court used the MPC test of insanity, as did more than half the states.[40] However, four states—Idaho, Montana, Utah, and Kansas—have abolished the insanity defense entirely.[41] Eight other states have abandoned the MPC test and gone back to *M'Naghten* or a tougher version. Currently, a significant majority of states with an insanity defense use some form of the *M'Naghten* test rather than the MPC test.[42]

---

38. Comprehensive Crime Control Act of 1984 (Insanity Defense Reform Act), Pub. L. No. 98-473, ch. IV.

39. Paul H. Robinson, Shima Baradaran Baughman, & Michael T. Cahill, Criminal Law: Case Studies and Controversies 728 (New York: Wolters Kluwer, 4th ed., 2017).

40. La Fond & Durham, supra n. 8, at 36.

41. Nevada also abolished the insanity defense in 1995, but the Nevada supreme court held that due process required a limited opportunity to present the defense. *Finger v. Nevada*, 27 P.3d 66 (2001).

42. Corrado, Responsibility and Control, 34 Hofstra L. Rev. 59 (2005).

Insanity Defense Myths and Facts

The insanity defense has been under heavy attack recently. The public becomes upset when individuals who intentionally engaged in harmful conduct are acquitted by reason of insanity. There are also common misconceptions about the use and consequences of this defense.

The insanity defense is not used very often. Criminal defendants use the insanity defense in less than 1 or 2 percent of all American criminal cases. When pleaded, the defense is usually not successful; only about one-third of insanity pleas succeed. Moreover, the defense is not used only by those charged with serious crimes such as murder. Defendants found NGRI have been charged with a wide variety of crimes, including felonies and misdemeanors. Minor property crimes are common among those found NGRI. Successful NGRIs are no more dangerous than criminals; they have re-arrest rates comparable to convicted felons.[43]

There is also risk in pleading insanity. NGRI defendants who successfully plead the insanity defense often spend significantly longer time in confinement for serious offenses than defendants convicted of similar offenses.[44]

The Guilty But Mentally Ill Defense

Historical Origin

In 1975, Michigan enacted a guilty but mentally ill defense (GBMI). At least 14 states have enacted the defense since then.[45]

Jury Options

The GBMI defense permits a jury to find a defendant who raises the insanity defense "guilty but mentally ill" rather than NGRI. In a few states that have abolished the insanity defense, the defendant may still raise a GBMI defense.[46] A GBMI verdict determines that the defendant is responsible for committing the crime but also recognizes that she was mentally ill at the time.

---

43. See La Fond & Durham, Cognitive Dissonance: Have Insanity Defense and Civil Commitment Reforms Made a Difference?, 39 Vill. L. Rev. 71 (1994).

44. Steadman, Empirical Research on the Insanity Defense, 477 Annals Am. Acad., Pol. & Soc. Sci. 58 (1985).

45. McGinley & Pasewark, National Survey of the Frequency and Success of the Insanity Plea and Alternate Pleas, 17 J. Psychiatry & L. 205 (1989); see also Current Application of the Insanity Defense http://criminal.findlaw.com/criminal-procedure/current-application-of-the-insanity-defense.html (last visited Dec. 9 2017).

46. Montana takes this approach. See *State v. Korell*, 690 P.2d 992 (1984).

Dispositional Consequences

The dispositional consequences of a GBMI verdict vary. Usually, a GBMI defendant may be sentenced to prison for up to the maximum authorized term. This keeps her under the control of the criminal justice system and ensures her confinement for a definite period of time. In some states, a verdict of GBMI requires a mental health evaluation of the defendant to determine if she needs treatment.

In a few states, a defendant found GBMI cannot be sentenced to imprisonment unless the trial judge specifically finds that the defendant was not suffering from a mental disease that rendered her unable to appreciate the criminality of her conduct or to conform her conduct to the requirements of law.[47] This approach effectively moves the issues raised by the insanity defense from the jury's consideration at the guilt phase to the judge's determination at sentencing. In other states, a GBMI verdict does not have any legal consequences for the defendant.[48] A defendant found GBMI may be sentenced to death.[49]

Arguments Pro and Con

Supporters argue that the defense enhances public safety by permitting dangerous mentally ill individuals to be confined in prison rather than prematurely released from mental health facilities. Critics claim that the GBMI defense requires the jury to consider an issue that is not relevant to guilt, sentencing, or release. Critics also claim that the GBMI defense confuses the jury and invites compromised verdicts, thereby allowing juries to avoid the difficult question of whether a mentally ill offender should be held criminally responsible.

The Empirical Consequences of the GBMI Defense

The GBMI defense was enacted to encourage juries not to find defendants NGRI. However, the impact of the GBMI defense on the insanity defense is mixed. It has not made much difference in the frequency of NGRI verdicts in Michigan. The number of NGRI verdicts actually increased in Illinois following enactment of the GBMI defense but declined in Georgia. On balance,

---

47. Id.

48. *See* Slobogin, The Guilty but Mentally Ill Verdict: An Idea Whose Time Should Not Have Come, 53 Geo. Wash. L. Rev. 494 (1985).

49. *Harris v. State*, 499 N.E. 723 (Ind. 1986); *People v. Crews*, 122 Ill. 2d 266, 522 N.E. 1167 (1988).

the GBMI defense does not seem to have achieved its goal of decreasing the number of successful insanity defenses.[50]

On the other hand, research indicates that GBMI offenders are more likely to go to prison, to receive life sentences, and to receive longer sentences for the same crime than neurotypical offenders.[51] Thus, defendants found GBMI may be treated as both "bad" and "mad."

Examples

1. Jason, who lives with his father and stepmother, is 22 years old and has suffered from schizophrenia for several years. Jason comes in and out of touch with reality. Often he does not recognize where he is, what day it is, or who is around him. In addition, he is deeply religious and reads the Bible often. He has been committed to the state psychiatric hospital on several occasions because of his irrational, delusional, and frightening behavior, though he has never actually harmed anyone.
   a. One day, he is sure he sees the Devil come into his bedroom to take away his soul. In fact, his stepmother has come into his bedroom and simply asked him to go to the store for her. Jason, fearing for his salvation, grabs the Devil by the throat and strangles him until he no longer moves. A few hours later, his father comes home and discovers his wife dead on the floor and Jason praying. Jason looks up and says, "I have just slain the Devil." He returns to his prayers.

      Presently, Jason is in touch with reality after taking psychotropic drugs. He is horrified by what he did because he loved his stepmother very much. He understands in general terms what a trial is, the role of the various participants, and what he is charged with. When asked about this event, however, Jason only remembers attacking the Devil, who was trying to take away his soul.
   b. One day, Jason hears the voice of God commanding him to slay his stepmother because she is in league with the Devil and must be destroyed as evil incarnate. Even though he knows that killing a human being is against the law, Jason obeys the divine command and strangles his stepmother to death, exclaiming, "Hallelujah, Lord!" throughout the episode.
   c. One day, Jason decides, based on his reading of the Bible, that his stepmother is a religious heretic who, according to his reading of scripture, must die for her sins. Jason strangles his stepmother to death.

      Is the insanity defense available in any of these examples?

50. La Fond & Durham, supra n. 8, at 138-139.

51. Callaghan et al., Measuring the Effects of the Guilty but Mentally Ill (GBMI) Verdict, 16 Law & Human Behavior 447, 452 (1992).

2. Peter Salli is 22 years old and has suffered from paranoid schizophrenia for several years. He is an extremely devout Catholic. Having believed for the past five years in a worldwide conspiracy to destroy the Catholic Church, Peter feels he is God's chosen defender of Catholicism from these conspiratorial forces. Acting more strangely than ever, Peter buys an automatic weapon and a large amount of ammunition. He also locates the addresses of several abortion clinics in his area.

   Shortly thereafter, Peter enters two separate abortion clinics, screaming, "Abortion is wrong! You should pray the rosary and stop this killing!" Peter then kills two clinic staff members and wounds several others. He flees and is apprehended while trying to avoid detection.

3. Sybil is 22 and suffers from dissociative identity disorder (DID). Physically and sexually abused by her mother during childhood, she has developed several different identities to cope with this stress. Each of these identities is a well-integrated personality (with its own pattern of perceiving, relating to, and thinking about the environment and one's self) within the primary or "host" personality. Each personality may at various times take full control of the individual's behavior.

   One of Sybil's alter egos, Bridget, is particularly troubling to Sybil's psychiatrist because Bridget is a pyromaniac, always setting fires. In fact, the psychiatrist has forced Gilda, another personality or alter ego, to stop smoking. The doctor does not want to risk that Bridget will emerge and find matches on Sybil's person. Sybil, the host personality, does not smoke.

   Much to her psychiatrist's dismay, Sybil is finally charged with arson for burning down a garage. Sybil, the host personality, doesn't recall the event at all. When the government psychiatrist talks to Bridget, she admits that she set the fire on purpose. "I knew it was against the law, but it looks cool!" Bridget is not remorseful about this act, and she understands that Sybil will go to prison.

   As prosecutor, you must decide whom to charge and whether you can convict Sybil for what Bridget did.

4. Daniel roamed the streets of a major city with his wife, Jean, preaching to the homeless about the necessity of joining God's new tribe on earth for eternal salvation. Daniel, diagnosed with schizophrenia, paranoid type, believed that God spoke to him directly, commanding him to take young brides and create God's new tribe here on earth. Jean, who was devoutly religious but did not suffer from any mental disorder, sincerely believed that Daniel was God's chosen instrument for salvation here on earth. Together, they forcibly and secretly took 15-year-old Sarah from her family late one night and took her to their apartment to begin God's new tribe.

5. Lucky bets on the horses. Lucky bets on the dogs. Lucky bets on football games. Lucky bets on everything—and usually loses! Lucky is a compulsive gambler, unable to stop his excessive and destructive betting.

   In fact, he has been diagnosed with "pathological gambling disorder," a disorder of impulse control recognized in 1980 by the mental health professions in the Diagnostic and Statistical Manual of Mental Disorders published by the American Psychiatric Association. These individuals have an overwhelming urge to gamble, and their compulsive gambling disrupts their family and work life. They always think the next bet is the "grand slam" that will finally put them ahead.

   Lucky knows. He owes his bookie so much that he secretly embezzled money from his job to place the grand slam bet. When he lost again, he wore a mask and robbed a bank to get money for his next bet. Arrested shortly thereafter, Lucky is charged with gambling, embezzling, and armed robbery. Can he plead insanity?

6. Amber Bates home-schooled four children, ages 2 to 7. After the birth of each child, Amber became extremely depressed. Diagnosed with a major recurrent depressive disorder, she had to be civilly committed from time to time to prevent her from committing suicide or hurting her children. Nonetheless, Rob, her husband, after each birth pressured her to have another child. For the past several years, Amber has continued to suffer from bouts of serious depression and periodically has had to be hospitalized. Amber was released again from a psychiatric hospital ten days ago at her husband's request. Despairing of her own worth as a mother and convinced that her children would be better off in heaven than in her home, Amber drowned each of her children in the bathtub. She then called the police and said, "Come quickly. I have done something terrible. I have killed my children."

7. At a young age, Eugene was diagnosed with schizophrenia. The illness caused him to have delusions that his life was in danger. On multiple occasions, his illness caused him to believe members of his family were trying to kill him, to which he responded violently to protect himself. He was eventually placed on medication, which, combined with weekly counseling, permitted him to lead a relatively normal life for years. However, the medication made him feel less like himself and he always hated it. One day, Eugene decided to stop taking his medication. Soon afterwards, Eugene is at his desk when he is overcome with the belief that his coworker, Allen, is trying to kill him. When Allen approaches Eugene at the cafeteria, Eugene is under the delusion that Allen is finally going to dispose of him. Afraid for his life, Eugene grabs a steak knife and attacks Allen, stabbing him repeatedly in the chest. Several people pull Eugene away, but amidst the chaos, Eugene stumbles backwards, falls, and hit his head on the corner of a table, causing serious injury to his head and brain.

Explanations

1a. Jason suffers from a serious mental disorder, schizophrenia, which causes significant distortions in perception and thinking. His medical history provides persuasive evidence of his long-standing illness.

Jason is competent to stand trial. He understands the nature of the charges and has a present ability to consult with his attorney with a reasonable degree of rational understanding. Though his factual recall is obviously incorrect in some important ways, he can recall what he thought he was doing and why he was doing it. A trial judge is likely to find Jason competent to stand trial on the murder charge.

This is a REALLY DIFFICULT case! It is not clear that the government can prove the mens rea of murder beyond a reasonable doubt. After all, Jason may not have intended to kill *another human being*. Rather, as a result of mental illness, he may honestly have believed he was killing "the Devil." Thus, the prosecutor's only alternative may be to seek involuntary civil commitment of Jason to a mental health facility where he will be confined and receive treatment until he is no longer mentally ill or dangerous.

If the jury does find the mens rea and actus reus of murder, then whether the state has an insanity defense becomes important. Under the M'*Naghten* test, Jason would be found not guilty by reason of insanity. As a result of his mental illness, Jason did not, at the time of the crime, understand the nature of his act, let alone that it was wrong. He actually perceived himself to be slaying the Devil. Because he did not realize he was killing a human being, there was no reason for him even to consider if what he was doing might be against the law or morally wrong. On the contrary, Jason undoubtedly thought he was doing the right thing. Punishing Jason will not deter others like him nor has he earned punishment by choosing to do a wrongful act. Jason will be confined in a secure mental health facility until he is no longer mentally ill or dangerous.

Under the MPC test, Jason would also be found NGRI. As a result of mental disease or defect, Jason lacked substantial capacity either to appreciate that his conduct was wrong or to obey the law by not killing someone he thought was the Devil. Again, most purposes of punishment would not be served by convicting Jason.

In a GBMI state, the jury could simply find Jason "guilty but mentally ill" rather than insane. This verdict establishes that the defendant committed a voluntary act with the required mens rea or culpability. In most states, the verdict has no significance. The defendant may be sentenced to prison for the maximum term and even sentenced to death for a capital offense. In a few states he will automatically be evaluated to see if he needs treatment. If he does, he may be sent to a mental health facility for treatment, and minimum sentences may be waived under certain circumstances.

Because some of these outcomes may be possible in states that have adopted the GBMI defense in many of the following examples, we will not repeat them for the rest of this section of Examples and Explanations.

1b. Though suffering from a serious mental illness, Jason knows that he is killing his stepmother. He also knows that killing another human being is against the law. In a number of jurisdictions, Jason would be held responsible for his acts and found guilty if he knew that his conduct was against the law. Some utilitarians would support this result, arguing that, because he knew he would be punished, Jason (and those like him) are deterrable. Some retributivists might argue that Jason chose to break the law and thus deserves his punishment.

Other jurisdictions permit a divine command exception and will not punish a mentally ill person who commits a harmful act thinking he is obeying a command from God. Not only is such person's ability to know in a relevant way disturbed; they may even be acting under duress. After all, one does not disobey a command from God lightly!

Some utilitarians would agree that many disturbed individuals would do what they thought God told them to do, regardless of the criminal law. Thus, it is very difficult to change their behavior even by a threat of incarceration. Some retributivists would also agree, concluding that these unfortunate individuals simply do not have the necessary ability to make a rational moral choice and, therefore, do not deserve punishment.

In the few states that have abolished the insanity defense, the only issues to be litigated at trial are the defendant's actus reus and mens rea. The defendant's mental illness might be relevant to his mens rea at the time of the crime. It will not be admitted to establish a claim of legal insanity.

1c. This is a more difficult case. In many ways, Jason is very much as he was in Examples 1a and 1b. However, in this example, his acts are based on a delusional religious belief system; he does not act because of a divine command. Some jurisdictions would permit conviction in this case, even though it is not clear whether Jason is deterrable or has made a meaningful choice to do wrong.

2. The defense will claim that, at the time of the killings, Peter suffered from a pronounced mental illness that made him perceive the world in a very distorted way. His perception of persecution may have put him in a very defensive position toward the world in general and in a state of constant vigilance.

Peter's perception of persecution, though grossly incorrect, may also have led him to believe he was acting in justifiable self-defense. This is an interesting question. Even if Peter's view of the threat was correct, he would not be justified in using deadly force because there is no threat of death or serious bodily injury. In this case, there is a good argument that Peter's response to his perception was inappropriate, even conceding his distorted view of the world. The insanity defense, however, does not require that the defendant's action be lawful if the facts were as the defendant thought them to be. His inability to gauge reality may also impair his ability to morally evaluate possible courses of action.

In a *M'Naghten* jurisdiction, the defense will assert that Peter's delusional sense of persecution, both of his church and of himself, left him unable to know that his act was wrong. This will be a close case, but if Peter knew that his conduct was against the law, he might be convicted. A jury may conclude that he is just like a conscientious objector who chooses to place his value system above society's and to disregard the criminal law. Or it may find Peter NGRI, concluding that Peter does not possess sufficient rationality to make a meaningful moral choice.

The result would not necessarily be any clearer in a jurisdiction that used the MPC test. This test lets the defense argue that, as a result of mental disease or defect, Peter lacked substantial capacity either to appreciate the criminality of his conduct or to conform his conduct to the requirements of law. The word "appreciate" may require a better understanding than simply "knowing" his conduct was wrong. It may also include some genuine emotional grasp that his conduct was wrong.

The prosecutor will retort that Peter may have been mentally ill, but he knew his act was against the law. She will claim that there is no evidence of compulsion in this case: no divine command, no delusional religious beliefs that killing, even in the defense of one's church, is appropriate. Moreover, there is abundant evidence of planning, preparation, and attempt to avoid detection and apprehension. Thus, she will argue that Peter should be convicted.

3. Now this is an interesting case! If one of the personalities within an individual suffering from DID knows what she is doing and appreciates that the conduct is criminal, can the "host" or "dominant" personality be held accountable for the actions of this other "alter" personality?

   One federal district court said no. The host personality must appreciate the wrongfulness of the conduct that is under the control of the alter personality. The court held that the insanity defense must be presented to the jury, even though the "acting" personality was *not* insane at the time of the offense.[52] Thus, Sybil cannot be found guilty of the crime

52. *United States v. Denny-Shaffer*, 2 F.3d 999 (10th Cir. 1993).

committed by Bridget because Sybil did not know what Bridget was doing or that it was wrong. The fact that Bridget, an alter ego, did know what she was doing and that it was wrong will not impose criminal responsibility on Sybil. Criminal responsibility depends on the mental status of the host personality.

Note, however, that some jurisdictions take a contrary approach and assess responsibility on the personality that is in control at that time[53] or refuse to recognize the defense altogether.[54] In jurisdictions that focus on the personality in control, the defense might prevail with an insanity defense if it uses the ALI test. Pyromania is a recognized impulse control disorder that substantially interferes with an individual's capacity to obey the law. Thus, "Bridget" may be successful pleading insanity.

4. In states that allow the defense of insanity, Daniel might be found not guilty by reason of insanity. At the time of the crime, he suffered from a serious mental disorder characterized by delusional beliefs and auditory hallucinations. He may honestly have believed that God had commanded him to take Sarah as his wife by whatever means necessary.

   Under the *M'Naghten* test, Daniel, as a result of his mental disorder, may not have known the nature of his act (he thought that he was simply taking a new wife) or that it was wrong (God does not command someone to do anything that is a crime or morally wrong). Under the ALI test, Daniel could also argue that he had no choice but to follow God's orders; thus, as a result of a mental disorder, he suffered from a significant volitional impairment.

   However, in states that have abolished the insanity defense, Daniel would not be allowed to raise this defense. Evidence of his mental illness would be relevant only to actus reus and mens rea. His lawyer would argue that Daniel understood his conduct to be taking a new wife. The prosecutor would disagree, pointing out that Daniel surely knew and intended to take a young girl from her family and bring her to his home without consent. That is why he did it secretly and used force. Thus, Daniel should be convicted of kidnapping.

   Jean's devout religious beliefs do not amount to a mental disorder. Thus, her "motive" for aiding and abetting Daniel would not be relevant to guilt or innocence but would be considered at sentencing.

5. In a *M'Naghten* jurisdiction, Lucky is out of luck. There is no evidence that he did not know what he was doing when he embezzled from his employer or robbed the bank, or that he did not know that these

---

53. See, e.g., *State v. Grimsley*, 3 Ohio App. 3d 265, 444 N.E.2d 1071 (1982); *Kirkland v. State*, 166 Ga. App. 478, 304 S.E.2d 561 (1983).
54. *State v. Greene*, 984 P.2d 1024 (Wash. 1999).

actions were wrong. To avoid apprehension, he tried to keep these crimes secret or his identity unknown. Thus, he would not succeed with a *M'Naghten* insanity defense.

In a jurisdiction that used the MPC test, Lucky just might get lucky. He suffers from "pathological gambling disorder." This impulse-control disorder substantially interferes with Lucky's capacity to "conform his conduct to the requirements of the law." Thus, he might be successful in using the MPC insanity defense to all charges, including not only the gambling charge, which is a "symptom" of his disorder, but also the other two charges involving crimes against property and persons committed to support his compulsive conduct.[55]

Defendants with a diagnosis of compulsive gambling have successfully used the MPC insanity defense to a charge of writing bad checks[56] and to a charge of first-degree larceny.[57] Other defendants have used the defense to charges like forgery, embezzlement, and armed bank robbery.[58] Some were successful; others were not.

6. Amber suffers from a serious mental disorder manifested by recurrent episodes of severe depression. At the time of her crime, she experienced an overwhelming sense of sadness and despair. Nonetheless, in a *M'Naghten* jurisdiction, Amber would probably be convicted of four counts of murder. Though she suffered from a serious mental disorder that clearly affected her mood, she knew what she was doing (killing her children) and that it was against the law and against society's morality. (She called the police and told them that she had done "something terrible" and they should come right away.) Her attorney could argue that "know" must include an emotional appreciation of the wrongfulness of her conduct, but most courts would not agree. Thus, she would probably be convicted in *M'Naghten* states. (In 2002, a Texas jury using the *M'Naghten* test convicted Andrea Yates under very similar facts. In a retrial after a successful appeal, another jury acquitted her in 2006. Close case.)

   Amber has a better chance of succeeding in an MPC jurisdiction. The defense would argue that as a result of her severe depression, clearly a mental disease or defect, Amber's capacity to *appreciate* the criminality of her conduct was *substantially impaired*. She might prevail if the jury concluded that "appreciate" included an ability to truly grasp the legal

55. See McGarry, Pathological Gambling: A New Insanity Defense, 11 Bull. Am. Acad. Psychiatry & L. 301 (1983).

56. *State v. Campanaro*, Nos. 632-679, 1309-1379, 514-580 & 707-789 (Superior Court of New Jersey Crim. Div., Union County, 1980).

57. *State v. Lafferty*, No. 44359 (Connecticut Superior Court, June 5, 1981). But see *United States v. Lyons*, 731 F.2d 243, 245 (5th Cir. 1982).

58. See McGarry, supra n. 48, and cases cited therein.

and moral significance of her conduct. On the other hand, since Amber called the police and literally confessed on the telephone, the jury may conclude that Amber understood that killing her children was against the law and social morality and that this basic comprehension is sufficient for criminal responsibility. Amber's ability to control her conduct did not appear impaired. She had to plan how to kill her children and deliberately repeat the homicidal act four times. This seems like a very deliberate choice to act. Despite the greater leeway provided by the MPC test, Amber would probably be convicted of murder.

Of course, in the four states that have abolished the insanity defense, Amber would almost certainly be convicted. Her mental disorder does not negate the voluntary act to drown each child or prevent her from acting with purpose.

Should Rob be considered an accomplice because he continually pressured her to have more children, knowing the impact that would have on Amber's mood and resulting dangerousness, and also requested Amber's discharge from the hospital? If Amber succeeded in using the insanity defense, should the criminal law hold Rob responsible as the last responsible human agent? Is it morally just to convict Amber?

7. Under the *M'Naghten* test, Eugene might argue that he did not know that his conduct was wrong. He certainly understood that he was engaging in violent, potentially lethal conduct. In fact, he meant to engage in such conduct, but he did not appreciate the wrongfulness of his conduct because he was under the delusion that his life was in danger. The criminal law has concluded that individuals are justified in defending themselves from harm. Eugene would argue that not only did not he know the wrongness of his conduct—he was convinced that he was doing the right and necessary thing, morally and legally. Thus, he would argue that he is not blameworthy for the killing because he did not know his conduct was wrong.

   Under the MPC, Eugene would likely qualify for the insanity defense. He would argue that because of his mental illness he lacked "substantial capacity . . . to appreciate the criminality [wrongfulness] of his conduct." This argument may look very similar to Eugene's argument under the *M'Naghten* test, but because the standard is lower under the MPC, he would likely qualify for the defense.

   Do not be distracted by the fact that Eugene affirmatively chose not to take his medication. Remember, the insanity defense looks at the defendant's state of mind at the time of the crime. At the time of the crime, Eugene's ability to perceive the wrongness of his actions was reduced. Some prosecutors have attempted to assert that mentally ill defendants who purposely fail to take their medication should bear responsibility for any crime they commit in the meantime. The argument is that because the mentally ill defendant knows of his mental illness and how it can cause him to act criminally, he purposely puts himself in a position to commit crimes if he fails to take his medication, and, thus, he should be held accountable for his criminal conduct. While few courts have addressed this argument, it has largely been held to be unpersuasive.[59] After all, not taking medication is not illegal and the defendant is not responsible for his mental illness.

Lastly, there may be a question of whether Eugene can stand trial. During the scuffle, as people attempted to intervene and stop him from stabbing Allen, Eugene suffered brain damage. Depending on the seriousness of the damage, Eugene may not be able to stand trial because he cannot understand what is happening in the trial and the significance of a guilty verdict.

INFANCY

Young children can commit harmful acts ranging from simple mischief, like setting off a firecracker in a mailbox, to serious havoc, like killing another person. Should they be held criminally responsible for such conduct?

The criminal law ordinarily requires more than harmful conduct before it will impose blame and punishment. In addition to requiring mens rea, the criminal law will not blame and punish individuals who are so very different from ordinary people that they are incapable of understanding the moral significance of their behavior.

Most young children do not have the intelligence, judgment, emotional maturity, and moral capacity to make the rational choices the criminal law requires. For this reason, the law does not hold very young children criminally responsible even for behavior designed to cause serious harm. This is accomplished by providing the defense of "infancy."

On the other hand, every "child" eventually becomes an "adult" and becomes responsible for his or her behavior. The criminal law has taken

59. This argument is similar to the one asserted against defendants who voluntarily consume alcohol or drugs and commit crimes. (See below). However, courts have refused to accept this argument. *Com v. Shin*, 16 N.E.3d 381, 389 (Mass. App. 2014) (the court stated that "[i]t strains the analysis considerably to apply it to a defendant such as this, because his mental illness is not *caused* by his failure to take medication. . . . The appropriate analysis was simply whether, at the time of the incident, the defendant was criminally responsible."); see also *State v. Edgar*, 398 P.3d 756 (Hawai'i 2017) ("the failure to take medication may not be considered in determining the defense of lack of penal responsibility due to a mental disease, disorder, or defect.").

different approaches to determining when a child can no longer assert the infancy defense and may be held criminally accountable for his behavior.

The Common Law

At very early common law, infancy was seemingly not a defense to a criminal prosecution. Instead, a young offender usually was pardoned for his crime.[60]

Over time, the common law developed the defense of infancy, which could be used to excuse children for crimes they had committed. The common law used chronological age at the time of the crime to determine when a child could be held criminally responsible.

Under Age 7

By the early fourteenth century, a child under the age of 7 was considered not to have the capacity to commit a crime. He was considered incapable of forming the mens rea necessary to commit a crime and was also considered undeterred by the threat of punishment. The common law used a conclusive presumption—that anyone under age 7 was incapable of committing a crime—to preclude criminal responsibility. The prosecutor could not in fact introduce evidence that a particular child under age 7 had the mental capacity and moral sensibility necessary for making rational choices sufficient to justify criminal blame and punishment.

Between Ages 7 and 14

Children between the ages of 7 and 14 were presumed incapable of committing a crime, but this presumption was not conclusive. It could be overcome by evidence establishing that the child understood what he was doing and that it was wrong. (Note the similarity of this test to the *M'Naghten* test for legal insanity. See pages 554-555, 558.) The prosecutor carried the burdens of production and persuasion, the latter probably beyond a reasonable doubt.

Over Age 14

Children over the age of 14 were considered capable of committing crimes and could be tried as adult offenders unless insane.

60. Kean, The History of the Criminal Liability of Children, 53 L.Q. Rev. 364 (1937).

The Model Penal Code

The Model Penal Code takes a very different approach to the age when children can be held fully responsible under the criminal law for criminal conduct. Section 4.10 provides a defense of "immaturity." Simply put, no one under the age of 16 can be tried and convicted of a crime. Children who are age 16 or 17 at the time of the crime can be tried in the juvenile court or, if the juvenile court waives jurisdiction over the offender and consents, in an adult court. Interestingly, the MPC does not establish a juvenile court system. It simply assumes that this system exists.

Contemporary Law

Juvenile Court Jurisdiction

Where a defendant succeeds on a defense of immaturity, he or she is generally transferred to juvenile court; in most cases, it does not mean the defendant is released.[61] All states have established juvenile court systems. They handle most cases involving children who engage in conduct that would be a crime if committed by an adult. Such conduct is often defined by statute as "delinquency."[62]

Most juvenile court laws do not set a minimum age for jurisdiction over delinquency cases, though they usually set under 18 as the maximum age of their jurisdiction. Thus, unless the state follows the common law approach, children under age 7 can be adjudged delinquent.

Juvenile courts were initially concerned primarily with the welfare of the child. Rehabilitation was their primary goal. Young offenders were channeled out of the adult criminal justice system and placed in special juvenile facilities designed to change their antisocial behavior and to restore them as productive members of society. Consequently, inquiry into a child's capacity to commit a crime was not considered relevant in a juvenile court proceeding.

Currently, many state legislatures have concluded that rehabilitation is not effective and that society needs to be protected from violent juvenile offenders. They have revised their juvenile court laws to emphasize responsibility rather than rehabilitation.[63]

---

61. Paul H. Robinson, Shima Baradaran Baughman, & Michael T. Cahill, Criminal Law: Case Studies and Controversies 774 (New York: Wolters Kluwer, 4th ed., 2017).

62. Juvenile courts also deal with other kinds of cases involving young people, including children in need of supervision and the termination of parental rights.

63. Walkover, The Infancy Defense in the New Juvenile Court, 31 UCLA L. Rev. 503 (1984); Ainsworth, Re-Imagining Childhood and Reconstructing the Legal Order: The Case for Abolishing the Juvenile Court, 69 N.C. L. Rev. 1083 (1991).

Juvenile court laws generally permit judges to waive or decline jurisdiction (often based on the offender's age and on the seriousness of the crime) if the best interests of the child or the public require. If the juvenile court declines to assert its jurisdiction, the defendant will be charged and tried as an adult offender in the regular criminal court system. If convicted, he will be sentenced to adult penal institutions and can serve the same sentences as adult offenders.

Criminal Responsibility

Many states follow some version of the common law. Their statutes set a minimum age of criminal responsibility, often 7 or 8 years old at the time of the crime. Children under the specified age are conclusively presumed incapable of committing a crime.

Some states, however, do not set a minimum chronological age. Instead, they presume young children under a specified age, such as 14 in California,[64] are incapable of committing a crime unless the state can prove the child knew what she was doing and that it was wrong. This approach focuses on the "mental age" of the child rather than her physical age.

In most states, older children, often between 7 or 8 and 12, 13, or 14 (depending on the specific statute), are *presumed* incapable of committing a crime. However, the prosecutor may introduce evidence that a young defendant within this age group understood the nature of her conduct and that it was wrong. If the prosecution carries the burden of persuasion on these issues, the child is considered to have sufficient mental and moral capacity to make rational choices sufficient for criminal responsibility. Consequently, she can be tried as an adult offender, usually subject to the juvenile court's declining its jurisdiction. If convicted, she can be punished just as severely as an adult offender.

In response to the growing number of juvenile offenders committing "adult crimes" at younger ages, many legislatures have lowered or eliminated the minimum age at which a juvenile can be tried as an adult. The empirical research supports this perceived trend of more juveniles committing more violent offenses. In 1994, persons under the age of 18 accounted for 11 percent of the willful killings cleared by law enforcement authorities nationally.[65] In addition, in 1990, there was a 27 percent increase over

64. Cal. Penal Code §26 (West 2009).

65. Federal Bureau of Investigations, U.S. Dept. of Justice, Uniform Crime Report 279 (1994).

1980 figures for juveniles arrested for violent crimes, and three out of four juveniles used guns to commit those crimes.[66]

Determining Capacity

As noted above, a minor who is under a certain age is presumed incapable of committing a crime, unless the prosecutor admits "clear and convincing" evidence that shows otherwise.[67] The determination of whether a child had the capacity to understand the wrongness of his or her conduct is fact-specific.[68] A number of factors are generally considered in the determination:

> (1) the nature of the crime, (2) the child's age and maturity, (3) whether the child evidenced a desire for secrecy, (4) whether the child told the victim (if any) not to tell, (5) prior conduct similar to that charged, (6) any consequences that attached to that prior conduct, and (7) whether the child had made an acknowledgment that the behavior is wrong and could lead to detention.[69]

Particularly, the seriousness of the crime can determine whether the defendant is prosecuted as an adult. Courts are generally more likely to find that a juvenile should be tried as an adult where the crime is violent and harmful toward another person.[70]

---

66. Federal Bureau of Investigations, U.S. Dept. of Justice, Uniform Crime Report 410 (1992). However, the rate of juvenile violent crime fell slightly in 1995 for the first time in almost a decade, and in that same year the rate of homicide by juveniles decreased for the second year in a row, down by 15.2 percent. After a Decade, Juvenile Crime Begins to Drop, New York Times, Aug. 9, 1996, at A1.

67. *State v. Ramer*, 86 P.3d 132, 114 (Wash. 2004).

68. *State v. Ramer*, 86 P.3d 132, 114 (Wash. 2004).

69. *State v. Ramer*, 86 P.3d 132, 114 (Wash. 2004); see also *Com v. Martz*, 118 A.3d 1175, 1183 (Penn. 2015). Some federal courts rely on a similar set of factors: "[1] the age and social background of the juvenile; [2] the nature of the alleged offense; [3] the extent and nature of the juvenile's prior delinquency record; [4] the juvenile's present intellectual development and psychological maturity; [5] the nature of past treatment efforts and the juvenile's response to such efforts; [and] [6] the availability of programs designed to treat the juvenile's behavioral problems." *United States v. Ramirez*, 297 *United States* F.3d 185, 193 (2d Cir. 2002).

70. *Ring v. State*, 894 S.W.2d 944, 947 (Ark. 1995) ("The serious and violent nature of an offense is a sufficient basis for trying a juvenile as an adult."); see also *United States v. Juvenile Male*, 754 F. Supp. 2d 569, 575 (E.D.N.Y. 2010) ("[t]he heinous nature of the crime of intentional murder . . . may be a factor entitled to special weight.") (quotations omitted)); but see *State v. Ramer*, 86 P.3d 132, 114 (Wash. 2004) (holding that for sex crimes, the State had a heavier burden of proving the minor's capacity).

EXAMPLES

Examples

1. Lem, aged 6, Ben, aged 7, and Jamal, aged 9, enter a neighbor's house to steal a tricycle while the parents are shopping. While in the house, Lem seeks out Matt, a 6-month-old baby, lying in a crib. He drags Matt out of the crib and drops him on the floor. He then kicks him repeatedly in the stomach and head, inflicting very serious injuries. He and the other two boys flee the house with the tricycle when they hear Gabriel, the 13-year-old babysitter, waking up from a nap in the bedroom. Gabriel sees Lem leaving Matt's bedroom.

   Matt is taken to the hospital where he is on life-support systems for several weeks. He eventually recovers but suffers serious long-term brain damage.

   The prosecutor has witnesses who will testify that Lem had threatened to kill Matt because he did not like "the way Matt's parents look at me." Gabriel will also testify that, shortly after the incident, Lem threatened to burn down Gabriel's house if she told the police about seeing Lem in Matt's house that day.

   Can the prosecutor charge Lem with aggravated assault and have him tried in an adult court? Or must Lem be tried in the juvenile justice system?

2. Haylee, who is 9 years old, breaks into an elementary school and steals food from the cafeteria. While in the school, someone sees Haylee and yells after her. Haylee immediately runs away. By the time she escapes the elementary school, the police have shown up and catch her fleeing. At first, when the police ask if she had broken into the school, Haylee lies. When she finally admits that she did, the police ask her whether she knows what she did was wrong, to which Haylee responds with, "I guess." Soon the police discover that the year before, Haylee had been transferred to juvenile court for breaking into someone's home. Should Haylee be tried as an adult? What facts are most relevant?

EXPLANATIONS

Explanation

1. In most states Lem could not be held criminally responsible for his attack on Matt. Because he was 6 years old at the time of the crime, Lem would be conclusively presumed incapable of committing a crime. Lem could probably be tried as a juvenile offender; he could not be tried and convicted as an adult for a criminal offense.

   Some states, however, do not set any minimum age of responsibility. Instead, they permit the prosecutor to introduce evidence that the defendant knew what he was doing and that it was wrong. Here the prosecutor might be able to prove that Lem had a motive to commit the crime and that the attack on Matt was premeditated and intentional.

Moreover, Gabriel's testimony might also establish that Lem knew that his behavior was wrong. By threatening Gabriel, Lem was trying to avoid detection. This indicates that Lem knew that attacking Matt was wrong. Lem might be tried for attempted murder in the first degree, subject to the juvenile court's jurisdiction in this state.

Whether Ben and Jamal can be tried and convicted for burglary and theft of the tricycle will be decided by the same analysis. Because Ben was 7 and Jamal was 9 when they went into Matt's house and stole the tricycle, it is more likely that the prosecutor would be able to try both as adults.

If successful in persuading a court that any of these young children should be tried as adult offenders, the prosecutor would also have to persuade the court that the defendants are competent to stand trial.[71] She would have to show that they understand the charges against them and the nature of the proceedings and that they could assist their attorneys.

Under the Model Penal Code, all of the defendants would have a valid defense of "immaturity" because they were under 16 years old at the time of the crime. Thus, none of the defendants could be tried and convicted of any crime. Instead, they would be dealt with in the juvenile court system.

2. Depending on the state, Haylee will likely be presumed to be incapable of committing a crime; however, the prosecution may rebut the presumption by presenting evidence that she had the capacity to understand the criminality of her conduct. First, the prosecution may note that Haylee attempted to conceal her criminal conduct by fleeing and lying to the police about what she had done. At the same time, when asked about the wrongness of what she did, Haylee did not admit she understood it to be wrong. Rather, she responded with, "I guess," which may be an indicator that Haylee did not really appreciate that her conduct was wrong. Nevertheless, Haylee's past conduct of breaking into a home may show that she knew what she was doing was wrong because she had been punished for similar behavior in the past. Still, the crime at issue was not violent; she did not cause bodily harm to anyone, so the court may be more inclined to permit adjudication of the crime in juvenile court to focus on the Haylee's rehabilitation, particularly given Haylee's age. The court (or prosecutor) may also consider the reason for her theft and her family situation in determining whether there was a lack of food at home or other difficult circumstances and not bring a charge at all.

   Under the MPC, Haylee would have a defense of "immaturity" because she is under the age of 16. Her case would be handled in juvenile court.

---

71. See pages 555-557 for a discussion of competency to stand trial.

INTOXICATION

From time immemorial most societies have enjoyed alcoholic beverages, but alcohol can change the way many people behave. It can loosen social and moral inhibitions, impair physical performance, and cloud judgment. Studies have consistently demonstrated a high correlation between alcohol consumption and crime.[72] Precisely because it may increase the frequency of harmful behavior, alcohol consumption poses special problems for the criminal law.

Early common law treated the inebriated offender and the sober offender in the same way. Intoxication was not relevant to criminal responsibility. Late common law modified this approach, permitting evidence of intoxication to reduce criminal responsibility for some crimes.

Except for occasional experiments with prohibition, contemporary criminal law has generally recognized that alcohol is a widely used and, some might argue, socially useful beverage. Because alcohol can seriously impair mental and physical abilities, however, the criminal law must impose its behavioral expectations on those who use it. The criminal law has developed doctrines that take into account the fact of intoxication in assessing responsibility but do not completely excuse crimes committed by people simply because they were intoxicated.

The law distinguishes between "voluntary intoxication" and "involuntary intoxication." *Voluntary intoxication* refers to individuals who know, or should know, that the substance they are consuming (e.g., alcohol, drugs, medication) is likely to produce intoxicating effects. *Involuntary intoxication* refers either to consuming such substances without realizing it or to an unanticipated and unforeseen response to these substances. This is treated differently from voluntary intoxication.

Frequently, the criminal law has struck an imperfect compromise. It holds voluntarily intoxicated offenders responsible but often allows them to be convicted and punished less severely than sober offenders. Not everyone is satisfied with this approach. The impact alcohol consumption should have on criminal responsibility remains a controversial subject.

---

72. One study showed that 64 percent of 882 felons arrested in a two-year period in Cincinnati were intoxicated. Many studies find a close association between the alcohol consumption rate and the homicide rate. Robert N. Parker & Randi S. Cartmill, Alcohol and Homicide in the United States, 1934-1995, 88 J. Crim. L. & Criminology 1369, 1374-1377 (1998). A study by the Drug Use Forecasting System found that from 53 percent to 79 percent of men arrested in twelve major cities tested positive for illegal drug use. Even excluding those who tested positive for marijuana, the results still ranged from 25 percent to 74 percent. Crime Study Finds Recent Drug Use in Most Arrested, New York Times, Jan. 22, 1988, at A1, col. 6.

The advent of drug use has complicated matters even more. Drugs can have many of the same consequences on behavioral controls as alcohol. In addition, some drugs are hallucinogenic and can severely distort the user's perceptions of reality.

In the common law tradition, courts generally analogized drug use to alcohol in deciding how the criminal law should respond to drugs. Because drug use is today much less socially accepted than drinking, the criminal law is less tolerant of those who commit crimes while under the influence of drugs. In our discussion here we include intoxication caused by alcohol, drug use, or prescription medicine unless otherwise indicated.

Intoxication as an Element

Many criminal laws forbid the use of intoxicating substances under certain circumstances. Thus, laws criminalize certain activity while intoxicated, such as driving while under the influence of alcohol or drugs. In these cases proof of intoxication is an element of the crime.[73] Hence, the prosecutor is allowed to introduce such evidence to establish a necessary element of her case. These cases are governed by ordinary criminal law rules governing proof of crime. The defendant may deny using intoxicating substances or, in the alternative, concede their use but maintain they did not adversely affect his mental or physical capabilities.

The Relevance of Voluntary Intoxication to Mens Rea or Culpability

The Common Law

Early common law held the intoxicated defendant to the same standard of responsibility as the sober defendant. Hale wrote that the intoxicated defendant "shall have no privilege by this voluntarily contracted madness, but shall have the same judgement as if he were in his right senses."[74] Indeed, some commentators stated the law viewed intoxication "as an *aggravation* of the offense, rather than an excuse for any criminal misbehavior" (emphasis added).[75] This approach was also adopted in early American common law, and evidence of intoxication was not admitted in criminal trials.

---

73. Many modern statutes criminalize drivers who operate a motor vehicle with a specified amount of alcohol in their blood. These statutes do not require any proof of intoxication.

74. 1 M. Hale, Pleas of the Crown *32-33.

75. 4 W. Blackstone, Commentaries *25-26.

During the nineteenth century, however, English courts modified this hard-line approach and permitted defendants to introduce evidence of voluntary intoxication in criminal trials. American courts followed suit, but judges did not want intoxicated offenders to avoid all criminal responsibility so they created "specific intent" crimes and admitted this evidence only when those crimes were charged (see Chapter 4). Such evidence was not admitted in "general intent" crimes. By the end of the nineteenth century most American jurisdictions allowed evidence of intoxication to be considered in determining whether the defendant was capable of forming the specific intent to commit the charged offense.[76] Thus, an intoxicated defendant, charged with assault with intent to commit rape, could present evidence of his intoxication to show that, because he was drunk, he thought the victim had consented and consequently he did not intend to rape her. If, however, he simply intended to assault the victim, he could not introduce evidence of intoxication to negate the elements of assault because assault is a "general intent" crime.

A defendant might argue that he would not have committed either crime if he were sober. Thus, his moral claim is that he is really being punished for getting drunk.[77] This is a plausible claim. Many people do things when intoxicated that they would not dream of doing while sober. However, the common law concluded that the act of getting drunk was itself a culpable act. By drinking, the defendant was "reckless" as to the effect alcohol might have on him.[78] Moral blameworthiness could at least be attributed to his decision to drink despite realizing the impact alcohol can have.

Limiting evidence of voluntary intoxication to specific intent offenses is criticized as arbitrary and illogical. If alcohol consumption is logically relevant to the presence or absence of mens rea (or, as we called it earlier, to "element negation," see Chapter 4), then it should be admissible *whenever* it tends to show the defendant did not act with the culpability required for commission of the charged offense. Critics point out that excluding relevant and probative evidence of mens rea simply because a court has characterized the charged offense as one of "general intent" defies both logic and experience. Indeed, this doctrine creates pressure on courts to characterize

---

76. Hall, Intoxication and Criminal Responsibility, 57 Harv. L. Rev. 1045 (1944).

77. There is some evidence that courts would not permit the defendant to introduce evidence of voluntary intoxication if he had formed his criminal intent *before* drinking and had consumed alcohol solely to summon up courage to commit the offense. *Roberts v. Michigan*, 19 Mich. 401 (1870).

78. Of course, the legislature could enact a law that punished the act of getting drunk more severely precisely because of this risk. A defendant could then be charged with this offense rather than a crime involving recklessness or negligence. However, this approach has been rejected.

a crime as one of "general intent" precisely so that evidence of intoxication will *not* be admissible to negate an element of the charged offense. See *People v. Hood*, 1 Cal. 3d 444, 462 P.2d 370 (1969). Policy concerns may override the logic of mens rea in such cases.

Supporters point out that the "specific intent only" approach ensures that the intoxicated defendant will usually be convicted of *some* crime because most specific intent offenses have lesser included general intent crimes. To allow evidence of intoxication in *every* case might lead to not convicting the intoxicated defendant of *any* crime. This result would be intolerable to most people. Individuals might simply put themselves beyond the reach of the criminal law by drinking and then committing their crimes while drunk. Public safety could be seriously damaged.

Thus, the common law eventually compromised. In specific intent crimes, which were usually punished more severely than general intent crimes, the intoxicated individual would "get a break." By introducing evidence of voluntary intoxication, he might reduce the seriousness of the conviction. However, he would usually not walk out of the courtroom a free man simply because he was drunk. In most cases, there was a general intent crime that covered his harmful behavior. A defendant can be charged with the (commonly lesser) general intent crime based on the theory that she acted *recklessly* when she consumed alcohol and became intoxicated.[79] Even then, this approach is flawed because many specific intent offenses do not include a lesser, general intent version.[80]

Note that under the later common law, voluntary intoxication is not a defense. Rather, it is a doctrine that permits the defendant to introduce evidence to negate an element. Thus, the prosecution does not have the burden of proving the defendant was not intoxicated nor does the defendant have the burden of proving voluntary intoxication. (Of course, the prosecutor still must prove the required mens rea.) However, the defendant will have the burden of producing evidence of voluntary intoxication if the jury is to consider it.

In *Montana v. Egelhoff*, 518 U.S. 37 (1996), the Supreme Court held that a Montana statute that precludes the jury from considering evidence of voluntary intoxication in determining the existence of *any* mental state that is an element of the charged crime does not violate due process. The Court concluded that the respondent did not carry his burden of showing that the more recent common law allowing such evidence was "so deeply rooted at the time of the Fourteenth Amendment (or perhaps has become so deeply

---

79. Paul H. Robinson, Shima Baradaran Baughman, & Michael T. Cahill, Criminal Law: Case Studies and Controversies 432 (New York: Wolters Kluwer, 4th ed., 2017).

80. Paul H. Robinson, Shima Baradaran Baughman, & Michael T. Cahill, Criminal Law: Case Studies and Controversies 432 (New York: Wolters Kluwer, 4th ed., 2017).

rooted since) as to be a fundamental principle which that Amendment enshrined."[81] Fourteen other states currently take the same basic approach as Montana.

About two-thirds of states allow evidence of intoxication on specific intent issues, like purpose or knowledge, but do not allow it on general intent issues, like recklessness or negligence. There is also an emerging trend to require that the intoxication be pronounced and that it significantly impair the defendant's faculties. Some states are more restrictive and admit evidence of intoxication only in first-degree murder cases.[82]

The Model Penal Code

The Model Penal Code provides more precise definitions than the common law did. *Intoxication* means a "disturbance of mental or physical capabilities resulting from the introduction of substances into the body." MPC §2.08(5)(a). *Self-induced intoxication* means taking substances one knows, or should know, have a tendency to cause intoxication unless taken pursuant to medical advice or when one would otherwise have a valid defense to a charge of crime, such as duress. Although the MPC does not use the term *involuntary intoxication*, it recognizes intoxication that is "not self-induced." *Pathological intoxication* means intoxication that is grossly excessive given the amount of intoxicant the actor consumed and assuming that she did not know of her special susceptibility.

Section 2.08 allows the defendant to introduce evidence of self-induced intoxication whenever it "negatives an element of the offense." Evidence of intoxication is admissible but only if the crime requires proof of intention, purpose, or knowledge. Section 2.08(2) excludes such evidence if the offense requires recklessness, and the actor is unaware of a risk he would have been aware of had he been sober. People now know the impact alcohol and other intoxicating substances can have on human behavior. Drinking or taking drugs in the face of this knowledge is treated as the moral equivalent of being reckless (and negligent) about risk.

Thus, a defendant charged with "knowingly entering the house of another" could present evidence of voluntary intoxication to establish that he thought he was breaking into his own house. Such evidence would negate the element of "knowingly entering the house of *another*" (emphasis added). The MPC is intended to be more permissive than the common law because

81. 518 U.S. at 37.

82. See Keiter, Just Say No Excuse: The Rise and Fall of the Intoxication Defense, 87 J. Crim. L & Criminology 482 (1997).

it does not exclude such evidence in "general intent" crimes.[83] Instead, it allows it in whenever it is logically relevant to the presence or absence of an element, except for recklessness or negligence. The MPC approach may lead to an outright acquittal, depending on the crime charged and its lesser included offenses.

The Relevance of Voluntary Intoxication to Defenses

Many defenses require the actor to perceive his situation reasonably and to respond to it reasonably. What, if any, impact should voluntary intoxication have on defenses?

Voluntary intoxication is not a defense. In fact, it often makes it more difficult for the defendant to prevail when he does present a defense because most defenses require the defendant to act as a reasonable person would in the situation. Several examples will illustrate this point. In many jurisdictions, a defendant who claims self-defense must *reasonably* believe that he is in imminent danger of death or serious bodily injury (see Chapter 16). If voluntary intoxication causes him to perceive such a threat when a sober individual would not, then the defense will fail. Likewise, voluntary manslaughter requires that the defendant acted in the "heat of passion upon *reasonable* provocation" (see Chapter 8). As already noted, the act of becoming voluntarily intoxicated is itself considered a kind of recklessness and negligence. Finally, the mistake of fact defense usually requires the defendant's mistake to be reasonable. Voluntary intoxication usually precludes this. Thus, voluntary intoxication undercuts most defenses because, in most cases, the defendant is held to the standard of a reasonable *sober* person.

There may be some limited exceptions. In jurisdictions that consider "fighting words" to be legally sufficient provocation (see Chapter 8), voluntary intoxication may be relevant if the provoking words relate to the defendant's condition of being intoxicated. For example, using words that demean an alcoholic and his condition of voluntary intoxication might be considered legally adequate provocation in some jurisdictions. (Even here, however, the defendant may be held to the standard of the reasonable alcoholic.) Generally speaking, however, the criminal law will hold an actor who is voluntarily intoxicated to the standard of the reasonably sober person when the actor asserts a defense.

---

83. If, however, crimes requiring "purpose, intent, and knowledge" are considered to be the functional equivalent of the common law's "specific intent crimes," then the MPC produces virtually the same result as the common law.

Involuntary Intoxication

People can also become involuntarily intoxicated. Thus, someone may drink a beverage without having the slightest inkling that it contains alcohol or other inebriating substances. Or someone may have an extremely unusual reaction to prescription drugs. The common law permitted defendants to introduce such evidence as an affirmative defense, regardless of the crime charged, to establish the defense of involuntary intoxication.[84]

The defendant must prove that he unwittingly consumed an intoxicating substance (or that he took medication and had a highly unlikely and unforeseeable reaction) that produced the same symptoms as required by the *M'Naghten* test of legal insanity; that is, he did not know what he was doing or that it was wrong. (See pages 554-555, 558.) Since the defendant was not at fault in becoming intoxicated, fairness requires the defendant to have an opportunity to present this defense in *all* cases. Because involuntary intoxication can be used for all criminal charges, it is broader than voluntary intoxication, which is generally limited to specific intent offenses at common law or to negate intent, purpose, or knowledge under the MPC.

However, the involuntary intoxication defense requires the defendant to establish that the involuntary intoxication caused very severe impairment of his cognitive ability. This seems unfair considering that the defendant was not to blame for consuming the substance or for not appreciating the risk of such an unusual reaction.

The Relevance of Voluntary Intoxication to Actus Reus

Defendants have also sought to introduce evidence of intoxication to show that they did not commit a voluntary act. The common law excluded this evidence because voluntary intoxication does not undermine the exercise of free will in human behavior.

It is possible, however, to argue that a defendant was so intoxicated that he could not have physically performed an act. Thus, if the defendant had passed out from drinking too much alcohol or using drugs, he could introduce this evidence to show that he could not have committed the voluntary act of the charged offense.

84. Reported cases of involuntary intoxication are extremely rare.

Alcoholism and Insanity

The Supreme Court has held that the constitutional prohibition on cruel and unusual punishment contained in the Eighth Amendment does not preclude punishing someone for appearing drunk in a public place even though the defendant claimed that, as an alcoholic, he could not control his drinking. *Powell v. Texas*, 392 U.S. 514 (1968). Though the Court has implicitly held that one cannot be punished for having the *status* of a chronic alcoholic, *Robinson v. California*, 370 U.S. 660 (1962), the Court concluded in *Powell* that a defendant may still be punished for *conduct* involving the use of alcohol if the behavior is not a symptom of the disease of alcoholism.

The Court noted that there was no medical consensus on whether alcoholism compelled a person to drink, thereby destroying an individual's free will. It therefore refused to strike down such laws as unconstitutional, preferring instead to permit states to experiment.

In some cases, heavy consumption of alcohol over an extended period can actually cause organic brain damage. A person suffering from this condition may actually raise the defense of legal insanity if his condition has become "settled" or "fixed" and results in the same cognitive or volitional impairments recognized by the insanity test used in the jurisdiction. Many such individuals suffer from delirium tremens, which can cause hallucinations. These individuals may raise the defense of insanity even if they were not intoxicated at the time of the crime.

It is not unusual to find that mental illness causally contributes to voluntary intoxication. Many people have the dual diagnosis of "mentally ill" and "substance abuser." The defenses of legal insanity and voluntary intoxication are available to these individuals in appropriate cases.

The Model Penal Code permits a defendant to introduce evidence of intoxication that is "not self-induced" (e.g., someone spiked the nonalcoholic punch) or "pathological" (e.g., someone has a very unusual reaction to prescribed medication for the first time) to negate recklessness. MPC §2.08(2).

It also permits the defendant to introduce this evidence to establish the special affirmative defense provided in §2.08(4). The defendant must prove by a preponderance of the evidence that, as a result of either involuntary or pathological intoxication, she lacked substantial capacity either to appreciate the criminality of her act or to conform her conduct to the requirements of law. (This is almost the same as the MPC's insanity defense but here is caused by intoxication that is "pathological" or is not "self-induced" rather than by a mental disease or defect. See pages 560-562. It is not an insanity defense because §2.08(3) states that "intoxication does not, in itself, constitute mental disease within the meaning of §4.01.") If established, this affirmative defense will excuse the defendant from criminal responsibility even if the prosecutor has proven all the elements of the charged offense.

Examples

1. Bo is drinking heavily in a bar. He meets Amanda, who also is drinking, and they dance and drink for several hours. Bo asks her if she would like to come to his apartment. Amanda readily agrees. At his apartment, they have several more drinks. Then . . .
   a. Bo undresses Amanda and is about to have intercourse with her when she begins screaming. An off-duty police officer, hearing her cry, bursts through the door and arrests Bo for assault with intent to rape Amanda.
   b. Same facts except the police officer does not hear Amanda's scream until after Bo has sexual intercourse with Amanda. He bursts through the door and arrests Bo for rape.
   c. Bo starts to undress Amanda, intending to have sex with her. Sometime later, he is awakened by an off-duty police officer who bursts through the door and arrests him for attempting to rape Amanda. Bo denies he ever initiated sexual intercourse, claiming he had passed out.

   Can Bo introduce evidence of his voluntary intoxication?

2a. Paul is at a party. Melissa offers him a Cuban cigar, which was illegally imported into this country. Unknown to Paul, it contains marijuana. After smoking the cigar, Paul becomes giddy and hyperactive. He goes to the adjacent house and opens the door without knocking. He then goes inside and invites "everyone to come join the party." The neighbors, an elderly couple, are not amused. They have Paul arrested and charged with criminal trespass.

2b. Paul is at a party. Melissa offers him a marijuana cigarette, which, unknown to Paul, contains "angel dust," a hallucinogenic drug. Paul smokes the cigarette and has a psychotic-like reaction. Believing Melissa to be Satan, he savagely beats her. He is arrested and charged with aggravated assault. Can he introduce evidence that he smoked a marijuana cigarette or that it was laced with "angel dust"?

3. Brent and Teresa had been dating for over a year, but had recently broken up. Extremely upset, Brent followed Teresa in his car after seeing her at a club. Brent had been drinking and was driving aggressively. Afraid, Teresa returned to the club to get help. She told the doorman about Brent. He came outside and asked Brent to leave. Brent drove straight into Teresa's car. He was charged with DUI and with the intentional destruction of another's property. Brent argues that he was unable to control his vehicle because of his intoxication and that his collision with Teresa's car was an accident. Does it matter if this state does not allow evidence of voluntary intoxication to negate a mens rea element?

4. Tubby drank incessantly. He was always being arrested for being drunk in public and other nuisance crimes. Finally, Tubby drank so much, he suffered organic brain damage. He began to hallucinate and to imagine terrible creatures were attacking him while he slept. One evening, a police officer tried to wake him after he had fallen asleep on a park bench; Tubby attacked the police officer, mistaking him for a giant spider. Can Tubby introduce this evidence in his trial on third-degree assault for attacking a police officer while in the performance of his duties?

5. Serena is a regular drinker. Recently, she was prescribed medication for a minor ailment. Her doctor informs her that on very rare occasions the medication can react badly with alcohol and that she needs to be careful. Serena is not worried, however, and when she gets home from work one day, she takes her medication and then makes herself a cocktail and kicks back like she always does at the end of the work day. After two drinks, Serena becomes extremely intoxicated—much more than usual after two drinks. She ventures out, so inebriated that she forgets to put on her shoes, and proceeds to run amok: She batters a man on the street, vandalizes both public and private property, and sets a residence on fire. In the morning, she wakes up in jail with no recollection of what she did or how she got there. It turns out that the medication and the alcohol reacted badly, causing her to become far more intoxicated than usual. Serena is charged with arson (specific intent), criminal battery (general intent), and criminal mischief (specific intent). Does she have a defense to any of the charges?

Explanations

EXPLANATIONS

1a. Because assault with intent to rape is a "specific intent" crime, later common law would allow Bo to introduce evidence of his drinking throughout the evening to prove that he thought Amanda had consented to have sexual intercourse with him. If believed by the jury, Bo would not be convicted of "assault with intent to rape" because his voluntary intoxication prevented him from acting with the "specific intent" of raping Amanda. He did *not intend* to have sexual intercourse with a female *without her consent*. He might be charged with a lesser included offense like assault, however, if it is one of "general intent."

The MPC would also allow Bo to present evidence of his voluntary intoxication that is logically relevant to negating any element of the charged offense. Thus, if the statute required that he "*knowingly* have intercourse without consent," evidence of his voluntary intoxication may negate "knowingly." If, however, a rape statute in this jurisdiction made *recklessness* with regard to consent an element of the crime, the

MPC would not permit Bo to use this evidence to negate such recklessness. By drinking so much, Bo decreased his ability to evaluate the risk that Amanda did not consent. The act of drinking is sufficiently blameworthy to satisfy the requirement of recklessness in the rape statute.

1b. In many jurisdictions, rape is considered a "general intent" offense. Thus, the common law would not allow Bo to introduce evidence of voluntary intoxication to negate the mens rea of rape. This may seem unfair to the defendant (though not to the victim who has been subjected to unwanted intercourse). After all, Bo's mental state was the same in both Examples 1a and 1b. Though influenced by the alcohol, Bo thought Amanda had consented to sexual intercourse in both cases. Yet, simply because a court has decided rape is a "general intent" crime, he will not be allowed to introduce evidence of voluntary intoxication in Example 1b.

Under the MPC, however, the analysis is essentially the same as in Example 1a. Bo could introduce this evidence if it tended to negate any element of the charged crime. If the rape statute requires the defendant to have acted intentionally, purposefully, or knowingly with respect to any element, then this evidence is admissible.

1c. Bo could introduce this evidence under both the common law and the MPC. The common law would let him argue that the evidence established he could not physically have performed the act of intercourse because he was unconscious. Likewise, the MPC would let him introduce the evidence because it is relevant to an "element" of the charged offense. He would argue that he could not, and therefore did not, engage in the voluntary act of sexual intercourse.

2a. Though Paul probably knew that the cigar was illegally imported, he had no idea it contained a prohibited substance or drug that could cause intoxication. If this were a case of *voluntary* intoxication, under the common law, Paul could use this evidence if he was charged with a specific intent crime. Criminal trespass, however, is probably not a specific intent offense. Thus, he probably cannot use this evidence to negate the element of "knowingly" entering another's house without permission. The MPC would allow Paul to use evidence of self-induced intoxication to negate any element of a charged offense. Paul would argue that this evidence negates that he "knowingly" (a) entered another person's house (b) without permission.

Unfortunately, this is more likely a case of *involuntary* intoxication. Paul had no idea he was consuming a substance that would, or was likely, to cause intoxication. To succeed under common law, he would have to prove that the marijuana made him unable to know what he was doing or that it was wrong. Paul probably did know that he was going into someone else's house and that he did not have permission. Thus, he would probably be convicted. Only if he was "really out of it" would he be acquitted. This is unjust. Ironically, Paul is probably in a better position under *voluntary* intoxication than he is under *involuntary* intoxication.

2b. This is a complicated case because it is, arguably, a case of both voluntary and involuntary intoxication. Paul knew that he was committing a crime—that is, smoking marijuana, an intoxicating substance. However, he did not know, or have reason to know, that he was consuming a far more powerful mind- and mood-altering drug. (See Chapter 6 for a review of the "greater crime" doctrine.)

Under common law, Paul can use evidence of *voluntary* intoxication to negate specific intent. If the aggravated assault statute proscribes an assault "with intent to inflict serious bodily injury" or other such language, it is probably a specific intent offense. If the court considered this a case of voluntary intoxication, Paul would be allowed to introduce this evidence to negate that specific intent. However, he could not use it in a general intent crime. Most likely, a general intent charge of assault is a lesser included offense, and the jury could not consider this evidence on that charge.

Under the MPC, however, Paul can use evidence of self-induced intoxication to negate any element of the charged crime except recklessness and negligence. Because a jury could consider this evidence on all charges, Paul has a better chance under the MPC than under common law.

If the jury considers this a case of *involuntary* intoxication, then both under common law and the MPC Paul can introduce this evidence to show that he did not know what he was doing (he thought he was attacking the devil) or that it was wrong. Thus, he may be better using involuntary intoxication as a defense. The problem, of course, is that the judge may rule that this is a case of voluntary intoxication because Paul knew that he was taking an illegal substance; therefore, he consciously disregarded the risk that he might consume another illegal substance.

3. If the state follows the Montana approach and excludes evidence of voluntary intoxication in determining mens rea or a culpability element (unless intoxication is an element of the charged offense), it will be much easier for the prosecutor to persuade a jury that Brent did, in fact, *intend* to damage Teresa's car. The jury could likely infer "intent" based on his conduct leading up to the incident without being allowed to consider the effect of his alcohol consumption on his judgment, perception, and motor skills. If, however, the state allows evidence of voluntary intoxication on the issue of mens rea or culpability, then Brent could introduce evidence of his drinking just prior to the event to support his claim that his collision with Teresa's car was accidental rather than intentional.

Ironically, even in a state that excludes evidence of voluntary intoxication on mens rea or culpability, the prosecutor could introduce evidence of Brent's drinking to prove that he was "driving under the influence" of alcohol because intoxication is an element of the charged offense. Thus, in some states, the prosecution could use this evidence to convict Brent of the DUI charge, while preventing Brent from using the same evidence to negate the mens rea of the intentional destruction of property charge. Is this consistent, logical, or fair?

4. Under the common law, Tubby could not introduce this evidence to negate mens rea because he is not charged with a specific intent offense. Because Tubby's extended drinking has actually caused organic brain damage with resulting impairment in his cognitive abilities, he may now also have a defense of legal insanity. Depending on the jurisdiction, this might be a successful defense, though it may also lead to mandatory commitment in a mental health facility if the jury finds Tubby "not guilty by reason of insanity."

   Under the MPC, Tubby could introduce this evidence if it negatives an element of the crime, including recklessness. Because Tubby was intoxicated and did not know that he was attacking a police officer while in the performance of his duties, this evidence should be admissible and Tubby may be acquitted.

   However, the MPC would not allow Tubby to raise the special affirmative defense of intoxication because his intoxication was self-induced. He may still have a defense of legal insanity if experts conclude that organic brain damage caused by excessive alcohol consumption is properly characterized as a "mental disease or defect" as used in the MPC.

5. Many jurisdictions permit evidence of intoxication on specific intent crimes. If Serena is allowed to admit evidence of her intoxication, she may have a defense against the arson and criminal mischief charges because both crimes require intent. If she can plead the defense successfully, she may get the arson charge down-graded to "reckless burning" or some other lesser crime. Similarly, she may get her criminal mischief down-graded or dismissed. However, Serena will not be able to introduce evidence of her intoxication on her criminal battery charge. Battery, unlike the other two charges, is a general intent crime and most jurisdictions do not permit evidence of intoxication against general intent crimes.

   Under the MPC, Serena might argue that her response to the drugs was *pathological*—that she became excessively and unexpectedly intoxicated because of the reaction between the medication and the alcohol. She could argue that she generally did not become so intoxicated after two drinks, something she knew from years of regular drinking.

The prosecution might argue that she cannot succeed on this defense because she was aware of her "special susceptibility" since her doctor had informed her that her medication and alcohol can react badly sometimes.

Under the MPC, Serena should be permitted to admit evidence of her intoxication to negate the mental state requirement for arson and criminal mischief because both crimes require intent. The MPC does not permit such evidence for crimes that require less than intent or knowledge to commit, so it is unlikely the evidence would be admitted on her charge of criminal battery.

Serena might even try to assert involuntary intoxication as an affirmative defense. While she was aware that the medication can react badly with alcohol, as her doctor informed her, such reactions are rare. She could argue that the rare reaction between the alcohol and the medication severely impaired her cognitive abilities. This may not work because the extreme intoxication was not a response she had to the medication alone, but one the medication and the alcohol caused together, a possibility Serena's doctor had raised.

DIMINISHED CAPACITY

The diminished capacity defense permits a more subjective inquiry into the blameworthiness of criminal defendants. The difference between the diminished capacity defense and the insanity defense is subtle at first, but can be readily distinguished by looking at the source of the disability.[85] The insanity defense is restricted to circumstances where the defendant's ability to perceive reality in a meaningful way or appreciate the wrongness of the criminal conduct is, depending on the test, totally or substantially reduced because of a mental disease or illness.[86] The diminished capacity defense, on the other hand, is not so restricted; it applies where the defendant's abilities are reduced by various conditions, such as immaturity, subnormality, duress, and more.[87]

The fact finder can take into account certain characteristics of the defendant, including mental illness and voluntary intoxication, in determining

85. Paul H. Robinson, Shima Baradaran Baughman, & Michael T. Cahill, Criminal Law: Case Studies and Controversies 764 (New York: Wolters Kluwer, 4th ed., 2017).

86. Paul H. Robinson, Shima Baradaran Baughman, & Michael T. Cahill, Criminal Law: Case Studies and Controversies 764 (New York: Wolters Kluwer, 4th ed., 2017).

87. Paul H. Robinson, Shima Baradaran Baughman, & Michael T. Cahill, Criminal Law: Case Studies and Controversies 764 (New York: Wolters Kluwer, 4th ed., 2017).

the degree of the defendant's culpability and the crime committed. Courts initially developed this doctrine to ameliorate the restrictiveness of the *M'Naghten* insanity test, to avoid imposing capital punishment on mentally disabled killers, and to individualize judgments of criminal responsibility.[88] Today, the diminished capacity defense also includes voluntary intoxication in many jurisdictions. See pages 582-587.

Despite its relatively young history, the diminished capacity defense has proven confusing and troublesome to courts, scholars, and law students alike. There are several reasons for this chaos. First, there are several versions of the defense, each with a fundamentally different conceptual basis. Second, it is not really a "defense" at all. Third, it may permit a broad range of expert testimony to be introduced that, arguably, is not relevant in determining criminal responsibility under the law.

There have been three primary versions of this defense: (1) the "diminished responsibility" defense used in Great Britain, (2) the "diminished capacity" defense used in California, and (3) the "diminished capacity" defense that is still used in a number of jurisdictions today.

A Brief History

The best way to understand this confusing area is to look at each of these versions.

The British Version: Diminished Responsibility

The diminished responsibility defense was a creation of Scottish common law. See *HM Advocate v. Dingwall*, [1867] J.C. 466 (Scot). In 1957, Great Britain enacted the defense in statutory form when capital punishment was still used in premeditated murder cases.[89] Under the British statute, a defendant could introduce evidence showing that, though not legally insane, he was nevertheless mentally disturbed at the time of the offense. If the jury found that mental retardation or mental illness "substantially impaired the [defendant's] mental responsibility" for the crime, it could find him guilty of manslaughter, even though the prosecution had actually proved all the elements of premeditated murder. Thus, mentally ill defendants who were not legally insane could avoid execution. In essence, the British doctrine of "diminished responsibility" is really a form of mitigation in punishment.

88. See Arenella, The Diminished Capacity and Diminished Responsibility Defenses: Two Children of a Doomed Marriage, 77 Colum. L. Rev. 827 (1977).
89. The Homicide Act of 1957, 5 & 6 Eliz. II, ch. II, §2(1).

The California Version

The California Supreme Court developed its version of the diminished capacity defense primarily to soften the perceived rigidity of the *M'Naghten* insanity defense. If a mentally ill offender was not found insane, he was held fully accountable under the criminal law. Initially, the California Court simply permitted mental health experts to testify that the defendant could not entertain the mens rea required for conviction of the charged offense. Thus, expert testimony could now be admitted not only on the insanity defense but also on the material element of mens rea or culpability. *People v. Wells*, 33 Cal. 2d 330 (1949).

In subsequent cases, however, the California Supreme Court began to use the diminished capacity defense to *redefine* the mens rea elements of homicide in California law. In *People v. Wolff*, 61 Cal. 2d 795, 394 P.2d 959 (1964), the court reversed the first-degree murder conviction of a schizophrenic 15-year-old who had planned and deliberately carried out the killing of his mother so he could realize his sexual fantasies of murder and rape. The court agreed that the jury had properly rejected his insanity defense under the *M'Naghten* test because the defendant knew that his acts were against the law. Nonetheless, it held that the undisputed psychiatric evidence admitted at trial established that the defendant was mentally ill and, consequently, could not "maturely and meaningfully reflect upon the gravity" of his contemplated act. The court thereupon reduced his conviction to second-degree murder.[90]

Later, in *People v. Conley*, 64 Cal. 2d 310 (1964), the court decided that the defendant was entitled to introduce evidence of mental illness and voluntary intoxication to reduce a charge of first-degree murder to voluntary manslaughter. The court concluded that such evidence could establish that the defendant did not act with "malice aforethought" because he was "unable to comprehend his duty to govern his actions in accord with the duty imposed by law."[91]

Then, in 1974, the California court held in *People v. Poddar* that "[i]f it is established that an accused, because he suffered a diminished capacity, was . . . *unable to act in accordance with the law*," he could only be convicted of manslaughter.[92] Under California's ever-expanding diminished capacity defense, volitional as well as cognitive impairment caused by mental illness could negate the "malice aforethought" necessary for conviction of both first- and second-degree murder.

The California Supreme Court had used the diminished capacity defense to infuse new meaning into the statutory elements for homicide. In so

90. 61 Cal. 2d 795, 821, 394 P.2d 959, 975, 40 Cal. Rptr. 271, 287 (1964).
91. 64 Cal. 2d 310, 322, 411 P.2d 911, 49 Cal. Rptr. 271 (1964).
92. 10 Cal. 3d 750, 758, 518 P.2d 342, 348 (1974) (emphasis added).

doing, the court had effectively created a "mini-insanity" defense.[93] It had changed homicide's mens rea terms from simple descriptive terms describing planning, motive, and manner of killing into normative terms requiring both subjective awareness of wrongdoing and ability to obey the law.[94]

The California approach enhanced the law's ability to take into account an individual's characteristics in assessing criminal responsibility. On the other hand, it was virtually impossible to apply the doctrine consistently and with an even hand. Juries returned different verdicts in very similar cases.[95] Moreover, once psychiatric evidence was admitted to negate mens rea in homicide cases, it became virtually impossible to exclude it in cases involving other crimes, such as burglary.[96] If a defendant was successful in using the diminished capacity defense, he would be convicted of a lesser included offense or, if there was no such offense, he would simply be acquitted and released immediately. Initially, the California Supreme Court tried to limit the availability of the defense to "specific intent" offenses,[97] but the court eventually permitted the defense to introduce any evidence seemingly relevant to the presence or absence of statutory mens rea.[98]

In 1978 Dan White, a former member of the San Francisco Board of Supervisors, shot and killed Mayor George Moscone, the popular mayor of the city, and Harvey Milk, a member of the Board of Supervisors, in what appeared to be a well-planned and calculated murder motivated by revenge. He was charged with two counts of first-degree murder. The jury accepted White's diminished capacity defense that, because of mental problems aggravated by erratic junk food binges, he did not act with "malice aforethought." It convicted him of voluntary manslaughter. The public was outraged. The verdict in this high-profile case, in which the claim of diminished capacity was quickly dubbed the "Twinkie defense" by its critics, provided strong impetus for changing the law. In 1982, the defense of diminished capacity was abolished by public initiative.[99]

The Rule of Evidence Approach

The simplest version of the diminished capacity defense is best understood as a rule of evidence. If evidence logically tends to establish or negate a mental state of the charged offense, then either the defendant or the government

93. See Morse, Undiminished Confusion in Diminished Capacity, 75 J. Crim. L. & Criminology 1 (1984).

94. G. Fletcher, Rethinking Criminal Law 250-259 (1978).

95. Note, A Punishment Rationale for Diminished Capacity, 18 UCLA L. Rev. 561 (1971).

96. *People v. Wetmore,* 22 Cal. 3d 318, 583 P.2d 1308 (1978).

97. See *People v. Hood,* 1 Cal. 3d 444, 462 P.2d 370 (1969).

98. *People v. Wetmore,* 22 Cal. 3d 318, 583 P.2d 1308 (1978).

99. Cal. Penal Code §25(a) (West 2012).

may introduce such evidence for the jury's consideration on the issue of mens rea. If a defendant's mental illness prevented him from acting with "premeditation," "intent," or whatever mental state is required for conviction, he may introduce expert testimony to establish that he did not have the necessary mens rea.

The form in which expert testimony is permitted can vary. In most jurisdictions, the expert will simply express an opinion as to whether the defendant, because of his mental disability, did or did not have the mental state of the charged offense. In other jurisdictions, the expert will testify as to whether the defendant, because of his mental disability, had the "capacity" to form this mental state. Note that, regardless of the form or content of the experts' opinions, the prosecution still must prove beyond a reasonable doubt that the defendant had the mens rea required for conviction.

Thus, a person suffering from an emotional disorder such as bipolar disorder (manic depression) that causes him to become very exhilarated and excited might introduce psychiatric testimony that he did not have the mental state necessary for fraud or theft, though he paid for a large purchase of clothing with a worthless check. The expert might conclude that, because of his mental condition, the defendant believed he had the money in his account or could readily get it in time to cover the check.

The rule of evidence version of the diminished capacity defense is still widely used in many jurisdictions. There is a strong argument that a defendant has a constitutional right to use evidence of mental illness if it is relevant to the presence or absence of mens rea.[100] Most federal courts and about half the states permit the use of psychiatric evidence when it is relevant to the mens rea of a specific intent crime. Some jurisdictions permit its use whenever it is relevant to the mens rea of *any* crime,[101] while others limit it to first-degree murder.

Increasingly, however, jurisdictions are concluding that psychiatric evidence should not be admitted on mens rea at all either because it is not relevant to mens rea or because it is too confusing for juries.[102] In these jurisdictions, mental illness that does not satisfy legal insanity will not be considered in determining guilt or innocence.

In *Clark v. Arizona*,[103] the Supreme Court approved this limitation. In this case, the defendant sought to have a mental health expert testify that, in his

---

100. See, e.g., *United States v. Pholot*, 827 F.2d 889 (3d Cir. 1987) (holding that the Federal Insanity Defense Reform Act of 1984 did not prevent defendants from using psychiatric evidence if relevant to the mens rea).

101. See, e.g., *United States v. Cameron*, 907 F.2d 1051 (10th Cir. 1990); *People v. Saille*, 54 Cal. 3d 1103, 820 P.2d 588 (1991).

102. See, e.g., *State v. Bouwman*, 328 N.W.2d 703 (Minn. 1982); *State v. Wilcox*, 70 Ohio St. 2d 182, 436 N.E.2d 523 (1982).

103. 548 U.S. 735 (2006).

opinion, Clark's paranoid schizophrenia rendered him unable to recognize that he was shooting a police officer rather than an alien disguised as a police officer. The Court determined that states can, without violating due process, exclude the testimony of mental health experts concluding that, as a result of a mental disorder, the defendant did not have a particular state of mind or the capacity to form mens rea. Thus, states are free to exclude opinion testimony of experts at trial on mens rea issues while admitting it on the defense of insanity, if they so choose.

The *Clark* case can be cogently criticized for denying the defendant the opportunity to present extremely relevant and reliable evidence (after all, it was admissible in the same case on the insanity defense) that could negate a material element of the charged crime. This evidentiary limitation effectively reduces the government's practical burden of proving that the defendant *knew* he was killing a police officer and, thus, intentionally killed a police officer acting in the line of duty.

The Model Penal Code

The Model Penal Code essentially adopts the rule of evidence approach and permits psychiatric evidence to be admitted whenever it is relevant to negate the mens rea of *any* crime: "Evidence that the defendant suffered from a mental disease or defect is admissible whenever it is relevant to prove that the defendant did or did not have a state of mind which is an element of the offense." §4.02(1).

The MPC concluded that psychiatric evidence should be treated just like any other relevant evidence. It argued: "If states of mind are accorded legal significance, psychiatric evidence should be admissible whenever relevant to prove or disprove their existence to the same extent as any other relevant evidence." If a defendant successfully used the diminished capacity defense to be acquitted of all charges, public safety could be adequately protected by involuntary civil commitment. See Model Penal Code and Commentaries, Comment to §4.02, at 219 (1985).

Summary

The diminished capacity defense today is best understood as a rule of evidence rather than a "defense." The doctrine simply permits courts to admit the opinions of mental health experts as evidence in a criminal trial if their testimony is relevant to the presence or absence of mens rea. Though such evidence has the potential for confusing juries and creating expert domination, it can, in appropriate cases, be relevant and useful to the jury's task of determining whether the defendant acted with the culpability required for conviction.

EXAMPLES

Examples

1. Hector suffers from paranoid schizophrenia. A uniformed officer in a patrol car with lights flashing responded to a neighbor's complaint about extremely loud music coming from Hector's house. As the officer approached his house, Hector opened the door, carefully looked at him, and shot him dead. The prosecutor has charged Hector with intentionally killing a police officer in the line of duty, and is seeking the death penalty.

   The defense seeks to introduce the evidence of a psychiatrist, who would testify that Hector suffers from a mental disorder known as "paranoid schizophrenia." He is extremely delusional, often hearing strange voices in his head threatening him with death, and believing that aliens (sometimes disguised as government agents) are trying to kill him. In the expert's opinion, Hector, as a result of this mental disorder, was psychotic or out of touch with reality at the time of the shooting, and believed that the victim was an alien disguised as a police officer who was about to kill him. The expert would also testify that paranoid schizophrenics often believe erroneously that they are being persecuted and even threatened with death. People diagnosed with this illness can also suffer from auditory hallucinations (hearing voices when no one is present), and they often play music very loudly to drown out these disturbing voices.

   The prosecutor argues that, based on a state statute, this testimony should be admitted only to establish legal insanity, and not to prove that, because of his illness, Hector did not intend to kill a police officer. He would, in turn, present a witness who heard Hector say that he wanted to kill police officers. The prosecutor intends to argue that Hector played his music loudly to lure a police officer to his home so he could kill him.

2a. Bertrand's wife, Lisu, recently divorced Bertrand, but he desperately wants to get back together. He has called her numerous times to no avail.

   Bertrand suffers from a minimal brain dysfunction with an associated explosive personality disorder with paranoid features. Minimal brain dysfunction is a biochemical imbalance in the brain that prevents Bertrand from maintaining control over his emotional impulses, especially in stressful situations.

   Finally, Bertrand visits Lisu at home, unannounced. She is very upset at Bertrand for his untimely visit and does not want to let him into the house, but finally does. She tries to explain that they cannot reconcile but he will not listen. When the discussion turns into a verbal fight, she tells him he is a "loser, incompetent, and sexually inadequate." Bertrand becomes extremely angry and upset. He grabs Lisu and indescribable violence ensues. Lisu ends up in the hospital in critical condition for her injuries. The prosecution charges Bertrand with attempted murder.

Bertrand seeks to present the testimony of a psychiatrist concerning his mental condition. The prosecution moves to exclude the evidence as irrelevant to legal insanity or to any other issue. Should the trial judge permit Bertrand to present the testimony of the psychiatrist, and, if so, on what issues?

2b. Same facts as above, except Bertrand's rage is caused by his drunkenness and not a minimal brain dysfunction. What about evidence he was drunk?

3. Linky has been plagued with a "passive aggressive personality" and "passive dependent personality" all his life. His dominating and overbearing father has humiliated and embarrassed him since he was a young boy. Finally, at 18, Linky decides to strike back. He pays Frank $500 to steal his father's pride and joy, a 1969 Ford Mustang. Linky calls Frank and meets with him to tell Frank dates and times when his father will be out of town. He also tells Frank to make sure he (Linky) isn't connected to the theft.

   Linky, empowered and liberated by this assertive act, feels fantastic after paying Frank to steal his father's car. He has finally "fought back." Linky moves out of his father's house, gets a job, and finds a girlfriend. Deciding that he no longer wants his father's car stolen, he telephones Frank and calls it off. Unfortunately, Frank is an undercover police officer. Linky is arrested and charged with conspiracy to steal a car. (This jurisdiction has adopted the unilateral approach to conspiracy. See Chapter 14.)

   A defense psychiatrist testifies at trial that, at the conscious level, Linky wanted his father's car to be stolen. But what Linky *really intended* at a subconscious level was to finally take control of his life by acting forcefully against the single overpowering person who had been controlling and dominating his life. The expert concludes that, in reality, Linky did not intend to commit a crime; he *intended* to obtain his psychological freedom by the act of hiring Frank to commit a crime. The fact that Linky called off the job after obtaining that psychological freedom is proof of what he "actually" intended.

4. Cedric is a veteran. While serving in the Marines, he was sent to Afghanistan where he witnessed combat. He has been out of the Corp. for five years but suffers from PTSD due to the experiences he had overseas. Cedric's PTSD manifests in numerous symptoms, including insomnia, headaches, depression, and extreme irritability. Cedric sees Dr. Fenton, a therapist who specializes in treating veterans with PTSD,

to help with his mental illness. Despite having no family or partner, Cedric has established a good support system in place. His best friend Rodger joined the Marines with him. Cedric gave Rodger a key to his apartment. One night, Rodger has been drinking and instead of driving home, he goes to Cedric's apartment close by, as he has done on multiple occasions before, even though Cedric has asked him not to due to Cedric's sleeping troubles. Before he goes to sleep on Cedric's couch, Rodger goes through the bedroom where Cedric is sleeping to get to the bathroom. Unknown to Rodger, Cedric is awake after not sleeping for two days. Enraged and deliriously sleep-deprived, Cedric hurriedly reaches for the revolver in the drawer of the nightstand next to his bed and shoots Rodger twice in the head. Cedric is charged with first degree murder. Cedric's lawyer moves to have expert testimony admitted to show that Cedric suffered from a mental illness. Analyze the issues.

Explanations

1. This example is based on the *Clark* case. The defense will argue that this evidence is crucial to assessing the defendant's criminal responsibility. It proves that, at the time of the shooting, his client suffered from a serious mental disorder that rendered him unable to know what he was doing or that it was wrong. Thus, under either the *M'Naghten* or MPC insanity tests, Hector should be acquitted.

   Counsel would also contend that expert psychiatric testimony on the defendant's mental illness and its impact on how he perceived the world around him is crucial to determining whether Hector acted with the intent to kill a *police officer*. The expert would testify that Hector was playing loud music to drown out these terrifying "voices," not to lure a police officer to his death. His professional opinion is that Hector perceived the approaching figure to be an alien disguised as a public official who was out to get him; thus, he did not *know* he was killing a police officer. Rather, he believed he was defending his life against an extraterrestrial attacker. This evidence is logically relevant to the presence or absence of mens rea and, without it, an innocent man may be convicted and executed.

   The prosecutor would argue that, under state law, this evidence is admissible on the insanity defense, but the defendant should not be allowed to use the "diminished capacity" defense. Otherwise, the defense will get "two bites at the apple"; that is, he will have two separate theories, legal insanity *and* lack of mens rea, available to avoid conviction and punishment for this very serious crime. The prosecutor will also claim that the opinion testimony of mental health experts can be very confusing to jurors and invite inappropriate sympathy for the defendant.

How should courts deal with this type of situation? Note that if a state does not have an insanity defense and does not allow the diminished capacity "rule of evidence" defense, expert evidence like this might be admissible only at sentencing. Even then, it might not have any impact.

2a. Although Bertrand suffers from a "minimal brain dysfunction," it probably does not prevent Bertrand from understanding the nature or quality of his act or that it was wrong to strike Lisu. Under the *M'Naghten* test, he is not legally insane.

If the jurisdiction used the MPC insanity test, Bertrand could introduce the testimony of a mental health expert to show that, at the time of the offense, he suffered from a mental disorder that substantially impaired his ability to conform his conduct to the requirements of the law. If the jury agreed, he might be found not guilty by reason of insanity.

But if the jury does not find Bertrand legally insane, it might still be able to consider the expert testimony in determining whether Bertrand intended to kill Lisu, if the jurisdiction permits the diminished capacity defense.

Because of the very serious injuries Lisu suffered, a jury might reasonably conclude that Bertrand intended to kill her rather than assault her. Thus, a jury might well convict him of attempted murder. Under the diminished capacity defense, Bertrand could introduce the expert's testimony on the mens rea. He would argue that his minimal brain dysfunction prevented him from forming the necessary mens rea for attempted murder; that is, he did not intend to cause Lisu's death. Rather, he was angry, stressed, and upset, and his brain dysfunction made him unable to control his impulses of rage. The testimony would help the jury understand that, though he may have intended seriously to hurt Lisu, Bertrand did not want to kill her. Even if this defense is successful on the mens rea element of attempted murder, Bertrand will not be fully acquitted. Rather, he will probably be convicted of a less serious crime, such as assault.

This example also illustrates that evidence concerning the defendant's mental condition at the time of the crime may be admissible on *both* the defense of legal insanity (particularly if the MPC test is used) and on the presence of mens rea if a diminished capacity defense is allowed.

2b. Whether Bertrand might be convicted of assault rather than attempted murder depends on whether this jurisdiction permits voluntary intoxication to support a diminished capacity defense.

Many states permit the defendant to present evidence of voluntary intoxication to negate intent or knowledge. (Usually, evidence of voluntary intoxication is *not* permitted to negate recklessness because voluntarily becoming intoxicated is itself considered a reckless act.) In such a jurisdiction Bertrand might be convicted of assault rather than attempted murder if a jury decided that, because he was drunk, Bertrand did not intend to kill Lisu.

Other jurisdictions hold voluntarily intoxicated individuals to the same standard of criminal responsibility as sober actors and do not permit a defendant to introduce evidence that he was drunk at the time of the crime. These jurisdictions assume everyone knows that excessive use of alcohol impairs perception, judgment, and volitional faculties. Bertrand must also be aware that alcohol will affect his mental faculties. The criminal law attributes moral responsibility to the defendant because he voluntarily drank and became intoxicated. As one court noted: "The moral blameworthiness lies in the voluntary impairment of one's mental faculties with knowledge that the resulting condition is a source of potential danger to others."[104]

Therefore, some jurisdictions do not permit defendants under a diminished capacity defense to introduce evidence of voluntary intoxication to negate mens rea.

3. Although Linky suffers from diagnosed psychological disorders, he will not prevail on his insanity defense whether under the *M'Naghten* or the MPC tests. He understood the nature of the act and that it was wrong. He also could control his behavior as evidenced by his first hiring and then firing Frank to do the job.

   Linky would also argue "diminished capacity" if this jurisdiction permitted this defense. He would claim that his mental illness prevented him from forming the mental state required for conviction of conspiracy or solicitation. However, mens rea elements like "intent" and "knowledge" do not require awareness of the unconscious influences that may influence a person's decision to commit a crime. They only require awareness of the behavior that constitutes the crime. Put simply, these criminal mental states only require that a person is aware of *what* he is doing; they do not require awareness of *why* he may be doing it.

   Linky has acted purposefully. He *intended* to come to an agreement with Frank and *intended* that Frank would commit a crime. Expert evidence on possible psychological reasons why Linky undertook this criminal enterprise will not be admitted under a diminished capacity defense because it is not relevant to the presence or absence of the mental states required for either conspiracy or solicitation. The defense may be able to use this evidence at sentencing.

---

104. *Hendershott v. People*, 653 P.2d 385, 396 (Colo. 1982).

4. Cedric's defense attorney will argue that expert testimony on Cedric's PTSD should be admitted because it relates to Cedric's state of mind. Specifically, the defense will argue that the expert testimony will show that Cedric did not act with premeditation due to his PTSD. The evidence will not likely show that Cedric is blameless—after all, Cedric knew that killing Rodger was wrong, but because of his PTSD and lack of sleep, he was not in a position to control his anger. The expert testimony will show the emotional distress Cedric was suffering and possibly demonstrate that he should be charged with a lesser homicide, one mitigated by "extreme emotional distress."

   If the jurisdiction uses the MPC for the insanity defense, the prosecution may make an argument similar to the one made in the Example 1.

ENTRAPMENT

Not all crimes are reported to the police, particularly so-called victimless crimes. These crimes usually involve willing participants engaged in activities that appear to involve no "real" victim. Prostitution, selling or purchasing drugs, and gambling are common examples of "victimless" crimes.

Because there is usually no incentive for the participants to notify the police when they commit these crimes, effective law enforcement often requires undercover police to engage in these criminal acts in order to detect and apprehend those who do. Thus, a police officer may buy crack cocaine to gather sufficient evidence to charge and convict drug dealers. (In many cases involving this defense, the police officer will also pretend to be an accomplice to the defendant's crime.[105])

This active involvement by the police in what would otherwise clearly be criminal activity if there were no legal authority for them to do so raises difficult public policy questions. After all, the role of the police is to detect and solve crime, not to manufacture crimes or to induce law-abiding citizens to commit them.

Entrapment is a defense that attempts to strike the balance between proper police undercover investigation and detection of crime and inappropriate police instigation of crime. The defense focuses both on (1) what the police did and (2) the defendant's predisposition to commit the crime. Because of this dual concern, the entrapment defense may be seen either as a rule of criminal procedure regulating police investigatory conduct or as a denial of true mens rea, claiming that the defendant did not really choose to commit a crime.

In some jurisdictions, entrapment is an affirmative defense. The defendant must produce evidence supporting the defense and must also establish

105. See Chapter 14.

it by a preponderance of the evidence. In other jurisdictions, the defendant has the burden of production, but the prosecution must establish that the defendant was predisposed to commit the offense. If successful, a claim of entrapment bars prosecution.

The History of the Entrapment Defense

American common law generally did not provide the defense of entrapment. As long as the defendant committed a crime, the police role in providing him with the opportunity to do so was simply not relevant to his guilt or innocence.

The primary impetus for recognizing this defense came from federal courts. In 1932, the Supreme Court held in *Sorrells v. United States*, 287 U.S. 435, that the defendant should have been allowed to use the entrapment defense to a charge of selling liquor to a government agent in violation of Prohibition laws. After refusing to sell liquor to the agent despite several requests, the defendant finally relented and sold him some. The Court defined the defense as follows: "Entrapment is the conception and planning of an offense by an officer, and his procurement of its commission by one who would not have perpetrated it except for the trickery, persuasion, or fraud of the officer."

One argument offered to support the entrapment defense is that of presumed legislative intent. Simply put, the legislature did not intend that enforcement of a criminal law should ensnare otherwise innocent people caught by abusive government inducement. (Of course, the legislature was silent on this question. This is really a classic judicial stratagem for reaching a decision based primarily on public policy grounds.)

Another rationale supporting the defense is to deter improper police conduct. The government will not be allowed to obtain a conviction if police investigatory methods improperly fabricated criminal activity. Thus, the defense is available only if law enforcement officials or their agents, such as informants, *induce*—rather than merely enable—the defendant to commit the crime.

The defense to federal crimes announced in *Sorrells* is not required by the Constitution. Nonetheless, today all states have adopted this defense, though there are two different approaches.

The Defense Today

The Subjective Approach

This two-step approach, used by federal courts and a majority of state courts, focuses both on the *nature of the police conduct* and on the *defendant's predisposition* to commit the offense.

The first requirement is that government conduct induce the commission of the crime. There is, as the *Sorrells* Court noted, a fine line between merely affording an opportunity to an "unwary criminal" to commit a crime and actually inducing an "unwary innocent" to commit a crime.[106]

The second requirement is that the defendant not be predisposed to commit the crime. This element shifts the analysis from what the government did to the character and criminal history of the defendant. It allows the government to argue that it was simply providing an opportunity for an "unwary criminal" to take the bait and commit a crime.

In *Jacobson v. United States*, 503 U.S. 540 (1992), the Supreme Court limited somewhat the targeting of criminal suspects. The defendant had subscribed to a magazine featuring nude pictures of boys under 18. After passage of a federal law criminalizing child pornography, the defendant stopped ordering the magazine. Government agents continually sent him material in the mail, including literature from a fake lobbying organization advocating repeal of the law and criticizing government censorship. The agents then sent him information for ordering magazines with titles indicating that they contained erotic pictures of young boys. Twenty-six months after receiving these various mailings, the defendant placed one order for two magazines that contained pornographic materials. After a controlled delivery to the defendant, he was arrested, charged, and convicted of possessing child pornography.

The majority held that the government had to establish that the defendant was predisposed to commit the crime and that *his predisposition was not the product of government conduct*. Because the defendant had never before ordered illegal material, the Court ruled as a matter of law that the government had not established this element.

Because the subjective approach allows the government to show that the defendant was predisposed to commit the crime, some critics believe this approach encourages the police to declare "open season" on individuals with a criminal history and to use any imaginable inducement to obtain their conviction. Using the defense is risky. A defendant's past criminal history usually becomes fair game, running the substantial risk of prejudicing the jury. And, in some states, the defendant must admit committing the crime.

The Objective Approach

This approach, adopted in the MPC and a minority of states, looks primarily at what the government did and assesses what its impact would be on

---

106. As a matter of causation, the criminal law usually does not look beyond the last causal agent. Yet, the defense of entrapment effectively permits the defendant to argue that the government "caused" him to commit the crime.

normally law-abiding people. It is less concerned with the criminal attitude or history of a particular offender than with controlling police conduct.

Under §2.13 of the MPC, the defense is established if a government agent, in order to gather evidence that a crime has been committed, "induces or encourages another person to engage [in an offense] either by (a) making knowingly false representations designed to induce the belief that such conduct is not prohibited; or (b) employing methods of persuasion or inducement which create a substantial risk that such an offense will be committed by persons other than those who are ready to commit it." The defendant's predispositions are irrelevant.

Because the MPC defense is phrased in general terms, its application depends on the facts of each case. Frequent entreaties over time despite initial refusals, continuing appeals to sympathy, promises of excessive profit, or other persuasive stratagems that might induce law-abiding individuals to commit a crime will support the claim. However, the MPC does not permit the claim of entrapment when "causing or threatening bodily injury" to someone other than the individual inducing the crime is an element of the charged offense.

Because the objective approach to entrapment focuses on whether the police behavior was appropriate and not on the characteristics of the offender, this formulation can be seen as an attempt to oversee how the police do their job. By creating disincentives for inappropriate police conduct, this substantive criminal law defense serves the same general purpose as a rule of criminal procedure, much like the *Miranda* exclusionary rule.

Critics of the objective approach point out that it is good police work to target individuals with a known criminal history. And, they add, it may take special inducements to persuade an experienced and savvy criminal to commit a crime.

Due Process

So far the Supreme Court has not held that constitutional due process requires the defense of entrapment. Thus, both Congress and other jurisdictions are free to do away with the defense.

Nonetheless, several Supreme Court cases suggest that, at least in cases involving outrageous police conduct, the Constitution *may* require the availability of the defense.[107] In *Russell*, a government informer had supplied the defendant with an indispensable ingredient (which was extremely difficult to obtain) for manufacturing methamphetamine ("speed"). In *Hampton*, the defendant obtained heroin from a government informant and then sold it to a government agent. Though the Court upheld convictions in both cases,

107. *United States v. Russell*, 411 U.S. 423 (1973); *United States v. Hampton*, 425 U.S. 484 (1976).

five Justices indicated that, in some cases of extremely outrageous government conduct, due process might require dismissal of the charges.[108]

Examples

1a. Linda, a prostitute, sees a man and asks if he needs a date. The man replies that Linda looks nice, but that he does not know if he can afford a date. Linda says that "a date" would only cost him $50, and they can have sex in her car parked just around the corner. The man then arrests Linda for soliciting prostitution.

1b. Linda occasionally engages in prostitution to raise extra money. One night she is walking home from a party, not intending to engage in prostitution. A man approaches Linda and asks her how much it would cost to have sex. Linda says she is not interested and keeps walking. The man follows her and says he will give her $1,000 to have sex with him in his car. Linda stops, thinks about it for a minute, and then agrees. The man, an undercover police officer, arrests her for prostitution.

Will the defense of entrapment succeed in either of these cases?

2. Lucy, a heroin addict, recently lost her job. Though she has saved some money, it is quickly running out. Unable to find her normal dealer, Lucy approaches someone else and asks to buy some heroin. The man says he will give her twice the amount if she will have sex with him in his car. Knowing she is short of cash and needs a fix, Lucy agrees. He arrests her for prostitution. Entrapment?

3. Al, a local car dealer, has a reputation for selling cars at a good price but only if buyers pay in cash or cash equivalents. Maria tells Al that she is a commodities broker and wants to buy a Jeep Cherokee for cash. Al tells her she can pay $9,000 in cash and the rest in bank checks under $10,000 each. He says she must obtain cashier checks just under $10,000 from several banks for the rest of the purchase price because, under federal law, the bank must report any transaction involving $10,000 or more to the government. Maria agrees.

A few days later she shows up to purchase the Cherokee with $9,000 cash and two bank checks for $9,900 each. Before signing the papers, Maria tells Al, "I really appreciate your telling me how to do this deal. In fact, I am a drug dealer and it's been difficult for me to spend the money I earn from dealing drugs without tipping off the cops." Al smiles and says, "Where there's a will, there is a way." After all the

108. At least one lower federal appellate court has held that the Constitution requires reversal of a conviction when government conduct was so outrageous as to violate due process. *United States v. Twigg*, 588 F.2d 373 (3d Cir. 1978). This is a minority view.

papers are signed, Maria arrests Al, who is subsequently charged with conducting a financial transaction involving property represented to be the proceeds of an illegal activity. Guilty or entrapped?

4a. An FBI agent poses as an Arab sheik and twice attempts to bribe a congressman. Both times the congressman rejects the bribes, telling the sheik, "This is neither the time nor the place. I need a place I am certain is secure so that I can't be caught." The "sheik" then arranges to meet the congressman in a hotel room. After the congressman hugs the sheik to make sure he is not "wired" with electronic recording devices, the congressman accepts the bribe. The event is recorded by secret cameras and microphones in the hotel room. Does the congressman have an entrapment claim?

4b. An FBI agent poses as an Arab sheik and twice attempts to bribe a congressman. Both times the congressman rejects the bribes, asserting they are unethical and illegal. On the third attempt the sheik says, "I fully understand your reasons for not accepting money. Will you accept a new kidney from my country for your daughter who, I understand, will die soon unless she gets a new kidney?" The congressman, knowing this is true, reluctantly agrees. The "sheik" then arrests him for accepting a bribe.

5. Shawn occasionally sells small amounts of marijuana to his friends. Oprah, a recent acquaintance, approaches Shawn and asks to buy some marijuana to relieve the pain she feels from her cancer. Shawn sympathizes with her plight, but declines. A week later, Oprah pleads with Shawn, saying her pain is getting worse. Again, Shawn declines. Finally, Oprah calls him on the telephone and, pretending to scream in agony, says: "For the love of God, sell me some marijuana. You're my only hope to ease my pain." Shawn, feeling sorry for Oprah and her suffering, sells her some marijuana. The next day he is arrested. Any defense?

6. Rashwana, pretending to be a battered wife whose husband often beats her severely, approaches Msumo and describes a powerful but false history of the violence she has suffered. Rashwana begs Msumo to kill her husband and offers him $4,000 for the job. Msumo, feeling sorry for Rashwana, agrees. He is then arrested for conspiracy to commit murder. Entrapment?

7. José, who had converted to Islam and had been homeless for several months, downloaded instructions on how to make a pipe bomb from a jihadist website at the public library, and showed it to Alex, who was a paid undercover informant for the NYC Police Department. José said: "Making this would be a great idea." Alex said: "Right and we could use it to bomb a police station or a police car." He told José that

he would find him an apartment where José could live and they could build the bomb together. José moved into an apartment Alex found for him. Alex then bought the necessary pipes, wires, and ignition device. José stole nails for shrapnel and dynamite from a construction site and started to build the bomb. José told Alex he did not have the drill bits necessary to drill the pipes and complete the bomb. Alex obtained them and together they completed the bomb. Alex then left. An hour later, the police arrested José in his apartment and charged him with plotting to build and detonate a bomb in New York.

8. Pete's Trucking has suffered great losses from thefts of valuable cargoes carried on his trucks. Seeking to find out the culprit, Pete arranges to have some particularly valuable fur coats shipped on each of his drivers' trucks. José's truck is selected to be the first. The furs are not packed in secure boxes nor is there any of the usual paperwork. José has never stolen a dime in his life. In fact, another driver has actually done all the stealing. José, who earns the minimum wage and has a family of seven children to support, suddenly realizes the golden opportunity that has presented itself. He stops the truck en route and off-loads the furs into his house, intending to sell them and use the money to support his poor family. Pete, who has been following José's truck from a distance, sees this and calls the police immediately. José is arrested and charged with theft. The prosecution moves to bar the defense of entrapment. Why?

9. Brenna is under investigation by the FBI. Her recent behavior suggests that she may be a terrorist threat to the United States but she has never committed any terrorists acts in the past and her criminal history is minimal. Thornton, an undercover informant for the FBI, contacts Brenna and eventually establishes a friendship with her. One day, Brenna says to Thornton, "I want to do something to America." But when Thornton asks for details, Brenna refuses to elaborate. The following week, Thornton brings up what Brenna said, urging her to explain what she meant, but Brenna again declines. Thornton then suggests that Brenna meant she wanted to detonate a bomb downtown, to which Brenna smiles but does not confirm. Over the next couple of months, Agent Thornton attempts to get Brenna to speak about what she meant, making remarks about how he has had thoughts of setting off bombs or "shooting up" the local mall. Brenna eventually becomes more comfortable and actively engages in the conversation, imagining out loud how she would carry out mass violence against the United States.

   Finally, Thornton asks, "So why don't you do it?" Brenna responds that she cannot. She explains that she needs to focus on getting money because she has been having financial difficulty lately. Thornton tells her that he could get her some money, as much as $100,000, if she can pull off the attack. Brenna agrees. Together, they start planning the attack. Thornton helps Brenna stake out a busy train terminal to target and provides her with fake bombs.

Over months of planning, Brenna develops a romantic affinity for Thornton, which Thornton uses against her. At one point, Brenna expresses doubt about carrying out the plan, but Thornton insists that it is the right thing to do. Brenna is unmoved by Agent Thornton at first, so he reminds her why she is doing this and how rewarding this will be. He tells her about the money and how they could use the money to "get away" together. Thornton then seduces Brenna, after which Brenna agrees to go through with the attack.

The day the attack is supposed to take place, Brenna loads up her car with the fake bombs and drives to Thornton's apartment where the FBI is waiting to arrest her. Brenna is charged with several counts of conspiracy and attempt to use weapons of mass destruction against the United States. Does she have an entrapment defense?

Explanations

1a. This is an easy case. The defendant approached the officer, initiated the discussion about sex for money, and provided a place for the crime. The government did no more than present an opportunity for an "unwary criminal" to commit a crime. In a jurisdiction adopting the subjective approach, the government could produce evidence of Linda's predisposition to commit prostitution, including any past convictions. Even under the objective approach, which focuses on the impact police conduct would have on a law-abiding citizen, Linda would not be successful. Ordinary citizens would not agree to commit an act of prostitution under these circumstances, so there is no risk of trapping the "unwary innocent."

1b. This case is more complicated. Under both the subjective and objective approaches the police instigated this criminal activity. The subjective approach looks not only at what the police did but also at the defendant's predisposition. Linda's past prostitution supports the prosecution's claim that she was predisposed to criminal activity even before the police embarked on the undercover operation. Here, the police officer initiated the criminal venture by asking Linda if she would commit prostitution.

Yet, Linda initially declined the offer. Only when the undercover officer offered an extremely high payment did she agree. Even though the police conduct was extremely persuasive, a judge or jury could well find that Linda was predisposed to commit prostitution if the price was right, thereby defeating her claim of entrapment.

The objective approach looks at what the police did and determines whether a reasonable law-abiding person would commit the offense. Under this approach, Linda's past history of occasional prostitution would be irrelevant. Nonetheless, even an offer of $1,000 would probably not induce a law-abiding citizen to commit an act of prostitution. Linda might well be convicted even under the objective approach.

2. Poor Lucy. Of course, she initiated a drug purchase; there can be little doubt about her predisposition to commit that crime. However, it was the undercover police officer who instigated prostitution. Moreover, he took advantage of her addiction. He offered her heroin—something she needed more desperately than money.

   There is no evidence indicating that Lucy was predisposed to commit prostitution. More important, the undercover officer used her addiction as a powerful incentive to induce Lucy to agree to prostitution. Is this appropriate police conduct? Is it entrapment? You decide.

3. Al would argue that the government entrapped him by providing an indispensable element of the offense—the cash and the checks represented to be proceeds of illegal activity. He would also point out that the government agent went beyond mere investigation to gather evidence of ongoing crime. She actually created the crime for which Al was charged.

   The prosecution would argue that Al clearly was predisposed to commit other crimes because he actually told the undercover agent how to avoid the $10,000 cash transaction-reporting law. All the police did was to provide Al an opportunity to commit a different crime; they offered no unusual incentives. In a similar case, the court concluded that the police conduct was not improper and dismissed the defense. See *United States v. Jensen*, 69 F.3d 906 (8th Cir. 1995).

4a. No. He rejected the bribe the first two times only because he was concerned about getting caught. When he thought he was in a secure place (even checking out the sheik for electronic surveillance), he readily accepted the bribe. Although the government did offer the bribe several times, this conduct did not reach a "level of outrageousness" sufficient to bar the prosecution. See *United States v. Kelly*, 707 F.2d 1460 (D.C. Cir. 1983).

4b. Wow! The congressman has not previously indicated a predisposition to accept the bribe. In fact, he actually refused it on ethical grounds (though he did not inform law enforcement officials of the attempted bribe). But an offer to save the life of your child is a very powerful inducement to which even a law-abiding citizen might succumb. You are the judge. How are you going to rule, using either test?

5. Clearly, the government initiated this criminal act by having Oprah ask Shawn to sell her marijuana. And there appears to be some basis for targeting Shawn as someone who occasionally sells marijuana. However, Shawn consistently refused to sell marijuana to Oprah until she appeared to be in extremely severe pain. The jury might well conclude that such callous manipulation of human sympathy for another suffering human being is so outrageous that the charge should be dismissed.

6. The government initiated this criminal activity and there is no basis for thinking Msumo was predisposed to commit a crime. Moreover, any law-abiding citizen might be sympathetic to Rashwana's plight. Nonetheless, entrapment is not available if an element of the charge includes inflicting bodily injury on another. Thus, Msumo cannot use this defense.

7. The prosecutor would argue that the idea to commit a crime originated with José. He downloaded the instructions and told Alex that it would be a great idea to build a pipe bomb. The defense of entrapment should not prevail because José was the "first mover" in this case by obtaining the plan from a jihadist website. He also obtained some of the vital bomb parts himself, clearly indicating his criminal intentions. Thus, under the subjective view, José had a prior personal desire to build a pipe bomb, an object which has no lawful use, and he acted on that pre-existing disposition by downloading plans and telling Alex what a great idea building the bomb was. The police conduct here was perfectly proper. Alex merely wanted to determine if José was willing to implement his plan and commit a crime.

   Defense counsel would point out that José simply downloaded plans to build a bomb, but he took no steps to build one. In fact, his client was homeless and in no position to do so. Thus, José did not have a subjective predisposition to actually build and detonate a bomb nor is there anything in his record that indicates he did. Moreover, the paid police informant here clearly has the motivation to manufacture crime and he did. Alex found José an apartment, provided most of the essential materials to build it, including drill bits critical to its completion, and actually suggested the targets. In sum, the police conduct in this case was outrageous and should not be encouraged.

   Under the MPC's objective approach, the prosecutor would argue that the police conduct here would not have persuaded a law-abiding citizen to commit this crime. She would note that Alex did not suggest the idea to José, but simply followed up on José's criminal inclination to build a pipe bomb that has no lawful use. Alex did not tell José the venture was legal nor did he have to use *any* persuasion—let alone persuasion that might create a substantial risk of inducing an otherwise law-abiding citizen to commit this crime—to induce José to undertake this venture. Alex should be commended for preventing a terrible crime that could have killed and maimed many innocent people.

Defense counsel would counter that a paid police agent turned a simple thought into action by doing everything necessary to persuade and enable José to commit a crime. José had absolutely no intention—let alone capacity or competence—to commit this crime until Alex actually planted the idea in his head and then went to extraordinary lengths to start implementing it. Thus, Alex actually caused José, an otherwise unwilling criminal, to commit a crime and did almost everything necessary for him to do so.

It might be a tougher defense for José under the MPC. Though the MPC focuses primarily on the government conduct, José would have to persuade a jury that Alex lied to José about the legality of the proposed conduct or that Alex used unusually powerful methods of persuasion that might induce anyone to commit this crime.

Is the defense of entrapment useless as a defense in terrorism cases in this post 9-11 era? Should it be?

8. Entrapment is available only if the *government* is involved. Because Pete is a private citizen, José will not be able to raise this defense.

9. These facts are based on the Second Circuit case *United States v. Cromitie*, 727 F.3d 194 (2013). Under the subjective test, the conduct of law enforcement (or an informant) must have induced the defendant to commit the crime and the defendant must not have been predisposed to commit the crime. First, she would argue that Thornton induced her to conspire to attack the United States. She would point to his continuously engaging in her conversations about it, urging her to do it, and convincing her to do it even after she expressed doubt. Moreover, she would argue that Thornton offering her money to execute the attack is more evidence that she was induced to carry out the attack. Brenna might also argue that Thornton induced her to act by providing all the necessary resources. Second, Brenna might argue that she was not predisposed to execute an attack. When she said she wanted "to do something to America" she did not necessarily mean that she wanted to execute an attack against the United States. In fact, she was not the first to mention it; Thornton was the one to bring up an attack and she did not go along with the idea until he had continuously engaged in her conversations about it.

   To Brenna's first argument, the government might argue it had "merely afforded" Brenna with the opportunity to conduct the attack by providing her with resources and information to do so. Second, the government might respond that even though she did not explain exactly what she meant by those words at the outset, the fact that she eventually participated in conversations about executing an attack after becoming more comfortable with Thornton shows that she was implying that she wanted to execute an attack, and therefore she was predisposed.

Under the MPC, an entrapment defense is viable if the police informant's conduct "induces or encourages another person to engage [in an offense] either by (a) making knowingly false representations designed to induce the belief that such conduct is not prohibited; or (b) employing methods of persuasion or inducement which create a substantial risk that such an offense will be committed by persons other than those who are ready to commit it."

Brenna would argue that Thornton used methods of persuasion that created a substantial risk that even an ordinary law-abiding person would commit the offense. She would emphasize the fact that Thornton repeatedly brought up the subject of committing an attack despite her initial unwillingness to discuss it. Thornton also repeatedly overcame her doubts about the attack and offered her a substantial sum of money to do it.

The government would likely stress the seriousness of the offense and argue that, despite Thornton's aggressive persuasion methods, an ordinary law-abiding person would not be tempted to commit such an offense. It would argue that an ordinary law-abiding person would not entertain so many conversations about committing the offense and that even a large sum of money would not be enough to convince most people to act as Brenna did.

Lastly, Brenna might argue that she was denied due process because Thornton's conduct was "outrageous." Specifically, Brenna might argue that Thornton's conduct was outrageous because he engaged in a romantic, sexual relationship with her to induce her into acting. Courts have indicated that engaging in a sexual relationship may be enough to find a due process violation, but it can be extremely difficult to prove.[109]

109. *United States v. Rabinowitz*, 645 Fed. Appx. 63, 65 (2d Cir. 2016). In the Second Circuit, the defendant must show: "(1) that the government consciously set out to use sex as a weapon in its investigatory arsenal, or acquiesced in such conduct for its own purposes upon learning that such a relationship existed; (2) that the government agent initiated a sexual relationship, or allowed it to continue to exist, to achieve governmental ends; and (3) that the sexual relationship took place during or close to the period covered by the indictment and was entwined with the events charged therein." *Id.* Even if the defendant can satisfy all three elements, she is only then entitled to a hearing to determine whether she was denied due process under the law. *Id.*

NEW EXCUSES: THE FUTURE IS UPON US

The law can treat claims of "new excuses" in at least three ways: (1) it can totally exclude them; (2) it can allow them as reductions of guilt, but not as full exculpations; (3) it can allow them in sentencing. For different claims, and at different historical moments, the path has been different, but it is not unusual to begin with the last approach and then move "up the chain" to a full defense. Consider, for example, duress. In the nineteenth century, duress was very narrowly restricted as a defensive claim; by the end of the twentieth century, the Model Penal Code had accepted it as a full defense even in homicide cases, and a number of courts or legislatures had recognized it as a mitigation to manslaughter in homicide cases.[110] Similarly, battered women who claimed self-defense prior to the 1970s framed their claims in "temporary insanity" or "heat of passion," because the law did not recognize "battered spouse syndrome" as a scientific theory. Today, in contrast, every state allows evidence of battered spouse syndrome in such cases. Many who agree with the law of battered spouses nevertheless caution against receiving new excuse claims precipitously, pointing to the arguments relating to XYY chromosomes (discussed infra) and to premenstrual syndrome (also discussed infra) as illustrations of the validity of the law's cautious pace.

To some, these new claims seem like nothing more than the last straw that an obviously guilty defendant will grasp. They characterize these claims as the "defense du jour" and talk about the "abuse excuse." Almost twenty years ago, Professor Alan Dershowitz, highly critical of most of these claims, listed over 50 such claims that have allegedly been made by defendants in criminal cases; many more have been raised since.[111] Although many of the excuses listed by Dershowitz have been rejected both by courts as a matter of law and by juries on resolution of fact, the argument he makes cannot be dismissed offhandedly.

Opponents of liberalizing the law of defensive claims have more than just precedent on their side. They aver that many of these new claims are based upon "junk science," and that there is no compelling evidence (yet) that these new findings show that criminal behavior is "caused" by such excuses. Moreover, to the extent that there is *some* evidence that such behavior is "influenced," opponents argue that it is the responsibility of an individual of good character to resist that influence, no matter how strong.

---

110. See also Kirchmeier, A Tear in the Eye of the Law: Mitigating Factors and the Progression Toward a Disease Theory of Criminal Justice, 83 Or. L. Rev. 631 (2004).

111. The Abuse Excuse (1994). See also J. Wilson, Moral Judgment (1997); Turk, Abuses and Syndromes: Excuses or Justifications?, 18 Whittier L. Rev. 901 (1997). But see Richard Singer, No Excuse for a Law Professor, 6 Crim. L. Forum 121 (1995).

Finally, some opponents argue eloquently that such claims will undermine the very premise of the criminal law, that of free will, and thus decimate the very concept of blameworthiness. *Even* if the claims are true, these persons argue, the criminal law must proceed *as* if they were not, for to admit them is to erode the very foundation of criminal liability.[112] As Lord Simon put it in *Lynch v. Director of Public Prosecutions*,[113] "Even the most devout predestinarian puts off his theology when he puts on legal robe."

Proponents contend that the law *should* respond to such evidence and reject the "parade of horribles" argument. They maintain that judges and juries can filter the relevant claims from the frivolous. The essence of criminal responsibility, they argue, requires the law to examine *any* claim that a defendant's power of control was undermined. As Professor Williams has declared:

> Once it is recognized that excuses are based on notions of justice, and show the law's consideration for the defendant's predicament in particular circumstances, it becomes obvious that the list of excuses need not be regarded as closed. [The Theory of Excuses, 1982 Crim. L. Rev. 732, 741-742.]

Usually, defendants will need, or certainly want, the testimony of an "expert" on the alleged excuse and its effects. Until very recently, most courts, following the lead of *Frye v. United States*, 293 F. 1013 (D. Cir. 1923), severely restricted the instances where expert testimony was allowed. In *Daubert v. Merrell Dow Pharmaceuticals, Inc.*, 509 U.S. 579 (1993), however, the United States Supreme Court adopted a more generous rule for federal civil cases.[114] Many state courts seem to be adopting a *Daubert*-like standard as well. Whether this trend will be followed in criminal cases is uncertain.

We will not discuss the merits or demerits of any of the new claims. Instead, we will simply catalog a few of the more persistent claims. How these will be treated by the courts in the coming years is highly uncertain. The struggle between empirical claims and the criminal law's assumptions of free will will be fought in many of these battlegrounds.

It is always dangerous—even under the best of circumstances and with a great deal of information—to try to "categorize" anything. This is certainly true of the new claims. The lines suggested here are tentative.

---

112. E.g., Justice Weintraub, concurring in *State v. Sikora*, 44 N.J. 453 (1965).

113. [1975] 1 All E.R. 913.

114. *Daubert* provided that judges must look to various factors to determine whether expert scientific testimony should be admitted. Among those factors listed are the (1) the empirical testability of the scientific methodology used by the expert; (2) whether the scientific theory or technique has been peer reviewed; (3) the "potential rate of error" of the technique utilized; and (4) the acceptance of the technique in the scientific community. *Daubert*, 509 U.S. 579, 594.

Thus, most "psychological" defense claims described below may later be treated as physiological in nature, if research increasingly indicates these conditions to be physiologically based.[115] Nevertheless, we shall make the attempt, in part because there may be similar issues surrounding one type of claim that do not surround others.

Physiologically (Biologically) Based Excuses for Criminality

At least since Ceaseare Lombroso[116] claimed to be able to determine a person's propensity for crime by feeling the bumps on his head,[117] both scientists and laymen have hoped that they could find a connection between biology and criminal behavior. After all, such persons might be "treatable," or if nontreatable, they could be incapacitated. In the early 1900s in this country and others, belief in such a biological connection led to a eugenics movement in which a number of state legislatures enacted statutes providing for the mandatory sterilization of criminals. Only after Hitler's "final solution" were these statutes repealed.[118]

Still, the search for a biological "cause" of crime continues, as controversial now as ever,[119] and again attacked on grounds that it supports racism.

115. For example, some geneticists now claim that there is good evidence that schizophrenia, a "psychologically based" claim already recognized under the common law "insanity" test, is really chromosomally and genetically influenced, if not determined.

116. See generally D. Denno, Biology and Violence (1990); D. Niehoff, The Biology of Violence (1999); Denno, Gender Issues and the Criminal Law: Gender, Crime and the Criminal Law Defenses, 85 J. Crim. L. & Criminality 80 (1994); Henry Fradella, What Role, if Any Should Biology Play in Criminal Cases, 45 Crim. L. Bull. (2009); Owen Jones and Timothy Goldsmith, Law and Behavioral Biology, 105 Colum. L. Rev. 405(2005).

117. C. Lombroso, Crime: Its Causes and Remedies (1911).

118. The United States Supreme Court considered the constitutionality of these statutes only once, in *Skinner v. Oklahoma ex rel. Williamson*, 316 U.S. 535 (1942). The Court found the statute unconstitutional on equal protection grounds: It did not sterilize *enough* criminals. Since, in *Buck v. Bell*, 274 U.S. 200 (1927), the Court had upheld a mandatory sterilization statute involving the mentally ill against an equal protection challenge, it is not clear what the Court might have done in the criminal context had the Oklahoma statute punished *all* thieves with sterilization.

119. In 1993, the National Institutes of Health funded a conference to assess the status of the investigation of the link between biology and crime, but withdrew the funds after public outcry. Two years later, however, the Institutes refunded the conference, which was held in late 1995.

Neuroscience and the Law — My Brain Made Me Do It

The most persistent[120] and daunting challenges to the theory of free will, and hence to the criminal law, are likely to come from neuroscience.[121] The advances made by this discipline in the past two decades are astounding — and growing exponentially. Neuroscientists now claim to know — more or less precisely — what parts of the brain control, or at least significantly affect, each part of our behavior.[122] For example, the amygdala is said to affect decisions on "flight or fight," while the prefrontal cortex has substantial impact on judgment. If there is physical damage to these areas of the brain, the function to which they are related is likely to be affected. Thus, persons with FLD (frontal lobe dysfunction) may lack the judgment that "normal" persons have, and may act more impulsively.[123] FLD defendants may then claim that their decision to act more "rashly" than others, particularly when confronted with what they (wrongly) perceive to be a threatening situation, should fully or partially exonerate them. Similarly, damage to the amygdala might result in a greater willingness to fight rather than retreat, even when there is a possibility of retreat.

---

120. Vanderbilt Law School has established an entire institute, funded by the MacArthur Foundation, on neuroscience and the law. See http://www.lawneuro.org. The work has grown exponentially. The fifth edition of this book cited an author who cited over two hundred articles written since 2000 on the subject of criminal law and neuroscience. Pustilnik, Violence on the Brain: A Critique of Neuroscience in Criminal Law, 44 Wake Forest L. Rev. 183, n.10 (2009). That information has now been broadened; for a general bibliography listing 565 articles on law and neuroscience, see Francis X. Shen, The Law and Neuroscience Bibliography: Navigating the Emerging Field of Neurolaw 38 Int'l J. L. Legal Info, 352 (2010). For even more recent information, see Blog, Neuroethics & Law, http://kolber.typepad.com. See also Susan A. Bandes, The Promise and Pitfalls of Neuroscience for Criminal Law and Procedure: Conclusion, 8 Ohio St. J. Crim. L. 119 (2010).

121. See O'Hanlon, Towards a More Reasonable Approach to Free Will in Criminal Law, 7 Cardozo Pub. L. Pol'y & Ethics 395 (2009).

122. The view that different parts of the brain are "primarily" responsible for specific kinds of conduct may seem to echo the views of psychiatrists in the nineteenth century. Current thinking, however, is that while one or two areas may be primarily responsible for conduct, every action and thought is affected by multiple sites in the brain. The claim is not that "all" judgment is lost if the prefrontal lobe is damaged, but that "some" or "a great deal" of judgment is affected. On the other hand, "numerous studies have suggested that one area, the ventromedial prefrontal cortex (VMPC), is predominantly responsible for moral behavior in humans." Steven K. Erickson, Blaming the Brain, 11 Minn. J.L. Sci & Tech. 27, 48, citing Michael Koenigs et al., Damage to the Prefrontal Cortex Increases Utilitarian Moral Judgments, 446 Nature 908, 908-910 (2007). See also Robert M. Sapolsky, The Frontal Cortex and the Criminal Justice System, 359 Phil. Trans. R. Soc. Lond. B 1787 (2004).

123. Redding, The Brain-Disordered Defendant: Neuroscience and Legal Insanity in the Twenty-First Century, 56 Am. U. L. Rev. 51 (2006).

As a general matter, these claims have not yet been accepted by courts, even those following the *Daubert* approach, as claims relevant to the defendant's guilt.[124] But numerous court decisions have grappled with the contention that the failure by counsel to raise, or by a court to allow, such a claim during the sentencing phase of a capital proceeding[125] may suggest that defendant's counsel was inadequate;[126] while many hold against the defendant, the issue will be continually raised.[127] While it is still several steps from those decisions to ones holding that these claims are relevant to guilt, these may be the first steps toward such holdings.[128]

On the other hand, the argument that this evidence is "scientific" is hardly resolved. Already a number of commentators are beginning to suggest that claims made—primarily by lawyers, not neuroscientists—that neuroscience will help "cure" violence are, like other claims made during the past two centuries,[129] significantly overblown and unsupportable. Specifically, the concerns are (1) that the current data do not support the notion of "locality"—that one portion of the brain is "responsible" for violence (or other misbehavior)—and (2) that the reliance on animal studies is too facile, ignoring or downplaying significant differences between the animals studied and humans.[130]

---

124. But see *State v. Anderson*, 79 S.W.3d 420 (Mo. 2002) (evidence allowed); see also *People v. Weinstein*, 591 N.Y.S.2d 715 (N.Y. Cty. 1992), (allowing PET scans of the defendant's frontal lobe even under the *Frye* test).

125. E.g., *State v. Mercer*, 381 S.C. 149 (2009) (clear, but not reversible, error not to allow doctor to testify at capital sentencing hearing about SPECT (brain scan) of defendant); *Hoskins v. State*, 735 So. 2d 202 (Fla. 1999) (ordering remand for purpose of having PET scan conducted on death penalty defendant). Laura Snodgrass and Brad Justice, "Death Is Different": Limits on the Imposition of the Death Penalty to Traumatic Brain Injuries, 26 Dev. Mental Health L. 81, 98 (2007).

126. There is also the possibility that cases that raise this issue are resolved by plea bargain. That occurred in the *Weinstein* case, supra n.102; after the court allowed the evidence in, the prosecution agreed to a bargain. See Snead, Neuroimaging and "Complexity" of Capital Punishment, 82 N.Y.U. L. Rev. 1265 (2007).

127. See *Forrest v. State*, 290 S.W.3d 704 (Mo. 2009) (failure to obtain PET scan of defendant's brain was not ineffective assistance). Pustilnik, supra n. 98, at fn. 9 (citing cases). See also Adequacy of defense counsel's representation of criminal client—pretrial conduct or conduct at unspecified time regarding issues of insanity, 72 A.L.R.5th 109.

128. This may overstate the strength of those cases. As a general rule, the United States Supreme Court has held that defendants must be allowed to present ANY evidence in a capital sentencing proceeding. But that holding is a far cry from decisions suggesting that defense failure to raise brain trauma could be ineffective assistance of counsel.

129. E.g., phrenology, biological determinism, eugenics, psychosurgery, and others.

130. For particularly strong critiques, see Morse, Brain Overclaim Syndrome and Criminal Responsibility: A Diagnostic Note, 3 Ohio St. J. Crim. L. 397 (2006) and Pustilnik, supra n. 98. For critiques of the current efficacy of some of the neuroscientific methods, see Tancredi & Brodie, The Brain and Behavior: Limitations in the Legal Use of Functional Magnetic Resonance Imaging, 33 Am. J.L. & Med. 271 (2007); Dumit, Objective Brains, Prejudicial

Genetics and Crime

Not far removed from the claim that brain disorders may affect behavior is the argument that genetic defects explain our (mis)behavior. Again, the view that there are "born criminals"[131] has been present for centuries. In 1988, Professor Deborah Denno wrote that "social science research has not successfully demonstrated sufficiently strong links between biological factors and criminal behavior to warrant major consideration in determining criminal responsibility."[132] But increasing evidence suggests that "significant genetic factors do appear to be influencing antisocial-behavior-related psychiatric disorder."[133]

One of the most (in)famous claims of genetic disorder is that of the XYY chromosomes.[134] In the 1960s, researchers announced that they had discovered that a vastly disproportionate percentage of prison inmates had an "extra" Y chromosome. The suggestion was that, since the Y chromosome is what makes a person a male (every person has two sex chromosomes, at least one of which is an X; if the other is also an X, the fetus is a female), the "extra" Y chromosome must "add to" the "maleness" of the individual. Since crime—and particularly violent crime—is mostly a male activity, the argument was that this extra Y chromosome "caused" (or at least strongly influenced) violence, which was viewed as synonymous with "super maleness." Since no individual can control his genetic makeup, it was argued that XYY men who committed crimes could not be blamed for those acts because they could not have done differently. Before the courts

---

Images, 12 Sci. Context 173 (1999). See generally Meyer, Brain, Gender, Law: A Cautionary Tale, 53 N.Y.L. Sch. L. Rev. 995 (2008/2009); Feldman, Law's Misguided Love Affair with Science, 10 Minn. J.L. Sci. & Tech. 95 (2009) ("We are constantly seduced into believing that some new science will provide answers to law's dilemmas, and we are constantly disappointed.").

131. Cf. the movie *Natural Born Killers*, starring Woody Harrelson.

132. Deborah Denno, Human Biology and Criminal Responsibility: Free Will or Free Ride, 137 U. Pa. L. Rev. 615, 617 (1988).

133. Baker, Bezdjian & Raine, Behavioral Genetics: The Science of Antisocial Behavior, 69 Law & Contemp. Prob. 724 (2006). This article is one of several in a symposium, entitled The Impact of Behavior Genetics on the Criminal Law: Behavioral Genetics: The Science of Antisocial Behavior, in this issue of the journal. See also M. Ridley, Nature via Nurture: Genes, Experience, and What Makes Us Human 185 (2003). Professor Denno found at least 58 criminal cases between 1994-2007 that relied on behavioral genetics, but most were capital sentencing cases; Deborah W. Denno, Behavioral Genetics Evidence in Criminal Cases: 1994-2007, in The Impact of Behavioral Sciences on Criminal Law 317, 318-319 (ed. Nita A. Farahany 2009).

134. See Burke, The "XYY" Syndrome: Genetics, Behavior and the Law, 46 Denv. L.J. 161 (1969).

were confronted with potentially hundreds of such cases,[135] the methodology of the research was thrown into disrepute. However, the issue raised by the experience will not merely survive but will certainly be raised again as biology purports to find more physical links to specific kinds of behavior. The law will inevitably have to confront the question: What *should* the criminal law do if a genetic link, of some reasonable strength, is shown to "cause" specific conduct?[136]

A more recent version of this claim contends:[137]

> Evolutionary psychologists understand that the general structure of our human genotype has evolved largely in response to, and as a part of, conditions in a world that no longer exists: an era in which day-to-day survival was the basic rule and long-term planning was unfathomable. Our genes continue to interact with the environment in important ways everyday, and humans share hardwiring for "social-emotional responses [a phenotype] we've inherited from our primate ancestors (due, presumably, to some adaptive advantages they conferred)."

Premenstrual Syndrome (PMS)

Premenstrual syndrome[138] is another biological condition alleged to affect behavior. While many women experience cramps, nausea, and other (often severe) discomfort just before their menstruation, the term PMS was always restricted to the small percentage (about 2-3 percent) who suffer such agony and pain or mood swings that they sometimes become severely violent.

Women who have raised this claim have been forced to fit it into existing categories of defenses recognized by the common law—for example, insanity, provocation, diminished responsibility. Provocation is unavailable, however, because the victim may have done nothing provocative at

---

135. At least one American court rejected the XYY chromosome argument. *Millard v. State*, 8 Md. App. 419 (1970). Because then-existing (and probably current) criminal law had no niche for the claim, the defendant argued that he was "insane" under the *M'Naghten* rules.

136. See Dreyfuss & Nelkin, The Jurisprudence of Genetics, 45 Vand. L. Rev. 313 (1992). See also Coffey, The Genetic Defense: Excuse or Explanation?, 35 Wm. & Mary L. Rev. 353 (1993); Friedland, The Criminal Law Implications of the Human Genome Project: Reimagining a Genetically Oriented Criminal Justice System, 86 Ky. L.J. 303 (1997-98).

137. Theodore Y. Blumoff, The Neuropsychology of Justifications and Excuses: Some Problematic Cases of Self-Defense, Duress and Provocation, 50 Jurimetrics J. 391 (2010).

138. Before the APA recognized PMDD, as discussed in the text, the literature was vast. See, for example, Lee Solomon, Premenstrual Syndrome: The Debate Surroundihng Criminal Defense, 54 Md. L. Rev. 571 (1995); Nicole R. Grosse, Premenstrual Dysphoric Disorder as a Mitigating Factor in Sentencing: Following the Lead of English Criminal Courts, 33 Val. U. L. Rev. 201 (1998).

all. The variations of insanity are usually not available because PMS is not considered to be a mental disease and because it is not permanent. In 1994, however, the American Psychiatric Association (APA) added premenstrual dysphoric disorder (PMDD), a severe form of premenstrual syndrome, to the list of depressive disorders in its Diagnostic and Statistical Manual (DSM-IV).[139] This might mean that (1) other women will be excluded from claiming PMS; (2) women who claim PMDD will be treated as suffering from a mental illness, with possible commitment after a successful defense.[140]

As with some of the other claims considered here, PMS raises other intriguing questions. For example, there are alleged "treatments" for PMDD. Could a woman who fails or refuses to undergo such treatment lose the claim on the basis of omission, much as did Decina (see Chapter 3)? How would such an argument take into consideration the fact that some of these treatments have potentially serious, long-run side effects? Is reasonableness the standard? And, if so, would that reasonableness be judged by the standard of (1) the reasonable woman; (2) the reasonable woman with PMDD; or (3) the reasonable woman with PMDD who feared such side effects (a) reasonably? (b) unreasonably? These questions may be precluded by the recognition of PMDD as a mental disorder, but perhaps not. After all, many women who do not fit the PMDD profile may still wish to argue that they were affected by PMS. There is no a priori reason why they should be prohibited from raising the facts just because the APA has declared some other women to be suffering from a mental illness.

Other Physiologically Based Claims

There is no end to the possible claims, but we list several more: hypoglycemia,[141] Alzheimer's disease,[142] neurotoxic damage,[143] and testosterone overload.[144]

---

139. The DSM expressly states that its classifications are not to be used in nonpsychiatric settings (e.g., in court), but lawyers have consistently relied on its authority in other types of cases in the past.

140. Connie Huang, It's a Hormonal Thing: Premenstrual Syndrome and Postpartum Psychosis as Criminal Defenses, 11 S. Cal. Rev. L. & Women's Stud. 345 (2002).

141. See *Regina v. Quick*, [1973] 3 W.L.R. 26 (Ct. of Crim. App.).

142. See Fred Cohen, Old Age as a Criminal Defense, 21 Crim. L. Bull. 5 (1985).

143. See Note, The Sevin Made Me Do It: Mental Non-Responsibility and the Neurotoxic Damage Defense, 14 Va. Envtl. L.J. 151 (1994).

144. Within the past few years, researchers have concluded that testosterone, a hormone found in much greater concentration in men than in women, does in fact affect "aggressive" behavior. See, e.g., Sullivan, the HE Hormone, New York Times Magazine, Apr. 2, 2000, p. 46. See also R. Sapolsky, The Trouble with Testosterone (1997); J. Dabbs, Heroes, Rogues and Lovers: Testosterone and Behavior (2000). While this may echo the "XYY" syndrome, the

Psychologically Based Excuses

Brainwashing

Many of the new claims of psychological causation and defense—diminished capacity, pathological behavior, post-traumatic stress disorder, temporary insanity, and the like—have already been considered in the section on insanity. At least one claim does not quite fit the usual psychiatric mode: brainwashing.[145] This phenomenon was first detected by studies of prisoners of war, but it became a criminal law issue in the bizarre case of Patty Hearst. As usual, truth is stranger than fiction.

Patty Hearst was an heiress to a fortune. By all accounts, she had little concern for political issues, much less for violent politics. Ms. Hearst was kidnapped in the 1970s by a militant group of terrorists in California, who demanded that her father take certain social measures (such as distributing free food to thousands of hungry poor people in several California cities). Months later, Ms. Hearst reappeared, dressed in black and carrying a machine gun, assisting the terrorists in robbing a California bank. She was arrested about a year later in San Francisco. When booked, she gave her name as Tanya, and her occupation as "revolutionary." (Not even Danielle Steele could concoct such a plot. But it all happened.)

At trial, Hearst (as she now called herself again) argued that it was not "she" but "Tanya" who had robbed the bank. During her captivity, she argued, she had been not merely tortured but indoctrinated. She had "become" another person, Tanya, and remained so until "deprogrammed" after her arrest.

The jury rejected Hearst's claim, but the judge allowed it to be presented. Clearly, it raises almost primordial questions. (1) When is a person "herself"? (2) Can that person "change" under psychological pressure and then revert back when the pressure is removed?[146] (3) "Who" is punished—the previous "person" or that person's "mind" (which, by hypoth-

---

research seems much more methodologically sound. Whether the "influence" is sufficient to warrant consideration by courts is unclear.

145. See Delgado, Ascription of Criminal States of Mind: Toward a Defense Theory for the Coercively Persuaded ("Brainwashed") Defendant, 63 Minn. L. Rev. 1 (1978); Dressler, Professor Delgado's "Brainwashing" Defense: Courting a Deterministic Legal System, 63 Minn. L. Rev. 335 (1979). Note that even Dressler's title poses the philosophical question—to what extent would recognition of such a claim "court" a deterministic view of human behavior (and how would the criminal law deal with such a view)?

146. Hearst had been out of the clutches of her captives for at least nine months before her arrest; police had destroyed the terrorist-robbers' hideout and killed virtually everyone there. Hearst had already disappeared before that event. She explained that merely being "away from" the terrorists was insufficient to allow "regression" back to her "real self"; it required professional assistance that was available only after her arrest.

esis, no longer exists)? (4) To what degree would an acceptance of the claim weaken the criminal law's moral stature? Some of these questions may also be raised in other contexts—for example, in dealing with "multiple personalities." But brainwashing raises all of them.

The brainwashing claim was more recently raised by Lee Malvo, a juvenile and one of the "Washington snipers" who, shortly after the 9/11 attacks, terrorized that city by randomly shooting victims. Malvo claimed that his cohort, much older than Malvo, had "created what (he) became just as surely as a potter molds clay." The jury convicted him, but refused to impose the death penalty.[147]

Mob Mentality

In a very famous (but not officially reported) incident, Damien Williams, a black resident of Los Angeles, joined a mob of rioters who were outraged by a jury verdict acquitting several white police officers charged with unlawfully beating a black man. The mob stopped a truck and its white driver, pulled him from the cab, and began beating him. Williams picked up a brick and hit the driver. Fortunately, the driver survived, but Williams was charged with attempted murder, aggravated assault, and several other offenses. At trial, Williams argued (among other things) that he had no intent to injure, much less kill, the driver, but that he was simply "swept up" in the emotions of the moment. The jury acquitted him of the most serious of these charges. Had the driver died, it is possible that Williams might have argued, at least under the Model Penal Code, that he was suffering from an "extreme emotional disturbance" that would lower his homicide from murder to manslaughter. However, the jury obviously sympathized with Williams' claim that he had been "caused" to act the way he did by influences beyond his power to control.

Cognitive Psychology, Law, and the Emotions

Scholars from a number of non-legal fields have suggested that the law should consider and adopt recent sophisticated studies of the emotions.[148] Professors Kahan and Nussbaum, in a landmark article,[149] urged the reconsideration of emotions with regard to provocation. Professor Reid Fontaine

147. Nolan, the Indoctrination Defense: From the Korean War to Lee Boyd Malvo, 11 Va. J. Soc. Pol'y & L. 435 (2004).

148. Terry A. Maroney, Law and Emotion: A Proposed Taxonomy of an Emerging Field, 30 Law & Hum. Behav. 119 (2006).

149. Dan H Kahan and Martha Nussbaum, Two Conceptions of Emotion in Criminal law, 96 Colum. L. Rev. 269 (1996).

has broadened the argument with a series of articles.[150] For example, he has pointed to "provocation interpretational bias," a condition that makes some persons more likely to react precipitously (and perhaps violently) to perceived insults. While some might respond that this is merely another way of saying the person is "short-fused,"[151] this may be an insufficient reaction if science demonstrates an inability, even over time, to control such a bias.[152] It may be too early for the law, particularly the criminal law, to absorb such findings, but it is clear that these arguments will be raised increasingly as the evidence for them becomes "harder."

Sociologically Based Claims

Many of the claims listed and criticized by Professor Dershowitz, while ultimately going to the defendant's blameworthiness, are currently cast in terms of "syndromes" caused by "abuses" of one sort or another (psychological, physical, sexual) that he suffered. Again, categorizing is both dangerous and simplistic. Nonetheless, one could distinguish between claims that these abuses led directly to criminality and those that argue that the abuse made the defendant more sensitive to indicia of imminent abuse.[153]

Criminogenic Causes: Rotten Social Background

Certainly one of the more controversial claims, still not raised in court,[154] has been the suggestion that persons raised in underserved environments

---

150. Reid Griffith Fontaine, On Passion's Potential to Undermine Rationality: A Reply, 43 U. Mich. J. L. Reform 207 (2009) (Fontaine I); Adequate (Non) Provocation and Heat of Passion as Excuse Not Justification, 43 U. Mich. J.L. Reform 27 (2009) (Fontaine II); The Wrongfulness of Wrongly Interpreting Wrongfulness: Provocation, Interpretation Bias, and Heat of Passion Homicide, 12 New Crim. L. Rev. 69 (2009) (Fontaine III); Reactive Cognition, Reactive Emotion: Toward a More Psychologically-Informed Understanding of Reactive Homicide, 14 Psychol. Pub. Pol'y & L. 243 (2008) (Fontaine IV).

151. Amir Pichhadze, Proposals for Reforming the Law of Self-Defence, 72 J. Crim. L. 409 (2008).

152. Theodore Y. Blumoff, The Neuropsychology of Justifications and Excuses: Some Problematic Cases of Self-Defense, Duress and Provocation, 50 Jurimetrics J. 391 (2010). See also Rebecca Hollander-Blumoff, Crime, Punishment and the Psychology of Self-Control, 61 Emory L.J. 501 (2012).

153. For a general discussion, see Falk, Novel Theories of Criminal Defense Based upon the Toxicity of the Social Environment: Urban Psychosis, Television Intoxication, and Black Rage, 74 N.C. L. Rev. 731 (1996).

154. The idea that someone's "rotten social background" could play a role in excusing or alleviating punishment for a crime was introduced in *United Status v. Alexander*, 471 F.2d 923 (D.C. Cir. 1972).

become hardened to the pain that crime inflicts on its victims and are therefore less "blameworthy" when they inflict such injury.[155] Furthermore, the argument runs, deprivation itself "creates" a "propensity to commit crimes." This is *not* merely an argument that poor people, or those living in a low-income neighborhood, are more likely to steal than people who are not poor—everyone likes material goods. It is, rather, an argument that constant deprivation affects the ability of the actor to assess the moral weight of his claim to goods (or bodily integrity) versus that of the "owner" of those goods.

Professor Erik Luna, tongue only slightly in cheek, has propagated the possibility of a "spoiled rotten social background" defense.[156] If this were a serious suggestion, it would be argued that a very wealthy child might simply not recognize that the "rules" applied to him.[157]

Urban Survival Syndrome and Black Rage

Although conceptually distinct, these two claims are suggested along with Rotten Social Background as fertile fields for defenses. The first argues that persons in tense urban settings are (much like battered women) more sensitive to, and therefore more able to comprehend than others, "signs" that suggest violence is imminent.[158] It has been rejected in the several cases that have raised it thus far. The second—possibly a variant of heat of passion—argues that minorities, especially black people, have so long been the victims of discrimination that their anger simply "erupts" against white people who are ostensibly unoffending, but who are seen as exemplars of the oppressing group.[159] This claim has been raised—and rejected—in several unreported cases.

Recap

It is easy to dismiss these claims as Dershowitz and many others do. But these claims touch directly the clash between the criminal law's assumption of free will and the scientific view that much human behavior is caused by

155. Delgado, "Rotten Social Background": Should the Criminal Law Recognize a Defense of Severe Environmental Deprivation? 3 Law & Inequality 9 (1985).
156. See 2 Ala. C.R. & C.L. L. Rev. 23 (2011).
157. Cf. Simon Baatz, For the Thrill of It: Leopold, Loeb, and the Murder That Shocked Chicago (2008).
158. See Liggins, Urban Survival Syndrome: Novel Concept or Recognized Defense?, 23 Am. J. Trial Advoc. 215 (1999).
159. See W. Grier & P. Cobbs, Black Rage (1968); Snierson, Black Rage and the Criminal Law: A Principled Approach to a Polarized Debate, 143 U. Pa. L. Rev. 2251 (1995).

physical or physiological factors we cannot control. How the criminal law responds to such claims, both specifically and generally, may become one measure of how evenhanded and fair it is. It is not necessarily an exaggeration to say that how the criminal law deals with such claims in the next century may well decide whether it continues to carry the moral weight it has always sought. As Professor Deborah Denno, a leading commentator on these questions, has said, "The criminal justice system still lacks a sound conceptual framework for handling genetics research no matter what it decides to do with it."[160]

Examples

1. Nrin Sok emigrated from Cambodia in 1996. He began work in scrap yards, where metal items were often melted down. He seldom wore a mask. In 1997, he brought home to his wife a set of "magic" fertility belts of zinc, silver, and lead. The couple wore the belts almost continuously, hoping to conceive a child. One night a year later, in their small apartment, he burned the belts in a hot pan, and fumes emitted into the room. Almost immediately after this, he killed his wife. A series of tests revealed that, shortly after his arrest, the defendant had toxic levels of lead, cadmium, and manganese in his blood. He was also found to be in acute renal failure when arrested and was treated for kidney failure and liver and heart damage. By the time of his trial for first degree murder, he had fully recovered physically. Sent to a mental hospital after his arrest, he had made a full recovery by the time of his trial. Is Sok guilty of murder? Of any crime?

2. Frank is a landscape gardener and has been exposed to pesticides for 15 years. Charged with first-degree murder, he seeks to introduce evidence that his exposure affected his mens rea. What result?

3. Lyle and Erik walked into the living room of their parents' home one night and shot both parents, who were eating ice cream and filling out college application forms for their sons, with a barrage of weapons. They seek to introduce evidence that they were sexually abused by their father as children. Should the evidence be admitted?

4. Julius is charged with first-degree murder. He admits having shot the victim, but claims that it was upon "impulse" and that "the," or at least "a," cause of his impulse was a low level of serotonin in his brain at the time of the shooting. He seeks to introduce (a) evidence from friends and relatives that he has consistently been

160. Revisiting the Legal Link Between Genetics and Crime, 69 Law and Contemp. Probs 209, 238 (2006).

subject to impulses, many of them violent, over his life; and (b) expert evidence from a neuropsychologist that low levels of serotonin "cause" "intermittent explosive disorder" and impair one's ability to resist impulses, violent and otherwise, and that Julius's brain shows such low levels of serotonin. Which of these types of evidence, if either, is admissible?

5. Jennifer's business had been going downhill for some time. On August 1, her financial officer, Elizabeth, refused to process the payroll. Jennifer went home, got her 9 mm Beretta semiautomatic pistol, returned to the plant, and shot Elizabeth four times. She wishes to introduce evidence that, beginning in January, friends noticed changes in her personality. In addition, she had not been able to sleep, she had lost weight, and on at least one occasion she had manifested suicidal intentions. She also wishes to show that these characteristics are related to "akathisia," a result of her taking Zoloft, a prescribed antidepressant medication. Is this evidence admissible?

6. Barry Stocks, a baseball player, strikes out, runs at the pitcher, and pummels him to death with the bat. Barry claims he was on anabolic steroids at the time, and that the homicidal act was a result of "'roid rage." What is the likely result?

7. Hume, 83, and Jessica, 79, have been married for 55 years. One day, Hume asks Jessica for a bagel. She brings him an onion roll. He "goes berserk" and axes Jessica to death. His attorney wants to argue to the jury that Hume's "old age" can account for his crime. To this end, he seeks to call several of Hume's friends and neighbors who will testify that over the past five to six years, Hume has seemed to "drift downhill" and become more easily irritated. He also wants to have a neurosurgeon show MRIs of Hume's brain, and testify that Hume's frontal lobe has deteriorated slightly, and that this may indicate he lacks full ability to control his impulses. The prosecutor seeks motion in limine to prevent either of these at trial. What should the trial court do?

8. College X and College Y have a longstanding rivalry. In the annual football game between the colleges' teams, College X destroys College Y after some questionable calls by the referee and wins the game 33 points to 0. The fans of College Y are so appalled by the loss that they start a riot outside the stadium. In a frenzy, the crowd starts vandalizing parts of the stadium and vehicles in the parking lot. Melanie is not a fan of either team but happened to attend the event with her friend, a self-proclaimed "College Y football fanatic." As she attempts to leave, her friend convinces her to follow him toward the rioting crowd. Melanie becomes swept up the frenzy and participates in the destruction.

She is later arrested and charged with criminal mischief. Does she have a defense? How does this square with the *Williams* case? If the judge ruled that evidence of a "mob mentality" defense could be admitted, do you think a jury would be as sympathetic toward Melanie?

Explanations

1. This instance of neurotoxicity from metal poisoning is detailed in Charell D. Arnold, At Nature's Mercy: the Uneasy Courtship of Criminal Defense and the Environment, 25 Tul. Envtl. L.J. 453 (2012). Any insanity claim that Sok might raise would confront the concern that mental illness is often permanent—while it may be treated, one is rarely "cured" of mental disease. (The misnomer "temporary insanity" is sometimes used by non-lawyers to refer to an "irresistible impulse" or to "heat of passion," but insanity is very rarely "temporary.")

   Nevertheless, in this instance, the prosecution agreed to recommend such a finding, and Sok was ultimately released. Did Sok create the condition of his own claim? Not knowingly. But see Chapter 16. For another example of neurotoxicity, see the case of Terrance Frank, who lived from childhood near a uranium mine and claimed organic brain damage caused him to kill two people. He was convicted of second (rather than first) degree murder.[161]

2. This too is a real case, *Commonwealth v. Garabedian*, 503 N.E.2d 1290 (Mass. 1987). The trial court admitted the evidence, but the jury rejected the claim. The defendant argued that his toxicological intoxication was *involuntary*, in the sense that he was unaware of the impact of the chemicals on his nervous (control) system. Many of these "toxicological damage" cases involve such a claim. Indeed, a defendant who is asked why he did not seek treatment or refrain from further exposure is likely to argue that the earlier exposure diminished or removed his capacity for self-assessment. In this regard, the claim is akin to insanity.

3. This is the famous Menendez brothers trial. At the first trial, the evidence was admitted. Separate juries, deliberating the fate of each brother, were unable to reach verdicts. The evidence was argued as relevant for any of several points: (a) the past abuse created a rage against their father that suddenly "exploded" into a killing spree; (b) the past abuse made them sensitive to "little signs" that their father was displeased with them and

161. See David B. Mcconnell, The Sevin Made Me Do It: Mental Non-Responsibility and the Neurotoxic Damage Defense, 14 Va. Envtl. L.J. 151 (1994). For a general discussion, see Deborah W. Denno, Considering Lead Poisoning as a Criminal Defense, 20 Fordham Urb. L.J. 377 (1993).

might abuse them again; (c) the past abuse, combined with this sensitivity, made them able to discern through "little signs" that their father (abetted by the mother) was about to kill them to prevent them from revealing the past abuse, and therefore went to a self-defense claim. The court admitted the evidence for at least the third purpose. At retrial, this evidence was barred, and both brothers were convicted.

4. This question would require a very long answer on an exam. We will only skim the surface here. First, Julius is *not* raising an insanity defense, because he does not suffer from a recognized mental disorder. If he is in a jurisdiction that does not recognize diminished capacity as a relevant claim, it is difficult to see how his claim would be relevant. He is not claiming that he did not "premeditate," which is the central issue for first-degree murder; he is instead arguing that he lacked the capacity to prevent himself from acting upon his premeditated decision. The problem with this claim, even assuming that the jury believes it, is that the "lay" evidence (a), which may well be the predicate for the expert evidence (b), strongly suggests that Julius *knew* he was unable to control such "impulses" but took no steps to remedy his lack of control. The prosecution would then argue that his failure to take such steps (such as asking a doctor how to address the problem) should preclude any evidence as to the genesis of his lack of control. The issue might then become whether Julius had a "duty" to recognize that his lack of control was physical (rather than "mental") and to take steps to deal with it (see Chapter 7).

   Furthermore, after *Clark v. Arizona*, discussed supra, pages 599-600, "complicated" expert evidence, and perhaps neuroscience in particular, might not be admissible because it could mislead the jury. Although *Clark* dealt with psychiatric evidence and the insanity claim, that decision could plausibly be applied to evidence of this kind as well. Although, hypothetically, this jurisdiction has not statutorily precluded neurological evidence, a trial court decision to do so might well be supported by *Clark*. Finally, there is the question of whether the evidence is sufficiently reliable or probative. In general neurology and cognitive behavioral science have become increasingly sophisticated, and there is increasing evidence that many neurological distinctions are genetically based.[162] Indeed, some courts have allowed evidence of low serotonin either at trial or at sentencing (in death cases).[163]

---

162. See S. Pinker, The Blank Slate (2003), it is not clear that this evidence has reached even the *Daubert* level of reliability. See *State v. Odom*, 137 S.W.3d 572 (Tenn. 2004).

163. See, e.g., *State v. Payne*, 2002 WL 31624813 (Tenn. Crim. App.); *Contra People v. Uncapher*, 2004 WL 790329 (Mich. App), *review denied*, 471 Mich. 901, (2004) (evidence of serotonin levels properly excluded because defendant did not raise insanity defense).

5. This is almost the direct reverse of Julius' situation in Example 4. Zoloft, Prozac, and Paxil, among others, are "selective serotonin reuptake inhibitors" (SSRIs), designed to increase the amount of serotonin in the brain (or, more accurately, to decrease the amount of serotonin not "absorbed" by brain cells, and therefore available for reducing depression). As in Julius' case, one issue will be whether there is sufficient agreement among physicians about the possible side effects of SSRIs.[164] Assuming Jennifer can surmount that obstacle, another issue here—in contrast, perhaps, to Julius' case—is that Jennifer may have an "involuntary intoxication" claim.[165] Some states have precluded claims of involuntary intoxication unless the intoxication was the result of "trick, artifice or force." That was obviously not the case here; there was no "trick" performed by Jennifer's doctors. But the side effects of Zoloft, and of Prozac, including depression, fatigue, and agitation, particularly at the initial stage of usage, were not clearly known—and certainly not known to Jennifer—when she followed the doctor's orders.[166] One source, however, says that of 80-plus cases raising the Prozac or Zoloft defense, only one has been successful.[167] A recent example where the claim failed involved a 12-year-old boy, convicted of killing both his grandparents and sentenced to 30 years in prison, who had been taking Zoloft for less than a month before the killings.[168] The FDA now requires SSRIs generally to carry warnings of increased risk of suicidal behavior among young people. If, rather than seeking an "involuntary intoxication" claim, Jennifer raises a claim of "temporary insanity" created by the drugs, she may run afoul, as might Julius, of the implications of *Clark v. Arizona*.[169]

6. This case is obviously similar to Jennifer's, with one possible exception: The effects of anabolic steroids on behavior have been well documented for some time.[170] The fact that the effect of SSRIs was well known was one of the reasons the defendant in *Shuman* (supra, Explanation 5) raised

164. See *Wood v. State*, 75 Ark. App. 22 (2001).

165. See, e.g., *People v. Hari*, 218 Ill. 2d 275, (2006).

166. Harris, Problems with Prozac: A Defective Product Responsible for Criminal Behavior? 10 J. Contemp. Legal Issues 359 (1999); *Commonwealth v. Shuman*, 445 Mass. 258 (2005).

167. Walker, Rx: Take Two of These and Sue Me in the Morning: The Emergence of Litigation Regarding Psychotropic Medication in the United States and Europe, 19 Ariz. J. Int'l & Comp. L. 775, n. 206 (2002).

168. New York Times, Feb. 16, 2005.

169. See *People v. Arteaga*, 2004 WL 811719 (Cal. Rules of Court, Rules 976, 977) (Cal. App. 4, 2004) (No. G031507).

170. See, e.g., Bidwill and Katz, Injecting New Life into an Old Defense: Anabolic Steroid—Induced Psychosis as a Paradigm of Involuntary Intoxication, 7 U. Miami Ent. & Sports L. Rev. 1 (1989).

in arguing that his counsel was ineffective. Indeed, failure to raise that issue has been suggested as constituting inadequate assistance of counsel.[171] If the court finds that these effects were known, it may be more difficult for Barry to successfully argue "involuntary" intoxication; it may be that he "should have known" of the risk posed by steroids, and if so, he would lose that claim.

7. This is a real event, recounted in Fred Cohen, Old Age as a Criminal Defense, 21 Crim. L. Bull. 5 (1985) (the prosecutor did not bring a charge). But the example raises both a "common sense" issue and a strict one of evidence. First, as to the "common sense," we have always recognized, simply as a matter of observation, that "young people" are less competent than adults. There has been no requirement that defendants "prove" this—it is simply understood, and now validated by our juvenile court system. Indeed, the United States Supreme Court, in holding, in *Atkins v. Virginia*, 536 U.S. 304 (2002), that persons under the age of 18 could not be criminally executed even if they had committed premeditated homicide, did not cite "scientific" evidence that persons under 18 are less morally culpable than those over that age—it simply concluded that, while some 17-year-olds might be more mature than some 18-year-olds, there was a need to draw an age line for the Constitution. So it would seem that Hume should be able to argue that he's "simply an old man." (On the other hand, don't we want older people to be more responsible, because they have learned over more years what "right" and "wrong" are?) But he wants to buttress that claim with "scientific" evidence on brain function generally and on frontal lobe dysfunction particularly. It is "well established that the brain undergoes considerable alterations during senescence . . . (including) an increase in the number of senile plaques and in the amount of neurofibrillary degeneration."[172] Courts have been reluctant to allow this evidence in at trial, either because it is not yet fully proven (even under the *Daubert* test) or because it might be too confounding to the jury (the *Clark* approach). (There is additionally the concern that an actual brain scan may be "so" persuasive to jurors as to be prejudicial against the state; there is some anecdotal evidence that such a phenomenon exists.) It is unlikely that Hume will be able to have the "scientific" evidence admitted, but he

171. See *Sallahdin v. Gibson*, 275 F.3d 1211 (10th Cir. 2004) ("evidence . . . regarding the potential of steroid use to cause severe personality changes . . . could have explained how (defendant) could have been transformed from an allegedly mild-mannered, law abiding individual into a person capable of committing the brutal murder"). But see *Pennington v. State*, 913 P.2d 156 (Okla. Crim. 1995) (insufficient evidence to establish that "'roid rage" is a valid scientific theory).

172. E. Busse & E. Pfeiffer, Behavior and Adaptation in Late Life 268 (1969).

almost surely would have the lay testimony admitted. Is that a good way to run a railroad?

8. Melanie could argue that her criminal conduct was the product of "mob mentality," and that she is not blameworthy, like the defendant in the *Williams* case. The jury may not be as sympathetic toward Melanie, however. The "mob" that Melanie was swept up in was, unlike the mob in the *Williams* case, simply upset fans. While some may take their football seriously, it is not as upsetting to lose a game as it is to witness apparent racial injustice in governmental institutions. Also, Melanie was not even a fan of the team that lost, so it is difficult to see why she would have been vulnerable to becoming swept away by the crowd of (presumably) true College Y fans.

Table of Cases

Index

Index